THE CATHOLIC ALMANAC'S

GUIDE TO THE CHURCH

MATTHEW BUNSON

Our Sunday Visitor Publishing Division
Our Sunday Visitor, Inc.
Huntington, Indiana 46750

ACKNOWLEDGMENTS:

*There are a great many persons to whom a special debt of gratitude is owed
for their kind assistance during the writing of this book. From Our Sunday Visitor:
Greg Erlandson; the Board of Directors for their confidence and faith that this project
would meet all of their hopes and expectations; Jackie Lindsey, for her vision, trust, and
encouragement; and Cathy Dee, for her endless patience. Also, Jane Cavolina;
Rev. Clyde Crews; Fr. Felician Foy, O.F.M.; Barbara Fraze; Brother Jeffrey Gros,
F.S.C.; Rev. Ronald Roberson, C.S.P.; William Ryan; Russell Shaw;
and Margaret Bunson for the magnificent illustrations.*

*Special thanks are owed to His Excellency Most Reverend John P. Foley,
President of the Pontifical Council for Social Communications, for his generosity
in taking the time to contribute the foreword to this book.*

Sources used in this text:

Catholic News Service, for coverage of news and documentary texts; *The Documents of Vatican II*,
ed. W. M. Abbott (Herder and Herder, America Press: New York 1966), for quotations of
Council documents; *Annuario Pontificio* (2001); *Statistical Yearbook of the Church* (2001);
L'Osservatore Romano (English editions); *The Official Catholic Directory* — Excerpts of statistical
data and other material, reprinted with permission of *The Official Catholic Directory*, © 2001 by
Reed Reference Publishing, a division of Reed Publishing (USA) Inc. Trademark used under
license from Reed Publishing (Nederland) B.V.; *The Papal Encyclicals*, 5 vols., ed. C. Carlen
(Pierian Press, Ann Arbor, Mich.); Newsletter of the U.S. Bishops' Committee on the Liturgy;
The United States Catholic Mission Assoc. (3029 Fourth St. N.E., Washington, D.C. 20017),
for U.S. overseas-mission compilations and statistics; *Catholic Press Directory* (2001);
Annuaire Directiore 2000-2001, Canadian Conference of Catholic Bishops, for latest available
Canadian Catholic statistics; Rev. Thomas J. Reese, S.J., for names of dioceses for which
U.S. bishops were ordained; other sources as credited in particular entries.

*Illustrations: Margaret Bunson
Interior designer: Sherri L. Hoffman
Cover design: Rebecca Heaston*

ISBN: 087973-914-2
LCCCN: 2001-130327

PRINTED IN THE UNITED STATES OF AMERICA

TABLE OF CONTENTS

FOREWORD

Archbishop John P. Foley, President, Pontifical Council for Social Communications

What is the Catholic Church?

Perhaps the shortest answer is that the Church represents the continuing presence of Jesus Christ in the world.

Who is Jesus Christ?

He is the God-man, the Messiah, the Savior promised by God to the patriarchs and prophets in the Hebrew Scriptures.

In fact, the name "Jesus" means "Savior," and the name "Christ" is a title rather than a name, and it signifies "anointed one" or Messiah.

On March 25, 2000, the Feast of the Annunciation, Pope John Paul II visited the grotto under the Church of the Annunciation in Nazareth that is believed to have been the house of Mary, where the Angel Gabriel appeared to the Virgin Mary and announced that she was to be the Mother of God. Mary understandably asked how such motherhood would occur, since she did not "know" man. After having been assured that the power of the Most High would overshadow her, she responded, "Be it done unto me according to Thy Word."

At that moment, we believe, Jesus Christ, the God-man, was conceived in the womb of the Blessed Virgin Mary and was born nine months later in Bethlehem.

The Great Jubilee of the Year 2000 thus marked the two-thousandth anniversary of the Incarnation and Birth of Jesus Christ, the Savior of the world.

God became man to show us how to live and to redeem us from our sins, our personal sins and the sin of our first parents, through His death and rising from the dead, so that we might enjoy a sharing in His divine life and might live forever with Him in heaven.

To make the fruits of His redemption and saving love available to all succeeding generations. Jesus chose from among His followers twelve apostles, a word which means "those sent," and He did indeed send them "to teach all nations." He bade them to baptize "in the name of the Father and of the Son and of the Holy Spirit."

From among the Apostles, Jesus chose one, Simon Peter, to be the leader: "You are Peter and on this rock I shall build my church and the gates of hell shall not prevail against it."

It is this Church, founded by Jesus Christ upon the rock of Peter, which does indeed represent the continuing presence of Jesus among us. It is this Church about which this excellent guide provides a brief history and explanation.

In an age of spiritual confusion, I pray that many will find in the saving love of Jesus the answer to all their longings. In an age of so much factual confusion and misinformation, I would hope that many will find in this guide the answer to many of their questions about what is the Catholic Church and about what it does and should mean for each one of us.

INTRODUCTION

The *Catholic Almanac Guide to the Catholic Church* is intended to present in a comprehensive, single-volume compendium a glimpse of the whole of the Catholic Church – including its history, institutional life, teachings, and laws – in a style that is accessible, easily consulted, and, hopefully, interesting. For readers of the annual reference work, *Our Sunday Visitor's Catholic Almanac*, there is much in the book that will seem familiar, in particular those sections on Doctrine, Revelation, and the Sacraments. At the same time, even the most dedicated reader of the *Almanac* will find a great deal of new information that is exclusive to this guide, including sections on Canon Law and the prayers of the Church.

One of the most consistently striking and remarkable facets of the *Catholic Almanac* is the way that it presents the Church throughout the world. It is possible, for example, to note quickly how many Cardinals there are in service at the moment, how many catechists are working in such distant countries as Paraguay, Vanuatu, and Namibia, or what the latest decrees might be on the translation of the liturgy. The universality, the rich diversity, and the labors of Catholics across the globe are sources of inspiration to all members of the Church. They remind us that we are not alone in our prayers, that we are all truly one, and that the Gospel of Christ is for all. As St. Irenaeus declared, "Just as God's creation, the sun, is one and the same the world over, so too does the Church's preaching shine everywhere to enlighten all who wish to come to a knowledge of the truth." It is hoped that this same spirit pervades this *Guide*.

How to Use this Book

For those who are picking up this book for the first time and with only a limited knowledge of the Church, there might be a few suggestions to follow for approaching the potentially intimidating material. After reviewing the table of contents, a reader should begin with the sections on doctrine and revelation. These are the heart of the *Guide* and the source for all of the information related in the other parts of the book. Next, a reader might examine the sections on the liturgy and sacraments, moving from there to the communion of saints, and especially Mary.

The institutional life of the Church is also given prominence in the *Guide*, with extensive coverage of the Holy See, the pontiffs of the twentieth century, and the Church hierarchy. From these topics, a reader might proceed to the long accounts of Church history. This background will place the historical life of the Church in a wider context and will permit the reader to see the important unity that exists between the teachings of the Church and the life of the Christian in the world. The study of canon law will also allow a reader to grasp theology in practice and how the laws of the Church serve not to limit or restrict, but to strengthen and give structure to the institutional life of the faith. Finally, after the grounding provided in the earlier sections, a reader might finish with the sections on ecumenism and interreligious dialogue to see how the Church is laboring to bring about the call of Christ, *ut unum sint* ("that all might be one").

Part 1

CHURCH HISTORY

Human history, marked as it is by the experience of sin, would drive us to despair if God had abandoned His creation to itself. But the divine promises of liberation, and their victorious fulfillment in Christ's death and resurrection, are the basis of the "joyful hope" from which the Christian community draws the strength to act resolutely and effectively in the service of love, justice and peace. The Gospel is a message of freedom and a liberating force which fulfills the hope of Israel based upon the words of the prophets. This hope relied upon the action of Yahweh, who even before He intervened as the "goel," liberator, Redeemer and Savior of His people, had freely chosen that people in Abraham.

"Instruction on Christian Freedom and Liberation," Sacred Congregation for the Doctrine of the Faith, *Libertatis Conscientia*, Chapter III.43.

CHRONOLOGY OF CATHOLIC HISTORY

FIRST CENTURY

c. 33: First Christian Pentecost; descent of the Holy Spirit upon the disciples; preaching of St. Peter in Jerusalem; conversion, baptism and aggregation of some 3,000 persons to the first Christian community.

St. Stephen, deacon, was stoned to death at Jerusalem; he is venerated as the first Christian martyr.

c. 34: St. Paul, formerly Saul the persecutor of Christians, was converted and baptized. After three years of solitude in the desert, he joined the college of the apostles; he made three major missionary journeys and became known as the Apostle to the Gentiles; he was imprisoned twice in Rome and was beheaded there between 64 and 67.

39: Cornelius (the Gentile) and his family were baptized by St. Peter; a significant event signaling the mission of the Church to all peoples.

42: Persecution of Christians in Palestine broke out during the rule of Herod Agrippa; St. James the Greater, the first apostle to die, was beheaded in 44; St. Peter was imprisoned for a short time; many Christians fled to Antioch, marking the beginning of the dispersion of Christians beyond the confines of Palestine. At Antioch, the followers of Christ were called Christians for the first time.

49: Christians at Rome, considered members of a Jewish sect, were adversely affected by a decree of Claudius which forbade Jewish worship there.

51: The Council of Jerusalem, in which all the apostles participated under the presidency of St. Peter, decreed that circumcision, dietary regulations, and various other prescriptions of Mosaic Law were not obligatory for Gentile converts to the Christian community. The crucial decree was issued in opposition to Judaizers who contended that observance of the Mosaic Law in its entirety was necessary for salvation.

64: Persecution broke out at Rome under Nero, the emperor said to have accused Christians of starting the fire that destroyed half of Rome.

64 or 67: Martyrdom of St. Peter at Rome during the Neronian persecution. He established his see and spent his last years there, after preaching in and around Jerusalem, establishing a see at Antioch, and presiding at the Council of Jerusalem.

70: Destruction of Jerusalem by Titus.

88-97: Pontificate of St. Clement I, third successor of St. Peter as bishop of Rome, one of the Apostolic Fathers. The First Epistle of Clement to the Corinthians, with which he has been identified, was addressed by the Church of Rome to the Church at Corinth, the scene of irregularities and divisions in the Christian community.

95: Domitian persecuted Christians, principally at Rome.

c. 100: Death of St. John, apostle and evangelist, marking the end of the Age of the Apostles and the first generation of the Church.

By the end of the century, Antioch, Alexandria and Ephesus in the East and Rome in the West were established centers of Christian population and influence.

SECOND CENTURY

c. 107: St. Ignatius of Antioch was martyred at Rome. He was the first writer to use the expression, "the Catholic Church."

112: Emperor Trajan, in a rescript to Pliny the Younger, governor of Bithynia, instructed him not to search out Christians but to punish them if they were publicly denounced and refused to do homage to the Roman gods. This rescript set a pattern for Roman magistrates in dealing with Christians.

117-38: Persecution under Hadrian. Many Acts of Martyrs date from this period.

c. 125: Spread of Gnosticism, a combination of elements of Platonic philosophy and Eastern mystery religions. Its adherents claimed that its secret-knowledge principle provided a deeper insight into Christian doctrine than divine revelation and faith. One gnostic thesis denied the divinity of Christ; others denied the reality of his humanity, calling it mere appearance (Docetism, Phantasiasm).

c. 144: Excommunication of Marcion, bishop and heretic, who claimed that there was total opposition and no connection at all between the Old Testament and the New Testament, between the God of the Jews and the God of the Christians; and that the Canon (list of inspired writings) of the Bible consisted only of parts of St. Luke's Gospel and ten letters of St. Paul. Marcionism was checked at Rome by 200 and was condemned by a council held there about 260, but the heresy persisted for several centuries in the East and had some adherents as late as the Middle Ages.

c. 155: St. Polycarp, bishop of Smyrna and disciple of St. John the Evangelist, was martyred.

c. 156: Beginning of Montanism, a form of religious extremism. Its principal tenets were the imminent second coming of Christ, denial of the divine nature of the Church and its power to forgive sin, and excessively rigorous morality. The heresy, preached by Montanus of Phrygia and others, was condemned by Pope St. Zephyrinus (199-217).

161-80: Reign of Marcus Aurelius. His persecution, launched in the wake of natural disasters, was more violent than those of his predecessors.

165: St. Justin, an important early Christian writer, was martyred at Rome.

c. 180: St. Irenaeus, bishop of Lyons and one of the great early theologians, wrote *Adversus Haereses*. He stated that the teaching and tradition of the Roman See was the standard for belief.

196: Easter Controversy, concerning the day of celebration — a Sunday, according to practice in the West, or the 14th of the month of Nisan (in the Hebrew calendar), no matter what day of the week, according to practice in the East. The controversy was not resolved at this time.

The *Didache*, whose extant form dates from the second century, is an important record of Christian belief, practice and governance in the first century.

Latin was introduced as a liturgical language in the West. Other liturgical languages were Aramaic and Greek.

The Catechetical School of Alexandria, founded about the middle of the century, gained increasing influence on doctrinal study and instruction, and interpretation of the Bible.

THIRD CENTURY

202: Persecution under Septimius Severus, who wanted to establish a simple common religion in the Empire.

206: Tertullian, a convert since 197 and the first great ecclesiastical writer in Latin, joined the heretical Montanists; he died in 230.

215: Death of Clement of Alexandria, teacher of Origen and a founding father of the School of Alexandria.

217-35: St. Hippolytus, the first antipope; he was reconciled to the Church while in prison during persecution in 235.

232-54: Origen established the School of Caesarea after being deposed in 231 as head of the School of Alexandria; he died in 254. A scholar and voluminous writer, he was one of the founders of systematic theology and exerted wide influence for many years.

c. 242: Manichaeism originated in Persia: a combination of errors based on the assumption that two supreme principles (good and evil) are operative in creation and life, and that the supreme objective of human endeavor is liberation from evil (matter). The heresy denied the humanity of Christ, the sacramental system, the authority of the Church (and state), and endorsed a moral code that threatened the fabric of society. In the 12th and 13th centuries, it took on the features of Albigensianism and Catharism.

249-51: Persecution under Decius. Many of those who denied the faith (*lapsi*) sought readmission to the Church at the end of the persecution in 251. Pope St. Cornelius agreed with St. Cyprian that *lapsi* were to be readmitted to the Church after satisfying the requirements of appropriate penance. Antipope Novatian, on the other hand, contended that persons who fell away from the Church under persecution and/or those guilty of serious sin after baptism could not be absolved and readmitted to communion with the Church. The heresy was condemned by a Roman synod in 251.

250-300: Neo-Platonism of Plotinus and Porphyry gained followers.

251: Novatian was condemned at Rome.

256: Pope St. Stephen I upheld the validity of baptism properly administered by heretics, in the Rebaptism Controversy.

257: Persecution under Valerian, who attempted to destroy the Church as a social structure.

258: St. Cyprian, bishop of Carthage, was martyred.

c. 260: St. Lucian founded the School of Antioch, a center of influence on biblical studies.

Pope St. Dionysius condemned Sabellianism, a form of modalism (like Monarchianism and Patripassianism). The heresy contended that the Father, Son and Holy Spirit are not distinct divine persons but are only three different modes of being and self-manifestations of the one God.

St. Paul of Thebes became a hermit.

261: Gallienus issued an edict of toleration which ended general persecution for nearly 40 years.

c. 292: Diocletian divided the Roman Empire into East and West. The division emphasized political, cultural and other differences between the two parts of the Empire and influenced different developments in the Church in the East and West. The prestige of Rome began to decline.

FOURTH CENTURY

303: Persecution broke out under Diocletian; it was particularly violent in 304.

305: St. Anthony of Heracles established a foundation for hermits near the Red Sea in Egypt.

c. 306: The first local legislation on clerical celibacy was enacted by a council held at Elvira, Spain; bishops, priests, deacons and other ministers were forbidden to have wives.

311: An edict of toleration issued by Galerius at the urging of Constantine the Great and Licinius officially ended persecution in the West; some persecution continued in the East.

313: The Edict of Milan issued by Constantine and Licinius recognized Christianity as a lawful religion in the Roman Empire.

314: A council of Arles condemned Donatism, declaring that baptism properly administered by heretics is valid, in view of the principle that sacraments have their efficacy from Christ, not from the spiritual condition of their human ministers. The heresy was condemned again by a council of Carthage in 411.

318: St. Pachomius established the first foundation of the cenobitic (common) life, as compared with the solitary life of hermits in Upper Egypt.

325: Ecumenical Council of Nicaea (I). Its principal action was the condemnation of Arianism, the most devastating of the early heresies, which denied the divinity of Christ.

The heresy was authored by Arius of Alexandria, a priest. Arians and several kinds of Semi-Arians propagandized their tenets widely, established their own hierarchies and churches, and raised havoc in the Church for several centuries. The council contributed to formulation of the Nicene Creed (Creed of Nicaea-Constantinople); fixed the date for the observance of Easter; passed regulations concerning clerical discipline; adopted the civil divisions of the Empire as the model for the jurisdictional organization of the Church.

326: With the support of St. Helena, the True Cross on which Christ was crucified was discovered.

337: Baptism and death of Constantine.

c. 342: Beginning of a 40-year persecution in Persia.

343-44: A council of Sardica reaffirmed doctrine formulated by Nicaea I and declared also that bishops had the right of appeal to the pope as the highest authority in the Church.

361-63: Emperor Julian the Apostate waged an unsuccessful campaign against the Church in an attempt to restore paganism as the religion of the Empire.

c. 365: Persecution of orthodox Christians under Emperor Valens in the East.

c. 376: Beginning of the barbarian invasion in the West.

379: Death of St. Basil, the Father of Monasticism in the East. His writings contributed greatly to the development of rules for the life of religious.

381: Ecumenical Council of Constantinople (I). It condemned various brands of Arianism as well as Macedonianism, which denied the divinity of the Holy Spirit; contributed to formulation of the Nicene Creed; approved a canon acknowledging Constantinople as the second see after Rome in honor and dignity.

382: The Canon of Sacred Scripture, the official list of the inspired books of the Bible, was contained in the Decree of Pope St. Damasus and published by a regional council of Carthage in 397; the Canon was formally defined by the Council of Trent in the 16th century.

382-c. 406: St. Jerome translated the Old and New Testaments into Latin; his work is called the Vulgate version of the Bible.

396: St. Augustine became bishop of Hippo in North Africa.

FIFTH CENTURY

410: Visigoths under Alaric sacked Rome and the last Roman legions departed Britain. The decline of imperial Rome dates approximately from this time.

430: St. Augustine, bishop of Hippo for 35 years, died. He was a strong defender of orthodox doctrine against Manichaeism, Donatism, and Pelagianism. The depth and range of his writings made him a dominant influence in Christian thought for centuries.

431: Ecumenical Council of Ephesus. It condemned Nestorianism, which denied the unity of the divine and human natures in the Person of Christ; defined Theotokos (Bearer of God) as the title of Mary, Mother of the Son of God made Man; condemned Pelagianism. The heresy of Pelagianism, proceeding from the assumption that Adam had a natural right to supernatural life, held that man could attain salvation through the efforts of his natural powers and free will; it involved errors concerning the nature of original sin, the meaning of grace, and other matters. Related Semi-Pelagianism was condemned by a council of Orange in 529.

432: St. Patrick arrived in Ireland. By the time of his death in 461 most of the country had been converted, monasteries founded, and the hierarchy established.

438: The Theodosian Code, a compilation of decrees for the Empire, was issued by Theodosius II; it had great influence on subsequent civil and ecclesiastical law.

451: Ecumenical Council of Chalcedon. Its principal action was the condemnation of Monophysitism (also called Eutychianism), which denied the humanity of Christ by holding that he had only one, the divine, nature.

452: Pope St. Leo the Great persuaded Attila the Hun to spare Rome.

455: Vandals under Genseric sacked Rome.

484: Patriarch Acacius of Constantinople was excommunicated for signing the *Henoticon*, a document which capitulated to the Monophysite heresy. The excommunication triggered the Acacian Schism, which lasted for 35 years.

494: Pope St. Gelasius I declared in a letter to Emperor Anastasius that the pope had power and authority over the emperor in spiritual matters.

496: Clovis, King of the Franks, was converted and became the defender of Christianity in the West. The Franks became a Catholic people.

SIXTH CENTURY

520: Irish monasteries flourished as centers for spiritual life, missionary training, and scholarly activity.

529: The Second Council of Orange condemned Semi-Pelagianism.

c. 529: St. Benedict founded the Monte Cassino Abbey. Some years before his death in 543 he wrote a monastic rule that exercised tremendous influence on the form and style of religious life. He is called the Father of Monasticism in the West.

533: John II became the first pope to change his name. The practice did not become general until the time of Sergius IV (1009).

533-34: Emperor Justinian promulgated the *Corpus Iuris Civilis* for the Roman world; like the Theodosian Code, it influenced subsequent civil and ecclesiastical law.

c. 545: Death of Dionysius Exiguus who was the first to date history from the birth of Christ, a practice that resulted in use of the B.C. and A.D. abbreviations. His calculations were at least four years late.

553: Ecumenical Council of Constantinople (II). It condemned the Three Chapters, Nestorian-tainted writings of Theodore of Mopsuestia, Theodoret of Cyrus, and Ibas of Edessa.

585: St. Columban founded an influential monastic school at Luxeuil.

589: The most important of several councils of Toledo was held. The Visigoths renounced Arianism, and St. Leander began the organization of the Church in Spain.

590-604: Pontificate of Pope St. Gregory I the Great. He set the form and style of the papacy that prevailed throughout the Middle Ages; exerted great influence on doctrine and liturgy; was strong in support of monastic discipline and clerical celibacy; authored writings on many subjects. Gregorian Chant is named in his honor.

596: Pope St. Gregory I sent St. Augustine of Canterbury and 40 monks to do missionary work in England.

597: St. Columba died. He founded an important monastery at Iona, established schools and did notable missionary work in Scotland. By the end of the century, monasteries of nuns were common; Western monasticism was flourishing; monasticism in the East, under the influence of Monophysitism and other factors, was losing its vigor.

SEVENTH CENTURY

613: St. Columban established the influential monastery of Bobbio in northern Italy; he died there in 615.

622: The *Hegira* (flight) of Mohammed from Mecca to Medina signaled the beginning of Islam which, by the end of the century, claimed almost all of the southern Mediterranean area.

628: Heraclius, Eastern Emperor, recovered the True Cross from the Persians.

649: A Lateran council condemned two erroneous formulas (Ecthesis and Type) issued by emperors Heraclius and Constans II as means of reconciling Monophysites with the Church.

664: Actions of the Synod of Whitby advanced the adoption of Roman usages in England, especially regarding the date for the observance of Easter. (See *Easter Controversy*.)

680-81: Ecumenical Council of Constantinople (III). It condemned Monothelitism, which held that Christ had only one will, the divine; censured Pope Honorius I for a letter to Sergius, bishop of Constantinople, in which he made an ambiguous but not infallible statement about the unity of will and/or operation in Christ.

692: Trullan Synod. Eastern-Church discipline on clerical celibacy was settled, permitting marriage before ordination to the diaconate and continuation in marriage afterwards, but prohibiting marriage following the death of the wife thereafter. Anti-Roman canons contributed to East-West alienation.

During the century, the monastic influence of Ireland and England increased in Western Europe; schools and learning declined; regulations regarding clerical celibacy became more strict in the East.

EIGHTH CENTURY

711: Muslims began the conquest of Spain.

726: Emperor Leo III, the Isaurian, launched a campaign against the veneration of sacred images and relics; called Iconoclasm (image-breaking), it caused turmoil in the East until about 843.

731: Pope Gregory III and a synod at Rome condemned Iconoclasm, with a declaration that the veneration of sacred images was in accord with Catholic tradition.

Venerable Bede issued his *Ecclesiastical History of the English People*.

732: Charles Martel defeated the Muslims at Poitiers, halting their advance in the West.

744: The Monastery of Fulda was established by St. Sturmi, a disciple of St. Boniface; it was influential in the evangelization of Germany.

754: A council of more than 300 Byzantine bishops endorsed Iconoclast errors. This council and its actions were condemned by the Lateran synod of 769.

Stephen II (III) crowned Pepin ruler of the Franks. Pepin twice invaded Italy, in 754 and 756, to defend the pope against the Lombards. His land grants to the papacy, called the Donation of Pepin, were later extended by Charlemagne (773) and formed part of the States of the Church.

c. 755: St. Boniface (Winfrid) was martyred. He was called the Apostle of Germany for his missionary work and organization of the hierarchy there.

781: Alcuin was chosen by Charlemagne to organize a palace school, which became a center of intellectual leadership.

787: Ecumenical Council of Nicaea (II). It condemned Iconoclasm, which held that the use of images was idolatry, and Adoptionism, which claimed that Christ was not the Son of God by nature but only by adoption. This was the last council regarded as ecumenical by Orthodox Churches.

792: A council at Ratisbon condemned Adoptionism.

The famous *Book of Kells* ("The Great Gospel of Columcille") dates from the early eighth or late seventh century.

NINTH CENTURY

800: Charlemagne was crowned Emperor by Pope Leo III on Christmas Day.

Egbert became king of West Saxons; he unified England and strengthened the See of Canterbury.

813: Emperor Leo V, the Armenian, revived Iconoclasm, which persisted until about 843.

814: Charlemagne died.

843: The Treaty of Verdun split the Frankish kingdom among Charlemagne's three grandsons.

844: A Eucharistic controversy involving the writings of St. Paschasius Radbertus, Ratramnus and Rabanus Maurus occasioned the development of terminology regarding the doctrine of the Real Presence.

846: Muslims invaded Italy and attacked Rome.

847-52: Period of composition of the False Decretals, a collection of forged documents attributed to popes from St. Clement (88-97) to Gregory II (714-731). The Decretals, which strongly supported the autonomy and rights of bishops, were suspect for a long time before being repudiated entirely about 1628.

848: The Council of Mainz condemned Gottschalk for heretical teaching regarding predestination. He was also condemned by the Council of Quierzy in 853.

857: Photius displaced Ignatius as patriarch of Constantinople. This marked the beginning of the Photian Schism, a confused state of East-West relations which has not yet been cleared up by historical research. Photius, a man of exceptional ability, died in 891.

865: St. Ansgar, apostle of Scandinavia, died.

869: St. Cyril died and his brother, St. Methodius (d. 885), was ordained a bishop. The Apostles of the Slavs devised an alphabet and translated the Gospels and liturgy into the Slavonic language.

869-70: Ecumenical Council of Constantinople (IV). It issued a second condemnation of Iconoclasm, condemned and deposed Photius as patriarch of Constantinople, and restored Ignatius to the patriarchate. This was the last ecumenical council held in the East. It was first called ecumenical by canonists toward the end of the 11th century.

871-c. 900: Reign of Alfred the Great, the only English king ever anointed by a pope at Rome.

TENTH CENTURY

910: William, duke of Aquitaine, founded the Benedictine Abbey of Cluny, which became a center of monastic and ecclesiastical reform, especially in France.

915: Pope John X played a leading role in the expulsion of Saracens from central and southern Italy.

955: St. Olga, of the Russian royal family, was baptized.

962: Otto I, the Great, crowned by Pope John XII, revived Charlemagne's kingdom, which became the Holy Roman Empire.

966: Mieszko, first of a royal line in Poland, was baptized; he brought Latin Christianity to Poland.

988: Conversion and baptism of St. Vladimir and the people of Kiev, which subsequently became part of Russia.

993: John XV was the first pope to decree the official canonization of a saint — Bishop Ulrich (Uldaric) of Augsburg — for the universal Church.

997: St. Stephen became ruler of Hungary. He assisted in organizing the hierarchy and establishing Latin Christianity in that country.

999-1003: Pontificate of Sylvester II (Gerbert of Aquitaine), a Benedictine monk and the first French pope.

ELEVENTH CENTURY

1009: Beginning of lasting East-West Schism in the Church, marked by dropping of the name of Pope Sergius IV from the Byzantine diptychs (the listing of persons prayed for during the liturgy). The deletion was made by Patriarch Sergius II of Constantinople.

1012: St. Romuald founded the Camaldolese Hermits.

1025: The Council of Arras, and other councils later, condemned the Cathari (Neo-Manichaeans, Albigenses).

1027: The Council of Elne proclaimed the Truce of God as a means of stemming violence; it involved armistice periods of varying length, which were later extended.

1038: St. John Gualbert founded the Vallombrosians.

1043-59: Constantinople patriarchate of Michael Cerularius, the key figure in a controversy concerning the primacy of the papacy. His and the Byzantine synod's refusal to acknowledge this primacy in 1054 widened and hardened the East-West Schism in the Church.

1047: Pope Clement II died; he was the only pope ever buried in Germany.

1049-54: Pontificate of St. Leo IX, who inaugurated a movement of papal, diocesan, monastic and clerical reform.

1054: Start of the Great Schism between the Eastern and Western Churches; it marked the separation of Orthodox Churches from unity with the pope.

1055: Condemnation of the Eucharistic doctrine of Berengarius.

1059: A Lateran council issued new legislation regarding papal elections; voting power was entrusted to the Roman cardinals.

1066: Death of St. Edward the Confessor, king of England from 1042 and restorer of Westminster Abbey.

Defeat, at Hastings, of Harold by William, Duke of Normandy (later William I), who subsequently exerted strong influence on the lifestyle of the Church in England.

1073-85: Pontificate of St. Gregory VII (Hildebrand). A strong pope, he carried forward programs of clerical and general ecclesiastical reform and struggled against German King Henry IV and other rulers to end the evils of lay investiture. He introduced the Latin liturgy in Spain and set definite dates for the observance of ember days.

1077: Henry IV, excommunicated and suspended from the exercise of imperial powers by Gregory VII, sought absolution from the pope at Canossa. Henry later repudiated this action and in 1084 forced Gregory to leave Rome.

1079: The Council of Rome condemned Eucharistic errors (denial of the Real Presence of Christ under the appearances of bread and wine) of Berengarius, who retracted.

1084: St. Bruno founded the Carthusians.

1097-99: The first of several Crusades undertaken between this time and 1265. Recovery of the Holy Places and free access to them for Christians were the original purposes, but these were diverted to less worthy objectives in various ways. Results included: a Latin Kingdom of Jerusalem, 1099-1187; a military and political misadventure in the form of a Latin Empire of Constantinople, 1204-1261; acquisition, by treaties, of visiting rights for Christians in the Holy Land. East-West economic and cultural relationships increased during the period. In the religious sphere, actions of the Crusaders had the effect of increasing the alienation of the East from the West.

1098: St. Robert founded the Cistercians.

TWELFTH CENTURY

1108: Beginnings of the influential Abbey and School of St. Victor in France.

1115: St. Bernard established the Abbey of Clairvaux and inaugurated the Cistercian Reform.

1118: Christian forces captured Saragossa, Spain; the beginning of the Muslim decline in that country.

1121: St. Norbert established the original monastery of the Praemonstratensians near Laon, France.

1122: The Concordat of Worms (*Pactum Callixtinum*) was formulated and approved by Pope Callistus II and Emperor Henry V to settle controversy concerning the investiture of prelates. The concordat provided that the emperor could invest prelates with symbols of temporal authority but had no right to invest them with spiritual authority, which came from the Church alone, and that the emperor was not to interfere in papal elections. This was the first concordat in history.

1123: Ecumenical Council of the Lateran (I), the first of its kind in the West. It endorsed provisions of the Concordat of Worms concerning the investiture of prelates and approved reform measures in 25 canons.

1139: Ecumenical Council of the Lateran (II). It adopted measures against a schism organized by antipope Anacletus and approved 30 canons related to discipline and other matters; one of the canons stated that holy orders is an invalidating impediment to marriage.

1140: St. Bernard met Abélard in debate at the Council of Sens. Abélard, whose rationalism in theology was condemned for the first time in 1121, died in 1142 at Cluny.

1148: The Synod of Rheims enacted strict disciplinary decrees for communities of women religious.

1152: The Synod of Kells reorganized the Church in Ireland.

1160: Gratian, whose *Decretum* became a basic text of canon law, died.

Peter Lombard, compiler of the Four Books of Sentences, a standard theology text for nearly 200 years, died.

1170: St. Thomas Becket, archbishop of Canterbury, who clashed with Henry II over church-state relations, was murdered in his cathedral.

1171: Pope Alexander III reserved the process of canonization of saints to the Holy See.

1179: Ecumenical Council of the Lateran (III). It enacted measures against Waldensianism and Albigensianism (see year 242 regarding Manichaeism); approved reform decrees in 27 canons; provided that popes be elected by a two-thirds vote of the cardinals.

1184: Waldenses and other heretics were excommunicated by Pope Lucius III.

THIRTEENTH CENTURY

1198-1216: Pontificate of Innocent III, during which the papacy reached its medieval peak of authority, influence and prestige in the Church and in relations with civil rulers.

1208: Innocent III called for a crusade, the first in Christendom itself, against the Albigensians; their beliefs and practices threatened the fabric of society in southern France and northern Italy.

1209: Verbal approval was given by Innocent III to a rule of life for the Order of Friars Minor, started by St. Francis of Assisi.

1212: The Second Order of Franciscans, the Poor Clares, was founded.

1215: Ecumenical Council of the Lateran (IV). It ordered annual reception of the sacraments of penance and the Eucharist; defined and made the first official use of the term transubstantiation to explain the change of bread and wine into the body and blood of Christ; adopted additional measures to counteract teachings and practices of the Albigensians and Cathari; approved 70 canons.

1216: Formal papal approval was given to a rule of life for the Order of Preachers, started by St. Dominic.

The Portiuncula Indulgence was granted by the Holy See at the request of St. Francis of Assisi.

1221: Rule of the Third Order Secular of St. Francis (Secular Franciscan Order) approved verbally by Honorius III.

1226: Death of St. Francis of Assisi.

1231: Pope Gregory IX authorized establishment of the Papal Inquisition for dealing with heretics. It was a creature of its time, when crimes against faith and heretical doctrines of extremists like the Cathari and Albigenses threatened the good of the Christian community, the welfare of the state and the very fabric of society. The institution, which was responsible for excesses in punishment, was most active in the second half of the century in southern France, Italy and Germany.

1245: Ecumenical Council of Lyons (I). It confirmed the deposition of Emperor Frederick II and approved 22 canons.

1247: Preliminary approval was given by the Holy See to a Carmelite rule of life.

1270: St. Louis IX, king of France, died. Beginning of papal decline.

1274: Ecumenical Council of Lyons (II). It accomplished a temporary reunion of separated Eastern Churches with the Roman Church; issued regulations concerning conclaves for papal elections; approved 31 canons. Death of St. Thomas Aquinas, Doctor of the Church, of lasting influence.

1280: Pope Nicholas III, who made the Breviary the official prayer book for clergy of the Roman Church, died.

1281: The excommunication of Michael Palaeologus by Pope Martin IV ruptured the union effected with the Eastern Church in 1274.

FOURTEENTH CENTURY

1302: Pope Boniface VIII issued the bull *Unam Sanctam*, concerning the unity of the Church and the temporal power of princes, against the background of a struggle with Philip IV of France; it was the most famous medieval document on the subject.

1309-77: For a period of approximately 70 years, seven popes resided at Avignon because of unsettled conditions in Rome and other reasons.

1311-12: Ecumenical Council of Vienne. It suppressed the Knights Templar and enacted a number of reform decrees.

1321: Dante Alighieri died a year after completing the *Divine Comedy*.

1324: Marsilius of Padua completed *Defensor Pacis*, a work condemned by Pope John XXII as heretical because of its denial of papal primacy and the hierarchical structure of the Church, and for other reasons. It was a charter for conciliarism (which asserted that an ecumenical council is superior to the pope in authority).

1337-1453: Period of the Hundred Years' War, a dynastic struggle between France and England.

1338: Four years after the death of Pope John XXII, who had opposed Louis IV of Bavaria in a years-long controversy, electoral princes declared at the Diet of Rhense that the emperor did not need papal confirmation of his title and right to rule. Charles IV later (1356) said the same thing in a *Golden Bull*, eliminating papal rights in the election of emperors.

1347-50: The Black Death swept across Europe, killing perhaps one-fourth to one-third of the total population; an estimated 40 per cent of the clergy succumbed.

1374: Petrarch, poet and humanist, died.

1377: Return of the papacy from Avignon to Rome. Beginning of the Western Schism.

FIFTEENTH CENTURY

1409: The Council of Pisa, without canonical authority, tried to end the Western Schism but succeeded only in complicating it by electing a third claimant to the papacy. (See *Western Schism.*)

1414-18: Ecumenical Council of Constance. It took successful action to end the Western Schism involving rival claimants to the papacy; rejected the teachings of Wycliff; condemned Hus as a heretic. One decree — passed in the earlier stages of the council but later rejected — asserted the superiority of an ecumenical council over the pope (conciliarism).

1431: St. Joan of Arc was burned at the stake.

1431-45: Ecumenical Council of Florence (also called Bâsle-Ferrara-Florence). It affirmed the primacy of the pope against the claims of conciliarists. It also formulated and approved decrees of union with several separated Eastern Churches — Greek, Armenian, Jacobite — which failed to gain general or lasting acceptance.

1438: The Pragmatic Sanction of Bourges was enacted by Charles VII and the French Parliament to curtail papal authority over the Church in France, in the spirit of conciliarism. It found expression in Gallicanism and had effects lasting at least until the French Revolution.

1453: The fall of Constantinople to the Turks.

c. 1456: Gutenberg issued the first edition of the Bible printed from movable type, at Mainz, Germany.

1476: Pope Sixtus IV approved observance of the feast of the Immaculate Conception on December 8 throughout the Church.

1478: Pope Sixtus IV, at the urging of King Ferdinand of Spain, approved establishment of the Spanish Inquisition for dealing with Jewish and Moorish converts accused of heresy. The institution, which was peculiar to Spain and its colonies in America, acquired jurisdiction over other cases as well and fell into disrepute because of its procedures, cruelty, and the manner in which it served the Spanish crown, rather than the accused and the good of the Church. Protests by the Holy See failed to curb excesses of the Inquisition, which lingered in Spanish history until early in the 19th century.

1492: Columbus discovered the Americas.

1493: Pope Alexander VI issued a Bull of Demarcation which determined spheres of influence for the Spanish and Portuguese in the Americas.

The Renaissance, a humanistic movement which originated in Italy in the 14th century, spread to France, Germany, the Low Countries, and England. A transitional period between the medieval world and the modern secular world, it introduced profound changes that affected literature and the other arts, general culture, politics, and religion.

SIXTEENTH CENTURY

1512-17: Ecumenical Council of the Lateran (V). It stated the relation and position of the pope with respect to an ecumenical council; acted to counteract the Pragmatic Sanction of Bourges and exaggerated claims of liberty by the Church in France; condemned erroneous teachings concerning the nature of the human soul; stated doctrine concerning indulgences. The council reflected concern for abuses in the Church and the need for reforms but failed to take decisive action in the years immediately preceding the Reformation.

1517: Martin Luther signaled the beginning of the Reformation by posting 95 theses at Wittenberg. Subsequently, he broke completely from doctrinal orthodoxy in discourses and three published works (1519 and 1520); was excommunicated on more than 40 charges of heresy (1521); remained the dominant figure in the Reformation in Germany until his death in 1546.

1519: Zwingli triggered the Reformation in Zurich and became its leading proponent there until his death in combat in 1531.

1524: Luther's encouragement of German princes in putting down the two-year Peasants' Revolt gained political support for his cause.

1528: The Order of Friars Minor Capuchin was approved as an autonomous division of the Franciscan Order; like the Jesuits, the Capuchins became leaders in the Counter-Reformation.

1530: The Augsburg Confession of Lutheran faith was issued; it was later supplemented by the Smalkaldic Articles, approved in 1537.

1533: Henry VIII divorced Catherine of Aragon, married Anne Boleyn, and was excommunicated. In 1534 he decreed the Act of Supremacy, making the sovereign the head of the Church in England, under which Sts. John Fisher and Thomas More were executed in 1535. Despite his rejection of papal primacy and actions against monastic life in England, he generally maintained doctrinal orthodoxy until his death in 1547.

1536: John Calvin, leader of the Reformation in Switzerland until his death in 1564, issued the first edition of *Institutes of the Christian Religion*, which became the classical text of Reformed (non-Lutheran) theology.

1540: The constitutions of the Society of Jesus (Jesuits), founded by St. Ignatius of Loyola, were approved.

1541: Start of the 11-year career of St. Francis Xavier as a missionary to the East Indies and Japan.

1545-63: Ecumenical Council of Trent. It issued a great number of decrees concerning doctrinal matters opposed by the Reformers, and mobilized the Counter-Reformation. Definitions covered the Canon of the Bible, the rule of faith, the nature of justification, grace, faith, original sin and its effects, the seven sacraments, the sacrificial nature of the Mass, the veneration of saints, use of sacred images, belief in purgatory, the doctrine of indulgences, the jurisdiction of the pope over the whole Church. It initiated many reforms for renewal in the liturgy and general discipline in the Church, the promotion of religious instruction, the education of the clergy through the foundation of seminaries, and other reforms. Trent ranks with Vatican II as the greatest ecumenical council held in the West.

1549: The first Anglican *Book of Common Prayer* was issued by Edward VI. Revised editions were published in 1552, 1559, and 1662, and later.

1553: Start of the five-year reign of Mary Tudor who tried to counteract actions of Henry VIII against the Roman Church.

1555: Enactment of the Peace of Augsburg, an arrangement of religious territorialism rather than toleration, which recognized the existence of Catholicism and Lutheranism in the German Empire and provided that citizens should adopt the religion of their respective rulers.

1558: Beginning of the reign (to 1603) of Queen Elizabeth I of England and Ireland, during which the Church of England took on its definitive form.

1559: Establishment of the hierarchy of the Church of England, with the consecration of Matthew Parker as archbishop of Canterbury.

1563: The first text of the 39 Articles of the Church of England was issued. Also enacted were a new Act of Supremacy and Oath of Succession to the English throne.

1570: Elizabeth I was excommunicated. Penal measures against Catholics subsequently became more severe.

1571: Defeat of the Turkish armada at Lepanto staved off the invasion of Eastern Europe.

1577: The Formula of Concord, the classical statement of Lutheran faith, was issued; it was, generally, a Lutheran counterpart of the canons of the Council of Trent. In 1580, along with other formulas of doctrine, it was included in the Book of Concord.

1582: The Gregorian Calendar, named for Pope Gregory XIII, was put into effect and was eventually adopted in most countries: England delayed adoption until 1752.

SEVENTEENTH CENTURY

1605: The Gunpowder Plot, an attempt by Catholic fanatics to blow up James I of England and the houses of Parliament, resulted in an anti-Catholic Oath of Allegiance.

1610: Death of Matteo Ricci, outstanding Jesuit missionary to China, pioneer in cultural relations between China and Europe.

Founding of the first community of Visitation Nuns by Sts. Francis de Sales and Jane de Chantal.

1611: Founding of the Oratorians.

1613: Catholics banned from Scandinavia.

1625: Founding of the Congregation of the Mission (Vincentians) by St. Vincent de Paul. He founded the Sisters of Charity in 1633.

1642: Death of Galileo, scientist, who was censured by the Congregation of the Holy Office for supporting the Copernican theory of the sun-centered planetary system. The case against him was closed in his favor in 1992.

Founding of the Sulpicians by Jacques Olier.

1643: Start of publication of the Bollandist *Acta Sanctorum*, a critical work on lives of the saints.

1648: Provisions in the Peace of Westphalia, ending the Thirty Years' War, extended terms of the Peace of Augsburg (1555) to Calvinists and gave equality to Catholics and Protestants in the 300 states of the Holy Roman Empire.

1649: Oliver Cromwell invaded Ireland and began a severe persecution of the Church there.

1653: Pope Innocent X condemned five propositions of Jansenism, a complex theory that distorted doctrine concerning the relations between divine grace and human freedom. Jansenism was also a rigoristic movement that seriously disturbed the Church in France, the Low Countries and Italy in this and the 18th century.

1673: The Test Act in England barred from public office Catholics who would not deny the doctrine of transubstantiation and receive Communion in the Church of England.

1678: Many English Catholics suffered death as a consequence of the Popish Plot, a false allegation by Titus Oates that Catholics planned to assassinate Charles II, land a French army in the country, burn London, and turn over the government to the Jesuits.

1682: The four Gallican articles, drawn up by Bossuet, asserted France's political and ecclesiastical immunities from papal control. The articles, which rejected the primacy of the pope, were declared null and void by Pope Alexander VIII in 1690.

1689: The Toleration Act granted a measure of freedom of worship to other English dissenters but not to Catholics.

EIGHTEENTH CENTURY

1704: Chinese Rites — involving the Christian adaptation of elements of Confucianism, veneration of ancestors, and Chinese terminology in religion — were condemned by Clement XI.

1720: The Passionists founded by St. Paul of the Cross.

1724: Persecution in China.

1732: The Redemptorists founded by St. Alphonsus Liguori.

1738: Freemasonry was condemned by Clement XII and Catholics were forbidden to join, under penalty of excommunication; the prohibition was repeated by Benedict XIV in 1751 and by later popes.

1760s: Josephinism, a theory and system of state control of the Church, was initiated in Austria; it remained in force until about 1850.

1764: Febronianism, an unorthodox theory and practice regarding the constitution of the Church and relations between Church and state, was condemned for the first of several times. Proposed by an auxiliary bishop of Trier using the pseudonym Justinus Febronius, it had the effects of minimizing the office of the pope and supporting national churches under state control.

1773: Clement XIV issued a brief of suppression against the Jesuits, following their expulsion from Portugal in 1759, from France in 1764, and from Spain in 1767. Political intrigue and unsubstantiated accusations were principal factors in these developments. The ban, which crippled the society, contained no condemnation of the Jesuit constitutions, particular Jesuits or Jesuit teaching. The society was restored in 1814.

1778: Catholics in England were relieved of some civil disabilities dating back to the time of Henry VIII, by an act which permitted them to acquire, own, and inherit property. Additional liberties were restored by the Roman Catholic Relief Act of 1791 and subsequent enactments of Parliament.

1789: Religious freedom in the United States was

guaranteed under the First Amendment to the Constitution.

Beginning of the French Revolution, which resulted in: the secularization of church property and the Civil Constitution of the Clergy in 1790; the persecution of priests, religious, and lay persons loyal to papal authority; invasion of the Papal States by Napoleon in 1796; renewal of persecution from 1797-1799; attempts to dechristianize France and establish a new religion; the occupation of Rome by French troops and the forced removal of Pius VI to France in 1798.

This century is called the age of Enlightenment or Reason because of the predominating rational and scientific approach of its leading philosophers, scientists, and writers with respect to religion, ethics and natural law. This approach downgraded the fact and significance of revealed religion. Also characteristic of the Enlightenment were subjectivism, secularism, and optimism regarding human perfection.

NINETEENTH CENTURY

1801: Concordat between Napoleon and Pope Pius VII is signed. It is soon violated by the Organic Articles issued by Napoleon in 1802.

1804: Napoleon crowns himself Emperor of the French with Pope Pius in attendance.

1809: Pope Pius VII was made a captive by Napoleon and deported to France, where he remained in exile until 1814. During this time he refused to cooperate with Napoleon, who sought to bring the Church in France under his own control, and other leading cardinals were imprisoned.

The turbulence in church-state relations in France at the beginning of the century recurred in connection with the Bourbon Restoration, the July Revolution, the second and third Republics, the Second Empire, and the Dreyfus case.

1814: The Society of Jesus, suppressed since 1773, was restored.

1817: Reestablishment of the Congregation for the Propagation of the Faith (Propaganda) by Pius VII was an important factor in increasing missionary activity during the century.

1820: Year s-long persecution, during which thousands died for the faith, ended in China. Thereafter, communication with the West remained cut off until about 1834. Vigorous missionary work got under way in 1842.

1822: The Pontifical Society for the Propagation of the Faith, inaugurated in France by Pauline Jaricot for the support of missionary activity, was established.

1829: The Catholic Emancipation Act relieved Catholics in England and Ireland of most of the civil disabilities to which they had been subject from the time of Henry VIII.

1832: Gregory XVI, in the encyclical *Mirari vos*, condemned indifferentism, one of the many ideologies at odds with Christian doctrine that were proposed during the century.

1833: Start of the Oxford Movement which affected the Church of England and resulted in some notable conversions, including that of John Henry Newman in 1845, to the Catholic Church.

Blessed Frederic Ozanam founded the Society of St. Vincent de Paul in France. The Society's objectives are works of charity.

1848: *The Communist Manifesto*, a revolutionary document symptomatic of socio-economic crisis, was issued.

1850: The hierarchy was reestablished in England and Nicholas Wiseman made the first archbishop of Westminster. He was succeeded in 1865 by Henry Manning, an Oxford convert and proponent of the rights of labor.

1853: The Catholic hierarchy was reestablished in Holland.

1854: Pius IX proclaimed the dogma of the Immaculate Conception in the bull *Ineffabilis Deus*.

1858: The Blessed Virgin Mary appeared to St. Bernadette at Lourdes, France.

1864: Pius IX issued the encyclical *Quanta cura* and the *Syllabus of Errors* in condemnation of some 80 propositions derived from the scientific mentality and rationalism of the century. The subjects in question had deep ramifications in many areas of thought and human endeavor; in religion, they explicitly and/or implicitly rejected divine revelation and the supernatural order.

1867: The first volume of *Das Kapital* was published. Together with the Communist First International, formed in the same year, it had great influence on the subsequent development of communism and socialism.

1869: The Anglican Church was disestablished in Ireland.

1869-70: Ecumenical Council of the Vatican (I). It defined papal primacy and infallibility in a dogmatic constitution on the Church; covered natural religion, revelation, faith, and the relations between faith and reason in a dogmatic constitution on the Catholic faith.

1870-71: Victor Emmanuel II of Sardinia, crowned king of Italy after defeating Austrian and papal forces, marched into Rome in 1870 and expropriated the Papal States after a plebiscite in which Catholics, at the order of Pius IX, did not vote. In 1871, Pius IX refused to accept a Law of Guarantees. Confiscation of church property and hindrance of ecclesiastical administration by the regime followed.

1871: The German Empire, a confederation of 26 states, was formed. Government policy launched a *Kulturkampf* whose May Laws of 1873 were designed to annul papal jurisdiction in Prussia and other states and to place the Church under imperial control. Resistance to the enactments and the persecution they legalized forced the government to modify its anti-Church policy by 1887.

1878: Beginning of the pontificate of Leo XIII, who was pope until his death in 1903. Leo is best known for the encyclical *Rerum novarum*, which greatly influenced the course of Christian social thought and the labor movement. His other accomplishments included promotion of Scholastic philosophy and the impetus he gave to scriptural studies.

1881: The first International Eucharistic Congress was held in Lille, France.

Alexander II of Russia was assassinated. His policies of Russification — as well as those of his two predecessors and a successor during the century — caused great suffering to Catholics, Jews, and Protestants in Poland, Lithuania, the Ukraine, and Bessarabia.

1882: Charles Darwin died. His theory of evolution by natural selection, one of several scientific highlights of the century, had extensive repercussions in the faith-and-science controversy.

1887: The Catholic University of America was founded in Washington, DC.

1893: The U.S. apostolic delegation was set up in Washington, D C.

TWENTIETH CENTURY

1901: Restrictive measures in France forced the Jesuits, Benedictines, Carmelites, and other religious orders to leave the country. Subsequently, 14,000 schools were suppressed; religious orders and congregations were expelled; the concordat was renounced in 1905; church property was confiscated in 1906. For some years the Holy See, refusing to comply with government demands for the control of bishops' appointments, left some ecclesiastical offices vacant.

1903-14: Pontificate of St. Pius X. He initiated the codification of canon law, 1904; removed the ban against participation by Catholics in Italian national elections, 1905; issued decrees calling upon the faithful to receive Holy Communion frequently and daily, and stating that children should begin receiving the Eucharist at the age of seven, 1905 and 1910, respectively; ordered the establishment of the Confraternity of Christian Doctrine in all parishes throughout the world, 1905; condemned Modernism in the decree *Lamentabili* and the encyclical *Pascendi*, 1907.

1908: The United States and England, long under the jurisdiction of the Congregation for the Propagation of the Faith as mission territories, were removed from its control and placed under the common law of the Church.

1910: Laws of separation were enacted in Portugal, marking a point of departure in church-state relations.

1911: The Catholic Foreign Mission Society of America — Maryknoll, the first U.S.-founded society of its type — was established.

1914: Start of World War I, which lasted until 1918.

1914-22: Pontificate of Benedict XV. Much of his pontificate was devoted to seeking ways and means of minimizing the material and spiritual havoc of World War I. In 1917 he offered his services as a mediator to the belligerent nations, but his pleas for settlement of the conflict went unheeded.

1917: The Blessed Virgin Mary appeared to three children at Fatima, Portugal.

A new constitution, embodying repressive laws against the Church, was enacted in Mexico. Its implementation resulted in persecution in the 1920s and 1930s.

Bolsheviks seized power in Russia and set up a communist dictatorship. The event marked the rise of communism in Russian and world affairs. One of its immediate, and lasting, results was persecution of the Church, Jews, and other segments of the population.

1918: The Code of Canon Law, in preparation for more than 10 years, went into effect in the Western Church.

1919: Benedict XV stimulated missionary work through the decree *Maximum Illud*, in which he urged the recruiting and training of native clergy in places where the Church was not firmly established.

1920-22: Ireland was partitioned by two enactments of the British government which (1) made the six counties of Northern Ireland part of the United Kingdom in 1920 and (2) gave dominion status to the Irish Free State in 1922. The Irish Free State became an independent republic in 1949.

1922-39: Pontificate of Pius XI. He subscribed to the Lateran Treaty, 1929, which settled the Roman Question created by the confiscation of the Papal States in 1871; issued the encyclical *Casti connubii*, 1930, an authoritative statement on Christian marriage; resisted the efforts of Benito Mussolini to control Catholic Action and the Church, in the encyclical

Non abbiamo bisogno, 1931; opposed various fascist policies; issued the encyclicals *Quadragesimo anno*, 1931, developing the social doctrine of Leo XIII's *Rerum novarum*, and *Divini Redemptoris*, 1937, calling for social justice and condemning atheistic communism; condemned anti-Semitism, 1937.

1926: The Catholic Relief Act repealed virtually all legal disabilities of Catholics in England.

1931: Leftists proclaimed Spain a republic and proceeded to disestablish the Church, confiscate church property, deny salaries to the clergy, expel the Jesuits, and ban teaching of the Catholic faith. These actions were preludes to the civil war of 1936-1939.

1933: Emergence of Adolf Hitler to power in Germany. By 1935 two of his aims were clear: the elimination of the Jews and control of a single national church. Six million Jews were killed in the Holocaust. The Church was subject to repressive measures, which Pius XI protested futilely in the encyclical *Mit brennender sorge* in 1937.

1936-39: Civil war in Spain between the leftist Loyalists and the forces of rightist leader Francisco Franco. The Loyalists were defeated and one-man, one-party rule was established. Many priests, religious, and lay persons fell victim to Loyalist persecution and atrocities.

1939-45: World War II.

1939-58: Pontificate of Pius XII. He condemned communism; proclaimed the dogma of the Assumption of Mary in 1950, in various documents and other enactments provided ideological background for many of the accomplishments of the Second Vatican Council. (See *Twentieth Century Popes*.)

1940: Start of a decade of communist conquest in more than 13 countries, resulting in conditions of persecution for a minimum of 60 million Catholics as well as members of other faiths.

Persecution diminished in Mexico because of non-enforcement of anti-religious laws still on record.

1950: Pius XII proclaimed the dogma of the Assumption of the Blessed Virgin Mary.

1957: The communist regime of China established the Patriotic Association of Chinese Catholics in opposition to the Church in union with the pope.

1958-63: Pontificate of John XXIII. His principal accomplishment was the convocation of the Second Vatican Council, the twenty-first ecumenical council in the history of the Church. (See *Popes of the Twentieth Century*.)

1962-65: Ecumenical Council of the Vatican (II).

It formulated and promulgated 16 documents — two dogmatic and two pastoral constitutions, nine decrees and three declarations — reflecting pastoral orientation toward renewal and reform in the Church, and making explicit the dimensions of doctrine and Christian life requiring emphasis for the full development of the Church and the better accomplishment of its mission in the contemporary world.

1963-78: Pontificate of Paul VI. His main purpose and effort was to give direction and provide guidance for the authentic trends of church renewal set in motion by the Second Vatican Council.

1978: The thirty-four-day pontificate of John Paul I.

Start of the pontificate of John Paul II.

1983: The revised Code of Canon Law, embodying reforms enacted by the Second Vatican Council, went into effect in the Church of Roman Rite.

1985: Formal ratification of a Vatican-Italy concordat replacing the Lateran Treaty of 1929.

1989-91: Decline and fall of communist influence and control in Middle and Eastern Europe and the Soviet Union.

1991: The Code of Canon Law for Eastern Churches went into effect.

The Gulf War was waged to eject Saddam Hussein from Kuwait.

1992: Approval of the new *Catechism of the Catholic Church*.

The Vatican officially closed the case against Galileo Galilei.

1994: Initiation of celebration preparations of the start of the third Christian millennium in the year 2000.

1997: Pope John Paul II issued an apology for any anti-Semitism by Catholics; a conference on anti-Semitism was also held in Rome and a number of Catholic leaders in Europe issued apologies for historical anti-Semitism.

1998: Pope John Paul II visited Cuba and secured the release of over 300 political prisoners.

The Vatican issued a white paper on Anti-Semitism, titled: *We Remember: A Reflection on the Shoah*.

Twentieth anniversary of the pontificate of Pope John Paul II; he became the longest reigning pontiff elected in the 20th century.

2000: The Catholic Church celebrated the Holy Year 2000 and the Jubilee; commencement of the third Christian millennium.

Pope John Paul II traveled to the Holy Land.

ECUMENICAL COUNCILS

An ecumenical council is an assembly of the college of bishops, with and under the presidency of the pope, which has supreme authority over the Church in matters pertaining to faith, morals, worship, and discipline.

The Second Vatican Council stated: "The supreme authority with which this college (of bishops) is empowered over the whole Church is exercised in a solemn way through an ecumenical council. A council is never ecumenical unless it is confirmed or at least accepted as such by the successor of Peter. It is the prerogative of the Roman Pontiff to convoke these councils, to preside over them, and to confirm them" (Dogmatic Constitution on the Church, *Lumen Gentium*, No. 22).

Pope Presides

The pope is the head of an ecumenical council; he presides over it either personally or through legates. Conciliar decrees and other actions have binding force only when confirmed and promulgated by him. If a pope dies during a council, it is suspended until reconvened by another pope. An ecumenical council is not superior to a pope; hence, there is no appeal from a pope to a council.

Collectively, the bishops with the pope represent the whole Church. They do this not as democratic representatives of the faithful in a kind of church parliament, but as the successors of the Apostles with divinely given authority, care, and responsibility over the whole Church.

All and only bishops are council participants with deliberative vote. The supreme authority of the Church can invite others and determine the manner of their participation.

Basic legislation concerning ecumenical councils is contained in Canons 337-41 of the Code of Canon Law. Basic doctrinal considerations were stated by the Second Vatican Council in the Dogmatic Constitution on the Church.

Background

Ecumenical councils had their prototype in the Council of Jerusalem in 51, at which the Apostles under the leadership of St. Peter decided that converts to the Christian faith were not obliged to observe all the prescriptions of Old Testament law (Acts 15). As early as the second century, bishops got together in regional meetings, synods, or councils to take common action for the doctrinal and pastoral good of their communities of faithful. The expansion of such limited assemblies to ecumenical councils was a logical and historical evolution, given the nature and needs of the Church.

Emperors Involved

Emperors were active in summoning or convoking the first eight councils, especially the first five and the eighth. Among reasons for intervention of this kind were the facts that the emperors regarded themselves as guardians of the faith; that the settlement of religious controversies, which had repercussions in political and social turmoil, served the cause of peace in the state; and that the emperors had at their disposal ways and means of facilitating gatherings of bishops. Imperial actions, however, did not account for the formally ecumenical nature of the councils.

Some councils were attended by relatively few bishops, and the ecumenical character of several was open to question for a time. However, confirmation and de facto recognition of their actions by popes and subsequent councils established them as ecumenical.

Role in History

The councils have played a highly significant role in the history of the Church by witnessing to and defining truths of revelation, by shaping forms of worship, and discipline, and by promoting measures for the ever-necessary reform and renewal of Catholic life. In general, they have represented attempts of the Church to mobilize itself in times of crisis for self-preservation, self-purification, and growth.

The first eight ecumenical councils were held in the East; the other 13 in the West. The majority of separated Eastern Churches — e.g., the Orthodox — recognize the ecumenical character of the first seven councils, which formulated a great deal of basic doctrine. Other separated Eastern Churches acknowledge only the first two or three ecumenical councils.

The 21 Councils

The 21 ecumenical councils in the history of the Church are listed below, with indication of their names or titles (taken from the names of the places where they were held); the dates; the reigning and/or approving popes; the emperors who were instrumental in convoking the eight councils in the East; the number of bishops who attended, when available; the number of sessions. Significant actions of the first 20 councils are indicated under appropriate dates in Dates and Events in Church History.

1. **Nicaea I**, 325: A council convened by Emperor Constantine the Great (d. 337) with the principal aim of resolving the Arian Controversy. Recognizing that Arianism had created a major storm in the eastern half of the Roman Empire, Constantine decided not to leave the matter in the hands of local Church councils but to summon bishops from all over. While advice was prob-

ably given by Hosius, bishop of Córdoba (Cordova), Constantine was most responsible for organizing the council, including the generous gesture of granting free transportation for the bishops who were attending. The site chosen was the imperial summer palace at Nicaea, on the Bosporus, in Bithynia. It was attended by over three hundred bishops, although the names of only two hundred twenty are known. The main Western representatives, besides Hosius, were the bishops of Milan, Dijon, and Carthage and the two papal delegates on behalf of Pope Sylvester I (r. 314-335). The traditionally accepted date for the start was May 20, 325. It went on until the end of August. The president was probably Bishop Hosius, although some historians argue that it may have been Eustathius, bishop of Antioch.

After a brief opening statement by Constantine, the Council Fathers set to work. It would appear that a creed of Arian disposition was proposed by Eusebius of Nicomedia and rejected; Eusebius of Caesarea then offered his own. With the insertion of the term *homoousios* this was adopted, although this was not the creed finally promulgated. Only two bishops, Theonas of Marmarica and Secundus of Ptolemais, refused to subscribe to the Nicene Creed and its anti-Arian anathemas, and both were deposed. The council then dealt with other pressing topics, including a resolution of the Melitian Schism and the fixing of the date of Easter for the Churches in the East and West (thus ending the Paschal Controversy), and the readmission of the Novatianists and Paulinians (followers of Paul of Samosata) to the Church. Privileges were also accorded to the sees of Alexandria, Antioch, and Jerusalem. While the council was supposed to bring a close to the Arian Controversy, this hope proved fleeting; the crisis would continue throughout the fourth century. Unfortunately, the acta of the council are lost. The only extant documents are the twenty canons it issued, the creed, and the synodal letter.

2. **Constantinople I**, 381: Convened by Emperor Theodosius I, this council sought to bring a sense of unity back to the Eastern Church after the divisiveness of the Arian Controversy. It was attended by one hundred fifty bishops under the presidency of Melitius, bishop of Antioch. It ratified the work of the Council of Nicaea (325) concerning the Nicene Creed and the doctrine of Christ, condemned Apollinarianism, and granted to Constantinople precedence over all churches save Rome. It is counted as the second ecumenical council.

3. **Ephesus**, 431: Held with the aim of bringing an end to the crises caused by Nestorianism. The specific cause for the need of the council had been the power granted St. Cyril of Alexandria in

August 430 by Pope St. Celestine I to excommunicate Nestorius, bishop of Constantinople, should he not recant his heretical position that there were two separate Persons in Christ, the divine and the human. Using his influence to prevent his immediate condemnation, Nestorius convinced Emperor Theodosius II to summon a general council. Organized with the full approval of the pope and under the presidency of Cyril, the council convened on June 22, 431, at Ephesus. In attendance were some two hundred bishops. Celestine was to be represented by two legates, Bishops Projectus and Arcadius, and the Roman priest Philip; but Cyril did not wait for their arrival before beginning the proceedings, nor did he delay for very long while awaiting the Syrian bishops under John, patriarch of Antioch, whom Cyril knew to be favorably disposed to Nestorius. Acting with the full authority as president and "as filling the place of the most holy blessed archbishop of the Roman Church, Celestine," Cyril maneuvered the majority of bishops into condemning Nestorius. The heresiarch was excommunicated and deposed, his doctrines formally condemned, and the Nicene Creed upheld.

The Eastern bishops, who had arrived and were immediately at odds with the council, were soon joined by a number of prelates, such as Theodoret, bishop of Cyrrhus, also unhappy with Cyril's driving the deliberations to such a precipitate conclusion. The rival bishops held their own council at which Cyril was excommunicated. Protracted negotiations followed, resulting in a compromise in 433 that brought a reconciliation between Cyril and John. Ephesus, however, had been a triumph for Orthodox Christianity. Through its seven sessions, Nestorianism had been clearly defeated in favor of Alexandrian theology, especially with the definition of the hypostatic union and the endorsement of the Marian title Theotokos, or Bearer of God.

4. **Chalcedon**, 451: Held from October 8 to November 1, 451, in the town of Chalcedon, in Asia Minor, just outside Constantinople. A major council in the history of Christology, it asserted once and for all the orthodox doctrine concerning the nature of Christ, namely that he is one Person with two distinct natures, divine and human; it brought to an end furious theological debate and controversy that had raged for much of the fifth century. In specific terms, the Council of Chalcedon was convened by Emperor Marcian to deal with the pressing crisis of the Eutychian heresy. The heresy argued that Christ had two natures but that these were so intimately connected that they became one, thereby resulting in the human nature being absorbed by the divine. The chief spokesman for this was Eutyches, the archimandrite of a monastery just

outside of Constantinople. He was soon opposed by orthodox theologians, and there ensued a bitter controversy, exacerbated by the Second Council of Ephesus (449), the Latrocinium (or Robber) Council, which was manipulated by Dioscorus, patriarch of Alexandria, who restored Eutyches, deposing Flavian, the patriarch of Constantinople, and refusing to allow the reading of the *Epistola Dogmatica* by Pope St. Leo I, the so-called Tome of Leo, elucidating the orthodox doctrine on the Incarnation. While condemned by the pope and opposed by most of the Church, the work of the Latrocinium stood unrepealed as long as Theodosius II, a patron of Eutyches, sat on the imperial throne. His sudden death in July 450, however, changed the complexion of the situation, as his sister Pulcheria succeeded him, marrying Marcian (r. 450-457); both were enemies of Eutyches and Dioscorus and thus sent to Pope Leo their approval for a new council to address the heresy.

The council opened at Chalcedon on October 8. In attendance were approximately 600 bishops (according to Pope Leo; other sources say 520 or even 630). All were from the East save for two who had come from Africa and the two papal legates, Boniface and Paschasinus, bishop of Lilybaeum (who also presided). The sessions were held in the Church of St. Euphemia, Martyr, directly opposite Constantinople. The work of the council was clear from the start and resulted in a complete triumph for the orthodox position. The decrees of the Latrocinium were annulled, Eutyches was condemned, Dioscorus deposed, and the Tome of Leo given full approval; the council delegates said of the epistle: "This is the faith of the Fathers and of the Apostles. This we all believe. Peter has spoken through Leo . . . anathema to him who teaches otherwise. . . ." In the fifth session (October 22), a formula or definition of dogma was written to make absolutely clear in a statement of faith: "One and the same Christ, Son, Lord, Only-begotten, known in two natures, without confusion, without change, without division, without separation." All of the canons were acceptable to the pope except for Canon 28, which proclaimed the see of Constantinople to be a patriarchate second only to Rome. Initially opposed by papal legates, the canon was rejected by Leo on the grounds that it was an insult to the older patriarchates; there were also political considerations involved, as the see of Constantinople had long harbored ambitions of eventual equal status with Rome.

5. **Constantinople II**, 553: Summoned by Emperor Justinian I, it was attended by 165 bishops under the presidency of Eutychius, patriarch of Constantinople. The council condemned Nestorianism; it also condemned the Three Chapters and anathematized their authors, and, because of Justinian's poor treatment of Pope Vigilius, it was not immediately recognized as an ecumenical council in the West.

6. **Constantinople III**, 680-681: Convoked by Emperor Constantine IV Pogonatos, it was intended to settle the Monothelite controversy in the Eastern Church. Attended by some 160 bishops, the council condemned Monothelitism, anathematized its leaders, and issued a dogmatic decree on the subject, essentially a reaffirmation of the declarations of the Council of Chalcedon (451) concerning the two natures of Christ.

7. **Nicaea II**, 787: Convened by Empress Irene in order to resolve the Iconoclastic Controversy. The proceedings were launched by the Byzantine empress at the behest of Tarasius, patriarch of Constantinople, who, at his election in December 784, had declared his request for a council. Both Empress Irene and Tarasius wrote to Pope Adrian I (r. 772-795) asking his support in the summoning of a council. He responded affirmatively and promised to send two legates, with the proviso that the false council of 753 be condemned – the Iconoclast Synod of Hieria.

On August 17, 786, the bishops gathered at the Church of the Apostles in Constantinople. They were soon dispersed, however, by an uprising of the Iconoclasts, assisted by some members of the army. Empress Irene suppressed the revolt, and the next year, on September 27, 787, with Tarasius presiding, the council finally met, in the church of St. Sophia in Nicaea. The patriarchs of Alexandria and Jerusalem could not attend, but their representatives proclaimed their full support of the condemnation of the Iconoclasts. Adrian's letter to Irene and Tarasius was read, and the council promulgated a decree stating that various kinds of images could be set up, but they were to be given veneration or honor and not worshiped, since the act of worship belongs only to God. The Iconoclasts were then condemned. There were also twenty-two disciplinary canons concerned with the clerical life of simplicity and diocesan administration.

8. **Constantinople IV**, 869-870: A council not recognized by the Eastern Church, convened by Emperor Basil I, and attended by over a hundred bishops. The council excommunicated Photius, patriarch of Constantinople, and restored St. Ignatius as the legal patriarch. The event was an important episode in the widening gulf between the Eastern and Western Churches. The Eastern Orthodox Church recognizes instead the council of 880 that supported Photius in his claims.

9. **Lateran I**, 1123: Summoned by Pope Callistus II to confirm the Concordat of Worms and thereby end the Investiture Controversy. The

council also promulgated twenty-two disciplinary canons.

10. **Lateran II**, 1139: Convened by Pope Innocent II to condemn the antipope Anacletus II and the followers of Arnold of Brescia after the schism that occurred with Innocent's election.

11. **Lateran III**, 1179: Convoked by Pope Alexander III to extirpate all trace of the schism of the antipope Callistus III. Most importantly, the council promulgated a decree concerning papal elections that provided for the election of the pope by the College of Cardinals, with a two-thirds majority required. A treaty with Frederick I Barbarossa was ratified and each bishopric was required to conduct a school for clerics.

12. **Lateran IV**, 1215: Convened by Pope Innocent III, considered one of the most important Church assemblies before the Council of Trent. Among its declarations were annual confession, a definition of the doctrine of transubstantiation, Communion during the Easter season, condemnation of the Cathars and Waldenses, and the requiring of Muslims and Jews to wear specific attire.

13. **Lyons I**, 1245: Summoned by Pope Innocent IV to address a number of problems facing the Church. This included the continued schism with the Byzantines, the invasion of Hungary by the Mongols (Tatars), the decline of morality among the clergy, and the troubled relations between the popes and Emperor Frederick II. The emperor was deposed by the council, an act that was based on four charges: sacrilege, disturbing the peace, suspicion of heresy, and perjury.

14. **Lyons II**, 1274: Convoked by Pope Gregory X to bring moral reform and a desired union of the Eastern and Western Churches. The main achievement of the council was the acceptance by the Byzantine delegates of Emperor Michael VIII Palaeologus of the supremacy of the pope and the articles of faith of the Western Churches. The union proved short-lived, however, as another rupture took place in 1289. Among those in attendance were 500 bishops and such notables as St. Bonaventure, St. Albertus Magnus, and Peter of Tarentaise (the future Innocent VI). St. Thomas Aquinas died en route to the council.

15. **Vienne**, 1311-1312: Held in Vienne, France, under Pope Clement V (r. 1305-1314). The council was summoned by the bull *Regnans in coelis* (1308) with the declared purpose of "making provision in regard to the Order of Knights Templar, both the individual members and its leaders, and in regard to other things in reference to the Catholic faith, the Holy Land, and the improvement of the Church and of ecclesiastical persons." The Templars were specifically commended to provide *defensores* (legal defense) and for the grand master (Jacques de Molay) to appear with all suitable officials from the order. Owing to the matter of the appeal of King Philip IV the Fair of France (r. 1285-1314) concerning his treatment of Pope Boniface VIII (r. 1294-1303), Clement postponed convening the council until October 16, 1311, when the first session was opened in the Cathedral of Vienne. At the opening, Clement restated his agenda: the controversy of the Templars (who were being accused of various crimes, especially by Philip, who coveted their wealth), aid to the Holy Land, and Church reform.

The commission charged with examining the case against the knights reached the conclusion that the Templars could not be condemned on the basis of the evidence and should thus be allowed to defend themselves. This was, of course, unsatisfactory to King Philip, who applied pressure on Clement, a pontiff residing at Avignon. To demonstrate his resolve, Philip appeared before the gate of Vienne in February 1312 to demand the suppression of the Templars. Clement yielded, issuing the bull of suppression *Vox clamantis* (March 22, 1312), which was promulgated at the second session, held on April 5. At the third session, convened on May 6, a letter from Philip was read in which he promised to go on a crusade within six years. A tithe was to be laid for the undertaking; in France, the money went to Philip, who used it for his war against Flanders. As it was, he never set sail and no crusade was ever launched. The council also issued a large number of decrees on the administration of the Inquisition, the question of Franciscan poverty, the Beguines, the observance of ecclesiastical hours, and various topics related to the clergy. These decrees were gathered together by Pope John XXII and issued on October 25, 1317; with the decrees not promulgated by Clement owing to his death in 1314, they were published in the *Clementiniae*.

16. **Constance**, 1414-1418: Held in forty-five sessions, ending the Great Schism that had divided the Church since 1378. Convened by the antipope John XXIII at the insistence of Emperor Sigismund, the council marked the high point of the conciliar movement and has been the subject of intense discussion concerning its legality and activities. The main purpose of the council was to bring about a solution to the division of the papacy into three camps, representing three papal claimants: Antipope John XXIII in Pisa, Antipope Benedict XIII in Avignon, and Pope Gregory XII in Rome. After a dispute arose over the procedures to be used for voting, a compromise was worked out by the cardinals by which one vote was given to the delegations from Italy,

England, France, Germany, and eventually Spain, while one vote was given to those cardinals acting together as a group. As deliberations proceeded, John, who had hoped to come out of the council as the only pontiff, grew increasingly concerned by the apparent willingness to remove all three popes and elect a new one for the entire Church. Scheming to force a legal end to the proceedings, John fled, but the council continued, urged on by Sigismund. John was deposed in May 1415, Gregory was convinced in July to resign, and, finally, in July 1417, Benedict was removed after months of diplomatic and political haggling. Oddone Colonna was then elected Pope Martin V in November, thereby ending the Great Schism.

Under the influence of Sigismund, the council issued the decree Sacrosancta, asserting the authority of the general council over the entire Church, including the papacy. The decree Frequens was passed to make frequent councils desirable by declaring that they were crucial for the good of the Church. Both decrees were hotly debated in the succeeding centuries and would prove ineffectual as the spirit and influence of conciliarism declined. The council also tried, convicted, and executed Jan Hus for heresy, condemned John Wycliffe, and attempted to institute other reforms.

17. **Florence** (also called Basel-Ferrara-Florence), 1431-c. 1445: Held at Ferrara and Florence, and also at Rome. Aside from the discussion of important doctrinal matters, the council had as its principal aim the possible reunion of the Eastern and Western Churches. While technically a continuation of the Council of Basel (convened in 1431) and held supposedly under the influence of conciliar ideas, Ferrara-Florence proved a major triumph for the papacy against the conciliar movement. The impetus for the discussions of reunion was given by the need of the Byzantines for assistance from the West against the Ottoman Turks, who were menacing Constantinople. In order to accommodate the large delegation (including Emperor John VIII Palaeologus, the patriarch of Constantinople, Joseph, and some 700 other Greek theologians and prelates), Pope Eugenius IV ordered the members of the Council of Basel to travel to Ferrara. Only those adherents of the pope agreed to go, but the council opened on January 8, 1438, with Eugenius in attendance, along with such notables as Cardinals Giuliano Cesarini and John Bessarion. Plague broke out in the city and, with the Florentines agreeing to pay the cost of the proceedings, Eugenius moved the council to Florence on January 10, 1439.

Long, protracted negotiations followed, resulting in July 1439 in an agreement by which a reunion was at last reached. The Eastern Church agreed to the basic tenets of Western doctrine, most importantly the *Filioque*, as well as the theological points of purgatory and the Eucharist. Further, Eugenius won recognition of papal primacy and was thus able to issue the bull *Laetentur Coeli*, which was signed on July 5, 1439, with only one Eastern prelate, Mark Eugenicus, metropolitan of Ephesus, dissenting. After the Greeks returned home, the council stayed in session to work toward reunion with the other schismatic Churches of the East and to resolve the schism that had erupted over the rump Council of Basel. Reunion was achieved with the Armenians and the Copts, and a little later with the Syrians and Chaldaeans. The recalcitrant members of the Council of Basel were excommunicated, and in the bull *Etsi non dubitemus* (April 20, 1441), Eugenius proclaimed his authority over the general council. From 1443, the council convened at Rome. Quite unpopular with the people of Constantinople, the reunion was soon repudiated by many of the Eastern bishops, dissatisfaction with the agreement only increasing as it became clear that no aid from the West was forthcoming. In 1453, Constantinople fell to the Turks, effectively ending the unity of Christendom.

18. **Lateran V**, 1512-1517: Summoned by Pope Julius II in response to the antipapal council summoned in Pisa by a number of cardinals opposed to Julius and through the influence of King Louis XII of France. The decrees of the Pisan Council were invalidated and a number of reforms were launched.

19. **Trent**, 1545-1563: The Council of Trent was one of the most important general councils in the history of the Church. The council had as its aims the refutation of the errors of the Protestant Reformers (Martin Luther, Huldrych Zwingli, and John Calvin), the clarification of Catholic teaching in the wake of the spread of Protestant teaching, and the advancing of authentic and genuinely needed reform for the entire Church. While Pope Clement VII (r. 1523-1534) had considered summoning a general council to deal with the crises of the moment, the pontiff had ultimately decided against it in order to prevent any possible outbreak of conciliarism and owing to the nationalist tendencies in Germany and the chronic warfare between Francis I of France and Emperor Charles V. The decision to convene a general council came under Pope Paul III (r. 1534-1549), part of his ambitious program to reform the Church. He declared in June 1536 that it should be held in Mantua, but Duke Federigo of Mantua refused to allow his city to be the site and, citing the war between Francis and Charles, he placed so many restrictions and demands on the pope that Paul moved the site in October 1537 to Vicenza. Fur-

ther obstacles were thrown before the pope by the Protestant princes who refused to send delegates. Paul thus adjourned the council on May 22, 1539. Exactly three years later, he summoned the council at Trent. This was now unacceptable to Francis, as the town was in the empire (now Italy). Only with the Peace of Crepy of 1544, ending the conflict between Francis and Charles, did the monarch agree (in a secret clause) to the Council of Trent.

Paul issued the bull *Laetare Jerusalem* (1544), formally summoning the council. It opened on December 13, 1545. While not ended until 1563, the council was to be plagued by constant delays and interruptions, a testament to the unsettled political state of affairs in Europe. The work was not continuous but took place in three periods: 1545-1547, 1551-1552, and 1562-1563. In all, there were twenty-five sessions in the three respective periods: Sessions I-VIII, Sessions IX-XIV, and Sessions XV-XXV.

The first session was attended by thirty Council Fathers, with three papal legates, Reginald Pole, Marcello Cervini, and Giovanni del Monte. It established the system by which the numerous doctrinal decrees would be promulgated in the form of treatises comprised of chapters and followed by a set of canons. Attached to the chapters, the canons were aimed specifically at refuting and condemning the errors of the Protestant Reformers. The first period wound down with the decision of some of the members to move to Bologna, ostensibly because of an outbreak of spotted fever in Trent but also to cut short any efforts by Emperor Charles to influence the proceedings. They were opposed by both Paul III and a minority of Spanish and other imperial cardinals. Paul struggled to bring the cardinals back to Trent, finally winning a compromise that no decrees should be issued by them. Active deliberations ended in February 1548. In November 1549, Paul suspended the council and died on November 10, 1549.

The second period, 1551-1552, was begun by Pope Julius III (r. 1550-1555) on November 14, 1550. Officially opened on May 1, 1551, it was under the presidency of Sebastiano Pighino and Luigi Lippomani and with the legate Marcello Crescenzio. It was handicapped by the absence of French bishops who acquiesced to the wishes of King Henry II of France. Present at the council were representatives of the Protestant princes who negotiated unsuccessfully with the Council Fathers and departed in 1552 when fighting erupted afresh in Germany between Protestant princes and Emperor Charles V. Pope Julius suspended the proceedings on April 28, 1552.

Eight years passed before the council could reconvene at the behest of Pope Pius IV (r. 1559-1565). The impetus for his call in November 1560 for the council to reconvene its work was the sudden rise of Calvinism in France. Both the new emperor, Ferdinand I, and King Charles IX of France opposed the pope's decision to continue the council, preferring to have him open a new one, since their Protestant leaders adamantly refused to acknowledge the first two periods of the Council at Trent. The council – which opened on January 18, 1562, under the presence of the papal legates Stanislaus Hosius, Girolamo Seripando, Giacomo Simonetta, and Ercole Gonzaga – was clear in its recognition that reconciliation with the Protestants was impossible. It was also much influenced by the Jesuits, whose theologians enjoyed a prominent place in the deliberations.

The council was closed solemnly on December 4, 1563, after the twenty-fifth session. The decrees were signed by the Council Fathers, including six cardinals, three patriarchs, twenty-five archbishops, and 169 bishops. These were given confirmation by Pope Pius IV on January 26, 1564, in the bull *Benedictus Deus*. The pope also published his famous creed, the *Professio Fidei Tridentina* (the Profession of the Tridentine Faith).

Of the twenty-five sessions of Trent, seventeen were concerned specifically with doctrine and reform. Among the important decrees promulgated by the council were: the two primary sources for revelation are the Scriptures and Tradition; justification is achieved by man's free cooperation with God's grace through faith, hope, charity, and good works; grace is granted to all and is not lost by mortal sin, although it is forced out by infidelity; there are seven sacraments, which produce their effect independent of faith and the virtue of the minister; the Eucharist is a true sacrament and Christ is present whole and entire under both species, bread and wine, and in each part of both species; the bread and wine are changed entirely into the substance of Christ's body and blood, with only the appearance of bread and wine remaining; and Mass is a true sacrifice. Among the disciplinary decrees were: the pope has the choice of bishops and cardinals; bishops, cardinals, archbishops, and patriarchs should reside in their dioceses; bishops are to visit parishes and take an interest in the welfare of all the souls of the faithful; pastors should be appointed only after consideration of qualifications and with the approval of the bishop; seminaries should be established in every diocese or region; secret marriages are prohibited; the Index of Forbidden Books should be revised; and members of religious orders should reside in their houses and follow their rules and vows.

The Council of Trent had a major impact upon the Church. It reaffirmed the teachings of the Catholic faith, bolstering and reviving Catholicism after serious crises and doubts had spread among the faithful as a result of the Reformation and its destructive wars. The Church also underwent a marked reform and renewal through discipline, the Roman Catechism of 1566, and the reformed missal of 1570. While the council failed in reconciling the Protestants, it left the Church significantly stronger in the years and even centuries to come when dealing with Protestantism and the social, political, and intellectual movements that would emerge across Europe.

20. **Vatican I**, 1869-1870: Convened by Pope Pius IX (r. 1846-1878), it was held between December 8, 1869, and September 1, 1870. Owing to the seizure of Rome by the troops of King Victor Emmanuel II, the council was adjourned by the pope indefinitely; it was never officially ended and never reconvened. The council was best known for two achievements: the dogmatic constitutions *Dei Filius* and *Pastor Aeternus*, the latter giving definition to papal infallibility.

Pope Pius recognized the desirability of holding a council. There had not been one since Trent (1545-1563), and the world had changed immeasurably in the intervening years. Further, the Church was confronted with the rise of liberalism, rationalism, and wide regard for sciences that many felt were dangers to the faith because of their promotion of rationalist criticism of Catholic doctrine and Scripture, religious indifference, hostility to many Christian tenets, and the questioning of the place of the Church in the modern world. A council was also desired to strengthen the authority and prestige of the papacy in the wake of the demise of the Papal States in 1860 by the Italians under Victor Emmanuel and the virtual extirpation of the centuries-old temporal power of the Holy See.

The announcement of his intention to summon a council was made by Pius to the cardinals of the Curia on December 4, 1864, two days before the publication of the Syllabus of Errors. In March 1865, Pius appointed a preparatory commission. The formal announcement of a council was made on June 29, 1867, and exactly one year later the pope issued the bull *Aeterni Patris*, which convoked the council. The opening at St. Peter's Basilica had about 700 prelates, assorted officials, and dignitaries; interestingly, this was the first council that did not send invitations to ambassadors and princes.

The first of the council's assemblies (called general congregations) was convened on December 10, 1869. Later that month, deliberations commenced on the dogmatic constitution on the faith. After spirited discussions and revisions, it was approved by final vote on April 24, 1870. *Dei Filius* was a profound reaffirmation of the teachings of the Church. Its chapters were concerned with: God as Creator; revelation; faith; and faith and reason — with attached canons to clarify important points and to condemn those who denied certain aspects of the faith (fideists, rationalists, naturalists, etc.). It vindicated human reason as sufficient to know God without revelation, stressed the reasonableness of faith, and elucidated the presence of the two kinds of knowledge, faith and reason.

While the question of infallibility was not specifically on Pius's planned list of topics, it was uppermost in the minds of many Fathers owing to the aspirations of the Ultramontanists to have it advanced and the concern of liberal Catholics that it should not be defined. In the period prior to the council, the matter had been the source of often bitter debate. The question was formally raised in January 1870 with a series of petitions supported by some 500 Council Fathers in favor of giving papal infallibility definition. The debate continued for several months, ending on July 4. Finally, on July 18, the fourth session gave solemn definition of the primacy and infallible authority of the Roman pontiff in the *Constitutio Dogmatica Prima de Ecclesia Christi* (First Dogmatic Constitution on the Church of Christ).

The majority of the Council Fathers departed the hot city of Rome for the summer, reassembling in late August. The last (eighty-ninth) general congregation was convened on September 1. One week later, Italian troops pushed across the papal frontier and moved against Rome, which fell on September 20. The papal lands had been left virtually defenseless when French protecting troops had departed the Eternal City with the start of the Franco-Prussian War. Pius suspended the council and it did not reassemble. When Pope John XXIII (r. 1958-1963) considered calling his own council, it was suggested to him that he simply reconvene the First Vatican Council; he chose to start a new one.

21. Vatican Council II

The Second Vatican Council, which was forecast by Pope John XXIII on January 25, 1959, was held in four sessions in St. Peter's Basilica. Pope John convoked it and opened the first session, which ran from October 11 to December 8, 1962. Following John's death on June 3, 1963, Pope Paul VI reconvened the council for the other three sessions which ran from September 29 to December 4, 1963; September 14 to November 21, 1964; September 14 to December 8, 1965.

Vatican II was only the second such assembly since the Council of Trent (1545-1563), the other being Vatican Council I (1869-1870). While a council had been considered by Pope Pius XII (r. 1939-1958), it had not come to any kind of fruition beyond the recognition of many in the Church that a council might be desirable to address the challenges confronting the faith in the radically changed world following the global conflict of World War II. It was Pius's successor, John XXIII (r. 1958-1963), who is given singular credit for deciding to summon another ecumenical gathering. That pontiff claimed the idea was the inspiration of the Holy Spirit. At first discouraged in the undertaking by members of the Curia, he persisted and, despite knowing that his health might not permit him to see its end, John gave the order for preparations to commence.

On May 16, 1959, Cardinal Domenico Tardini was appointed the head of the first preparatory commission with the task of consulting with the prelates of the Church throughout the globe and the esteemed theologians of the Catholic universities. On June 29, Pope John issued the encyclical *Ad Petri cathedram* in which he gave formal explanation of the purpose of the council. The next year, he wrote the *motu proprio Superno Dei nutu* (June 5, 1960), by which he announced the appointment of a preparatory commission and other ancillary and subordinate commissions and secretariats. John himself headed the central commission and appointed curial cardinals to preside over the others; the one exception was the Secretariat on Communications Media, under Archbishop Martin O'Connor, rector of the North American College (1946-1964, later nuncio to Malta, 1965-1969, and head of the Pontifical Commission for Social Communication, 1964-1969).

These commissions initiated their work in November 1960 and were finished in June 1962. The previous year, on Christmas Day, John published the apostolic constitution *Humanae salutis*, instructing the council to begin in 1962. By the *motu proprio Concilium* (February 2, 1962), he placed the opening of the proceedings at October 2, 1962. After commending the assembly to the protection of St. Joseph, on July 1, 1962, he asked all Catholics to do penance in anticipation of the work of the Council Fathers through the encyclical *Paenitentiam agere*.

John had as his stated goals the renewal of the Church and its modernization to facilitate the accomplishment of its mission in the modern world and thereby to foster the unity of all Christians. He used the term *aggiornamento* (updating) to describe the aim of his program and hopes. At the opening session (October 11), attended by 2,540 prelates, the pope stressed the distinctly positive nature of his call.

The council was given its organization by the *motu proprio Appropinquante concilio* (August 2, 1962). There were to be three types of meetings: commissions of twenty-four members; general congregations where first votes and discussions would be held; and public sessions, headed by the pope, at which final votes on the assorted documents would be taken. The commissions and secretariats were: Doctrinal Commission for the Faith and Morals; Commission for the Eastern Churches; Commission for the Discipline of the Sacraments; Commission for the Discipline of the Clergy and Christian People; Commission for Religious; Commission for the Missions; Commission for the Liturgy; Commission for Seminaries, Studies, and Catholic Schools; Commission for the Apostolate of the Laity, Press, and Entertainment; and Secretariat for the Promotion of Christian Unity.

The work of the council was carried out in four sessions: Session I (October 11-December 8, 1962), Session II (September 29-December 4, 1963), Session III (September 14-November 21, 1964), and Session IV (September 14-December 8, 1965). At the first congregation of December 13, 1962, in Session I, two cardinals, Joseph Frings of Cologne and Achille Liénart of Lille, requested that the Council Fathers should adjourn until December 16 so as to familiarize themselves with possible candidates for the commissions and be granted the right to choose their own commission members instead of the ones picked by the Curia. This move, approved by John, significantly altered the atmosphere, proceedings, and direction of the commissions and the council itself.

After the close of the first session, the remaining deliberations were presided over by a new pontiff. Increasingly ill, John had attended the last meeting of the session with difficulty. His health deteriorated over the early part of 1963, and he died on June 3.

In the resulting conclave, the cardinals chose Cardinal Giovanni Montini, archbishop of Milan, on June 21, 1963, Pope Paul VI. Montini had been a clear favorite on entering the conclave and had been used extensively by John in the preparation for the council. Besides being considered the chosen successor of John, Montini also clearly desired to continue the council in the Johannine tradition (although he later confessed that he would not have summoned a council on his own). His eulogy of Pope John – declaring that the council must continue on the path chosen by John – and his own statements of approval were said by many observers to have been critical to his election.

Work resumed on September 29, 1963, and the sessions went on for two years. The result was embodied in the sixteen documents promulgated by the council, two dogmatic and two pastoral constitutions (the heart of the reforms), nine decrees, and three declarations. Pope Paul solemnly closed the council on December 8, 1965. Since that time, the Church has been faced with the major challenge in implementing the reforms and processes of modernization while maintaining Tradition and interpreting in an authentic way both the specific commands and the spirit of the council. Toward that end, both Popes Paul VI and John Paul II have issued hundreds of decrees and statements on the proper interpretation of its acts and decrees. John Paul II has been a determined champion of the authentic meaning of Vatican II and has warned against interpretations that fail to consider the continuity of Tradition or de-emphasize or even denigrate the preconciliar Church.

Documents of Vatican Council II

Lumen Gentium (Dogmatic Constitution on the Church), November 21, 1964: One of the two dogmatic constitutions published by the council (with *Dei Verbum*), it is to be distinguished from the "Pastoral Constitution on the Church in the Modern World" (*Gaudium et Spes*), released on December 7, 1965, whose purpose is to make clear the nature of the Church as "a sacramental sign and an instrument of intimate union with God, and of the unity of all mankind" (No. 42). *Lumen Gentium* (Latin for "Light of the Nations") is organized into a number of chapters, from "The Mystery of the Church" to "The Role of the Blessed Virgin Mary, Mother of God, in the Mystery of Christ and the Church." To the conciliar document was added a "Prefatory Note of Explanation" at the order of Pope Paul VI. Its aim is to give additional clarification on collegiality by reemphasizing the essential requirement of communion with and dependence on the Bishop of Rome for the full exercise of authority by the bishops. Additional interpretation was given by a number of postconciliar documents, including *Ministeria Quaedam* (1973), the declaration of the Congregation for the Faith *Mysterium Ecclesiae* (1973), and *Ad Pascendum* (1973).

Dei Verbum (Dogmatic Constitution on Divine Revelation), November 18, 1965: Its focus is on the nature of divine revelation, its transmission, inspiration, and interpretation, and the place of Scripture in the life of the Church. *Dei Verbum* is generally considered to be a successor or complimentary document to the "Dogmatic Constitution on Catholic Faith," *Dei Filius*, that had been issued by Vatican Council I (1869-1870). It is divided into the following related categories: Revelation, Transmission or Revelation, Inspiration

and Interpretation, the Old Testament, the New Testament, and Scripture in Church Life.

God chose to give to humanity a fundamental revelation of himself and to make known to us the hidden purpose of his will (or the mystery of his will).

In examining the transmission of revelation, *Dei Verbum* observes that "Christ the Lord, in whom the full revelation of the supreme God is brought to completion. . . , commissioned the apostles to preach to all men that gospel which is the source of all saving truth and moral teaching, . . . But in order to keep the gospel forever whole and alive within the Church, the apostles left bishops as their successors, 'handing over their own teaching role' to them. This sacred tradition, therefore, and sacred Scripture of both the Old and New Testament are like a mirror in which the pilgrim Church on earth looks at God" (No. 7).

The "Dogmatic Constitution on Divine Revelation" (Nos. 9, 10) then traces the development of doctrine, elaborating upon the "close connection and communication between sacred tradition and sacred Scripture," which "form one sacred deposit of the word of God, which is committed to the Church." It adds, however, the important element of the magisterium, the teaching authority of the Church, declaring that all three – Sacred Scripture, Sacred Tradition, and the Magisterium – "are so linked and joined together that one cannot stand without the others, and that all together and each in its own way under the action of the one Holy Spirit contribute effectively to the salvation of souls."

In examining both inspiration and interpretation, *Dei Verbum* states that "Holy Mother Church, relying on the belief of the apostles, holds that the books of both the Old and New Testament in their entirety, with all their parts, are sacred and canonical because, having been written under the inspiration of the Holy Spirit . . . they have God as their author and have been handed on as such to the Church herself" (No. 11). It then studies the questions of inerrancy, literary forms, and the analogy of faith.

Both the Old and New Testaments are given their place in the "planning and preparing the salvation of the whole human race" (No. 14). The Old Testament is described as having as its primary purpose "to prepare for the coming both of Christ, the universal Redeemer, and of the messianic kingdom, . . . the books of the Old Testament with all their parts, caught up into the proclamation of the gospel, acquire and show forth their full meaning in the New Testament" (Nos. 15, 16). The New Testament, written under the inspiration of the Holy Spirit, gives confirmation of "those matters which concern Christ the Lord" and "His true teaching is more and more fully stated, the saving power of the divine work of Christ is preached, the story is told of the beginnings of the Church and her marvelous growth, and her glorious fulfillment is foretold" (No. 20). Finally, the role of Scripture in Church life is emphasized, exhorting that ease of "access to sacred Scripture should be provided for all the Christian faithful" and calling for biblical studies to progress "under the watchful care of the sacred teaching office of the Church," adding that the careful study of Sacred Scripture is "the soul of sacred theology" (Nos. 22-24).

Sacrosanctum Concilium (Constitution on the Sacred Liturgy), December 4, 1963: Its aim was to introduce a process of liturgical renewal. The desire for a careful examination of the liturgy did not simply commence with the deliberations of the council but had as its basis the ongoing study and research of the question for many years by the Holy See. For example, Pope St. Pius X (r. 1903-1914) instituted a number of directives aimed at liturgical renewal, such as the restoration of Sunday as the center of the liturgical observance each week, and, most importantly, urging the reception of Communion early and often in the lives of all Catholics. Pope Pius XII (r. 1939-1958) issued the important encyclical *Mediator Dei*, calling the liturgy the foundation of the Church's spiritual life, and stressing the Mass as the Church's primary or principal prayer. He also gave encouragement to heightened participation by the congregation through vocal prayer and frequent Communion and the reading of the Divine Office, which he considered a complementary activity to the Mass. It was thus both inevitable and desirable that the Second Vatican Council should take up the vitally important work of liturgical renewal as part of its wider considerations and endeavors.

The final decree, issued under Pope Paul VI, began with "General Principles for the Restoration and Promotion of the Sacred Liturgy" (ch. 1), including "I. The Nature of the Sacred Liturgy and Its Importance in the Church's Life"; "II. The Promotion of Liturgical Instruction and Active Participation"; "III. The Reform of the Sacred Liturgy" (with its general principles, principles drawn from the hierarchical and communal nature of the liturgy, and principles for adapting the liturgy to the culture and traditions of nations); "IV. The Promotion of Liturgical Life in Diocese and Parish"; and "V. The Promotion of Pastoral-Liturgical Action." The constitution then concerned itself with "The Most Sacred Mystery of the Eucharist" (ch. 2); "The Other Sacraments and the Sacramentals" (ch. 3); "The Divine Office" (ch. 4); "The Liturgical Year" (ch.

5); "Sacred Music" (ch. 6); and "Sacred Art and Sacred Furnishings" (ch. 7).

As with many other enactments of Vatican Council II, *Sacrosanctum Concilium* has been the subject of considerable debate concerning its implementation and the direction that such a process has taken. In his apostolic letter on the constitution, dated December 4, 1988, Pope John Paul II celebrated the twenty-fifth anniversary of its promulgation by noting the continuing importance of liturgical renewal that has begun "in accordance with the conciliar principles of fidelity to tradition and openness to legitimate development." The pope, however, made note at that time of the very real problem of abuses and liberties taken with the liturgy on the one hand, and the stubborn refusal of some to accept liturgical reforms as they were formally intended by the Church authority on the other. His Holiness observed that the liturgical renewal, authentically interpreting the constitution through a harmonious dialogue between competent authorities in Rome and the local conferences of bishops, is not the source of the problem in the liturgical controversy, but it is the result of indifference on the part of many members of the faith, a rejection of the meaning and correct interpretation of the constitution, and unacceptable and outlandish innovations in the liturgy. The Holy Father has stressed the need for the liturgy to provide a ritual experience.

Gaudium et Spes (Pastoral Constitution on the Church in the Modern World), December 7, 1965: The longest document of the council and the one with the broadest purpose, namely to provide an extensive final presentation of the aims and hopes of the council while offering guidance to humanity on a variety of pressing subjects. *Gaudium et Spes*, so called from the opening words of the document ("The joy and hope"), is evenly divided into two main parts: the Church's teaching on humanity in the modern era and urgent problems of the times.

The first part starts out: "The joys and the hopes, the griefs and the anxieties of this age" (No. 1) – a clear indication that the Council Fathers were aware both of the positive nature of the modern world and its many dangers and travails. Further, the council places great emphasis throughout on human existence, a stress that was quite innovative in its presentation: "According to the almost unanimous opinion of believers and unbelievers alike, all things on earth should be related to man as their center and crown" (No. 12). Having developed an analysis of humanity, the document then offered a thorough summary of traditional Church teaching on human life, complete with discussion of sin, the union of body and soul, and the moral conscience.

There is, as well, a genuinely realistic appraisal of contemporary society, noting the pervasiveness of atheism, adding that its spread can be attributed in part to the fault and carelessness of those within the Church whose actions and failures "must be said to conceal rather than reveal the authentic face of God and religion" (No. 19). Toward the fuller understanding of the place of the Church in the modern world, *Gaudium et Spes* emphasizes the harmony that should exist between the Catholic faith and scientific progress because "earthly matters and the concerns of faith derive from the same God" (No. 36). This does not mean, however, that there ought to be no qualifying elements or restraints to science; the Council Fathers add to this positive statement the provision that such research, "within every branch of learning," must be "carried out in a genuinely scientific manner and in accord with moral norms" (No. 36). Finally, the first part makes an ecumenical gesture, noting that the Church "holds in high esteem the things which other Christian Churches or ecclesial communities have done. . ." (No. 40).

Part Two offers the practical application of the Church's teaching and message enunciated in Part One. Most pressing is the council's concern for the family, and its treatment of family life and marriage is the most detailed and extensive in the history of the councils of the Church. This leads to study of the deeply troubling presence of contraception. The council reiterates Church instruction in an affirmation of opposition to contraception that would receive even fuller expression in three years in the encyclical *Humanae vitae*. In the matter of abortion, the document states clearly: ". . . from the moment of its conception life must be guarded with the greatest care, while abortion and infanticide are unspeakable crimes" (No. 51). In its study of culture, in which the council reminds all humanity that culture and civilization are creations of man, it points out his responsibility over it and his duty to seek that which is above, which entails an "obligation to work with all men in constructing a more human world" (No. 57). Here we have a powerful preface or introduction to the next concerns voiced in *Gaudium et Spes*: the questions of economic life, political systems, and war. In building upon earlier social encyclicals, *Gaudium et Spes* discusses economics as vital to human progress and social development, striking the important balance (developed so masterfully in the later writings of Pope John Paul II) between the rights of an individual to possess goods and the obligation to aid the poor (Nos. 63–72). While declaring the autonomous and independent nature of the Church and politics, the Council Fathers do acknowledge: "There are, indeed, close links between earthly affairs and those aspects of man's condition which transcend this world. The Church herself employs the things of time to the degree that her own proper mission demands" (No. 76). The document goes on to state that "the arms race is an utterly treacherous trap for humanity" (No. 81) and "it is our clear duty, then, to strain every muscle as we work for the time when all war can be completely outlawed by international consent" (No. 82).

Christus Dominus (Decree on the Bishops' Pastoral Office in the Church), October 28, 1965: It discusses the numerous roles of bishops in the Church, in their own dioceses, and in cooperation with each other. *Christus Dominus* placed special emphasis on the collegiality of the bishops. The decree tells us: "As lawful successors of the apostles and as members of the episcopal college, bishops should always realize that they are linked one to the other, and should show concern for all the churches. . . . They should be especially concerned about those parts of the world where the Word of God has not yet been proclaimed or where . . . the faithful are in danger of departing from the precepts of the Christian life, and even of losing the faith itself"; in light of this, it exhorts bishops to "make every effort to have the faithful actively support and promote works of evangelization and the apostolate" (No. 6).

Ad Gentes (Decree on the Church's Missionary Activity), December 7, 1965: A reaffirmation of the important missionary nature of the Catholic Church, founded on the biblical idea of the people of God. The decree, in six chapters with an introduction, examined specifically the doctrine of the Church's activities in missions, the nature of the work, the need for new churches, the role of missionaries, the organization of missionary planning, and the utilization of Church resources in missionary work. The decree also called for a thorough reappraisal and reform of so-called Christian or Catholic imperialism, the teaching of Christianity in a purely Western (or Eurocentric) fashion, thus theoretically alienating many in the native African or Asian communities. Pope Paul VI issued *Ecclesia Sancta III* on August 16, 1966, to establish the means of actually implementing *Ad Gentes*.

Unitatis Redintegratio (Decree on Ecumenism), November 21, 1964: It elaborated the principles guiding Catholic participation in ecumenism and clarifying the Catholic view concerning the status and position of other faiths separate from the Roman Catholic Church. Considered one of the most important documents related to the Church's role in ecumenism, the decree was additionally clarified and supported by *Lumen Gentium* ("Dogmatic Constitution on the Church"), *Gaudium et Spes* ("Pastoral Constitution on the Church in the Modern World"), and *Orientalium Ecclesiarum* ("Decree on Eastern Catholic Churches").

Unitatis Redintegratio (Nos. 1, 3) from the outset makes clear that the Catholic Church as "established by Christ the Lord is, indeed, one and unique," although "from her very beginnings there arose in this one and only Church of God certain rifts." However, the decree goes on to point out, the fault for the schism that separated many from the Church in the Reformation of the sixteenth century lies not merely with the Protestants but with Catholics as well. Nor should those born in these communities be condemned. Rather, they should be given "respect and affection as brothers," for they too were brought up in the Christian faith. While granting the often misunderstood recognition that the gifts of the Holy Spirit (e.g., the life of grace and the theological virtues) are obtainable to those Christians not of the Catholic faith, *Unitatis Redintegratio* makes the vital distinction that "it is through Christ's Catholic Church alone, which is the all-embracing means of salvation, that the fullness of the means of salvation can be obtained" (No. 3). The decree then calls on all Christians to pray and labor toward the unity of the Church, but it makes the important point that this reconciliation, or reunion, is possible only by placing hope entirely in Christ.

Orientalium Ecclesiarum (Decree on Eastern Catholic Churches), November 21, 1964: The decree has, among its goals, the declaration of the full rights and equality of the Eastern communities of the Catholic Church, while at the same time making positive statements toward the separated Eastern Churches (the Orthodox Christian Churches). Members of the Eastern Catholic communities are given encouragement to remain steadfast in their faith and to preserve always their customs and proper liturgical rites. The council sought to give reassurance of the full intention of the Church in the West to have the utmost respect for their brethren in the Eastern Church and that Catholics in the West would be urged to study and become acquainted with the other rites of the Catholic Church. Beyond these broad assurances, the decree covers such legal matters as: the declaration as valid of all marriages between Eastern Catholic and non-Catholic Christians, when performed by a validly ordained priest;

the reception of non-Catholic Christians into the Catholic Church with the simple profession of faith; the points of shared worship between the Catholic and non-Catholic Eastern Churches. The simplifying of the process of reception would have important ramifications for the rebirth of the Catholic Church in Ukraine in the early 1990s following the collapse of the Soviet Union. *Orientalium Ecclesiarum* also makes clear the hope of the council that a reunion between the Catholic and Orthodox Churches will one day take place.

Presbyterorum Ordinis (Decree on the Ministry and Life of Priests), December 7, 1965: Stresses the important share of priests in Christ's ministry and calls upon all priests to remain devoted to the ministry. Accordingly, they should remain in obedience and a state of charity with their bishop; strive to make the word of God central to their very being; administer the sacraments and prayer with diligence; celebrate the Eucharist every day; promote the role of laypeople in the Church; and, in keeping with the example of Christ, remain devoted to their vows of priestly celibacy. The decree was careful to confirm the vows of celibacy in the Latin Church, although it added provision for those priests lawfully married and noted that the nature of the priesthood does not demand celibacy. The spirit and intention of the decree was elaborated upon by the 1990 Synod of Bishops, which gave the "The Formation of Priests in the Circumstances of the Present Day." On April 7, 1992, Pope John Paul II issued his apostolic exhortation *Pastores Dabo Vobis* ("I Will Give You Shepherds") on the subjects covered by the synod.

Optatam Totius (Decree on Priestly Formation), October 28, 1965: Concerned with the training of priests and the fostering of priestly vocations. Stressing the need for a priesthood that is "vitalized by the spirit of Christ" (Preface), the decree calls for care in preparation of potential members of the priestly ministry. Among suggested steps to achieve this are recognizing the importance of stable seminaries, revising and updating the program of studies, and the continuation of studies by priests after ordination. Above all, the decree hopes to facilitate the preparation of priests full of "that truly Catholic spirit by which they can transcend the borders of their own diocese, nation, or rite, be accustomed to consulting the needs of the whole Church, and be ready in spirit to preach the gospel everywhere" (No. 20). It has been the subject of ongoing debates as to the effectiveness of the actual implementation of the decree. Pope John Paul II examined the continuing process of priestly formation in his *Pastores Dabo Vobis* (1992), a postsynodal apostolic exhortation, "To the Bishops, Clergy, and Faithful on the Formation of Priests in the Circumstances of the Present Day."

Perfectae Caritatis (Decree on the Appropriate Renewal of the Religious Life), October 28, 1965: Concerned with adapting the religious life to the demands and conditions of modern times; it also calls for the renewal of the religious orders but without the loss of the essential elements of the consecrated life and role of the religious. A number of important points were to be followed in bringing this about: the Gospels are to serve as the central guide in renewal; the spirit and intention of the founders of each of the religious orders should be reemphasized; the members of the religious orders should each be fully aware of the problems and challenges facing the contemporary Church; each religious institute should participate in the active life of the Church to the degree established by its charter; and all members of the institutes must remember that their lives as religious are to be guided by the principle of charity, obedience, and poverty, and that to be a religious is not a career or activity but a complete way of life. *Perfectae Caritatis* has been the source of considerable debate within the Church over its implementation. Questions about it led to the formation of the *Consortium Perfectae Caritatis* in 1971 to assist women religious in the formation of the religious life in keeping with the intention of *Perfectae Caritatis* and in obedience to the teachings of the Church.

Apostolicam Actuositatem (Decree on the Apostolate of the Laity), November 18, 1965: Defining the mission to which all laity (or laypeople) are called, by virtue of their baptism into the faith. Known in English as the "Decree on the Apostolate of the Laity," it promotes the right of the laity to establish and participate in associations that help carry out the lay apostolate, encouraging and charging the hierarchy to provide spiritual assistance and guidance to ensure the common good and to preserve doctrinal purity.

Inter Mirifica (Decree on the Instruments of Social Communication), December 4, 1963: Concerned with the nature and proper application of the communications media. The document first defines the media as those forms of communication "which by their very nature can reach and influence . . . the whole of society" (No. 1). It then examines how the media

should be used in a responsible manner and proclaims the right of the Church to use them as it sees fit – for the care of souls and pastoral formation. The document also declared that "the matter communicated [must] always be true, and as complete as charity and justice allow" (No. 5). To give direction to social communication, the council said that "a pastoral instruction [should] be drawn up. . . . Experts from various countries should assist in this effort. In this way, all the principles and norms enunciated by this council concerning the instruments of social communication may achieve their effect" (No. 23). The result of this call was the publication of *Communio et progressio*, the "Pastoral Instruction on the Means of Social Communication" (January 29, 1971). Currently, the Church is aided by the Pontifical Council for Social Communication, a Vatican council intended to put into practice the furthering of the Church's message of salvation through all the relevant media. First instituted by Pope Pius XII in 1948, it was soon reorganized and then given permanent form in 1959 by Pope John XXIII as a commission. Pope John Paul II made it a council with specified duties in June 1988.

Dignitatis Humanae (Declaration on Religious Freedom), December 7, 1965: A powerful statement on the fundamental rights of all persons to enjoy freedom of worship, a right to be guaranteed and reaffirmed by civil law, the Vatican decree was the result of extensive deliberation both on the nature of religious freedom and the way it should be defined. In the end, the declaration proclaimed: "This Vatican Synod declares that the human person has a right to religious freedom. This freedom means that all men are to be immune from coercion on the part of individuals or of social groups and of any human power, in such wise that in matters religious no one is to be forced to act in a manner contrary to his own beliefs. Nor is anyone to be restrained from acting in accordance with his own beliefs, whether privately or publicly, whether alone or in association with others, within limits" (No. 2). The basis of this right is the inherent dignity of the human person, as an individual and as a social being. This reality is revealed by the Word of God and also by reason.

The declaration also examines the rights of the family, especially in choosing schools, noting that many states violate "the rights of parents" (No. 5) when they compel children to attend a single system of education. Further, certain limits on freedom are recognized, when the need for public order and morality require it, but "the freedom of man [must] be respected as far as possible, and curtailed only when and in so far as necessary" (No. 7). In its conclusion, *Dignitatis Humanae* observed that many constitutions of government throughout the world contain specific rights of religious freedom, but there are other governments that do not; the Council "greets with joy the first of these two facts, as among the signs of the times. With sorrow, however, it denounces the other fact, as only to be deplored" (No. 15).

Nostra Aetate (Declaration on the Relationship of the Church to Non-Christian Religions), October 28, 1965: While positively affirming the common solidarity of humanity and rejecting all forms of intolerance and prejudice, the Council Fathers specifically discussed and praised the other world's major faiths, including Buddhism, Islam, and Hinduism. Special attention, however, was paid to Judaism, in recognition of the people of the Old Testament, the historical roots of Christianity in the Jewish faith, and the age-old and often pervasive anti-Semitism found within the culture of the West. The decree refuted in certain terms such claims as a collective guilt for the crucifixion and death of Christ. Anti-Semitism in all of its forms was utterly rejected. The docu-

ment was especially embraced by the German bishops.

Gravissimum Educationis (Declaration on Christian Education), October 28, 1965: The Council Fathers used the decree to proclaim the inalienable rights of all children to receive education. Among the most important points are: the very grave obligation on parents to ensure a proper education for their family; the need for parents to have freedom of choice in schools, without restrictions, regulations, and coercion; the place of society in imparting a proper education; the obligation of the Church to provide its children with education so that the very lives of the young might be given inspiration by Christ, while offering its assistance in promoting the development of well-balanced individuals; the place of catechetical instruction; the praiseworthy work of teachers, those individuals who labor on behalf of the community through their teaching career; the crucial role of Catholic schools; and the devotion of much attention by the Church to higher education, calling upon all Catholic universities and faculties to be known not for their numbers but their high standards.

UNITED STATES CATHOLIC HISTORY

U.S. CATHOLIC HISTORY

The starting point of the mainstream of Catholic history in the United States was in Baltimore at the end of the Revolutionary War. Long before that time, however, Catholic explorers had traversed much of the country and missionaries had done considerable work among Indians in the Southeast, Northeast, and Southwest.

Spanish and French Missions

Missionaries from Spain evangelized Indians in Florida (which included a large area of the Southeast), New Mexico, Texas, and California. Franciscan Juan de Padilla, killed in 1542 in what is now central Kansas, was the first of numerous martyrs among the early missionaries. The city of St. Augustine, settled by the Spanish in 1565, was the first permanent settlement in the United States and also the site of the first parish, established the same year with secular Father Martin Francisco Lopez de Mendoza Grajales as pastor. Italian Jesuit Eusebio Kino (1645-1711) established Spanish missions in lower California and southern Arizona, where he founded San Xavier

del Bac mission in 1700. Blessed Junípero Serra (1713-84), who established nine of the famous chain of 21 Franciscan missions in California, was perhaps the most noted of the Spanish missionaries. He was beatified in 1988.

Jesuit Eusebio Kino and
San Xavier del Bac Mission

French missionary efforts originated in Canada and extended to parts of Maine, New York ,and areas around the Great Lakes and along the Mississippi River as far south as Louisiana. Sts. Isaac Jogues, René Goupil and John de Brébeuf, three of eight Jesuit missionaries of New France martyred between 1642 and 1649 (canonized in 1930), met their deaths near Auriesville, New York. Jesuit explorer Jacques Marquette (1637-75), who founded St. Ignace Mission at the Straits of Mackinac in 1671, left maps and a diary of his exploratory trip down the Mississippi River with Louis Joliet in 1673. Claude Allouez (1622-89), another French Jesuit, worked for 32 years among Indians in the Midwest, baptizing an estimated 10,000. French Catholics founded the colony in Louisiana in 1699. In 1727, Ursuline nuns from France founded a convent in New Orleans, the oldest in the United States.

Archbishop John Carroll (1735–1815)

English Settlements

Catholics were excluded by penal law from English settlements along the Atlantic coast.

The only colony established under Catholic leadership was Maryland, granted to George Calvert (Lord Baltimore) as a proprietary colony in 1632; its first settlement at St. Mary's City was established in 1634 by a contingent of Catholic and Protestant colonists who had arrived from England on the *Ark* and the *Dove*. Jesuits Andrew White and John Altham, who later evangelized Indians of the area, accompanied the settlers. The principle of religious freedom on which the colony was founded was enacted into law in 1649 as the Act of Toleration. It was the first such measure passed in the colonies and, except for a four-year period of Puritan control, remained in effect until 1688, when Maryland became a royal colony, and the Anglican Church was made the official religion in 1692. Catholics were disenfranchised and persecuted until 1776.

The only other colony where Catholics were assured some degree of freedom was Pennsylvania, founded by the Quaker William Penn in 1681.

One of the earliest permanent Catholic establishments in the English colonies was St. Francis Xavier Mission, Old Bohemia, in northern Maryland, founded by the Jesuits in 1704 to serve Catholics of Delaware, Maryland, and southeastern Pennsylvania. Its Bohemia Academy, established in the 1740s, was attended by sons of prominent Catholic families in the area.

Catholics and the Revolution

Despite their small number, which accounted for about one percent of the population, Catholics made significant contributions to the cause for independence from England.

Father John Carroll (1735-1815), who would later become the first bishop of the American hierarchy, and his cousin, Charles Carroll (1737-1832), a signer of the Declaration of Independence, were chosen by the Continental Congress to accompany Benjamin Franklin and Samuel Chase to Canada to try to secure that country's neutrality. Father Pierre Gibault (1737-1804) gave important aid in preserving the Northwest Territory for the revolutionaries. Thomas FitzSimons (1741-1811) of Philadelphia gave financial support to the Continental Army, served in a number of campaigns, and later, with Daniel Carroll of Maryland, became one of the two Catholic signers of the Constitution. John Barry (1745-1803), commander of the Lexington, the first ship commissioned by Congress, served valiantly and is considered a founder of the U.S. Navy. There is no record of the number of Catholics who served in Washington's armies, although 38 to 50 percent had Irish surnames.

Casimir Pulaski (1748-79) and Thaddeus Kosciuszko (1746-1817) of Poland served the cause of the Revolution. Assisting also were the Catholic nations of France, with a military and naval force, and Spain, with money and the neutrality of its colonies.

Acknowledgment of Catholic aid in the war and the founding of the Republic was made by General Washington in his reply to a letter from prominent Catholics seeking justice and equal rights: "I presume your fellow citizens of all denominations will not forget the patriotic part which you took in the accomplishment of our Revolution and the establishment of our government or the important assistance which they received from a nation [France] in which the Roman Catholic faith is professed."

In 1789, religious freedom was guaranteed under the First Amendment to the Constitution. Discriminatory laws against Catholics remained in force in many of the states, however, until well into the 19th century.

Beginning of Organization

Father John Carroll's appointment as superior of the American missions on June 9, 1784, was the first step toward organization of the Church in this country. According to a report he made to Rome the following year, there were 24 priests and approximately 25,000 Catholics, mostly in Maryland and Pennsylvania, in a general population of four million. Many of them had been in the Colonies for several generations. For the most part, however, they were an unknown minority laboring under legal and social handicaps.

Establishment of the Hierarchy

Father Carroll was named the first American bishop in 1789 and placed in charge of the Diocese of Baltimore, whose boundaries were coextensive with those of the United States. He was ordained in England on August 15, 1790, and installed in his see the following December 12.

Ten years later, Father Leonard Neale became his coadjutor and the first bishop ordained in the United States. Bishop Carroll became an archbishop in 1808 when Baltimore was designated a metropolitan see and the new dioceses of Boston, New York, Philadelphia, and Bardstown (now Louisville) were established. These jurisdictions were later subdivided, and by 1840 there were, in addition to Baltimore, 15 dioceses, 500 priests and 663,000 Catholics in the general population of 17 million.

Priests and First Seminaries

The original number of 24 priests noted in Bishop Carroll's 1785 report was gradually augmented with the arrival of others from France and other countries. Among arrivals from France after the Civil Constitution of the Clergy went into effect in 1790 were Jean Louis Lefebvre de Cheverus and Sulpicians Ambrose Maréchal, Benedict Flaget, and William Dubourg, who later became bishops.

The first seminary in the country was St. Mary's, established in 1791 in Baltimore, and placed under the direction of the Sulpicians. French seminarian Stephen T. Badin (1768-1853), who fled to the U.S. in 1792 and became a pioneer missionary in Kentucky, Ohio, and Michigan, was the first priest ordained (1793) in the U.S. Demetrius Gallitzin (1770-1840), a Russian prince and convert to Catholicism who did pioneer missionary work in western Pennsylvania, was ordained to the priesthood in 1795; he was the first to receive all his orders in the U.S. By 1815, St. Mary's Seminary had 30 ordained alumni.

Two additional seminaries — Mt. St. Mary's at Emmitsburg, Maryland, and St. Thomas at Bardstown, Kentucky — were established in 1809 and 1811, respectively. These and similar institutions founded later played key roles in the development and growth of the American clergy.

Early Schools

Early educational enterprises included the establishment in 1791 of a school at Georgetown which later became the first Catholic university in the U.S.; the opening of a secondary school for girls, conducted by Visitation Nuns, in 1799 at Georgetown; and the start of a similar school in the first decade of the 19th century at Emmitsburg, Maryland, by Sr. Elizabeth Ann Bayley Seton.

By the 1840s, which saw the beginnings of the present public school system, more than 200 Catholic elementary schools, half of them west of the Alleghenies, were in operation. From this start, the Church subsequently built the greatest private system of education in the world.

Sisterhoods

Institutes of women religious were largely responsible for the development of educational and charitable institutions. Among them were Ursuline Nuns in Louisiana from 1727 and Visitation Nuns at Georgetown in the 1790s.

The first contemplative foundation in the country was established in 1790 at Fort Tobacco, Maryland, by three American-born Carmelites trained at an English convent in Belgium.

The first community of American origin was that of the Sisters of Charity of St. Joseph,

Rose Philippine Duchesne (1796–1852)

founded in 1808 at Emmitsburg, MD, by Mother Elizabeth Ann Seton (canonized in 1975). Other early American communities were the Sisters of Loreto and the Sisters of Charity of Nazareth, both founded in 1812 in Kentucky, and the Oblate Sisters of Providence, a black community founded in 1829 in Baltimore by Mother Mary Elizabeth Lange.

Among pioneer U.S. foundresses of European communities were Mother Rose Philippine Duchesne (canonized in 1980), who established the Religious of the Sacred Heart in Missouri in 1818, and Mother Theodore Guérin, who founded the Sisters of Providence of St.-Mary-of-the-Woods in Indiana in 1840.

The number of sisters' communities, most of them branches of European institutes, increased apace with needs for their missions in education, charitable service, and spiritual life.

Trusteeism

The initial lack of organization in ecclesiastical affairs, nationalistic feeling among Catholics, and the independent action of some priests were factors involved in several early crises.

In Philadelphia, some German Catholics, with the reluctant consent of Bishop Carroll, founded Holy Trinity, the first national parish in the U.S. They refused to accept the pastor appointed by the bishop and elected their own. This and other abuses led to formal schism in 1796, a condition that existed until 1802 when they returned to canonical jurisdiction. Philadelphia was also the scene of the Hogan Schism, which developed in the 1820s when Father William Hogan, with the aid of lay trustees, seized control of St. Mary's Cathedral. His movement, for churches and parishes controlled by other than canonical procedures and run in extralegal ways, was nullified by a decision of the Pennsylvania Supreme Court in 1822.

Similar troubles seriously disturbed the peace of the Church in other places, principally New York, Baltimore, Buffalo, Charleston, and New Orleans.

Dangers arising from the exploitation of lay control were gradually diminished with the extension and enforcement of canonical procedures and with changes in civil law around the middle of the 19th century.

Anti-Catholicism

Bigotry against Catholics waxed and waned during the 19th century and into the 20th. The first major campaign of this kind, which developed in the wake of the panic of 1819 and lasted for about 25 years, was mounted in 1830 when the number of Catholic immigrants began to increase to a noticeable degree. Nativist anti-Catholicism generated a great deal of violence, represented by climaxes in loss of life and property in Charlestown, Massachusetts, in 1834, and in Philadelphia 10 years later. Later bigotry was fomented by the Know-Nothings in the 1850s; the Ku Klux Klan, from 1866; the American Protective Association, from 1887, and the Guardians of Liberty. Perhaps the last eruption of virulently overt anti-Catholicism occurred during the campaign of Alfred E. Smith for the presidency in 1928. Observers feel the issue was muted to a considerable extent in the political area with the election of John F. Kennedy to the presidency in 1960.

The Catholic periodical press had its beginnings in response to the attacks of bigots. The *U.S. Catholic Miscellany* (1822-61), the first Catholic newspaper in the U.S., was founded by Bishop John England of Charleston to answer critics of the Church. This remained the character of most of the periodicals published in the 19th and into the 20th century.

Growth and Immigration

Between 1830 and 1900, the combined factors of natural increase, immigration and conversion raised the Catholic population to 12 million. A large percentage of the growth figure represented immigrants: some 2.7 million, largely from Ireland, Germany, and France, between 1830 and 1880; and another 1.25 million during the 1880s when Eastern and Southern Europeans came in increasing numbers. By the 1860s the Catholic Church, with most of its members concentrated in urban areas, was probably the largest religious body in the country.

The efforts of progressive bishops to hasten the acculturation of Catholic immigrants occasioned a number of controversies, which generally centered around questions concerning national or foreign-language parishes. One of them, called Cahenslyism, arose from complaints that German Catholic immigrants were not being given adequate pastoral care.

Eastern-Rite Catholics

The immigration of the 1890s included large numbers of Eastern-Rite Catholics with their own liturgies and tradition of a married clergy, but without their own bishops. The treatment of their clergy and people by some of the U.S. (Latin-Rite) hierarchy and the prejudices they encountered resulted in the defection of thousands from the Catholic Church.

In 1907, Basilian monk Stephen Ortynsky was ordained the first bishop of Byzantine-rite Catholics in the U.S. Eventually jurisdictions were established for most Byzantine- and other Eastern-rite Catholics in the country.

Councils of Baltimore

The bishops of the growing U.S. dioceses met at Baltimore for seven provincial councils between 1829 and 1849.

In 1846, they proclaimed the Blessed Virgin Mary patroness of the United States under the title of the Immaculate Conception, eight years before the dogma was proclaimed in Rome.

After the establishment of the Archdiocese of Oregon City in 1846 and the elevation to metropolitan status of St. Louis, New Orleans, Cincinnati, and New York, the first of the three plenary councils of Baltimore was held.

The first plenary assembly was convoked on May 9, 1852, with Archbishop Francis P. Kenrick of Baltimore as papal legate. The bishops drew up regulations concerning parochial life, matters of church ritual and ceremonies, the administration of church funds and the teaching of Christian doctrine.

The second plenary council, meeting from October 7 to 21, 1866, under the presidency of Archbishop Martin J. Spalding, formulated a condemnation of several current doctrinal errors and established norms affecting the organization of dioceses, the education and conduct of the clergy, the management of ecclesiastical property, parochial duties, and general education.

Archbishop (later Cardinal) James Gibbons called into session the third plenary council which lasted from November 9 to December 7, 1884. Among highly significant results of actions taken by this assembly were the preparation of the line of Baltimore catechisms which became a basic means of religious instruction in this country; legislation that fixed the pattern of Catholic education by requiring the building of elementary schools in all parishes; the establishment of the Catholic University of America in Washington, DC, in 1889; and the determination of six holy days of obligation for observance in this country.

The enactments of the three plenary councils have had the force of particular law for the Church in the United States.

The Holy See established the Apostolic Delegation in Washington, DC, on January 24, 1893.

Slavery

In the Civil War period, as before, Catholics reflected attitudes of the general population with respect to the issue of slavery. Some supported it, some opposed it, but none were prominent in the Abolition Movement. Gregory XVI had condemned the slave trade in 1839, but no contemporary pope or American bishop published an official document on slavery itself. The issue did not split Catholics in schism as it did Baptists, Methodists, and Presbyterians.

Catholics fought on both sides in the Civil War. Five hundred members of 20 or more sisterhoods served the wounded of both sides.

One hundred thousand of the four million slaves emancipated in 1863 were Catholics; the highest concentrations were in Louisiana, about 60,000, and Maryland, 16,000. Three years later, their pastoral care was one of the subjects covered in nine decrees issued by the Second Plenary Council of Baltimore. The measures had little practical effect with respect to integration of the total Catholic community, predicated as they were on the proposition that individual bishops should handle questions regarding segregation in churches and related matters as best they could in the pattern of local customs.

Long entrenched segregation practices continued in force through the rest of the 19th century and well into the 20th. The first effective efforts to alter them were initiated by Cardinal Joseph Ritter of St. Louis in 1947, Cardinal (then Archbishop) Patrick O'Boyle of Washington in 1948, and Bishop Vincent Waters of Raleigh in 1953.

Friend of Labor

The Church became known during the 19th century as a friend and ally of labor in seeking justice for the working man. Cardinal Gibbons journeyed to Rome in 1887, for example, to defend and prevent a condemnation of the Knights of Labor by Leo XIII. The encyclical *Rerum Novarum* (1891) was hailed by many American bishops as a confirmation, if not vindication, of their own theories. Catholics have always formed a large percentage of union membership, and some have served unions in positions of leadership.

Americanism

Near the end of the century some controversy developed over what was characterized as Americanism or the phantom heresy. It was alleged that Americans were discounting the importance of contemplative virtues, exalting the practical virtues, and watering down the purity of Catholic doctrine for the sake of facilitating convert work.

The French translation of Father Walter Elliott's *Life of Isaac Hecker*, which fired the controversy, was one of many factors that led to the issuance of Leo XIII's *Testem Benevolentiae* in January 1899, in an attempt to end the matter. It was the first time the orthodoxy of the Church in the U.S. was called into question.

Schism

In the 1890s, serious friction developed between Poles and Irish in Scranton, Buffalo and

Chicago, resulting in schism and the establishment of the Polish National Catholic Church. A central figure in the affair was Father Francis Hodur, who was excommunicated by Bishop William O'Hara of Scranton in 1898. Nine years later, his ordination by an Old Catholic Archbishop of Utrecht gave the new Church its first bishop.

Another schism of the period led to formation of the American Carpatho-Russian Orthodox Greek Catholic Church.

Coming of Age

In 1900, there were 12 million Catholics in the total U.S. population of 76 million, 82 dioceses in 14 provinces, and 12,000 priests and members of about 40 communities of men religious. Many sisterhoods, most of them of European origin and some of American foundation, were engaged in Catholic educational and hospital work, two of their traditional apostolates.

The Church in the United States was removed from mission status with promulgation of the apostolic constitution *Sapienti Consilio* by Pope St. Pius X on June 29, 1908.

Before that time, and even into the early 1920s, the Church in this country received financial assistance from mission-aid societies in France, Bavaria, and Austria. Already, however, it was making increasing contributions of its own. At the present time, it is one of the major national contributors to the worldwide Society for the Propagation of the Faith.

American foreign missionary personnel increased from 14 or less in 1906 to an all-time high in 1968 of 9,655 priests, brothers, sisters, seminarians, and lay persons. The first missionary seminary in the U.S. was in operation at Techny, Illinois, in 1909, under the auspices of the Society of the Divine Word. Maryknoll, the first American missionary society, was established in 1911 and sent its first priests to China in 1918. Despite these contributions, the Church in the U.S. has not matched the missionary commitment of some other nations.

Bishops' Conference

A highly important apparatus for mobilizing the Church's resources was established in 1917 under the title of the National Catholic War Council. Its name was changed to National Catholic Welfare Conference several years later, but its objectives remained the same: to serve as an advisory and coordinating agency of the American bishops for advancing works of the Church in fields of social significance and impact — education, communications, immigration, social action, legislation, youth and lay organizations.

The forward thrust of the bishops' social thinking was evidenced in a program of social

reconstruction they recommended in 1919. By 1945, all but one of their 12 points had been enacted into legislation — including many later social security programs.

The NCWC was renamed the United States Catholic Conference (USCC) in November 1966, when the hierarchy also organized itself as a territorial conference with pastoral-juridical authority under the title, National Conference of Catholic Bishops. The USCC carried on the functions of the former NCWC until July 2001 when it merged with the National Conference of Catholic Bishops to create the USCCB.

Catholic Press

The establishment of the National Catholic News Service (NC) — now the Catholic News Service (CNS) — in 1920 was an important event in the development of the Catholic press, which had its beginnings about a hundred years earlier. Early in the 20th century there were 63 weekly newspapers. The 2001 *Catholic Press Directory*, published by the Catholic Press Association, reported a total of 648 periodicals in North America, with a circulation of 26.5 million. The figures included 218 newspapers, 252 magazines, 135 newsletters, and 43 other-language periodicals (newspapers and magazines).

Lay Organizations

A burst of lay organizational growth occurred from the 1930s onwards with the appearance of Catholic Action types of movements and other groups and associations devoted to special causes, social service, and assistance for the poor and needy. Several special apostolates developed under the aegis of the National Catholic Welfare Conference (now the United States Catholic Conference); the outstanding one was the Confraternity of Christian Doctrine.

Nineteenth-century organizations of great influence included: The St. Vincent de Paul Society, whose first U.S. office was set up in 1845 in St. Louis; the Catholic Central Union (*Verein*), dating from 1855; the Knights of Columbus, founded in 1882; the Holy Name Society, organized in the U.S. in 1870; the Rosary Society (1891) and scores of chapters of the Sodality of the Blessed Virgin Mary.

Pastoral Concerns

The potential for growth of the Church in this country by immigration was sharply reduced but not entirely curtailed after 1921 with the passage of restrictive federal legislation. As a result, the Catholic population became more stabilized and, to a certain extent and for many reasons, began to acquire an identity of its own.

Some increase from outside has taken place in

the past fifty years, however – from Canada, from Central and Eastern European countries, and from Puerto Rico and Latin American countries since World War II. This influx, while not as great as that of the 19th century and early 20th, has enriched the Church here with a sizable body of Eastern-Rite Catholics for whom twelve ecclesiastical jurisdictions have been established. It has also created a challenge for pastoral care of millions of Hispanics in urban centers and in agricultural areas where migrant workers are employed.

The Church continues to grapple with serious pastoral problems in rural areas, where about 600 counties have no priests in ministry. The National Catholic Rural Life Conference was established in 1922 in an attempt to make the Catholic presence felt on the land, and the Glenmary Society has devoted itself to this single apostolate since its foundation in 1939. Religious communities and diocesan priests are similarly engaged.

Other challenges lie in the cities and suburbs where seventy-five percent of the Catholic population lives. Conditions peculiar to each segment of the metropolitan area have developed in recent years as the flight to the suburbs has not only altered some traditional aspects of parish life but has also, in combination with many other factors, left behind a complex of special problems in inner-city areas.

A Post-War World

In the year after the Second World War, Catholics increasingly assumed a mainline role in American life. This was evidenced especially in the 1960 election of John F. Kennedy as the nation's first Catholic president. Catholic writers and thinkers were making a greater impact in the nation's life. One example of this was Trappist Thomas Merton's runaway best-selling book of 1948, *The Seven Storey Mountain*; another was the early television success of Bishop Fulton Sheen's "Life is Worth Living" series, begun in 1952. Meanwhile, lay leader Dorothy Day, founder of the Catholic Worker movement, continued to challenge American society with her views on pacifism and evangelical poverty.

A Post-Conciliar World

Catholic life in the United States was profoundly affected by the Second Vatican Council (1962-65). In the post-conciliar generation, American Catholicism grew both in numbers and complexity. Lay ministry and participation expanded; extensive liturgical changes (including the use of English) were implemented; and the numbers of priests, vowed religious and seminarians declined.

The Church has taken a high profile in many social issues. This has ranged from opposition to abortion, capital punishments, and euthanasia to support for civil rights, economic justice, and international peace and cooperation. Meanwhile Catholics have been deeply involved in inter-faith and ecumenical relationships. And the bishops have issued landmark pastoral statements, including "The Challenge of Peace" (1983) and "Economic Justice for All" (1986).

In these years after the Council, Catholics in America have known something of alienation, dissent and polarity. They have also found new intensity and maturity. New U.S. saints have been declared by the universal church, such as Elizabeth Ann Seton (1975), John Nepomucene Neumann (1977), and Rose Philippine Duchesne (1988). Especially at the time of visits to America by Pope John Paul II (e.g., in 1979, 1987, 1993, and 1999), U.S. Catholics have given evidence – in their personal and corporate lives – of the ongoing power of faith, liturgy, and the primal call of the Gospel in its many dimensions.

EARLY KEY DATES IN U.S. CATHOLIC CHRONOLOGY

Dates here refer mostly to earlier "firsts" and developments of Catholic history in the United States until the promulgation of the apostolic constitution Sapienti Consilio *by Pope St. Pius X (June 29, 1908) by which the Church in the United States was removed from mission status.*

Alabama

1540: Priests crossed the territory with De Soto's expedition.

1560: Five Dominicans in charge of mission at Santa Cruz des Nanipacna.

1682: La Salle claimed territory for France.

1704: First parish church established at Fort Louis de la Mobile under the care of diocesan priests.

1829: Mobile diocese established (redesignated Mobile-Birmingham, 1954-69).

1830: Spring Hill College, Mobile, established.

1834: Visitation Nuns established an academy at Summerville.

Alaska

1779: Mass celebrated for first time on shore of Port Santa Cruz on lower Bucareli Bay on May 13 by Franciscan Juan Riobo.

1868: Alaska placed under jurisdiction of Vancouver Island.

1879: Father John Althoff became first resident missionary.

1886: Archbishop Charles J. Seghers, "Apostle of Alaska," murdered by a guide; had surveyed southern and northwest Alaska in 1873 and 1877.

Sisters of St. Ann, first nuns in Alaska.

1887: Jesuits enter Alaska territory.

1894: Alaska made prefecture apostolic.

1902: Sisters of Providence opened hospital at Nome.

Arizona

1539: Franciscan Marcos de Niza explored the state.

1540: Franciscans Juan de Padilla and Marcos de Niza accompanied Coronado expedition through the territory.

1629: Spanish Franciscans began work among Moqui Indians.

1632: Franciscan Martin de Arvide killed by Indians.

1680: Franciscans José de Espeleta, Augustin de Santa Maria, José de Figueroa, and José de Trujillo killed in Pueblo Revolt.

1700: Jesuit Eusebio Kino, who first visited the area in 1692, established mission at San Xavier del Bac, near Tucson. In 1783, under Franciscan administration, construction was begun of the Mission Church of San Xavier del Bac near the site of the original mission; it is still in use as a parish church.

1767: Jesuits expelled; Franciscans took over 10 missions.

1828: Spanish missionaries expelled by Mexican government.

1863: Jesuits returned to San Xavier del Bac briefly.

1869: Sisters of Loreto arrived to conduct schools at Bisbee and Douglas.

1897: Tucson diocese established.

Arkansas

1541: Priests accompanied De Soto expedition through the territory.

1673: Marquette visited Indians in East.

1686: Henri de Tonti established trading post, first white settlement in territory.

1700-1702: Fr. Nicholas Foucault working among Indians.

1805: Bishop Carroll of Baltimore appointed Administrator Apostolic of Arkansas.

1838: Sisters of Loreto opened first Catholic school.

1843: Little Rock diocese established. There were about 700 Catholics in state, two churches, one priest.

1851: Sisters of Mercy founded St. Mary's Convent in Little Rock.

California

1542: Cabrillo discovered Upper (Alta) California; name of priest accompanying expedition unknown.

1602: On November 12, Carmelite Anthony of the Ascension offered first recorded Mass in California on shore of San Diego Bay.

1697: Missionary work in Lower and Upper Californias entrusted to Jesuits.

1767: Jesuits expelled from territory. Spanish Crown confiscated their property, including the Pious Fund for Missions. Upper California missions entrusted to Franciscans.

1769: Franciscan Junípero Serra, missionary in Mexico for 20 years, began establishment of Franciscan missions in California, in present San Diego. He was beatified in 1988.

1775: Franciscan Luis Jayme killed by Indians at San Diego Mission.

1779: Diocese of Sonora, Mexico, which included Upper California, established.

1781: On September 4, an expedition from San Gabriel Mission founded present city of Los Angeles — Pueblo "de Nuestra Senora de los Angeles."

Franciscans Francisco Hermenegildo Garces, Juan Antonio Barreneche, Juan Marcello Diaz, and José Matias Moreno killed by Indians.

1812: Franciscan Andres Quintana killed at Santa Cruz Mission.

1822: Dedication on December 8, of Old Plaza Church, "Assistant Mission of Our Lady of the Angels."

1833: Missions secularized, finally confiscated.

1840: Pope Gregory XVI established Diocese of Both Californias.

1846: Peter H. Burnett, who became first governor of California in 1849, received into Catholic Church.

1848: Mexico ceded California to the United States.

1850: Monterey diocese erected; redesignated Monterey-Los Angeles, 1859, and Los Angeles-San Diego, 1922.

1851: University of Santa Clara chartered.

Sisters of Notre Dame de Namur opened women's College of Notre Dame at San José; chartered in 1868; moved to Belmont, 1923.

1852: Baja California detached from Monterey diocese.

1853: San Francisco archdiocese established.

1855: Negotiations inaugurated to restore confiscated California missions to Church.

1868: Grass Valley diocese established; transferred to Sacramento in 1886. (Grass Valley was reestablished as a titular see in 1995.)

Colorado

1858: First parish in Colorado established.

1864: Sisters of Loreto at the Foot of the Cross, first nuns in the state, established academy at Denver.

1868: Vicariate Apostolic of Colorado and Utah established.

1887: Denver diocese established.

1888: Regis College (now University) founded.

Connecticut

1651: Probably first priest to enter state was Jesuit Gabriel Druillettes; ambassador of Governor of Canada, he participated in a New England Colonial Council at New Haven.

1756: Catholic Acadians, expelled from Nova Scotia, settled in the state.

1791: Rev. John Thayer, first native New England priest, offered Mass at the Hartford home of Noah Webster, his Yale classmate.

1808: Connecticut became part of Boston diocese.

1818: Religious freedom established by new constitution, although the Congregational Church remained, in practice, the state church.

1829: Father Bernard O'Cavanaugh became first resident priest in state.
Catholic Press of Hartford established.

1830: First Catholic church in state dedicated at Hartford.
Father James Fitton (1805-81), New England missionary, was assigned to Hartford for six years. He ministered to Catholics throughout the state.

1843: Hartford diocese established

1882: Knights of Columbus founded by Father Michael J. McGivney.

Delaware

1730: Mount Cuba, New Castle County, the scene of Catholic services.

1750: Jesuit mission at Apoquiniminck administered from Maryland.

1772: First permanent parish established at Coffee Run.

1792: French Catholics from Santo Domingo settled near Wilmington.

1816: St. Peter's Church, later the cathedral of the diocese, erected at Wilmington.

1830: Daughters of Charity opened school and orphanage at Wilmington.

1868: Wilmington diocese established.

1869: Visitation Nuns established residence in Wilmington.

District of Columbia

1641: Jesuit Andrew White evangelized Anacosta Indians.

1774: Father John Carroll ministered to Catholics.

1789: Georgetown, first Catholic college in U.S., established.

1791: Pierre Charles L'Enfant designed the Federal City of Washington. His plans were not fully implemented until the early 1900s.

1792: James Hoban designed the White House.

1794: Father Anthony Caffrey began St. Patrick's Church, first parish church in the new Federal City.

1801: Poor Clares opened school for girls in Georgetown.

1802: First mayor of Washington, appointed by President Jefferson, was Judge Robert Brent.

1889: Catholic University of America founded.

1893: Apostolic Delegation established; became an Apostolic Nunciature in 1984 with the establishment of full diplomatic relations between the U.S. and the Holy See.

Florida

1513: Ponce de León discovered Florida.

1521: Missionaries accompanying Ponce de León and other explorers probably said first Masses within present limits of U.S.

1528: Franciscans landed on western shore.

1539: Twelve missionaries landed with De Soto at Tampa Bay.

1549: Dominican Luis Cancer de Barbastro and two companions slain by Indians near Tampa Bay.

1565: City of St. Augustine, oldest in U.S., founded by Pedro Menendez de Aviles, who was accompanied by four secular priests.
America's oldest mission, Nombre de Dios, was established.
Father Martin Francisco Lopez de Mendoza Grajales became the first parish priest of St. Augustine, where the first parish in the U.S. was established.

1572: St. Francis Borgia, general of the Society, withdrew Jesuits from Florida.

1606: Bishop Juan de las Cabeyas de Altamirano, O.P., conducted the first episcopal visitation in the U.S.

1620: The chapel of Nombre de Dios was dedicated to Nuestra Senora de la Leche y Buen Parto (Our Nursing Mother of the Happy Delivery); oldest shrine to the Blessed Mother in the U.S.

1704: Destruction of Florida's northern missions by English and Indian troops led by Governor James Moore of South Carolina. Franciscans Juan de Parga, Dominic Criodo,

Tiburcio de Osorio, Augustine Ponze de León, Marcos Delgado, and two Indians, Anthony Enixa and Amador Cuipa Feliciano, were slain by the invaders.

1735: Bishop Francis Martinez de Tejadu Diaz de Velasco, auxiliary of Santiago, was the first bishop to take up residence in U.S., at St. Augustine.

1793: Florida and Louisiana were included in Diocese of New Orleans.

1857: Eastern Florida made a vicariate apostolic.

1870: St. Augustine diocese established.

Georgia

1540: First priests to enter were chaplains with De Soto. They celebrated first Mass within territory of 13 original colonies.

1566: Pedro Martinez, first Jesuit martyr of the New World, was slain by Indians on Cumberland Island.

1569: Jesuit mission was opened at Guale Island by Father Antonio Sedeno.

1572: Jesuits withdrawn from area.

1595: Five Franciscans assigned to Province of Guale.

1597: Five Franciscan missionaries (Fathers Pedro de Corpa, Blas de Rodriguez, Miguel de Anon, Francisco de Berascolo, and Brother Antonio de Badajoz) killed in coastal missions. Their cause for beatification was formally opened in 1984.

1606: Bishop Altamirano, O.P., conducted visitation of the Georgia area.

1612: First Franciscan province in U.S. erected under title of Santa Elena; it included Georgia, South Carolina, and Florida.

1655: Franciscans had nine flourishing missions among Indians.

1742: Spanish missions ended as result of English conquest at Battle of Bloody Marsh.

1796: Augustinian Father Le Mercier was first post-colonial missionary to Georgia.

1798: Catholics granted right of refuge.

1800: First church erected in Savannah on lot given by city council.

1810: First church erected in Augusta on lot given by State Legislature.

1850: Savannah diocese established; became Savannah-Atlanta, 1937; divided into two separate sees, 1956.

1864: Father Emmeran Bliemel, of the Benedictine community of Latrobe, PA, was killed at the battle of Jonesboro while serving as chaplain of the Confederate 10th Tennessee Artillery.

Hawaii

1825: Pope Leo XII entrusted missionary efforts in Islands to Sacred Hearts Fathers.

1827: The first Catholic missionaries arrived – Fathers Alexis Bachelot, Abraham Armand, and Patrick Short, along with three lay brothers. After three years of persecution, the priests were forcibly exiled.

1836: Father Arsenius Walsh, SS. CC., a British subject, was allowed to remain in Islands but was not permitted to proselytize or conduct missions.

1839: Hawaiian government signed treaty with France granting Catholics freedom of worship and same privileges as Protestants.

1844: Vicariate Apostolic of Sandwich Islands (Hawaii) erected.

1873: Father Damien de Veuster of the Sacred Hearts Fathers arrived in Molokai and spent the remainder of his life working among lepers. He was beatified in 1995.

Idaho

1840: Jesuit Pierre de Smet preached to the Flathead and Pend d'Oreille Indians; probably offered first Mass in state.

1842: Jesuit Nicholas Point opened a mission among Coeur d'Alene Indians near St. Maries.

1863: Secular priests sent from Oregon City to administer to incoming miners.

1867: Sisters of Holy Names of Jesus and Mary opened first Catholic school at Idaho City.

1868: Idaho made a vicariate apostolic.

1870: First church in Boise established.

Church lost most of missions among Indians of Northwest Territory when Commission on Indian Affairs appointed Protestant missionaries to take over.

1893: Boise diocese established.

Illinois

1673: Jesuit Jacques Marquette, accompanying Joliet, preached to Indians.

1674: Father Marquette set up a cabin for saying Mass in what later became city of Chicago.

1675: Father Marquette established Mission of the Immaculate Conception among Kaskaskia Indians, near present site of Utica; transferred to Kaskaskia, 1703.

1679: La Salle brought with him Franciscans Louis Hennepin, Gabriel de la Ribourde, and Zenobius Membre.

1680: Father Ribourde was killed by Kickapoo Indians.

1689: Jesuit Claude Allouez died after 32 years of missionary activity among Indians of Midwest; he had evangelized Indians of 20 different tribes. Jesuit Jacques Gravier succeeded Allouez as vicar general of Illinois.

1699: Mission established at Cahokia, first permanent settlement in state.

1730: Father Gaston, a diocesan priest, was killed at the Cahokia Mission.

1763: Jesuits were banished from the territory.

1778: Father Pierre Gibault championed Colonial cause in the Revolution and aided greatly in securing states of Ohio, Indiana, Illinois, Michigan, and Wisconsin for Americans.

1827: The present St. Patrick's Parish at Ruma, oldest English-speaking Catholic congregation in state, was founded.

1833: Visitation Nuns established residence in Kaskaskia.

1843: Chicago diocese established.

1853: Quincy diocese established; transferred to Alton, 1857; Springfield, 1923; Quincy and Alton were reestablished as titular sees in 1995.

1860: Quincy College founded.

1877: Peoria diocese established.

1880: Chicago made archdiocese.

1887: Belleville diocese established.

1894: Franciscan Sisters of Blessed (now Saint) Kunegunda (now the Franciscan Sisters of Chicago) founded by Mother Marie Therese (Josephine Dudzik).

1908: Rockford diocese established.
First American Missionary Congress held in Chicago.

Indiana

1679: Recollects Louis Hennepin and Gabriel de la Ribourde passed through state.

1686: Land near present Notre Dame University at South Bend given by French government to Jesuits for mission.

1749: Beginning of the records of St. Francis Xavier Church, Vincennes. These records continue with minor interruptions to the present.

1778: Father Gibault aided George Rogers Clark in campaign against British in conquest of Northwest Territory.

1824: Sisters of Charity of Nazareth, Kentucky, opened St. Clare's Academy in Vincennes.

1825: Laying of cornerstone of third church of St. Francis Xavier, which later (from 1834-98) was the cathedral of the Vincennes diocese. The church was designated a minor basilica in 1970 and is still in use as a parish church.

1834: Vincennes diocese established with Simon Gabriel Bruté as bishop; title transferred to Indianapolis, 1898. (Vincennes was reestablished as a titular see in 1995.)

1840: Sisters of Providence founded St. Mary-of-the-Woods College for women.

1842: University of Notre Dame founded by Holy Cross Father Edward Sorin and Brothers of St. Joseph on land given the diocese of Vincennes by Father Stephen Badin.

1854: First Benedictine community established in state at St. Meinrad. It became an abbey in 1870 and an archabbey in 1954.

1857: Fort Wayne diocese established; changed to Fort Wayne-South Bend, 1960.

Iowa

1673: A Peoria village on Mississippi was visited by Father Marquette.

1679: Fathers Louis Hennepin and Gabriel de la Ribourde visited Indian villages.

1836: First permanent church, St. Raphael's, founded at Dubuque by Dominican Samuel Mazzuchelli.

1837: Dubuque diocese established.

1838: St. Joseph's Mission founded at Council Bluffs by Jesuit Father De Smet.

1843: Sisters of Charity of the Blessed Virgin Mary was first sisterhood in state.
Sisters of Charity opened Clarke College, Dubuque.

1850: First Trappist Monastery in state, Our Lady of New Melleray, was begun.

1881: Davenport diocese established.

1882: St. Ambrose College (now University), Davenport, established.

1893: Dubuque made archdiocese.

1902: Sioux City diocese established.

Kansas

1542: Franciscan Juan de Padilla, first martyr of the United States, was killed in central Kansas.

1858: St. Benedict's College (now Benedictine College) founded.

1863: Sisters of Charity opened orphanage at Leavenworth, and St. John's Hospital in following year.

1877: Leavenworth diocese established; transferred to Kansas City in 1947; Leavenworth was reestablished as a titular see in 1995.

1887: Dioceses of Wichita and Concordia established. Concordia was transferred to Salina in 1944, but reestablished as a titular see in 1995.

1888: Oblate Sisters of Providence opened an orphanage for African-American boys at Leavenworth, first west of Mississippi.

Kentucky

1775: First Catholic settlers came to Kentucky.

1787: Father Charles Maurice Whelan, first resident priest, ministered to settlers in the Bardstown district.

1793: Father Stephen T. Badin began missionary work in Kentucky.

1806: Dominican Fathers built Priory at St. Rose of Lima.

1808: Bardstown diocese established with

Benedict Flaget as its first bishop; see transferred to Louisville, 1841; Bardstown was reestablished as a titular see in 1995.

1811: Rev. Guy I. Chabrat first priest ordained west of the Allegheny Mountains.
St. Thomas Seminary founded.

1812: Sisters of Loreto founded by Rev. Charles Nerinckx; first religious community in the United States without foreign affiliation.
Sisters of Charity of Nazareth founded, the second native community of women founded in the West.

1814: Nazareth College for women established.

1816: Cornerstone of St. Joseph's Cathedral, Bardstown, laid.

1822: First foundation of Dominican Sisters in the U.S. established near Springfield.

1836: Hon. Benedict J. Webb founded *Catholic Advocate*, first Catholic weekly newspaper in Kentucky.

1848: Trappist monks took up residence in Gethsemani.

1849: Cornerstone of Cathedral of the Assumption laid at Louisville.

1853: Covington diocese established.

1855: Know-Nothing troubles in state.

Louisiana

1682: La Salle's expedition, accompanied by two priests, completed discoveries of De Soto at mouth of Mississippi. LaSalle named territory Louisiana.

1699: French Catholics founded colony of Louisiana.
First recorded Mass offered March 3, by Franciscan Father Anastase Douay.

1706: Father John Francis Buisson de St. Cosmé was killed near Donaldsonville.

1717: Franciscan Anthony Margil established first Spanish mission in north central Louisiana.

1718: City of New Orleans founded by Jean Baptiste Le Moyne de Bienville.

1720: First resident priest in New Orleans was the French Recollect Prothais Boyer.

1725: Capuchin Fathers opened school for boys.

1727: Ursuline Nuns founded convent in New Orleans, oldest convent in what is now U.S.; they conducted a school, hospital and orphan asylum.

1793: New Orleans diocese established.

1842: Sisters of Holy Family, a black congregation, founded at New Orleans by Henriette Delille and Juliette Gaudin.

1850: New Orleans made archdiocese.

1853: Natchitoches diocese established; transferred to Alexandria in 1910; became Alexandria-Shreveport in 1977; redesignated Alexandria, 1986; Natchitoches diocese reestablished as a titular see in 1995.

Maine

1604: First Mass in territory celebrated by Father Nicholas Aubry, accompanying De Monts' expedition which was authorized by King of France to begin colonizing region.

1605: Colony founded on St. Croix Island; two secular priests served as chaplains.

1613: Four Jesuits attempted to establish permanent French settlement near mouth of Kennebec River.

1619: French Franciscans began work among settlers and Indians; driven out by English in 1628.

1630: New England made a prefecture apostolic in charge of French Capuchins.

1633: Capuchin Fathers founded missions on Penobscot River.

1646: Jesuits established Assumption Mission on Kennebec River.

1688: Church of St. Anne, oldest in New England, built at Oldtown.

1704: English soldiers destroyed French missions.

1724: English forces again attacked French settlements, killed Jesuit Sebastian Rale.

1853: Portland diocese established.

1854: Know-Nothing uprising resulted in burning of church in Bath.

1856: Anti-Catholic feeling continued; church at Ellsworth burned.

1864: Sisters of Congregation of Notre Dame from Montréal opened academy at Portland.

1875: James A. Healy, first African-American bishop consecrated in U.S., became second Bishop of Portland.

Maryland

1634: Maryland established by Lord Calvert. Two Jesuits among first colonists.
First Mass offered on Island of St. Clement in Lower Potomac by Jesuit Father Andrew White.
St. Mary's City founded by English and Irish Catholics.

1641: St. Ignatius Parish founded by English Jesuits at Chapel Point, near Port Tobacco.

1649: Religious Toleration Act passed by Maryland Assembly. It was repealed in 1654 by Puritan-controlled government.

1651: Cecil Calvert, second Lord Baltimore, gave Jesuits 10,000 acres for use as Indian mission.

1658: Lord Baltimore restored Toleration Act.

1672: Franciscans came to Maryland under leadership of Father Massius Massey.

1688: Maryland became royal colony as a result of the Revolution in England; Anglican Church became the official religion (1692);

Toleration Act repealed; Catholics disenfranchised and persecuted until 1776.

1704: Jesuits founded St. Francis Xavier Mission, Old Bohemia, to serve Catholics of Delaware, Maryland, and southeastern Pennsylvania; its Bohemia Academy established in the 1740s was attended by sons of prominent Catholics in the area.

1784: Father John Carroll appointed prefect apostolic for the territory embraced by new Republic.

1789: Baltimore became first diocese established in U.S., with John Carroll as first bishop.

1790: Carmelite Nuns founded convent at Port Tobacco, the first in the English-speaking Colonies.

1791: First Synod of Baltimore held.

St. Mary's Seminary, first seminary in U.S., established.

1793: Rev. Stephen T. Badin first priest ordained by Bishop Carroll.

1800: Jesuit Leonard Neale became first bishop consecrated in present limits of U.S.

1806: Cornerstone of Assumption Cathedral, Baltimore, was laid.

1808: Baltimore made archdiocese.

1809: St. Joseph's College, Emmitsburg, founded (closed in 1973).

Sisters of Charity of St. Joseph founded by St. Elizabeth Ann Seton; first native American sisterhood.

1821: Assumption Cathedral, Baltimore, formally opened.

1829: Oblate Sisters of Providence, first congregation of black sisters, established at Baltimore by Mother Mary Elizabeth Lange.

First Provincial Council of Baltimore held; six others followed, in 1833, 1837, 1840, 1843, 1846, and 1849.

1836: Roger B. Taney appointed Chief Justice of Supreme Court by President Jackson.

1852: First of the three Plenary Councils of Baltimore convened. Subsequent councils held in 1866 and 1884.

1855: German Catholic Central Verein founded.

1886: Archbishop James Gibbons of Baltimore made cardinal by Pope Leo XIII.

Massachusetts

1630: New England made a prefecture apostolic in charge of French Capuchins.

1647: Massachusetts Bay Company enacted an anti-priest law.

1688: Hanging of Ann Glover, an elderly Irish Catholic widow, who refused to renounce her Catholic religion.

1732: Although Catholics were not legally admitted to colony, a few Irish families were in Boston; a priest was reported working among them.

1755-56: Acadians landing in Boston were denied services of a Catholic priest.

1775: General Washington discouraged Guy Fawkes Day procession in which pope was carried in effigy, and expressed surprise that there were men in his army "so void of common sense as to insult the religious feelings of the Canadians with whom friendship and an alliance are being sought."

1780: The Massachusetts State Constitution granted religious liberty, but required a religious test to hold public office and provided for tax to support Protestant teachers of piety, religion, and morality.

1788: First public Mass said in Boston on November 2 by Abbé de la Poterie, first resident priest.

1803: Church of Holy Cross erected in Boston with financial aid given by Protestants headed by John Adams.

1808: Boston diocese established.

1831: Irish Catholic immigration increased.

1832: St. Vincent's Orphan Asylum, oldest charitable institution in Boston, opened by Sisters of Mercy.

1834: Ursuline Convent in Charlestown burned by a Nativist mob.

1843: Holy Cross College founded.

1855: Catholic militia companies disbanded; nunneries' inspection bill passed.

1859: St. Mary's, first parochial school in Boston, opened.

1860: Portuguese Catholics from Azores settled in New Bedford.

1870: Springfield diocese established.

1875: Boston made archdiocese.

1904: Fall River diocese established.

Michigan

1641: Jesuits Isaac Jogues and Charles Raymbaut preached to Chippewas; named the rapids Sault Sainte Marie.

1660: Jesuit René Menard opened first regular mission in Lake Superior region.

1668: Father Marquette founded Sainte Marie Mission at Sault Sainte Marie.

1671: Father Marquette founded St. Ignace Mission on north shore of Straits of Mackinac.

1701: Fort Pontchartrain founded on present site of Detroit and placed in command of Antoine de la Mothe Cadillac. The Chapel of Sainte-Anne-de-Detroit founded.

1706: Franciscan Father Delhalle killed by Indians at Detroit.

1823: Father Gabriel Richard elected delegate to Congress from Michigan territory; he was

Bishop Baraga (1797–1868)

the first priest chosen for the House of Representatives.

1833: Father Frederic Baraga celebrated first Mass in present Grand Rapids.
Detroit diocese established, embracing whole Northwest Territory.

1843: *Western Catholic Register* founded at Detroit.

1845: St. Vincent's Hospital, Detroit, opened by Sisters of Charity.

1848: Cathedral of Sts. Peter and Paul, Detroit, consecrated.

1853: Vicariate Apostolic of Upper Michigan established.

1857: Sault Ste. Marie diocese established; later transferred to Marquette; Sault Ste. Marie reestablished as a titular see in 1995.

1877: University of Detroit founded.

1882: Grand Rapids diocese established.

1897: Nazareth College for women founded.

Minnesota

1680: Falls of St. Anthony discovered by Franciscan Louis Hennepin.

1727: First chapel, St. Michael the Archangel, erected near town of Frontenac and placed in charge of French Jesuits.

1732: Fort St. Charles built; Jesuits ministered to settlers.

1736: Jesuit Jean Pierre Aulneau killed by Indians.

1839: Swiss Catholics from Canada settled near Fort Snelling; Bishop Loras of Dubuque, accompanied by Father Pellamourgues, visited the Fort and administered sacraments.

1841: Father Lucian Galtier built Church of St. Paul, thus forming nucleus of modern city of same name.

1850: St. Paul diocese established.

1851: Sisters of St. Joseph arrived in state.

1857: St. John's University founded.

1888: St. Paul made archdiocese; name changed to St. Paul and Minneapolis in 1966.

1889: Duluth, St. Cloud, and Winona dioceses established.

Mississippi

1540: Chaplains with De Soto expedition entered territory.

1682: Franciscans Zenobius Membre and Anastase Douay preached to Taensa and Natchez Indians. Father Membre offered first recorded Mass in the state on March 29, Easter Sunday.

1698: Priests of Québec Seminary founded missions near Natchez and Fort Adams.

1702: Father Nicholas Foucault murdered by Indians near Fort Adams.

1721: Missions practically abandoned, with only Father Juif working among Yazoos.

1725: Jesuit Mathurin de Petit carried on mission work in northern Mississippi.

1729: Indians tomahawked Jesuit Paul du Poisson near Fort Rosalie; Father Jean Souel shot by Yazoos.

1736: Jesuit Antoine Senat and seven French officers burned at stake by Chickasaws.

1822: Vicariate Apostolic of Mississippi and Alabama established.

1825: Mississippi made a separate vicariate apostolic.

1837: Natchez diocese established; became Natchez-Jackson in 1956; transferred to Jackson in 1977. (Natchez was established as a titular see.)

1848: Sisters of Charity opened orphan asylum and school in Natchez.

Missouri

1700: Jesuit Gabriel Marest established a mission among Kaskaskia Indians near St. Louis.

1734: French Catholic miners and traders settled Old Mines and Sainte Genevieve.

1750: Jesuits visited French settlers.

1762: Mission established at St. Charles.

1767: Carondelet mission established.

1770: First church founded at St. Louis.

1811: Jesuits established Indian mission school at Florissant.

1818: Bishop Dubourg arrived at St. Louis, with Vincentians Joseph Rosati and Felix de Andreis. St. Louis University, the diocesan (Kenrick) seminary and the Vincentian Seminary in Perryville trace their origins to them. Rose Philippine Duchesne arrived at St. Charles; founded first American convent of the Society of the Sacred Heart; missionary; beatified 1940; canonized 1988.

1826: St. Louis diocese established.

1828: Sisters of Charity opened first hospital west of the Mississippi at St. Louis.

1832: *The Shepherd of the Valley*, first Catholic paper west of the Mississippi.

1845: First conference of Society of St. Vincent de Paul in U.S. founded at St. Louis.

1847: St. Louis made archdiocese.

1865: A Test Oath Law passed by State Legislature (called Drake Convention) to crush Catholicism in Missouri. Law declared unconstitutional by Supreme Court in 1866.

1867: College of St. Teresa for women founded at Kansas City.

1868: St. Joseph diocese established.

1880: Kansas City diocese established.

Montana

1743: Pierre and Francois Verendrye, accompanied by Jesuit Father Coquart, may have explored territory.

1833: Indian missions handed over to care of Jesuits by Second Provincial Council of Baltimore.

1840: Jesuit Pierre De Smet began missionary work among Flathead and Pend d'Oreille Indians.

1841: St. Mary's Mission established by Father De Smet and two companions on the Bitter Root River in present Stevensville.

1845: Jesuit Antonio Ravalli arrived at St. Mary's Mission; Ravalli County named in his honor.

1859: Fathers Point and Hoecken established St. Peter's Mission near the Great Falls.

1869: Sisters of Charity founded a hospital and school in Helena.

1884: Helena diocese established.

1904: Great Falls diocese established; redesignated Great Falls-Billings in 1980.

Nebraska

1541: Coronado expedition, accompanied by Franciscan Juan de Padilla, reached the Platte River.

1673: Father Marquette visited Nebraska Indians.

1720: Franciscan Juan Miguel killed by Indians near Columbus.

1855: Father J. F. Tracy administered to Catholic settlement of St. Patrick and to Catholics in Omaha.

1856: Land was donated by Governor Alfred Cumming for a church in Omaha.

1857: Nebraska vicariate apostolic established.

1878: Creighton University established.

1881: Poor Clares, first contemplative group in state, arrived in Omaha.
Duchesne College established.

1885: Omaha diocese established.

1887: Lincoln diocese established.

Nevada

1774: Franciscan missionaries passed through Nevada on way to California missions.

1860: First parish, serving Genoa, Carson City, and Virginia City, established.

1862: Rev. Patrick Manogue appointed pastor of Virginia City; he established a school for boys and girls, an orphanage, and hospital.

1871: Church erected at Reno.

New Hampshire

1630: Territory made part of a prefecture apostolic embracing all of New England.

1784: State Constitution included a religious test which barred Catholics from public office; local support was provided for public Protestant teachers of religion.

1818: The Barber family of Claremont was visited by their son Virgil (converted to Catholicism in 1816) accompanied by Father Charles French, O.P. The visit led to the conversion of the entire Barber family.

1823: Father Virgil Barber, minister who became a Jesuit priest, built first Catholic church and school at Claremont.

1830: Church of St. Aloysius dedicated at Dover.

1853: New Hampshire made part of the Portland diocese.

1858: Sisters of Mercy began to teach school at St. Anne's, Manchester.

1877: Catholics obtained full civil liberty and rights.

1884: Manchester diocese established.

1893: St. Anselm's College opened; St. Anselm's Abbey canonically erected.

New Jersey

1668: William Douglass of Bergen was refused a seat in General Assembly because he was a Catholic.

1672: Fathers Harvey and Gage visited Catholics in Woodbridge and Elizabethtown.

1701: Tolerance granted to all but "papists."

1744: Jesuit Theodore Schneider of Pennsylvania visited German Catholics of New Jersey.

1762: Fathers Ferdinand Farmer and Robert Harding working among Catholics in state.

1765: First Catholic community organized in New Jersey at Macopin in Passaic County.

1776: State Constitution tacitly excluded Catholics from office.

1799: Foundation of first Catholic school in state, St. John's at Trenton.

1814: First church in Trenton erected.

1820: Father Richard Bulger, of St. John's, Paterson, first resident pastor in state.

1844: Catholics obtained full civil liberty and rights.

1853: Newark diocese established.

1856: Seton Hall University established.

1878: John P. Holland, teacher at St. John's School, Paterson, invented first workable submarine.

1881: Trenton diocese established.

New Mexico

1539: Territory explored by Franciscan Marcos de Niza.

1581: Franciscans Agustin Rodriguez, Juan de Santa Maria, and Francisco Lopez named the region "New Mexico"; they later died at hands of Indians.

1598: Juan de Onate founded a colony at Chamita, where first chapel in state was built.

1609-10: Santa Fe founded.

1631: Franciscan Pedro de Miranda was killed by Indians.

1632: Franciscan Francisco Letrado was killed by Indians.

1672: Franciscan Pedro de Avila y Ayala was killed by Indians.

1675: Franciscan Alonso Gil de Avila was killed by Indians.

1680: Pueblo Indian revolt; 21 Franciscan missionaries massacred; missions destroyed.

1692: Franciscan missions refounded and expanded.

1696: Indians rebelled, five more Franciscan missionaries killed.

1850: Jean Baptiste Lamy appointed head of newly established Vicariate Apostolic of New Mexico.

1852: Sisters of Loreto arrived in Santa Fe.

1853: Santa Fe diocese established.

1859: Christian Brothers arrived, established first school for boys in New Mexico (later St. Michael's College).

1865: Sisters of Charity started first orphanage and hospital in Santa Fe. It was closed in 1966.

1875: Santa Fe made archdiocese.

New York

1524: Giovanni da Verrazano was first white man to enter New York Bay.

1642: Jesuits Isaac Jogues and Rene Goupil were mutilated by Mohawks; Rene Goupil was killed by them shortly afterwards. Dutch Calvinists rescued Father Jogues.

1646: Jesuit Isaac Jogues and John Lalande were martyred by Iroquois at Ossernenon, now Auriesville.

1654: The Onondagas were visited by Jesuits from Canada.

1655: First permanent mission established near Syracuse.

1656: Church of St. Mary erected on Onondaga Lake, in first French settlement within state.

Kateri Tekakwitha, "Lily of the Mohawks," was born at Ossernenon, now Auriesville (d. in Canada, 1680). She was beatified in 1980.

1658: Indian uprisings destroyed missions among Cayugas, Senecas, and Oneidas.

1664: English took New Amsterdam. Freedom of conscience allowed by the Duke of York, the new Lord Proprietor.

1667: Missions were restored under protection of Garaconthie, Onondaga chief.

1678: Franciscan Louis Hennepin, first white man to describe Niagara Falls, celebrated Mass there.

1682: Thomas Dongan appointed governor by Duke of York.

1683: English Jesuits came to New York, later opened a school.

1700: Although Assembly enacted a bill calling for religious toleration of all Christians in 1683, other penal laws were now enforced against Catholics; all priests were ordered out of the province.

1709: French Jesuit missionaries obliged to give up their central New York missions.

1741: Because of an alleged popish plot to burn city of New York, four whites were hanged and 11 blacks burned at stake.

1774: Elizabeth Bayley Seton, foundress of the American Sisters of Charity, was born in New York City on August 28. She was canonized in 1975.

1777: State Constitution gave religious liberty, but the naturalization law required an oath to renounce allegiance to any foreign ruler, ecclesiastical as well as civil.

Blessed Kateri Tekakwitha
"Lily of the Mohawks"

**John Cardinal McCloskey
First American Cardinal**

1785: Cornerstone was laid for St. Peter's Church, New York City, first permanent structure of Catholic worship in state.
Trusteeism began to cause trouble at New York.

1806: Anti-Catholic 1777 Test Oath for naturalization repealed.

1808: New York diocese established.

1823: Father Felix Varela of Cuba, educator, theologian, and social reformer, arrived in New York; established churches and charitable organizations; published journals and philosophical works.

1828: New York State Legislature enacted a law upholding sanctity of seal of confession.

1834: First native New Yorker to become a secular priest, Rev. John McCloskey, was ordained.

1836: John Nepomucene Neumann arrived from Bohemia and was ordained a priest in Old St. Patrick's Cathedral, New York City. He was canonized in 1977.

1841: Fordham University and Manhattanville College established.

1847: Albany and Buffalo dioceses established.

1850: New York made archdiocese.

1853: Brooklyn diocese established.

1856: Present St. Bonaventure University and Christ the King Seminary founded at Allegany.

1858: Cornerstone was laid of second (present) St. Patrick's Cathedral, New York City. The cathedral was completed in 1879.

1868: Rochester diocese established.

1872: Ogdensburg diocese established.

1875: Archbishop John McCloskey of New York made first American cardinal by Pope Pius IX.

1878: Franciscan Sisters of Allegany were first native American community to send members to foreign missions.

1880: William R. Grace was first Catholic mayor of New York City.

1886: Syracuse diocese established.

1889: Mother Frances Xavier Cabrini arrived in New York City to begin work among Italian immigrants. She was canonized in 1946.

North Carolina

1526: The Ayllon expedition attempted to establish a settlement on Carolina coast.

1540: De Soto expedition, accompanied by chaplains, entered state.

1776: State Constitution denied office to "those who denied the truths of the Protestant religion."

1805: The few Catholics in state were served by visiting missionaries.

1821: Bishop John England of Charleston celebrated Mass in the ballroom of the home of William Gaston at New Bern, marking the start of organization of the first parish, St. Paul's, in the state.

1835: William Gaston, State Supreme Court Justice, succeeded in having the article denying religious freedom repealed.

1852: First Catholic church erected in Charlotte.

1868: North Carolina vicariate apostolic established.
Catholics obtained full civil liberty and rights.

1874: Sisters of Mercy arrived, opened an academy, several schools, hospitals, and an orphanage.

1876: Benedictine priory and school (later Belmont Abbey College) founded at Belmont; priory designated an abbey in 1884.

North Dakota

1742: Pierre and Francois Verendrye, accompanied by Jesuit Father Coquart, explored territory.

1818: Canadian priests ministered to Catholics in area.

1840: Jesuit Father De Smet made first of several trips among Mandan and Gros Ventre Indians.

1848: Father George Belcourt, first American resident priest in territory, reestablished Pembina Mission.

1874: Grey Nuns arrived at Fort Totten to conduct a school.

1889: Jamestown diocese established; transferred to Fargo in 1897; Jamestown was reestablished as a titular see in 1995.

1893: Benedictines founded St. Gall Monastery at Devil's Lake (moved to Richardton in 1899 and became an abbey in 1903.)

Ohio

1749: Jesuits in expedition of Céleron de Blainville preached to Indians.
First religious services were held within

present limits of Ohio. Jesuit Joseph de Bonnecamps celebrated Mass at mouth of Little Miami River and in other places.

1751: First Catholic settlement founded among Huron Indians near Sandusky by Jesuit Father de la Richardie.

1790: Benedictine Pierre Didier ministered to French immigrants.

1812: Bishop Flaget of Bardstown visited and baptized Catholics of Lancaster and Somerset Counties.

1818: Dominican Father Edward Fenwick (later first bishop of Cincinnati) built St. Joseph's Church.

1821: Cincinnati diocese established.

1830: At request of Bishop Fenwick Dominican Sisters from Kentucky established second Dominican foundation in U.S. at Somerset (transferred to Columbus in 1868).

1831: Xavier University founded.

1843: Members of Congregation of Most Precious Blood arrived in Cincinnati from Switzerland.

1845: Cornerstone laid for St. Peter's Cathedral, Cincinnati.

1847: Cleveland diocese established.

1850: Cincinnati made archdiocese.
Marianists opened St. Mary's Institute, now University of Dayton.

1865: Sisters of Charity opened hospital in Cleveland, first institution of its kind in city.

1868: Columbus diocese established.

1871: Ursuline College for women opened at Cleveland.

Oklahoma

1540: De Soto expedition, accompanied by chaplains, explored territory.

1541: Coronado expedition, accompanied by Franciscan Juan de Padilla, explored state.

1630: Spanish Franciscan Juan de Salas labored among Indians.

1700: Scattered Catholic families were visited by priests from Kansas and Arkansas.

1874: First Catholic church built by Father Smyth at Atoka.

1876: Prefecture Apostolic of Indian Territory established with Benedictine Isidore Robot as its head.

1886: First Catholic day school for Choctaw and white children opened by Sisters of Mercy at Krebs.

1891: Vicariate Apostolic of Oklahoma and Indian Territory established.

1905: Oklahoma diocese established; title changed to Oklahoma City and Tulsa, 1930.

Oregon

1603: Vizcaino explored northern Oregon coast.

1774: Franciscan missionaries accompanied Juan Perez on his expedition to coast, and Heceta a year later.

1811: Catholic Canadian trappers and traders with John J. Astor expedition founded first American settlement at Astoria.

1834: Indian missions in Northwest entrusted to Jesuits by Holy See.

1838: Abbe Blanchet appointed vicar general to Bishop of Québec with jurisdiction over area which included Oregon Territory.

1839: First Mass celebrated at present site of St. Paul.

1843: Oregon vicariate apostolic established.
St. Joseph's College for boys opened.

1844: Jesuit Pierre De Smet established Mission of St. Francis Xavier near St. Paul.
Sisters of Notre Dame de Namur, first to enter Oregon, opened an academy for girls.

1846: Vicariate made an ecclesiastical province with Bishop Blanchet as first Archbishop of Oregon City (now Portland).

1847: First priest was ordained in Oregon.

1848: First Provincial Council of Oregon.

1857: Death of Dr. John McLoughlin, "Father of Oregon."

1865: Rev. H. H. Spalding, a Protestant missionary, published the Whitman Myth to hinder work of Catholic missionaries.

1874: Catholic Indian Mission Bureau established.

1875: St. Vincent's Hospital, first in state, opened at Portland.

1903: Baker diocese established.

Pennsylvania

1673: Priests from Maryland ministered to Catholics in the Colony.

1682: Religious toleration was extended to members of all faiths.

1729: Jesuit Joseph Greaton became first resident missionary of Philadelphia.

1734: St. Joseph's Church, first Catholic church in Philadelphia, was opened by Father Greaton.

1741: Jesuit Fathers Schneider and Wappeler ministered to German immigrants.
Conewego Chapel, a combination chapel and dwelling, was built by Father William Wappeler, S.J., a priest sent to minister to the German Catholic immigrants who settled in the area in the 1730s.

1782: St. Mary's Parochial School opened at Philadelphia.

1788: Holy Trinity Church, Philadelphia, was incorporated; first exclusively national church organized in U.S.

1797: Augustinian Matthew Carr founded St. Augustine parish, Philadelphia.

1799: Prince Demetrius Gallitzin (Father Augustine Smith) built church in western Pennsylvania, at Loreto.

1808: Philadelphia diocese established.

1814: St. Joseph's Orphanage was opened at Philadelphia; first Catholic institution for children in U.S.

1842: University of Villanova founded by Augustinians.

1843: Pittsburgh diocese established.

1844: Thirteen persons killed, two churches and a school burned in Know-Nothing riots at Philadelphia.

1846: First Benedictine Abbey in New World founded near Latrobe by Father Boniface Wimmer.

1852: Redemptorist John Nepomucene Neumann became fourth bishop of Philadelphia. He was beatified in 1963 and canonized in 1977.

1853: Erie diocese established.

1868: Scranton and Harrisburg dioceses established.

1871: Chestnut Hill College, first for women in state, founded.

1875: Philadelphia made archdiocese.

1876: Allegheny diocese established by division of Pittsburgh diocese; reunited to Pittsburgh 1877, with resignation of its first and only bishop; suppressed in 1889; later reestablished as a titular see.

1891: Katharine Drexel founded Sisters of Blessed Sacrament for Indians and Colored Peoples. She was beatified in 1988.

1901: Altoona-Johnstown diocese established.

Rhode Island

1663: Colonial Charter granted freedom of conscience.

1719: Laws denied Catholics the right to hold public office.

1829: St. Mary's Church, Pawtucket, was first Catholic church in state.

1837: Parochial schools inaugurated in state.

St. Katharine Drexel

First Catholic church in Providence was built.

1851: Sisters of Mercy began work in Rhode Island.

1872: Providence diocese established.

1900: Trappists took up residence in state.

South Carolina

1569: Jesuit Juan Rogel was the first resident priest in the territory.

1573: First Franciscans arrived in southeastern section.

1606: Bishop Altamirano conducted visitation of area.

1655: Franciscans had two missions among Indians; later destroyed by English.

1697: Religious liberty granted to all except "papists."

1790: Catholics given right to vote.

1820: Charleston diocese established.

1822: Bishop England founded *U.S. Catholic Miscellany*, first Catholic paper of a strictly religious nature in U.S.

1830: Sisters of Our Lady of Mercy, first in state, took up residence at Charleston.

1847: Cornerstone of Cathedral of St. John the Baptist, Charleston, was laid.

1861: Cathedral and many institutions destroyed in Charleston fire.

South Dakota

1842: Father Augustine Ravoux began ministrations to French and Indians at Fort Pierre, Vermilion, and Prairie du Chien; printed devotional book in Sioux language the following year.

1867: Parish organized among the French at Jefferson.

1878: Benedictines opened school for Sioux children at Fort Yates.

1889: Sioux Falls diocese established.

1902: Lead diocese established; transferred to Rapid City, 1930; Lead was reestablished as a titular see in 1995.

Tennessee

1541: Cross planted on shore of Mississippi by De Soto; accompanying the expedition were Fathers John de Gallegos and Louis De Soto.

1682: Franciscan Fathers Membre and Douay accompanied La Salle to present site of Memphis; may have offered the first Masses in the territory.

1800: Catholics were served by priests from Bardstown, Kentucky.

1822: Non-Catholics assisted in building church in Nashville.

1837: Nashville diocese established.

1843: Sisters of Charity opened a school for girls in Nashville.

1860: Sisters of St. Dominic from Somerset, Ohio, arrived in Nashville to open a school for girls.

1871: Christian Brothers opened a school for boys in Memphis; it later became Christian Brothers College (now University).

Texas

1541: Missionaries with Coronado expedition probably entered territory.

1553: Dominicans Diego de la Cruz, Hernando Mendez, Juan Ferrer, Brother Juan de Mina killed by Indians.

1675: Bosque-Larios missionary expedition entered region; Father Juan Larios offered first recorded high Mass.

1682: Mission Corpus Christi de Isleta (Ysleta) founded by Franciscans near El Paso, first mission in present-day Texas.

1690: Mission San Francisco de los Tejas founded in east Texas.

1703: Mission San Francisco de Solano founded on Rio Grande; rebuilt in 1718 as San Antonio de Valero or the Alamo.

1717: Franciscan Antonio Margil founded six missions in northeast.

1720: San José y San Miguel de Aguayo Mission founded by Fray Antonio Margil de Jesus.

1721: Franciscan Brother José Pita killed by Indians at Carnezeria.

1728: Site of San Antonio settled.

1738: Construction of San Fernando Cathedral at San Antonio.

1744: Mission church of the Alamo built.

1750: Franciscan Francisco Xavier was killed by Indians; so were José Ganzabal in 1752, and Alonzo Ferrares and José San Esteban in 1758.

1793: Mexico secularized missions.

1825: Governments of Cohuila and Texas secularized all Indian missions.

1838-39: Irish priests ministered to settlements of Refugio and San Patricio.

1841: Vicariate of Texas established.

1847: Ursuline Sisters established their first academy in territory at Galveston.
Galveston diocese established.

1852: Oblate Fathers and Franciscans arrived in Galveston to care for new influx of German Catholics.
St. Mary's College (now University) founded at San Antonio.

1854: Know-Nothing Party began to stir up hatred against Catholics.
Oldest Polish settlement in Texas established December 24; settlers named the area Panna Maria (Virgin Mary in Polish).

1858: Texas Legislature passed law entitling all schools that granted free scholarships and met state requirements to share in school fund.

1874: San Antonio diocese established.
Vicariate of Brownsville established.

1881: St. Edward's College founded; became first chartered college in state in 1889.
Sisters of Charity founded Incarnate Word College at San Antonio.

1890: Dallas diocese established; changed to Dallas-Ft. Worth, 1953; made two separate dioceses, 1969.

Utah

1776: Franciscans Silvestre de Escalante and Atanasio Dominguez reached Utah (Salt) Lake; first white men known to enter the territory.

1858: Jesuit Father De Smet accompanied General Harney as chaplain on expedition sent to settle troubles between Mormons and U.S. government.

1866: On June 29 Father Edward Kelly offered first Mass in Salt Lake City in Mormon Assembly Hall.

1886: Utah vicariate apostolic established.

1891: Salt Lake City diocese established.

Vermont

1609: Champlain expedition passed through territory.

1666: Captain La Motte built fort and shrine of St. Anne on Isle La Motte; Sulpician Father Dollier de Casson celebrated first Mass.

1668: Bishop Laval of Québec (beatified in 1980), administered confirmation in region; this was the first area in northeastern U.S. to receive an episcopal visit.

1710: Jesuits ministered to Indians near Lake Champlain.

1793: Discriminatory measures against Catholics were repealed.

1830: Father Jeremiah O'Callaghan became first resident priest in state.

1853: Burlington diocese established.

1854: Sisters of Charity of Providence arrived to conduct St. Joseph's Orphanage at Burlington.

1904: St. Michael's College founded.

Virginia

1526: Dominican Antonio de Montesinos offered first Mass on Virginia soil.

1561: Dominicans visited the coast.

1571: Father John Baptist de Segura and seven Jesuit companions killed by Indians.

1642: Priests outlawed and Catholics denied right to vote.

1689: Capuchin Christopher Plunket was captured and exiled to a coastal island where he died in 1697.

1776: Religious freedom granted.

1791: Father Jean Dubois arrived at Richmond with letters from Lafayette; the House of Delegates was placed at his disposal for celebration of Mass.
A church was built in Norfolk (St. Mary of the Immaculate Conception); it was designated a minor basilica in 1991.

1796: A church was built at Alexandria.

1820: Richmond diocese established.

1822: Trusteeism created serious problems in diocese; Bishop Patrick Kelly resigned the see.

1848: Sisters of Charity opened an orphan asylum at Norfolk.

1866: School Sisters of Notre Dame and Sisters of Charity opened academies for girls at Richmond.

Washington

1774: Spaniards explored the region.

1838: Fathers Blanchet and Demers, "Apostles of the Northwest," were sent to territory by Archbishop of Québec.

1840: Cross erected on Whidby Island, Puget Sound.

1843: Vicariate Apostolic of Oregon, including Washington, was established.

1844: Mission of St. Paul founded at Colville. Six Sisters of Notre Dame de Namur began work in area.

1846: Walla Walla diocese established; suppressed in 1850 (reestablished later as a titular see).

1850: Nesqually diocese established; transferred to Seattle, 1907; Nesqually reestablished as a titular see in 1995.

1856: Providence Academy, the first permanent Catholic school in the Northwest, was built at Fort Vancouver by Mother Joseph Pariseau of the Sisters of Charity of Providence.

1887: Gonzaga University founded.

West Virginia

1749: Father Joseph de Bonnecamps, accompanying the Bienville expedition, may have offered first Mass in the territory.

1821: First Catholic church in Wheeling.

1838: Sisters of Charity founded school at Martinsburg.

1848: Visitation Nuns established academy for girls in Wheeling.

1850: Wheeling diocese established; name changed to Wheeling-Charleston, 1974.
Wheeling Hospital incorporated, the oldest Catholic charitable institution in territory.

1955: Wheeling College established.

Wisconsin

1661: Jesuit René Menard, first known missionary in the territory, was killed or lost in the Black River district.

1665: Jesuit Claude Allouez founded Mission of the Holy Ghost at La Pointe Chegoimegon, now Bayfield; was the first permanent mission in region.

1673: Father Marquette and Louis Joliet traveled from Green Bay down the Wisconsin and Mississippi rivers.

1762: Suppression of Jesuits in French Colonies closed many missions for 30 years.

1843: Milwaukee diocese established.

1853: St. John's Cathedral, Milwaukee, was built.

1864: State charter granted for establishment of Marquette University; first students admitted, 1881.

1868: Green Bay and La Crosse dioceses established.

1875: Milwaukee made archdiocese.

1905: Superior diocese established.

Wyoming

1840: Jesuit Pierre De Smet offered first Mass near Green River.

1851: Father De Smet held peace conference with Indians near Fort Laramie.

1867: Father William Kelly, first resident priest, arrived in Cheyenne and built first church a year later.

1873: Father Eugene Cusson became first resident pastor in Laramie.

1875: Sisters of Charity of Leavenworth opened school and orphanage at Laramie.

1884: Jesuits took over pastoral care of Shoshone and Arapaho Indians.

1887: Cheyenne diocese established.

Puerto Rico

1493: Island discovered by Columbus on his second voyage; he named it San Juan de Borinquen (the Indian name for Puerto Rico).

1509: Juan Ponce de León, searching for gold, colonized the island and became its first governor; present population descended mainly from early Spanish settlers.

1511: Diocese of Puerto Rico established as suffragan of Seville, Spain; Bishop Alonso Manso, sailing from Spain in 1512, became first bishop to take up residence in New World.

1645: Synod held in Puerto Rico to regulate frequency of Masses according to distances people had to walk.

1898: Puerto Rico ceded to U.S. (became self-governing Commonwealth in 1952); inhabitants granted U.S. citizenship in 1917.

MISSIONARIES TO THE AMERICAS

An asterisk with a feast date indicates that the saint or blessed is listed in the General Roman Calendar or the proper calendar for U.S. dioceses.

Allouez, Claude Jean (1622-1689): French Jesuit; missionary in Canada and midwestern U.S.; preached to 20 different tribes of Indians and baptized over 10,000; vicar general of Northwest.

Altham, John (1589-1640): English Jesuit; missionary among Indians in Maryland.

Anchieta, José de, Blessed (1534-1597): Portuguese Jesuit, born Canary Islands; missionary in Brazil; writer; beatified 1980; feast, June 9.

Andreis, Felix de (1778-1820): Italian Vincentian; missionary and educator in western U.S.

Aparicio, Sebastian, Blessed (1502-1600): Franciscan brother, born Spain; settled in Mexico, c. 1533; worked as road builder and farmer before becoming Franciscan at about the age of 70; beatified, 1787; feast, February 25.

Badin, Stephen T. (1768-1853): French missioner; came to U.S., 1792, when Sulpician seminary in Paris was closed; ordained, 1793, Baltimore, the first priest ordained in U.S.; missionary in Kentucky, Ohio, and Michigan; bought land on which Notre Dame University now stands; buried on its campus.

Baraga, Frederic (1797-1868): Slovenian missionary bishop in U.S.; studied at Ljubljana and Vienna, ordained, 1823; came to U.S., 1830; missionary to Indians of Upper Michigan; first bishop of Marquette, 1857-1868; wrote Chippewa grammar, dictionary, prayer book, and other works.

Bertran, Louis, St. (1526-1581): Spanish Dominican; missionary in Colombia and Caribbean, 1562-69; canonized, 1671; feast, October 9.

Betancur, Pedro de San José, Blessed (1626-1667): Secular Franciscan, born Canary Islands; arrived in Guatemala, 1651; established hospital, school, and homes for poor; beatified 1980; feast, April 25.

Bourgeoys, Marguerite, St. (1620-1700): French foundress, missionary; settled in Canada, 1653; founded Congregation of Notre Dame, 1658; beatified, 1950; canonized 1982; feast, January 12.

Brébeuf, Jean de, St. (1593-1649): French Jesuit; missionary among Huron Indians in Canada; martyred by Iroquois, March 16, 1649; canonized, 1930; one of Jesuit North American martyrs; feast, October 19* (U.S.).

Cancer de Barbastro, Luis (1500-1549):

Spanish Dominican; began missionary work in Middle America, 1533; killed at Tampa Bay, FL.

Castillo, John de, St. (1596-1628): Spanish Jesuit; worked in Paraguay Indian mission settlements (reductions); martyred; beatified, 1934; canonized, 1988; feast, November 16.

Catala, Magin (1761-1830): Spanish Franciscan; worked in California mission of Santa Clara for 36 years.

Chabanel, Noël, St. (1613-1649): French Jesuit; missionary among Huron Indians in Canada; murdered by renegade Huron, December 8, 1649; canonized, 1930; one of Jesuit North American martyrs; feast, October 19* (U.S.).

Chaumonot, Pierre Joseph (1611-1693): French Jesuit; missionary among Indians in Canada.

Claver, Peter, St. (1581-1654): Spanish Jesuit; missionary among Blacks of South America and West Indies; canonized, 1888; patron of Catholic missions among black people; feast, September 9*.

Daniel, Anthony, St. (1601-1648): French Jesuit; missionary among Huron Indians in Canada; martyred by Iroquois, July 4, 1648; canonized, 1930; one of Jesuit North American martyrs; feast, October 19* (U.S.).

De Smet, Pierre Jean (1801-1873): Belgian-born Jesuit; missionary among Indians of northwestern U.S.; served as intermediary between Indians and U.S. government; wrote on Indian culture.

Duchesne, Rose Philippine, St. (1769-1852): French nun; educator and missionary in the U.S.; established first convent of the Society of the Sacred Heart in the U.S., at St. Charles, MO; founded schools for girls; did missionary work among Indians; beatified, 1940; canonized, 1988; feast, November 18* (U.S.).

Farmer, Ferdinand (family name, Steinmeyer) (1720-1786): German Jesuit; missionary in Philadelphia, where he died; one of the first missionaries in New Jersey.

Flaget, Benedict J. (1763-1850): French Sulpician bishop; came to U.S., 1792; missionary and educator in U.S.; first bishop of Bardstown, Kentucky (now Louisville), 1810-32; 1833-50.

Gallitzin, Demetrius (1770-1840): Russian prince, born The Hague; convert, 1787; ordained priest at Baltimore, 1795; frontier missionary, known as Father Smith; Gallitzin, Pennsylvania, named for him.

Garnier, Charles, St. (c. 1606-1649): French Jesuit; missionary among Hurons in Canada; martyred by Iroquois, December 7, 1649; canonized, 1930; one of Jesuit North American martyrs; feast, October 19* (U.S.).

Gibault, Pierre (1737-1804): Canadian missionary in Illinois and Indiana; aided in securing states of Ohio, Indiana, Illinois, Michigan, and Wisconsin for the Americans during Revolution.

Gonzalez, Roch, St. (1576-1628): Paraguayan Jesuit; worked in Paraguay Indian mission settlements (reductions); martyred; beatified, 1934; canonized, 1988; feast, November 16.

Goupil, René, St. (1607-1642): French lay missionary; had studied surgery at Orleans, France; missionary companion of St. Isaac Jogues among the Hurons; martyred, September 29, 1642; canonized, 1930; one of Jesuit North American martyrs; feast, October 19* (U.S.).

Gravier, Jacques (1651-1708): French Jesuit; missionary among Indians of Canada and midwestern U.S.

Hennepin, Louis (d. c. 1701): Belgian-born Franciscan missionary and explorer of Great Lakes region and Upper Mississippi, 1675-81, when he returned to Europe.

Jesuit North American Martyrs: Isaac Jogues, Anthony Daniel, John de Brébeuf, Gabriel Lalemant, Charles Garnier, Noël Chabanel (Jesuit priests), and René Goupil and John Lalande (lay missionaries), who were martyred between September 29, 1642, and December 9, 1649, in the missions of New France; canonized June 29, 1930; feast, October 19* (U.S.).

Jogues, Isaac, St. (1607-1646): French Jesuit; missionary among Indians in Canada; martyred near present site of Auriesville, New York, by Mohawks, October 18, 1646; canonized, 1930; one of Jesuit North American martyrs; feast, October 19* (U.S.).

Kino, Eusebio (1645-1711): Italian Jesuit; missionary and explorer in U.S.; arrived Southwest, 1681; established 25 Indian missions, took part in 14 exploring expeditions in northern Mexico, Arizona and southern California; helped develop livestock raising and farming in the area. He was selected in 1965 to represent Arizona in Statuary Hall.

Lalande, John, St. (d. 1646): French lay missionary, companion of Isaac Jogues; martyred by Mohawks at Auriesville, New York, October 19, 1646; canonized, 1930; one of Jesuit North American martyrs; feast, October 19* (U.S.).

Lalemant, Gabriel, St. (1610-1649): French Jesuit; missionary among the Hurons in Canada; martyred by the Iroquois, March 17, 1649; canonized, 1930; one of Jesuit North American martyrs; feast, October 19* (U.S.).

Lamy, Jean Baptiste (1814-1888): French prelate; came to U.S., 1839; missionary in Ohio and Kentucky; bishop in Southwest from 1850; first bishop (later archbishop) of Santa Fe,

1850-1885. He was nominated in 1951 to represent New Mexico in Statuary Hall.

Las Casas, Bartolomé (1474-1566): Spanish Dominican; missionary in Haiti, Jamaica, and Venezuela; reformer of abuses against Indians and black people; bishop of Chalapas, Mexico, 1544-47; historian.

Laval, Françoise de Montmorency, Blessed (1623-1708): French-born missionary bishop in Canada; named vicar apostolic of Canada, 1658; first bishop of Québec, 1674; jurisdiction extended over all French-claimed territory in New World; beatified 1980; feast, May 6.

Manogue, Patrick (1831-1895): Missionary bishop in U.S., born Ireland; migrated to U.S.; miner in California; studied for priesthood at St. Mary's of the Lake, Chicago, and St. Sulpice, Paris; ordained, 1861; missionary among Indians of California and Nevada; coadj. bishop, 1881-84, and bishop, 1884-86, of Grass Valley; first bishop of Sacramento, 1886-1895, when see was transferred there.

Margil, Antonio, Ven. (1657-1726): Spanish Franciscan; missionary in Middle America; apostle of Guatemala; established missions in Texas.

Marie of the Incarnation, St. (Marie Guyard Martin) (1599-1672): French widow; joined Ursuline Nuns; arrived in Canada, 1639; first superior of Ursulines in Québec; missionary to Indians; writer; beatified 1980; feast, April 30.

Marquette, Jacques (1637-1675): French Jesuit; missionary and explorer in America; sent to New France, 1666; began missionary work among Ottawa Indians on Lake Superior, 1668; accompanied Joliet down the Mississippi to mouth of the Arkansas, 1673, and returned to Lake Michigan by way of Illinois River; made a second trip over the same route; his diary and map are of historical significance. He was selected in 1895 to represent Wisconsin in Statuary Hall.

Massias (Macias), John de, St. (1585-1645): Dominican brother, a native of Spain; entered Dominican Friary at Lima, Peru, 1622; served as doorkeeper until his death; beatified, 1837; canonized 1975; feast, September 16.

Mazzuchelli, Samuel C. (1806-1864): Italian Dominican; missionary in midwestern U.S.; called builder of the West; writer. A decree advancing his beatification cause was promulgated July 6, 1993.

Membre, Zenobius (1645-1687): French Franciscan; missionary among Indians of Illinois; accompanied LaSalle expedition down the Mississippi (1681-1682) and Louisiana colonizing expedition (1684) which landed in Texas; murdered by Indians.

Mozcygemba, Leopold (1824-1891): Polish Franciscan priest and missionary, the patriarch of American Polonia; labored as a missionary in Texas and 11 other states for nearly 40 years; co-founded the Polish seminary of Sts. Cyril and Methodius in Detroit (1885) and served as confessor at Vatican Council I.

Nerinckx, Charles (1761-1824): Belgian priest; missionary in Kentucky; founded Sisters of Loreto at the Foot of the Cross.

Nobrega, Manoel (1517-1570): Portuguese Jesuit; leader of first Jesuit missionaries to Brazil, 1549.

Padilla, Juan de (d. 1542): Spanish Franciscan; missionary among Indians of Mexico and southwestern U.S.; killed by Indians in Kansas; protomartyr of the U.S.

Palou, Francisco (c. 1722-1789): Spanish Franciscan; accompanied Junípero Serra to Mexico, 1749; founded Mission Dolores in San Francisco; wrote history of the Franciscans in California.

Pariseau, Mother Mary Joseph (1833-1902): Canadian Sister of Charity of Providence; missionary in state of Washington from 1856; founded first hospitals in northwest territory; artisan and architect. Represents Washington in National Statuary Hall.

Peter of Ghent (d. 1572): Belgian Franciscan brother; missionary in Mexico for 49 years.

Porres, Martin de, St. (1579-1639): Peruvian Dominican oblate; his father was a Spanish soldier and his mother a black freedwoman from Panama; called wonder worker of Peru; beatified, 1837; canonized, 1962; feast, November 3*.

Quiroga, Vasco de (1470-1565): Spanish missionary in Mexico; founded hospitals; bishop of Michoacan, 1537.

Ravalli, Antonio (1811-1884): Italian Jesuit; missionary in far-western United States, mostly Montana, for 40 years.

Raymbaut, Charles (1602-1643): French Jesuit; missionary among Indians of Canada and northern U.S.

Richard, Gabriel (1767-1832): French Sulpician; missionary in Illinois and Michigan; a founder of University of Michigan; elected delegate to Congress from Michigan, 1823; first priest to hold seat in the House of Representatives.

Rodriguez, Alfonso, St. (1598-1628): Spanish Jesuit; missionary in Paraguay; martyred; beatified, 1934; canonized, 1988; feast, November 16.

Rosati, Joseph (1789-1843): Italian Vincentian; missionary bishop in U.S. (vicar apostolic of Mississippi and Alabama, 1822; coadj. of Louisiana and the Two Floridas, 1823-26; administrator of New Orleans, 1826-29; first bishop of St. Louis, 1826-1843).

Sahagun, Bernardino de (c. 1500-1590): Spanish Franciscan; missionary in Mexico for over 60 years; expert on Aztec archaeology.

Seelos, Francis X. (1819-1867): Redemptorist missionary, born Bavaria; ordained, 1844, at Baltimore; missionary in Pittsburgh and New Orleans.

Seghers, Charles J. (1839-1886): Belgian missionary bishop in North America; Apostle of Alaska; archbishop of Oregon City (now Portland), 1880-1884; murdered by berserk companion while on missionary journey.

Serra, Junípero, Blessed (1713-1784): Spanish Franciscan, born Majorca; missionary in America; arrived Mexico, 1749, where he did missionary work for 20 years; began work in Upper California in 1769 and established nine of the 21 Franciscan missions along the Pacific coast; baptized some 6,000 Indians and confirmed almost 5,000; a cultural pioneer of California. Represents California in Statuary Hall. He was declared venerable May 9, 1985, and was beatified September 25, 1988; feast, July 1* (U.S.).

Solanus, Francis, St. (1549-1610): Spanish Franciscan; missionary in Paraguay, Argentina, and Peru; wonder worker of the New World; canonized, 1726; feast, July 14.

Sorin, Edward F. (1814-1893): French priest; member of Congregation of Holy Cross; sent to U.S. in 1841; founder and first president of the University of Notre Dame; missionary in Indiana and Michigan.

Todadilla, Anthony de (1704-1746): Spanish Capuchin; missionary to Indians of Venezuela; killed by Motilones.

Turibius de Mogrovejo, St. (1538-1606): Spanish archbishop of Lima, Peru, c. 1580-1606; canonized 1726; feast, March 23*.

Twelve Apostles of Mexico (early 16th century): Franciscan priests; arrived in Mexico, 1524: Fathers Martin de Valencia (leader), Francisco de Soto, Martin de la Coruna, Juan Suares, Antonio de Ciudad Rodrigo, Toribio de Benevente, Garcia de Cisneros, Luis de Fuensalida, Juan de Ribas, Francisco Ximenes; Brothers Andres de Coroboda, Juan de Palos.

Valdivia, Luis de (1561-1641): Spanish Jesuit; defender of Indians in Peru and Chile.

Vasques de Espiñosa, Antonio (early 17th century): Spanish Carmelite; missionary and explorer in Mexico, Panama, and western coast of South America.

Vieira, Antonio (1608-1687): Portuguese Jesuit; preacher; missionary in Peru and Chile; protector of Indians against exploitation by slave owners and traders; considered foremost prose writer of 17th-century Portugal.

White, Andrew (1579-1656): English Jesuit; missionary among Indians in Maryland.

Wimmer, Boniface (1809-1887): German

Benedictine; missionary among German immigrants in the U.S.

Youville, Marie Marguerite d', St. (1701-1771): Canadian widow; foundress of Sisters of Charity (Grey Nuns), 1737, at Montréal; beatified, 1959; canonized 1990, first native Canadian saint; feast, December 23.

Zumarraga, Juan de (1468-1548): Spanish Franciscan; missionary; first bishop of Mexico; introduced first printing press in New World, published first book in America, a catechism for Aztec Indians; extended missions in Mexico and Central America; vigorous opponent of exploitation of Indians; approved of devotions at Guadalupe; leading figure in early church history in Mexico.

FRANCISCAN MISSIONS

The 21 Franciscan missions of Upper California were established during the 54-year period from 1769 to 1822. Located along the old El Camino Real, or King's Highway, they extended from San Diego to San Francisco and were the centers of Indian civilization, Christianity, and industry in the early history of the state.

Junípero Serra (beatified 1988) was the great pioneer of the missions of Upper California. He and his successor as superior of the work, Fermin Lasuen, each directed the establishment of nine missions. One hundred and forty-six priests of the Order of Friars Minor, most of them Spaniards, labored in the region from 1769 to 1845; sixty-seven of them died at their posts, two as martyrs. The regular time of mission service was 10 years.

The missions were secularized by the Mexican government in the 1830s but were subsequently restored to the Church by the U.S. government. They are now variously used as the sites of parish churches, a university, houses of study, and museums.

The names of the missions and the order of their establishment were as follows:

San Diego de Alcala, San Carlos Borromeo (El Carmelo), San Antonio de Padua, San Gabriel Arcangel, San Luis Obispo de Tolosa, San Francisco de Asis (Dolores), San Juan Capistrano; Santa Clara de Asis, San Buenaventura, Santa Barbara, La Purisima Concepcion de Maria Santisima, Santa Cruz, Nuestra Señora de la Soledad, San José de Guadalupe, San Juan Bautista, San Miguel Arcangel, San Fernando Rey de España, San Luis Rey de Francia, Santa Iñes, San Rafael Arcangel, San Francisco Solano de Sonoma (Sonoma).

AMERICAN CATHOLICS OF THE PAST

A

Abbelin, Peter (1843-1917): Priest, monsignor, and vicar general of the Milwaukee archdiocese; adherent of the German language and culture and the separateness of German Catholics.

Alemany, Joseph Sadoc, O.P. (1814-88): Bishop of Monterey, 1850-53 and first archbishop of San Francisco (1853-84); labored in American missions in Ohio, Kentucky, and Tennessee; attended Vatican Council I and the Third Plenary Council of Baltimore.

Allen, Fred (1894-1956): Entertainer; after a successful stage career, moved to radio in 1932 and became best known for *The Fred Allen Show* and the *Texaco Star Theater.*

Allen, Gracie (d. 1964): Entertainer and wife of George Burns, with whom she had a long and successful career; enjoyed success on stage, radio, and in films; one of the most popular entertainers of her generation.

Allouez, Claude Jean: See under *Missionaries to the Americas.*

Altham, John: See under *Missionaries to the Americas.*

Amat, Thaddeus, C.M. (1811-78): Missionary bishop; born in Spain; bishop of Monterey, California, 1854-59, and bishop of Monterey-Los Angeles, 1859-78; founded the cathedral of St. Vibiana and directed the expansion of the Church in California.

Andreis, Felix de: See under *Missionaries to the Americas.*

Anchieta, José de, Blessed: See under *Missionaries to the Americas.*

Aparicio, Sebastian, Blessed: See under *Missionaries to the Americas.*

Avery, Martha (1851-1929): Catholic lay writer and lecturer; one-time Socialist, convert to Catholicism in 1904; supported social reform and papal encyclical *Rerum Novarum;* founder of the Catholic Truth Guild.

B

Badin, Stephen T.: See *Missionaries to the Americas.*

Baker, Josephine (1906-75): African-American dancer and entertainer; worked her way out of poverty as a dancer in Philadelphia, Boston, and Harlem; moved to Paris in the 1920s; success allowed her to open *Chez Josephine*, her own nightclub, in 1926; French citizen in 1937; worked with the Red Cross and the French Resistance during World War II; granted the *Croix de Guerre* and *Legion d'Honneur* with the rosette of the Resistance; took part in the Civil Rights Movement in the 1960s.

Baraga, Frederic: See under *Missionaries to the Americas*.

Barry, John (1745-1803): Father of the U.S. Navy; born in Ireland; went to sea at a young age and eventually became a wealthy ship owner in the American colonies; supported the American Revolution and was made captain of the brig *Lexington*; the first American naval officer to engage the vaunted British Navy at sea; assisted the new republic in building a fleet.

Barry, Leonora (1849-1930): Lay leader of the Knights of Labor; helped pass the Pennsylvania Factory Inspection Act in 1889; supporter of the suffrage movement and prohibition.

Barrymore, Ethel (1879-1959): Actress and member of the famed Barrymore family; educated by the Sisters of Notre Dame de Namur; enjoyed a brilliant career on stage and screen; won Academy Award for best Supporting Actress in 1944 for *None But the Lonely Heart*.

Bauer, Mother Benedicta (1803-65): German-born Dominican missionary sister; founded convents in Brooklyn, Ohio, Tennessee, and Green Bay, and began the Dominican motherhouse in Racine, Wisconsin.

Beauregard, Pierre (1818-93) Confederate general in the Civil War; directed the bombardment of Fort Sumter in 1861; participated in the battles of First Manassas (Bull Run) and Shiloh; defended Charleston in 1863.

Benson, William (1891-1957): Admiral; graduated Naval Academy, 1877; served on various assignments and taught at the Academy, 1890-93; appointed commandant of the Philadelphia Naval Yard, 1913-15; first chief of naval operations, 1915; admiral, 1916; first president of the National Council of Catholic men, 1921-25; devout Catholic.

Bernardin, Joseph L. (1928-96): Archbishop of Chicago, 1982-96 and Cardinal from 1983; auxiliary bishop of Atlanta, 1966-72 and Archbishop of Cincinnati, 1972-82; became renowned for the grace with which he bore a scurrilous accusation of sexual misconduct and his suffering from terminal cancer; authored a best-selling book on dying in Christ.

Bertran, Louis, St.: See under *Missionaries to the Americas*.

Betancur, Pedro de San José, Blessed: See under *Missionaries to the Americas*.

Bishop, William (1885-1953): Priest and founder of the Glenmary Home Missioners.

Black Elk (1866-1950): Native American, called the Holy Man of the Oglala; as a young man, he lived with his tribe in Montana at the time of Custer's death at Little Big Horn and took part in the tragic Wounded Knee Massacre of 1890; converted in 1904 and known as a zealous catechist.

Blanc, Anthony (1792-1860): The first archbishop of New Orleans, 1850-60; bishop of New Orleans in 1835.

Blanchet, Francis N. (1795-1883): First archbishop of Oregon City (now Portland); his brother, Augustin Blanchet (1797-1887), was first bishop of Nesqually (now Seattle) from 1850-84.

Bohachevsky, Constantine (1884-1961): First metropolitan of the Byzantine Rite archeparchy of Philadelphia.

Bonaparte, Charles Joseph (1851-1921): Secretary of the Navy and U.S. Attorney General; the grandson of Jerome Bonaparte (brother to Napoleon Bonaparte); supporter and friend of Theodore Roosevelt; aggressively pursued Roosevelt's antitrust policy.

Bourgeoys, Marguerite, St.: See under *Missionaries to the Americas*.

Brady, Mathew (c.1823-96) Photographer; photographed Lincoln; best known for his photographic record of the Civil War, now in the Library of Congress.

Brébeuf, Jean de, St.: See under *Missionaries to the Americas*.

Brennan, Francis J. (1894-1968): Cardinal and American prelate who served for many years in Rome; judge, 1940-59, and dean, 1959-67, of the Roman Rota in Rome; bishop in 1967; cardinal in 1967.

Brennan, William (1906-98): Associate justice of the U.S. Supreme Court, 1956-90; justice on the New Jersey supreme court, 1952-56; the most influential liberal during the 1980s and a supporter of abortion.

Brent, Margaret (1601-c.1671): The first woman in Maryland to own land; migrated to Maryland in 1638 and granted land by Lord Baltimore; named executrix for Governor Leonard Calvert.

Brown, Fr. Raymond, S.S. (d. 1998): Scripture scholar and professor of biblical studies at Union Theological Seminary in New York; author of over 37 books on Scripture and co-editor of two editions of *The Jerome Biblical Commentary*.

Brownson, Orestes (1803-76): Journalist, author, and one of the leading lay theologians of the 19th century.

Burke, John (1875-1936): Paulist priest, social reformer, and editor of *Catholic World* (1903-22); coordinated the National Catholic War Council to advance Catholic perspectives during World War I; general secretary of the National Catholic Welfare Conference (NCWC); worked to promote a settlement of the Church-State conflict in Mexico.

Byrne, Andrew (1802-62): First bishop of Little Rock, Arkansas; worked to establish the new diocese in the face of numerous obstacles, including a chronic shortage of priests; avoided involvement in assorted controversies, especially slavery.

C

Cabot, John (c. 1450-98): Explorer; born in Italy; won the support of King Henry VII of England to find an all-water route to the East; set out to find the "Northwest Passage" but only reached Newfoundland; later made a voyage along the eastern coast of North America in the search for Japan; gave to England much of its claim to North America.

Cabrini, Frances Xavier: See under *Saints of the Church.*

Calvert, Cecil (1606-75): Second Lord Baltimore and a major figure in early Maryland; eldest son of Lord George Calvert, first Lord of Baltimore; inherited his father's control of Maryland in 1632; strove to make the colony a model for religious toleration and protected Catholics from Puritan persecution through "The Act of Concerning Religion," following the execution of King Charles I in 1649.

Calvert, Charles (1628-1714): Third Lord Baltimore and second Lord Proprietary of Maryland; his period as Lord Baltimore marked the decline in the fortunes of the Calverts in Maryland; his eldest son, Benedict Calvert, abjured Catholicism in 1713.

Calvert, George (1580-1632): Founder of the Maryland colony and first Lord Baltimore; petitioned for a charter to found a colony in Maryland; his son, Cecil, inherited the title of Lord Baltimore.

Cancer de Barbastro, Luis: See under *Missionaries to the Americas.*

Capra, Frank (1897–1991): Academy-Award-winning film director best known for such classics as *It Happened One Night* (1934), *Mr. Deeds Goes to Town* (1936), *You Can't Take It with You* (1938), and *It's a Wonderful Life* (1946).

Carberry, John J. (1904-98): Archbishop of St. Louis, 1968-79, and cardinal from 1969.

Carey, Mathew (1760-1839): American publisher and banker; co-founder of *Columbian Magazine* (1786) and *American Museum* (1787), the first nationally read American literary journal; launched the country's largest publishing house; served on the board of the bank of Pennsylvania, helped establish the Hibernian Society (for Irish immigrants).

Carroll, Austin (1835-1909): Sister of Mercy and caretaker of the poor.

Carroll, Charles (1737-1834): Called "First Citizen," one of the most prominent Catholic leaders in the cause of American independence; U.S. Senator, 1789-92; last surviving signer of the Declaration of Independence.

Carroll, Daniel (1733-96): Elder brother of Archbishop John Carroll and a Catholic leader during the American Revolution and the creation of the Constitution; supported the ratification of the Constitution; one of four Catholics chosen to represent American Catholics in congratulating George Washington on his election as president.

Carroll, John (1735-1815): First bishop and archbishop of Baltimore and the architect of the Church in the United States; a member of the Carroll family of Maryland; entered the Jesuits in Europe but returned to America after the suppression of the order; missionary priest in Maryland from 1774-83; named Superior of American missions in 1784; appointed bishop of Baltimore in 1789 with his diocese extending across the whole of the United States; promoted in 1808 to Archbishop of Baltimore; supported religious liberty and tolerance and established the Church on a firm administrative and spiritual footing in the new country.

Carson, Christopher "Kit" (1809-68): Trapper, guide, and frontiersman; convert to Catholicism under the influence of Padre Antonio José Martinez; active as a soldier in California against the Mexican army in 1846-47; served as Indian agent to the Utes and helped negotiate peace with the Cheyenne, Arapaho, and Navaho; later waged several campaigns against the Apaches and Navahos.

Cartier, Jacques (1491-1557): French explorer; sailed up the St. Lawrence River in the hopes of finding a route to the East; entered the Gulf of St. Lawrence and encountered the native tribes; his explorations opened up the wilderness of North America to further French exploration.

Casey, Robert (1932-2000): Governor of Pennsylvania and an outspoken supporter of the Pro-Life cause in the Democratic Party; as governor of Pennsylvania from 1986 to 1994 he was a strong Pro-Life advocate and had his named attached to a lawsuit that became the 1992 Supreme Court abortion case, *Planned Parenthood vs. Casey*, which challenged the constitutionality of 1989's Pennsylvania Abortion Control Act; in 1992 and 1996 he was refused permission to address the Democratic National Convention because of his stand on abortion; in 1996, his speech at Cooper Union College in New York (where Abraham Lincoln had given a famous address on slavery in 1860) was prevented by pro-abortion activists.

Casey, Solanus, O.F.M., Cap. (1870-1957): Capuchin friar and noted healer; after failing academically in the seminary of St. Francis de Sales, entered the Capuchins and was finally ordained as a priest simplex, in which he was not given faculties to hear confessions or to preach; acquired a reputation for holiness and miracles, with a special devotion to the Eucharist and the B.V.M.; his cause was opened in 1982 and given formal recognition in 1992.

Castillo, John de, St.: See under *Missionaries to the America*s.

Catala, Magin: See under *Missionaries to the Americas*.

Chabanel, Noël, St.: See under *Missionaries to the America*s.

Champlain, Samuel de (1567-1635): French explorer and governor; established a fort at Quebec and explored Lakes Huron and Ontario, making possible the further exploration of the Mississippi Valley; established French relations with the Huron.

Charlot, Chief (c. 1831-1910): Native American chief of the Kalispel in Idaho; known properly as Little-Claw-of-the-Grizzly-Bear; became chief in 1870 and attempted to negotiate with the Federal Government to adhere to the terms of earlier treaties; continued white violations of Indian territory brought gradual destitution of the tribe; moved in 1889 to the Flathead reservation in Montana.

Chaumonot, Pierre Joseph: See under *Missionaries to the Americas*.

Chavez, Cesar (1927-93): Founder of the United Farmworkers (UFW) and social activist; established the National Farmworkers Association (NFWA) for migrant farmworkers; joined with the Agricultural Workers Organizing Committee (AWOC) to form the United Farmworkers Organizing Committee (UFWOC), the foundation for the UFWA; led a famous strike against the agricultural industry in the 1960s.

Cheverus, Jean Lefebvre de (1768-1836): Missionary, cardinal and bishop of Boston from 1810-23; born and ordained in France, he left his native country in the face of the Revolution; served as a priest in Boston from 1796-1808; established the diocese on a firm footing before departing for France in 1823; made a cardinal in 1836.

Cody, John P. (1907-82): Archbishop of Chicago, 1965-82, and Cardinal from 1967; headed the largest archdiocese in America during the

turbulent post-conciliar period; Archbishop of New Orleans, 1964-65; his time in Chicago was marked by numerous challenges to authority; also an advocate of civil rights.

Connolly, John, O.P. (1750-1825): Dominican friar and the second bishop of New York, 1814-25; born in Ireland; served in Rome during the turbulent days of the French occupation; became the second bishop of New York; worked to advance the cause of the Church in the city.

Conway, Katherine (1853-1927): Editor and novelist; trustee of the Boston Public Library; opposed extension of full suffrage to women.

Conwell, Henry (1748-1842): Bishop of Philadelphia, 1820-42; his time was marked by the difficulties of the Hogan Schism and trusteeism; summoned to Rome over diocesan management; coadj. bishop, Francis Kenrick, was appointed in 1830, and Conwell held the see in name only until his death.

Cooke, Terence J. (1921-83): Archbisop of New York, 1968-83, and Cardinal from 1969; work also included efforts to promote the Military Vicariate; his cause for canonization is currently being promoted.

Corcoran, James (1820-89): A priest and theologian; advised the Baltimore Provincial Councils and the Baltimore Plenary Councils; theological advisor to Vatican Council I (1869-70); a staunch supporter of antebellum Southern culture, separation of Church and State, and Ultramontane Catholicism.

Corrigan, Michael A. (1839-1902): Archbishop of New York from 1885-1902; one of the most vocal leaders of conservative Catholicism and a vigorous opponent of Americanism; complained to Rome about the Knights of Labor and supported Pope Leo XIII's encyclical *Testem Benevolentiae*, condemning the errors of Americanism.

Coughlin, Fr. Charles (1891-1979): Priest and famous radio preacher who enjoyed national prominence during the Great Depression; founded the National Union for Social Justice to promote social justice, but both his writings and radio program were increasingly anti-Semitic; forced from the air in 1942.

Crétin, Joseph (1799-1857): Missionary bishop; born in France; worked in the Dubuque missions; preached among the Winnebago Indians; appointed the first bishop of St. Paul, 1851-57; heavily promoted the Church in the region, founding 26 churches, 24 schools, and a hospital.

Crosby, "Bing" (1903-77): Singer and entertainer; called Bing after his fondness for "The Bingville Bungle" comic strip; became famous as a singer from 1932 and starred in over 70 films, including the popular "Road" series with Bob

Hope; among his most beloved films was *Going My Way* (1944), in which he played a priest; two songs, "White Christmas" and "Silent Night," became all-time classics.

Crowley, Patrick (1911-74): Lawyer and co-founder of the Christian Family Movement in the 1940s with his wife Patricia; helped establish the International Confederation of the Christian Family Movement (ICCFM) in 1966 and served on the Papal Commission on Birth Control from 1964-67.

Curley, James (1796-1889): Massachusetts politician; the model for Edwin O'Connor's novel *The Last Hurrah*; served in the U.S. House of Representatives, 1910-14; elected mayor of Boston for the first of several times in 1914; elected governor of Massachusetts in 1934.

Curran, John (1859-1936): Labor priest and supporter of mine workers; a friend of Theodore Roosevelt and John Mitchell, head of the United Mine Workers; involved himself in a variety of labor disputes.

Cushing, Richard J. (1895-1970): Archbishop of Boston, 1944-70, and Cardinal from 1958; auxiliary bishop of Boston, 1939-44; close friend of the Kennedy family and one of the most respected and beloved Catholic leaders in the United States; supported reforms of Vatican Council II.

D

Daley, Richard (1902-76): Mayor of Chicago, 1955-76; oversaw one of the most efficient political machines in American politics; campaigned vigorously for John F. Kennedy and proved essential in his victory in 1960; presided over the city during the 1968 Democratic National Convention; his son, Richard M. Daley, subsequently served as mayor of Chicago and Secretary of Commerce in the Clinton administration.

Damien de Veuster, S.S.C.C. (1840-89) "The Leper Priest of Molokai"; born in Belgium; entered the Sacred Hearts Fathers and replaced his brother Pamphile in the Hawaiian missions; after labors on the Big Island, went to Molokai to work among the lepers from 1873; established orphanages, hospitals, and houses for the lepers; diagnosed with leprosy in 1884; honored with the rank of Knight Commander of the Royal Order of Kalakaua, 1881; beatified by Pope John Paul II in 1995.

Daniel, Anthony, St.: See under *Missionaries to the Americas.*

David, Jean Baptiste, S.S. (1761-1841): Missionary, Sulpician, and coadj. bishop of Bardstown, 1819-41; the first bishop consecrated in the West (in 1819), he resisted appointment as bishop of Bardstown in 1832; assisted in the founding of the Sisters of Charity of Nazareth.

Davis, Thurston, S.J. (1913-86): Jesuit priest, professor, and editor; editor of *America* from 1953-68; founder of La Farge Institute to promote the study of religious traditions.

Day, Dorothy (1897-1980): Social activist and founder of the Catholic Worker movement; after a socialist youth marked by an abortion, she converted to Catholicism in 1927, following the birth and baptism of her daughter that same year; met Peter Maurin in 1932 and launched *The Catholic Worker* in 1933; created the first of many houses of hospitality in New York, 1935; opposed World War II, the Korean War, and Vietnam; arrested in 1973 with Cesar Chavez during a farm workers' demonstration; one of the most influential lay Catholics of the 20th century.

Dearden, John F. (1907-88): Archbishop of Detroit, 1958-80, and Cardinal from 1969; bishop of Pittsburgh, 1950-58; president of the NCCB from 1966-71.

De Cheverus, John L.: See *Cheverus, John.*

De Smet, Pierre Jean: See under *Missionaries to the Americas.*

Dietz, Peter (1878-1947): Labor priest and editor; editor of *Central Blatt* and *Social Justice* from 1909-10; secretary of Social Service Commission of American Federation of Catholic Societies, 1911-18; founder of American Academy for Christian Democracy for Women, 1915.

DiMaggio, Joe (1914-1999): Legendary baseball player, called "Joltin' Joe" and the "Yankee Clipper"; spent his entire career (1936-51) with the New York Yankees; set a major-league record in 1941 by hitting safely in 56 straight games; married briefly to Marilyn Monroe; inducted in 1955 into the Baseball Hall of Fame; raised millions for the Joe DiMaggio Children's Hospital.

Dohen, Dorothy (1923-84): Writer and social worker; editor of *Integrity* from 1952-56; professor, Fordham University, 1960-84; author on Catholic lay spirituality.

Doherty, Catherine de Hueck (1896-1985): Social activist and spiritual writer; born in Russia and fled during the Bolshevik Revolution; established Friendship House to care for those in need of food, shelter, and clothing; subsequently established Madonna House to promote spirituality of a Western and Eastern inspiration.

Dooley, Thomas (1927-61): Physician, activist, and one of the most popular Catholics in the 1950s; enlisted in the U.S. Navy after graduating from medical school; worked to care for the North Vietnamese refugees who fled their homes following Dienbienphu; supported the South Vietnamese government; authored numerous popular books on his work; in 1959, he was one of the most admired men in America (the only other Catholic on the list was John F. Kennedy).

Dorsey, John (1874-1926): Missionary and the first African-American Josephite priest ordained in the United States; supporter of Catholic missions among African-Americans, including pastoral assignments in Nashville and Memphis; assaulted in 1924 and left paralyzed; endured humiliations, persecutions, and violence for the Catholic faith.

Dougherty, Dennis (1865-1951): Archbishop of Philadelphia, 1918-51, and cardinal from 1921; bishop of Nueva Segovia, PI, from 1903-08; bishop of Jaro, P.I., from 1908-15; bishop of Buffalo, from 1915-18; served as Archbishop in the long period of the Great Depression and World War II.

Drexel, Katharine: See under *Saints of the Church.*

Drossaerts, Arthur J. (1862-1940): The first Archbishop of San Antonio, 1926-40; native of Holland; ordained on June 15, 1889; bishop of San Antonio 1918-26.

Dubois, Jean, S.S. (1764-1842): Bishop of New York from 1826-42; born in France, journeyed to labor in the missions of the United States.

Dubourg, Louis William, S.S. (1766-1833): Bishop of Louisiana and the Two Floridas (now New Orleans), 1815-25; born in Santo Domingo; ordained in 1788; later returned to France, serving as bishop of Montauban, 1826-33, and Archbishop of Besançon in 1833.

Duchesne, Rose Philippine, St.: See under *Missionaries to the Americas.*

Duffy, Fr. Francis (1871-1932): Chaplain and educator; served for 14 years as a teacher at Dunwoodie Seminary; served as a chaplain during World War I from 1917-20; promoted ecumenism and supported Alfred E. Smith.

Durante, Jimmy (1893-1980): Comedian best known for his hoarse voice, ample nose, and time-worn hat; starred in numerous films and Broadway shows, including *Red, Hot, and Blue* (1936).

E

Elliott, Walter (1842-1928): Priest, missionary, and editor; Civil War veteran; joined the Paulists in 1868 and ordained in 1872; labored among non-Catholics and established the Apostolic Mission House for home mission work; founding editor of the *Missionary*; author of famous biography on Isaac Hecker, 1891, that helped spark the Americanist controversy and the issue of the encyclical *Testem Benevolentiae.*

Ellis, John Tracy (1905-92): Historian and educator, for many years the dean of Catholic Church historians in the U.S.; ordained in 1938; professor at Catholic University of America from 1938-64; earned praise for his many writings; president of the American Catholic Historical Society and American Society of Church History.

England, John (1786-1842): First Bishop of Charleston, SC, 1820-42; born in Ireland; president of College of St. Mary, in Cork, Ireland, from 1812-17; ardent supporter of the compatibility between Catholicism and American democracy; founded the first national Catholic newspaper, the U.S. Catholic Miscellany; invited in 1926 to address the U.S. Congress, the first Catholic clergyman so honored; apostolic delegate to Haiti, 1833-37.

F

Farley, John (1842-1918): Archbishop of New York, 1902-18 and Cardinal from 1911; born in Ireland; auxiliary bishop of New York from 1895-1902; promoted education.

Farmer, Ferdinand: See under *Missionaries to the Americas.*

Feehan, Patrick (1829-1902): First Archbishop of Chicago, 1880-92; born in Ireland and ordained in St. Louis in 1852; bishop of Nashville from 1865-80; renowned preacher and promoter of education; later years troubled by poor relations with Polish Catholics and internal conflicts among the Irish priests.

Fenton, Joseph (1906-69): American theologian, priest, and supporter of neo-Scholasticism; professor and dean of theology at Catholic University of America; cofounder of Catholic Theological Society of America, 1946; cofounder of Mariological Society, 1949; *peritus* at Vatican Council II, 1962-65.

Fenwick, Edward D., O.P. (1768-1832): First Bishop of Cincinnati from 1822-32; founder of the *Catholic Telegraph-Register*, 1831; efforts at education and missions prompted a Protestant counter-reaction, including Lyman Beecher's *Plea for the West.*

Fink, Michael, O.S.B. (1834-1904): First Bishop of Leavenworth (now Kansas City), from 1877-1904; born in Germany; coadj. vicar apostolic from 1871-74, and vicar apostolic from 1874-77, of the Kansas and Indian Territory.

Fitzsimmons, Thomas (1741-1811): Signer of the U.S. Constitution; born in Ireland; founded the Friendly Sons of St. Patrick in America; assisted the cause of the American Revolution; was one of two Catholic delegates (with Daniel Carroll) to the Constitutional convention in 1787; served in the House of Representatives, 1788-95; grandfather of General Gordon B. Meade, victor of the Battle of Gettysburg in 1863.

Flaget, Benedict J.: See under *Missionaries to the Americas.*

Flanagan, Edward (1886-1948): Founder of Father Flanagan's Boys' Town; born in Ireland and ordained in 1912; served in Omaha, Nebraska, founded Boys' Town in 1917 to care for homeless boys; the home became internationally known.

Floersh, John (1886-1968): First Archbishop of Louisville from 1937-67; coadj. bishop of Louisville from 1923-24; bishop of Louisville from 1924-37.

Ford, John (1895-1973): Motion picture director and anticommunist; a director of some 130 films, he won five Academy Awards for Best Director, including *Stagecoach* (1939), *The Grapes of Wrath* (1940), *How Green Was My Valley* (1941), and *The Quiet Man* (1952); received the Presidential Medal of Freedom.

Friess, Mother Caroline (1824-92): Mother superior, School Sisters of Notre Dame in America from 1850-92; born in France; by 1892, her sisters had founded 265 parochial schools in 16 states and taught 70,000 pupils.

Furfrey, Paul (1897-1992): Priest, sociologist, and social justice reformer; professor and chairman of Sociology department, Catholic University of America, 1934-66; director, Juvenile Delinquency Evaluation Project, 1956-61; spokesperson for Christian personalism; supporter of Catholic Worker Movement and anti-war activist during Vietnam.

G

Gallitzin, Demetrius: See under *Missionaries to the Americas*.

Garnier, Charles, St.: See under *Missionaries to the Americas*.

Gaston, William (1778-1844): Catholic layperson and prominent leader in North Carolina; first Catholic to serve in the North Carolina state legislature and supreme court; served in U.S. House of Representatives; although a slaveholder, advocated abolition.

Gibault, Pierre: See under *Missionaries to the Americas*.

Gibbons, James (1834-1921): Archbishop of Baltimore, 1877-1921, the second American cardinal from 1886, and one of the foremost American prelates of the 19th century; vicar apostolic for North Carolina, 1868-72; bishop of Richmond, 1872-77; coadj. bishop of Baltimore, May-October, 1877; defended the Knights of Labor and was a famed champion of the poor and working class; promoted the Americanization of the Church; immensely popular in the country among Catholics and non-Catholics.

Glennon, John J. (1862-1946): Archbishop of St. Louis, 1903-46 and Cardinal from 1946; born in Ireland; coadj. bishop of Kansas City, Missouri, from 1896-1903; coadj. of St. Louis from April-October, 1903; promoted Catholic social work; founded schools, hospitals, and a new seminary; first cardinal from the see of St. Louis.

Goldstein, David (1870-1958): Convert from Judaism and prominent Catholic layperson; born in England and raised in a Jewish family and as a Socialist; converted in 1905 and became opponent of Socialism; cofounder (with Martha Moore Avery) of the Catholic Truth Guild in 1917; founder, Catholic Campaigners for Christ, 1936.

Gonzalez, Roch, St.: See under *Missionaries to the Americas*.

Goupil, René, St.: See under *Missionaries to the Americas*.

Gravier, Jacques: See under *Missionaries to the Americas*.

Guérin, Mother Theodore (1798-1856): Beati and founding superior of the Sisters of Providence, St. Mary-of-the-Woods, Indiana, 1840-56; beatified on October 25, 1998 by Pope John Paul II.

Guiney, Louise (1861-1920): Essayist, poet, and scholar; a major figure in the literary revival in the United States of the late 19th century.

H

Haas, Francis (1899-1953): Priest, professor, sociologist, and editor; supporter of labor, and social and racial justice; named to the Civil Rights Commission by Harry Truman.

Hallinan, Paul (1911-68): Priest, chaplain, and Archbishop of Atlanta from 1962-68; served as army chaplain from 1942-45; president of National Association of Newman Club Chaplains from 1952-58; bishop of Charleston from 1958-62; as Archbishop, he supported civil rights.

Hayes, Carlton (1882-1964): Diplomat and historian; earned a doctorate in history from Columbia University; noted historian; co-founded the National Association of Christians and Jews; ambassador to Spain from 1942-45.

Hayes, Helen (1900-93): Actress; enjoyed a career of 60 years, winner of two Academy Awards, as well as Emmy Awards and Tony Awards; beloved figure on the Broadway stage; authored autobiography, *My Life in Three Acts* (1990).

Hayes, Patrick J. (1867-1938): Archbishop of New York, 1919-38, and Cardinal from 1924; auxiliary bishop of New York, 1914-19; Military Ordinary for Catholic American chaplains during World War I; founded Catholic Charities of the Archdiocese of New York and did much to promote social welfare; wielded much influence in local politics (his private residence was termed "The Powerhouse").

Healy, James (1830-1900): Bishop of Portland from 1875-1900; son of an Irish father and an African-American mother; founded 60 parishes, 68 mission stations, and 18 schools and convents; also served as consultant to the U.S. Bureau of Indian Affairs.

Hecker, Isaac (1819-88): Priest, theologian, and founder of the Paulists; convert in 1844; entered the Redemptorists; missionary in the U.S.,

1851-57; founder and superior of the Congregation of Missionary Priests of St. Paul the Apostle (Paulists), 1858-88; developed an apologetic that stressed the benefits of American culture and political traditions; following his death, the story of his life by Walter Elliott was the cause of the Americanist controversy that sparked the papal encyclical *Testem Benevolentiae*, 1899, by Pope Leo XIII, condemning assorted ideas connected with Hecker.

Heeney, Cornelius (1754-1848): Philanthropist; born in Ireland and emigrated to New York; partner for a time of John Jacob Astor in fur trading; helped establish old St. Patrick's Cathedral; patron of John McCloskey, the future cardinal Archbishop of New York; devoted time and money to Catholic charities.

Hennepin, Louis (1626-after 1701): Missionary and member of the Recollect Order of Friars Minor; traveled to the Mississippi River and was captured by the Sioux; rescued by the French explorer Daniel Graysolon Du Lhut.

Henni, John M. (1805-81): First Archbishop of Milwaukee from 1875-81; born in Switzerland; first bishop of Milwaukee from 1844-75.

Heuser, Herman (1852-1933): Priest, professor, and editor; born in Germany; founding editor of *American Ecclesiastical Review*, 1899-1914; founding editor of the *Dolphin*, 1900-08.

Hildebrand, Dietrich von (1889-1977): Philosopher; born in Florence; converted in 1914; fled Germany in 1933 to escape the Nazis and later joined Fordham University in 1941; ranked as one of the most prominent and devoutly Catholic philosophers of the second half of the 20th century.

Hitchcock, Alfred (1899–1980) Anglo-American film director; considered a true master of suspense films; directed such films as *The Lady Vanishes* (1938), *Notorious* (1946), *Strangers on a Train* (1951), *Psycho* (1960), and *Frenzy* (1972).

Hogan, John J. (1829-1913): First Bishop of Kansas City, 1880-1913; born in Ireland; first bishop of St. Joseph from 1868-80.

Hughes, John J. (1797-1864): First Archbishop of New York, 1850-64; born in Ireland and ordained in 1826 in New York; coadj. bishop of New York from 1837-42; bishop of New York from 1842-50; opposed anti-Catholic riots in 1844; one of the foremost Catholic leaders in the U.S.; addressed Congress in 1847; traveled to Europe to promote the Union cause during the Civil War; championed the cause of immigrants.

I

Ireland, John (1838-1918): First archbishop of St. Paul from 1888-1918; born in Ireland and ordained in 1861 in St. Paul; coadj. bishop of St. Paul from 1875-84; bishop of St. Paul from 1884-88; promoted the Catholic University of America and was an ardent support of Americanizing the Church in the U.S., the Knights of Labor and a controversial school plan; leading figure in the Americanist controversy.

Ireland, Mother Seraphine (1842-1930): Mother Superior of the Sisters of St. Joseph, province of St. Paul, 1882-1921; sister of Archbishop John Ireland; helped to promote the Sisters of St. Joseph Carondelet in the Midwest of the U.S.

Ives, Levi (1797-1867): Convert to Catholicism who was raised as an Episcopalian, he became bishop of North Carolina in 1831; a member of the Tractarian movement, he entered the Catholic Church in 1852; worked as a promoter of Catholic Charities from 1854-67.

J

Jackson, Carol (1911-37): Catholic convert and editor; raised an atheist, she converted in 1941; influenced by Catholic Worker Movement; cofounder and coeditor of *Integrity* magazine from 1946-52.

Jesuit North American Martyrs: See under *Missionaries to the Americas*.

Jogues, Isaac, St.: See under *Missionaries to the Americas*.

Jolliet, Louis (1645-1700): French explorer; after brief studies to be a priest, he became a fur trader; set out in 1673 with Fr. Jacques Marquette to explore the copper mines of Lake Superior; reached the Mississippi, Ohio, and Arkansas Rivers; had positive dealing with local native Americans.

Jones, Mother Mary (c.1830-1930): Irish-born labor union organizer and political activist; operated dressmaking business in 1861; founder of the Social Democratic Party in 1898; organizer of the United Mine Workers of America in 1900; a founder of the Industrial Workers of the World in 1905; known as "mother" among the male labor workers.

K

Keane, John J. (1839-1918): Archbishop of Dubuque from 1900-11 and a defender of the Americanist movement; born in Ireland; bishop of Richmond from 1878-88; rector of the Catholic University of America from 1888-97; consultor of Congregation for Propagation of the Faith, 1897-1900; opposed the condemnation of the Knights of Labor and was an ally of the work of John Ireland and John Gibbons.

Kelley, Francis (1870-1948): Priest and founder of the Catholic Church Extension Society; founder and editor of *Extension Magazine* from 1905-24; bishop of Oklahoma City-Tulsa from 1924-28.

Kelly, Grace (1929-82): Actress and Princess Consort of Monaco; after a start in television and on stage, she launched a major film career in *High Noon* (1951) and won the Academy Award for *The Country Girl* (1954); met Prince Rainier III of Monaco at the Cannes Film Festival in 1954 and married him in 1956; died, after a car crash, on September 14, 1982.

Kennedy, John F. (1917-63): President of the United States; born into the powerful Kennedy family of Massachusetts, he became a hero during World War II for his command of PT109; served in U.S. Congress and then U.S. Senate (1952-60); married Jacqueline Bouvier in 1953; elected the first Catholic president in 1960; domestic policy included programs of tax cuts, civil rights, and social security; foreign policy distinguished by the Bay of Pigs and the Cuban Missile Crisis; assassinated on November 22, 1963.

Kennedy, Joseph (1888-1969): Diplomat, businessman, and patriarch of the Kennedy family; born into the family of a ward boss in Boston, he earned his first million by the age of 30; involved in banking, shipbuilding, and motion pictures; named chairman of the Securities and Exchange Commission in 1934 by Franklin Roosevelt; ambassador to Great Britain from 1937-40; devoted his later years to pushing his children's political advancement.

Kennedy, Robert (1925-68): U.S. Senator and Attorney General; third son of Joseph Kennedy and brother of John F. Kennedy; managed his brother's successful presidential bid in 1960 and was named Attorney General; served as JFK's foremost advisor and was a strong force in the passing of the Civil Rights Act (1964); elected Senator from New York in 1964; launched campaign for president in 1968, during which he was assassinated.

Kenrick, Francis P. (1796-1863): Archbishop of Baltimore from 1851-63; born in Ireland and educated in Rome; labored in Bardstown, Kentucky and defended the Catholic faith; coadj. of Philadelphia from 1830-42, with the task of repairing diocesan unity after trustee crisis; bishop of Philadelphia from 1842-51; founded St. Charles Borromeo Seminary in 1832 and promoted education; organized and presided over the first Plenary Council of Baltimore in 1852; promoted the foundation of the North American College.

Kenrick, Peter (1806-96): Brother of Francis Kenrick and first archbishop of St. Louis from 1847-95; born in Ireland; after service in Ireland, invited by his brother to Philadelphia; rector of the cathedral and president of St. Charles Borromeo Seminary from 1833-41; coadj. bishop of St. Louis from 1841-43; bishop from 1843-47; took part in Vatican Council I and opposed the definition of papal infallibility.

Kerby, William (1870-1936): Priest and founder of the national Conference of Catholic Charities; founded and organized the national Conference of Catholic Charities in 1910; co-founder of the National Catholic School of Social Service in 1918; editor of *American Ecclesiastical Review* from 1927-36; promoted social justice issues.

Kilmer, Joyce (1886-1918): Poet; born Alfred Kilmer, he converted to Catholicism in 1913 with his wife; a popular poet in the United States and Europe; killed in World War I during the Second Battle of the Marne.

Kino, Eusebio: See under *Missionaries to the Americas*.

Kohlmann, Anthony (1771-1836): Jesuit and theologian; born in Alsace; joined the Russian Jesuit chapter in 1803; sent to the United States; pastor and administrator of the diocese of New York from 1808-15; won "The Catholic Question," a controversy over the seal of confession in 1812; consultor to Vatican congregations in Rome from 1824-36.

Kosciuszko, Thaddeus (1746-1817): Polish soldier; a member of the minor Polish aristocracy, he volunteered for the American Revolution in 1776; commissioned as a colonel, he designed West Point and helped in the victory at Saratoga and Ticonderoga; retired to Poland and fought against the Russians in a doomed effort to win Polish independence.

Kreisler, Fritz (1875-62): Composer and violinist; born in Austria, debuted in New York as a virtuoso violinist and toured from 1888-89; opposed the Nazis and was forced to leave Europe in 1939; American citizen in 1943.

Krol, John Joseph (1910-96): Archbishop of Philadelphia from 1961-88 and Cardinal from 1967; auxiliary bishop of Cleveland from 1953-61; one of the most devoted supporters of Pope John Paul II among the American hierarchy.

L

L'Enfant, Pierre (1754-1825): Architect; born in France; submitted plans in 1791 for the new capital city at Washington at George Washington's request; eventually dismissed because of various personality differences; in 1889 the plans were recovered from the archives, and the capital was developed in 1901 along his vision.

La Farge, John (1880-1963): Priest, reformer, and editor; founded the Cardinal Gibbons Institute in 1924, to educate African-Americans in Maryland; editor on the staff of *America* from 1926-63; founded the Laymen's Union in 1934 to promote spiritual formation among African-Americans.

Lafayette, Marquis de (1757-1834): French soldier and statesman; a member of a French noble family, he joined the Continental Army in 1777 and received a position on George Washington's staff; instrumental in winning support for the American cause in Europe; a leading figure in the early days of the French Revolution, he was condemned by the Jacobins in 1792 and fled France; returned in 1797 and resumed a public life in 1814.

Lalemant, Gabriel, St.: See under *Missionaries to the Americas*.

Lamy, Jean Baptiste: See under *Missionaries to the Americas*.

Lange, Mary (1784-1882): Founding mother superior of the Oblate Sisters of Providence in Baltimore from 1829-32; born in the Santo Domingo, Haiti, her family emigrated to Cuba and then the U.S.; taught Haitian children in Baltimore; founded the Oblate Sisters of Providence to educate African-American children; served among the poor, the sick, and the dying, especially during the cholera epidemics in Baltimore.

Las Casas, Bartolome: See under *Missionaries to the Americas*.

Lathrop, Rose Hawthorne (1851-1926): Cofounder of the Dominican Congregation of St. Rose of Lima in 1900; the third daughter of Nathaniel Hawthorne; married George Parsons Lathrop, with whom she entered the Church in 1891; separated from her husband because of his alcoholism (he died in 1898); established the Dominican Congregation of St. Rose of Lima (Servants of Relief for Incurable Cancer), to care for those dying and neglected; pioneered hospice work in the United States for the terminally ill.

Laval, Françoise de Montmorency, Blessed: See under *Missionaries to the Americas*.

Lewis, Edmonia (1845-after 1909): First African-American sculptress; daughter of an African-American father and an Ojibwe mother; studied at Oberlin College, Ohio, and Boston; emigrated to Rome where she remained for the rest of her life; Pope Pius XI visited her studio; her work was displayed in Europe and the United States, including the National Museum of American Art.

Ligutti, Luigi (1885-1983): Priest and leading figure in the Catholic rural life movement; born in Italy; after pastoral service became executive secretary and director of the National Catholic Rural Life Conference from 1938-58; editor of *Land and Home* from 1942-47; editor of *Christian Farmer News Letter* in 1947; director of international affairs for the NCRLC from 1958-70; founded the Agrimissio in Rome, to promote agriculture in the developing parts of the world.

Lombardi, Vince (1913–70): American football coach; born in New York City; head coach of the Green Bay Packers from 1959-69 and won five championships; head coach briefly of the Washington Redskins, from 1969-70.

Lombardo, Guy (1902-77): Canadian born band leader; led the band of the Royal Canadians, debuting in New York in 1929; was best known for his New Year's Eve performances in New York City.

Longstreet, James (1821-1904): Confederate general during the Civil War; graduated from West point in 1842 and fought in the Mexican War; one of the most competent corps commanders under Robert E. Lee; after the war, he joined the Republican Party and served in assorted posts; converted in 1877.

Loras, Matthias (1792-1858): First bishop of Dubuque from 1837-58; born in France, he was a friend and schoolmate of St. Jean Vianney; after a distinguished career in France, he went to America in 1828; as bishop, he promoted a seminary, missionary activity on the Mississippi River, German and Irish immigration.

Lord, Daniel (1888-1955): Jesuit priest and writer; author of 30 books, 50 plays, 12 musicals, and six pageants; assisted Cecil B. DeMille on the film *King of Kings*; helped draft Motion Picture Production Code; director of the Sodality of the Blessed Virgin from 1948-55, the largest Catholic youth organization in the U.S.

Luce, Clare Boothe (1903-87): Author, playwright, ambassador, and politician; wife of Henry C. Luce (publisher of *Time*, *Fortune*, and *Sports Illustrated*); converted to Catholicism in 1946 under the influence of then Msgr. Fulton J. Sheen; keynote speaker at the 1944 Republican National Convention; leading woman Catholic politician, serving in the U.S. House from 1942-46; U.S. ambassador to Italy from 1953-57.

Lucey, Robert E. (1891-1977): Archbishop of San Antonio from 1941-69; pastoral work in Los Angeles, especially among the homeless from 1916-34; bishop of Amarillo from 1934-41; supported CCD programs and the policies of Lyndon Johnson on poverty and the Vietnam War.

Lynch, Patrick N. (1817-82): Bishop of Charleston from 1858-82 and a leading Catholic in the South during the Civil War; born in Ireland; sent twice to Europe to plead the Southern cause; returned to the U.S. after the war following a presidential pardon; took part in Vatican Council I and was in favor of papal infallibility.

M

McCarthy, Joseph (1908-57): American politician; U.S. senator from Wisconsin (1947-57); rose to national prominence through the permanent subcommittee on investigations that looked into the threat of Communism against the country; held public hearings in which he accused army officials, members of the media, and public figures of being Communists; his charges were never proved, and he was censured by the Senate in 1954.

McCloskey, John (1810-85): Archbishop of New York from 1864-85 and the first U.S. Cardinal from 1875; coadj. bishop of New York from 1843-47; first bishop of Albany from 1847-64; attended Vatican Council I (1869-70); promoted harmony and growth of the Church in New York; completed St. Patrick's Cathedral, an important symbol of Catholicism's progress in the city and the prosperity of its members; made cardinal in recognition of his work and the prominence of the New York archdiocese.

McGinley, Phyllis (1905-78): Writer and poet; her first book of poetry was published in 1934; she won the Pulitzer Prize in 1961 for *Times Three*; won numerous other literary awards.

McIntyre, James F. (1886-1979): Archbishop of Los Angeles from 1948-70 and Cardinal from 1953; aux. bishop of New York from 1941-46; coadj. Archbishop of New York from 1946-48; oversaw the rapid and extensive expansion of the Church in Los Angeles; by 1970, there were 318 parishes and 350 schools; supported CCD programs and seminary education.

McKenzie, Fr. John (1910-91): Jesuit priest and biblical scholar; first Catholic president of the Society of Biblical Literature; eventually left the Jesuits.

McMaster, James (1820-86): Journalist; converted in 1845, he studied briefly with the Redemptorists; launched a career in journalism in 1846; editor of the *Freeman's Journal* which became a powerful voice in American Catholicism; imprisoned briefly in 1861-62 for his opposition to Lincoln and the Civil War; inaugurated the first American pilgrimage to Rome.

McQuaid, Bernard (1823-1909): First bishop of Rochester from 1868-1909; promoted Americanization and education; predicted suffrage for women.

Mack, Connie (1862-1956): Baseball player and manager of the Philadelphia Athletics from 1901-51; he led the A's to nine American League pennants and five World Series championships between 1902 and 1930; managed until 1951.

Machebeuf, Joseph P. (1812-89): First bishop of Denver, 1887-89; born in France; vicar apostolic to Colorado and Utah from 1868-87; established 102 churches and chapels, ten hospitals, nine academies, and a college.

Manning, Timothy (1909-89): Archbishop of Los Angeles, 1970-85 and Cardinal from 1973; born in Ireland; American citizen, 1944; aux. bishop of Los Angeles from 1946-67; first bishop of Fresno, 1967-69; coadj. archbishop of Los Angeles from 1969-70.

Manogue, Patrick: See under *Missionaries to the Americas.*

Marechal, Ambrose, S.S. (1766-1828): Archbishop of Baltimore from 1817-28; born in France; member of the Sulpicians, taught in French seminaries and St. Mary's Seminary, Baltimore; period as Archbishop was marked by a transition in the life of the Church as growth of the Irish influence was increasingly felt.

Margil, Antonio: See under *Missionaries to the Americas.*

Marie of the Incarnation, Blessed: See under *Missionaries to the Americas.*

Markoe, William (1892-1969): Jesuit priest and advocate of interracial justice; as a priest, authored articles in America promoting social justice for African-Americans; editor of *Chronicale/Interracial Review* from 1930-33; served as a missionary in the Jesuit mission band in Missouri province from 1948-51.

Marquette, Jacques: See under *Missionaries to the Americas.*

Marty, Martin (1834-96): Missionary, Benedictine, and bishop; born in Switzerland; arrived in St. Meinrad, Indiana, in 1860; first abbot, 1870; chose himself as a missionary to the Dakota (Sioux) Indians, 1876, and encountered initial refusal from the local pastor as he did not bear a *celebret*; labored among the Native Americans; vicar apostolic of the Dakota Territory, 1880-89; first bishop of Sioux Falls, 1889-94; bishop of St. Cloud, 1894-96; called "Black Robe Lean Chief" among the Native Americans.

Massias (Macias), John de, St.: See under *Missionaries to the Americas.*

Maurin, Aristide Peter (1877-1949): Lay activist and cofounder with Dorothy Day of the Catholic Worker Movement; born in France; embraced a Franciscan spirit of poverty; met Day in 1932; founded with her *The Catholic Worker*, 1933; his obituary was reported in *The New York Times* and *L'Osservatore Romano*.

Mazzuchelli, Samuel C.: See under *Missionaries to the Americas.*

Meany, William George (1894-80): Labor leader and president of the American Federation of Labor and Congress of Industrial Organizations (1955-79); a plumber; secretary-treasurer of the AFL, 1939-52; president, AFL, 1952-55; head of the new federation after the merger of the AFL and CIO from 1955; denounced economic policies of Jimmy Carter.

Medeiros, Humberto S. (1915-83): Archbishop of Boston from 1970-83 and cardinal from 1973; born in the Azores and a U.S. citizen from 1940; bishop of Brownsville from 1966-70; Archbishop during a turbulent period in modern U.S. Catholic history; took part in the 1978 papal conclaves.

Membre, Zenobius: See under *Missionaries to the Americas*.

Merton, Thomas (1915-68): Trappist monk and influential spiritual writer; after a famed conversion entered the Trappists; authored *Seven Storey Mountain, Seeds of Contemplation, Mystics and Zen Masters, The New Man*.

Mestrovic, Ivan (1883-1962): Sculptor; born in Croatia; studied in Vienna; exhibited throughout Europe and inspired a nationalist movement among the Croats and Serbs; imprisoned by the Fascists, 1941 (released through Vatican intervention); emigrated to the U.S., 1947; citizen, 1953; taught at Syracuse University and Notre Dame; first sculptor to be honored with a one-man show at the Metropolitan Museum of Art.

Meyer, Albert (1903-65): Archbishop of Chicago, 1958-65, and Cardinal from 1959; bishop of Superior from 1946-53; Archbishop of Milwaukee, 1953-58; worked for civil rights and promoted ecumenism.

Michel, Virgil (1890-1938): Liturgist; considered the founder of the American Catholic liturgical movement.

Monaghan, John (1889-1961): Priest and social activist; born in Ireland; taught at cathedral College, New York, 1922-38; co-founder of the Association of Catholic Trade Unionist (ACTU) to inform Catholic trade unionists of Catholic social teaching; beloved pastor of St. Margaret Mary parish, 1939-54 and St. Michael's parish, 1954-61.

Mooney, Edward (1882-1958): First archbishop of Detroit, 1937-58 and Cardinal from 1946; apostolic delegate to India from 1926-31; apostolic delegate Japan from 1931-33; bishop of Rochester from 1933-37; brilliant diplomat; curtailed the activities of Fr. Charles Coughlin.

Moylan, Stephen (1737-1811): Revolutionary era general and businessman; born in Ireland; quartermaster general of the Continental Army and distinguished soldier during the war.

Mudd, Samuel (1833-83): Physician and supposed member of the conspiracy against Abraham Lincoln in 1865; imprisoned from 1865-69; pardoned by Andrew Johnson.

Muench, Aloysius (1889-1962): Cardinal from 1959, and the first American to hold office in the Curia; bishop of Fargo from 1935-59; apostolic visitator to Germany, 1946, and nuncio to Germany from 1951-59.

Mundelein, George (1872-1939): Archbishop of Chicago from 1915-39 and Cardinal from 1924; auxiliary bishop of Brooklyn from 1909-15; first cardinal in the Midwest; supporter of Franklin Roosevelt.

Murray, John Courtney (1904-67): Jesuit priest and influential theologian; professor of theology and philosophy, *peritus* at Vatican Council

II, and editor of *Theological Studies* from 1941-67; studied the Church's relationship to society and the state.

N

Nerinckx, Charles: See under *Missionaries to the Americas*.

Neumann, St. John: See under *Saints of the Church*.

Noll, John F. (1875-1956): Bishop of Fort Wayne, 1925-56, personal titular Archbishop in 1953, and publisher; established *Our Sunday Visitor* in 1912.

O

O'Boyle, Patrick A. (1896-1987): Archbishop of Washington, DC, 1948-73, and Cardinal from 1967; director of the Catholic War Relief Services and War relief Services of the National Catholic Welfare Conference; champion of civil rights.

O'Connell, Denis (1849-1927): Bishop of Richmond, 1912-26; friend of Cardinal James Gibbons; rector of the North American College; rector of the Catholic University of America; opposed anti-Catholicism in Virginia.

O'Connell, William H. (1859-1944): Archbishop of Boston, 1907-44, and Cardinal from 1911; bishop of Portland, 1901-06; coadj. bishop of Boston (Constantia), 1906-07; prominent figure in American Catholic life and politics.

O'Connor, Edwin (1918-68): Author; columnist for the *Boston Herald* under the pseudonym "Roger Swift"; author of *The Oracle* (1951), *The Last Hurrah* (1958), *The Edge of Sadness* (1961), *I Was Dancing* (1964), and *All in the Family* (1966).

O'Connor, Flannery (1925-64): Author; novels included *Wise Blood* (1952) and *The Violent Bear It Away* (1960), and short stories, collected in such works as *A Good Man is Hard to Find* (1955).

O'Connor, John J. (1920-2000): Archbishop of New York from 1984-2000 and Cardinal from 1985; born in Philadelphia, PA; ordained a priest in1945; joined U.S. Navy and Marine Corps as a chaplain, 1952; overseas posts included service in South Korea and Vietnam; U.S. Navy chief of chaplains, 1975; retired from Navy June 1, 1979, with rank of rear admiral; aux. of military vicariate (Curzola), 1979-83; bishop of Scranton, 1983-84; one of the most prominent of all American Church leaders and a powerful spokesman for the Pro-Life cause.

O'Hara, Edwin (1881-1956): Bishop of Great Falls, 1930-56, and social activist; promoter of social justice, including workers' rights and rural life; named personal archbishop in 1954.

O'Hara, John F., C.S.C. (1888-1960): Arch-

John Cardinal O'Connor

bishop of Philadelphia, 1951-60 and Cardinal from 1958; delegate of U.S. military vicar, 1940-45; bishop of Buffalo, 1945-51; promoted concern for Native Americans, Hispanics, and African-Americans, and education.

O'Neill, Thomas (Tip) (1912-94): Speaker of the House of Representatives from 1977-87; first elected to Congress in 1952, winning JFK's old seat; majority whip of House Democrats, 1971-73; majority leader, 1973-77; advanced liberal agenda throughout his career; followed the maxim, "All politics is local."

O'Reilly, John (1844-90): Poet, author, and editor; editor of the *Pilot*, 1870, for Catholic and Irish interests; authored volumes of poetry and the novel *Moondyne* (1875).

O'Sullivan, Mary (1864-1943): Reformer and labor organizer; national organizer for women of the AFL, 1892; founded the National Women's Trade League.

P

Pace, Edward (1861-1938): Priest and scholar; founder and dean of Philosophy department of Catholic University of America; founding editor of *Catholic Encyclopedia*; early leader in experimental psychology.

Padilla, Juan de: See under Missionaries to the Americas.

Palladino, Laurence, S.J. (1837-1927): Jesuit missionary, the last pioneer missionary of the Northwest; born in Italy; sent to Montana Territory, 1867; built the first church in the Helena Mission (later the first cathedral); director of diocesan schools, 1889-92; president of Gonzaga College, 1894.

Palou, Francisco: See under *Missionaries to the Americas.*

Pariseau, Mother Mary Joseph: See under *Missionaries to the Americas.*

Percy, Walker (1916–90): Novelist; author of *The Moviegoer* (1961), *Love in the Ruins* (1971),

and *The Second Coming* (1980); expressed a rich understanding of change in the South.

Peter, Carl J. (1932-91): Priest and theologian; chairman of Department of Theology, Catholic University of America, 1975-77; ranked as one of CUA's greatest scholars; served on International Theological Commission.

Peyton, Fr. Patrick (1909-92): Holy Cross priest and evangelist; established Family Rosary Crusade, 1947, to promote the rosary among families; coined the motto, "The family that prays together, stays together."

Powderly, Terence (1849-1924): Labor leader and director of the Knights of Labor, a secret organization that repudiated strikes; reached his period of greatest influence from 1879-93; source of controversy in the Church.

Powers. J.F. (1917-99): Author and novelist; taught at Marquette University and University of Michigan; member of the American Academy and Institute of Arts and Letters; notable works included *Morte d'Urban* (1962, winner of the National Book Award and Thormod Monsen award), *Wheat That Springeth Green* (1988, National Book Award and National Book Critics Circle finalist, Wethersfield Institute Award); considered one of the most prominent Catholic writers of the 1950s and 1960s.

Pulaski, Casimir (1748-79): Polish soldier during the American Revolution; joined staff of General Washington, 1777; fought in numerous battles and killed at Savannah.

Purcell, John B. (1783-1883): First archbishop of Cincinnati, 1850-83; born in Ireland; bishop of Cincinnati, 1833-50; supported the Union during the Civil War; last years marked by financial troubles.

Q

Quigley, Martin (1890-1964): Editor and publisher; founded motion picture trade magazines; devised the Motion Picture Production Code; helped found the Legion of Decency.

Quiroga, Vasco de: See under *Missionaries to the Americas.*

R

Rappe, Louis Amadeus (1801-77): First bishop of Cleveland, 1847-70; born in France; established parishes, missions, hospitals, and missions.

Ravalli, Antonio (1811-84): Italian Jesuit; missionary in far-western United States, mostly Montana, for 40 years.

Raymbaut, Charles (1602-43): French Jesuit; missionary among Indians of Canada and northern U.S.

Reedy, William (1925-83): Priest and editor; editor of *Ave Maria*, for Catholic families; columnist for *Our Sunday Visitor.*

Repplier, Agnes (1855-1950): Author of essays and biographies; wrote for *Atlantic Monthly*.

Résé, Frederic (1791-1871): First bishop of Detroit, 1833-71; born in Germany; inactive from 1841 because of ill health; remained in Europe from 1838.

Richard, Gabriel: See under *Missionaries to the Americas*.

Riepp, Benedicta (1825-62): Benedictine nun; born in Bavaria; established first monastery of women Benedictines in North America.

Ritter, Cardinal Joseph E. (1892-1967): Archbishop of St. Louis, 1946-67 and Cardinal from 1961; aux. bishop of Indianapolis, 1933-34; bishop of Indianapolis, 1934-44; first Archbishop Indianapolis, 1944-46; promoted national episcopal conference and Catholic charities; active at Vatican Council II.

Rockne, Knute (1888–1931): Football coach; born in Norway; head coach of Notre Dame (1918- 31); died in a plane crash.

Rosati, Joseph: See under *Missionaries to the Americas*.

Rosecrans, William (1819-98): Union general; campaigned in West Virginia and Mississippi; defeated at the battle of Chickamauga, Georgia (1863), and relieved of duties.

Rudd, Daniel (1854-1933): Journalist and civil rights leader; founded the *Ohio Star Tribune* (*American Catholic Tribune*), 1886, for African-American Catholics; founded African-American Catholic lay congress.

Russell, Mother Mary (1829-98): Superior of the Order of Sisters of Mercy; invited to San Francisco by Archbishop Joseph Alemany; founded St. Mary's Hospital, first Catholic hospital on the west coast.

Ruth, Babe (1895-1948): Baseball player, known as "the Sultan of Swat"; pitcher for the Boston Red Sox (1915-19) and outfielder for the New York Yankees (1920-35); hit 714 home runs, played in 10 World Series, and held 54 major-league records; inducted into the Baseball Hall of Fame in 1936.

Ryan, James H. (1886-1947): First archbishop of Omaha, 1945-47; rector of the Catholic University of America, 1928-35; titular bishop of Modra, 1933-35; bishop of Omaha, 1935-45; promoter of education; supported the New Deal and policies of FDR.

Ryan, John (1869-1945): Priest, influential social reformer, and educator; the leading Catholic voice in the U.S. on social issues in the first half of the 20th century.

Ryan, Thomas (1851-1928): Financier and philanthropist; founder of the American Tobacco Company and National Bank of Commerce; donated over $20 million to Catholic charities.

S

Sadlier, Mary (1820-1903): Novelist; born in Ireland; author of over 30 novels and books focusing on contemporary issues; editor of *The Tablet*; noted Catholic philanthropist.

Seattle, Chief (1786-1866): Native American chief of the Suquamish of Puget Sound; baptized a Catholic at the age of 54; maintained excellent relations with the white settlers; his daughter, Princess Angeline, was also a Catholic.

Seelos, Francis X.: See under *Missionaries to the Americas*.

Seghers, Charles J.: See under *Missionaries to the Americas*.

Serra, Junipero, Blessed: See under *Missionaries to the Americas*.

Seton, Elizabeth: See under *Saints of the Church*.

Shea, John Gilmary (1826-92): Editor and the "Father of American Catholic historians"; editor and author of over 200 publications and supporter of the U.S. bishops.

Sheed, Francis "Frank" (1897-1981): Author and apologist; co-founded the influential publisher Sheed and Ward, 1933; lectured and wrote in defense of the Catholic faith.

Sheen, Fulton J. (1895-1979): Archbishop, radio and television personality, and educator; internationally famous as a preacher on radio and television; aux. bishop of New York, 1951-66; bishop of Rochester, 1966-69; titular Archbishop of Newport; national director of the Society for the Propagation for the Faith; perhaps the most popular and socially influential American Catholic of the 20th century.

Shehan, Lawrence J. (1898-1984): Archbishop of Baltimore, 1961-74, and cardinal from 1965; aux. bishop of Baltimore and Washington, 1945-53; first bishop of Bridgeport, 1953-61; coadj. Archbishop of Baltimore, September-December, 1961; supported the civil rights movement and took part in Martin Luther King's March on Washington, 1963; Archbishop during a time of deep social unrest.

Sheil, Bernard (1886-1969): Archbishop and social activist; aux. bishop of Chicago, 1928-69; titular Archbishop of Selge, 1959-69; formed the Catholic Youth Organization (CYO), 1931; supported organized Labor and FDR; opposed Fr. Coughlin and Sen. Joseph McCarthy.

Sheridan, Philip (1831-88) Union general; took part in the Chattanooga (1863) and Wilderness (1864) campaigns; defeated the Confederate forces at the Battle of Five Forks (1865); brilliant cavalry leader.

Shields, James (1806-79): Union general and U.S. Senator; member of the Illinois Supreme Court, 1843-45; brigadier general during Civil

War; the only person to represent three states in the U.S. Senate (Illinois, Minnesota, Missouri).

Shields, Thomas (1862-1921): Priest, psychologist, and educator; professor at Catholic University of America; promoted dialogue between theology and modern science and philosophy.

Shuster, George (1894-1977): Author, editor, and educator; president of Hunter College, 1940-69.

Siuwheem, Louise (d. c. 1850): Native American, member of the Couer d'Alene tribe in Idaho; known for her zeal and care for the sick; a friend of Fr. Pierre De Smet.

Slattery, John (1851-1926): Priest and advocate for civil rights; member of the Mill Hill missions and sought to have a Mill Hill community in the U.S.; supported African American rights and vocations.

Smith, Alfred E. (1873-1944): Four-time governor of New York (1919-20, 1923-28) and presidential candidate in 1928; as governor, he was responsible for numerous reforms; the Democratic nominee for president, he was the first Roman Catholic candidate for the White House; defeated by Herbert Hoover, primarily because of the Catholic issue and Prohibition.

Solanus, Francis, St.: See under *Missionaries to the Americas.*

Sorin, Edward F.: See under *Missionaries to the Americas.*

Spalding, Catherine (d. 1858): Co-foundress of the Sisters of Charity of Nazareth, Kentucky; her sisters cared for orphans, educated the poor, and eventually expanded into health care.

Spalding, John (1840-1916): First bishop of Peoria from 1877-1908; supporter of separation of Church and State; authored numerous books and articles; helped found the Catholic University of America.

Spalding, Martin (1810-72): Archbishop of Baltimore, 1864-72; perhaps the most influential Catholic apologist of the 19th century; bishop of Louisville, 1850-64; supported the Confederacy during the Civil War; promoted evangelization among the former slaves; favored papal infallibility at Vatican Council I; ranked as one of the foremost prelates in the American Church, esp. for his work in shaping and directing the immigrant influx.

Spellman, Francis J. (1889-1967): Archbishop of New York, 1939-67, and Cardinal from 1946; studies in Rome led to appointment to the Vatican Secretariat of State; arranged for publication of the anti-fascist encyclical, *Non Abbiamo Bisogno*, 1931, in Paris; auxiliary bishop of Boston, 1932-39; good friend of Cardinal Eugenio Pacelli (the future Pope Pius XII); reorganized diocesan finances and centralized authority; Military Vicar for the Armed Forces, 1939-67; staunch anti-Commu-

nist and supporter of the Vietnam War; supported the Vatican II Declaration on Religious Liberty and modern biblical scholarship; the most influential American prelate from 1939-58.

Stritch, Samuel (1887-1958): Archbishop of Chicago, 1939-58, and Cardinal from 1946; bishop of Toledo, 1921-30; Archbishop of Milwaukee, 1930-39; active in the National Catholic Welfare Conference and Catholic Action; named proprefect of the Congregation for the Propagation of the Faith, 1958; died in Rome.

Sullivan, John L. (1858–1918) Boxer; won the bare-knuckles heavyweight championship over Paddy Ryan in 1882; called the "Great John L."; won the last bare-knuckles title bout over Jake Kilrain in 1889; defeated, using gloves, in 1892, by James J. Corbett.

T

Talbot, Francis X., S.J. (1889-1953): Editor and author; editor-in-chief of *America*, 1936-44; founded Catholic Poetry Society of America; author of numerous books; president of Loyola College, Baltimore, 1947-51.

Taney, Roger (1777-1864): Chief Justice of the U.S. Supreme Court, 1836-64; Attorney General of the U.S., 1831-34; participated in over 300 decisions, but is remembered for the Dred Scott decision, 1857, in which he ruled that slaves and their descendants had no rights as citizens; disagreed with Lincoln over several actions during the Civil War.

Tekakwitha, Kateri: See under *Saints of the Church.*

Timon, John, C.M. (1797-1867): First bishop of Buffalo, 1847-67; superior of the Vincential province of the U.S., 1835-39; prefect apostolic for the Republic of Texas, 1839-47.

Todadilla, Anthony de: See under *Missionaries to the Americas.*

Tolton, Augustus (1854-97): First African-American priest in the U.S.; escaped from slavery with his mother to Illinois and discerned a vocation; studied in Rome when no American seminary would take him; ordained, 1886; pastor in Quincy and Chicago, Illinois; encountered racism, especially from fellow priests.

Toscanini, Arturo (1867–1957): Italian conductor; began his career as conductor of the Rio de Janeiro opera; returned to Italy and conducted the premieres of Leoncavallo's *Pagliacci* (1892) and Puccini's *La Bohème* (1896); later musical director at La Scala, Milan; in the U.S., conducted at the Metropolitan Opera, 1908–14, the New York Philharmonic, 1926–36, and the NBC Symphony, which was formed for him, 1937–54.

Toussaint, Pierre, Venerable (1766-1853): Former slave and businessman; born into slavery in Haiti; served as a domestic servant and permitted to learn French (studied Catholic books and sermons); given his freedom in 1807; became a successful hairdresser; devout Catholic; cause opened in 1990 by Cardinal John O'Connor, declared venerable in 1997 by Pope John Paul II.

Tracy, Spencer (1900-67) Film actor; won Academy Awards as Best Actor for *Captains Courageous* (1937) and *Boys' Town* (1938); other films include *Adam's Rib* (1949), *The Last Hurrah* (1958), and *Guess Who's Coming to Dinner* (1967).

Tunney, Gene (1898-1978): Boxer; won, 1922, the light-heavyweight title over Battling Levinsky, but lost it that same year (to Harry Greb) in his only defeat as a professional; defeated Jack Dempsey in 1926 for the heavyweight championship; retired as champion in 1928.

Turibius de Mongrovejo, St.: See under *Missionaries to the Americas.*

Turner, Thomas (1877-1978): Educator and civil rights leader; professor of biology at Howard University, 1913; acting dean of the School of Education at Howard University, 1914-20; worked against discrimination, especially in the Church, through the Federated Colored Catholics (FCC).

Twelve Apostles of Mexico: See under *Missionaries to the Americas.*

U-V

Valdivia, Luis de: See under *Missionaries to the Americas.*

Varela, Féliz (1788-1853): Cuban patriot and scholar; promoter of Thomistic philosophy, the abolition of slavery in Cuba, and education; founded in 1825 in Philadelphia the newspaper *El Habanero*, the first Spanish Catholic magazine in the U.S.; vicar general of the diocese of New York from 1829; founder of *The Protestant's Abridger and Annotator*, 1830, and *Catholic Expositor and Literary Magazine*, 1841-43, the first pastoral magazine and the first literary magazine respectively for Catholics in the U.S.

Vasques de Espiñosa, Antonio: See under *Missionaries to the Americas.*

Verot, Augustin, S.S. (1805-76): Bishop and vocal participant at Vatican Council I; vicar apostolic of Florida, 1856-61; bishop of Savannah, 1861-70; bishop of St. Augustine, 1870-76; known as the "rebel bishop" during the Civil War for his support of the Confederacy; spoke frequently and loudly at the Vatican Council, calling for recognition of those of African descent, vindication of Galileo, and ecumenical dialogue; opposed papal infallibility, but signed the conciliar document.

Verrazano, Giovanni da (1484-1528): Explorer and navigator; searched for a westward route to Cathay and reached the coast of North America; explored Newfoundland and the east coast; killed by Caribbean Indians.

Vespucci, Amerigo (1451-1512): Explorer; journeyed with European explorers between 1497-1502; coined the phrase, "New World"; his name was used by the German cartographer Martin Waldseemüller in a 1507 map designating the area called "South America."

Vieira, Antonio: See under *Missionaries to the Americas.*

W

Wagner, Robert (d. 1953): U.S. Senator from New York, 1926-49; born in Germany; elected to state senate, 1911; member of the commission that investigated the notorious Triangle Shirtwaist Co. (in which 147 women died); elected to the N.Y. Supreme Court, 1918; converted to Catholicism in 1946.

Walker, James (Jimmy) (1881-1946): Flamboyant New York City mayor, 1926-32; rose through New York City's political world, the son of a state legislator; also dabbled in the theater and song writing; after initial success as mayor, suffered severe scandals and resigned in 1932; reconciled to the Church before his death.

Walsh, James A., M.M. (1867-1936): Co-founder (with Thomas F. Price) of Maryknoll, the first U.S. established foreign mission society and first sponsor of a U.S. foreign mission seminary; superior of Maryknoll, 1911-36; titular bishop, 1933-36.

Walsh, James E., M.M. (1891-1981): Bishop, religious superior, and missionary; after ordination in 1915 was sent as one of four Maryknoll missionaries to China; vicar apostolic of Kongmoon, China, 1927-36; superior of Maryknoll, 1936-46; general secretary, Catholic Central Bureau, Shanghai, China, 1948; imprisoned by Chinese communists, 1958-70.

Walsh, Robert (1784-1859): Journalist and author; founded *The American Review of History and Politics*, 1811, American Register, 1817, and, with William Frye, the *National Gazette and Literary Register*; dedicated Federalist and patriot.

Walworth, Clarence (1820-1900): Priest and social activist; converted in 1845 and entered the Redemptorists; worked with Isaac Hecker and served for a time as a Paulist (he left in 1865 over disagreements with Hecker); promoted social justice and the temperance movement; authored numerous books and articles.

Ward, Maisie (1889-1975): Publisher, street preacher, and activist; wife of Francis Sheed, with whom she co-founded the publishing firm of Sheed and Ward; author of 27 books; supported numerous social reform organizations, including the Catholic Worker, Friendship House, and land reform in India.

Warde, Mary (1810-84): Mercy Sister; born in Ireland; entered the Sisters of Mercy and was sent to Pittsburgh; opened houses, boarding schools for girls, and eventually cared for the sick and orphans in New England, encountering much resistance from the Know-Nothings.

Weigel, Gustave, S.J. (1906-64): Jesuit priest and ecumenist; professor of theology at the Catholic University of Chile, 1937-48; professor at Woodstock College, 1949-64; lecturer and supporter of the ecumenical movement.

White, Andrew: See under *Missionaries to the Americas.*

Whitfield, James (1770-1834): Archbishop of Baltimore, 1828-34; born in England; coadj. bishop of Baltimore, 1828.

Williams, John J. (1822-1907): First archbishop of Boston, 1875-1907; bishop of Boston, 1866-75; worked to accommodate the waves of Catholic immigrants into the archdiocese; established many new parishes and found priests to speak in a host of different languages.

Williams, Mary Lou (d. 1981): Jazz musician and composer; taught herself music and the piano; worked with many other famous Jazz musicians, including Dizzy Gillespie, Benny Goodman, and Duke Ellington; composed Jazz for sacred music; founded the Pittsburgh Jazz Festival; a devout Catholic and one of the foremost Jazz artists in the U.S,

Williams, Michael (1877-1950): Author, editor, and leading lay Catholic during and after World War I; belonged briefly to the utopian colony of Upton Sinclair; assistant director of the National Catholic War Council during WWI; founder and editor of *Commonweal*, a journal by and for lay Catholics, 1924-37.

Wimmer, Boniface: See under *Missionaries to the Americas.*

Wolff, Madeleva (1877-1964): Educator, author, poet, religious, and the first woman religious to receive a doctorate from the University of California at Berkeley; president of St. Mary's College, Notre Dame, Indiana, 1934-61, she was responsible for numerous innovations and the rise of the school to national prominence.

Wood, James F. (1813-83): First Archbishop of Philadelphia, 1875-83; convert in 1836; coadj. bishop of Philadelphia, 1857-60; bishop of Philadelphia, 1860-75.

Wright, John J. (1909-79): Cardinal from 1969 and prefect of the Congregation of the Clergy, 1969-79; aux. bishop of Boston, 1947-50; first bishop of Worcester, 1950-59; bishop of Pittsburgh, 1959-69; the first American to head a congregation in Rome with global duties.

Wynne, John, S.J. (1859-1925): Jesuit priest and author; editor of *Messenger of the Sacred Heart*, 1892-1909; founder of *America*, 1909, the foremost Jesuit journal of opinion in the U.S.; vice-postulator of the causes of the Jesuit North American Martyrs (beatified in 1925 and canonized in 1930).

X, Y, Z

Yorke, Peter (1864-1925): Priest, editor, and social activist; born in Ireland; chancellor of the archdiocese of San Francisco and editor of the archdiocesan newspaper; opposed anti-Catholicism in San Francisco; supported the Teamsters in the strike of 1901; founded the Irish newspaper, *The Leader*, 1902; a well-known spiritual figure in the Bay Area.

Youville, Marie Marguerite d', St.: See under *Missionaries to the Americas.*

Zahm, John (1851-1921): Holy Cross priest, theologian, and scientist; professor of physics at Notre Dame, 1875-92; sought to reconcile modern science and the Catholic faith; American provincial for the Congregation of the Holy Cross; traveled with Theodore Roosevelt to South America.

Zumarraga, Juan de: See under *Missionaries to the Americas.*

CATHOLICS IN THE U.S. GOVERNMENT

Catholics In Presidents' Cabinets

From 1789 to 1940, nine Catholics were appointed to cabinet posts by six of 32 presidents. The first was Roger Brooke Taney (later named first Catholic Supreme Court Justice) who was appointed in 1831 by Pres. Andrew Jackson. Catholics have been appointed to cabinet posts from the time of Pres. Franklin D. Roosevelt to the present.

Listed below in chronological order are the presidents, their Catholic cabinet officials, posts held, dates.

Andrew Jackson — Roger B. Taney, Attorney General, 1831-33, Secretary of Treasury, 1833-34.

Franklin Pierce — James Campbell, Postmaster General, 1853-57.

James Buchanan — John B. Floyd, Secretary of War, 1857-61.

William McKinley — Joseph McKenna, Attorney General, 1897-98.

Theodore Roosevelt — Robert J. Wynne, Postmaster General, 1904-05; Charles Bonaparte, Secretary of Navy, 1905-06, Attorney General, 1906-09.

Franklin D. Roosevelt — James A. Farley, Postmaster General, 1933-40; Frank Murphy, Attorney General, 1939-40; Frank C. Walker, Postmaster General, 1940-45.

Harry S. Truman — Robert E. Hannegan, Postmaster General, 1945-47; J. Howard McGrath, Attorney General, 1949-52; Maurice J. Tobin, Secretary of Labor, 1948-53; James P. McGranery, Attorney General, 1952-53.

Dwight D. Eisenhower — Martin P. Durkin, Secretary of Labor, 1953; James P. Mitchell, Secretary of Labor, 1953-61.

John F. Kennedy — Robert F. Kennedy, Attorney General, 1961-63; Anthony Celebrezze, Secretary of Health, Education and Welfare, 1962-63; John S. Gronouski, Postmaster General, 1963.

Lyndon B. Johnson — (Robert F. Kennedy, 1963-64, Anthony Celebrezze, 1963-65, and John S. Gronouski, 1963-65, reappointed to posts held in Kennedy Cabinet, see above.) John T. Connor, Secretary of Commerce, 1965-67; Lawrence O'Brien, Postmaster General, 1965-68.

Richard M. Nixon — Walter J. Hickel, Secretary of Interior, 1969-71; John A. Volpe, Secretary of Transportation, 1969-72; Maurice H. Stans, Secretary of Commerce, 1969-72; Peter J. Brennan, Secretary of Labor, 1973-74; William E. Simon, Secretary of Treasury, 1974.

Gerald R. Ford — (Peter J. Brennan, 1974-75, and William E. Simon, 1974-76, reappointed to posts held above.)

Jimmy Carter — Joseph Califano, Jr., Secretary of Health, Education and Welfare, 1977-79; Benjamin Civiletti, Attorney General, 1979-81; Moon Landrieu, Secretary of Housing and Urban Development, 1979-81; Edmund S. Muskie, Secretary of State, 1980-81.

Ronald Reagan — Alexander M. Haig, Secretary of State, 1981-82; Raymond J. Donovan, Secretary of Labor, 1981-84; Margaret M. Heckler, Secretary of Health and Human Services, 1983-85; William J. Bennett, Secretary of Education, 1985-88; Ann Dore McLaughlin, Secretary of Labor, 1988-89; Lauro F. Cavazos, Secretary of Education, 1988-89; Nicholas F. Brady, Secretary of Treasury, 1988-89.

George Bush — Lauro F. Cavazos (reappointed), Secretary of Education, 1989-90; Nicholas F. Brady (reappointed), Secretary of Treasury, 1989-93; James D. Watkins, Secretary of Energy, 1989-93; Manuel Lujan, Jr., Secretary of Interior, 1989-93; Edward J. Derwinski, Secretary of Veteran Affairs, 1989-92; Lynn Martin, Secretary of Labor, 1990-93; Edward Madigan, Secretary of Agriculture, 1991-93; William P. Barr, Attorney General, 1991-93.

Bill Clinton – Henry G. Cisneros, Secretary of Housing and Urban Development, 1993-97; Federico F. Peña, Secretary of Transportation, 1993-97; Donna Shalala, Secretary of Health and Human Services, 1993-2001; William M. Daley, Secretary of Commerce, 1997-2001; Andrew Cuomo, Secretary of Housing and Urban Development, 1997-2001; Alexis H. Herman, Secretary of Labor, 1997-2001.

George W. Bush — Paul O'Neill, Secretary of the Treasury, 2001-; Tommy Thompson, Secretary of Health and Human Services, 2001-; Mel Martinez, Secretary of Housing and Urban Development, 2001-; Anthony Principi, Secretary of Veterans Affairs, 2001-.

Cabinet members who became Catholics after leaving their posts were: Thomas Ewing, Secretary of Treasury under William A. Harrison, and Secretary of Interior under Zachary Taylor; Luke E. Wright, Secretary of War under Theodore Roosevelt; Albert B. Fall, Secretary of Interior under Warren G. Harding.

Catholic Supreme Court Justices

Roger B. Taney, Chief Justice 1836-64; app. by Andrew Jackson.

Edward D. White, Associate Justice 1894-1910, app. by Grover Cleveland; Chief Justice 1910-21, app. by William H. Taft.

Joseph McKenna, Associate Justice 1898-1925; app. by William McKinley.

Pierce Butler, Associate Justice 1923-39; app. by Warren G. Harding.

Frank Murphy, Associate Justice 1940-49; app. by Franklin D. Roosevelt.

William Brennan, Associate Justice 1956-90; app. by Dwight D. Eisenhower.

Antonin Scalia, Associate Justice 1986-; app. by Ronald Reagan.

Anthony M. Kennedy, Associate Justice 1988-; app. by Ronald Reagan.

Clarence Thomas, Associate Justice 1991- ; app. by George Bush.

Sherman Minton, Associate Justice from 1949 to 1956, became a Catholic several years before his death in 1965.

Catholics In Statuary Hall

Statues of 13 Catholics deemed worthy of national commemoration are among those enshrined in National Statuary Hall and other places in the U.S. Capitol. The Hall, formerly the chamber of the House of Representatives, was erected by Act of Congress July 2, 1864.

Donating states, names and years of placement are listed.

Arizona: Rev. Eusebio Kino, S. J., missionary, 1965.

California: Rev. Junípero Serra, O. F. M. missionary, 1931. (Beatified 1988.)

Hawaii: Father Damien, missionary, 1969. (Beatified 1995.)

Illinois: Gen. James Shields, statesman, 1893.

Louisiana: Edward D. White, Justice of the U.S. Supreme Court (1894-1921), 1955.

Maryland: Charles Carroll, statesman, 1901.

Nevada: Patrick A. McCarran, statesman, 1960.

New Mexico: Dennis Chavez, statesman, 1966. (Archbishop Jean B. Lamy, pioneer prelate of Santa Fe, was nominated for Hall honor in 1951.)

North Dakota: John Burke, U.S. treasurer, 1963.

Oregon: Dr. John McLoughlin, pioneer, 1953.

Washington: Mother Mary Joseph Pariseau, pioneer missionary and humanitarian.

West Virginia: John E. Kenna, statesman, 1901.

Wisconsin: Rev. Jacques Marquette, S.J., missionary, explorer, 1895.

CHURCH-STATE RELATIONS IN THE UNITED STATES

Church-State Decisions of the Supreme Court

(Among sources of this selected listing of U.S. Supreme Court decisions was The Supreme Court on Church and State, *Joseph Tussman, editor; Oxford University Press, New York, 1962.)*

Watson v. Jones, 13 Wallace 679 (1872): The Court declared that a member of a religious organization may not appeal to secular courts against a decision made by a church tribunal within the area of its competence.

Reynolds v. United States, 98 US 145 (1879); Davis v. Beason, 133 US 333 (1890); Church of Latter-Day Saints v. United States, 136 US 1 (1890): The Mormon practice of polygamy was at issue in three decisions and was declared unconstitutional:.

Bradfield v. Roberts, 175 US 291 (1899): The Court denied that an appropriation of government funds for an institution (Providence Hospital, Washington, D.C.) run by Roman Catholic sisters violated the No Establishment Clause of the First Amendment.

Pierce v. Society of Sisters, 268 US 510 (1925): The Court denied that a state can require children to attend public schools only. The Court held that the liberty of the Constitution forbids standardization by such compulsion, and that the parochial schools involved had claims to protection under the Fourteenth Amendment.

Cochran v. Board of Education, 281 US 370 (1930): The Court upheld a Louisiana statute providing textbooks at public expense for children attending public or parochial schools. The Court held that the children and state were beneficiaries of the appropriations, with incidental secondary benefit going to the schools.

United States v. MacIntosh, 283 US 605 (1931): The Court denied that anyone can place allegiance to the will of God above his allegiance to the government since such a person could make his own interpretation of God's will the decisive test as to whether he would or would not obey the nation's law. The Court stated that the nation, which has a duty to survive, can require citizens to bear arms in its defense.

Everson v. Board of Education, 330 US 1 (1947): The Court upheld the constitutionality of a New Jersey statute authorizing free school bus transportation for parochial as well as public school students. The Court expressed the opinion that the benefits of public welfare legislation, included under such bus transportation, do not run contrary to the concept of separation of Church and State.

McCollum v. Board of Education, 333 US 203 (1948): The Court declared unconstitutional a program for releasing children, with parental consent, from public school classes so they could receive religious instruction on public school premises from representatives of their own faiths.

Zorach v. Clauson, 343 US 306 (1952): The Court upheld the constitutionality of a New York statute permitting, on a voluntary basis, the release during school time of students from public school classes for religious instruction given off public school premises.

Torcaso v. Watkins, 367 US 488 (1961): The Court declared unconstitutional a Maryland requirement that one must make a declaration of belief in the existence of God as part of the oath of office for notaries public.

McGowan v. Maryland, 81 Sp Ct 1101; Two Guys from Harrison v. McGinley, 81 Sp Ct 1135; Gallagher v. Crown Kosher Super Market, 81 Sp Ct 1128; Braunfield v. Brown, 81 Sp Ct 1144 (1961): The Court ruled that Sunday closing laws do not violate the No Establishment of Religion Clause of the First Amendment, even though the laws were religious in their inception and still have some religious overtones. The Court held that, "as presently written and administered, most of them, at least, are of a secular rather than of a religious character, and that presently they bear no relationship to establishment of religion as those words are used in the Constitution of the United States."

Engel v. Vitale, 370 US 42 (1962): The Court declared that the voluntary recitation in public schools of a prayer composed by the New York State Board of Regents is unconstitutional on the ground that it violates the No Establishment of Religion Clause of the First Amendment.

Abington Township School District v. Schempp and Murray v. Curlett, 83 Sp Ct 1560 (1963): The Court ruled that Bible reading and recitation of the Lord's Prayer in public schools, with voluntary participation by students, are unconstitutional on the ground that they violate the No Establishment of Religion Clause of the First Amendment.

Chamberlin v. Dade County, 83 Sp Ct 1864 (1964): The Court reversed a decision of the Florida Supreme Court concerning the constitutionality of prayer and devotional Bible reading in public schools during the school day, as sanctioned by a state statute which specifically related the practices to a sound public purpose.

Board of Education v. Allen, No. 660 (1968): The Court declared constitutional the New York school book loan law which requires local school boards to purchase books with state funds and lend them to parochial and private school students.

Walz v. Tax Commission of New York (1970): The Court upheld the constitutionality of a New York statute exempting church-owned property from taxation.

Earle v. DiCenso, Robinson v. DiCenso, Lemon v. Kurtzman, Tilton v. Richardson (1971): In Earle v. DiCenso and Robinson v. DiCenso, the Court ruled unconstitutional a 1969 Rhode Island statute that provided salary supplements to teachers of secular subjects in parochial schools; in Lemon v. Kurtzman, the Court ruled unconstitutional a 1968 Pennsylvania statute that authorized the state to purchase services for the teaching of secular subjects in nonpublic schools. The principal argument against constitutionality in these cases was that the statutes and programs at issue entailed excessive entanglement of government with religion. In Tilton v. Richardson, the Court held that this argument did not apply to a prohibitive degree with respect to federal grants, under the Higher Education Facilities Act of 1963, for the construction of facilities for nonreligious purposes by four church-related institutions of higher learning, three of which were Catholic, in Connecticut.

Yoder, Miller and Yutzy (1972): In a case appealed on behalf of Yoder, Miller and Yutzy, the Court ruled that Amish parents were exempt from a Wisconsin statute requiring them to send their children to school until the age of 16. The Court said in its decision that secondary schooling exposed Amish children to attitudes, goals, and values contrary to their beliefs, and substantially hindered "the religious development of the Amish child and his integration into the way of life of the Amish faith-community at the crucial adolescent state of development."

Committee for Public Education and Religious Liberty, et al., v. Nyquist, et al., No. 72-694 (1973): The Court ruled that provisions of a 1972 New York statute were unconstitutional on the grounds that they were violative of the No Establishment Clause of the First Amendment and had the "impermissible effect" of advancing the sectarian activities of church-affiliated schools. The programs ruled unconstitutional concerned: (1) maintenance and repair grants, for facilities and equipment, to ensure the health, welfare and safety of students in nonpublic, non-profit elementary and secondary schools serving a high concentration of students from low income families; (2) tuition reimbursement ($50 per grade school child, $100 per high school student) for parents (with income less than $5,000) of children attending nonpublic elementary or secondary schools; tax deduction from adjusted gross income for parents failing to qualify under the above reimbursement plan, for each child attending a nonpublic school.

Sloan, Treasurer of Pennsylvania, et al., v. Lemon, et al., No. 72-459 (1973): The Court ruled unconstitutional a Pennsylvania Parent Reimbursement Act for Nonpublic Education which provided funds to reimburse parents (to a maximum of $150) for a portion of tuition expenses incurred in sending their children to nonpublic schools. The Court held that there was no significant difference between this and the New York tuition reimbursement program (above), and declared that the Equal Protection Clause of the Fourteenth Amendment cannot be relied upon to sustain a program held to be violative of the No Establishment Clause.

Levitt, et al., v. Committee for Public Education and Religious Liberty, et al., No. 72-269 (1973): The Court ruled unconstitutional the Mandated Services Act of 1970 under which New York provided $28 million ($27 per pupil from first to seventh grade, $45 per pupil from seventh to twelfth grade) to reimburse nonpublic schools for testing, recording, and reporting services required by the state. The Court declared that the act provided "impermissible aid" to religion in contravention of the No Establishment Clause.

In related decisions handed down June 25, 1973, the Court: (1) affirmed a lower court decision against the constitutionality of an Ohio tax credit law benefiting parents with children in nonpublic schools; (2) reinstated an injunction against a parent reimbursement program in New Jersey; (3) affirmed South Carolina's right to grant construction loans to church-affiliated colleges, and (4) dismissed an appeal contesting its right to provide loans to students attending church-affiliated colleges (Hunt v. McNair, Durham v. McLeod).

Wheeler v. Barrera (1974): The Court ruled that nonpublic school students in Missouri must share in federal funds for educationally deprived students on a comparable basis with public school students under Title I of the Elementary and Secondary Education Act of 1965.

Norwood v. Harrison (93 S. Ct. 2804): The Court ruled that public assistance which avoids the prohibitions of the "effect" and "entanglement" tests (and which therefore does not substantially promote the religious mission of sectarian schools) may be confined to the secular functions of such schools.

Wiest v. Mt. Lebanon School District (1974): The Court upheld a lower court ruling that invocation and benediction prayers at public high school commencement ceremonies do not violate the principle of separation of Church and State.

Meek v. Pittenger (1975): The Court ruled unconstitutional portions of a Pennsylvania law providing auxiliary services for students of nonpublic schools; at the same time, it ruled in favor of provisions of the law permitting textbook loans to students of such schools. In denying the constitutionality of auxiliary services, the Court held that they had the "primary effect of establishing religion" and involved "excessive entanglement" of Church and state officials with respect to supervision; objection was also made against providing such services only on the premises of nonpublic schools and only at the request of such schools.

TWA, Inc., v. Hardison, 75-1126; International Association of Machinists and Aero Space Workers v. Hardison, 75-1385 (1977): The Court ruled that federal civil rights legislation does not require employers to make more than minimal efforts to accommodate employees who want a particular working day off as their religion's Sabbath Day, and that an employer cannot accommodate such an employee by violating seniority systems determined by a union collective bargaining agreement. The Court noted that its ruling was not a constitutional judgment but an interpretation of existing law.

Wolman v. Walter (1977): The Court ruled constitutional portions of an Ohio statute providing tax-paid textbook loans and some auxiliary services (standardized and diagnostic testing, therapeutic and remedial services, off school premises) for nonpublic school students. It decided that other portions of the law, providing state funds for nonpublic school field trips and instructional materials (audio-visual equipment, maps, tape recorders), were unconstitutional.

Byrne v. Public Funds for Public Schools (1979): The Court decided against the constitutionality of a 1976 New Jersey law providing state income tax deductions for tuition paid by parents of students attending parochial and other private schools.

Student Bus Transportation (1979): The Court upheld a Pennsylvania law providing bus transportation at public expense for students to nonpublic schools up to 10 miles away from the boundaries of the public school districts in which they lived.

Reimbursement (1980): The Court upheld the constitutionality of a 1974 New York law providing direct cash payment to nonpublic schools for the costs of state-mandated testing and record-keeping.

Ten Commandments (1980): The Court struck down a 1978 Kentucky law requiring the posting of the Ten Commandments in public school classrooms in the state.

Widmar v. Vincent (1981): The Court ruled that the University of Missouri at Kansas City could not deny student religious groups the use of campus facilities for worship services. The Court also, in Brandon v. Board of Education of Guilderland Schools, declined without comment to hear an appeal for reversal of lower court decisions denying a group of New York high school students the right to meet for prayer on public school property before the beginning of the school day.

Lubbock v. Lubbock Civil Liberties Union (1983): By refusing to hear an appeal in this case, the Court upheld a lower court ruling against a public policy of permitting student religious groups to meet on public school property before and after school hours.

Mueller v. Allen (1983): The Court upheld a Minnesota law allowing parents of students in public and nonpublic (including parochial) schools to take a tax deduction for the expenses of tuition, textbooks and transportation. Maximum allowable deductions were $500 per child in elementary school and $700 per child in grades seven through twelve.

Lynch v. Donnelly (1984): The Court ruled 5-to-4 that the First Amendment does not mandate "complete separation of church and state," and that, therefore, the sponsorship of a Christmas nativity scene by the City of Pawtucket, Rhode Island, was not unconstitutional. The case involved a scene included in a display of Christmas symbols sponsored by the city in a park owned by a non-profit group. The majority opinion said "the Constitution (does not) require complete separation of church and state; it affirmatively mandates accommodation, not merely tolerance, of all religions and forbids hostility toward any. Anything less" would entail callous indifference not intended by the Constitution. Moreover, "such hostility would bring us into 'war with our national tradition as embodied in the First Amendment's guaranty of the free exercise of religion.' " (The additional quotation was from the 1948 decision in McCollum v. Board of Education.)

Christmas Nativity Scene (1985): The Court upheld a lower court ruling that the Village of Scarsdale, New York, must make public space available for the display of privately sponsored nativity scenes.

Wallace v. Jaffree, No. 83-812 (1985): The Court ruled against the constitutionality of a 1981 Alabama law calling for a public-school moment of silence that specifically included optional prayer.

Grand Rapids v. Ball, No. 83-990, and **Aguilar v. Felton, No. 84-237** (1985): The Court ruled against the constitutionality of programs in Grand Rapids and New York City allowing public school teachers to teach remedial entitlement subjects (under the Elementary and Secondary Education Act of 1965) in private schools, many of which were Catholic.

Bender v. Williamsport Area School District (1986): The Court let stand a lower federal court decision allowing a public high school Bible study group the same "equal access" to school facilities as that enjoyed by other extracurricular clubs. A similar decision was handed down in 1990 in Board of Education v. Mergens, involving Westside High School in Omaha.

County of Allegheny v. American Civil Liberties Union (1989): The Court ruled (1) that display of a Christmas nativity scene in the Allegheny County Courthouse in Pittsburgh, Pennsylvania, violated the principle of separation of church and state because it appeared to be a government-sponsored endorsement of Christian belief. (2) and that the display of a Hanukkah menorah outside the Pittsburgh-Allegheny city-county building was constitutional because of its "particular physical setting" with secular symbols.

Unemployment Division v. Smith (1990): The Court ruled that religious use of the hallucinogenic cactus peyote is not covered by the First Amendment protection of religious freedom.

Lee v. Weisman (1992): The Court banned officially-organized prayer at public school graduation ceremonies.

Lamb's Chapel v. Center Moriches Union School District (1993): The Court reversed a ruling by the 3rd U.S. Circuit Court of Appeals, declaring that the school district was wrong in prohibiting the congregation of Lamb's Chapel from using public school meeting space after hours to show a film series addressing family problems from

a religious perspective. In view of the variety of organizations permitted to use school property after school hours, said the Court's opinion: "There would have been no realistic danger that the community would think that the district was endorsing religion or any particular creed, and any benefit to religion or to the church would have been no more than incidental."

5th U.S. Circuit Court of Appeals (1993): The Court let stand a ruling by the 5th U.S. Circuit Court of Appeals, permitting students in Texas, Mississippi, and Louisiana to include student-organized and student-led prayers in graduation exercises.

Church of Lukumi Babalu Aye v. City of Hialeah (1993): The Court ruled that municipal laws that effectively prohibit a single church from performing its religious rituals are unconstitutional. The ordinances at issue singled out one religion, Santeria, for the purpose of restricting its members from the practice of ritual animal sacrifices.

Zobrest v. Catalina Foothills School District (1993): The Court ruled that a public school district may provide a sign-language interpreter for a deaf student attending a Catholic school without violating constitutional separation of church and state. The majority opinion said: "Handicapped children, not sectarian schools, are the primary beneficiaries of the Disabilities Education Act; to the extent sectarian schools benefit at all from (the act), they are only incidental beneficiaries."

Fairfax County, Virginia, school district (1994): The Court upheld lower court rulings against a Fairfax County, Virginia, school district's practice of charging churches more rent than other entities for the use of school buildings.

Board of Education of Kiryas Joel Village School District v. Grumet (1994): In, the Court ruled in 1994 that a school district created to meet the special education needs of an Hasidic Jewish community violated the Establishment Clause of the Constitution. The Court said the New York Legislature effectively endorsed a particular religion when it established a public school district for the Satmar Hasidic Village of Kiryas Joel.

Agostino v. Felton (1997): The court reversed, 5-to-4, its 1985 Aguilar v. Felton ruling, which had declared it unconstitutional for teachers employed by public school districts to hold Title I remedial programs for low-income students on the property of church-related schools.

Boerne v. Flores (1997): The court ruled, 6-to-3, that the Religious Freedom Restoration Act (1993) was unconstitutional because Congress overstepped its constitutional authority in enacting the law. Congress "has been given the power to 'enforce,' not the power to determine what constitutes a constitutional violation," said the majority opinion.

Mitchell v. Helms (2000): The court ruled, 6-to-3, that a Louisiana parish can distribute money for instructional equipment – including computers, books, maps, and film strip projectors – to private schools as long as it's done in a "secular, neutral and nonideological" way. The court's decision overturns two previous Supreme Court bans on giving public materials to parochial schools.

Santa Fe Independent School District v. Doe (2000): The court affirmed a lower court ruling that said prayer in public schools must be private and that such prayers at high school football games violate the constitutionally required separation of church and state. At issue in the Santa Fe case was a Texas school policy which permitted students selected by their peers to deliver an inspirational message of their own design at football games and the graduation ceremony. In 1999, the Santa Fe policy was struck down by the U.S. Court of Appeals for the Fifth Circuit. The Court of Appeals held that the policy violated the Establishment Clause of the First Amendment, even though the government played no role in creating the message or selecting the messenger.

RELIGION IN PUBLIC SCHOOLS

(Based on a Catholic News Service article by Carol Zimmermann.)

A diverse group of religious and civil rights organizations issued a joint statement April 13, 1995, in an effort to clarify the confusing issue of prayer and religious observances or discussions in public schools. Their six-page statement outlines what is and what is not currently permissible in expressing religious beliefs in public schools.

The statement says, for example: "Students have the right to pray individually or in groups, or to discuss their religious views with their peers so long as they are not disruptive." But, the statement specifies that such prayers or discussions do not include "the right to have a captive audience listen or to compel other students to participate."

Prayer at Graduations

Regarding prayer at graduation ceremonies, the document says school officials may not mandate or organize prayer, but hardly sets the record straight about student-led prayer at these services.

"The courts have reached conflicting conclusions under the federal Constitution" in this area, says the statement, recommending that schools consult their lawyers for the rules that apply to them, "until the issue is authoritatively resolved."

Since the Supreme Court's 1992 Lee v. Weisman opinion prohibited school authorities from even arranging for a speaker to present a prayer, lower courts in different states have made various rulings about student-led prayer at commencement exercises.

In Virginia, the state's Attorney General and the Board of Education proposed guidelines in mid-April to allow student-led prayer at graduations, despite a 1994 ruling by a U.S. district judge banning all prayer at graduations.

Religion in the Classroom

"It is both permissible and desirable to teach objectively about the role of religion in the history of the United States and other countries," but public school teachers may not specifically teach religion.

The same rules apply to the recurring controversy surrounding theories of evolution. Teachers may discuss explanations of the beginnings of life, but only within the confines of classes on religion or social studies. Public school teachers are required, according to the statement, to teach only scientific explanations of life's beginnings in science classes. And, just as teachers may not advance a religious view, they should not ridicule a student's religious belief.

Constitutional Protection

The statement says that students' expressions of religious beliefs in reports, homework or artwork are constitutionally protected. Likewise, students have the right to speak to and attempt to persuade their peers on religious topics. "But school officials should intercede to stop student religious speech if it turns into religious harassment aimed at a student or a small group of students."

The statement also says:
- Students have the right to distribute religious literature to their schoolmates, subject to reasonable restrictions for any non-school literature.
- Student religious clubs in secondary schools "must be permitted to meet and to have equal access" to school media for announcing their events.
- Religious messages on T-shirts and the like cannot be singled out for suppression.
- Schools can use discretion about dismissing students for off-site religious instruction.

The 35 organizations that endorsed the statement included the National Association of Evangelicals, the American Jewish Congress, the Christian Legal Society, the National Council of Churches, the Baptist Joint Committee on Public Affairs, the American Muslim Council, the Presbyterian Church (USA), and the American Civil Liberties Union.

Purpose of the Statement

"By making this document available," said Phil Baum, executive director of the American Jewish Congress, "the organizations are attempting to clarify what has become one of the most divisive issues of our time: religion in the public schools."

He said the document attempts to "ensure that the rights of all students are respected in the public schools."

Baum noted that the American Jewish Congress, which initiated the effort to draft the statement, had a long-standing commitment to ensuring that public schools are themselves religiously neutral.

"We believe, however, that it is inconsistent with that historic commitment to ask the public schools to root out private expressions of religious faith."

CHURCH TAX EXEMPTION

The exemption of church-owned property was ruled constitutional by the U.S. Supreme Court May 4, 1970, in the case of Walz v. The Tax Commission of New York.

Suit in the case was brought by Frederick Walz, who purchased in June 1967, a 22-by-29-foot plot of ground in Staten Island valued at $100 and taxable at $5.24 a year. Shortly after making the purchase, Walz instituted a suit in New York State, contending that the exemption of church property from taxation authorized by state law increased his own tax rate and forced him indirectly to support churches in violation of his constitutional right to freedom of religion under the First Amendment. Three New York courts dismissed the suit, which had been instituted by mail. The Supreme Court, judging that it had probable jurisdiction, then took the case.

In a 7-to-1 decision affecting Church-state relations in every state in the nation, the Court upheld the New York law under challenge.

For and Against

Chief Justice Warren E. Burger, who wrote the majority opinion, said that Congress from its earliest days had viewed the religion clauses of the Constitution as authorizing statutory real estate tax exemption to religious bodies. He declared: "Nothing in this national attitude toward religious tolerance and two centuries of uninterrupted freedom from taxation has given the remotest sign of leading to an established church or religion, and on the contrary it has operated affirmatively to help guarantee the free exercise of all forms of religious beliefs."

Justice William O. Douglas wrote in dissent that the involvement of government in religion as typified in tax exemption may seem inconsequential but: "It is, I fear, a long step down the establishment path. Perhaps I have been misinformed. But, as I read the Constitution and the philosophy, I gathered that independence was the price of liberty."

Burger rejected Douglas' "establishment" fears. If tax exemption is the first step toward establishment, he said, "the second step has been long in coming."

The basic issue centered on the following question: Is there a contradiction between federal constitutional provisions against the establishment of religion, or the use of public funds for religious purposes, and state statutes exempting church property from taxation? In the Walz decision, the Supreme Court ruled that there is no contradiction.

Legal Background

The U.S. Constitution makes no reference to tax exemption. There was no discussion of the issue in the Constitutional Convention nor in debates on the Bill of Rights.

In the Colonial and post-Revolutionary years, some churches had established status and were state-supported. This changed with enactment of the First Amendment, which laid down no-establishment as the federal norm. This norm was adopted by the states which, however, exempted churches from tax liabilities.

No establishment, no hindrance, was the early American view of Church-State relationships.

This view, reflected in custom law, was not generally formulated in statute law until the second half of the 19th century, although specific tax exemption was provided for churches in Maryland in 1798, in Virginia in 1800, and in North Carolina in 1806.

The first major challenge to church property exemption was initiated by the Liberal League in the 1870s. It reached the point that President Grant included the recommendation in a State of the Union address in 1875, stating that church property should bear its own proportion of taxes.

The plea fell on deaf ears in Congress, but there was some support for the idea at state levels. The exemption, however, continued to survive various challenges.

About 36 state constitutions contain either mandatory or permissive provisions for exemption. Statutes provide for exemption in all other states.

There has been considerable litigation challenging this exemption, but most of it focused on whether a particular property satisfied statutory requirements. Few cases before Walz focused on the strictly constitutional question, whether directly under the First Amendment or indirectly under the Fourteenth.

Objections

Objectors to the tax exempt status of churches feel that churches should share, through taxation, in the cost of the ordinary benefits of public services they enjoy, and/or that the amount of "aid" enjoyed through exemption should be proportionate to the amount of social good they do.

According to one opinion, exemption is said to weaken the independence of churches from the political system that benefits them by exemption.

In another view, exemption is said to involve the government in decisions regarding what is and what is not religion.

The Wall of Separation

Thomas Jefferson, in a letter written to the Danbury (CN) Baptist Association January 1, 1802, coined the metaphor, "a wall of separation between Church and State," to express a theory concerning interpretation of the religion clauses of the First Amendment: "Congress shall make no law respecting an establishment of religion or prohibiting the free exercise thereof."

The metaphor was cited for the first time in judicial proceedings in 1879, in the opinion by Chief Justice Waite in Reynolds v. United States.

It did not, however, figure substantially in the decision.

Accepted as Rule

In 1947 the wall of separation gained acceptance as a constitutional rule, in the decision handed down in Everson v. Board of Education. Associate Justice Black, in describing the principles involved in the No Establishment Clause, wrote:

"Neither a state nor the Federal Government can set up a church. Neither can pass laws which aid one religion, aid all religions, or prefer one religion over another. Neither can force nor influence a person to go to or to remain away from church against his will or force him to profess a belief or disbelief in any religion. No person can be punished for entertaining or professing religious beliefs or disbeliefs, for church attendance or non-attendance. No tax in any amount, large or small, can be levied to support any religious activities or institutions, whatever they may be called, or whatever form they may adopt to teach or practice religion. Neither a state nor the Federal Government can, openly or secretly, participate in the affairs of any religious organizations or groups and vice versa. In the words of Jefferson, the clause against establishment of religion by law was intended to erect 'a wall of separation between Church and State.' "

Mr. Black's associates agreed with his statement of principles, which were framed without reference to the Freedom of Exercise Clause. They disagreed, however, with respect to application of the principles, as the split decision in the case indicated. Five members of the Court held that the benefits of public welfare legislation — in this case, free bus transportation to school for parochial as well as public school students — did not run contrary to the concept of separation of Church and State embodied in the First Amendment.

CANADIAN CATHOLIC HISTORY

Background

The first date in the remote background of the Catholic history of Canada was July 7, 1534, when a priest in the exploration company of Jacques Cartier celebrated Mass on the Gaspé Peninsula.

Successful colonization and the significant beginnings of the Catholic history of the country date from the foundation of Québec in 1608 by Samuel de Champlain and French settlers. Montréal was established in 1642.

The earliest missionaries were Franciscan Récollets (Recollects) and Jesuits who arrived in 1615 and 1625, respectively. They provided some pastoral care for the settlers but worked mainly among the 100,000 Indians — Algonquins, Hurons and Iroquois — in the interior and in the Lake Ontario region. Eight of the Jesuit missionaries, killed in the 1640s, were canonized in 1930. (See Index: Jesuit North American Martyrs.) Sulpician Fathers, who arrived in Canada late in the 1640s, played a part in the great missionary period which ended about 1700.

Kateri Tekakwitha, "Lily of the Mohawks," who was baptized in 1676 and died in 1680, was declared "Blessed" June 22, 1980.

The communities of women religious with the longest histories in Canada are the Canonesses of St. Augustine and the Ursulines, since 1639; and the Hospitallers of St. Joseph, since 1642. Communities of Canadian origin are the Congregation of Notre Dame, founded by St. Marguerite Bourgeoys in 1658, and the Grey Nuns, formed by St. Marie Marguerite d'Youville in 1737.

Mother Marie (Guyard) of the Incarnation, an Ursuline nun, was one of the first three women missionaries to New France; called "Mother of the Church in Canada," she was declared "Blessed" June 22, 1980.

Start of Church Organization

Ecclesiastical organization began with the appointment in 1658 of François De Montmorency-Laval, "Father of the Church in Canada," as vicar apostolic of New France. He was the first bishop of Québec from 1674 to 1688, with jurisdiction over all French-claimed territory in North America. He was declared "Blessed" June 22, 1980.

In 1713, the French Canadian population numbered 18,000. In the same year, the Treaty of Utrecht ceded Acadia, Newfoundland, and the Hudson Bay Territory to England. The Acadians were scattered among the American Colonies in 1755.

The English acquired possession of Canada and its 70,000 French-speaking inhabitants in virtue of the Treaty of Paris in 1763. Anglo-French and Anglican-Catholic differences and tensions developed. The pro-British government at first refused to recognize the titles of church officials, hindered the clergy in their work, and tried to install a non-Catholic educational system. Laws were passed that guaranteed religious liberties to Catholics (Québec Act of 1774, Constitutional Act of 1791, legislation approved by Queen Victoria in 1851), but it took some time before actual respect for these liberties matched the legal enactments. The initial moderation of government antipathy toward the Church was caused partly by the loyalty of Catholics to the Crown during the American Revolution and the War of 1812.

Growth

The 15 years following the passage in 1840 of the Act of Union, which joined Upper and Lower Canada, were significant. New communities of men and women religious joined those already in the country. The Oblates of Mary Immaculate, missionaries par excellence in Canada, advanced the penetration of the West which had been started in 1818 by Abbé Provencher. New jurisdictions were established, and Québec became a metropolitan see in 1844. The first Council of Québec was held in 1851. The established Catholic school system enjoyed a period of growth.

Laval University was inaugurated in 1854 and canonically established in 1876.

Archbishop Elzear-Alexandre Taschereau of Québec was named Canada's first cardinal in 1886.

The apostolic delegation to Canada was set up in 1899. It became a nunciature October 16, 1969, with the establishment of diplomatic relations with the Vatican.

Early in this century, Canada had eight ecclesiastical provinces, 23 dioceses, three vicariates apostolic, 3,500 priests, 2 million Catholics, about 30 communities of men religious, and 70 or more communities of women religious. The Church in Canada was phased out of mission status and removed from the jurisdiction of the Congregation for the Propagation of the Faith in 1908.

Diverse Population

The greatest concentration of Catholics is in the eastern portion of the country. In the northern and western portions, outside metropolitan centers, are some of the most difficult parish and mission areas in the world. Bilingual (English-French) differences in the general population are reflected in the Church, for example, in the parallel structures of the Canadian Conference of Catholic Bishops, which was established in 1943. Québec is the center of French cultural influence. Many language groups are represented among Catholics, who include more than 257,000 members of Eastern Rites in one metropolitan see, seven eparchies and an apostolic exarchate.

Education, a past source of friction between the Church and the government, is administered by the civil provinces in a variety of arrangements authorized by the Canadian Constitution. Denominational schools have tax support in one way in Québec and Newfoundland, and in another way in Alberta, Ontario, and Saskatchewan. Several provinces provide tax support only for public schools, making private financing necessary for separate church-related schools.

MEXICAN CATHOLIC HISTORY

BACKGROUND

Start of Church Organization

The history of the Catholic Church in Mexico began in 1519 with the capture of Mexico's native civilization, the Aztec Empire, by the Spanish *conquistadores* under Hernándo Cortés. The Spanish army besieged the Aztec capital of Tenochtitlan, massacred most of the inhabitants, strangled the Aztec emperor Montezuma, and crushed the rest of the empire. Mexico City became the chief city of New Spain and the cultural and religious center of colonial Mexico; it was declared a diocese in 1530.

The record of Colonial Spanish treatment of the native peoples of Mexico is a grim one. The Indians suffered exploitation, slavery, and rapid depletion of their population from disease; they were forced to labor in inhuman conditions in mines and endured servitude in the *encomienda* system.

In sharp contrast to the treatment of the natives by the government was the effort to evangelize Mexico by the religious orders who followed the command of Pope Alexander VI in the 1494 Treaty of Tordesillas to convert all peoples who should be encountered in the coming age of exploration. A papal bull, dated April 25, 1521, gave to the Franciscans the permission of the Holy See to preach in New Spain. They were joined by the Dominicans and, later, by the Jesuits. The missionary orders soon distinguished themselves by their resistance to the brutal enslavement of the Indians, their mastery of native languages, and their willingness to endure enormous hardships in bringing the faith to the distant corners of Mexico.

As the Church became more established, however, the missionary priests and friars came increasingly into conflict with the secular clergy, who desired full control over ecclesiastical affairs, resented the extensive powers of the religious orders, and normally identified closely with the interests of the crown. The government thus decreed that the missionaries were to have ten years in which to convert the Indians after which control should pass to the diocesan clergy. This was protested by the missionary orders, and the conflict was resolved in favor of the diocesan priests finally in 1640 thanks to the efforts of Bishop Juan de Palafox de Mendoza of Puebla.

The alliance of the secular clergy with the government was a reflection of the control enjoyed by the Spanish crown over the Church in Mexico. The Holy See had granted to the kings of Spain royal patronage over the Church in Mexico, and the practice of the *Patronato Real* meant that the king nominated all Church officials in New Spain and held authority over the Church's temporal concerns. A major element in this policy was the forced conversion of the local peoples. Coerced into adopting the faith, many Indians were insincere or hesitant to embrace a faith that was forced upon them. To insure the full embrace of the faith, Spanish authorities received permission from King Philip II in 1569 to introduce the Inquisition to Mexico. Indians who had survived the mines, diseases, and brutality of the colonial rulers were now subjected to tribunals to test their faith. This practice was eventually ended when authorities decided that the natives were not culpable because of limited intelligence. Nevertheless, the close identification of the diocesan clergy with the interests and policies of the Spanish crown created a hostility toward the Church in Mexico by the lower classes that endures even today.

On the positive side, the Church did much through its missionaries to save many Indians from death and enslavement and to preserve vital portions of Mesoamerican culture, art, and history. Equally, friars traveled to northern Mexico and beyond, bringing the faith into California, Texas, and New Mexico.

The native peoples were given a profound encouragement to embrace the Catholic faith in 1531 by the appearance of Our Lady of Guadalupe to the farmer Juan Diego (beatified in 1990 by Pope John Paul II) on the Tepeyac hill just outside of Mexico City. The shrine built in her honor remains the most important religious site in Mexico. Enshrined within it is the mantle brought by Juan Diego to Bishop Zumaragga to convince him of the genuine nature of the apparition. Miraculously emblazoned upon it is the life-size image of the Virgin Mary.

Mexican Independence

The Spanish domination of Mexico endured for nearly three centuries, deteriorating gradually throughout the 1700s as the gulf widened between the Spanish ruling class and the native classes that were joined by the *mestizos* and *creoles* (descendants of Native Americans and Europeans). Unrest broke out into a full-scale rebellion in 1810 with the uprising of many priests led by

Father Miguel Hidalgo y Costilla and, after his execution, by Father José Maria Morelos y Pavón. While suppressed in 1816 by the colonial regime, with the support of the upper classes and most of the diocesan clergy, it proved only the first of several revolts, culminating in the 1821 declaration of Mexican independence. By the terms of the independence, the Church received a special status and had enormous sway in political life.

A republic was proclaimed in 1834 and various liberal regimes came to power. Anticlericalism became commonplace, made even more strident by the lingering hostility over the Church's activities with Spanish colonial government. Much influenced by the ideals of the European revolutions then taking place, the Mexican republican movements were strongly anti-Catholic. For more than a decade, power was in the hands of Antonio López de Santa Anna (of the Alamo fame) and Valentin Gómez Farías. After the Mexican-American War (1846-1848), the political instability led to the dictatorship of Santa Anna.

Santa Anna was toppled in 1855 by a liberal regime whose anti-Church legislation sparked an armed struggle called the War of the Reform (1858-1861). The laws issued by the government included the *Ley Juárez*, abolishing all ecclesiastical courts, and the *Ley Lerdo*, forcing the Church to sell all of its lands. Deprived of its properties, the Church lost control of education and schools, and Mexico's educational system became often bitterly anti-Catholic.

While the liberal forces won the War of the Reform, the conflict had so debilitated Mexico that the French were able to intervene in 1861 and install their puppet, the Austrian duke Maximilian, on the Mexican throne. As the United States was embroiled in its own civil war from 1861-1865, it was unable to respond to French imperialist ambitions in Mexico. Maximilian initially enjoyed the support of the conservative elements and the Church, but his liberal reforms alienated the mistrustful conservatives and he soon clung to power only with French support. When France finally withdrew its troops in 1867, Maximilian was deposed by republican forces and executed.

Modern Mexico

The fall of Emperor Maximilian signaled a restoration of the anticlerical constitution of 1857 and the elevation of Benito Juárez – the republican leader long recognized by the United States – as president. His successor, Sebastián Lerdo de Tijada, was toppled in 1876 by Porfirio Diáz who remained dictator for thirty-four years. A civil war ended his regime, and more bloodshed ensued. Finally, a constitution was issued in 1917 that placed severe restrictions on the Church:

there could be no criticism of the government, only Mexicans could be clergy, the Church was not permitted to own property, and any privileges were stripped away.

The situation became worse from 1923 when the papal legate was expelled. The administration of Plutarco Calles (1924-1928) launched a wave of persecution that sparked a popular but ultimately unsuccessful uprising called the Cristero Rebellion. Coupled with the repressive measures of local governments, the Calles regime and its successors forced the Church into very difficult circumstances, with only a few priests remaining in the country. The tragedy was deepened by the execution of dozens of priests and nuns by republican forces for assorted and imaginary crimes or for speaking out on behalf of the poor or oppressed Catholics. A number of the executed clergy have been beatified and canonized since the tragedy, most so during the pontificate of Pope John Paul II. The persecution prompted Pope Pius XI to issue the encyclicals *Iniquis afflictisque* (1926) and *Acerba animi* (1932).

An easing of the situation began in 1940 as the rigid anticlerical laws ceased to be enforced with enthusiasm. A rapprochement was visible in the 1958 elections, when the Church received conciliatory gestures from the ruling Revolutionary Party and its presidential candidate, Adolfo López Mateos. The Church continued to exist under numerous legal disabilities and was oppressed in a number of the Mexican states.

Gradual improvement in relations between Mexico and the Holy See led to the exchange in 1990 of personal representatives between the Mexican president and Pope John Paul II. The Holy Father's efforts to build a further diplomatic bridge culminated in the establishment of full diplomatic ties in 1992. This was followed by the final easing of many of the handicaps under which the Church had long suffered.

The faith of the Mexican people is profoundly deep, as was seen in the nearly frenzied greeting given to Pope John Paul II in 1979, 1990, 1993, and 1999. However, social unrest, poverty, economic challenges, the violence of drug cartels, and corruption still plague the country. Church leaders – especially religious orders – have been outspoken in their criticism against government human rights abuses and corruption. During the mid-1990s, the Jesuits said they were the target of a "campaign of intimidation" because of their human rights work.

On May 24, 1993, Cardinal Juan Jesus Posadas Ocampo of Guadalajara was killed during a supposed shoot-out among rival drug cartels. The murder remained unsolved, although Cardinal Posadas' successor, Cardinal Juan

Sandoval Íñiguez, continued to claim that high-ranking officials, including the Mexican attorney general at the time, lied to protect others involved in a plot.

In the 1970s and 1980s, one of Mexico's most prominent proponents of liberation theology was Bishop Samuel Ruiz Garcia of San Cristobal de las Casas. In the early 1990s the Vatican began investigating his views, but because he had the trust of indigenous peasants, in 1994 he was thrown into the role of mediator between the government and the mostly native Zapatista National Liberation Army in Chiapas. He continued that role until 1998, when he resigned after accusing the government of "dismantling any possible means or effort to solve the crisis in Chiapas." Mexico's bishops said at that time that they would provide support to the peace process but would not seek to mediate the conflict. Currently, the Church in Mexico faces threats of defections among Catholics to Evangelical Protestant sects and religious indifference.

On July 2, 2000, the Mexican Presidential election was won by Vicente Fox Quesada, head of the National Action Party, marking the first time since 1929 that power in the country was not in the hands of the Institutional Revolutionary Party (PRI). Mexicans hungry for political change gave the National Action Party candidate 43% of the vote and just 36% to his PRI rival, Francisco Labastida.

The election of Fox, often described as a conservative populist, presented a serious opportunity for substantive changes in the relationship between the Church and State, a cessation of decades of anti-Church hostility, and the reform of laws that sharply curtailed Church activities. Aside from his promises of sweeping governmental and economic reforms, Fox also declared his commitment to freedom of religion. He also had no plans to change Mexico's standing laws prohibiting abortion.

The 2000 election represents a major change in the political landscape of Mexico, offering the best opportunity in seven decades for an end to the long-standing repression of the Church. Throughout the campaign, Fox called for religious freedom and equality of treatment of Christian churches in Mexico. He promised to ease restrictions on Catholic schools and on religious activity in public schools.

Church leaders were optimistic about the possibilities for Mexican Catholics, but they were also realistic. Auxiliary Bishop Abelardo Alvarado Alcantara of Mexico City, general secretary of the Mexican bishops' conference, told a post-election news conference that Church leaders congratulated Fox, but that the Church "did not expect privileges or need them, nor was it asking for them."

Bishop Alvarado added that, "We do desire that there be religious teaching, not precisely in the schools, but rather that there be an awareness of the necessity to educate in religious and moral values. We are not asking for this at this time, but it is up to the society, parents, and the executive and legislative branches to decide in their time."

The bishops' conference was pleased that the election was carried out in relative peace and order. Conference president Archbishop Luis Morales of San Luis Potosi expressed his thanks to God that the peaceful election was "one of the advances achieved by the people of Mexico in recent years, the construction of a more participatory democracy."

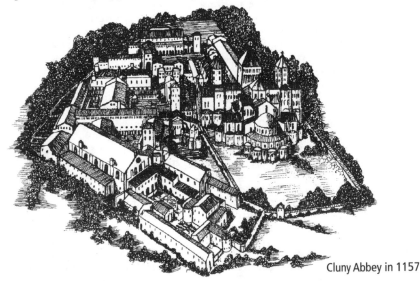

Cluny Abbey in 1157

Part 2

THE PAPACY AND THE HOLY SEE

POPE JOHN PAUL II
(Courtesy of Russell Shaw.)

Cardinal Karol Wojtyla of Cracow was elected Bishop of Rome and 263rd successor of St. Peter as Supreme Pastor of the Universal Church on October 16, 1978. He chose the name John Paul II in honor of his predecessor, Pope John Paul I, as well as Popes John XXIII and Paul VI. He was invested with the pallium, symbol of his office, on October 22 in ceremonies attended by more than 250,000 people in St. Peter's Square.

From the start, Pope John Paul II has labored to keep the Church faithful to its tradition and to the teaching and spirit of Vatican Council II, while positioning it to meet the challenges of the Third Millennium. He is a staunch defender of the sanctity of human life — "from conception to natural death," he often says — and of marriage and the family. Opposition to totalitarianism and support for human rights make this activist, long-reigning pope a major figure on the world political scene.

He is the first non-Italian pope since Adrian VI (1522-23) and the first Polish pope ever. At his election, he was the youngest pope since Pius IX (1846-78). On May 24, 1998, he became the longest-reigning pope elected in the 20th century, surpassing the 19 years, seven months and seven days of Pius XII (1939-58). (Leo XIII, who died in 1903, was pope for 25 years.)

He is the most-traveled pope in history. Through July 2001, he had covered nearly 800,000 miles during 94 pastoral visits outside Italy and over 137 within Italy. In all, he has visited 126 countries and has held talks with 846 heads of state or government. Certainly he is the pope most prolific in literary output, having issued (through May 2000) 13 encyclicals, 14 apostolic exhortations, ten apostolic constitutions, and 37 apostolic letters.

By his 81st birthday, John Paul II had canonized over 300 saints and declared over 1,000 persons blessed; his 17 predecessors from Pope Clement VIII to Pope Paul VI canonized a total of 296 people. He had held seven consistories in which he created 157 cardinals, not including two *in pectore* (or secret, from the Latin, "in the heart") announced along with 20 others on January 18, 1998. As of May 2000, the Holy Father had presided at 15 synods: the Particular Synod of Bishops of the Netherlands in 1980; five ordinary

synods (1980, 1983, 1987, 1990, 1994); one extraordinary (1985) and eight special (1980, 1991, 1994, 1995, 1997, two in 1998, and the 2nd synod for Europe in October 1999). A synod that assembled in October 2001 was on the topic, "The Bishop: Servant of the Gospel of Jesus Christ for the Hope of the World."

Early Life

Karol Josef Wojtyla was born May 18, 1920, in Wadowice, an industrial town near Cracow. His parents were Karol Wojtyla, who had been an adminstrative officer in the Austrian army and was a lieutenant in the Polish army until his retirement in 1927, and Emilia Kaczorowska Wojtyla. His mother died in 1929 of kidney and heart failure. His sister died a few days after birth; his older brother Edmund, a physician, died in 1932, and his father in 1941.

He attended schools in Wadowice and in 1938 enrolled in the faculty of philosophy of the Jagiellonian University in Cracow, moving there with his father that summer. At the university he also was active in the Studio 38 experimental theater group.

For young Wojtyla, as for countless others, life changed forever on September 1, 1939, when World War II began. Nazi occupation forces closed the Jagiellonian University and the young man had to work in a quarry as a stone cutter and later in a chemical plant to avoid deportation to Germany. In February 1940 he met Jan Tryanowski, a tailor who became his spiritual mentor and introduced him to the writings of St. John of the Cross and St. Teresa of Ávila. He also participated in underground theater groups, including the Rhapsodic Theater of Mieczyslaw Kotlarczyk.

In October 1942 he began studies for the priesthood in the underground seminary maintained by Cardinal Adam Sapieha of Cracow. He was struck by an automobile February 29, 1944, and hospitalized until March 12. In August of that year Cardinal Sapieha transferred him and the other seminarians to the Archbishop's Residence, where they lived and studied until war's end. Ordained a priest by the Cardinal on November 1, 1946, he left Poland November 15 to begin advanced studies in Rome at the

Angelicum University (the Pontifical University of St. Thomas Aquinas). He subsequently earned doctorates in theology and philosophy and was a respected moral theologian and ethicist.

Bishop and Cardinal

On July 4, 1958, Pope Pius XII named him Auxiliary Bishop to Archbishop Eugeniusz Baziak, Apostolic Administrator of Cracow. His book *Love and Responsibility* was published in 1960. (Earlier, he published poetry and several plays.) Following Archbishop Baziak's death in 1962, he became Vicar Capitular and then on January 13, 1964, Archbishop of Cracow—the first residential head of the See permitted by the communist authorities since Cardinal Sapieha's death in 1951.

Archbishop Wojtyla attended all four sessions of the Second Vatican Council, from 1962 to 1965, and helped draft Schema XIII, which became *Gaudium et Spes*, the Pastoral Constitution on the Church in the Modern World. He also contributed to *Dignitatis Humanae* (the Declaration on Religious Freedom) and on the theology of the laity.

Pope Paul VI created him a cardinal in the consistory of June 28, 1967, with the titular Roman church of S. Cesario in Palatio. Although scheduled to attend the first general assembly of the Synod of Bishops in September and October of that year, Cardinal Wojtyla did not go, as a sign of solidarity with Cardinal Stefan Wyszynski of Warsaw, Poland's primate, whom the communist government refused a passport. In October, 1969, however, he participated in the first extraordinary assembly of the synod. Earlier that year, with approval of the statutes of the Polish bishops' conference, he became its vice president.

In 1971 he took part in the second general assembly of the synod and was elected to the council of the secretary general of the synod. He continued to participate in synod assemblies and to serve on the synod council until his election as pope. May 8, 1972, saw the opening of the archdiocesan of synod of Cracow, which he had convened and would see conclude during his visit to Poland as Pope in 1979. Also in 1972 he published *Foundations of Renewal: A Study on the Implementation of the Second Vatican Council.*

Pope Paul died August 6, 1978. Cardinal Wojtyla participated in the conclave that chose Cardinal Albino Luciani of Venice his successor on August 26. When the new Pope, who had taken the name John Paul I, died unexpectedly on September 28, Cardinal Wojtyla joined 110 other cardinals in that year's second conclave. He emerged on the second day of voting, October 16, as Pope John Paul II.

Pontificate

Pope John Paul set out the major themes and program of his pontificate in his first encyclical, *Redemptor Hominis (The Redeemer of Man)*, dated March 4, 1979, and published March 15. "The Redeemer of Man, Jesus Christ, is the center of the universe and of history," he wrote. Throughout his pontificate he has emphasized preparation for the year 2000—which he proclaimed a Jubilee Year—and for the Third Millennium of the Christian era, with the aim of fostering a renewed commitment to evangelization among Catholics. He also has produced a significant body of magisterial teaching in such areas as Christian anthropology, sexual morality, and social justice, while working for peace and human rights throughout the world.

His pontificate has been uncommonly active and filled with dramatic events. Among the most dramatic are those associated with the fall of communism in Eastern Europe. Many students of that complex event credit John Paul with a central role. His visits to his Polish homeland in 1979 (June 2-10) and 1983 (June 16-23) bolstered Polish Catholicism and kindled Polish resistance to communism, while his determined support for the Solidarity labor movement gave his countrymen a vehicle for their resistance. The result was a growing nonviolent liberation movement leading to the dramatic developments of 1989—the collapse of communist regimes and the emergence of democracy in Poland and other countries, the fall of the Berlin Wall—and in time to the breakup of the Soviet Union and the end of the Cold War.

Dramatic in a much different way was the 1981 attempt on the Pope's life. At 5:19 p.m. on May 13, as he greeted crowds in St. Peter's Square before his Wednesday general audience, a Turkish terrorist named Mehmet Ali Agca shot John Paul at close range. Whether the assassin acted alone or at the behest of others—and which others—remain unanswered questions. Following a six-hour operation, John Paul was hospitalized for 77 days at Gemelli Hospital. He visited Ali Agca in the Rebibbia prison on December 27, 1983.

Although he resumed his activities vigorously after his recuperation, the Pope's health and strength have declined over the years. In July 1992, he had colon surgery for the removal of a non-cancerous tumor; in November 1993, his shoulder was dislocated in a fall; he suffered a broken femur in another fall in April 1994; and in October 1996, he had an appendectomy. For several years, too, the effects have been apparent of what the Vatican acknowledges to be a neurological condition (many observers take the ailment to be Parkinson's disease). John Paul nevertheless maintains what is by any standards a highly demanding schedule. Clearly, he wished to lead the Church into the new millennium.

Foreign Pastoral Visits

As noted, his pastoral visits have been a striking feature of his pontificate. Many have been to nations in the Third World. His 94 trips outside Italy (through September 2001) are as follows.

1979 Dominican Republic and Mexico, January 5-February 1; Poland, June 2-10; Ireland and the United States, September 29-October 7; Turkey, November 28-30.

1980 Africa (Zaire, Congo Republic, Kenya, Ghana, Upper Volta, Ivory Coast), May 2-12; France, May 30-June 2; Brazil (13 cities), June 30-July 12; West Germany, November 15-19.

1981 Philippines, Guam, and Japan, with stopovers in Pakistan and Alaska, February 16-27.

1982 Africa (Nigeria, Benin, Gabon, Equatorial Guinea), February 12-19; Portugal, May 12-15; Great Britain, May 28-June 2; Argentina, June 11-12; Switzerland, June 15; San Marino, August 29; Spain, October 31-November 9.

1983 Central America (Costa Rica, Nicaragua, Panama, El Salvador, Guatemala, Belize, Honduras) and Haiti, March 2-10; Poland, June 16-23; Lourdes, France, August 14-15; Austria, September 10-13.

1984 South Korea, Papua New Guinea, Solomon Islands, Thailand, May 12; Switzerland, June 12-17; Canada, September 9-20; Spain, Dominican Republic, and Puerto Rico, October 10-12.

1985 Venezuela, Ecuador, Peru, Trinidad and Tobago, January 26-February 6; Belgium, The Netherlands, and Luxembourg, May 11-21; Africa (Togo, Ivory Coast, Cameroon, Central African Republic, Zaire, Kenya, and Morocco), August 8-19; Liechtenstein, September 8.

1986 India, February 1-10; Colombia and Saint Lucia, July 1-7; France, October 4-7; Oceania (Australia, New Zealand, Bangladesh, Fiji, Singapore, and Seychelles), November 18-December 1.

1987 Uruguay, Chile, and Argentina, March 31-April 12; West Germany, April 30-May 4; Poland, June 8-14; the United States and Canada, September 10-19.

1988 Uruguay, Bolivia, Peru, and Paraguay, May 7-18; Austria, June 23-27; Africa (Zimbabwe, Botswana, Lesotho, Swaziland, and Mozam-bique), September 10-19; France, October 8-11.

1989 Madagascar, Reunion, Zambia, and Malawi, April 28-May 6; Norway, Iceland, Finland, Denmark, and Sweden, June 1-10; Spain, August 19-21; South Korea, Indonesia, East Timor, and Mauritius, October 6-16.

1990 Africa (Cape Verde, Guinea Bissau, Mali, and Burkna Faso), January 25-February 1; Czechoslovakia, April 21-22; Mexico and Curaçao, May 6-13; Malta, May 25-27; Africa (Tanzania, Burundi, Rwanda, and Ivory Coast), September 1-10.

1991 Portugal, May 10-13; Poland, June 1-9; Poland and Hungary, August 13-20; Brazil, October 12-21.

1992 Africa (Senegal, The Gambia, Guinea), February 10-26; Africa (Angola, São Tome, and Principe), June 4-10; Dominican Republic, October 10-14.

1993 Africa (Benin, Uganda, Sudan), February 2-10; Albania, April 25; Spain, June 12-17; Jamaica, Mexico, Denver (U.S.A.), August 9-15; Lithuania, Latvia, Estonia, September 4-10.

1994 Zagreb, Croatia, September 10.

1995 Philippines, Papua New Guinea, Australia, Sri Lanka, January 12-21; Czech Republic and Poland, May 20-22; Belgium, June 3-4; Slovakia, June 30-July 3; Africa (Cameroon, South Africa, Kenya), September 14-20; United Nations and United States, October 4-8.

1996 Central America (Guatemala, Nicaragua, El Salvador), February 5-11; Tunisia, April 17; Slovenia, May 17-19; Germany, June 21-23; Hungary, September 6-7; France, September 19-22.

1997 Sarajevo, April 12-13; Czech Republic, April 25-27; Lebanon, May 10-11; Poland, May 31-June 10; France, August 21-24; Brazil, October 2-5.

1998 Cuba, January 21-25; Nigeria, March 21-23; Austria, June 19-21; Croatia, October 3-4.

1999 Mexico, January 22-25; St. Louis (USA), January 26-27; Romania, May 2-5; Poland June, 5-17; Slovenia, September 19; India, November 6-7; Georgia, November 8-9.

2000 Egypt and Mount Sinai, February 24-26; Holy Land, March 20-26; Fátima, May 12-13.

2001 Greece, Syria, and Malta, May 4-9; Ukraine, June 23-27;

Notable among the Pope's pastoral visits have been journeys to celebrate World Youth Day with young people.

Encyclicals and Other Writings

As noted above, Pope John Paul's first encyclical, *Redemptor Hominis* (1979), set the tone for and in general terms indicated the subject matter of many of the documents to follow. These are infused with the Pope's distinctive personalism, which emphasizes the dignity and rights of the human person, most truly understood in the light of Christ, as the norm and goal of human endeavor.

His other encyclical letters to date are: *Dives in Misericordia* (*On the Mercy of God*), 1980; *Laborem Exercens* (*On Human Work*), 1981; *Slavorum Apostoli* (*The Apostles of the Slavs*, honoring Sts. Cyril and Methodius), 1985; *Dominum et Vivificantem* (*Lord and Giver of Life*, on the Holy Spirit), 1986; *Redemptoris Mater* (*Mother of the Redeemer*), 1987; *Sollicitudo Rei Socialis* (*On Social Concerns*), 1988; *Redemptoris Missio* (*Mission of the Redeemer*) and *Centesimus Annus* (*The Hundredth Year*, on the anniversary of Leo XIII's *Rerum Novarum*), both 1991; *Veritatis Splendor* (*The Splendor of Truth*), 1993; *Evangelium Vitae* (*The Gospel of Life*) and *Ut Unum Sint* (*That All May Be One*), 1995; *Fides et Ratio* (*Faith and Reason*), 1998.

Among his other publications are: *Catechesi Tradendae*, a post-synodal apostolic exhortation on catechesis, 1979; apostolic letter proclaiming Sts. Cyril and Methodius, together with St. Benedict, patrons of Europe, 1980; post-synodal apostolic exhortation *Familiaris Consortio*, on the family, 1981; apostolic letter *Caritatis Christi*, for the Church in China, 1982; letter for the 500th anniversary of the birth of Martin Luther, 1983; apostolic letter *Salvifici Doloris* ("On the Christian Meaning of Suffering"), apostolic exhortation *Redemptionis Donum*, to men and women religious, apostolic letters *Redemptionis Anno*, on Jerusalem, and *Les Grands Mysteres*, on Lebanon, and post-synodal apostolic exhortation *Reconciliatio et Poenitentia* ("Reconciliation and Penance"), all 1984.

Also: apostolic letter *Dilecti Amici*, on the occasion of the United Nations' International Year of Youth, 1985; apostolic letter *Euntes in Mundum*, for the millennium of Christianity in Kievan Rus', and apostolic letter *Mulieris Dignitatem* ("On the Dignity and Vocation of Women"), all 1988; post-synodal apostolic exhortation *Christifideles Laici* ("The Lay Members of Christ's Faithful People") and apostolic exhortation *Redemptoris Custos* ("On St. Joseph"), 1989; post-synodal apostolic exhortation *Pastores Dabo Vobis* ("I Give You Shepherds"), 1992; *Letter to Families*, for the International Year of the Family, Letter on the International Conference on Population and Development in Cairo, apostolic letter *Ordinatio Sacerdotalis* ("On Reserving Priestly Ordination to Men Alone"), apostolic letter *Tertio Millennio Adveniente*, on preparation

for the Jubilee Year 2000, and *Letter to Children in the Year of the Family*, all 1994.

Also: apostolic letter *Orientale Lumen* ("The Light of the East"), on Catholic-Orthodox relations, *Letter to Women*, post-synodal apostolic exhortation *Ecclesia in Africa*, and apostolic letter for the fourth centenary of the Union of Brest, all 1995; apostolic constitution *Universi Dominici Gregis* ("On the Vacancy of the Apostolic See and the Election of the Roman Pontiff"), post-synodal apostolic exhortation *Vita Consecrata* ("On the Consecrated Life and Its Mission in the Church and in the World"), and apostolic letter on the 350th anniversary of the Union of Uzhorod, all 1996; post-synodal apostolic exhortation, *A New Hope for Lebanon*, 1997; *Incarnationis Mysterium*, Bull of Indiction of the Great Jubilee of the Year 2000, 1998.

In his years as Pope he also has published two books: *Crossing the Threshold of Hope* (1994) and *Gift and Mystery: On the Fiftieth Anniversary of My Priestly Ordination* (1996).

Issues and Activities

Doctrinal Concerns: The integrity of Catholic doctrine has been a major concern of Pope John Paul. On November 25, 1981, he appointed Archbishop—later, Cardinal—Joseph Ratzinger of Munich-Freising, a prominent theologian, Prefect of the Congregation for the Doctrine of the Faith. The congregation under Cardinal Ratzinger has published important documents on bioethics, on liberation theology (1984 and 1986), and on the Church's inability to ordain women as priests, the latter affirming that the teaching on this matter has been "set forth infallibly" (1995).

Catechism: One of Pope John Paul's most important initiatives is the *Catechism of the Catholic Church*. The idea for this up-to-date compendium was broached at the extraordinary assembly of the Synod of Bishops held in 1985 to evaluate the implementation of Vatican Council II. The Pope approved, and the project went forward under a commission of cardinals headed by Cardinal Ratzinger. Published in 1992 by authorization of John Paul II (the original was in French, with the English translation appearing in 1994 and the authoritative Latin *editio typica* in 1997), this first catechism for the universal Church in four centuries is crucial to the hoped-for renewal of catechesis.

Canon Law: John Paul oversaw the completion of the revision of the Code of Canon Law begun in 1959 at the direction of Pope John XXIII. He promulgated the new code on January 25, 1983; it went into effect on November 27 of that year. In *Sacrae Disciplinae Leges*, the apostolic constitution accompanying the revised code, the Pope says it has "one and the same intention" as Vatican Council II — whose convening John XXIII announced at the same time — namely, "the renewal of Christian living."

On April 18, 1990, John Paul promulgated the Code of Canons for the Eastern Churches. Although particular sections of the Eastern code appeared at various times dating back to 1949, this was the first time an integrated code of law for the Eastern Churches had been issued in its entirety.

Ecumenical and Interreligious Relations: Ecumenical and interreligious relations have received much attention from Pope John Paul II. Two of his major documents, the encyclical *Ut Unum Sint* and the apostolic letter *Orientale Lumen*, both published in 1995, deal with these matters. He has met frequently with representatives of other religious bodies, has spoken frequently about the quest for unity, and has called for Catholics and others to pray and work to this end.

Among the important actions in this area have been the signings of common declarations with the Ecumenical Patriarch of Constantinople His Holiness Dimitrios (December 7, 1987) and his successor Bartholomew I (June 29, 1995), with the Archbishop of Canterbury and Primate of the Anglican Communion, Dr. Robert Runcie (May 29, 1982, in Canterbury Cathedral and again October 2, 1989, in Rome) and his successor Dr. George Leonard Carey (December 6, 1996), with the Supreme Patriarch and Catholicos of All Armenians, His Holiness Karekin I (December 14, 1996), and with His Holiness Aram I Keshishian, Catholicos of Cilicia of the Armenians (January 26, 1997). On October 5, 1991, for the first time since the Reformation, two Lutheran bishops joined the Pope and the Catholic bishops of Stockholm and Helsinki in an ecumenical prayer service in St. Peter's Basilica marking the sixth centenary of the canonization of St. Bridget of Sweden.

Pope John Paul II has had Jewish friends since boyhood, and he has worked hard to strengthen Catholic-Jewish ties. The Holy See formally initiated diplomatic relations with the State of Israel at the level of apostolic nunciature and embassy on June 15, 1994. In March, 1998, the Commission for Religious Relations with the Jews published an important document on the roots of the World War II Jewish Holocaust entitled *We Remember: A Reflection on the 'Shoah.'* In a letter dated March 12 to the commission chairman, Cardinal Edward Idris Cassidy, the Pope expressed "fervent hope" that it would "help to heal the wounds of past misunderstandings and injustices."

On Sunday, March 12, 2000, Pope John Paul II presided over a day of pardon for those sins committed by members of the Church over the centuries. The Holy Father issued a formal apology for the misdeeds of the members of the Church in the past, including a renewed apology for all anti-Semitic actions by Catholics. This apology was given even greater depth by the Holy Father's trip to the Holy Land in March 2000. During his historic visit to Israel, the pope placed a written apology to the Jewish people in the Wailing Wall in Jerusalem. He made further efforts at ecumenical dialogue with the Orthodox Churches during his visits to Greece, Syria, and Ukraine in 2001.

Women's Concerns: Pope John Paul's insistence that, in fidelity to the will of Christ, the Church is unable to ordain women as priests has put him at odds with some feminists, as has his opposition to abortion and contraception. But it is clear from his writings that he is unusually sensitive to women's issues, and he is a strong defender of women's dignity and rights, about which he often has spoken. In 1995 he appointed a woman, Professor Mary Ann Glendon of the Harvard University law school, head of the Holy See's delegation to the fourth United Nations conference on women, held in Beijing September 4-15, the first time a woman had been named to such a post.

World Affairs: At least since January 1979, when he accepted a request for mediation in a border conflict between Argentina and Chile, John Paul II has worked for peace in many parts of the world. He has supported efforts to achieve reconciliation between conflicting parties in troubled areas like Lebanon, the Balkans, and the Persian Gulf, where he sought to avert the Gulf War of 1991. He has advocated religious liberty and human rights during pastoral visits to many countries, including Cuba and Nigeria in 1998. Among the notable ecumenical and interreligious events of the pontificate was the World Day of Prayer for Peace on October 27, 1986, which he convoked in Assisi and attended

St. Peter's Square

along with representatives of numerous other churches and religious groups.

In 1984 the Holy See and the United States established diplomatic relations. (The Pope has met with Presidents Jimmy Carter, Ronald Reagan, George Bush, and Bill Clinton.) Relations with Poland were re-established in 1989. Diplomatic relations were established with the Soviet Union in 1990 and with the Russian Federation in 1992. Relations also have been established with other Eastern European countries and countries that were part of the former Soviet Union, with Mexico, and with other nations including Jordan, South Africa, and Libya. Working contacts of a "permanent and official character" were begun with the Palestine Liberation Organization in 1994.

Administration: Under Pope John Paul II the long-term financial problems of the Holy See have been addressed and brought under control. Finances were on the agenda at the first plenary assembly of the College of Cardinals, November 5-9, 1979, and subsequent meetings of that body. A council of cardinals for the study of organizational and economic problems of the Holy See was established in 1981. In 1988, the Holy See's financial report (for 1986) was published for the first time, along with the 1988 budget. In April 1991 a meeting of the presidents of episcopal conferences was held to discuss ways of increasing the Peter's Pence Collection taken in support of the Pope.

A reorganization of responsibilities of Vatican offices was carried out in 1984, and in 1988 an apostolic constitution, *Pastor Bonus*, on reform of the Roman Curia was issued. A Vatican labor office was instituted in 1989. Pope John Paul established a new Pontifical Academy of Social Sciences in 1994 and Pontifical Academy for Life in 1995. On April 8, 1994, he celebrated Mass in the Sistine Chapel for the unveiling of the Michelangelo frescoes, which had been painstakingly cleaned and restored. The opening presentation of the Holy See's Internet site took place March 24, 1997.

As Bishop of Rome, John Paul presided over a diocesan synod that concluded May 29, 1993. He also has visited numerous Roman parishes — 270 out of 328 by the time of his 78th birthday.

POPES OF THE ROMAN CATHOLIC CHURCH

Information includes the name of the pope, in many cases his name before becoming pope, his birthplace or country of origin, the date of accession to the papacy, and the date of the end of reign which, in all but a few cases, was the date of death. Double dates indicate date of election and date of solemn beginning of ministry as Pastor of the universal Church.

Source: Annuario Pontificio.

St. Peter (Simon Bar-Jona): Bethsaida in Galilee; d. c. 64 or 67.
St. Linus: Tuscany; 67-76.
St. Anacletus (Cletus): Rome; 76-88.
St. Clement: Rome; 88-97.
St. Evaristus: Greece; 97-105.
St. Alexander I: Rome; 105-115.
St. Sixtus I: Rome; 115-125.
St. Telesphorus: Greece; 125-136.
St. Hyginus: Greece; 136-140.
St. Pius I: Aquileia; 140-155.
St. Anicetus: Syria; 155-166.
St. Soter: Campania; 166-175.
St. Eleutherius: Nicopolis in Epirus; 175-189.
Up to the time of St. Eleutherius, the years indicated for the beginning and end of pontificates are not absolutely certain. Also, up to the middle of the 11th century, there are some doubts about the exact days and months given in chronological tables.

St. Victor I: Africa; 189-199.
St. Zephyrinus: Rome; 199-217.
St. Callistus I: Rome; 217-222.
St. Urban I: Rome; 222-230.
St. Pontian: Rome; July 21, 230, to September 28, 235.
St. Anterus: Greece; November 21, 235, to January 3, 236.
St. Fabian: Rome; January 10, 236, to January 20, 250.
St. Cornelius: Rome; March 251, to June 253.
St. Lucius I: Rome; June 25, 253, to March 5, 254.
St. Stephen I: Rome; May 12, 254, to August 2, 257.
St. Sixtus II: Greece; August 30, 257, to August 6, 258.
St. Dionysius: birthplace unknown; July 22, 259, to December 26, 268.
St. Felix I: Rome; January 5, 269, to December 30, 274.
St. Eutychian: Luni; January 4, 275, to December 7, 283.
St. Caius: Dalmatia; December 17, 283, to April 22, 296.
St. Marcellinus: Rome; June 30, 296, to October 25, 304.
St. Marcellus I: Rome; May 27, 308, or June 26, 308, to January 16, 309.

St. Eusebius: Greece; April 18, 309, to August 17, 309 or 310.

St. Melchiades (Miltiades): Africa; July 2, 311, to January 11, 314.

St. Sylvester I: Rome; January 31, 314, to December 31, 335.

Most of the popes before St. Sylvester I were martyrs.

St. Marcus: Rome; January 18, 336, to October 7, 336.

St. Julius I: Rome; February 6, 337, to April 12, 352.

Liberius: Rome; May 17, 352, to September 24, 366.

St. Damasus I: Spain; October 1, 366, to December 11, 384.

St. Siricius: Rome; December 15, 22 or 29, 384, to November 26, 399.

St. Anastasius I: Rome; November 27, 399, to December 19, 401.

St. Innocent I: Albano; December 22, 401, to March 12, 417.

St. Zozimus: Greece; March 18, 417, to December 26, 418.

St. Boniface I: Rome; December 28 or 29, 418, to September 4, 422.

St. Celestine I: Campania; September 10, 422, to July 27, 432.

St. Sixtus III: Rome; July 31, 432, to August 19, 440.

St. Leo I (the Great): Tuscany; September 29, 440, to November 10, 461.

St. Hilary: Sardinia; November 19, 461, to February 29, 468.

St. Simplicius: Tivoli; March 3, 468, to March 10, 483.

St. Felix III (II): Rome; March 13, 483, to March 1, 492.

He should be called Felix II, and his successors of the same name should be numbered accordingly. The discrepancy in the numerical designation of popes named Felix was caused by the erroneous insertion in some lists of the name of St. Felix of Rome, a martyr.

St. Gelasius I: Africa; March 1, 492, to November 21, 496.

Anastasius II: Rome; November 24, 496, to November 19, 498.

St. Symmachus: Sardinia; November 22, 498, to July 19, 514.

St. Hormisdas: Frosinone; July 20, 514, to August 6, 523.

St. John I, Martyr: Tuscany; August 13, 523, to May 18, 526.

St. Felix IV (III): Samnium; July 12, 526, to September 22, 530.

Boniface II: Rome; September 22, 530, to October 17, 532.

John II: Rome; January 2, 533, to May 8, 535.

John II was the first pope to change his name. His given name was Mercury.

St. Agapitus I: Rome; May 13, 535, to April 22, 536.

St. Silverius, Martyr: Campania; June 1 or 8, 536, to November 11, 537 (d. December 2, 537).

St. Silverius was violently deposed in March, 537, and abdicated November 11, 537. His successor, Vigilius, was not recognized as pope by all the Roman clergy until his abdication.

Vigilius: Rome; March 29, 537, to June 7, 555.

Pelagius I: Rome; April 16, 556, to March 4, 561.

John III: Rome; July 17, 561, to July 13, 574.

Benedict I: Rome; June 2, 575, to July 30, 579.

Pelagius II: Rome; November 26, 579, to February 7, 590.

St. Gregory I (the Great): Rome; September 3, 590, to March 12, 604.

Sabinian: Blera in Tuscany; September 13, 604, to February 22, 606.

Boniface III: Rome; February 19, 607, to November 12, 607.

St. Boniface IV: Abruzzi; August 25, 608, to May 8, 615.

St. Deusdedit (Adeodatus I): Rome; October 19, 615, to November 8, 618.

Boniface V: Naples; December 23, 619, to October 25, 625.

Honorius I: Campania; October 27, 625, to October 12, 638.

Severinus: Rome; May 28, 640, to August 2, 640.

John IV: Dalmatia; December 24, 640, to October 12, 642.

Theodore I: Greece; November 24, 642, to May 14, 649.

St. Martin I, Martyr: Todi; July, 649, to September 16, 655 (in exile from June 17, 653).

St. Eugene I: Rome; August 10, 654, to June 2, 657.

St. Eugene I was elected during the exile of St. Martin I, who is believed to have endorsed him as pope.

St. Vitalian: Segni; July 30, 657, to January 27, 672.

Adeodatus II: Rome; April 11, 672, to June 17, 676.

Donus: Rome; November 2, 676, to April 11, 678.

St. Agatho: Sicily; June 27, 678, to January 10, 681.

St. Leo II: Sicily; August 17, 682, to July 3, 683.

St. Benedict II: Rome; June 26, 684, to May 8, 685.

John V: Syria; July 23, 685, to August 2, 686.

Conon: birthplace unknown; October 21, 686, to September 21, 687.

St. Sergius I: Syria; December 15, 687, to September 8, 701.

John VI: Greece; October 30, 701, to January 11, 705.

John VII: Greece; March 1, 705, to October 18, 707.

Sisinnius: Syria; January 15, 708, to February 4, 708.

Constantine: Syria; March 25, 708, to April 9, 715.

St. Gregory II: Rome; May 19, 715, to February 11, 731.

St. Gregory III: Syria; March 18, 731, to November, 741.

St. Zachary: Greece; December 10, 741, to March 22, 752.

Stephen II (III): Rome; March 26, 752, to April 26, 757.

> After the death of St. Zachary, a Roman priest named Stephen was elected but died (four days later) before his consecration as bishop of Rome, which would have marked the beginning of his pontificate. Another Stephen was elected to succeed Zachary as Stephen II. (The first pope with this name was St. Stephen I, 254–57.) The ordinal III appears in parentheses after the name of Stephen II because the name of the earlier elected but deceased priest was included in some lists. Other Stephens have double numbers.

St. Paul I: Rome; April (May 29), 757, to June 28, 767.

Stephen III (IV): Sicily; August 1 (7), 768, to January 24, 772.

Adrian I: Rome; February 1 (9), 772, to December 25, 795.

St. Leo III: Rome; December 26 (27), 795, to June 12, 816.

Stephen IV (V): Rome; June 22, 816, to January 24, 817.

St. Paschal I: Rome; January 25, 817, to February 11, 824.

Eugene II: Rome; February (May) 824, to August, 827.

Valentine: Rome; August 827, to September 827.

Gregory IV: Rome; 827 to January 844.

Sergius II: Rome; January, 844 to January 27, 847.

St. Leo IV: Rome; January (April 10), 847, to July 17, 855.

Benedict III: Rome; July (September 29), 855, to April 17, 858.

St. Nicholas I (the Great): Rome; April 24, 858, to November 13, 867.

Adrian II: Rome; December 14, 867, to December 14, 872.

John VIII: Rome; December 14, 872, to December 16, 882.

Marinus I: Gallese; December 16, 882, to May 15, 884.

St. Adrian III: Rome; May 17, 884, to September 885. Cult confirmed June 2, 1891.

Stephen V (VI): Rome; September 885, to September 14, 891.

Formosus: Bishop of Porto; October 6, 891, to April 4, 896.

Boniface VI: Rome; April 896, to April 896.

Stephen VI (VII): Rome; May 896, to August 897.

Romanus: Gallese; August 897, to November 897.

Theodore II: Rome; December 897, to December 897.

John IX: Tivoli; January 898, to January 900.

Benedict IV: Rome; January (February) 900 to July 903.

Leo V: Ardea; July 903 to September 903.

Sergius III: Rome; January 29, 904, to April 14, 911.

Anastasius III: Rome; April 911 to June 913.

Landus: Sabina; July, 913, to February, 914.

John X: Tossignano (Imola); March 914 to May 928.

Leo VI: Rome; May 928 to December 928.

Stephen VII (VIII): Rome; December 928 to February 931.

John XI: Rome; February (March) 931 to December 935.

Leo VII: Rome; January 3, 936, to July 13, 939.

Stephen VIII (IX): Rome; July 14, 939, to October 942.

Marinus II: Rome; October 30, 942, to May 946.

Agapitus II: Rome; May 10, 946, to December 955.

John XII (Octavius): Tusculum; December 16, 955, to May 14, 964 (date of his death).

Leo VIII: Rome; December 4 (6), 963, to March 1, 965.

Benedict V: Rome; May 22, 964, to July 4, 966. Confusion exists concerning the legitimacy of claims to the pontificate by Leo VIII and Benedict V. John XII was deposed December 4, 963, by a Roman council. If this deposition was invalid, Leo was an antipope. If the deposition of John was valid, Leo was the legitimate pope and Benedict was an antipope.

John XIII: Rome; October 1, 965, to September 6, 972.

Benedict VI: Rome; January 19, 973, to June 974.

Benedict VII: Rome; October 974 to July 10, 983.

John XIV (Peter Campenora): Pavia; December 983, to August 20, 984.

John XV: Rome; August 985 to March 996.

Gregory V (Bruno of Carinthia): Saxony; May 3, 996, to February 18, 999.

Sylvester II (Gerbert): Auvergne; April 2, 999, to May 12, 1003.

John XVII (Siccone): Rome; June 1003 to December, 1003.

John XVIII (Phasianus): Rome; January 1004 to July 1009.

Sergius IV (Peter): Rome; July 31, 1009, to May 12, 1012.

The custom of changing one's name on election to the papacy is generally considered to date from the time of Sergius IV. Before his time, several popes had changed their names. After his time, this became a regular practice, with few exceptions; e.g., Adrian VI and Marcellus II.

Benedict VIII (Theophylactus): Tusculum; May 18, 1012, to April 9, 1024.

John XIX (Romanus): Tusculum; April (May) 1024, to 1032.

Benedict IX (Theophylactus): Tusculum; 1032, to 1044.

Sylvester III (John): Rome; January 20, 1045, to February 10, 1045.

Sylvester III was an antipope if the forcible removal of Benedict IX in 1044 was not legitimate.

Benedict IX (second time): April 10, 1045, to May 1, 1045.

Gregory VI (John Gratian): Rome; May 5, 1045, to December 20, 1046.

Clement II (Suitger, Lord of Morsleben and Hornburg): Saxony; December 24 (25), 1046, to October 9, 1047.

If the resignation of Benedict IX in 1045 and his removal at the December 1046, synod were not legitimate, Gregory VI and Clement II were antipopes.

Benedict IX (third time): November 8, 1047, to July 17, 1048 (d. c. 1055).

Damasus II (Poppo): Bavaria; July 17, 1048, to August 9, 1048.

St. Leo IX (Bruno): Alsace; February 12, 1049, to April 19, 1054.

Victor II (Gebhard): Swabia; April 16, 1055, to July 28, 1057.

Stephen IX (X) (Frederick): Lorraine; August 3, 1057, to March 29, 1058.

Nicholas II (Gerard): Burgundy; January 24, 1059, to July 27, 1061.

Alexander II (Anselmo da Baggio): Milan; October 1, 1061, to April 21, 1073.

St. Gregory VII (Hildebrand): Tuscany; April 22 (June 30), 1073, to May 25, 1085.

Blessed Victor III (Dauferius; Desiderius): Benevento; May 24, 1086, to September 16, 1087. Cult confirmed July 23, 1887.

Blessed Urban II (Otto di Lagery): France; March 12, 1088, to July 29, 1099. Cult confirmed July 14, 1881.

Paschal II (Raniero): Ravenna; August 13 (14), 1099, to January 21, 1118.

Gelasius II (Giovanni Caetani): Gaeta; January 24 (March 10), 1118, to January 28, 1119.

Callistus II (Guido of Burgundy): Burgundy; February 2 (9), 1119, to December 13, 1124.

Honorius II (Lamberto): Fiagnano (Imola); December 15 (21), 1124, to February 13, 1130.

Innocent II (Gregorio Papareschi): Rome; February 14 (23), 1130, to September 24, 1143.

Celestine II (Guido): Citta di Castello; September 26 (October 3), 1143, to March 8, 1144.

Lucius II (Gerardo Caccianemici): Bologna: March 12, 1144, to February 15, 1145.

Blessed Eugene III (Bernardo Paganelli di Montemagno): Pisa; February 15 (18), 1145, to July 8, 1153. Cult confirmed October 3, 1872.

Anastasius IV (Corrado): Rome; July 12, 1153, to Dec. 3, 1154.

Adrian IV (Nicholas Breakspear): England; December 4 (5), 1154, to September 1, 1159.

Alexander III (Rolando Bandinelli): Siena; September 7 (20), 1159, to August 30, 1181.

Lucius III (Ubaldo Allucingoli): Lucca; September 1 (6), 1181, to September 25, 1185.

Urban III (Uberto Crivelli): Milan; November 25 (December 1), 1185, to October 20, 1187.

Gregory VIII (Alberto de Morra): Benevento; October 21 (25), 1187, to December 17, 1187.

Clement III (Paolo Scolari): Rome; December 19 (20), 1187, to March 1191.

Celestine III (Giacinto Bobone): Rome; March 30 (April 14), 1191, to January 8, 1198.

Innocent III (Lotario dei Conti di Segni): Anagni; January 8 (February 22), 1198, to July 16, 1216.

Honorius III (Cencio Savelli): Rome; July 18 (24), 1216, to March 18, 1227.

Gregory IX (Ugolino, Count of Segni): Anagni; March 19 (21), 1227, to August 22, 1241.

Celestine IV (Goffredo Castiglioni): Milan; October 25 (28), 1241, to November 10, 1241.

Innocent IV (Sinibaldo Fieschi): Genoa; June 25 (28), 1243, to December 7, 1254.

Alexander IV (Rinaldo, House of Ienne): Ienne (Rome); December 12 (20), 1254, to May 25, 1261.

Urban IV (Jacques Pantal,on): Troyes; August 29 (September 4), 1261, to October 2, 1264.

Clement IV (Guy Foulques or Guido le Gros): France; February 5 (15), 1265, to November 29, 1268.

Blessed Gregory X (Teobaldo Visconti): Piacenza; September 1, 1271 (March 27, 1272), to January 10, 1276. Cult confirmed September 12, 1713.

Blessed Innocent V (Peter of Tarentaise): Savoy; January 21 (February 22), 1276, to June 22, 1276. Cult confirmed March 13, 1898.

Adrian V (Ottobono Fieschi): Genoa: July 11, 1276, to August 18, 1276.

John XXI (Petrus Juliani or Petrus Hispanus):

Portugal; September 8 (20), 1276, to May 20, 1277.

There is confusion in the numerical designation of popes named John. The error dates back to the time of John XV.

Nicholas III (Giovanni Gaetano Orsini): Rome; November 25 (December 26), 1277, to August 22, 1280.

Martin IV (Simon de Brie): France; February 22 (March 23), 1281, to March 28, 1285.

The names of Marinus 1 (882-84) and Marinus II (942-46) were construed as Martin. In view of these two pontificates and the earlier reign of St. Martin I (649-55), this pope was called Martin IV.

Honorius IV (Giacomo Savelli): Rome; April 2 (May 20), 1285, to April 3, 1287.

Nicholas IV (Girolamo Masci): Ascoli; February 22, 1288, to April 4, 1292.

St. Celestine V (Pietro del Murrone): Isernia; July 5 (August 29), 1294, to December 13, 1294; d. May 19, 1296. Canonized May 5, 1313.

Boniface VIII (Benedetto Caetani): Anagni; December 24, 1294 (January 23, 1295), to October 11, 1303.

Blessed Benedict XI (Niccolo Boccasini): Treviso; October 22 (27), 1303, to July 7, 1304. Cult confirmed April 24, 1736.

Clement V (Bertrand de Got): France; June 5 (November 14), 1305, to April 20, 1314. (First of Avignon popes.)

John XXII (Jacques d'Euse): Cahors; August 7 (September 5), 1316, to December 4, 1334.

Benedict XII (Jacques Fournier): France; December 20, 1334 (January 8, 1335), to April 25, 1342.

Clement VI (Pierre Roger): France; May 7 (19), 1342, to December 6, 1352.

Innocent VI (Etienne Aubert): France; December 18 (30), 1352, to September 12, 1362.

Blessed Urban V (Guillaume de Grimoard): France; September 28 (November 6), 1362, to December 19, 1370. Cult confirmed March 10, 1870.

Gregory XI (Pierre Roger de Beaufort): France; December 30, 1370 (January 5, 1371), to March 26, 1378. (Last of Avignon popes.)

Urban VI (Bartolomeo Prignano): Naples; April 8 (18), 1378, to October 15, 1389.

Boniface IX (Pietro Tomacelli): Naples; November 2 (9), 1389, to October 1, 1404.

Innocent VII (Cosma Migliorati): Sulmona; October 17 (November 11), 1404, to November 6, 1406.

Gregory XII (Angelo Correr): Venice; November 30 (December 19), 1406, to July 4, 1415, when he voluntarily resigned from the papacy to permit the election of his successor. He died October 18, 1417.

Martin V (Oddone Colonna): Rome; November 11 (21), 1417, to February 20, 1431.

Eugene IV (Gabriele Condulmer): Venice; March 3 (11), 1431, to February 23, 1447.

Nicholas V (Tommaso Parentucelli): Sarzana; March 6 (19), 1447, to March 24, 1455.

Callistus III (Alfonso Borgia): Jativa (Valencia); April 8 (20), 1455, to August 6, 1458.

Pius II (Enea Silvio Piccolomini): Siena; August 19 (September 3), 1458, to August 14, 1464.

Paul II (Pietro Barbo): Venice; August 30 (September 16), 1464, to July 26, 1471.

Sixtus IV (Francesco della Rovere): Savona; August 9 (25), 1471, to August 12, 1484.

Innocent VIII (Giovanni Battista Cibo): Genoa; August 29 (September 12), 1484, to July 25, 1492.

Alexander VI (Rodrigo Borgia): Jativa (Valencia); August 11 (26), 1492, to August 18, 1503.

Pius III (Francesco Todeschini-Piccolomini): Siena; September 22 (October 1, 8), 1503, to October 18, 1503.

Julius II (Giuliano della Rovere): Savona; October 31 (November 26), 1503, to February 21, 1513.

Leo X (Giovanni de' Medici): Florence; March 9 (19), 1513, to December 1, 1521.

Adrian VI (Adrian Florensz): Utrecht; January 9 (August 31), 1522, to September 14, 1523.

Clement VII (Giulio de' Medici): Florence; November 19 (26), 1523, to September 25, 1534.

Paul III (Alessandro Farnese): Rome; October 13 (November 3), 1534, to November 10, 1549.

Julius III (Giovanni Maria Ciocchi del Monte): Rome; February 7 (22), 1550, to March 23, 1555.

Marcellus II (Marcello Cervini): Montepulciano; April 9 (10), 1555, to May 1, 1555.

Paul IV (Gian Pietro Carafa): Naples; May 23 (26), 1555, to August 18, 1559.

Pius IV (Giovan Angelo de' Medici): Milan; December 25, 1559 (January 6, 1560), to December 9, 1565.

St. Pius V (Antonio-Michele Ghislieri): Bosco (Alexandria); January 7 (17), 1566, to May 1, 1572. Canonized May 22, 1712.

Gregory XIII (Ugo Buoncompagni): Bologna; May 13 (25), 1572, to April 10, 1585.

Sixtus V (Felice Peretti): Grottammare (Ripatransone); April 24 (May 1), 1585, to August 27, 1590.

Urban VII (Giambattista Castagna): Rome; September 15, 1590, to September 27, 1590.

Gregory XIV (Niccolo Sfondrati): Cremona; December 5 (8), 1590, to October 16, 1591.

Innocent IX (Giovanni Antonio Facchinetti): Bologna; October 29 (November 3), 1591, to December 30, 1591.

Clement VIII (Ippolito Aldobrandini): Florence; January 30 (February 9), 1592, to March 3, 1605.

Leo XI (Alessandro de' Medici): Florence; April 1 (10), 1605, to April 27, 1605.

Paul V (Camillo Borghese): Rome; May 16 (29), 1605, to January 28, 1621.

Gregory XV (Alessandro Ludovisi): Bologna; February 9 (14), 1621, to July 8, 1623.

Urban VIII (Maffeo Barberini): Florence; August 6 (September 29), 1623, to July 29, 1644.

Innocent X (Giovanni Battista Pamfili): Rome; September 15 (October 4), 1644, to January 7, 1655.

Alexander VII (Fabio Chigi): Siena; April 7 (18), 1655, to May 22, 1667.

Clement IX (Giulio Rospigliosi): Pistoia; June 20 (26), 1667, to December 9, 1669.

Clement X (Emilio Altieri): Rome; April 29 (May 11), 1670, to July 22, 1676.

Blessed Innocent XI (Benedetto Odescalchi): Como; September 21 (October 4), 1676, to August 12, 1689. Beatified October 7, 1956.

Alexander VIII (Pietro Ottoboni): Venice; October 6 (16), 1689, to February 1, 1691.

Innocent XII (Antonio Pignatelli): Spinazzola (Venosa); July 12 (15), 1691, to September 27, 1700.

Clement XI (Giovanni Francesco Albani): Urbino; November 23, 30 (December 8), 1700, to March 19, 1721.

Innocent XIII (Michelangelo dei Conti): Rome; May 8 (18), 1721, to March 7, 1724.

Benedict XIII (Pietro Francesco Vincenzo Maria Orsini): Gravina (Bari); May 29 (June 4), 1724, to February 21, 1730.

Clement XII (Lorenzo Corsini): Florence; July 12 (16), 1730, to February 6, 1740.

Benedict XIV (Prospero Lambertini): Bologna; August 17 (22), 1740, to May 3, 1758.

Clement XIII (Carlo Rezzonico): Venice; July 6 (16), 1758, to February 2, 1769.

Clement XIV (Giovanni Vincenzo Antonio Lorenzo Ganganelli): Rimini; May 19, 28 (June 4), 1769, to September 22, 1774.

Pius VI (Giovanni Angelo Braschi): Cesena; February 15 (22), 1775, to August 29, 1799.

Pius VII (Barnaba Gregorio Chiaramonti): Cesena; March 14 (21), 1800, to August 20, 1823.

Leo XII (Annibale della Genga): Genga (Fabriano); September 28 (October 5), 1823, to February 10, 1829.

Pius VIII (Francesco Saverio Castiglioni): Cingoli; March 31 (April 5), 1829, to November 30, 1830.

Gregory XVI (Bartolomeo Alberto Mauro Cappellari): Belluno; February 2 (6), 1831, to June 1, 1846.

Blessed Pius IX (Giovanni M. Mastai-Ferretti): Senigallia; June 16 (21), 1846, to February 7, 1878.

Leo XIII (Gioacchino Pecci): Carpineto (Anagni); February 20 (March 3), 1878, to July 20, 1903.

St. Pius X (Giuseppe Sarto): Riese (Treviso); August 4 (9), 1903, to August 20, 1914. Canonized May 29, 1954.

Benedit XV (Giacomo della Chiesa): Genoa; September 3 (6), 1914, to January 22, 1922.

Pius XI (Achille Ratti): Desio (Milan); February 6 (12), 1922, to February 10, 1939.

Pius XII (Eugenio Pacelli): Rome; March 2 (12), 1939, to October 9, 1958.

Blessed John XXIII (Angelo Giuseppe Roncalli): Sotto il Monte (Bergamo); October 28 (November 4), 1958, to June 3, 1963.

Paul VI (Giovanni Battista Montini): Concessio (Brescia); June 21 (30), 1963, to August 6, 1978.

John Paul I (Albino Luciani): Forno di Canale (Belluno); August 26 (September 3), 1978, to September 28, 1978.

John Paul II (Karol Wojtyla): Wadowice, Poland; October 16 (22), 1978.

ANTIPOPES

This list of men who claimed or exercised the papal office in an uncanonical manner includes names, birthplaces and dates of alleged reigns.

Source: Annuario Pontificio

St. Hippolytus: Rome; 217-235; was reconciled before his death.

Novatian: Rome; 251.

Felix II: Rome; 355 to November 22, 365.

Ursinus: 366-367.

Eulalius: December 27 or 29, 418, to 419.

Lawrence: 498; 501-505.

Dioscorus: Alexandria; September 22, 530, to October 14, 530.

Theodore: ended alleged reign, 687.

Paschal: ended alleged reign, 687.

Constantine: Nepi; June 28 (July 5), 767, to 769.

Philip: July 31, 768; retired to his monastery on the same day.

John: ended alleged reign, January 844.

Anastasius: August 855 to September 855; d. 880.

Christopher: Rome; July or September 903 to January 904.

Boniface VII: Rome; June 974 to July 974; August 984 to July 985.

John XVI: Rossano; April 997 to February 998.

Gregory: ended alleged reign, 1012.

Benedict X: Rome; April 5, 1058, to January 24, 1059.

Honorius II: Verona; October 28, 1061, to 1072.

Clement III: Parma; June 25, 1080 (March 24, 1084), to September 8, 1100.

Theodoric: ended alleged reign, 1100; d. 1102.

Albert: ended alleged reign, 1102.

Sylvester IV: Rome; November 18, 1105, to 1111.

Gregory VIII: France; March 8, 1118, to 1121.

Celestine II: Rome; ended alleged reign, December 1124.

Anacletus II: Rome; February 14 (23), 1130, to January 25, 1138.

Victor IV: March, 1138, to May 29, 1138; submitted to Pope Innocent II.

Victor IV: Montecelio; September 7 (October 4), 1159, to April 20, 1164; he did not recognize his predecessor (Victor IV, above).

Paschal III: April 22 (26), 1164, to September 20, 1168.

Callistus III: Arezzo; September 1168 to August 29, 1178; submitted to Pope Alexander III.

Innocent III: Sezze; September 29, 1179, to 1180.

Nicholas V: Corvaro (Rieti); May 12 (22), 1328, to August 25, 1330; d. October 16, 1333.

Four antipopes of the Western Schism:

Clement VII: September 20 (October 31), 1378, to September 16, 1394.

Benedict XIII: Aragon; September 28 (October 11), 1394, to May 23, 1423.

Alexander V: Crete; June 26 (July 7), 1409, to May 3, 1410.

John XXIII: Naples; May 17 (25), 1410, to May 29, 1415; (date of deposition by Council of Constance which ended the Western Schism; d. November 22, 1419.)

Felix V: Savoy; November 5, 1439 (July 24, 1440), to April 7, 1449; d. 1451.

AVIGNON PAPACY

Avignon was the residence (1309-77) of a series of French popes (Clement V, John XXII, Benedict XII, Clement VI, Innocent VI, Urban V, and Gregory XI). Prominent in the period were power struggles over the mixed interests of Church and state with the rulers of France (Philip IV, John II), Bavaria (Louis IV), England (Edward III); factionalism of French and Italian churchmen; political as well as ecclesiastical turmoil in Italy, a factor of significance in prolonging the stay of popes in Avignon. Despite some positive achievements, the Avignon papacy was a prologue to the Western Schism, which began in 1378.

GREAT WESTERN SCHISM

The Great Western Schism was a confused state of affairs which divided Christendom into two and then three papal obediences from 1378 to 1417.

It occurred some 50 years after Marsilius theorized that a general (not ecumenical) council of bishops and other persons was superior to a pope and nearly 30 years before the Council of Florence stated definitively that no kind of council had such authority.

It was a period of disaster preceding the even more disastrous period of the Reformation.

Urban VI, following the return of the papal residence to Rome after approximately 70 years at Avignon, was elected pope April 8, 1378, and reigned until his death in 1389. He was succeeded by Boniface IX (1389-1404), Innocent VII (1404-1406), and Gregory XII (1406-1415). These four are considered the legitimate popes of the period.

Some of the cardinals who chose Urban pope, dissatisfied with his conduct of the office, declared that his election was invalid. They proceeded to elect Clement VII, who claimed the papacy from 1378 to 1394. He was succeeded by Benedict XIII.

Prelates seeking to end the state of divided papal loyalties convoked the Council of Pisa (1409) which, without authority, found Gregory XII and Benedict XIII, in absentia, guilty on 30-odd charges of schism and heresy, deposed them, and elected a third claimant to the papacy, Alexander V (1409-1410). He was succeeded by John XXIII (1410-1415).

The schism was ended by the Council of Constance (1414-1418). Although originally called into session in an irregular manner, the council acquired authority after being convoked by Gregory XII in 1415. In its early irregular phase, it deposed John XXIII, whose election to the papacy was uncanonical anyway. After being formally convoked, it accepted the abdication of Gregory in 1415 and dismissed the claims of Benedict XIII two years later, thus clearing the way for the election of Martin V on November 11, 1417. The Council of Constance also rejected the theories of John Wycliff and condemned Jan Hus as a heretic.

POPES OF THE TWENTIETH CENTURY

LEO XIII

Leo XIII (Gioacchino Vincenzo Pecci) was born May 2, 1810, in Carpineto, Italy. Although all but three years of his life and pontificate were of the 19th century, his influence extended well into the 20th century.

He was educated at the Jesuit college in Viterbo, the Roman College, the Academy of Noble Ecclesiastics, and the University of the Sapienza. He was ordained to the priesthood in 1837.

He served as an apostolic delegate to two States of the Church, Benevento from 1838 to 1841 and Perugia in 1841 and 1842. Ordained titular archbishop of Damietta, he was papal nuncio to Belgium from January 1843 until May 1846; in the post, he had controversial relations with the government over education issues and acquired his first significant experience of industrialized society.

He was archbishop of Perugia from 1846 to 1878. He became a cardinal in 1853 and chamberlain of the Roman Curia in 1877. He was elected to the papacy February 20, 1878. He died July 20, 1903.

Canonizations: He canonized 18 saints and beatified a group of English martyrs.

Church Administration: He established 300 new dioceses and vicariates; restored the hierarchy in Scotland, set up an English, as contrasted with the Portuguese, hierarchy in India; approved the action of the Congregation for the Propagation of the Faith in reorganizing missions in China.

Encyclicals: He issued 86 encyclicals, on subjects ranging from devotional to social. In the former category were *Annum Sacrum*, on the Sacred Heart, in 1899, and 11 letters on Mary and the Rosary.

Social Questions: Much of Leo's influence stemmed from social doctrine stated in numerous encyclicals, concerning liberalism, liberty, the divine origin of authority; socialism, in *Quod Apostolici Muneris*, 1878; the Christian concept of the family, in *Arcanum*, 1880; socialism and economic liberalism, relations between capital and labor, in *Rerum Novarum*, 1891. Two of his social encyclicals were against the African slave trade.

Interfaith Relations: He was unsuccessful in unity overtures made to Orthodox and Slavic Churches. He declared Anglican orders invalid in the apostolic bull *Apostolicae Curae* September 13, 1896.

International Relations: Leo was frustrated in seeking solutions to the Roman Question arising from the seizure of church lands by the Kingdom of Italy in 1870. He also faced anticlerical situations in Belgium and France and in the *Kulturkampf* policies of Bismarck in Germany.

Studies: In the encyclical *Aeterni Patris* of August 4, 1879, he ordered a renewal of philosophical and theological studies in seminaries along scholastic, and especially Thomistic, lines, to counteract influential trends of liberalism and Modernism. He issued guidelines for biblical exegesis in *Providentissimus Deus* November 18, 1893, and established the Pontifical Biblical Commission in 1902.

In other actions affecting scholarship and study, he opened the Vatican Archives to scholars in 1883 and established the Vatican Observatory.

United States: He authorized establishment of the apostolic delegation in Washington, DC, January 24, 1893. He refused to issue a condemnation of the Knights of Labor. With a document entitled *Testem Benevolentiae*, he eased resolution of questions concerning what was called an American heresy in 1899.

ST. PIUS X

St. Pius X (Giuseppe Melchiorre Sarto) was born in 1835 in Riese, Italy. Educated at the college of Castelfranco and the seminary at Padua, he was ordained to the priesthood September 18, 1858. He served as a curate in Trombolo for nine years before beginning an eight-year pastorate at Salzano. He was chancellor of the Treviso diocese from November 1875, and bishop of Mantua

Pope St. Pius X

from 1884 until 1893. He was cardinal-patriarch of Venice from that year until his election to the papacy by the conclave held from July 31 to August 4, 1903.

Aims: Pius' principal objectives as pope were "to restore all things in Christ, in order that Christ may be all and in all," and "to teach (and defend) Christian truth and law."

Canonizations, Encyclicals: He canonized four saints and issued 16 encyclicals. One of the encyclicals was issued in commemoration of the 50th anniversary of the proclamation of the dogma of the Immaculate Conception of Mary.

Catechetics: He introduced a whole new era of religious instruction and formation with the encyclical *Acerbo Nimis* of April 15, 1905, in which he called for vigor in establishing and conducting parochial programs of the Confraternity of Christian Doctrine.

Catholic Action: He outlined the role of official Catholic Action in two encyclicals in 1905 and 1906. Favoring organized action by Catholics themselves, he had serious reservations about interconfessional collaboration.

He stoutly maintained claims to papal rights in the anticlerical climate of Italy. He authorized bishops to relax prohibitions against participation by Catholics in some Italian elections.

Church Administration: With the *motu proprio Arduum Sane* of March 19, 1904, he inaugurated the work which resulted in the Code of Canon Law; the code was completed in 1917 and went into effect in the following year. He reorganized and strengthened the Roman Curia with the apostolic constitution *Sapienti Consilio* of June 29, 1908.

While promoting the expansion of missionary work, he removed from the jurisdiction of the Congregation for the Propagation of the Faith the Church in the United States, Canada, Newfoundland, England, Ireland, Holland, and Luxembourg.

International Relations: He ended traditional prerogatives of Catholic governments with respect to papal elections in 1904. He opposed anti-Church and anticlerical actions in several countries: Bolivia in 1905, because of anti-religious legislation; France in 1906, for its 1901 action in annulling its concordat with the Holy See, and for the 1905 Law of Separation by which it decreed separation of Church and State, ordered the confiscation of church property, and blocked religious education and the activities of religious orders; Portugal in 1911, for the separation of Church and State and repressive measures which resulted in persecution later.

In 1912 he called on the bishops of Brazil to work for the improvement of conditions among Indians.

Liturgy: "The Pope of the Eucharist," he strongly recommended the frequent reception of Holy Communion in a decree dated December 20, 1905; in another decree, *Quam Singulari*, of August 8, 1910, he called for the early reception of the sacrament by children. He initiated measures for liturgical reform with new norms for sacred music and the start of work on revision of the Breviary for recitation of the Divine Office.

Modernism: Pius was a vigorous opponent of "the synthesis of all heresies," which threatened the integrity of doctrine through its influence in philosophy, theology, and biblical exegesis. In opposition, he condemned 65 of its propositions as erroneous in the decree *Lamentabili* July 3, 1907; issued the encyclical *Pascendi* in the same vein September 8, 1907; backed both of these with censures; and published the Oath against Modernism in September, 1910, to be taken by all the clergy. Ecclesiastical studies suffered to some extent from these actions, necessary as they were at the time.

Pius followed the lead of Leo XIII in promoting the study of scholastic philosophy. He established the Pontifical Biblical Institute May 7, 1909.

His death, August 20, 1914, was hastened by the outbreak of World War I. He was beatified in 1951 and canonized May 29, 1954. His feast is observed August 21.

BENEDICT XV

Benedict XV (Giacomo della Chiesa) was born November 21, 1854, in Pegli, Italy.

He was educated at the Royal University of Genoa and Gregorian University in Rome. He was ordained to the priesthood December 21, 1878.

He served in the papal diplomatic corps from 1882 to 1907; as secretary to the nuncio to Spain from 1882 to 1887, as secretary to the papal secretary of state from 1887, and as undersecretary from 1901.

He was ordained archbishop of Bologna December 22, 1907, and spent four years completing a pastoral visitation there. He was made a cardinal just three months before being elected to the papacy September 3, 1914. He died January 22, 1922. Two key efforts of his pontificate were for peace and the relief of human suffering caused by World War I.

Canonizations: Benedict canonized three saints; one of them was Joan of Arc.

Canon Law: He published the Code of Canon Law, developed by the commission set up by St. Pius X, May 27, 1917; it went into effect the following year.

Curia: He made great changes in the personnel of the Curia. He established the Congregation for the Oriental Churches May 1, 1917, and founded the Pontifical Oriental Institute in Rome later in the year.

Encyclicals: He issued 12 encyclicals. Peace was the theme of three of them. In another, published two years after the cessation of hostilities, he wrote about child victims of the war. He followed the lead of Leo XIII in *Spiritus Paraclitus*, September 15, 1920, on biblical studies.

International Relations: He was largely frustrated on the international level because of the events and attitudes of the war period, but the number of diplomats accredited to the Vatican nearly doubled, from 14 to 26, from his accession to the papacy and his death.

Peace Efforts: Benedict's stance in the war was one of absolute impartiality but not of uninterested neutrality. Because he would not take sides he was suspected by both sides and the seven-point peace plan he offered to all belligerents August 1, 1917, was turned down. The points of the plan were: recognition of the moral force of right; disarmament; acceptance of arbitration in cases of dispute; guarantee of freedom of the seas; renunciation of war indemnities; evacuation and restoration of occupied territories; examination of territorial claims in dispute.

Relief Efforts: Benedict assumed personal charge of Vatican relief efforts during the war. He set up an international missing persons bureau for contacts between prisoners and their families, but was forced to close it because of the suspicion of warring nations that it was a front for espionage operations. He persuaded the Swiss government to admit into the country military victims of tuberculosis.

Roman Question: Benedict prepared the way for the meetings and negotiations which led to settlement of the question in 1929.

PIUS XI

Pius XI (Ambrogio Damiano Achille Ratti) was born May 31, 1857, in Desio, Italy.

Educated at seminaries in Seviso and Milan, and at the Lombard College, Gregorian University and Academy of St. Thomas in Rome, he was ordained to the priesthood in 1879.

He taught at the major seminary of Milan from 1882 to 1888. Appointed to the staff of the Ambrosian Library in 1888, he remained there until 1911, acquiring a reputation for publishing works on paleography and serving as director from 1907 to 1911. He then moved to the Vatican Library, of which he was prefect from 1914 to 1918. In 1919, he was named apostolic visitor to Poland in April, nuncio in June, and was made titular archbishop of Lepanto October 28. He was made archbishop of Milan and cardinal June

13, 1921, before being elected to the papacy February 6, 1922. He died February 10, 1939.

Aim: The objective of his pontificate, as stated in the encyclical *Ubi Arcano*, December 23, 1922, was to establish the reign and peace of Christ in society.

Canonizations: He canonized 34 saints, including the Jesuit Martyrs of North America, and conferred the title of Doctor of the Church on Sts. Peter Canisius, John of the Cross, Robert Bellarmine and Albertus Magnus.

Eastern Churches: He called for better understanding of the Eastern Churches in the encyclical *Rerum Orientalium* of September 8, 1928, and developed facilities for the training of Eastern Rite priests. He inaugurated steps for the codification of Eastern-Church law in 1929. In 1935 he made Syrian Patriarch Tappouni a cardinal.

Encyclicals: His first encyclical, *Ubi Arcano*, in addition to stating the aims of his pontificate, blueprinted Catholic Action and called for its development throughout the Church. *In Quas Primas*, December 11, 1925, he established the feast of Christ the King for universal observance. Subjects of some of his other encyclicals were: Christian education, in *Rappresentanti in Terra*, December 31, 1929; Christian marriage, in *Casti Connubii*, December 31, 1930; social conditions and pressure for social change in line with the teaching in *Rerum Novarum*, in *Quadragesimo Anno*, May 15, 1931; atheistic Communism, in *Divini Redemptoris*, March 19, 1937; the priesthood, in *Ad Catholici Sacerdotii*, December 20, 1935.

Missions: Following the lead of Benedict XV, Pius called for the training of native clergy in the pattern of their own respective cultures, and

Pope Pius XI

promoted missionary developments in various ways. He ordained six native bishops for China in 1926, one for Japan in 1927, and others for regions of Asia, China, and India in 1933. He placed the first 40 mission dioceses under native bishops, saw the number of native priests increase from about 2,600 to more than 7,000 and the number of Catholics in missionary areas more than double from nine million.

In the apostolic constitution *Deus Scientiarum Dominus* of May 24, 1931, he ordered the introduction of missiology into theology courses.

Interfaith Relations: Pius was negative to the ecumenical movement among Protestants but approved the Malines Conversations, 1921 to 1926, between Anglicans and Catholics.

International Relations: Relations with the Mussolini government deteriorated from 1931 on, as indicated in the encyclical *Non Abbiamo Bisogno*, when the regime took steps to curb liberties and activities of the Church; they turned critical in 1938 with the emergence of racist policies. Relations deteriorated also in Germany from 1933 on, resulting finally in condemnation of the Nazis in the encyclical *Mit Brennender Sorge*, March 1937. Pius sparked a revival of the Church in France by encouraging Catholics to work within the democratic framework of the Republic rather than foment trouble over restoration of a monarchy. Pius was powerless to influence developments related to the civil war which erupted in Spain in July 1936, sporadic persecution and repression by the Calles regime in Mexico, and systematic persecution of the Church in the Soviet Union. Many of the 10 concordats and two agreements reached with European countries after World War I became casualties of World War II.

Roman Question: Pius negotiated for two and one-half years with the Italian government to settle the Roman Question by means of the Lateran Agreement of 1929. The agreement provided independent status for the State of Vatican City; made Catholicism the official religion of Italy, with pastoral and educational freedom and state recognition of Catholic marriages, religious orders and societies; and provided a financial payment to the Vatican for expropriation of the former States of the Church.

PIUS XII

Pius XII (Eugenio Maria Giovanni Pacelli) was born March 2, 1876, in Rome.

Educated at the Gregorian University and the Lateran University, in Rome, he was ordained to the priesthood April 2, 1899.

He entered the Vatican diplomatic service in 1901, worked on the codification of canon law, and was appointed secretary of the Congrega-tion for Ecclesiastical Affairs in 1914. Three years later he was ordained titular archbishop of Sardis and made apostolic nuncio to Bavaria. He was nuncio to Germany from 1920 to 1929, when he was made a cardinal, and took office as papal secretary of state in the following year. His diplomatic negotiations resulted in concordats between the Vatican and Bavaria (1924), Prussia (1929), Baden (1932), Austria and the German Republic (1933). He took part in negotiations which led to settlement of the Roman Question in 1929.

He was elected to the papacy March 2, 1939. He died October 9, 1958, at Castel Gandolfo, after the 12th longest pontificate in history.

Canonizations: He canonized 34 saints, including Mother Frances X. Cabrini, the first U.S. citizen-Saint.

Cardinals: He raised 56 prelates to the rank of cardinal in two consistories held in 1946 and 1953. There were 57 cardinals at the time of his death.

Church Organization and Missions: He increased the number of dioceses from 1,696 to 2,048. He established native hierarchies in China (1946), Burma (1955), and parts of Africa, and extended the native structure of the Church in India. He ordained the first black bishop for Africa.

Communism: In addition to opposing and condemning Communism on numerous occasions, he decreed in 1949 the penalty of excommunication for all Catholics holding formal and willing allegiance to the Communist Party and its policies. During his reign the Church was persecuted in some 15 countries, which fell under communist domination.

Doctrine and Liturgy: He proclaimed the dogma of the Assumption of the Blessed Virgin Mary November 1, 1950 (apostolic constitution, *Munificentissimus Deus*).

In various encyclicals and other enactments, he provided background for the *aggiornamento* introduced by his successor, John XXIII: by his formulations of doctrine and practice regarding the Mystical Body of Christ, the liturgy, sacred music and biblical studies; by the revision of the Rites of Holy Week; by initiation of the work that led to the calendar-missal-breviary reform ordered into effect January 1, 1961; by the first of several modifications of the Eucharistic fast; by extending the time of Mass to the evening. He instituted the feasts of Mary, Queen, and of St. Joseph the Worker, and clarified teaching concerning devotion to the Sacred Heart.

His 41 encyclicals and nearly 1,000 public addresses made Pius one of the greatest teaching popes. His concern in all his communications was to deal with specific points at issue and/

or to bring Christian principles to bear on contemporary world problems.

Peace Efforts: Before the start of World War II, he tried unsuccessfully to get the contending nations — Germany and Poland, France and Italy — to settle their differences peaceably. During the war, he offered his services to mediate the widened conflict, spoke out against the horrors of war and the suffering it caused, mobilized relief work for its victims, proposed a five-point program for peace in Christmas messages from 1939 to 1942, and secured a generally open status for the city of Rome. He has been criticized in some quarters for not doing enough to oppose the Holocaust. (See *below.*) After the war, he endorsed the principles and intent of the United Nations and continued efforts for peace.

United States: Pius appointed more than 200 of the 265 American bishops resident in the U.S. and abroad in 1958, erected 27 dioceses in this country, and raised seven dioceses to archiepiscopal rank.

The Holocaust Issue

Revered in his lifetime for having worked for peace and the relief of human suffering, Pope Pius XII today is the subject of an ugly controversy over his policies and actions before and during World War II. Critics say that he helped the Nazis consolidate power by weakening the Church in Germany on behalf of his own program to centralize authority in the papacy, that he was anti-Semitic, and that he failed to speak out against persecution of the Jews. Defenders say that he was a conscientious pope who protested Nazi cruelties as much as prudence allowed and saved many thousands of Jewish and other lives, that his record contains no evidence of anti-Semitism, and that he was a force for decency and spiritual values in violent times.

Attacks began in 1963 with the production of *The Deputy*, a play by a German writer, Rolf Hochhuth. It depicted him, another papal critic said, as "a ruthless cynic, interested more in the Vatican's stockholdings than in the fate of the Jews."

In response to the resulting controversy, Pope Paul VI commissioned four Jesuit historians to compile documents from the Vatican archives relevant to the wartime record of the late Pope and the Holy See. The four were Fathers Angelo Martini, S.J., Burkhardt Schneider, S.J., Robert A. Graham, S.J., and Pierre Blet, S.J. *Acts and Documents of the Holy See Relating to the Second World War* was published in twelve volumes between 1965 and 1981. The historian Eamon Duffy says it "decisively established the falsehood of Hochhuth's specific allegations." But questioning of Pius XII's record continued.

The controversy flared up in March 1998, with the publication of "We Remember: A Reflection on the Shoah," a document prepared by the Vatican's Commission for Religious Relations with the Jews at the direction of Pope John Paul II. Although generally welcomed by Jewish sources, it also was criticized on various grounds, including what it said about Pius XII, whom it credited with saving "hundreds of thousands of Jewish lives." A typical negative reaction from a Jewish source was that of Robert S. Wistrich, professor of history at the University of Jerusalem, who challenged the statement that hundreds of thousands of Jews were saved and spoke of the "ambiguity" of the Pope's record.

Why, critics demand, did not the Pope speak out more often and more forcefully? The reason, defenders reply, lies in the record of Nazi reprisals when churchmen did speak out. This happened, for example, in 1942 in Holland, where the bishops strongly protested the deportation of Jews; in response, the Nazis began seizing and deporting Jewish converts to Christianity, who previously had been spared. Among them was Carmelite Sister Teresa Benedicta of the Cross – Edith Stein. Overall, some 100,000 Jews, eighty percent of the Jewish population of The Netherlands, were killed.

After the war many Jewish groups and individuals praised and thanked Pope Pius. These included the secretary general of the World Jewish Congress, the National Jewish Welfare Board, the president of the Union of Italian Jewish Communities, the president of the Anglo-Jewish Association, the Grand Rabbi of Jerusalem, and others. In 1955 Italian Jews proclaimed April 17 a "Day of Gratitude" and thousands went to the Vatican to pay tribute to Pius XII while the Israeli Philharmonic performed a special concert there. At the time of his death, Golda Meir, Israeli representative at the United Nations and future prime minister of Israel, said: "During the ten years of the Nazi terror . . . the Pope raised his voice to condemn the persecutors and to commiserate with their victims." Other Jewish leaders expressed similar sentiments.

Although the figure is disputed, Jewish historian and diplomat Pinchas E. Lapide estimated that 860,000 Jews were saved by the efforts of Pope Pius XII. The wartime British ambassador to the Holy See, Francis Osborne, said: "So far from being a cool (which, I suppose, implies cold-blooded and inhumane) diplomatist, Pius XII was the most warmly humane, kind, generous, sympathetic (and incidentally saintly) character that it has been my privilege to meet in the course of a long life."

BLESSED JOHN XXIII

Blessed John XXIII (Angelo Roncalli) was born November 25, 1881, at Sotte il Monte, Italy.

He was educated at the seminary of the Bergamo diocese and the Pontifical Seminary in Rome, where he was ordained to the priesthood August 10, 1904.

He spent the first nine or ten years of his priesthood as secretary to the bishop of Bergamo and as an instructor in the seminary there. He served as a medic and chaplain in the Italian army during World War I. Afterwards, he resumed duties in his own diocese until he was called to Rome in 1921 for work with the Society for the Propagation of the Faith.

He began diplomatic service in 1925 as titular archbishop of Areopolis and apostolic visitor to Bulgaria. A succession of offices followed: apostolic delegate to Bulgaria (1931-1935); titular archbishop of Mesembria, apostolic delegate to Turkey and Greece, administrator of the Latin vicariate apostolic of Istanbul (1935-1944); apostolic nuncio to France (1944-1953). On these missions, he was engaged in delicate negotiations involving Roman, Eastern-Rite and Orthodox relations; the needs of people suffering from the consequences of World War II; and unsettling suspicions arising from wartime conditions.

He was made a cardinal January 12, 1953, and three days later was appointed patriarch of Venice, the position he held until his election to the papacy October 28, 1958. He died of stomach cancer June 3, 1963. Pope John Paul II beatified him on September 3, 2000, on the same day as Pope Pius IX.

Second Vatican Council: John announced January 25, 1959, his intention of convoking the 21st ecumenical council in history to renew life in the Church, to reform its structures and institutions, and to explore ways and means of promoting unity among Christians. Through the council, which completed its work two and one-half years after his death, he ushered in a new era in the history of the Church.

Canon Law: He established a commission March 28, 1963, for revision of the Code of Canon Law. The revised Code was promulgated in 1983.

Canonizations: He canonized 10 saints and beatified Mother Elizabeth Ann Seton, the first native of the U.S. ever so honored. He named St. Lawrence of Brindisi a Doctor of the Church.

Cardinals: He created 52 cardinals in five consistories, raising membership of the College of Cardinals above the traditional number of 70; at one time in 1962, the membership was 87. He made the college more international in representation than it had ever been, appointing the first cardinals from the Philippines, Japan, and Africa. He ordered episcopal ordination for all cardinals. He relieved the suburban bishops of Rome of ordinary jurisdiction over their dioceses so they might devote all their time to business of the Roman Curia.

Eastern Rites: He made all Eastern-Rite patriarchs members of the Congregation for the Oriental Churches.

Ecumenism: He assigned to the Second Vatican Council the task of finding ways and means of promoting unity among Christians. He established the Vatican Secretariat for Promoting Christian Unity June 5, 1960. He showed his desire for more cordial relations with the Orthodox by sending personal representatives to visit Patriarch Athenagoras I June 27, 1961; approved a mission of five delegates to the General Assembly of the World Council of Churches which met in New Delhi, India, in November, 1961; removed a number of pejorative references to Jews in the Roman-Rite liturgy for Good Friday.

Encyclicals: Of the eight encyclicals he issued, the two outstanding ones were *Mater et Magistra* ("Christianity and Social Progress"), in which he recapitulated, updated, and extended the social doctrine stated earlier by Leo XIII and Pius XI; and *Pacem in Terris* ("Peace on Earth"), the first encyclical ever addressed to all men of good will as well as to Catholics, on the natural-law principles of peace.

Liturgy: In forwarding liturgical reforms already begun by Pius XII, he ordered a calendar-missal-breviary reform into effect January 1, 1961. He authorized the use of vernacular languages in the administration of the sacraments and approved giving Holy Communion to the sick in afternoon hours. He selected the liturgy as the first topic of major discussion by the Second Vatican Council.

Pope John XXIII

Missions: He issued an encyclical on the missionary activity of the Church; established native hierarchies in Indonesia, Vietnam, and Korea; and called on North American superiors of religious institutes to have one-tenth of their members assigned to work in Latin America by 1971.

Peace: John spoke and used his moral influence for peace in 1961 when tension developed over Berlin, in 1962 during the Algerian revolt from France, and later the same year in the Cuban missile crisis. His efforts were singled out for honor by the Balzan Peace Foundation. In 1963, he was posthumously awarded the U.S. Presidential Medal of Freedom.

PAUL VI

Paul VI (Giovanni Battista Montini) was born September 26, 1897, at Concesio in northern Italy. Educated at Brescia, he was ordained to the priesthood May 29, 1920. He pursued additional studies at the Pontifical Academy for Noble Ecclesiastics and the Pontifical Gregorian University. In 1924 he began 30 years of service in the Secretariat of State; as undersecretary from 1937 until 1954, he was closely associated with Pius XII and was heavily engaged in organizing informational and relief services during and after World War II. He declined the offer of the cardinalate by Pope Pius XII.

Ordained archbishop of Milan December 12, 1954, he was inducted into the College of Cardinals December 15, 1958, by Pope John XXIII. Trusted by John, he was a key figure in organizing the first session of Vatican Council II and was elected to the papacy June 21, 1963, two days after the conclave began. He died of a heart attack August 6, 1978.

Second Vatican Council: He reconvened the Second Vatican Council after the death of John XXIII, presided over its second, third, and fourth sessions, formally promulgated the 16 documents it produced, and devoted the whole of his pontificate to the task of putting them into effect throughout the Church. The main thrust of his pontificate — in a milieu of cultural and other changes in the Church and the world — was toward institutionalization and control of the authentic trends articulated and set in motion by the council.

Canonizations: He canonized 84 saints. They included groups of 22 Ugandan martyrs and 40 martyrs of England and Wales, as well as two Americans — Elizabeth Ann Seton and John Nepomucene Neumann.

Cardinals: He created 144 cardinals, and gave the Sacred College a more international complexion than it ever had before. He limited participation in papal elections to 120 cardinals under the age of 80.

Collegiality: He established the Synod of Bishops in 1965 and called it into session five times. He stimulated the formation and operation of regional conferences of bishops, and of consultative bodies on other levels.

Creed and Holy Year: On June 30, 1968, he issued a Creed of the People of God in conjunction with the celebration of a Year of Faith. He proclaimed and led the observance of a Holy Year from Christmas Eve of 1974 to Christmas Eve of 1975.

Diplomacy: He met with many world leaders, including Soviet President Nikolai Podgorny in 1967, Marshal Tito of Yugoslavia in 1971, and President Nicolas Ceausescu of Romania in 1973. He worked constantly to reduce tension between the Church and the intransigent regimes of Eastern European countries by means of a detente type of policy called *Ostpolitik*. He agreed to significant revisions of the Vatican's concordat with Spain and initiated efforts to revise the concordat with Italy. More than 40 countries established diplomatic relations with the Vatican during his pontificate.

Encyclicals: He issued seven encyclicals, three of which are the best known. In *Populorum Progressio* ("Development of Peoples") he appealed to wealthy countries to take "concrete action" to promote human development and to remedy imbalances between richer and poorer nations; this encyclical, coupled with other documents and related actions, launched the Church into a new depth of involvement as a public advocate for human rights and for humanizing social, political, and economic policies. In *Sacerdotalis Caelibatus* ("Priestly Celibacy") he reaffirmed the strict observance of priestly celibacy throughout the Western Church. In *Humanae Vitae* ("Of Human Life") he con-

Pope Paul VI

demned abortion, sterilization, and artificial birth control, in line with traditional teaching and in "defense of life, the gift of God, the glory of the family, the strength of the people."

Interfaith Relations: He initiated formal consultation and informal dialogue on international and national levels between Catholics and non-Catholics — Orthodox, Anglicans, Protestants, Jews, Muslims, Buddhists, Hindus, and unbelievers. He and Greek Orthodox Patriarch Athenagoras I of Constantinople nullified in 1965 the mutual excommunications imposed by their respective churches in 1054.

Liturgy: He carried out the most extensive liturgical reform in history, involving a new Order of the Mass effective in 1969, a revised church calendar in 1970, revisions and translations into vernacular languages of all sacramental rites and other liturgical texts.

Ministries: He authorized the restoration of the permanent diaconate in the Roman Rite and the establishment of new ministries of lay persons.

Peace: In 1968, he instituted the annual observance of a World Day of Peace on New Year's Day as a means of addressing a message of peace to all the world's political leaders and the peoples of all nations. The most dramatic of his many appeals for peace and efforts to ease international tensions was his plea for "No more war!" before the United Nations October 4, 1965.

Pilgrimages: A "Pilgrim Pope," he made pastoral visits to the Holy Land and India in 1964, the United Nations and New York City in 1965, Portugal and Turkey in 1967, Colombia in 1968, Switzerland and Uganda in 1969, and Asia, Pacific islands and Australia in 1970. While in Manila in 1970, he was stabbed by a Bolivian artist.

Roman Curia: He reorganized the central administrative organs of the Church in line with provisions of the apostolic constitution, *Regimini Ecclesiae Universae*, streamlining procedures for more effective service and giving the agencies a more international perspective by drawing officials and consultors from all over the world. He also instituted a number of new commissions and other bodies. Coupled with curial reorganization was a simplification of papal ceremonies.

JOHN PAUL I

John Paul I (Albino Luciani) was born October 17, 1912, in Forno di Canale (now Canale d'Agordo) in northern Italy. Educated at the minor seminary in Feltre and the major seminary of the Diocese of Belluno, he was ordained to the priesthood July 7, 1935. He pursued further studies at the Pontifical Gregorian University in Rome and was awarded a doctorate in theology. From 1937 to 1947 he was vice rector of the Belluno seminary, where he taught dogmatic and moral theology, canon law and sacred art. He was appointed vicar general of his diocese in 1947 and served as director of catechetics.

Ordained bishop of Vittorio Veneto December 27, 1958, he attended all sessions of the Second Vatican Council, participated in three assemblies of the Synod of Bishops (1971, 1974 and 1977), and was vice president of the Italian Bishops' Conference from 1972 to 1975.

He was appointed archbishop and patriarch of Venice December 15, 1969, and was inducted into the College of Cardinals March 5, 1973.

He was elected to the papacy August 26, 1978, on the fourth ballot cast by the 111 cardinals participating in the largest and one of the shortest conclaves in history. The quickness of his election was matched by the brevity of his pontificate of 33 days, during which he delivered 19 addresses. He died of a heart attack September 28, 1978.

JOHN PAUL II

See separate entry.

PAPAL ENCYCLICALS — BENEDICT XIV (1740) TO JOHN PAUL II

(Source: The Papal Encyclicals [5 vols.], Claudia Carlen, I.H.M.; Pieran Press, Ann Arbor, Mich. Used with permission.)

An encyclical letter is a pastoral letter addressed by a pope to the whole Church. In general, it concerns matters of doctrine, morals or discipline, or significant commemorations. Its formal title consists of the first few words of the official text. Some encyclicals, notably *Pacem in Terris* by John XXIII, *Ecclesiam Suam*, by Paul VI and several by John Paul II, have been addressed to people of good will in general as well as to bishops and the faithful in communion with the Church.

An encyclical epistle resembles an encyclical letter but is addressed only to part of the Church. The authority of encyclicals was stated by Pius XII in the encyclical *Humani generis* August 12, 1950: "Nor must it be thought that what is contained in encyclical letters does not of itself demand assent, on the pretext that the popes do not exercise in them the supreme power of their teaching authority. Rather, such teachings belong to the ordinary magisterium, of which it is true to say: 'He who hears you, hears me' (Lk. 10:16); for the most part, too, what is expounded and inculcated in encyclical letters already appertains to Catholic doctrine for other reasons."

The Second Vatican Council declared: "Religious submission of will and of mind must be shown in a special way to the authentic teaching authority of the Roman Pontiff, even when he is not speaking *ex cathedra*. That is, it must be shown in such a way that his supreme magisterium is acknowledged with reverence, the judgments made by him are sincerely adhered to, according to his manifest mind and will. His mind and will in the matter may be known chiefly either from the character of the documents (one of which could be an encyclical), from his frequent repetition of the same doctrine, or from his manner of speaking" (Dogmatic Constitution on the Church, *Lumen Gentium*, No. 25).

The following list contains the titles and indicates the subject matter of encyclical letters and epistles. The latter are generally distinguishable by the limited scope of their titles or contents.

Benedict XIV

(1740-1758)

1740: *Ubi primum* (On the duties of bishops), December 3.

1741: *Quanta cura* (Forbidding traffic in alms), June 30.

1743: *Nimiam licentiam* (To the bishops of Poland: on validity of marriages), May 18.

1745: *Vix pervenit* (To the bishops of Italy: on usury and other dishonest profit), November 1.

1748: *Magnae Nobis* (To the bishops of Poland: on marriage impediments and dispensations), June 29.

1749: *Peregrinantes* (To all the faithful: proclaiming a Holy Year for 1750), May 5.
Apostolica Constitutio (On preparation for the Holy Year), June 26.

1751: *A quo primum* (To the bishops of Poland: on Jews and Christians living in the same place), June 14.

1754: *Cum Religiosi* (To the bishops of the States of the Church: on catechesis), June 26.
Quod Provinciale (To the bishops of Albania: on Christians using Mohammedan names), August 1.

1755: *Allatae sunt* (To missionaries of the Orient: on the observance of Oriental rites), July 26.

1756: *Ex quo primum* (To bishops of the Greek rite: on the Euchologion), March 1.
Ex omnibus (To the bishops of France: on the apostolic constitution, *Unigenitus*), October 16.

Clement XIII

(1758-1769)

1758: *A quo die* (Unity among Christians), September 13.

1759: *Cum primum* (On observing canonical sanctions), September 17.
Appetente Sacro (On the spiritual advantages of fasting), December 20.

1761: *In Dominico agro* (On instruction in the faith), June 14.

1766: *Christianae republicae* (On the dangers of anti-Christian writings), November 25.

1768: *Summa quae* (To the bishops of Poland: on the Church in Poland), January 6.

Clement XIV

(1769-1774)

1769: *Decet quam maxime* (To the bishops of Sardinia: on abuses in taxes and benefices), September 21.
Inscrutabili divinae sapientiae (To all Christians: proclaiming a universal jubilee), December 12.
Cum summi (Proclaiming a universal jubilee), December 12.

1774: *Salutis nostra* (To all Christians: proclaiming a universal jubilee), April 30.

Pius VI

(1775-1799)

1775: *Inscrutabile* (On the problems of the pontificate), December 25.

1791: *Charitas* (To the bishops of France: on the civil oath in France), April 13.

Pius VII

(1800-1823)

1800: *Diu satis* (To the bishops of France: on a return to Gospel principles), May 15.

Leo XII

(1823-1829)

1824: *Ubi primum* (To all bishops: on Leo XII's assuming the pontificate), May 5.
Quod hoc ineunte (Proclaiming a universal jubilee), May 24.

1825: *Charitate Christi* (Extending jubilee to the entire Church), December 25.

Pius VIII

(1829-1830)

1829: *Traditi humilitati* (On Pius VIII's program for the pontificate), May 24.

Gregory XVI

(1831-1846)

1832: *Summo iugiter studio* (To the bishops of Bavaria: on mixed marriages), May 27.
Cum primum (To the bishops of Poland: on civil obedience), June 9.
Mirari vos (On liberalism and religious indifferentism), August 15.

1833: *Quo graviora* (To the bishops of the

Rhineland: on the "pragmatic Constitution"), October 4.

1834: *Singulari Nos* (On the errors of Lammenais), June 25.

1835: *Commissum divinitus* (To clergy of Switzerland: on Church and State), May 17.

1840: *Probe nostis* (On the Propagation of the Faith), September 18.

1841: *Quas vestro* (To the bishops of Hungary: on mixed marriages), April 30.

1844: *Inter praecipuas* (On biblical societies), May 8.

Blessed Pius IX

(1846-1878)

1846: *Qui pluribus* (On faith and religion), November 9.

1847: *Praedecessores Nostros* (On aid for Ireland), March 25.

Ubi primum (To religious superiors: on discipline for religious), June 17.

1849: *Ubi primum* (On the Immaculate Conception), February 2.

Nostis et Nobiscum (To the bishops of Italy: on the Church in the Pontifical States), December 8.

1851: *Exultavit cor Nostrum* (On the effects of jubilee), November 21.

1852: *Nemo certe ignorat* (To the bishops of Ireland: on the discipline for clergy), March 25.

Probe noscitis Venerabiles (To the bishops of Spain: on the discipline for clergy), May 17.

1853: *Inter multiplices* (To the bishops of France: pleading for unity of spirit), March 21.

1854: *Neminem vestrum* (To clergy and faithful of Constantinople: on the persecution of Armenians), February 2.

Optime noscitis (To the bishops of Ireland: on the proposed Catholic university for Ireland), March 20.

Apostolicae Nostrae caritatis (Urging prayers for peace), August 1.

1855: *Optime noscitis* (To the bishops of Austria: on episcopal meetings), November 5.

1856: *Singulari quidem* (To the bishops of Austria: on the Church in Austria), March 17.

1858: *Cum nuper* (To the bishops of the Kingdom of the Two Sicilies: on care for clerics), January 20.

Amantissimi Redemptoris (On priests and the care of souls), May 3.

1859: *Cum sancta mater Ecclesia* (Pleading for public prayer), April 27.

Qui nuper (On Pontifical States), June 18.

1860: *Nullis certe verbis* (On the need for civil sovereignty), January 19.

1862: *Amantissimus* (To bishops of the Oriental rite: on the care of the churches), April 8.

1863: *Quanto conficiamur moerore* (To the bishops of Italy: on promotion of false doctrines), August 10.

Incredibili (To the bishops of Bogota: on persecution in New Granada), September 17.

1864: *Maximae quidem* (To the bishops of Bavaria: on the Church in Bavaria), August 18.

Quanta cura (Condemning current errors), December 8.

1865: *Meridionali Americae* (To the bishops of South America: on the seminary for native clergy), September 30.

1867: *Levate* (On the afflictions of the Church), October 27.

1870: *Respicientes* (Protesting the taking of the Pontifical States), November 1.

1871: *Ubi Nos* (To all bishops: on Pontifical States), May 15.

Beneficia Dei (On the twenty-fifth anniversary of his pontificate), June 4.

Saepe Venerabiles Fratres (On thanksgiving for twenty-five years of pontificate), August 5.

1872: *Quae in Patriarchatu* (To bishops and people of Chaldea: on the Church in Chaldea), November 16.

1873: *Quartus supra* (To bishops and people of the Armenian rite: on the Church in Armenia), January 6.

Etsi multa (On the Church in Italy, Germany, and Switzerland), November 21.

1874: *Vix dum a Nobis* (To the bishops of Austria: on the Church in Austria), March 7.

Gravibus Ecclesiae (To all bishops and faithful: proclaiming a jubilee for 1875), December 24.

1875: *Quod nunquam* (To the bishops of Prussia: on the Church in Prussia), February 5.

Graves ac diuturnae (To the bishops of Switzerland: on the Church in Switzerland), March 23.

Leo XIII

(1878-1903)

1878: *Inscrutabili Dei consilio* (On the evils of society), April 21.

Quod Apostolici muneris (On socialism), December 28.

1879: *Aeterni Patris* (On the restoration of Christian philosophy), August 4.

1880: *Arcanum* (On Christian marriage), February 10.

Grande munus (On Sts. Cyril and Methodius), September 30.

Sancta Dei civitas (On mission societies), December 3.

1881: *Diuturnum* (On the origin of civil power), June 29.

Licet multa (To the bishops of Belgium: on Catholics in Belgium), August 3.

1882: *Etsi Nos* (To the bishops of Italy: on conditions in Italy), February 15.
Auspicato concessum (On St. Francis of Assisi), September 17.
Cum multa (To the bishops of Spain: on conditions in Spain), December 8.

1883: *Supremi Apostolatus officio* (On devotion to the Rosary), September 1.

1884: *Nobilissima Gallorum gens* (To the bishops of France: on the religious question), February 8.
Humanum genus (On Freemasonry), April 20.
Superiore anno (On the recitation of the Rosary), August 30.

1885: *Immortale Dei* (On the Christian constitution of states), November 1.
Spectata fides (To the bishops of England: on Christian education), November 27.
Quod auctoritate (Proclamation of extraordinary Jubilee), December 22.

1886: *Iampridem* (To the bishops of Prussia: on Catholicism in Germany), January 6.
Quod multum (To the bishops of Hungary: on the liberty of the Church), August 22.
Pergrata (To the bishops of Portugal: on the Church in Portugal), September 14.

1887: *Vieben noto* (To the bishops of Italy: on the Rosary and public life), September 20.
Officio sanctissimo (To the bishops of Bavaria: on the Church in Bavaria), December 22.

1888: *Quod anniversarius* (On his sacerdotal jubilee), April 1.
In plurimis (To the bishops of Brazil: on the abolition of slavery), May 5.

Libertas (On the nature of human liberty), June 20.
Saepe Nos (To the bishops of Ireland: on boycotting in Ireland), June 24.
Paterna caritas (To the Patriarch of Cilicia and the archbishops and bishops of the Armenian people: on reunion with Rome), July 25.
Quam aerumnosa (To the bishops of America: on Italian immigrants), December 10.
Etsi cunctas (To the bishops of Ireland: on the Church in Ireland), December 21.
Exeunte iam anno (On the right ordering of Christian life), December 25.

1889: *Magni Nobis* (To the bishops of the United States: on the Catholic University of America), March 7.
Quamquam pluries (On devotion to St. Joseph), August 15.

1890: *Sapientiae Christianae* (On Christians as citizens), January 10.
Dall'alto Dell'Apostolico seggio (To the bishops and people of Italy: on Freemasonry in Italy), October 15.
Catholicae Ecclesiae (On slavery in the missions), November 20.

1891: *In ipso* (To the bishops of Austria: on episcopal reunions in Austria), March 3.
Rerum novarum (On capital and labor), May 15.
Pastoralis (To the bishops of Portugal: on religious union), June 25.
Pastoralis officii (To the bishops of Germany and Austria: on the morality of dueling), September 12.
Octobri mense (On the Rosary), September 22.

1892: *Au milieu des sollicitudes* (To the bishops, clergy and faithful of France: on the Church and State in France), February 16.
Quarto abeunte saeculo (To the bishops of Spain, Italy, and the two Americas: on the Columbus quadricentennial), July 16.
Magnae Dei Matris (On the Rosary), September 8.
Inimica vis (To the bishops of Italy: on Freemasonry), December 8.
Custodi di quella fede (To the Italian people: on Freemasonry), December 8.

1893: *Ad extremas* (On seminaries for native clergy), June 24.
Constanti Hungarorum (To the bishops of Hungary: on the Church in Hungary), September 2.
Laetitiae sanctae (Commending devotion to the Rosary), September 8.
Non mediocri (To the bishops of Spain: on the Spanish College in Rome), October 25.

Pope Leo XIII

Providentissimus Deus (On the study of Holy Scripture), November 18.

1894: *Caritatis* (To the bishops of Poland: on the Church in Poland), March 19.

Inter graves (To the bishops of Peru: on the Church in Peru), May 1.

Litteras a vobis (To the bishops of Brazil: on the clergy in Brazil), July 2.

Iucunda semper expectatione (On the Rosary), September 8.

Christi nomen (On the propagation of the Faith and Eastern churches), December 24.

1895: *Longinqua* (To the bishops of the United States: on Catholicism in the United States), January 6.

Permoti Nos (To the bishops of Belgium: on social conditions in Belgium), July 10.

Adiutricem (On the Rosary), September 5.

1896: *Insignes* (To the bishops of Hungary: on the Hungarian millennium), May 1.

Satis cognitum (On the unity of the Church), June 29.

Fidentem piumque animum (On the Rosary), September 20.

1897: *Divinum illud munus* (On the Holy Spirit), May 9.

Militantis Ecclesiae (To the bishops of Austria, Germany, and Switzerland: on St. Peter Canisius), August 1.

Augustissimae Virginis Mariae (On the Confraternity of the Holy Rosary), September 12.

Affari vos (To the bishops of Canada: on the Manitoba school question), December 8.

1898: *Caritatis studium* (To the bishops of Scotland: on the Church in Scotland), July 25.

Spesse volte (To the bishops, priests, and people of Italy: on the suppression of Catholic institutions), August 5.

Quam religiosa (To the bishops of Peru: on civil marriage law), August 16.

Diuturni temporis (On the Rosary), September 5.

Quum diuturnum (To the bishops of Latin America: on Latin American bishops' plenary council), December 25.

1899: *Annum Sacrum* (On consecration to the Sacred Heart), May 25.

Depuis le jour (To the archbishops, bishops, and clergy of France: on the education of the clergy), September 8.

Paternae (To the bishops of Brazil: on the education of the clergy), September 18.

1900: *Omnibus compertum* (To the Patriarch and bishops of the Greek-Melkite rite: on unity among the Greek Melkites), July 21.

Tametsi futura prospicientibus (On Jesus Christ the Redeemer), November 1.

1901: *Graves de communi re* (On Christian democracy), January 18.

Gravissimas (To the bishops of Portugal: on religious orders in Portugal), May 16.

Reputantibus (To the bishops of Bohemia and Moravia: on the language question in Bohemia), August 20.

Urbanitatis Veteris (To the bishops of the Latin church in Greece: on the foundation of a seminary in Athens), November 20.

1902: *In amplissimo* (To the bishops of the United States: on the Church in the United States), April 15.

Quod votis (To the bishops of Austria: on the proposed Catholic University), April 30.

Mirae caritatis (On the Holy Eucharist), May 28.

Quae ad Nos (To the bishops of Bohemia and Moravia: on the Church in Bohemia and Moravia), November 22.

Fin dal principio (To the bishops of Italy: on the education of the clergy), December 8.

Dum multa (To the bishops of Ecuador: on marriage legislation), December 24.

St. Pius X

(1903-1914)

1903: *E supremi* (On the restoration of all things in Christ), October 4.

1904: *Ad diem illum laetissimum* (On the Immaculate Conception), February 2.

Iucunda sane (On Pope Gregory the Great), March 12.

1905: *Acerbo nimis* (On teaching Christian doctrine), April 15.

Il fermo proposito (To the bishops of Italy: on Catholic Action in Italy), June 11.

1906: *Vehementer Nos* (To the bishops, clergy, and people of France: on the French Law of Separation), February 11.

Tribus circiter (On the Mariavites or Mystic Priests of Poland), April 5.

Pieni l'animo (To the bishops of Italy: on the clergy in Italy), July 28.

Gravissimo officio munere (To the bishops of France: on French associations of worship), August 10.

1907: *Une fois encore* (To the bishops, clergy, and people of France: on the separation of Church and State), January 6.

Pascendi dominici gregis (On the doctrines of the Modernists), September 8.

1909: *Communium rerum* (On St. Anselm of Aosta), April 21.

1910: *Editae saepe* (On St. Charles Borromeo), May 26.

1911: *Iamdudum* (On the Law of Separation in Portugal), May 24.

1912: *Lacrimabili statu* (To the bishops of Latin

America: on the Indians of South America), June 7.

Singulari quadam (To the bishops of Germany: on labor organizations), September 24.

Benedict XV

(1914-1922)

1914: *Ad beatissimi Apostolorum* (Appeal for peace), November 1.

1917: *Humani generis Redemptionem* (On preaching the Word of God), June 15.

1918: *Quod iam diu* (On the future peace conference), December 1.

1919: *In hac tanta* (To the bishops of Germany: on St. Boniface), May 14.

Paterno iam diu (On children of central Europe), November 24.

1920: *Pacem, Dei munus pulcherrimum* (On peace and Christian reconciliation), May 23.

Spiritus Paraclitus (On St. Jerome), September 15.

Principi Apostolorum Petro (On St. Ephrem the Syrian), October 5.

Annus iam plenus (On children of central Europe), December 1.

1921: *Sacra propediem* (On the Third Order of St. Francis), January 6.

In praeclara summorum (To professors and students of fine arts in Catholic institutions of learning: on Dante), April 30.

Fausto appetente die (On St. Dominic), June 29.

Pius XI

(1922-1939)

1922: *Ubi arcano Dei consilio* (On the peace of Christ in the Kingdom of Christ), December 23.

1923: *Rerum omnium perturbationem* (On St. Francis de Sales), January 26.

Studiorum Ducem (On St. Thomas Aquinas), June 29.

Ecclesiam Dei (On St. Josaphat), November 12.

1924: *Maximam gravissimamque* (To the bishops, clergy, and people of France: on French diocesan associations), January 18.

1925: *Quas primas* (On the feast of Christ the King), December 11.

1926: *Rerum Ecclesiae* (On Catholic missions), February 28.

Rite expiatis (On St. Francis of Assisi), April 30.

Iniquis afflictisque (On the persecution of the Church in Mexico), November 18.

1928: *Mortalium animos* (On religious unity), January 6.

Miserentissimus Redemptor (On reparation to the Sacred Heart), May 8.

Rerum Orientalium (On the promotion of Oriental Studies), September 8.

1929: *Mens Nostra* (On the promotion of Spiritual Exercises), December 20.

Quinquagesimo ante (On his sacerdotal jubilee), December 23.

Rappresentanti in terra (On Christian education), December 31. [Latin text, *Divini illius magistri*, published several months later with minor changes.]

1930: *Ad salutem* (On St. Augustine), April 20.

Casti connubii (On Christian Marriage), December 31.

1931: *Quadragesimo anno* (Commemorating the fortieth anniversary of Leo XIII's *Rerum novarum*: on reconstruction of the soical order), May 15.

Non abbiamo bisogno (On Catholic Action in Italy), June 29.

Nova impendet (On the economic crisis), October 2.

Lux veritatis (On the Council of Ephesus), December 25.

1932: *Caritate Christi compulsi* (On the Sacred Heart), May 3.

Acerba animi (To the bishops of Mexico: on persecution of the Church in Mexico), September 29.

1933: *Dilectissima Nobis* (To the bishops, clergy, and people of Spain: on oppression of the Church in Spain), June 3.

1935: *Ad Catholici sacerdotii* (On the Catholic priesthood), December 20.

1936: *Vigilanti cura* (To the bishops of the United States: on motion pictures), June 29.

1937: *Mit brennender Sorge* (To the bishops of Germany: on the Church and the German Reich), March 14.

Divini Redemptoris (On atheistic communism), March 19.

Nos es muy conocida (To the bishops of Mexico: on the religious situation in Mexico), March 28

Ingravescentibus malis (On the Rosary) September 29.

Pius XII

(1939-1958)

1939: *Summi Pontificatus* (On the unity of human society), October 20.

Sertum laetitiae (To the bishops of the United States: on the 150th anniversary of the establishment of the hierarchy in the United States), November 1.

1940: *Saeculo exeunte octavo* (To the bishops of Portugal and its colonies: on the eighth centenary of the independence of Portugal), June 13.

1943: *Mystici Corporis Christi* (On the Mystical Body of Christ), June 29.

Divino afflante Spiritu (On promoting biblical studies, commemorating the fiftieth anniversary of *Providentissimus Deus*), September 30.

1944: *Orientalis Ecclesiae* (On St. Cyril, Patriarch of Alexandria), April 9.

1945: *Communium interpretes dolorum* (To the bishops of the world: appealing for prayers for peace during May), April 15.

Orientales omnes Ecclesias (On the 350th anniversary of the reunion of the Ruthenian Church with the Apostolic See), December 23.

1946: *Quemadmodum* (Pleading for the care of the world's destitute children), January 6.

Deiparae Virginis Mariae (To all bishops: on the possibility of defining the Assumption of the Blessed Virgin Mary as a dogma of faith), May 1.

1947: *Fulgens radiatur* (On St. Benedict), March 21.

Mediator Dei (On the sacred liturgy), November 20.

Optatissima pax (Prescribing public prayers for social and world peace), December 18.

1948: *Auspicia quaedam* (On public prayers for world peace and solution of the problem of Palestine), May 1.

In multiplicibus curis (On prayers for peace in Palestine), October 24.

1949: *Redemptoris nostri cruciatus* (On the holy places in Palestine), April 15.

1950: *Anni Sacri* (On the program for combating atheistic propaganda throughout the world), March 12.

Summi maeroris (On public prayers for peace), July 19.

Humani generis (Concerning some false opinions threatening to undermine the foundations of Catholic doctrine), August 12.

Mirabile illud (On the crusade of prayers for peace), December 6.

1951: *Evangelii praecones* (On the promotion of Catholic missions), June 2.

Sempiternus Rex Christus (On the Council of Chalcedon), September 8.

Ingruentium malorum (On reciting the Rosary), September 15.

1952: *Orientales Ecclesias* (On the persecuted Eastern Church), December 15.

1953: *Doctor Mellifluus* (On St. Bernard of Clairvaux, the last of the fathers), May 24.

Fulgens corona (Proclaiming a Marian Year to commemorate the centenary of the definition of the dogma of the Immaculate Conception), September 8.

1954: *Sacra virginitas* (On consecrated virginity), March 25.

Ecclesiae fastos (To the bishops of Great Britain, Germany, Austria, France, Belgium, and Holland: on St. Boniface), June 5.

Ad Sinarum gentem (To the bishops, clergy, and people of China: on the supranationality of the Church), October 7.

Ad Caeli Reginam (Proclaiming the Queenship of Mary), October 11.

1955: *Musicae sacrae* (On sacred music), December 25.

1956: *Haurietis aquas* (On devotion to the Sacred Heart), May 15.

Luctuosissimi eventus (Urging public prayers for peace and freedom for the people of Hungary), October 28.

Laetamur admodum (Renewing exhortation for prayers for peace for Poland, Hungary, and especially for the Middle East), November 1.

Datis nuperrime (Lamenting the sorrowful events in Hungary and condemning the ruthless use of force), November 5.

1957: *Fidei donum* (On the present condition of the Catholic missions, especially in Africa), April 21.

Invicti athletae (On St. Andrew Bobola), May 16.

Le pelerinage de Lourdes (Warning against materialism on the centenary of the apparitions at Lourdes), July 2.

Miranda prorsus (On the communications field: motion picture, radio, television), September 8.

1958: *Ad Apostolorum Principis* (To the bishops of China; on Communism and the Church in China), June 29.

Meminisse iuvat (On prayers for persecuted Church), July 14.

Blessed John XXIII

(1958-1963)

1959: *Ad Petri Cathedram* (On truth, unity, and peace, in a spirit of charity), June 29.

Sacerdotii Nostri primordia (On St. John Vianney), August 1.

Grata recordatio (On the Rosary: prayer for the Church, missions, international and social problems), September 26.

Princeps Pastorum (On the missions, native clergy, lay participation), November 28.

1961: *Mater et Magistra* (On Christianity and social progress), May 15.

Aeterna Dei sapientia (On fifteenth centenary of the death of Pope St. Leo I: the see of Peter as the center of Christian unity), November 11.

1962: *Paenitentiam agere* (On the need for the practice of interior and exterior penance), July 1.

1963: *Pacem in terris* (On establishing universal

peace in truth, justice, charity, and liberty), April 11.

Paul VI

(1963-1978)

1964: *Ecclesiam Suam* (On the Church), August 6.

1965: *Mense maio* (On prayers during May for the preservation of peace), April 29.
Mysterium Fidei (On the Holy Eucharist), September 3.

1966: *Christi Matri* (On prayers for peace during October), September 15.

1967: *Populorum progressio* (On the development of peoples), March 26.
Sacerdotalis caelibatus (On the celibacy of the priest), June 24.

1968: *Humanae vitae* (On the regulation of birth), July 25.

John Paul II

(1978-)

1979: *Redemptor hominis* (On redemption and dignity of the human race), March 4

1980: *Dives in misericordia* (On the mercy of God), November 30.

1981: *Laborem exercens* (On human work), September 14.

1985: *Slavorum Apostoli* (Commemorating Sts. Cyril and Methodius, on the eleventh centenary of the death of St. Methodius), June 2.

1986: *Dominum et Vivificantem* (On the Holy Spirit in the life of the Church and the world), May 18.

1987: *Redemptoris Mater* (On the role of Mary in the mystery of Christ and her active and exemplary presence in the life of the Church), March 25.
Sollicitudo Rei Socialis (On social concerns, on the twentieth anniversary of *Populorum progressio*), December 30.

1991: *Redemptoris missio* (On the permanent validity of the Church's missionary mandate), January 22.
Centesimus annus (Commemorating the centenary of *Rerum novarum* and addressing the social question in a contemporary perspective), May 1.

1993: *Veritatis Splendor* (Regarding fundamental questions on the Church's moral teaching), August 6.

1995: *Evangelium Vitae* (On the value and inviolability of human life), March 25.
Ut Unum Sint (On commitment to ecumenism), May 25.

1998: *Fides et Ratio* (On Faith and Reason), October 1, 1998.

CANONIZATIONS BY LEO XIII AND HIS SUCCESSORS

Canonization (see entry in *Glossary*) is an infallible declaration by the pope that a person who suffered martyrdom and/or practiced Christian virtue to a heroic degree is in glory with God in heaven and is worthy of public honor by the universal Church and of imitation by the faithful.

Leo XIII

(1878-1903)

1881: Clare of Montefalco (d. 1308); John Baptist de Rossi (1698-1764); Lawrence of Brindisi (d. 1619).

1883: Benedict J. Labre (1748-1783).

1888: Seven Holy Founders of the Servite Order; Peter Claver (1581-1654); John Berchmans (1599-1621); Alphonsus Rodriguez (1531-1617).

1897: Anthony M. Zaccaria (1502-1539); Peter Fourier of Our Lady (1565-1640).

1900: John Baptist de La Salle (1651-1719); Rita of Cascia (1381-1457).

St. Pius X

(1903-1914)

1904: Alexander Sauli (1534-1593); Gerard Majella (1725-1755).

1909: Joseph Oriol (1650-1702); Clement M. Hofbauer (1751-1820).

Benedict XV

(1914-1922)

1920: Gabriel of the Sorrowful Mother (1838-1862); Margaret Mary Alacoque (1647-1690); Joan of Arc (1412-1431).

Pius XI

(1922-1939)

1925: Thérèse of Lisieux (1873-1897); Peter Canisius (1521-1597); Mary Magdalen Postel (1756-1846); Mary Magdalen Sophie Barat (1779-1865); John Eudes (1601-1680); John Baptist Vianney (Curé of Ars) (1786-1859).

1930: Lucy Filippini (1672-1732); Catherine Tomas (1533-1574); Jesuit North American Martyrs; Robert Bellarmine (1542-1621); Theophilus of Corte (1676-1740).

1931: Albert the Great (1206-1280) (equivalent canonization).

1933: Andrew Fournet (1752-1834); Bernadette Soubirous (1844-1879).

1934: Joan Antida Thouret (1765-1826); Mary Michaeli (1809-1865); Louise de Marillac

(1591-1660); Joseph Benedict Cottolengo (1786-1842); Pompilius M. Pirotti, priest (1710-1756); Teresa Margaret Redi (1747-1770); John Bosco (1815-1888); Conrad of Parzham (1818-1894).

1935: John Fisher (1469-1535); Thomas More (1478-1535).

1938: Andrew Bobola (1592-1657); John Leonardi (c. 1550-1609); Salvatore of Horta (1520-1567).

Pius XII

(1939-1958)

1940: Gemma Galgani (1878-1903); Mary Euphrasia Pelletier (1796-1868).

1943: Margaret of Hungary (d. 1270) (equivalent canonization).

1946: Frances Xavier Cabrini (1850-1917).

1947: Nicholas of Flüe (1417-1487); John of Britto (1647-1693); Bernard Realini (1530-1616); Joseph Cafasso (1811-1860); Michael Garicoits (1797-1863); Jeanne Elizabeth des Ages (1773-1838); Louis Marie Grignon de Montfort (1673-1716); Catherine Labouré (1806-1876).

1949: Jeanne de Lestonnac (1556-1640); Maria Josepha Rossello (1811-1880).

1950: Émily de Rodat (1787-1852); Anthony Mary Claret (1807-1870); Bartolomea Capitanio (1807-1833); Vincenza Gerosa (1784-1847) Jeanne de Valois (1461-1504); Vincenzo M. Strambi (1745-1824); Maria Goretti (1890-1902); Mariana Paredes of Jesus (1618-1645).

1951: Maria Domenica Mazzarello (1837-1881); Emilie de Vialar (1797-1856); Anthony M. Gianelli (1789-1846); Ignatius of Laconi (1701-1781); Francis Xavier Bianchi (1743-1815).

1954: Pope Pius X (1835-1914); Dominic Savio (1842-1857); Maria Crocifissa di Rosa (1813-1855); Peter Chanel (1803-1841); Gaspar del Bufalo (1786-1837); Joseph M. Pignatelli (1737-1811).

1958: Herman Joseph, O. Praem. (1150-1241) (equivalent canonization).

Blessed John XXIII

(1958-1963)

1959: Joaquina de Vedruna de Mas (1783-1854); Charles of Sezze (1613-1670).

1960: Gregory Barbarigo (1625-1697) (equivalent canonization); John de Ribera (1532-1611).

1961: Bertilla Boscardin (1888-1922).

1962: Martin de Porres (1579-1639); Peter Julian Eymard (1811-1868); Anthony Pucci, priest (1819-1892); Francis Mary of Camporosso (1804-1866).

1963: Vincent Pallotti (1795-1850).

Paul VI

(1963-1978)

1964: Charles Lwanga and Twenty-One Companions, Martyrs of Uganda (d. between 1885-1887).

1967: Benilde Romacon (1805-1862).

1969: Julia Billiart (1751-1816).

1970: Maria Della Dolorato Torres Acosta (1826-1887); Leonard Murialdo (1828-1900); Thérèse Couderc (1805-1885); John of Ávila (1499-1569); Nicholas Tavelic, Deodatus of Aquitaine, Peter of Narbonne, and Stephen of Cuneo, martyrs (d. 1391); Forty English and Welsh Martyrs (d. 16th century).

1974: Teresa of Jesus Jornet Ibars (1843-1897).

1975: Vicenta Maria Lopez y Vicuna (1847-1890); Elizabeth Ann Bayley Seton (1774-1821); John Masias (1585-1645); Oliver Plunket (1629-1681); Justin de Jacobis (1800-1860); John Baptist of the Conception (1561-1613).

1976: Beatrice da Silva (1424 or 1426-1490); John Ogilvie (1579-1615).

1977: Rafaela Maria Porras y Ayllon (1850-1925); John Nepomucene Neumann (1811-1860); Sharbel Makhlouf (1828-1898).

John Paul II

(1978-)

1982: Crispin of Viterbo (1668-1750); Maximilian Kolbe (1894-1941); Marguerite Bourgeoys (1620-1700); Jeanne Delanoue (1666-1736).

1983: Leopold Mandic (1866-1942).

1984: Paola Frassinetti (1809-1892); 103 Korean Martyrs (d. between 1839-1867); Miguel Febres Cordero (1854-1910).

1986: Francis Anthony Fasani (1681-1742); Giuseppe Maria Tomasi (1649-1713).

Pope John Paul II

1987: Giuseppe Moscati (d. 1927); Lawrence (Lorenzo) Ruiz and Fifteen Companions, Martyrs of Japan (d. 1630s).

1988: Eustochia Calafato (1434-1485); 117 Martyrs of Vietnam (96 Vietnamese, 11 Spanish, 10 French; included 8 bishops, 50 priests, 1 seminarian, 58 lay persons); Roque Gonzalez (1576-1628), Alfonso Rodriguez (1598-1628) and Juan de Castillo (1596-1628), Jesuit martyrs of Paraguay; Rose Philippine Duchesne (1796-1852); Simon de Rojas (1552-1624); Magdalen of Canossa (1774-1835); Maria Rosa Molas y Vollve (d. 1876).

1989: Clelia Barbieri (1847-1870); Gaspar Bertoni (1777-1853); Richard Pampuri, religious (1897-1930); Agnes of Bohemia (1211-1282); Albert Chmielowski (1845-1916); Mutien-Marie Wiaux (1841-1917).

1990: Marguerite D'Youville (1701-1777).

1991: Raphael (Jozef) Kalinowski (1835-1907).

1992: Claude La Colombiere (1641-1682); Ezequiel Moreno y Diaz (1848-1905).

1993: Marie of St. Ignatius (Claudine Thevenet) (1774-1837); Teresa "de los Andes" (Juana Fernandez Solar) (1900-1920); Enrique de Ossó y Cervelló (1840-1896).

1995: Jan Sarkander (1576-1620), Zdislava of Lemberk (d. 1252); Marek Krizin (1588-1619), Stefan Pongracz (1582-1619), Melichar Grodziecky (1584-1619), martyrs of Kosice; Eugene de Mazenod (1782-1861).

1996: Jean-Gabriel Perboyre (1802-1840), Juan Grande Roman (1546-1600) and Bro. Egidio Maria of St. Joseph (1729-1812).

1997: Hedwig (1371-1399); John Dukla, O.F.M. (d. 1484).

1998: Edith Stein (d. 1942).

1999: Marcellin Joseph Benoit Champagnat (1789-1840), Giovanni Calabria (1873-1954), Agostina Livia Pietrantonio (1864-1894), Sr. Kunegunda Kinga (1224-1292); Cirilo Bertrán and eight companion Brothers of the Christian Schools (d. October 9, 1934); Inocencio de la Immaculada (d. October 9, 1934); St. Jaime Hilario Barbal (1889-1937); Benedetto Menni (1841-1914); Tommaso da Cori (1655-1729).

2000: Mary Faustina Kowalska (1905-1938); Augustine Chao and Other Martyrs of China; María Josefa of the Heart of Jesus Sancho de Guerra (1842-1912); Cristóbal Magallanes and 24 Companions (d. 1915-1928); José Maria de Yermo y Parres (1851-1904); Maria de Jesús Sacramentado Venegas (1868-1959); Katherine Drexel (1858-1955); Josephine Bakhita (d. 1947).

2001: Luigi Scrosoppi (1804-1884); Agostino Roscelli (1818-1902); Bernardo da Corleone (1605-1667); Teresa Eustochio Verzeri (1801-1852); Rafqa Petra Choboq Ar-Rayes (1832-1914).

BEATIFICATIONS BY POPE JOHN PAUL II, 1979-2001

1979: Margarret Ebner (February 24); Francis Coll, O.P., Jacques Laval, S.S.Sp. (April 29); Enrique de Ossó y Cervelló (October 14).

1980: José de Anchieta, Peter of St. Joseph Betancur, Francois de Montmorency Laval, Kateri Tekakwitha, Marie Guyart of the Incarnation (June 22); Don Luigi Orione, Bartolomea Longo, Maria Anna Sala (October 26).

1981: Sixteen Martyrs of Japan (Lorenzo Ruiz and Companions) (February 18; canonized October 18, 1987); Maria Repetto, Alan de Solminihac, Richard Pampuri, Claudine Thevenet, Aloysius (Luigi) Scrosoppi (October 4).

1982: Peter Donders, C.SS.R., Marie Rose Durocher, Andre Bessette, C.S.C., Maria Angela Astorch, Marie Rivier (May 23); Fra Angelico (equivalent beatification) (July); Jeanne Jugan, Salvatore Lilli and 7 Armenian Companions (October 3); Sr. Angela of the Cross (November 5).

1983: Maria Gabriella Sagheddu (January 25); Luigi Versiglia, Callisto Caravario (May 15);

Ursula Ledochowska (June 20); Raphael (Jozef) Kalinowski, Bro. Albert (Adam Chmielowski), T.O.R. (June 22); Giacomo Cusmano, Jeremiah of Valachia, Domingo Iturrate Zubero (October 30); Marie of Jesus Crucified (Marie Bouardy) (November 13).

1984: Fr. William Repin and 98 Companions (Martyrs of Angers during French Revolution), Giovanni Mazzucconi (February 19); Marie Leonie Paradis (September 11); Federico Albert, Clemente Marchisio, Isidore of St. Joseph (Isidore de Loor), Rafaela Ybarra de Villalongo (September 30); José Manyanet y Vives, Daniel Brottier, C.S.Sp., Sr. Elizabeth of the Trinity (Elizabeth Catez) (November 25).

1985: Mercedes of Jesus (February 1); Ana de los Angeles Monteagudo (February 2); Pauline von Mallinckrodt, Catherine Troiani (April 14); Benedict Menni, Peter Friedhofen (June 23); Anwarite Nangapeta (August 15); Virginae Centurione Bracelli (September 22); Diego Luis de San Vitores, S.J., Jose M. Rubio y Peralta, S.J., Francisco Garate, S.J. (October 6); Titus Brandsma, O.Carm. (November 3); Pio Campidelli, C.P., Marie Teresa of Jesus Gerhardinger, Rafqa Ar-Rayes (November 17).

1986: Alphonsa Mattathupandatu of the Immaculate Conception, Kuriakose Elias Chavara (February 8); Antoine Chevrier (October 4); Teresa Maria of the Cross Manetti (October 19).

1987: Maria Pilar of St. Francis Borgia, Teresa of the Infant Jesus, Maria Angeles of St. Joseph, Cardinal Marcellis Spinola y Maestre, Emmanuel Domingo y Sol (March 29); Teresa of Jesus "de los Andes" (April 3); Edith Stein (Teresa Benedicta of the Cross) (May 1); Rupert Meyer, S.J. (May 3); Pierre-Francois Jamet, Cardinal Andrea Carlo Ferrari, Benedicta Cambiagio Frassinello, Louis Moreau (May 10); Carolina Kozka, Michal Kozal (June 10); George Matulaitis (Matulewicz) (June 28); Marcel Callo, Pierino Morosini, Antonia Mesina (October 4); Blandina Marten, Ulricke Nische, Jules Reche (Bro. Arnold) (November 1); 85 Martyrs (d. between 1584-1689) of England, Scotland and Wales (November 22).

1988: John Calabria, Joseph Nascimbeni (April 17); Pietro Bonilli, Kaspar Stangassinger, Francisco Palau y Quer, Savina Petrilli (April 24), Laura Vicuna (September 3); Joseph Gerard (September 11); Miguel Pro, Giuseppe Benedetto Dusmet, Francisco Faa di Bruno, Junipero Serra, Frederick Jansoone, Josefa Naval Girbes (September 25); Bernardo Maria Silvestrelli, Charles Houben, Honoratus Kozminski (October 16); Niels Stensen (Nicolaus Steno) (October 23); Katharine Drexel, 3 Missionary Martyrs of Ethiopia (Liberato Weiss, Samuel Marzorati, Michele Pio Fasoli) (November 20).

1989: Martin of Saint Nicholas, Melchior of St. Augustine, Mary of Jesus of the Good Shepherd, Maria Margaret Caiani, Maria of Jesus Siedliska, Maria Catherine of St. Augustine (April 23); Victoria Rasoamanarivo (April 30); Bro. Scubilionis (John Bernard Rousseau) (May 2); Elizabeth Renzi, Antonio Lucci (June 17); Niceforo de Jesus y Maria (Vicente Diez Tejerina and 25 Companions, martyred in Spain), Lorenzo Salvi, Gertrude Caterina Comensoli, Francisca Ana Cirer Carbonell (October 1); 7 Martyrs from Thailand (Philip Sipong, Sr. Agnes Phila, Sr. Lucia Khambang, Agatha Phutta, Cecilia Butsi, Bibiana Khampai, Maria Phon), Timothy Giaccardo, Mother Maria of Jesus Deluil-Martiny (October 22); Giuseppe Baldo (October 31).

1990: 9 Martyrs of Astoria during Spanish Civil War (De la Salle Brothers Cyrill Bertran, Marciano Jose, Julian Alfredo, Victoriano Pio, Benjamin Julian, Augusto Andres, Benito de Jesus, Aniceto Adolfo; and Passionist priest Innocencio Inmaculada), Mercedes Prat, Manuel Barbal Cosan (Brother Jaime), Philip Rinaldi (April 29); Juan Diego (confirmation of April 9 decree), 3 Child Martyrs (Cristobal, Antonio and Juan), Fr. Jose Maria de Yermo y Parres (May 6); Pierre Giorgio Frassati (May 20); Hanibal Maria Di Francia, Joseph Allamano (October 7); Marthe Aimee LeBouteiller, Louise Therese de Montaignac de Chauvance, Maria Schinina, Elisabeth Vendramini (November 4).

1991: Annunciata Cocchetti, Marie Therese Haze, Clara Bosatta (April 21); Jozef Sebastian Pelczar (June 2); Boleslava Lament (June 5); Rafael Chylinski (June 9); Angela Salawa (August 13); Edoardo Giuseppe Rosaz (July 14, Susa, Italy); Pauline of the Heart of Jesus in Agony Visentainer (October 18, Brazil); Adolph Kolping (October 27).

1992: Josephine Bakhita, Josemaria Escriva de Balaguer (May 17); Francesco Spinelli (June 21, Caravaggio, Italy); 17 Irish Martyrs, Rafael Arnáiz Barón, Nazaria Ignacia March Mesa, Léonie Françoise de Sales Aviat, and Maria Josefa Sancho de Guerra (September 27); 122 Martyrs of Spanish Civil War, Narcisa Martillo Morán (October 25); Cristóbal Magellanes and 24 Companions, Mexican Martyrs, and Maria de Jesús Sacramentado Venegas (November 22).

1993: Dina Belanger (March 20); John Duns Scotus (March 20, cult solemnly recognized); Mary Angela Truszkowska, Ludovico of Casoria, Faustina Kowalska, Paula Montal Fornés (April 18); Stanislaus Kazimierczyk (April 18, cult solemnly recognized); Maurice Tornay, Marie-Louise Trichet, Columba Gabriel and Florida Cevoli (May 16); Giuseppe Marello (September 26); Eleven Martyrs of Almeria, Spain, during Spanish Civil War (2 bishops, 7 brothers, 1 priest, 1 lay person); Victoria Diez y Bustos de Molina, Maria Francesca (Anna Maria) Rubatto; Pedro Castroverde, Maria Crucified (Elisabetta Maria) Satellico (October 10).

1994: Isidore Bakanja, Elizabeth Canori Mora; Dr. Gianna Beretta Molla (April 24); Nicolas Roland, Alberto Hurtado Cruchaga, Maria Rafols, Petra of St. Joseph Perez Florida; Josephine Vannini (October 16); Magdalena Caterina Morano (November 5); Hyacinthe Marie Cormier, Marie Poussepin, Agnes de Jesus Galand, Eugenia Joubert, Claudio Granzotto (November 20).

1995: Peter ToRot (January 17); Mother Mary

of the Cross MacKillop (January 19); Joseph Vaz (January 21); Rafael Guizar Valencia, Modestino of Jesus and Mary, Genoveva Torres Morales, Grimoaldo of the Purification (January 29); Johann Nepomuk von Tschiderer (April 30); Maria Helena Stollenwerk, Maria Alvarado Cordozo, Giuseppina Bonino, Maria Domenica Brun Barbantini, Agostino Roscelli (May 7); Damien de Veuster (June 4); 109 Martyrs (64 from French Revolution – Martyrs of La Rochelle – and 45 from Spanish Civil War), Anselm Polanco Fontecha, Felipe Ripoll Morata, and Pietro Casini (October 1); Mary Theresa Scherer, Maria Bernarda Butler and Marguerite Bays (October 29).

1996: Daniel Comboni and Guido Maria Conforti (March 17); Cardinal Alfredo Ildefonso Schuster, O.S.B., Filippo Smaldone and Gennaro Sarnelli (priests) and Candida Maria de Jesus Cipitria y Barriola, Maria Raffaella Cimatti, Maria Antonia Bandres (religious) (May 12), Bernhard Lichtenberg and Karl Leisner (June 23), Wincenty Lewoniuk and 12 Companions, Edmund Rice, Maria Ana Mogas Fontcuberta and Marcelina Darowska (Oct 6); Otto Neururer, Jakob Gapp and Catherine Jarrige (November 24).

1997: Bishop Florentino Asensio Barroso, Sr. Maria Encarnacion Rosal of the Sacred Heart, Fr. Gaetano Catanoso, Fr. Enrico Rebuschini and Ceferino Gimenez Malla, first gypsy beatified (May 4); Bernardina Maria Jablonska, Maria Karlowska (June 6); Frédéric Ozanam (August 22); Bartholomew Mary Dal Monte (September 27); Elías del Socorro Nieves, Domenico Lentini, Giovanni Piamarta, Emilie d'Hooghvorst, Maria Teresa Fasce (October 12); John Baptist Scalabrini, Vilmos Apor, María Vicenta of St. Dorothy Chávez Orozco (November 9).

1998: Bishop Vincent Bossilkov, María Sallés, Brigida of Jesus (March 15); Fr. Cyprian Tansi (March 22); Nimatullah al-Hardini, 11 Spanish nuns (May 10); Secondo Polla (May 23); Giovanni Maria Boccardo, Teresa Grillo Chavez, Teresa Bracco (May 24); Jakob Kern, Maria Restituta Kafka, and Anton Schwartz (June 21); Giuseppe Tovini (September 20); Cardinal Alojzije Stepinac (October 3); Antônio de Sant'Anna Galvão, Faustino Miguez, Zeferino Agostini, Mother Theodore Guérin (October 25).

1999: Vicente Soler, and six Augustinian Recollect Companions, Manuel Martin Sierra, Nicolas Barre, Anna Schaeffer (March 7); Padre Pio (May 2); Fr. Stefan Wincenty, Frelichowski (June 7); 108 Polish Martyrs, Regina Protmann, Edmund Bojanowski (June 13); Bishop Anton Slomsek (September 19); Ferdinando Maria Baccilieri, Edward Maria Joannes Poppe, Arcangelo Tadini, Mariano da Roccacasale, Diego Oddi, Nicola da Gesturi (October 3).

2000: André de Soveral, Ambrósio Francisco Ferro and 28 Companions, Nicolas Bunkerd Kitbamrung, Maria Stella Mardosewicz and 10 Companions, Pedro Calungsod and Andrew of Phú Yên (March 5); Mariano de Jesus Euse Hoyos, Francis Xavier Seelos, Anna Rosa Gattorno, Maria Elisabetta Hesselblad, Mariam Thresia Chiramel Mankidiyan (April 9); Jacinta and Francisco Marto of Fatima (May 13); Pope Pius IX, Pope John XXIII, Tommaso Reggio, Guillaume-Joseph Chaminade, Columba Marmion (September 3).

2001: José Aparicio Sanz and 232 Companions of the Spanish Civil War (March 11); Manuel Gonzalez Garcia, Marie-Anne Blondin, Caterina Volpicelli, Caterina Cittadini, Carlos Manuel Cecilio Rodriguez Santiago (April 29); George Preca, Ignatius Falzon, Maria Adeodata Pisani (May 9).

THE ROMAN CURIA

The Roman Curia is the Church's network of central administrative agencies (called dicasteries) serving the Vatican and the local churches, with authority granted by the Pope.

The Curia evolved gradually from advisory assemblies or synods of the Roman clergy with whose assistance the popes directed church affairs during the first eleven centuries. Its original office was the Apostolic Chancery, established in the fourth century to transmit documents. The antecedents of its permanently functioning agencies and offices were special commissions of cardinals and prelates. Its establishment in a form

resembling what it is now dates from the second half of the 16th century.

Pope Paul VI initiated a four-year reorganization study in 1963 which resulted in the constitution *Regimini Ecclesiae Universae*. The document was published August 18, 1967, and went into full effect in March 1968. Pope John Paul II, in the apostolic constitution *Pastor Bonus*, published June 28, 1988, and effective March 1, 1989, ordered modifications of the Curia based on the broad outline of Paul VI's reorganization.

In accordance with Pope John Paul II's reform effective March 1, 1989, and later revisions, the Curia consists of the Secretariat of State, nine congregations (governing agencies), three tribunals (judicial agencies), 11 councils (promotional agencies) and three offices (specialized service agencies). All have equal juridical status with authority granted by the pope.

SECRETARIAT OF STATE

The Secretariat of State provides the pope with the closest possible assistance in the care of the universal Church. It is administered by the Cardinal Secretary of State with the assistance of the Deputy for General Affairs and Secretary for Relations with States (both archbishops).

Background: Evolved gradually from secretarial offices (dating back to the 15th century) and the Congregation for Extraordinary Ecclesiastical Affairs (dating back to 1793; restructured as the Council for the Public Affairs of the Church by Paul VI in 1967). John Paul II gave it its present form in his June 28, 1988, reform of the Curia.

The Secretariat consists of two sections:

The Section for General Affairs assists the Pope in expediting daily business of the Holy See. It coordinates curial operations; prepares drafts of documents entrusted to it by the pope; has supervisory duties over the *Acta Apostolicae Sedis, Annuario Pontificio,* the Vatican Press Office, and the Central Statistics Office.

The Section for Relations with States (formerly the Council for Public Affairs of the Church, a separate body) handles diplomatic and other relations with civil governments. Attached to it is a Council of Cardinals and Bishops.

CONGREGATIONS

Congregation for the Doctrine of the Faith. The Congregation has responsibility to safeguard the doctrine of faith and morals. Accordingly, it examines doctrinal questions; promotes studies thereon; evaluates theological opinions and, when necessary and after prior consultation with concerned bishops, reproves those regarded as opposed to principles of the faith; examines books on doctrinal matters and can reprove such works, if the contents so warrant, after giving authors the opportunity to defend themselves. It examines matters pertaining to the Privilege of Faith (Petrine Privilege) in marriage cases, and safeguards the dignity of the sacrament of penance. Attached to the congregation are the Pontifical Biblical Commission and the Theological Commission.

Background: At the beginning of the 13th century, legates of Innocent III were commissioned as the Holy Office of the Inquisition to combat heresy; the same task was entrusted to

the Dominican Order by Gregory IX in 1231 and to the Friars Minor by Innocent IV from 1243 to 1254. On July 21, 1542 (apostolic constitution *Licet*), Paul III instituted a permanent congregation of cardinals with supreme and universal competence over matters concerning heretics and those suspected of heresy. Pius IV, St. Pius V, and Sixtus V further defined the work of the congregation. St. Pius X changed its name to the Congregation of the Holy Office. Paul VI (*motu proprio Integrae Servandae,* December 7, 1965) began reorganization of the Curia with this body, to which he gave the new title, Congregation for the Doctrine of the Faith. Its orientation is not merely negative, in the condemnation of error, but positive, in the promotion of orthodox doctrine.

Congregation for the Oriental Churches. The Congregation has competence in matters concerning the persons and discipline of Eastern Catholic Churches. It has jurisdiction over territories in which the majority of Christians belong to Eastern Churches (i.e., Egypt, the Sinai Peninsula, Eritrea, Northern Ethiopia, Southern Albania, Bulgaria, Cyprus, Greece, Iran, Iraq, Lebanon, Palestine, Syria, Jordan, Turkey, Afghanistan); also, over minority communities of Eastern Church members no matter where they live.

Background: Established by Pius IX January 6, 1862 (apostolic constitution *Romani Pontifices*), and united with the Congregation for the Propagation of the Faith. The congregation was made autonomous by Benedict XV May 1, 1917 (*motu proprio Dei Providentis*), and given wider authority by Pius XI March 25, 1938 (*motu proprio Sancta Dei Ecclesia*).

Congregation for Divine Worship and the Discipline of the Sacraments. The Congregation supervises everything pertaining to the promotion and regulation of the liturgy, primarily the sacraments, without prejudice to the competencies of the Congregation for the Doctrine of the Faith. Attached to the congregation are special commissions treating causes of nullity of sacred ordinations and dispensations from obligations of sacred ordination of deacons and priests.

Background: Originally two separate congregations: the Congregation for Divine Worship (instituted by Paul VI, May 8, 1969) and the Congregation for the Discipline of the Sacraments (established by St. Pius X, June 29, 1908, to replace the Congregation of Rites instituted by Pope Sixtus V in 1588). They were united by Paul VI, July 11, 1975, as the Congregation for the Sacraments and Divine Worship; reestablished as separate congregations by John Paul II in an autograph letter of April 5, 1984, and reunited anew by the same Pope, June 28, 1988 (apostolic constitution *Pastor Bonus*) as the Congregation for Divine Worship and the Discipline of the Sacraments.

Congregation for the Causes of Saints. The Congregation handles matters connected with beatification and canonization causes (in accordance with revised procedures decreed in 1983), and the preservation of relics.

Background: Established by Sixtus V in 1588 as the Congregation of Rites; affected by legislation of Pius XI in 1930; title changed and functions defined by Paul VI, 1969 (apostolic constitution *Sacra Rituum Congregatio*). It was restructured and canonization procedures were revised by John Paul II in 1983 (apostolic constitution *Divinus Perfectionis Magister*).

Congregation for Bishops. The Congregation has functions related in one way or another to bishops and the jurisdictions in which they serve. It supervises the Pontifical Commission for Latin America. Attached to the congregation are a central coordinating office for Military Vicars (established February 2, 1985) and an office for coordinating *ad limina* visits (established June 29, 1988).

Background: Established by Sixtus V January 22, 1588 (apostolic constitution *Immensa*); given an extension of powers by St. Pius X June 20, 1908, and Pius XII August 1, 1952 (apostolic constitution *Exsul Familia*); given present title (was known as Consistorial Congregation) by Paul VI (August 1, 1967); competencies redefined by John Paul II, June 28, 1988.

Congregation for the Evangelization of Peoples. The Congregation directs and coordinates missionary work throughout the world. Accordingly, it has competence over those matters which concern all the missions established for the spread of Christ's kingdom without prejudice to the competence of other congregations. These include: fostering missionary vocations; assigning missionaries to fields of work; establishing ecclesiastical jurisdictions and proposing candidates to serve them as bishops and in other capacities; encouraging the recruitment and development of indigenous clergy; mobilizing spiritual and financial support for missionary activity.

To promote missionary cooperation, the congregation has a Supreme Council for the Direction of Pontifical Missionary Works composed of the Missionary Union of the Clergy and Religious, the Society for the Propagation of the Faith, the Society of St. Peter the Apostle for Native Clergy, the Society of the Holy Childhood, and the International Center of Missionary Animation.

Background: Originated as a commission of cardinals by St. Pius V and Gregory XII for missions in East and West Indies, Italo-Greeks, and for ecclesiastical affairs in Protestant territories of Europe; Clement VIII instituted a Congregation of the Propagation of the Faith in 1599 which ceased to exist after several years. Erected as a stable congregation by Gregory XV June 22, 1622 (apostolic constitution *Inscrutabili Divinae*); its functions were redefined by John Paul II, June 28, 1988.

Congregation for the Clergy. The Congregation has three offices with competencies concerning the life, discipline, rights, and duties of the clergy; the preaching of the Word, catechetics, norms for religious education of children and adults; preservation and administration of the temporal goods of the Church. Attached to it are the International Council for Catechetics (established in 1973 by Paul VI) and the Institute *Sacrum Ministerium* for the permanent formation of the clergy (established in line with John Paul II's 1992 apostolic exhortation *Pastores Dabo Vobis*).

Background: Established by Pius IV August 2, 1564 (apostolic constitution *Alias Nos*), under the title Congregation of the Cardinals Interpreters of the Council of Trent; affected by legislation of Gregory XIII and Sixtus V; known as Congregation of the Council until August 15, 1967, when Paul VI renamed it the Congregation for the Clergy and redefined its competency; John Paul II gave it added responsibilities June 28, 1988.

Congregation for Institutes of Consecrated Life and Societies of Apostolic Life. The Congregation has competence over institutes of religious, secular institutes, societies of the apostolic life, and third (secular) orders. With two sections, the congregation has authority in matters related to the establishment, general direction and suppression of the various institutes; general discipline in line with their rules and constitutions; the movement toward renewal and adaptation of institutes in contemporary circumstances; the setting up and encouragement of councils and conferences of major religious superiors for intercommunication and other purposes.

Background: Founded by Sixtus V May 27, 1586, with the title Congregation for Consultations of Regulars; confirmed by the apostolic constitution *Immensa* January 22, 1588; made part of the Congregation for Consultations of Bishops and other Prelates in 1601; made autonomous by St. Pius X in 1908 as Congregation of Religious; title changed to Congregation for Religious and Secular Institutes by Paul VI in 1967; given present title by John Paul II, June 28, 1988.

Congregation for Catholic Education (for Seminaries and Institutes of Study)

The Congregation has supervisory competence over institutions and works of Catholic education. It carries on its work through three offices. One office handles matters connected with the direction, discipline and temporal administration of seminaries, and with the education of diocesan clergy, religious and members of secular institutes. A second office oversees Catholic universities, faculties of study and other institutions of higher learning inasmuch as they depend on the authority of the Church; encourages cooperation and mutual assistance among Catholic institutions, and the establishment of Catholic hospices and centers on campuses of non-Catholic institutions. A third office is concerned in various ways with all Catholic schools below the college-university level, with general questions concerning education and studies, and with the cooperation of conferences of bishops and civil authorities in educational matters. The congregation supervises Pontifical Works for Priestly Vocations.

Background: The title (Congregation of Seminaries and Universities) and functions of the congregation were defined by Benedict XV November 4, 1915; Pius XI, in 1931 and 1932, and Pius XII, in 1941 and 1949, extended its functions; Paul VI changed its title to Congregation for Catholic Education in 1967; given its present title by Pope John Paul II, June 28, 1988. Its work had previously been carried on by two other congregations erected by Sixtus V in 1588 and Leo XII in 1824.

Inter-Agency Curia Commissions

In accordance with provisions of the apostolic constitution *Pastor Bonus,* John Paul II established the following interdepartmental permanent commissions to handle matters when more than one agency of the Curia is involved in activities:

• For matters concerning appointments to local Churches and the setting up and alteration of them and their constitution (March 22, 1989). Members include officials of the Secretariat of State and Congregation for Bishops.

• For matters concerning members, individually or as a community, of Institutes of Consecrated Life founded or working in mission territories (March 22, 1989). Members include officials of the Congregations for the Evangelization of Peoples and for Institutes of Consecrated Life and Societies of Apostolic Life.

• For the formation of candidates for Sacred Orders (March 22, 1989). Members include officials of the Congregations for Catholic Education, for Institutes of Consecrated Life and Societies of Apostolic Life, for Evangelization of Peoples, for Oriental Churches.

• For promoting a more equitable distribution of priests throughout the world (July 20, 1991). Members include secretaries of congregations for Evangelization of Peoples, for the Clergy, Catholic Education, for the Institutes of Consecrated Life and Societies of Apostolic Life; and vice-president of Commission for Latin America.

• For the Church in Eastern Europe (January 15, 1993), replacing the Pontifical Commission for Russia which was terminated. The commission is concerned with both Latin and Eastern-rite churches in territories of the former Soviet Union and other nations affected by the historical circumstances resulting from atheistic communism. It is responsible for promoting the apostolic mission of the Church and fostering ecumenical dialogue with the Orthodox and other Churches of the Eastern tradition. Members, under presidency of Cardinal Secretary of State, include the secretary and undersecretary of the Section for Relations with States and secretaries of Congregations for the Oriental Churches, for the Clergy, for Institutes of Consecrated Life and Societies of Apostolic Life, secretary of the Pontifical Council for Promoting Christian Unity.

TRIBUNALS

Apostolic Penitentiary. The Penitentiary has jurisdiction for the internal forum only (sacramental and non-sacramental). It issues decisions on questions of conscience; grants absolutions, dispensations, commutations, sanations and condonations; has charge of non-doctrinal matters pertaining to indulgences.

It is under the direction of a Cardinal serving as major penitentiary; he is assisted by an archbishop serving as regent.

Background: Origin dates back to the twelfth century; affected by the legislation of many popes; radically reorganized by St. Pius V in 1569; jurisdiction limited to the internal forum by St. Pius X; Benedict XV annexed the Office of Indulgences to it March 25, 1917.

Apostolic Signatura. The supreme court of the Church, its principal concerns are to resolve questions concerning juridical procedure and to supervise the observance of laws and rights at the highest level. It decides the jurisdictional competence of lower courts and has jurisdiction in cases involving personnel and decisions of the Rota. It is the supreme court of the State of Vatican City.

Background: A permanent office of the Signatura has existed since the time of Eugene IV in the 15th century; affected by the legislation of many popes; reorganized by St. Pius X in 1908 and made the supreme tribunal of the Church.

Roman Rota. The ordinary court of appeal for cases appealed to the Holy See, the Rota is best known for its competence and decisions in cases involving the validity of marriage. It is headed by a dean.

Background: Originated in the Apostolic Chancery; affected by the legislation of many popes; reorganized by St. Pius X in 1908; further revised by Pius XI in 1934; new norms approved and promulgated by John Paul II in 1982 and 1987.

PONTIFICAL COUNCILS

Pontifical Council for the Laity. The Council has competence over the apostolate of the laity and their participation in the life and mission of the Church. Members are mostly lay people from different parts of the world and involved in different apostolates.

Background: Established on an experimental basis by Paul VI January 6, 1967; given permanent status December 10, 1976 (*motu proprio Apostolatus Peragendi*).

Pontifical Council for Promoting Christian Unity. The Council handles relations with members of other Christian ecclesial communities; deals with the correct interpretation and execution of the principles of ecumenism; initiates or promotes Catholic ecumenical groups and coordinates on national and international levels the efforts of those promoting Christian unity; undertakes dialogue regarding ecumenical questions and activities with churches and ecclesial communities separated from the Apostolic See; sends Catholic observer-representatives to Christian gatherings, and invites to Catholic gatherings observers of other churches; orders into execution conciliar decrees dealing with ecumenical affairs. The Commission for Religious Relations with the Jews is attached to the secretariat.

Background: Established by John XXIII June 5, 1960, as a preparatory secretariat of the Second Vatican Council; raised to commission status during the first session of the council in the fall of 1962; status as a secretariat confirmed and functions defined by Paul VI in 1966 and 1967; made a pontifical council by John Paul II, June 28, 1988.

Pontifical Council for the Family. The Council is concerned with promoting the pastoral care of families so they may carry out their educative, evangelizing, and apostolic mission and make their influence felt in areas such as defense of human life and responsible procreation according to the teachings of the Church. Members, chosen by the Pope, are married couples and men and women from all parts of the world and representing different cultures. They meet in general assembly at least once a year.

Background: Instituted by John Paul II May 9, 1981, replacing the Committee for the Family established by Paul VI January 11, 1973.

Pontifical Council for Justice and Peace. The Council's primary competence is to promote justice and peace in the world according to the Gospels and social teaching of the Church.

Background: Instituted by Paul VI January 6, 1967, on an experimental basis; reconstituted and made a permanent commission December 10, 1976; its competence was redefined and it was made a pontifical council June 28, 1988, by John Paul II.

Pontifical Council "*Cor Unum*." The Council's principal aims are to provide informational and coordinating services for Catholic aid and human development organizations and projects on a worldwide scale. Attached to the council are the John Paul II Foundation for the Sahel and *"Populorum Progressio."*

Background: Instituted by Paul VI July 15, 1971.

Pontifical Council for Pastoral Care of Migrants and Itinerant Peoples. The Council is concerned with pastoral assistance to migrants, nomads, tourists, sea and air travelers.

Background: Instituted by Paul VI and placed under general supervision of Congregation for Bishops, March 19, 1970; made autonomous as a pontifical council and renamed by John Paul II, June 28, 1988.

Pontifical Council for Pastoral Assistance to Health Care Workers. The Council's functions are to stimulate and foster the work of formation, study and action carried out by various international Catholic organizations in the health care field.

Background: Established in 1985 as a commission by John Paul II; made a council June 28, 1988.

Pontifical Council for the Interpretation of Legislative Texts. The Council's primary function is the authentic interpretation of the universal laws of the Church.

Background: Established by John Paul II, January 2, 1984, as the Pontifical Commission for the Authentic Interpretation of the Code of Canon Law; name changed and given additional functions June 28, 1988. Its competency was extended in 1991 to include interpretation of Code of Canon Law of Oriental Church which was promulgated in 1990.

Pontifical Council for Interreligious Dialogue. The Council's function is to promote studies and dialogue for the purpose of increasing mutual understanding and respect between Christians and non-Christians. The Commission for Religious Relations with Muslims is attached to the council.

Background: Established by Paul VI May 19, 1964, as the Secretariat for Non-Christians; given present title and functions by John Paul II, June 28, 1988.

Pontifical Council for Culture. The Council's functions are to foster the Church's and the Holy See's relations with the world of culture and to establish dialogue with those who do not believe in God or who profess no religion provided they are open to sincere cooperation. It consists of two sections: (1) faith and culture; (2) dialogue with cultures. Attached to it is the Coordinating Council for Pontifical Academies.

Background: Present council with expanded functions was instituted by John Paul II (*motu proprio* of March 25, 1993) through the merger of the Pontifical Council for Culture (established May 20, 1982, by John Paul II) and the Pontifical Council for Dialogue with Non-Believers (established by Paul VI April 9, 1965, as the secretariat for Non-Believers).

Pontifical Council for Social Communications. The Council is engaged in matters pertaining to instruments of social communication so that through them the message of salvation and human progress is fostered and carried forward in civil culture and mores.

Background: Instituted on an experimental basis by Pius XII in 1948; reorganized three times in the 1950s; made permanent commission by John XXIII February 22, 1959; established as council and functions restated by John Paul II June 28, 1988.

OFFICES

Apostolic Camera. The Apostolic Chamber administers the temporal goods and rights of the Holy See between the death of one pope and the election of another, in accordance with special laws. It is headed by the chamberlain of the Holy Roman Church, a Cardinal termed the *Camerlengo*, who remains in office (with the Grand Penitentiary) during the *sede vacante* between the death of a pontiff and the election by conclave of his successor.

Background: Originated in the eleventh century; reorganized by Pius XI in 1934; functions redefined (especially of camerlengo) by subsequent legislation in 1945, 1962, and 1975.

Administration of the Patrimony of the Apostolic See. The APSA handles the estate of the Apostolic See under the direction of papal del-

egates acting with ordinary or extraordinary authorization.

Background: Some of its functions date back to 1878; established by Paul VI August 15, 1967.

Prefecture for the Economic Affairs of the Holy See. A financial office, the Prefecture coordinates and supervises administration of the temporalities of the Holy See. Membership includes Cardinal Roger M. Mahony.

Background: Established by Paul VI August 15, 1967; functions redefined by John Paul II June 28, 1988.

Other Curia Agencies

Prefecture of the Papal Household. The Prefecture oversees the papal chapel — which is at the service of the pope in his capacity as spiritual head of the Church — and the pontifical family — which is at the service of the pope as a sovereign. It arranges papal audiences, has charge of preparing non-liturgical elements of papal ceremonies, makes all necessary arrangements for papal visits and trips outside the Vatican, and settles questions of protocol connected with papal audiences and other formalities. The office is headed by a Prefect.

Background: Established by Paul VI August 15, 1967, under the title, Prefecture of the Apostolic Palace; it supplanted the Sacred Congregation for Ceremonies founded by Sixtus V January 22, 1588. The office was updated and reorganized under the present title by Paul VI, March 28, 1968.

Office for Liturgical Celebrations of the Supreme Pontiff. Prepares everything necessary for liturgical and other sacred celebrations by the Pope or in his name; directs everything in accordance with prescriptions of liturgical law. The office is headed by a Master of Ceremonies.

Background: Evolved gradually from the early office of Apostolic Master of Ceremonies; affected by legislation of Pope Paul IV in 1563 and Benedict XV in 1917; restructured by Paul VI in 1967; given its present title (formerly known as Prefecture of Pontifical Ceremonies) and con-

Rare Vatican Stamps

stituted as an autonomous agency of the Roman Curia by John Paul II, June 28, 1988.

Vatican Press Office. Established February 29, 1968, the office replaced service agencies formerly operated by *L'Osservatore Romano* and an office created for press coverage of the Second Vatican Council. New directives were issued in 1986.

Vatican Information Service (VIS). Established March 28, 1990, within the framework but distinct from the Vatican Press Office, the Service furnishes information, in English, French and Spanish, on pastoral and magisterial activity of the Pope through electronic mail and fax.

Central Statistics Office. Established by Paul VI August 15, 1967, the Office is attached to the Secretariat of State. Compiles, systematizes and analyzes information on the status and condition of the Church.

COMMISSIONS AND COMMITTEES

Listed below are non-curial institutes which assist in the work of the Holy See. Some are attached to curial agencies, as indicated.

Pontifical Commission for the Cultural Heritage of the Church: Established by John Paul II, June 28, 1988, as Pontifical Commission for Preserving the Church' s Patrimony of Art and History and attached to the Congregation for the Clergy; made autonomous and given present title March 25, 1993.

Pontifical Commission for Sacred Archeology: Instituted by Pius IX Jan, 6, 1852.

Pontifical Biblical Commission: Instituted by Leo XIII October 30, 1902; completely restructured by Paul VI June 27, 1971; attached to the Congregation for the Doctrine of the Faith. The Cardinal Prefect for the Doctrine of the Faith is president.

Pontifical Commission for Latin America: Instituted by Pius XII April 19, 1958; attached to the Congregation for Bishops July, 1969; restructured by John Paul II in 1988. The Prefect of the Congregation for Bishops is president.

Pontifical Commission for the Revision and Emendation of the Vulgate: Established in 1984 by John Paul II to replace the Abbey of St. Jerome instituted by Pius XI in 1933.

Pontifical Commission *"Ecclesia Dei"*: Established by John Paul II July 2, 1988, to facilitate the return to full ecclesial communion of priests, seminarians and religious who belonged to the fraternity founded by Marcel Lefebvre.

International Theological Commission: Instituted by Paul VI April 11, 1969, as an advisory adjunct of no more than 30 theologians to the Congregation for the Doctrine of the Faith; definitive statutes promulgated by John Paul II, August 6, 1982.

Commission for Religious Relations with the Jews: Instituted by Paul VI, October 22, 1974, to promote and foster relations of a religious nature between Jews and Christians; attached to the Council for Promoting Christian Unity.

Commission for Religious Relations with Muslims: Instituted by Paul VI, October 22, 1974, to promote, regulate and interpret relations between Catholics and Muslims; attached to the Council for Interreligious Dialogue. The head of the Council for Interreligious Dialogue is president.

Pontifical Committee for International Eucharistic Congresses: Instituted 1879, by Pope Leo XIII; established as a pontifical committee with new statutes by John Paul II, February 11, 1986.

Pontifical Committee for Historical Sciences: Instituted by Pius XII April 7, 1954, as a continuation of a commission dating from 1883.

Vatican II Archives: Preserves the documents of the Second Vatican Council.

Disciplinary Commission of the Roman Curia: A Commission to oversee the discipline of the members of the Curia.

Council of Cardinals for Study of Organizational and Economic Problems of the Holy See: Council established in 1981 by Pope John Paul II; composed of approximately 15 cardinals from countries throughout the world to maintain vigilance over the financial challenges facing the Holy See.

Commission for the Protection of the Historical and Artistic Monuments of the Holy See: Instituted by Pius XI in 1923, reorganized by Paul VI in 1963.

Institute for Works of Religion: The so-called Vatican Bank, the Institute was established by Pius XII June 27, 1942, to bank and administer funds for works of religion; replaced an earlier administration established by Leo XIII in 1887; reorganized by John Paul II (chirograph, or papal decree, of March 1, 1990).

Fabric of St. Peter: Administration, care and preservation of Vatican Basilica. The Fabric is headed the Cardinal Archpriest of the Patriarchal Vatican Basilica.

Office of Papal Charities (Apostolic Almoner): Distributes alms and aid to those in need in the name of the Pope.

Labor Office of the Apostolic See (ULSA - *Ufficio del Lavoro della Sede Apostolica*): The office has competence in regard to those who work for the Apostolic See; charged with settling labor issues. Instituted by John Paul II (*motu proprio* of January 1, 1989); functions reaffirmed and definitive text of statutes approved by John Paul II (*motu proprio* of September 30, 1994).

VATICAN CITY STATE

The State of Vatican City (*Stato della Città del Vaticano*) is the territorial seat of the papacy. The smallest sovereign state in the world, it is situated within the city of Rome, embraces an area of 108.7 acres, and includes within its limits the Vatican Palace, museums, art galleries, gardens, libraries, radio station, post office, bank, astronomical observatory, offices, apartments, service facilities, St. Peter's Basilica, and neighboring buildings between the Basilica and Viale Vaticano. The extraterritorial rights of Vatican City extend to more than 10 buildings in Rome, including the major basilicas and office buildings of various congregations of the Roman Curia, and to the papal villas at **Castel Gandolfo** 15 miles southeast of the City of Rome. Castel Gandolfo is the summer residence of the Holy Father.

The government of Vatican City is in the hands of the reigning pope, who has full executive, legislative and judicial power. The administration of affairs, however, is handled by the **Pontifical Commission for the State of Vatican City** under Cardinal Edmund Casimir Szoka. The legal system is based on Canon Law; in cases where this code does not obtain, the laws of the City of Rome apply. The City is an absolutely neutral state and enjoys all the rights and privileges of a sovereign power. The citizens of Vatican City, and they alone, owe allegiance to the pope as a temporal head of state.

Cardinals of the Roman Curia residing outside Vatican City enjoy the privileges of extraterritoriality. The Secretary General for the Governatorate of the Vatican City State administers the affairs of the city state.

The normal population is approximately 1,000. While the greater percentage is made up of priests and religious, there are several hundred lay persons living in Vatican City. They are housed in their own apartments in the City and are engaged in secretarial, domestic, trade and service occupations. About 3,400 lay persons are employed by the Vatican.

Services of honor and order are performed by the Swiss Guards, who have been charged with responsibility for the personal safety of popes since 1506. Additional police and ceremonial functions are under the supervision of a special office. These functions were formerly handled by the Papal Gendarmes, the Palatine Guard of Honor, and the Guard of Honor of the Pope (Pontifical Noble Guard) which Pope Paul VI disbanded September 14, 1970.

The **Basilica of St. Peter**, built between 1506 and 1626, is the largest church in Christendom (with the exception of the Basilica of Our Lady Queen of Peace in Ivory Coast) and the site of most papal ceremonies. The pope's own patriarchal basilica, however, is St. John Lateran, whose origins date back to 324.

St. Ann's, staffed by Augustinian Fathers, is the parish church of Vatican City. Its pastor is appointed by the pope following the recommendation of the prior general of the Augustinians and the archpriest of the Vatican Basilica.

The Church of Santa Susanna was designated as the national church for Americans in Rome by Pope Benedict XV January 10, 1922, and entrusted to the Paulist Fathers, who have served there continuously since then except for several years during World War II.

Pastoral care in Vatican City State, which is separate from the diocese of Rome, is entrusted to the archpriest of St. Peter's Basilica, who is also vicar general for Vatican City and the papal villas at Castel Gandolfo (chirograph of Pope John Paul II, January 14, 1991). Cardinal Virgilio Noè was appointed to the posts, July 1, 1991.

The Vatican Library (00120 Vatican City) is oe of the most famous collections anywhere in the world. It has among its holdings 150,000 manuscripts, about 1,000,000 printed books, and 7,500 incunabula. The **Vatican Secret Archives** containing central church documents dating back to the time of Innocent III (1198-1216), was opened to scholars by Leo XIII in 1881, contain central church documents dating back to the time of Innocent III (1198-1216). The Library is headed by the librarian and archivist of the Holy Roman Church.

The independent temporal power of the pope, which is limited to the confines of Vatican City and small areas outside, was for many centuries more extensive than it is now. As late as the nineteenth century, the pope ruled 16,000 square miles of Papal States across the middle of Italy, with a population of over 3,000,000. In 1870 forces of the Kingdom of Italy occupied these lands which, with the exception of the small areas surrounding the Vatican and Lateran in Rome and the Villas of Castel Gandolfo, became part of the Kingdom by Italian law on May 13, 1871.

The **Roman Question**, occasioned by this seizure and the voluntary confinement of the pope to the Vatican, was settled with ratification of the Lateran Agreement June 7, 1929, by the Italian government and Vatican City. The agreement recognized Catholicism as the religion of Italy and provided, among other things, a financial indemnity to the Vatican in return for the former Papal States; it became Article 7 of the Italian Constitution March 26, 1947.

The Lateran Agreement was superseded by a new concordat given final approval by the Italian Chamber of Deputies March 20 and formally ratified June 3, 1985.

Papal Flag

The papal flag consists of two equal vertical stripes of yellow and white, charged with the insignia of the papacy on the white stripe — triple crown or tiara over two crossed keys, one of gold and one of silver, tied with a red cord and two tassels. The divisions of the crown represent the teaching, sanctifying, and ruling offices of the pope. The keys symbolize his jurisdictional authority.

The papal flag is a national flag inasmuch as it is the standard of the Supreme Pontiff as the sovereign of the state of Vatican City. It is also universally accepted by the faithful as a symbol of the supreme spiritual authority of the Holy Father.

Vatican Radio

The declared purpose of Vatican Radio Station HVJ is "that the voice of the Supreme Pastor may be heard throughout the world by means of the ether waves, for the glory of Christ and the salvation of souls." Designed by Guglielmo Marconi, the inventor of radio, and supervised by him until his death, the station was inaugurated by Pope Pius XI in 1931. The original purpose has been extended to a wide variety of programming.

Vatican Radio operates on international wave lengths, transmits programs in 37 languages, and serves as a channel of communication between the Vatican, church officials, and listeners in general in many parts of the world. The station broadcasts about 400 hours a week throughout the world.

The daily English-language program for North America is broadcast on 6095, 7305, 9600 kilohertz as well as via satellite INTELSAT 325,5° East (Atlantic) — 4097.75 Mhz — LHCP polarization.

Frequencies, background information, and audio files can be obtained via the world wide web homepages www.wrn.org/vatican-radio and www.vatican.va.

The staff of 415 broadcasters and technicians includes 30 Jesuits. Studios and offices are at Palazzo Pio, Piazza Pia, 3, 00193 Rome. The transmitters are situated at Santa Maria di Galeria, a short distance north of Rome.

Vatican Television

Vatican Television Center (*Centro Televisivo Vaticano*, CTV), Palazzo Belvedere, 00120 Vatican City: Instituted by John Paul II October 23, 1983, with the rescript, *Ex Audentia.*

Vatican Web Site

Vatican Web Site. The Holy See manages its own extensive web site. The site offers links to the biographies of the popes, offices of the Curia, the Vatican City State, and the Vatican Museum. The Holy See also offers a daily Internet news servive via the VIS (Vatican Information Service). The address for the site is www.vatican.va.

Vatican Stamps and Coins

The Vatican Philatelic and Numismatic Office (00120 Vatican City) issues a variety of stamps and coins each year. These include stamps, postal stationery, postcards, the publication *Vaticano 2000* and coins. The coins are issued in assorted values (e.g., L. 10, 20, 50, 100, 200, 500, 1,000 two metal, 1,000 — silver) and with specific subjects. There are also gold coins, and celebrative L. 500 and 2000 silver coins with subjects.

Papal Audiences

General audiences are scheduled weekly, on Wednesday.

In Vatican City, they are held in the Audience Hall on the south side of St. Peter's Basilica or, weather permitting, in St. Peter's Square. The hall, which was opened in 1971, has a seating capacity of 6,800 and a total capacity of 12,000. Audiences have been held during the summer at Castel Gandolfo when the pope is there on a working vacation.

General audiences last from about 60 to 90 minutes, during which the pope gives a talk and his blessing. A résumé of the talk, which is usually in Italian, is given in several languages. Arrangements for papal audiences are handled by an office of the Prefecture of the Apostolic Household.

American visitors can obtain passes for general audiences by applying to the Bishops' Office for United States Visitors to the Vatican, Casa Santa Maria, Via dell'Umilita, 30, 00187 Rome. Private and group audiences are reserved for dignitaries of various categories and for special occasions.

Publishing Activities

Vatican Press, 00120 Vatican City: The official printing plant of the Vatican. The Vatican press was conceived by Marcellus II and Pius IV but was actually founded by Sixtus V on April 27, 1587, to print the Vulgate and the writings of the Fathers of the Church and other authors. A Polyglot Press was established in 1626 by the Congregation for the Propagation of the Faith to serve the needs of the Oriental Church. St. Pius X merged both presses under the title Vatican Polyglot Press. It was renamed Vatican Press July 1, 1991, by John Paul II following restructuring. The plant has facilities for the printing of a wide variety of material in about 30 languages.

Vatican Publishing House (*Libreria Editrice Vaticana*), Piazza S. Pietro, 00120 Vatican City: Formerly an office of the Vatican Press to assist in the circulation of the liturgical and juridical publications of the Apostolic See, the congregations and later the *Acta Apostolicae Sedis*. In 1926, with the expansion of publishing activities and following the promulgation of the 1917 Code, the office was made an independent entity. An administrative council and editorial commission were instituted in 1983; in 1988 the papal document *Pastor Bonus*, which launched a reform of the Curia, listed it among institutes joined to the Holy See; new statutes were approved by the Secretariat of State July 1, 1991.

The Holy See each year issues several important publications:

Acta Apostolicae Sedis, 00120 Vatican City: The only "official commentary" of the Holy See; was established in 1908 for the publication of activities of the Holy See, laws, decrees and acts of congregations and tribunals of the Roman Curia. The first edition was published in January, 1909. St. Pius X made AAS an official organ in 1908. Laws promulgated for the Church ordinarily take effect three months after the date of their publication in this commentary. The publication, mostly in Latin, is printed by the Vatican Press. The immediate predecessor of this organ was *Acta Sanctae Sedis*, founded in 1865 and given official status by the Congregation for the Propagation of the Faith in 1904.

Annuario Pontificio, 00120 Vatican City: The yearbook of the Holy See. It is edited by the Central Statistics Office of the Church and is printed in Italian, with some portions in other languages, by the Vatican Press. It covers the worldwide organization of the Church, lists members of the hierarchy, and includes a wide range of statistical information. The publication of a statistical yearbook of the Holy See dates back to 1716, when a volume called *Notizie* appeared. Publication under the present title began in 1860, was suspended in 1870, and resumed again in 1872 under the title *Catholic Hierarchy*. This volume

was printed privately at first, but has been issued by the Vatican Press since 1885. The title *Annuario Pontificio* was restored in 1912, and the yearbook was called an "official publication" until 1924.

L'Osservatore Romano, Via del Pellegrino, 00120 Vatican City: The daily newspaper of the Holy See. It began publication July 1, 1861, as an independent enterprise under the ownership and direction of four Catholic laymen headed by Marcantonio Pacelli, vice minister of the interior under Pope Pius IX and a grandfather of the late Pius XII. Leo XIII bought the publication in 1890, making it the "pope's" own newspaper.

The only official material in *L'Osservatore Romano* is that which appears under the heading, "*Nostre Informazioni*." This includes notices of appointments by the Holy See, the texts of papal encyclicals and addresses by the Holy Father and others, various types of documents, accounts of decisions and rulings of administrative bodies, and similar items. Additional material includes news and comment on developments in the Church and the world. Italian is the language most used. A staff of about 15 reporters covers Rome news sources. A corps of correspondents provides foreign coverage.

A weekly roundup edition in English was inaugurated in 1968. Other weekly editions are printed in French (1949), Italian (1950), Spanish (1969), Portuguese (1970) and German (1971). The Polish edition (1980) is published monthly. *L'Osservatore della Domenica* is published weekly as a supplement to the Sunday issue of the daily edition.

Activities of the Holy See: An annual documentary volume covering the activities of the pope and of the congregations, commissions, tribunals and offices of the Roman Curia.

Statistical Yearbook of the Church: Issued by the Central Statistics Office of the Church, it contains principal data concerning the presence and work of the Church in the world. The first issue was published in 1972 under the title *Collection of Statistical Tables, 1969*. It is printed in corresponding columns of Italian and Latin. Some of the introductory material is printed in other languages.

DIPLOMATIC ACTIVITIES OF THE HOLY SEE

The Holy See enjoys diplomatic relations with countries throughout the entire world. Its diplomatic activities are centered on advancing the concerns of the Holy See in matters of peace, justice, and charity. Papal representatives serve

as a direct representative of the Supreme Pontiff to the Church in the countries to which they are assigned. They also are always in the forefront of promoting peace and safeguarding the value of life.

REPRESENTATIVES OF THE HOLY SEE

Representatives of the Holy See and their functions were the subject of a document entitled *Sollicitudo Omnium Ecclesiarum* which Pope Paul VI issued on his own initiative under the date of June 24, 1969.

Delegates and Nuncios

Papal representatives "receive from the Roman Pontiff the charge of representing him in a fixed way in the various nations or regions of the world. "When their legation is only to local churches, they are known as apostolic delegates. When to this legation, of a religious and ecclesial nature, there is added diplomatic legation to states and governments, they receive the title of nuncio, pro-nuncio, and internuncio." An apostolic nuncio has the diplomatic rank of ambassador extraordinary and plenipotentiary. Traditionally, because the diplomatic service of the Holy See has the longest uninterrupted history in the world, a nuncio has precedence among diplomats in the country to which he is accredited and serves as dean of the diplomatic corps on state occasions. Since 1965 pro-nuncios, also of ambassadorial rank, have been assigned to countries in which this prerogative is not recognized. In recent years, the Vatican started to phase out the title of pro-nuncio. The title of nuncio has been given to the majority of appointments of ambassadorial rank. In many countries the papal nuncio is dean of the diplomatic corps.

Service and Liaison

Representatives, while carrying out their general and special duties, are bound to respect the autonomy of local churches and bishops. Their service and liaison responsibilities include the following:

- Nomination of Bishops: To play a key role in compiling, with the advice of ecclesiastics and lay persons, and submitting lists of names of likely candidates to the Holy See with their own recommendations.
- Bishops: To aid and counsel local bishops without interfering in the affairs of their jurisdictions.
- Episcopal Conferences: To maintain close relations with them and to assist them in every possible way. (Papal representatives do not belong to these conferences.)
- Religious Communities of Pontifical Rank: To advise and assist major superiors for the purpose of promoting and consolidating conferences of men and women religious and to coordinate their apostolic activities.
- Church-State Relations: The thrust in this area is toward the development of sound relations with civil governments and collaboration in work for peace and the total good of the whole human family. The mission of a papal representative begins with appointment and assignment by the pope and continues until termination of his mandate. He acts "under the guidance and according to the instructions of the cardinal secretary of state to whom he is directly responsible for the execution of the mandate entrusted to him by the Supreme Pontiff." Normally representatives are required to retire at age 75.

The office of Delegate for Papal Legations was established in 1973 to coordinate papal diplomatic efforts throughout the world. The office entails responsibility for "following more closely through timely visits the activities of papal representatives . . . and encouraging their rapport with the central offices" of the Secretariat of State.

U.S. - HOLY SEE RELATIONS

Papal Representatives to the U.S.

A Nuncio represents the Holy Father to both the hierarchy and Church of a particular nation and to that nation's civil government. The U.S. Apostolic Nunciature is located at 3339 Massachusetts Ave., N.W., Washington, D.C. 20008-3687.

From 1893 to 1984, papal representatives to the Church in the U.S. were apostolic delegates (all archbishops): Francesco Satolli (1893-96), Sebastiano Martinelli, O.S.A., (1896-1902), Diomede Falconio, O.F.M. (1902-1911), Giovanni Bonzano (1911-22), Pietro Fumasoni-Biondi (1922-33), Amleto Cicognani (1933-58), Egidio Vagnozzi (1958-67), Luigi Raimondi (1967-73), Jean Jadot (1973-80), and Pio Laghi (1980-90) who was the first to hold the title Pro-Nuncio, beginning in 1984 (See *Index: U.S.-Vatican Relations*). Archbishop Agostino Cacciavillan was Pro-Nuncio and permanent observer to the Organization of American States from 1990 to 1998. As of July 30, 2001, the representative of the Pope to the Church in the United States is Archbishop Gabriel Montalvo, J.C.D.

History of Relations

The United States and the Holy See announced January 10, 1984, the establishment of full diplomatic relations, thus ending a period of 117 years in which there was no formal diplomatic relationship. The announcement followed

action by the Congress in November, 1983, to end a prohibition on diplomatic relations enacted in 1867.

PONTIFICAL ACADEMIES

Pontifical Academy Of Sciences

The Pontifical Academy of Sciences was constituted in its present form by Pius XI October 28, 1936, in virtue of *In Multis Solaciis*, a document issued on his own initiative.

The academy is the only supranational body of its kind in the world with a pope-selected, life-long membership of outstanding mathematicians and experimental scientists regardless of creed from many countries. The normal complement of 70 members was increased to 80 in 1985-86 by John Paul II. There are additional honorary and supernumerary members.

The academy traces its origin to the *Linceorum Academia* (Academy of the Lynxes — its symbol) founded in Rome August 17, 1603. Pius IX reorganized this body and gave it a new name — *Pontificia Accademia dei Nuovi Lincei* — in 1847. It was taken over by the Italian state in 1870 and called the *Accademia Nazionale dei Lincei*. Leo XIII reconstituted it with a new charter in 1887. Pius XI designated the Casina of Pope Pius IV in the Vatican Gardens as the site of academy headquarters in 1922 and gave it its present title and status in 1936. In 1940, Pius XII gave the title of Excellency to its members; John XXIII

extended the privilege to honorary members in 1961.

Pontifical Academy of Social Sciences

Founded by John Paul II, January 1, 1994 (*motu proprio Socialium scientiarum investigationes*) to promote the study and the progress of social sciences, to advise the Vatican on social concerns and to foster research aimed at improving society. The number of members is not less than 20 nor more than 40. Address: Casino Pio IV, Vatican Gardens.

Pontifical Academy for Life

Established by John Paul II, February 11, 1994 (*motu proprio Vitae Mysterium*) "to fulfill the specific task of study, information and formation on the principal problems of biomedicine and law relative to the promotion and defense of life, especially in the direct relationship they have with Christian morality and the directives of the Church's magisterium." Members, appointed by the Pope without regard to religion or nationality, represent the various branches of "the biomedical sciences and those that are most closely related to problems concerning the promotion and protection of life." Address: Via della Conciliazione, 3, 00193 Rome, Italy.

HIERARCHY OF THE CATHOLIC CHURCH

ORGANIZATION AND GOVERNMENT

As a structured society, the Catholic Church is organized and governed along lines corresponding mainly to the jurisdictions of the pope and bishops. The pope is the supreme head of the Church. He has primacy of jurisdiction as well as honor over the entire Church. Bishops, in union with and in subordination to the pope, are the successors of the Apostles for care of the Church and for the continuation of Christ's mission in the world. They serve the people of their own dioceses, or particular churches, with ordinary authority and jurisdiction. They also share, with the pope and each other, common concern and effort for the general welfare of the whole Church.

Bishops of exceptional status are patriarchs of Eastern Catholic Churches who, subject only

to the pope, are heads of the faithful belonging to their rites throughout the world.

Subject to the Holy Father and directly responsible to him for the exercise of their ministry of service to people in various jurisdictions or divisions of the Church throughout the world are: resident archbishops and metropolitans (heads of archdioceses), diocesan bishops, vicars and prefects apostolic (heads of vicariates apostolic and prefectures apostolic), certain abbots and prelates, apostolic administrators. Each of these, within his respective territory and according to the provisions of canon law, has ordinary jurisdiction over pastors (who are responsible for the administration of parishes), priests, religious and lay persons.

Also subject to the Holy Father are titular archbishops and bishops, religious orders and congregations of pontifical right, pontifical institutes and faculties, papal nuncios and apostolic delegates.

Assisting the pope and acting in his name in the central government and administration of the Church are cardinals and other officials of the Roman Curia.

THE HIERARCHY

The ministerial hierarchy is the orderly arrangement of the ranks and orders of the clergy to provide for the spiritual care of the faithful, the government of the Church, and the accomplishment of the Church's total mission in the world.

Persons belong to this hierarchy by virtue of ordination and canonical mission.

The term hierarchy is also used to designate an entire body or group of bishops; for example, the hierarchy of the Church, the hierarchy of the United States.

Hierarchy of Order: Consists of the pope, bishops, priests and deacons. Their purpose, for which they are ordained to holy orders, is to carry out the sacramental and pastoral ministry of the Church.

Hierarchy of Jurisdiction: Consists of the pope and bishops by divine institution, and other church officials by ecclesiastical institution and mandate, who have authority to govern and direct the faithful for spiritual ends.

THE POPE

His Holiness the Pope is the Bishop of Rome, Vicar of Jesus Christ, successor of St. Peter, Prince of the Apostles, Supreme Pontiff of the Universal Church, Patriarch of the West, Primate of Italy, Archbishop and Metropolitan of the Roman Province, Sovereign of the State of Vatican City, Servant of the Servants of God.

CARDINALS

(See *below*)

PATRIARCHS

Patriarch, a term which had its origin in the Eastern Church, is the title of a bishop who, second only to the pope, has the highest rank in the hierarchy of jurisdiction. He is the incumbent of one of the sees listed below. Subject only to the pope, a patriarch of the Eastern Church is the head of the faithful belonging to his rite throughout the world. The patriarchal sees are so called because of their special status and dignity in the history of the Church.

The Council of Nicaea (325) recognized three patriarchs — the Bishops of Alexandria and Antioch in the East, and of Rome in the West. The First Council of Constantinople (381) added the bishop of Constantinople to the list of patriarchs and gave him rank second only to that of the pope, the bishop of Rome and patriarch of the West; this action was seconded by the Council of Chalcedon (451) and was given full recognition by the Fourth Lateran Council (1215). The Council of Chalcedon also acknowledged patriarchal rights of the bishop of Jerusalem.

Eastern patriarchs are as follows: one of Alexandria, for the Copts; three of Antioch, one each for the Syrians, Maronites and Greek Melkites (the latter also has the personal title of Greek Melkite patriarch of Alexandria and of Jerusalem). The patriarch of Babylonia, for the Chaldeans, and the patriarch of Sis, or Cilicia, for the Armenians, should be called, more properly, *Katholikos* — that is, a prelate delegated for a universality of causes. These patriarchs are elected by bishops of their churches: they receive approval and the pallium, symbol of their office, from the pope.

Latin Rite patriarchates were established for Antioch, Jerusalem, Alexandria and Constantinople during the Crusades; afterwards, they became patriarchates in name only. Jerusalem, however, was reconstituted as a patriarchate by Pius IX, in virtue of the bull *Nulla Celebrior* of July 23, 1847. In 1964, the Latin titular patriarchates of Constantinople, Alexandria, and Antioch, long a bone of contention in relations with Eastern Churches, were abolished.

MAJOR ARCHBISHOPS

An archbishop with the prerogatives but not the title of a patriarch. As of May 15, 2000, there were two major archbishops: the major archbishop of Lviv of the Ukrainian Catholic Church (Ukraine) and the major archbishop of Ernakulam-Angomaly of the Syro-Malabar Church (India).

ARCHBISHOPS, METROPOLITANS

Archbishop: A bishop with the title of an archdiocese.

Coadjutor Archbishop: An assistant archbishop with right of succession.

Metropolitan: Archbishop of the principal see, an archdiocese, in an ecclesiastical province consisting of several dioceses. He has the full powers of bishop in his own archdiocese and limited supervisory jurisdiction and influence over the other (suffragan) dioceses in the province.

The pallium, conferred by the pope, is the symbol of his status as a metropolitan.

Titular Archbishop: Has the title of an archdiocese that formerly existed in fact but now exists in title only. He does not have ordinary jurisdiction over an archdiocese. Examples are archbishops in the Roman Curia, papal nuncios, apostolic delegates.

Archbishop *ad personam:* A title of personal honor and distinction granted to some bishops. They do not have ordinary jurisdiction over an archdiocese.

Primate: A title of honor given to the ranking prelate of some countries or regions.

BISHOPS

Diocesan Bishop: A bishop in charge of a diocese.

Coadjutor Bishop: An assistant (auxiliary) bishop to a diocesan bishop, with right of succession to the see.

Titular Bishops: A bishop with the title of a diocese which formerly existed in fact but now exists in title only; an assistant (auxiliary) bishop to a diocesan bishop.

Episcopal Vicar: An assistant, who may or may not be a bishop, appointed by a residential bishop as his deputy for a certain part of a diocese, a determined type of apostolic work, or the faithful of a certain rite.

Eparch, Exarch: Titles of bishops of Eastern churches.

Nomination of Bishops: Nominees for episcopal ordination are selected in several ways. Final appointment and/or approval in all cases is subject to decision by the pope.

In the U.S., bishops periodically submit the names of candidates to the archbishop of their province. The name are then considered at a meeting of the Bishops of the province, and those receiving a favorable vote are forwarded to the pro-nuncio for transmission to the Holy See. Normally, three names are submitted. Bishops are free to seek the counsel of priests, religious, and lay persons with respect to nominees.

Eastern Catholic churches have their own procedures and synodal regulations for nominating and making final selection of candidates for episcopal ordination. Such selection is subject to approval by the pope. The Code of Canon Law concedes no rights or privileges to civil authorities with respect to the election, nomination, presentation, or designation of candidates for the episcopate.

Ad Limina Visit: Diocesan bishops and apostolic vicars are obliged to make an ad limina visit ("to the threshold" of the Apostles) every five years to the tombs of Sts. Peter and Paul, have audience with the Holy Father, and consult with appropriate Vatican officials. They are required to send a report on conditions in their jurisdiction to the Congregation for bishops approximately six — and not less than three — months in advance of the scheduled visit.

OTHERS WITH ORDINARY JURISDICTION

Ordinary: One who has the jurisdiction of an office: the pope, diocesan bishops, vicars general, prelates of missionary territories, vicars apostolic prefects apostolic, vicars capitular during the vacancy of a see, superiors general, abbots primate, and other major superiors of men religious.

Some prelates and abbots, with jurisdiction like that of diocesan bishops, are pastors of the people of God in territories (prelatures and abbacies) not under the jurisdiction of diocesan bishops.

Vicar Apostolic: Usually a titular bishop who has ordinary jurisdiction over a mission territory.

Prefect Apostolic: Has ordinary jurisdiction over a mission territory.

Apostolic Administrator: Usually a bishop appointed to administer an ecclesiastical jurisdiction temporarily. Administrators of lesser rank are also appointed on occasion and have more restricted supervisory duties.

Vicar General: A bishop's deputy for the administration of a diocese. Such a vicar does not have to be a bishop.

PRELATES WITHOUT JURISDICTION

The title of protonotary apostolic was originally given by the fourth century or earlier to clergy who collected accounts of martyrdom and other church documents, or who served the Church with distinction in other ways. Other titles — e.g., domestic prelate, papal chamberlain, prelate of honor — are titles of clergy in service to the pope and the papal household, or of clergy honored for particular reasons. All prelates without jurisdiction are appointed by the pope, have designated ceremonial privileges and the title of Rev. Monsignor.

SYNOD OF BISHOPS

The Synod of Bishops was chartered by Pope Paul VI September 15, 1965, in a document he issued on his own initiative under the title, *Apostolica Sollicitudo*. Provisions of this *motu proprio* are contained in Canons 342 to 348 of the Code of Canon Law. According to major provisions of the Synod charter:

- The purposes of the Synod are: "to encourage close union and valued assistance between the Sovereign Pontiff and the Bishops of the entire world; to insure that direct and real information is provided on questions and situations touching upon the internal action of the Church and its necessary activity in the world of today; to facilitate agreement on essential points of doctrine and on methods of procedure in the life of the Church."
- The Synod is a central ecclesiastical institution, permanent by nature.
- The Synod is directly and immediately subject to the Pope, who has authority to assign its agenda, to call it into session, and to give its members deliberative as well as advisory authority.
- In addition to a limited number of ex officio members and a few heads of male religious institutes, the majority of the members are elected by and representative of national or regional episcopal conferences. The Pope reserved the right to appoint the general secretary, special secretaries and no more than 15 percent of the total membership.

The Pope is president of the Synod, and the secretary general is a Cardinal.

An advisory council of 15 members (12 elected, three appointed by the pope) provides the secretariat with adequate staff for carrying on liaison with episcopal conferences and for preparing the agenda of synodal assemblies. Cardinal William H, Keeler, archbishop of Baltimore, is a member of the secretariat.

ASSEMBLIES

1. First Assembly: The first assembly was held from September 29 to October 29, 1967. Its objectives, as stated by Pope Paul VI, were "the preservation and strengthening of the Catholic faith, its integrity, its force, its development, its doctrinal and historical coherence." One result was a recommendation for the establishment of an international commission of theologians to assist the Congregation for the Doctrine of the Faith and to broaden approaches to theological research. Pope Paul set up the commission in 1969.

2. Pope-Bishop Relations: The second assembly held October 11 to 28, 1969, was extraordinary in character. It opened the way toward greater participation by bishops with the pope and each other in the governance of the Church. Proceedings were oriented to three main points: (1) the nature and implications of collegiality; (2) the relationship of bishops and their conferences to the pope; (3) the relationships of bishops and their conferences to each other.

3. Priesthood and Justice: The ministerial priesthood and justice in the world were the principal topics under discussion at the second ordinary assembly, September 30 to November 6, 1971. In one report, the Synod emphasized the primary and permanent dedication of priests in the Church to the ministry of word, sacrament and pastoral service as a full-time vocation. In another report, the assembly stated: "Action on behalf of justice and participation in the transformation of the world fully appear to us as a constitutive dimension of the preaching of the Gospel; or, in other words, of the Church's mission for the redemption of the human race and its liberation from every oppressive situation."

4. Evangelization: The assembly of September 27 to October 26, 1974, produced a general statement on evangelization of the modern world, covering the need for it and its relationship to efforts for total human liberation from personal and social evil. The assembly observed: "The Church does not remain within merely political, social and economic limits (elements which she must certainly take into account) but leads towards freedom under all its forms — liberation from sin, from individual or collective selfishness — and to full communion with God and with men who are like brothers. In this way the Church, in her evangelical way, promotes the true and complete liberation of all men, groups and peoples."

5. Catechetics: The fourth ordinary assembly, September 30 to October 29, 1977, focused attention on catechetics, with special reference to children and young people. The participants issued a "Message to the People of God," the first synodal statement issued since inception of the body, and also presented to Pope Paul VI a set of 34 related propositions and a number of suggestions.

6. Family: "A Message to Christian Families in the Modern World" and a proposal for a "Charter of Family Rights" were produced by the assembly held September 26 to October 25, 1980. The assembly reaffirmed the indissolubility of marriage and the contents of the encyclical letter *Humanae Vitae* (see *separate entry*), and urged married couples who find it hard to live up to "the difficult but loving demands" of Christ not to be discouraged but to avail themselves of the aid of divine grace. In response to synodal recommendation, Pope John Paul issued a charter of family rights late in 1983.

7. Reconciliation: Penance and reconciliation in the mission of the Church was the theme of the assembly held September 29 to October 29, 1983. Sixty-three propositions related to this theme were formulated on a wide variety of subjects, including: personal sin and so-called systemic or institutional sin; the nature of serious sin; the diminished sense of sin and of the need of redemption, related to decline in the administration and reception of the sacrament of penance; general absolution; individual and social reconciliation; violence and violations of human rights; reconciliation as the basis of peace and justice in society. In a statement issued October 27, the Synod stressed the need of the world to become, increasingly, "a reconciled community of peoples," and said that "the Church, as sacrament of reconciliation to the world, has to be an effective sign of God's mercy."

8. Vatican II Review: The second extraordinary assembly was convened November 24 to December 8, 1985, for the purposes of: (1) recalling the Second Vatican Council; (2) evaluating the implementation of its enactments during the 20 years since its conclusion; (3) seeking ways and means of promoting renewal in the Church in accordance with the spirit and letter of the council. At the conclusion of the assembly the bishops issued two documents. In "A Message to the People of God," they noted the need for greater appreciation of the enactments of Vatican II and for greater efforts to put them into effect, so that all members of the Church might discharge their responsibility of proclaiming the good news of salvation. In a "Final Report," the first of its kind published by a synodal assembly, the bishops reflected on lights and shadows since Vatican II, stating that negative developments had come from partial and superficial interpretations of conciliar enactments and from incomplete or ineffective implementation thereof. The report also covered a considerable number of subjects discussed during the assembly, including the mystery of the Church, inculturation, the preferential (but not exclusive) option for the poor, and a suggestion for the development of a new universal catechism of the Catholic faith.

9. Vocation and Mission of the Laity in the Church and in the World 20 years after the Second Vatican Council: The seventh ordinary assembly, October 1 to 30, 1987, said in a "Message to the People of God": "The majority of the Christian laity live out their vocation as followers and disciples of Christ in all spheres of life which we call 'the world': the family, the field of work, the local community and the like. To permeate this day-to-day living with the spirit of Christ has always been the task of the lay faithful; and it should be with still greater force their challenge today. It is in this way that they sanctify the world and collaborate in the realization of the kingdom of God." The assembly produced a set of fifty-four propositions which were presented to the Pope for consideration in the preparation of a document of his own on the theme of the assembly. He responded with the apostolic exhortation *Christifideles Laici*, "The Christian Faithful Laity," released by the Vatican January 30, 1989.

10. Formation of Priests in Circumstances of the Present Day: The eighth general assembly, September 30 to October 28, 1990, dealt principally with the nature and mission of the priesthood; the identity, multi-faceted formation and spirituality of priests; and, in a Message to the People of God, the need on all levels of the Church for the promotion of vocations to the priesthood. Forty-one proposals were presented to the Pope for his consideration in preparing a document of his own on the theme of the assembly. Pope John Paul issued an apostolic exhortation entitled *Pastores Dabo Vobis* ("I Will Give You Shepherds") April 7, 1992, in response to the Synod's recommendations.

11. The Consecrated Life and Its Role in the Church and in the World: The ninth general assembly was held October 2 to 29, 1994. Pope John Paul's reflections on the proceedings of the assembly and the recommendations of the Bishops were the subjects of his apostolic exhortation entitled *Vita Consecrata* ("Consecrated Life"), issued March 25, 1996. The document dealt with various forms of consecrated life: contemplative institutes, apostolic religious life, secular institutes, societies of apostolic life, mixed institutes and new forms of evangelical life.

12. The Tenth Ordinary General Assembly: The synod assembled in October, 2001 on the topic, "The Bishop: Servant of the Gospel of Jesus Christ for the Hope of the World."

Recent special assemblies of the Synod of Bishops: Special Synods have been held for Europe (November 28 to December 14, 1991; on the theme "So that we might be witnesses of Christ who has set us free"); for Africa (April 10 to May 8, 1994; on the theme "The Church in Africa and Her Evangelizing Mission Towards the Year 2000: 'You Shall Be My Witnesses' (Acts 1:8)"); for Lebanon (November 27 to December 14, 1995; on the theme "Christ is Our Hope:

Renewed by His Spirit, in Solidarity We Bear Witness to His Love"); the Americas (November 16 to December 12, 1997; on the theme, "Encounter with the Living Jesus Christ: Way to Conversion, Community and Solidarity"); for Asia (April 19 to May 14, 1998 on the theme "Jesus Christ the Savior and His Mission of Love and Service in Asia: '. . . That They May Have Life, and Have it Abundantly' (Jn 10:10)"); for Oceania (November 12 to December 12, 1998, with the theme "Jesus Christ and the Peoples of Oceania: Walking His Way, Telling His Truth, Living His Life"); and a special assembly for Europe (October 1-23, 1999), on the theme "Jesus Christ, Alive in His Church, Source of Hope for Europe."

COLLEGE OF CARDINALS

Cardinals are chosen by the pope to serve as his principal assistants and advisers in the central administration of church affairs. Collectively, they form the College of Cardinals. Provisions regarding their selection, rank, roles and prerogatives are detailed in Canons 349 to 359 of the Code of Canon Law.

History of the College

The College of Cardinals was constituted in its present form and categories of membership in the 12th century. Before that time the pope had a body of advisers selected from among the bishops of dioceses neighboring Rome, priests and deacons of Rome. The college was given definite form in 1150, and in 1179 the selection of cardinals was reserved exclusively to the pope. Sixtus V fixed the number at 70, in 1586. John XXIII set aside this rule when he increased membership at the 1959 and subsequent consistories. The number was subsequently raised by Paul VI and by John Paul II. The number of cardinals entitled to participate in papal elections was limited to 120 by Paul VI in 1973. Pope John Paul II twice increased membership beyond the limit, in 1998 and 2001.

In 1567 the title of cardinal was reserved to members of the college; previously it had been used by priests attached to parish churches of Rome and by the leading clergy of other notable churches. The Code of Canon Law promulgated in 1918 decreed that all cardinals must be priests. Previously there had been cardinals who were not priests (e.g., Cardinal Giacomo Antonelli, d. 1876, Secretary of State to Pius IX, was a deacon). John XXIII provided in the *motu proprio Cum Gravissima* April 15, 1962, that cardinals would henceforth be bishops; this provision is included in the revised Code of Canon Law.

Age Limits

Pope Paul VI placed age limits on the functions of cardinals in the apostolic letter *Ingravescentem Aetatem,* dated November 21, 1970, and effective as of January 1, 1971. At 80, they cease to be members of curial departments and offices, and become ineligible to take part in papal elections. They retain membership in the College of Cardinals, however, with relevant rights and privileges.

Three Categories

All cardinals except Eastern patriarchs are aggregated to the clergy of Rome. This aggregation is signified by the assignment to each cardinal, except the patriarchs, of a titular church in Rome. The three categories of members of the college are cardinal Bishops, cardinal priests and cardinal deacons.

Cardinal Bishops include the six titular bishops of the suburbicarian sees and Eastern patriarchs. First in rank are the titular bishops of the suburbicarian sees, neighboring Rome: Ostia, Palestrina, Porto-Santa Rufina, Albano, Velletri-Segni, Frascati, Sabina-Poggio Mirteto. The dean of the college holds the title of the See of Ostia as well as his other suburbicarian see. These cardinal Bishops are engaged in full-time service in the central administration of church affairs in departments of the Roman Curia.

Full recognition is given in the revised Code of Canon Law to the position of Eastern patriarchs as the heads of sees of apostolic origin with ancient liturgies. They are assigned rank among the cardinals in order of seniority, following the suburbicarian titleholders.

Cardinal priests, who were formerly in charge of leading churches in Rome, are bishops whose dioceses are outside Rome.

Cardinal deacons, who were formerly chosen according to regional divisions of Rome, are titular bishops assigned to full-time service in the Roman Curia.

The dean and sub-dean of the college are elected by the cardinal bishops — subject to approval by the pope — from among their number. The dean, or the sub-dean in his absence, presides over the college as the first among equals. There is also a Secretary to the College of Cardinals.

Selection and Duties

Cardinals are selected by the pope and are inducted into the college in appropriate ceremonies. Cardinals under the age of 80: elect the pope when the Holy See becomes vacant and are major administrators of church affairs, serving in one or more departments of the Roman Curia. Cardinals in charge of agencies of the Roman Curia and Vatican City are asked to submit their resignation from office to the pope on reaching the age of 75. All cardinals enjoy a number of special rights and privileges. Their title, while symbolic of high honor, does not signify any extension of the powers of holy orders. They are called princes of the Church.

A cardinal *in pectore (petto)* is one whose selection has been made by the pope but whose name has not been disclosed; he has no title, rights or duties until such disclosure is made, at which time he takes precedence from the time of the secret selection.

Ineligible to Vote

Those cardinals who reach the age of 80 are ineligible to participate in the conclave in keeping with the apostolic letter *Ingravescentem Aetetem* effective January 1, 1971, which limited the functions of cardinals after completion of their 80th year.

Cardinals of the United States

U.S. Cardinals (according to year of elevation; for biographical data on deceased cardinals, see American Catholics of the Past):

1875: John McCloskey; 1886: James Gibbons; 1911: John Farley, William O'Connell; 1921: Dennis Dougherty; 1924: Patrick Hayes, George Mundelein; 1946: John Glennon, Edward Mooney, Francis Spellman, Samuel Stritch; 1953: James F. McIntyre; 1958: John O'Hara, C.S.C., Richard Cushing; 1959: Albert Meyer, Aloysius Muench; 1961: Joseph Ritter; 1965:

Lawrence J. Shehan; 1967: Francis Brennan, John P. Cody, Patrick A. O'Boyle, John J. Krol; 1969: John J. Wright, Terence J. Cooke, John F. Dearden, John J. Carberry; 1973: Humberto S. Medeiros, Timothy Manning; 1983: Joseph L. Bernardin; 1985: John J. O'Connor.

[Myroslav Lubachivsky (d. Dec. 14, 2000), major Archbishop of Lviv of the Ukrainians (Ukraine), was made a cardinal in 1985. He was a citizen of the United States and was metropolitan of the Philadelphia Ukrainian Rite Archeparchy, from 1979-81.]

Prelates who became cardinals after returning to their native countries: John Lefebvre de Chevrus, first bishop of Boston (1808-23) and apostolic administrator of New York (1810-15), elevated to the cardinalate, 1836, in France. Ignatius Persico, O.F.M. Cap., bishop of Savannah (1870-72), elevated to the cardinalate, 1893, in Italy; Diomede Falconio, O.F.M. ord. a priest in Buffalo, N.Y.; missionary in U.S.; apostolic delegate to the U.S. (1902-11), elevated to cardinalate, 1911, in Italy.

As of August 30, 2001, the following cardinals were in service, according to their years of elevation:

1976: **William W. Baum** (major penitentiary); 1985: **Bernard F. Law** (Archbishop of Boston); 1988: **James A. Hickey** (Archbishop of Washington), **Edmund C. Szoka** (governor of the Vatican City State); 1991: **Roger M. Mahony** (Archbishop of Los Angeles), **Anthony M. Bevilacqua** (Archbishop of Philadelphia); 1994: **William H. Keeler** (Archbishop of Baltimore), **Adam J. Maida** (Archbishop of Detroit); 1998: **Francis E. George**, **O.M.I.** (Archbishop of Chicago), **James F. Stafford** (president of the Pontifical Council for the Laity); 2001: **Edward M. Egan** (abp. of New York), **Theodore McCarrick** (abp. of Washington), **Avery Dulles, S.J.** (theologian).

ELECTING THE POPE: THE CONCLAVE

One of the primary duties of the Cardinals of the Catholic Church is the election of the Bishop of Rome who becomes thereby the Supreme Pontiff of the Church. The election is held in what is termed the conclave. The name is derived from the Latin *cum* (with) and *clavis* (key), and implies the fact that the cardinals are locked together in a room until a new pontiff has been chosen. This form of papal election began in 1274 and is considered the third period in the historical evolution of choosing the successor to St. Peter. Central to the full understanding of the conclave is the firm belief that the entire process of election is guided by the Holy Spirit.

In the early Church, new Bishops of Rome were chosen in the manner customarily used in the other dioceses, that is, the clergy, with the

people of the diocese, elected or chose the new bishop in the presence of the other bishops in the province. This was a simple method, but it became impractical as the Christian population grew in size and there arose rival claimants and a certain hostility between the upper classes (the patricians) and the lower classes (the plebeians), each of whom had their own candidates. This situation created considerable upheaval in Rome as demonstrated by the riots accompanying the contested elections of Pope St. Damasus I (366-384) and the antipope Ursinus in 366. Such was the violence that the prefect of the city was called in to restore order.

On the basis of these disturbances, the Roman emperors began to involve themselves in the elections by guaranteeing proper procedure and ensuring free voting by the clergy in cases where two claimants had emerged. This intervention launched a long period of secular interference that would continue, to various degrees, until 1903. The so-called barbarian kings often supervised elections until the sixth century when the Byzantines reconquered Italy. The emperors not only demanded tribute from the popes but also retained the right of confirmation, a practice that routinely created long delays, as word would have to be sent to Constantinople (later Ravenna) to request approval. The last pope to seek confirmation from imperial authorities was Gregory III in 731. After this time, the popes sought the protection of the Franks, and in 769, Pope Stephen III convened a synod at Rome that confirmed the decree of 502 (under Symmachus) that laypeople should no longer vote for the popes and that only higher clerics should be considered eligible.

While making elections more efficient, the decrees did not remove the troublesome Roman nobility and their ambitions toward the papacy from 843 that resulted from the decline of the Frankish Empire and the end of imperial protection of Rome. The next centuries saw such ruthless families as the Crescentii and Tusculani scheme to have their candidates elected, freely murdering those popes who displeased them and deposing others. A major reform was achieved in 1059 when Pope Nicholas II decreed that the cardinal bishops should choose the popes, a procedure modified by the Third Lateran Council (1179), which declared an end to distinctions among the three orders of cardinals in terms of voting, and requiring that a candidate receive a two-thirds majority.

The new need of a majority complicated many elections as a two-thirds plurality would often be quite difficult to reach owing to competing international interests among the cardinals. Vacancies were prolonged by squabbles, and sickly candidates were picked as compromises while negotiations would take place among the factions. After the death of Pope Clement IV in 1268, for example, three years passed until the eighteen cardinals gathered at Viterbo could agree on Pope Gregory X (r. 1271-1276), and this only after the citizens of the city reduced them to bread and water and tore the roof off the palace in which they were residing. Gregory introduced changes through the Second Council of Lyons (1272) to speed up elections, inaugurating the system of the conclave. It remained essentially unchanged until 1975. In that year, Pope Paul VI issued the apostolic constitution *Romano Pontifici Eligendo* (October 1) which stipulated various requirements for the conclave. Among these were: only cardinals may be electors; their number is limited to one hundred twenty, with each cardinal allowed to bring two or three assistants; while not essential for validity, it is the recognized form of election; three forms are acceptable: acclamation (*acclamatio*), compromise (by which certain cardinals are named delegates and are given power to act on behalf of the others); and balloting; if the person chosen is not a bishop, he is to be ordained to the episcopacy immediately (if a bishop, he is pope at once); secrecy is to be carefully observed; all ecumenical councils are immediately adjourned; and, if no one is elected after three days, one day is to be spent in prayer and meditation. New legislation regarding papal elections and church government during a vacancy of the Holy See was promulgated by Pope John Paul II on February 23, 1996, in the apostolic constitution *Universi Dominici Gregis* ("Shepherd of the Lord's Whole Flock"). Among the changes that were introduced was the call for heightened security in preventing electronic surveillance and the provision that after a set number of unsuccessful ballots, the cardinals may elect the new pope by a simple majority vote.

The last election not held in the Vatican (the Sistine Chapel) was in 1846 (Pius IX), which took place at the Quirinal Palace. The last pope not a cardinal at the time of his election was Urban VI (1378-1389); the last by compromise was John XXII (r. 1316-1334); and the last by acclamation was Gregory XV (1621-1623).

Pope Pius XII

Part 3
EASTERN CATHOLIC CHURCHES

The Second Vatican Council, in its Decree on Eastern Catholic Churches (*Orientalium Ecclesiarum*), stated the following points regarding Eastern heritage, patriarchs, sacraments and worship.

Venerable Churches: The Catholic Church holds in high esteem the institutions of the Eastern Churches, their liturgical rites, ecclesiastical traditions, and Christian way of life. For, distinguished as they are by their venerable antiquity, they are bright with that tradition which was handed down from the Apostles through the Fathers, and which forms part of the divinely revealed and undivided heritage of the universal Church (No. 1). That Church, Holy and Catholic, which is the Mystical Body of Christ, is made up of the faithful who are organically united in the Holy Spirit through the same faith, the same sacraments, and the same government and who, combining into various groups held together by a hierarchy, form separate Churches or rites. It is the mind of the Catholic Church that each individual Church or rite retain its traditions whole and entire, while adjusting its way of life to the various needs of time and place (No. 2).

Such individual Churches, whether of the East or of the West, although they differ somewhat among themselves in what are called rites (that is, in liturgy, ecclesiastical discipline, and spiritual heritage) are, nevertheless, equally entrusted to the pastoral guidance of the Roman Pontiff, the divinely appointed successor of St. Peter in supreme government over the universal Church. They are consequently of equal dignity, so that none of them is superior to the others by reason of rite (No. 3).

Eastern Heritage: Each and every Catholic, as also the baptized of every non-Catholic Church or community who enters into the fullness of Catholic communion, should everywhere retain his proper rite, cherish it, and observe it to the best of his ability (No. 4). The Churches of the East, as much as those of the West, fully enjoy the right, and are in duty bound, to rule themselves. Each should do so according to its proper and individual procedures (No. 5). All Eastern-rite members should know and be convinced that they can and should always preserve their lawful liturgical rites and their established way of life, and that these should not be altered except by way of an appropriate and organic development (No. 6)

Patriarchs: The institution of the patriarchate has existed in the Church from the earliest times and was recognized by the first ecumenical Synods. By the name Eastern Patriarch is meant the bishop who has jurisdiction over all bishops (including metropolitans), clergy, and people of his own territory or rite, in accordance with the norms of law and without prejudice to the primacy of the Roman Pontiff (No. 7). Though some of the patriarchates of the Eastern Churches are of later origin than others, all are equal in patriarchal dignity. Still the honorary and lawfully established order of precedence among them is to be preserved (No. 8). In keeping with the most ancient tradition of the Church, the Patriarchs of the Eastern Churches are to be accorded exceptional respect, since each presides over his patriarchate as father and head.

This sacred Synod, therefore, decrees that their rights and privileges should be re-established in accord with the ancient traditions of each Church and the decrees of the ecumenical Synods. The rights and privileges in question are those which flourished when East and West were in union, though they should be somewhat adapted to modern conditions.

The Patriarchs with their synods constitute the superior authority for all affairs of the patriarchate, including the right to establish new eparchies and to nominate bishops of their rite within the territorial bounds of the patriarchate, without prejudice to the inalienable right of the Roman Pontiff to intervene in individual cases (No. 9).

What has been said of Patriarchs applies as well, under the norm of law, to major archbishops, who preside over the whole of some individual Church or rite (No. 10).

Sacraments: This sacred Ecumenical Synod endorses and lauds the ancient discipline of the sacraments existing in the Eastern Churches, as also the practices connected with their celebration and administration (No. 12).

With respect to the minister of holy chrism (confirmation), let that practice be fully restored which existed among Easterners in most ancient times. Priests, therefore, can validly confer this sacrament, provided they use chrism blessed by a Patriarch or bishop (No. 13).

In conjunction with baptism or otherwise, all Eastern-Rite priests can confer this sacrament validly on all the faithful of any rite, including the Latin; licitly, however, only if the regulations of both common and particular law are observed. Priests of the Latin Rite, to the extent of the faculties they enjoy for administering this sacrament, can confer it also on the faithful of Eastern Churches, without prejudice to rite. They do so licitly if the regulations of both common and particular law are observed (No. 14).

The faithful are bound on Sundays and feast days to attend the divine liturgy or, according to the regulations or custom of their own rite, the celebration of the Divine Praises. That the faithful may be able to satisfy their obligation more easily, it is decreed that this obligation can be fulfilled from the Vespers of the vigil to the end of the Sunday or the feast day (No. 15). Because of the everyday intermingling of the communicants of diverse Eastern Churches in the same Eastern region or territory, the faculty for hearing confession, duly and unrestrictedly granted by his proper bishop to a priest of any rite, is applicable to the entire territory of the grantor, also to the places and the faithful belonging to any other rite in the same territory, unless an Ordinary of the place explicitly decides otherwise with respect to the places pertaining to his rite (No. 16).

This sacred Synod ardently desires that where it has fallen into disuse the office of the permanent diaconate be restored. The legislative authority of each individual church should decide about the subdiaconate and the minor orders (No. 17).

By way of preventing invalid marriages between Eastern Catholics and baptized Eastern non-Catholics, and in the interests of the permanence and sanctity of marriage and of domestic harmony, this sacred Synod decrees that the canonical "form" for the celebration of such marriages obliges only for lawfulness. For their validity, the presence of a sacred minister suffices, as long as the other requirements of law are honored (No. 18).

Worship: Henceforth, it will be the exclusive right of an ecumenical Synod or the Apostolic See to establish, transfer, or suppress feast days common to all the Eastern Churches. To establish, transfer, or suppress feast days for any of the individual Churches is within the competence not only of the Apostolic See but also of a patriarchal or archiepiscopal synod, provided due consideration is given to the entire region and to other individual Churches (No. 19). Until such time as all Christians desirably concur on a fixed day for the celebration of Easter, and with a view meantime to promoting unity among the Christians of a given area or nation, it is left to the Patriarchs or supreme authorities of a place to reach a unanimous agreement, after ascertaining the views of all concerned, on a single Sunday for the observance of Easter (No. 20). With respect to rules concerning sacred seasons, individual faithful dwelling outside the area or territory of their own rite may conform completely to the established custom of the place where they live. When members of a family belong to different rites, they are all permitted to observe sacred seasons according to the rules of any one of these rites (No. 21). From ancient times the Divine Praises have been held in high esteem among all Eastern Churches. Eastern clerics and religious should celebrate these Praises as the laws and customs of their own traditions require. To the extent they can, the faithful too should follow the example of their forebears by assisting devoutly at the Divine Praises (No. 22).

Restoration of Ancient Practices

An "Instruction for the Application of the Liturgical Prescriptions of the Code of Canons of the Eastern Churches" was published in Italian by the Congregation for Eastern-Rite Churches in January, 1996. Msgr. Alan Detscher, executive director of the U.S. bishops' Secretariat for the Liturgy, said it was the first instruction on liturgical renewal of the Eastern Catholic Churches since the Second Vatican Council (1962-65).

JURISDICTIONS AND FAITHFUL OF THE EASTERN CATHOLIC CHURCHES

Introduction

The Church originated in Palestine, whence it spread to other regions of the world where certain places became key centers of Christian life with great influence on the local churches in their respective areas. These centers developed into the ancient patriarchates of Constantinople, Alexandria, Antioch and Jerusalem in the East, and Rome in the West. The main lines of Eastern Church patriarchal organization and usages were drawn before the Roman Empire became two empires, East (Byzantine) and West (Roman), in 292.

Other churches with distinctive traditions grew up beyond the boundaries of the Roman Empire in Persia, Armenia, Syria, Egypt, Ethiopia, and India. The "Nestorian" church in Persia, known today as the Assyrian Church of the East, broke communion with the rest of the Church in the wake of the Council of Ephesus (431) whose teachings it did not accept. The "monophysite" churches of Armenia, Syria, Egypt, Ethiopia, Eritrea, and India (known today as the Oriental Orthodox Churches) did not accept the christological teachings of the Council of

Chalcedon (451) and so broke away from the church within the Roman Empire. And finally, in the wake of the mutual excommunications of 1054 between the Patriarch of Constantinople and the papal legate, the church within the empire divided into what would become the Catholic Church in the West and the Orthodox Church in the East. This was a lengthy process of estrangement that culminated only in 1204 and the sack of Constantinople by the Latin Crusaders.

In the following centuries, attempts to overcome these divisions took place, most notably at the Second Council of Lyons in 1274 and the Council of Ferrara-Florence in 1438-39. Both failed. Subsequently, the Catholic Church began to send missionaries to work with separated Eastern Christians, and some groups within those churches spontaneously asked to enter into full communion with Rome. Thus began the formation of the Eastern Catholic Churches, which retained most of the liturgical, canonical, spiritual and theological patrimony of their non-Catholic counterparts.

The Code of Canons of the Eastern Churches groups these churches today into four categories: patriarchal, major archepiscopal, metropolitan, and other churches *sui iuris*.

ALEXANDRIAN

The liturgical tradition of Egypt, in particular that of the early Greek Patriarchate of Alexandria. In the Egyptian desert monasteries the rite evolved in a distinctive way and eventually became that of the Coptic Orthodox Church. The Greek Patriarchate of Alexandria adopted the Byzantine rite by the twelfth century. The Coptic rite, with its Alexandrian origins, spread to Ethiopia in the fourth century where it underwent substantial modifications under strong Syrian influence. The Catholic Churches in this group are:

The Coptic Catholic Church (Patriarchate): Six dioceses in Egypt.

Catholic missionaries were present since the seventeenth century. The Patriarchate was established first in 1824 and renewed in 1895. Liturgical languages are Coptic and Arabic.

The Ethiopian Catholic Church (Metropolitanate): Two dioceses in Ethiopia and three in Eritrea. Catholic missionary activity began in the nineteenth century, and the present ecclesiastical structure dates from 1961. The liturgical languages are Ge'ez and Amharic.

ANTIOCHENE

The liturgical tradition of Antioch, one of the great centers of the early Christian world, also known as West Syrian. In Syria it developed under strong influence of Jerusalem, especially the Liturgy of St. James, into the form used by today's Syrian Orthodox and Catholics in the Middle East and India. The Maronites of Lebanon developed their own liturgical traditions under the influence of both the Antiochene and Chaldean rites.

The Catholic Churches of this group are:

The Syro-Malankara Catholic Church (Metropolitanate): Four diocese in India. Began in 1930 when two bishops, a priest, a deacon and a layman of the Malankara Orthodox Church were received into full communion with Rome. The liturgical language is Malayalam.

The Maronite Catholic Church (Patriarchate): Ten dioceses in Lebanon, three in Syria, two in the United States, and one each in Cyprus, Egypt, Argentina, Brazil, Australia, Canada, and Mexico, plus patriarchal exarchates in Jordan and Jerusalem.

Founded by St. Maron in the fourth century, the Maronites claim to have always been in communion with Rome. They have no counterpart among the separated Eastern churches. The patriarchate dates to the eighth century, and was confirmed by Pope Innocent III in 1216. Liturgical language is Arabic.

The Syrian Catholic Church (Patriarchate): Four dioceses in Syria, two in Iraq, and one each in Lebanon, Egypt, and North America, and patriarchal exarchates in Turkey and Iraq/Kuwait.

Catholic missionary activity among the Syrian Orthodox began in the 17th century, and there has been an uninterrupted series of Catholic patriarchs since 1783. The liturgical languages are Syriac/Aramaic and Arabic.

ARMENIAN

The liturgical tradition of the Armenian Apostolic and Catholic Churches. It contains elements of the Syriac, Jerusalem, and Byzantine rites. From the 5th to the 7th centuries there was strong influence from Syria and Jerusalem. More Byzantine usages were adopted later, and in the Middle Ages elements of the Latin tradition were added.

The Armenian Catholic Church (Patriarchate): Two dioceses in Syria, one each in Lebanon, Iran, Iraq, Egypt, Turkey, Ukraine, France and Argentina. Apostolic Exarchate for the United States, and Ordinariates in Greece, Romania, and Eastern Europe (Armenia).

Catholic missionaries had been working among the Armenians since the fourteenth century, and an Armenian Catholic patriarchate was established in Lebanon in 1742. The liturgical language is classical Armenian.

BYZANTINE

The tradition of the Eastern Orthodox and Byzantine Catholic Churches which originated in the Orthodox Patriarchate of Constantinople (Byzantium). Its present form is a synthesis of Constantinopolitan and Palestinian elements that took place in the monasteries between the ninth and fourteenth centuries. It is by far the most widely used Eastern liturgical tradition. The Catholic Churches of this group are:

Albanians: One apostolic administration in southern Albania. Very small groups of Albanian Orthodox became Catholic in 1628 and again in 1900; liturgical language is Albanian.

Belarussians (formerly Byelorussian, also known as White Russian): No hierarchy. Most Belarusan Orthodox became Catholic with the Union of Brest in 1595-6, but this union was short lived. A modest revival has taken place since the end of communism. The liturgical language is Belarusan.

The Bulgarian Catholic Church: One apostolic exarchate in Bulgaria. Originated with a group of Bulgarian Orthodox who became Catholic in 1861; liturgical language is Old Slavonic.

Eparchy of Krizevci: One diocese located in Croatia with jurisdiction over all of former Yugoslavia.

A bishop for former Serbian Orthodox living in Catholic Croatia was first appointed in 1611; liturgical languages are Old Slavonic and Croatian.

The Greek Catholic Church: Apostolic exarchates in Greece and Turkey. Catholic missionaries in Constantinople formed a small group of Byzantine Catholics there in the mid-nineteenth century. Most of them moved to Greece in the 1920s. The liturgical language is Greek.

The Hungarian Catholic Church: One diocese and one apostolic exarchate in Hungary.

Descendants of groups of Orthodox in Hungary who became Catholic in the seventeenth century and after. The liturgical language is Hungarian.

The Italo-Albanian Catholic Church: Two dioceses, one territorial abbey in Italy.

Descended mostly from Albanian Orthodox who came to southern Italy and Sicily in the 15th century and eventually became Catholic; liturgical languages are Greek and Italian.

The Melkite Greek Catholic Church (Patriarchate): Five dioceses in Syria, seven in Lebanon, one each in Jordan, Israel, Brazil, US, Canada, Mexico, and Australia. Apostolic Exarchate in Venezuela, and patriarchal exarchates in Iraq and Kuwait.

Catholic missionaries began work within the Greek Orthodox Patriarchate of Antioch in the mid-seventeenth century. In 1724 it split into Catholic and Orthodox counterparts, the Catholics becoming known popularly as Melkites. Liturgical languages are Greek and Arabic.

The Romanian Greek Catholic Church (Metropolitanate): Five dioceses in Romania and one in the US.

Romanian Orthodox in Transylvania formally entered into union with Rome in 1700; the liturgical language is Romanian.

Russians: No hierarchy. An apostoic exarchate was established for Russia in 1917 and for Russians in China in 1928, but neither is functioning today. Five parishes exist in the diaspora.

The Ruthenian Catholic Church (Metropolitanate in the United States): One diocese in Ukraine, four in the United States, and an apostolic exarchate in the Czech Republic. Originated with the reception of 63 Orthodox priests into the Catholic Church at the Union of Uzhhorod in 1646. Liturgical languages are Old Slavonic and English.

The Slovak Catholic Church: One diocese and one apostolic exarchate in Slovakia, and one diocese in Canada.

Also originated with the Union of Uzhhorod in 1646; diocese of Presov was established for them in 1818. Liturgical languages are Old Slavonic and Slovak.

The Ukrainian Greek Catholic Church (Major Archbishopric): Six dioceses and one archepiscopal exarchate in Ukraine, two dioceses in Poland, five dioceses in Canada, four in the United States, one each in Australia, Brazil, and Argentina, apostolic exarchates in Great Britain, Germany, and France.

Originated with the Union of Brest between the Orthodox Metropolitanate of Kiev and the Catholic Church in 1595-6. Liturgical languages are Old Slavonic and Ukrainian.

CHALDEAN

Also called East Syrian, the liturgical tradition of the Chaldean Catholic and Syro-Malabar Catholic Churches as well as the Assyrian Church of the East. Descends from the ancient rite of the church of Mesopotamia in the Persian Empire. It is celebrated in the eastern dialect of classical Syriac. The Catholic Churches of this tradition are:

The Chaldean Catholic Church (Patriarchate): Ten dioceses in Iraq, three in Iran, one each in Lebanon, Egypt, Syria, Turkey, and the U.S.

A group of disaffected members of the ("nestorian") Assyrian Church of the East asked for union with Rome in 1553. In that year Pope Julius III ordained their leader a bishop and named him Patriarch; liturgical languages are Syriac, Arabic.

The Syro-Malabar Catholic Church (Major Archbishopric): 22 dioceses in India.

Descended from Thomas Christians of India who became Catholic in the wake of Portuguese colonization; the diocese of Ernakulam-Angamaly was raised to Major Archepiscopal status in 1993; the liturgical language is Malayalam.

EASTERN JURISDICTIONS

For centuries Eastern Churches were identifiable with a limited number of nationality and language groups in certain countries of the Middle East, Eastern Europe, Asia, and Africa. The persecution of religion in the former Soviet Union since 1917 and in communist-controlled countries for more than 40 years following World War II — in addition to decimating and destroying the Church in those places — resulted in the emigration of many Eastern Catholics from their homelands. This forced emigration, together with voluntary emigration, has led to the spread of Eastern Churches to many other countries.

EUROPE

(Apostolic visitors serve Armenian Catholics in Western Europe who do not have their own bishop, Chaldeans in Europe, and Maronites in Western and Northern Europe.)

Albania: Byzantine apostolic administration.
Austria: Byzantine ordinariate.
Bulgaria: Bulgarian apostolic exarchate
Croatia: Eparchy of Krizevci.
Czech Republic: Ruthenian apostolic exarchate.
France: Ukrainian apostolic exarchate. Armenian eparchy (1986). Ordinariate for all other Eastern Catholics.
Germany: Ukrainian apostolic exarchate.
Great Britain: Ukrainian apostolic exarchate.
Greece: Byzantine apostolic exarchate. Armenian ordinariate.
Hungary: Hungarian Byzantine eparchy, apostolic exarchate
Italy: Two Italo-Albanian eparchies, one abbacy.
Poland: Ukrainian metropolitan see (1996), one eparchy. Ordinariate for all other Eastern Catholics.
Romania: Romanian Byzantine metropolitan, four eparchies; Armenian ordinariate.
Russia: Russian apostolic exarchate (for Byzantine Catholics in Moscow).
Slovakia: Slovak Byzantine eparchy, one apostolic exarchate.
Ukraine: Armenian archeparchy; Ruthenian eparchy; Ukrainian major archbishopric, five eparchies.

ASIA

Armenia: Armenian ordinariate (for Armenians of Eastern Europe).
China: Russian Byzantine apostolic exarchate.
Cyprus: Maronite archeparchy.
India: Syro-Malankara metropolitan see, three eparchies.

Syro-Malabar major archbishopric (1993), three metropolitan sees (1995), 18 eparchies.
Iran: Two Chaldean metropolitan sees, one archeparchy, one eparchy; Armenian eparchy.
Iraq: Two Syrian archeparchies; Melkite patriarchal exarchate; Chaldean patriarchate, two metropolitan sees, three archeparchies and five eparchies; Armenian archeparchy.
Israel (including Jerusalem): Syrians patriarchal exarchate; Maronite archeparchy; Melkite archeparchy, patriarchal exarchate; Chaldean patriarchal exarchate; Armenian patriarchal exarchate.
Jordan: Melkite archeparchy.
Kuwait: Melkite patriarchal exarchate; Lebanon Maronite patriarchate, four archeparchies and six eparchies; Syrian patriarchate, patriarchal exarchate; two Melkite metropolitan and five archeparchal sees; Chaldean eparchy; Armenian patriarchate, metropolitan see.
Syria: Two Maronite archeparchies, one eparchy; two Syrian metropolitan and two archeparchal sees; Melkite patriarchate, four metropolitan sees, one archeparchy; Chaldean eparchy; Armenian archeparchy, one eparchy.

Turkey: Syrian patriarchal exarchate; Greek apostolic exarchate; Chaldean archeparchy; Armenian archeparchy.

OCEANIA

Australia: Ukrainian eparchy; Melkite eparchy (1987); Maronite eparchy.

AFRICA

Egypt: Coptic patriarchate, five eparchies; Maronite eparchy; Syrian eparchy; Melkite patriarchal dependency; Chaldean eparchy; Armenian eparchy.
Eritrea: Three Ethiopian eparchies.
Ethiopia: Ethiopian metropolitan see, one eparchy.
Sudan: Melkite patriarchal dependency.

NORTH AMERICA

Canada: One Ukrainian metropolitan, four eparchies; Slovak eparchy; Melkite eparchy; Armenian apostolic exarchate for Canada and the U.S. (New York is see city); Maronite eparchy.
United States: Two Maronite eparchies; Syrian eparchy (1995); one Ukrainian metropolitan see, three eparchies; one Ruthenian metropolitan see, three eparchies; Melkite eparchy; Romanian eparchy; Belarusan apostolic visitor; Armenian apostolic exarchate for Canada and U.S. (New York is see city); Chaldean eparchy; other Eastern Catholics are under the jurisdiction of local Latin bish-

ops. (See Eastern Catholics in the United States.)

Mexico: Melkite eparchy; Maronite eparchy (1995).

SOUTH AMERICA

Armenian Catholics in Latin America (including Mexico and excluding Argentina) are under the jurisdiction of an apostolic exarchate (see city, Buenos Aires, Argentina).

Argentina: Ukrainian eparchy; Maronite eparchy; Armenian eparchy; ordinariate for all other Eastern Catholics.

Brazil: Maronite eparchy; Melkite eparchy; Ukrainian eparchy; ordinariate for all other Eastern Catholics.

Venezuela: Melkite apostolic exarchate.

SYNODS, ASSEMBLIES

These assemblies are collegial bodies which have pastoral authority over members of the Eastern Catholic Churches. (Canons 102-113, 152-153, 322 of Oriental Code of Canon Law.)

Patriarchal Synods: Synod of the Catholic Coptic Church: patriarch of Alexandria of the Copts.

Synod of the Greek-Melkite Catholic Church: Patriarch of Antioch of the Greek Catholics-Melkites.

Synod of the Syrian Catholic Church: Patriarch of Antioch of the Syrians.

Synod of the Maronite Church: Patriarch of Antioch of the Maronites.

Synod of the Chaldean Church: Patriarch of Babylonia of the Chaldeans.

Synod of the Armenian Catholic Church: Patriarch of Cilicia of the Armenians.

MAJOR ARCHIEPISCOPAL SYNODS

The Synod of the Ukrainian Catholic Church (raised to major archiepiscopal status December 23, 1963): the major archbishop of Lviv of the Ukrainians is president.

The Synod of the Syro-Malabar Church (raised to major archiepiscopal status, January 29, 1993): the major archbishop of Ernakulam-Angamaly of the Syro-Malabars is president.

COUNCILS, ASSEMBLIES, CONFERENCES

Council of Ethiopian Churches
Council of Romanian Churches
Council of Ruthenian Churches, U.S.A.
Council of Syro-Malankarese Churches
Assembly of the Catholic Hierarchy of Egypt (December 5, 1983)
Assembly of Catholic Patriarchs and Bishops of Lebanon
Assembly of Ordinaries of the Syrian Arab Republic
Assembly of Catholic Ordinaries of the Holy Land (January 27, 1992)
Interritual Union of the Bishops of Iraq
Iranian Episcopal Conference (August 11, 1977)
Episcopal Conference of Turkey (November 30, 1987)

EASTERN CATHOLIC CHURCHES IN U.S.

BYZANTINE TRADITION

Ukrainians: There were four jurisdictions in the U.S.: the metropolitan see of Philadelphia (1924, metropolitan 1958) and the suffragan sees of Stamford, Connecticut (1956), St. Nicholas of Chicago (1961) and St. Josaphat in Parma (1983).

Ruthenians: There were four jurisdictions in the U.S.: the metropolitan see of Pittsburgh (est. 1924 at Pittsburgh; metropolitan and transferred to Munhall, 1969; transferred to Pittsburgh, 1977) and the suffragan sees of Passaic, New Jersey (1963), Parma, Ohio (1969) and Van Nuys, Calif. (1981). Hungarian and Croatian Byzantine Catholics in the U.S. are also under the jurisdiction of Ruthenian bishops.

Melkites: There was a jurisdiction of the Melkite eparchy of Newton, Massachusetts (established as an exarchate, 1965; eparchy, 1976).

Romanians: There were 15 Romanian Catholic Byzantine Rite parishes in the U.S., under the jurisdiction of the Romanian eparchy of St. George Martyr, Canton, Ohio (established as an exarchate, 1982; eparchy, 1987).

Belarusans: Have one parish in the U.S. — Christ the Redeemer, Chicago, Illinois.

Russians: Have parishes in California (St. Andrew, El Segundo, and Our Lady of Fatima Center, San Francisco); New York (St. Michael's Chapel of St. Patrick's Old Cathedral). They are under the jurisdiction of local Latin bishops.

ALEXANDRIAN TRADITION

Copts: Have a Catholic Chapel—Resurrection, in Brooklyn, New York.

ANTIOCHENE TRADITION

Maronites: There were two jurisdictions in the U.S.: the eparchy of St. Maron, Brooklyn (established at Detroit as an exarchate, 1966;

eparchy, 1972; transferred to Brooklyn, 1977) and the eparchy of Our Lady of Lebanon of Los Angeles (established March 1, 1994).

Syrians: The eparchy of Our Lady of the Deliverance of Newark was established in 1995 for Syrian Catholics of the U.S. and Canada.

Malankarese: Have a mission in Chicago.

ARMENIAN TRADITION

An apostolic exarchate for Canada and the United States (see in New York) was established July 3, 1981.

CHALDEAN TRADITION

Chaldeans: There was a jurisdiction of the eparchy of St. Thomas Apostle of Detroit (established as an exarchate, 1982; eparchy, 1986).

Syro-Malabarese (Malabar): There is a jurisdiction of the eparchy of St. Thomas of Chicago (established in 2001).

EASTERN CATHOLIC ASSOCIATES

Eastern Catholic Associates is the association of all Eastern Catholic bishops and their equivalents in law in the United States, representing the Armenian, Chaldean, Maronite, Melkite, Syriac, Romanian, Ruthenian and Ukrainian churches. The Syro-Malabar and Russian churches are also represented even though they do not have bishops in the U.S.

The association meets at the same time as the National Conference of Catholic Bishops in the fall of each year.

BYZANTINE DIVINE LITURGY

The Divine Liturgy in all rites is based on the consecration of bread and wine by the narration-reactualization of the actions of Christ at the Last Supper, and the calling down of the Holy Spirit. Aside from this fundamental usage, there are differences between the Roman (Latin) Rite and Eastern Rites, and among the Eastern Rites themselves. Following is a general description of the Byzantine Divine Liturgy which is in widest use in the Eastern Churches.

In the Byzantine, as in all Eastern Rites, the bread and wine are prepared at the start of the Liturgy. The priest does this in a little niche or at a table in the sanctuary. Taking a round loaf of leavened bread stamped with religious symbols, he cuts out a square host and other particles while reciting verses expressing the symbolism of the action. When the bread and wine are ready, he says a prayer of offering and incenses the oblations, the altar, the icons, and the people.

Liturgy of the Catechumens: At the altar, a litany for all classes of people is sung by the priest. The congregation answers, "Lord, have mercy." The Little Entrance comes next. In procession, the priest leaves the sanctuary carrying the Book of the Gospels, and then returns. He sings prayers especially selected for the day and the feast. These are followed by the solemn singing of the prayer, "Holy God, Holy Mighty One, Holy Immortal One." The Epistle follows. The Gospel is sung or read by the priest facing the people at the middle door of the sanctuary.

An interruption after the Liturgy of the Catechumens, formerly an instructional period for those learning the faith, is clearly marked. Catechumens, if present, are dismissed with a prayer. Following this are a prayer and litany for the faithful.

Great Entrance: The Great Entrance or solemn Offertory Procession then takes place. The priest first says a long silent prayer for himself, in preparation for the great act to come. Again he incenses the oblations, the altar, the icons, and people. He goes to the table on the Gospel side for the veil-covered paten and chalice. When he arrives back at the sanctuary door, he announces the intention of the Mass in the prayer: "May the Lord God remember all of you in his kingdom, now and forever." After another litany, the congregation recites the Nicene Creed.

Consecration: The most solemn portion of the sacrifice is introduced by the preface, which is very much like the preface of the Roman Rite. At the beginning of the last phrase, the priest raises his voice to introduce the singing of the Sanctus. During the singing he reads the introduction to the words of consecration. The words of consecration are sung aloud, and the people sing "Amen" to both consecrations. As the priest raises the Sacred Species in solemn offering, he sings: "Thine of Thine Own we offer unto Thee in behalf of all and for all." A prayer to the Holy Spirit is followed by the commemorations, in which special mention is made of the all-holy, most blessed and glorious Lady, the Mother of God and ever-Virgin Mary. The dead are remembered and then the living.

Holy Communion: A final litany for spiritual gifts precedes the Our Father. The Sacred Body and Blood are elevated with the words, "Holy Things for the Holy." The Host is then broken and commingled with the Precious Blood. The priest recites preparatory prayers for Holy Communion, consumes the Sacred Species, and distributes Holy Communion to the people under the forms of both bread and wine. During this time a communion verse is sung by the choir or congregation.

The Liturgy closes quickly after this. The consecrated Species of bread and wine are removed to the side table to be consumed later by the priest. A prayer of thanksgiving is recited, a prayer for all the people is said in front of the icon of Christ, a blessing is invoked upon all, and the people are dismissed.

BYZANTINE CALENDAR

The Byzantine calendar has many distinctive features of its own, although it shares common elements with the Roman calendar — e.g., general purpose, commemoration of the mysteries of faith and of the saints, identical dates for some feasts. Among the distinctive things are the following. The liturgical year begins on September 1, the Day of Indiction, in contrast with the Latin or Roman start on the First Sunday of Advent late in November or early in December. The Advent season begins on December 10.

Cycles of the Year

As in the Roman usage, the dating of feasts follows the Gregorian Calendar. Formerly, until well into this century, the Julian Calendar was used. (The Julian Calendar, which is now about 13 days late, is still used by some Eastern Churches.) The year has several cycles, which include proper seasons, the feasts of saints, and series of New Testament readings. All of these elements of worship are contained in liturgical books of the rite. The ecclesiastical calendar, called the *Menologion,* explains the nature of feasts, other observances and matters pertaining to the liturgy for each day of the year. In some cases, its contents include the lives of saints and the history and meaning of feasts.

The Divine Liturgy (Mass) and Divine Office for the proper of the saints, fixed feasts, and the Christmas season are contained in the *Menaion.* The *Triodion* covers the pre-Lenten season of preparation for Easter; Lent begins two days before the Ash Wednesday observance of the Roman Rite. The Pentecostarion contains the liturgical services from Easter to the Sunday of All Saints, the first after Pentecost. The *Evangelion* and *Apostolos* are books in which the Gospels, and Acts of the Apostles and the Epistles, respectively, are arranged according to the order of their reading in the Divine Liturgy and Divine Office throughout the year.

The cyclic progression of liturgical music throughout the year, in successive and repetitive periods of eight weeks, is governed by the *Oktoechos,* the *Book of Eight Tones.*

Sunday Names

Many Sundays are named after the subject of the Gospel read in the Mass of the day or after the name of a feast falling on the day — e.g., Sunday of the Publican and Pharisee, of the Prodigal Son, of the Samaritan Woman, of St. Thomas the Apostle, of the Fore-Fathers (Old Testament Patriarchs).

Other Sundays are named in the same manner as in the Roman calendar e.g., numbered Sundays of Lent and after Pentecost.

Holy Days

The calendar lists about 28 holy days. Many of the major holy days coincide with those of the Roman calendar, but the feast of the Immaculate Conception is observed on December 9 instead of December 8, and the feast of All Saints falls on the Sunday after Pentecost rather than on November 1. Instead of a single All Souls' Day, there are five All Souls' Saturdays. According to regulations in effect in the Byzantine (Ruthenian) Archeparchy of Pittsburgh and its suffragan sees of Passaic, Parma, and Van Nuys, holy days are obligatory, solemn and simple, and attendance at the Divine Liturgy is required on five obligatory days —the feasts of the Epiphany, the Ascension, Sts. Peter and Paul, the Assumption of the Blessed Virgin Mary, and Christmas. Although attendance at the liturgy is not obligatory on 15 solemn and seven simple holy days, it is recommended. In the Byzantine (Ukrainian) Archeparchy of Philadelphia and its suffragan sees of St. Josaphat in Parma, St. Nicholas (Chicago) and Stamford, the obligatory feasts are the Circumcision, Epiphany, Annunciation, Easter, Ascension, Pentecost, Dormition (Assumption of Mary), Immaculate Conception and Christmas.

Lent

The first day of Lent — the Monday before Ash Wednesday of the Roman Rite — and Good Friday are days of strict abstinence for persons in the age bracket of obligation. No meat, eggs, or dairy products may be eaten on these days. All persons over the age of fourteen must abstain from meat on Fridays during Lent, Holy Saturday, and the vigils of the feasts of Christmas and Epiphany; abstinence is urged, but is not obligatory, on Wednesdays of Lent. The abstinence obligation is not in force on certain "free" or "privileged" Fridays.

Synaxis

An observance without a counterpart in the Roman calendar is the synaxis. This is a commemoration, on the day following a feast, of persons involved with the occasion for the feast —

e.g., September 9, the day following the feast of the Nativity of the Blessed Virgin Mary, is the Synaxis of Joachim and Anna, her parents.

Holy Week

In the Byzantine Rite, Lent is liturgically concluded with the Saturday of Lazarus, the day before Palm Sunday, which commemorates the raising of Lazarus from the dead. On the following Monday, Tuesday, and Wednesday, the Liturgy of the Presanctified is prescribed.

On Holy Thursday, the Liturgy of St. Basil the Great is celebrated together with Vespers.

The Divine Liturgy is not celebrated on Good Friday. On Holy Saturday, the Liturgy of St. Basil the Great is celebrated along with Vespers.

BYZANTINE FEATURES

Art: Named for the empire in which it developed, Byzantine art is a unique blend of imperial Roman and classic Hellenic culture with Christian inspiration. The art of the Greek Middle Ages, it reached a peak of development in the tenth or eleventh century. Characteristic of its products, particularly in mosaic and painting, are majesty, dignity, refinement and grace. Its sacred paintings, called icons, are reverenced highly in all the Eastern Churches of the Byzantine tradition.

Church Building: The classical model of Byzantine church architecture is the Church of the Holy Wisdom (*Hagia Sophia*), built in Constantinople in the first half of the sixth century and still standing. The square structure, extended in some cases in the form of a cross, is topped by a distinctive onion-shaped dome and surmounted by a triple-bar cross. The altar is at the eastern end of building, where the wall bellies out to form an apse. The altar and sanctuary are separated from the body of the church by a fixed or movable screen, the iconostas, to which icons or sacred pictures are attached (see below).

Clergy: The Byzantine Churches have married as well as celibate priests. In places other than the U.S., where married candidates have not been accepted for ordination since about 1929, men already married can be ordained to the diaconate and priesthood and can continue in marriage after ordination. Celibate deacons and priests cannot marry after ordination; neither can a married priest remarry after the death of his wife. Bishops must be unmarried.

Iconostas: A large screen decorated with sacred pictures or icons which separates the sanctuary from the nave of a church; its equivalent in the Roman Rite, for thus separating the sanctuary from the nave, is an altar rail. An iconostas has three doors through which the sacred ministers enter the sanctuary during the Divine Liturgy: smaller (north and south) Deacons' Doors and a large central Royal Door. The Deacons' Doors usually feature the icons of Sts. Gabriel and Michael; the Royal Door, the icons of the Evangelists—Matthew, Mark, Luke, and John. To the right and left of the Royal Door are the icons of Christ the Teacher and of the Blessed Virgin Mary with the Infant Jesus. To the extreme right and left are the icons of the patron of the church and St. John the Baptist (or St. Nicholas of Myra). Immediately above the Royal Door is a picture of the Last Supper. To the right are six icons depicting the major feasts of Christ, and to the left are six icons portraying the major feasts of the Blessed Virgin Mary. Above the picture of the Last Supper is a large icon of Christ the King. Some icon screens also have pictures of the Twelve Apostles and the major Old Testament prophets surmounted by a crucifixion scene.

Liturgical Language: In line with Eastern tradition, Byzantine practice has favored the use of the language of the people in the liturgy. Two great advocates of the practice were Sts. Cyril and Methodius, apostles of the Slavs, who devised the Cyrillic alphabet and pioneered the adoption of Slavonic in the liturgy.

Sacraments: Baptism is administered by immersion, and confirmation (Chrismation) is conferred at the same time. The Eucharist is administered by intinction, i.e., by giving the communicant a piece of consecrated leavened bread which has been dipped into the consecrated wine. When giving absolution in the sacrament of penance, the priest holds his stole over the head of the penitent. Distinctive marriage ceremonies include the crowning of the bride and groom. Ceremonies for anointing the sick closely resemble those of the Roman Rite. Holy orders are conferred by a bishop.

Sign of the Cross: The sign of the cross in conjunction with a deep bow expresses reverence for the presence of Christ in the Blessed Sacrament. (See also entry in Glossary.)

VESTMENTS, APPURTENANCES

Antimension: A silk or linen cloth laid on the altar for the Liturgy; it may be decorated with a picture of the burial of Christ and the instruments of his passion; the relics of martyrs are sewn into the front border.

Asteriskos: Made of two curved bands of gold or silver which cross each other to form a double arch; a star depends from the junction, which forms a cross; it is placed over the *diskos* holding the consecrated bread and is covered with a veil.

Diskos: A shallow plate, which may be elevated on a small stand, corresponding to the Roman Rite paten.

Eileton: A linen cloth which corresponds to the Roman Rite corporal.

Epimanikia: Ornamental cuffs; the right cuff symbolizing strength, the left, patience and good will.

Epitrachelion: A stole with ends sewn together, having a loop through which the head is passed; its several crosses symbolize priestly duties.

Lance: A metal knife used for cutting up the bread to be consecrated during the Liturgy.

Phelonion: An ample cape, long in the back and sides and cut away in front; symbolic of the higher gifts of the Holy Spirit.

Poterion: A chalice or cup which holds the wine and Precious Blood.

Spoon: Used in administering Holy Communion by intinction; consecrated leavened bread is dipped into consecrated wine and spooned onto the tongue of the communicant.

Sticharion: A long white garment of linen or silk with wide sleeves and decorated with embroidery; formerly the vestment for clerics in minor orders, acolytes, lectors, chanters, and subdeacons; symbolic of purity.

Veils: Three are used, one to cover the *poterion*, the second the *diskos*, and the third both.

Zone: A narrow clasped belt made of the same material as the *epitrachelion*; symbolic of the wisdom of the priest, his strength against enemies of the Church, and his willingness to perform holy duties.

Katchkar Cross 12th century

Part 4

THE CODE OF CANON LAW

Canon Law is the term that denotes the body of laws governing the Catholic Church. The name is derived from the Greek word *kanon* (rule, i.e., rule of practical direction), which, from the fourth century, was used to denote the ordinances and regulations promulgated by the various Church councils that were convened to discuss problems or important topics. The actual term "canon law" (*ius canonicum*) came into use in the 1100s and was intended to differentiate ecclesiastical law from civil law (*ius civile*).

HISTORY OF CANON LAW

In a practical sense, the laws and regulations began to take shape as early as apostolic times and were evident in their nascent form in the Didache, the Didascalia and the Apostolic Tradition. Owing to the persecution of the Church, however, there was little effort to gather laws together, and certainly less time was devoted to systematizing them.

The fourth century brought the Church freedom from persecution and the resulting rapid growth in membership that was a concomitant of the favors bestowed upon the faith by the rulers of the Roman Empire. New laws were naturally needed and desired. Local regulations were soon established through the decrees of the councils, although these most often had only a local authority and adherence. The general (or ecumenical) councils made laws for the whole Church, and the custom developed of carrying on the decrees of previous assemblies by having them read before the start of a new council. Collections of these laws or canons were then undertaken, but these did not bear the weight of being an official code as they were gathered under private authority.

The earliest efforts at collecting Church laws were centered around the private compilation of the decrees of the Eastern councils to which were added those of the Western Church. The councils of the African Church also made lasting contributions, the most significant coming out of the Seventeenth Council of Carthage (419), which accepted the book of canons later adopted into the canon law of both the Eastern and Western Churches. An official Code of Canon Law was recognized in the seventh century under the Isidorian Collection. Other important influences were the writings of monks in England and Ireland. The monks compiled lists of sins and various offenses to which confessors applied the proper fines or penances. The resulting books were called Penitentials, and they offer scholars an invaluable glimpse into the state of Church law in early medieval England and the development of moral theology.

The Carolingian Reforms of the Church under Charlemagne facilitated the enactment of much legislation that was beneficial to the faith, but it also signaled a long period of secular interference in ecclesiastical affairs. Two by-products of this lay intrusion were the creation of the forged but interesting False Decretals (collections of false canons and decrees of the popes used to falsify the Church's position) and the application of legal arguments by Churchmen that could protect the Church from abuse. Efforts at revitalization would become heightened under the Gregorian Reform, in particular with the reign of Pope St. Gregory VII (1073-1085). From that time, throughout the Middle Ages, laws from the Church would be centered in and produced by the papacy, assisted in running the administration of the Church by the Roman Curia.

Gradually, legal experts collected the decrees of popes, enactments of councils, and sources of older, ancient canons. To these were added glosses, or commentaries, to assist in the teaching of the details of the subject. Still, the study of canon law was severely handicapped by the sheer number of collections, the contradiction between many points of law, and the inability to find specific laws because of the chronological arrangements of the material. Thus can be seen the major significance of the *Decretum* of Gratian, published around 1148 in Bologna. Compiled by the legal expert Gratian, the *Decretum* (in full, *Concordantia discordantum canonum*) was not a formal collection of canons but sought to provide a juridical system for its readers. Toward this end, though, Gratian examined (and excerpted) virtually every canon ever published. The *Decretum* was quickly adopted as the textbook of canon law, despite the fact that it was a private collection and not codified.

Over the next centuries, the popes added to the body of laws by giving rulings to those questions posed to them by bishops from around the Church. These decretal letters were then brought together and, for purposes of comprehensiveness, added to the *Decretum Gratiani*. The most important of these was the *Liber extra*, the collection made by St. Raymond Peñafort for Pope Gregory IX. This received official approval and was to be a vital source for the *Corpus Juris Canonici*. Other remarkable contributors to canon law in the late Middle Ages were Zenzelinus de Cassanis, Jean Chappuis, Guido de Baysio, John the Teuton (or Joannes Teutonicus), Stephen of Tournai, and most of all, Joannes Andreae (d. 1348).

Considerable activity was initiated by the Council of Trent (1545-1563), which sought to reform and reinvigorate the Church in the wake of the Protestant Reformation. The same century brought the formation in 1588 of the Sacred Congregation of the Curia by Pope Sixtus V (r. 1585-1590), which became the main means of implementing new laws and examining facets of established ones.

The final decision to codify the laws of the Church was made by Pope St. Pius X who, in 1903, issued *Arduum*, the *motu proprio* ordering the complete reform and codification of all canon law. It was completed and promulgated in 1917 as the *Codex Juris Canonici*, the first official guide to the laws of the Catholic Church. A new Code of Canon Law was issued by Pope John Paul II in 1983, the final result of a call for a new code dating back to Pope John XXIII (r. 1958-1963) and continued by Pope Paul VI (r. 1963-1978).

The 1983 Code of Canon Law

Pope John Paul II promulgated a revised Code of Canon Law for the Latin Rite on January 25, 1983, with the apostolic constitution *Sacrae Disciplinae Legis* ("Of the Sacred Discipline of Law") and ordered it into effect the following November 27. Promulgation of the Code marked the completion of the last major reform in the Church stemming from the Second Vatican Council.

The 1983 Code of Canon Law replaced the one which had been in effect since 1918. The new Code incorporates into law the insights of Vatican Council II. These 1,752 canons focus on the People of God and the threefold ministries of sanctifying, teaching, and governance. Also included are general norms, temporalities, sanctions, and procedures.

Guiding Principles

When Pope John XXIII announced on January 25, 1959, that he was going to convoke the Second Vatican Council, he also called for a revision of the existing Code of Canon Law. His successor, Paul VI, appointed a commission for this purpose in 1963 and subsequently enlarged it. The commission, which began its work after the conclusion of the Council in 1965, was instructed by the 1967 Synod of Bishops to direct its efforts in line with ten guiding principles. The bishops said the revised Code should:

- be juridical in character, not just a set of broad moral principles;
- be intended primarily for the external forum (regarding determinable fact, as opposed to the internal forum of conscience);
- be clearly pastoral in spirit;
- incorporate most of the faculties bishops need in their ministry;
- provide for subsidiarity or decentralization;
- be sensitive to human rights;
- state clear procedures for administrative processes and tribunals;
- be based on the principle of territoriality;
- reduce the number of penalties for infraction of law;
- have a new structure.

The commission carried out its mandate with the collegial collaboration of bishops all over the world and in consultation and correspondence with individuals and experts in canon law, theology, and related disciplines. The group finished its work in 1981 and turned its final draft over to Pope John Paul II at its final plenary meeting in October of that year.

Features

The revised code is shorter (1,752 canons) than the one it has replaced (2,414 canons) and has a number of important features:

It is more pastoral and flexible, as well as more theologically-oriented than the former Code.

It gives greater emphasis than its predecessor to a number of significant facets and concepts in church life.

In the apostolic constitution with which he promulgated the Code, Pope John Paul II called attention to its nature and some of its features, as follows:

"This Code has arisen from a single intention, that of restoring Christian living. All the work of the (Second Vatican) Council actually drew its norms and its orientation from such an intention.

"A . . . question . . . arises about the very nature of the Code of Canon Law. In order to answer this question well, it is necessary to recall the distant heritage of law contained in the books of the Old and New Testaments, from which, as from its first spring, the whole juridical legislation of the Church derives.

"Christ the Lord did not in fact will to destroy the very rich heritage of the law and the prophets which had been forming over the course of the history and experience of the People of God in the Old Testament. On the contrary, He gave fulfillment to it (cf. Mt. 5:17). Thus, in a new more lofty way, it became part of the inheritance of the New Testament."

"Therefore although, when expounding the paschal mystery, St. Paul teaches that justification is not obtained through the works of the law but through faith (cf. Rom. 3:28; Gal. 2:16), he does not thereby exclude the obligatory force of the Decalogue (cf. Rom. 13:28; Gal. 5:13-25 and 6:2), nor does he deny the importance of discipline in the Church of God (cf. 1Cor. 5 and 6). The writings of the New Testament, therefore allow us to understand the importance of discipline even better and to understand better how discipline is more closely connected with the salvific character of the Gospel message itself."

Prime Legislative Document

"Since this is so, it seems clear enough that the Code in no way has its scope to substitute for faith, grace, the charisms, and especially charity in the life of the Church of the faithful. On the contrary, its end is rather to create such order in ecclesial society that, assigning primacy to love, grace and charisms, it at the same time renders more active their organic developments in the life both of the ecclesial society and of the individuals belonging to it. "Inasmuch as it is the Church's prime legislative document, based on the juridical and legislative heritage of revelation and tradition, the Code must be regarded as the necessary instrument whereby due order is preserved in both individual and social life and in the Church's activity. Therefore, besides containing the fundamental elements of the hierarchical and organic structure of the Church, laid down by her divine Founder and founded on apostolic or at any rate most ancient tradition, and besides outstanding norms concerning the carrying out of the task mandated to the Church herself, the Code must also define a certain number of rules and norms of action."

Suits the Nature of the Church

"The instrument the Code is fully suits the Church's nature, for the Church is presented, especially through the magisterium of the Second Vatican Council, in her universal scope, and especially through the Council's ecclesiological teaching. In a certain sense, indeed, this new Code may be considered as a great effort to transfer that same ecclesiological or conciliar doctrine into canonical language. And, if it is impossible for the image of the Church described by the Council's teaching to be perfectly converted into canonical language, the Code nonetheless must always be referred to that very image, as the primary pattern whose outline the Code ought to express as well as it can by its own nature.

"From this derive a number of fundamental norms by which the whole of the new Code is ruled, of course within the limits proper to it as well as the limits of the very language befitting the material.

"It may rather be rightly affirmed that from this comes that note whereby the Code is regarded as a complement to the magisterium expounded by the Second Vatican Council.

"The following elements are most especially to be noted among those expressing a true and genuine image of the Church: the doctrine whereby the Church is proposed as the People of God and the hierarchical authority is propounded as service; in addition, the doctrine which shows the Church to be a 'communion' and from that lays down the mutual relationships which ought to exist between the particular and universal Church and between collegiality and primacy; likewise, the doctrine whereby all members of the People of God, each in the manner proper to him, share in Christ's threefold office of priest, prophet and king; to this doctrine is also connected that regarding the duties and rights of the Christian faithful, particularly the laity; then there is the effort which the Church has to make for ecumenism."

Code Necessary for the Church

"Indeed, the Code of Canon Law is extremely necessary for the Church . . . The Church needs it for her hierarchichal and organic structure to be visible: so that exercise of the offices and tasks divinely entrusted to her, especially her sacred power and administration of the sacraments, should be rightly ordered; so that mutual relations of the Christian faithful may be carried out according to justice based on charity, with the rights of all being safeguarded and defined; so that we may then prepare and perform our common tasks, and that these, undertaken in order to live a Christian life more perfectly, may be fortified by means of the canonical laws.

"Thus, canonical laws need to be observed because of their very nature. Hence it is of the greatest importance that the norms be carefully expounded on the basis of solid juridical, canonical and theological foundations."

BOOKS OF THE CODE

Book I, General Norms (Canons 1-203):

Canons in this book cover Church laws, in general, custom and law, general decrees and instructions, administrative acts, statutes, physical and juridical persons, juridical acts, the power of governing, ecclesiastical offices, prescription (statutes of limitations), the reckoning of time.

Book II, The People of God (Canons 204-746):

Canons in Part I cover the obligations and rights of all the faithful, the obligations and rights of lay persons, sacred ministers and clerics, personal prelatures, and associations of the faithful.

Canons in Part II cover the hierarchic constitution of the Church under the headings: the supreme authority of the Church and the college of bishops, diocesan churches and the authority constituted in them, councils of diocesan churches and the internal order of diocesan churches.

Canons in Part III cover institutes of consecrated life and societies of apostolic life.

Book III: The Teaching Office of the Church (Canons 747-833):

Canons under this heading cover the ministry of the divine word, the missionary action of the Church, Catholic education, the instruments of social communication and books in particular, and the profession of faith.

Book IV, The Sanctifying Office of the Church (Canons 834-1252):

Canons under this heading cover each of the seven sacraments – baptism, confirmation, the Eucharist, penance, anointing of the sick, holy orders and matrimony; other acts of divine worship including sacramentals, the Liturgy of the Hours, ecclesiastical burial; the veneration of saints, sacred images and relics, vows and oaths.

Book V, Temporal Goods of the Church (Canons 1254-1310):

Canons under this heading cover the acquisition and administration of goods, contracts, the alienation of goods, wills and pious foundations.

Book VI, Sanctions in the Church (Canons 1311-1399):

Canons in Part I cover crimes and penalties in general: the punishment of crimes in general, penal law and penal precept, persons subject to penal sanctions, penalties and other punishments, the application and cessation of penalties.

Canons in Part II cover penalties for particular crimes: crimes against religion and the unity of the Church; crimes against the authority of Church and the liberty of the Church; the usurpation of Church offices and crimes in exercising office; false accusation of a confessor; crimes against special obligations; crimes against human life and liberty; a general norm regarding the punishment of external violations of divine law not specifically covered in the Code.

Book VII, Procedures (Canons 1400-1752):

Judicial proceedings are the principal subjects of canons under this heading: tribunals and their personnel, parties to proceedings, details regarding litigation and the manner in which it is conducted, special proceedings – with emphasis on matrimonial cases.

RIGHTS AND OBLIGATIONS OF ALL THE FAITHFUL

The following rights are listed in Canons 208-223 of the revised Code of Canon Law; additional rights are specified in other canons.

- Because of their baptism and regeneration, there is equality regarding dignity and action for the building up of the Body of Christ.
- They are bound always to preserve communion with the Church.
- According to their condition and circumstances, they should strive to lead a holy life and promote the growth and holiness of the Church.
- They have the right and duty to work for the spread of the divine message of salvation to all peoples of all times and places.
- They are bound to follow with Christian obedience those things which the bishops, as they represent Christ, declare as teachers of the faith or establish as rulers of the Church.
- They have the right to make known their needs, especially their spiritual needs, to pastors of the Church.
- They have the right, and sometimes the duty, of making known to pastors and others of the faithful their opinions about things pertaining to the good of the Church.
- They have the right to receive help from their pastors, from the spiritual goods of the Church and especially from the word of God and the sacraments.
- They have the right to divine worship performed according to prescribed rules of their rite, and to follow their own form of spiritual life in line with the doctrine of the Church.
- They have the right to freely establish and

control associations for good and charitable purposes, to foster the Christian vocation in the world, and to hold meetings related to the accomplishment of these purposes.

- They have the right to promote and support apostolic action but may not call it "Catholic" unless they have the consent of competent authority.
- They have a right to a Christian education.
- They have a right to freedom of inquiry in sacred studies, in accordance with the teaching authority of the Church.
- They have a right to freedom in the choice of their state of life.
- No one has the right to harm the good name of another person or to violate his or her right to maintain personal privacy.
- They have the right to vindicate the rights they enjoy in the Church, and to defend themselves in a competent ecclesiastical forum.
- They have the obligation to provide for the needs of the Church, with respect to things pertaining to divine worship, apostolic and charitable works, and the reasonable support of ministers of the Church.
- They have the obligation to promote social justice and to help the poor from their own resources.
- In exercising their rights, the faithful should have regard for the common good of the Church and for the rights and duties of others.
- Church authority has the right to monitor the exercise of rights proper to the faithful, with the common good in view.

RIGHTS AND OBLIGATIONS OF LAY PERSONS

In addition to rights and obligations common to all the faithful and those stated in other canons, lay persons are bound by the obligations and enjoy the rights specified in these canons (224-231).

- Lay persons, like all the faithful, are called by God to the apostolate in virtue of their baptism and confirmation. They have the obligation and right, individually or together in associations, to work for the spread and acceptance of the divine message of salvation among people everywhere; this obligation is more urgent in those circumstances in which people can hear the Gospel and get to know Christ only through them (lay persons).
- They are bound to bring an evangelical spirit to bear on the order of temporal things and to give Christian witness in carrying out their secular pursuits.
- Married couples are obliged to work for the building up of the people of God through their marital and family life.
- Parents have the most serious obligation to provide for the Christian education of their children according to the doctrine handed down by the Church.
- Lay persons have the same civil liberty as other citizens. In the use of this liberty, they should take care that their actions be imbued with an evangelical spirit. They should attend to the doctrine proposed by the magisterium of the Church but should take care that, in questions of opinion, they do not propose their own opinion as the doctrine of the Church.
- Qualified lay persons are eligible to hold and perform the duties of ecclesiastical offices open to them in accord with the provisions of law.
- Properly qualified lay persons can assist pastors of the Church as experts and counselors.
- Lay persons have the obligation and enjoy the right to acquire knowledge of doctrine commensurate with their capacity and condition.
- They have the right to pursue studies in the sacred sciences in pontifical universities or facilities and in institutes of religious sciences, and to obtain academic degrees.
- If qualified, they are eligible to receive from ecclesiastical authority a mandate to teach sacred sciences.
- Laymen can be invested by liturgical rite and in a stable manner in the ministries of lector and acolyte.
- Lay persons, by temporary assignment, can fulfill the office of lector in liturgical actions; likewise, all lay persons can perform the duties of commentator or cantor.
- In cases of necessity and in the absence of the usual ministers, lay persons — even if not lectors or acolytes — can exercise the ministry of the word, lead liturgical prayers, confer baptism and distribute Communion, according to the prescripts of law.
- Lay persons who devote themselves permanently or temporarily to the service of the Church are obliged to acquire the formation necessary for carrying out their duties in a proper manner.
- They have a right to remuneration for their service which is just and adequate to provide for their own needs and those of their families; they also have a right to insurance, social security, and health insurance.

Part 5

THE TEACHINGS OF THE CATHOLIC CHURCH

APOSTLES' CREED

I believe in God, the Father almighty, creator of heaven and earth; and in Jesus Christ, his only Son, our Lord; who was conceived of the Holy Spirit, born of the Virgin Mary, suffered under Pontius Pilate, was crucified, died and was buried.

He descended into hell; on the third day he rose again from the dead. He ascended into heaven, and

is seated at the right hand of the Father. From thence he shall come again to judge the living and the dead.

I believe in the Holy Spirit, the Holy Catholic Church, the communion of saints, the forgiveness of sins, the resurrection of the body, and life everlasting. Amen.

THE CATECHISM OF THE CATHOLIC CHURCH
(By Russell Shaw)

"The *Catechism of the Catholic Church* . . . is a statement of the Church's faith and of Catholic doctrine, attested to or illumined by Sacred Scripture, the Apostolic Tradition, and the Church's Magisterium. I declare it to be a sure norm for teaching the faith and thus a valid and legitimate instrument for ecclesial communion."

Thus Pope John Paul II in the Apostolic Constitution *Fidei Depositum* (The Deposit of Faith) formally presented the first official catechism or compendium of doctrine for the universal Church to have been published since the sixteenth century.

Fidei Depositum is dated October 11, 1992, the thirtieth anniversary of the opening of the Second Vatican Council (1962-65), and that date is significant. The predecessor of the *Catechism of the Catholic Church* is the *Roman Catechism* or *Catechism of the Council of Trent*, which was published by Pope St. Pius V in 1566 following the great reforming council held from 1545 to 1563. As the *Roman Catechism* sets forth the doctrine of the Church in light of the Council of Trent, so the *Catechism of the Catholic Church* sets forth the Church's teaching against the background of Vatican Council II.

HISTORY OF THE CATECHISM

In development since 1986, the definitive text of the *Catechism of the Catholic Church* was officially approved by Pope John Paul on June 25, 1992, with December 8 the date of formal promulgation.

Nine separate drafts of the *Catechism* were prepared. The document was written in French.

In November, 1989, the commission of cardinals sent a draft text to all the bishops of the world asking for their comments and suggestions. Although this consultation produced a reaction generally favorable to the text, more than 24,000 individual amendments were submitted by the bishops, and these were reviewed by the commission, and helped to shape the further revision of the document.

The pope in *Fidei Depositum* described the Catechism as "a sure and authentic reference text" both for the teaching of Catholic doctrine and particularly for the preparation of local catechisms; he said the catechism was presented to "all the Church's Pastors and the Christian faithful" with these ends in view. Other purposes mentioned included helping Catholics to deepen their knowledge of the faith, supporting ecumenical efforts by "showing carefully the content and wondrous harmony of the catholic faith," and providing authoritative answers to anyone who wishes to know "what the Catholic Church believes."

STRUCTURE AND CONTENTS OF THE CATECHISM

The *Catechism* adopts the four-fold division of the *Roman Catechism*. The four parts or "pillars" deal with the Creed; the Sacred Liturgy, with special emphasis on the sacraments; the Christian way of life, analyzed according to the Ten Commandments; and Prayer, considered in the framework of the petitions of the Our Father.

Describing this organizational scheme, Pope John Paul said: "The four parts are related one to another: the Christian mystery is the object of faith (first part); it is celebrated and communicated in liturgical actions (second part); it is present to enlighten and sustain the children of God in their actions (third part); it is the basis of our prayer, the privileged expression of which is the Our Father, and it represents the object of our supplication, our praise and our intercession (fourth part)."

The pope also stressed the Christocentric nature of Christian faith as it is presented in the *Catechism*. "In reading the *Catechism of the Catholic Church* we can perceive the wonderful unity of the mystery of God, his saving will, as well as the central place of Jesus Christ, the only-begotten Son of God, sent by the Father, made man in the womb of the Blessed Virgin Mary by the power of the Holy Spirit, to be our Savior. Having died and risen, Christ is always present in his Church, especially in the sacraments; he is the source of our faith, the model of Christian conduct, and the Teacher of our prayer."

The text of the *Catechism of the Catholic Church*, with extensive cross-references and sectional summaries, consists of 2,865 numbered paragraphs. Passages in large print set out its more substantive contents, while passages in small print provide background information and explanations; there are numerous cross-references in the margins directing readers to other passages that treat the same theme or related themes. Among the features of the catechism are the "In Brief" sections found throughout, which sum up the teaching of the preceding unit.

OUTLINE OF THE CATECHISM

Prologue (1-25). The nature of catechesis is described, along with the aim of the present catechism and its intended readership, its structure, its use, and the desirability of adaptations for different cultures, age groups, etc.

PART ONE: The Profession of Faith (26-1065)

Section One discusses the nature of faith. "Faith is man's response to God, who reveals himself and gives himself to man, at the same time bringing man a superabundant light as he searches for the ultimate meaning of his life. Thus we shall consider first that search (Chapter One), then the divine Revelation by which God comes to meet man (Chapter Two), and finally the response of faith (Chapter Three)" (26). The topics discussed include knowledge of God; Divine Revelation and its transmission; Sacred Scripture; and faith as the human response to God. "We do not believe in formulas, but in those realities they express, which faith allows us to touch. . . . All the same, we do approach these realities with the help of formulations of the faith

which permit us to express the faith and to hand it on, to celebrate it in community, to assimilate and live on it more and more" (170).

Section Two deals with the profession of Christian faith, with the treatment organized according to the articles of the Creed. The Creed used is the Apostles' Creed; its "great authority," says the *Catechism*, quoting St. Ambrose, arises from its being "the Creed of the Roman Church, the See of Peter, the first of the apostles" (194). Among the doctrines covered in the three chapters of this section are the Trinity, creation, the angels, the creation of man, original sin, the Incarnation, the virgin birth, redemption, the Resurrection of Christ, the work of the Holy Spirit, the Church, the hierarchical constitution of the Church, the communion of saints, the Virgin Mary as Mother of Christ and Mother of the Church, the resurrection of the dead, judgment, heaven, and hell. "[T]he Creed's final 'Amen' repeats and confirms its first words: 'I believe.' To believe is to say 'Amen' to God's words, promises and commandments; to entrust oneself completely to him who is the 'Amen' of infinite love and perfect faithfulness. The Christian's everyday life will then be the 'Amen' to the 'I believe' of our baptismal profession of faith" (1064).

PART TWO: The Celebration of the Christian Mystery (1066-1690)

Section One considers the sacramental economy. It explains that in this present "age of the Church," begun on Pentecost, "Christ now lives and acts in his Church, in a new way appropriate to this new age. He acts through the sacraments in what the common Tradition of the East and the West calls 'the sacramental economy'. . . the communication (or 'dispensation') of the fruits of Christ's Paschal Mystery in the celebration of the Church's 'sacramental' liturgy" (1076). Topics treated here are the Paschal Mystery and its sacramental celebration.

Section Two covers the seven sacraments of the Church. "Christ instituted the sacraments of the new law. . . . The seven sacraments touch all the stages and all the important moments of Christian life: they give birth and increase, healing and mission to the Christian's life of faith. There is thus a certain resemblance between the stages of natural life and the stages of the spiritual life" (1210). The presentation is organized in four chapters. These are: the sacraments of Christian initiation (baptism, confirmation, the eucharist) in chapter one; the sacraments of healing (penance and reconciliation, the anointing of the sick) in chapter two; the "sacraments at the service of communion" (holy orders and matrimony) in chapter three; and sacramentals and Christian funerals in chapter four.

PART THREE: Life in Christ (1691-2557)

Section One is entitled "Man's Vocation: Life in the Spirit." Its three chapters discuss the dignity of the human person, the human community, and "God's Salvation: Law and Grace" (the moral law, grace and justification, the Church as teacher of moral truth). "Catechesis has to reveal in all clarity the joy and the demands of the way of Christ. . . . The first and last point of reference of this catechesis will always be Jesus Christ himself, who is 'the way, and the truth, and the life' " (1697-1698).

Section Two reflects on the contents of Christian moral life. The treatment is organized according to the Ten Commandments, with a chapter devoted to each commandment and its concrete applications. While the commandments admit of what is traditionally called light matter (venial sin), nevertheless, the text says: "Since they express man's fundamental duties towards God and towards his neighbor, the Ten Commandments reveal, in their primordial content, grave obligations. They are fundamentally immutable, and they oblige always and everywhere. No one can dispense from them. The Ten Commandments are engraved by God in the human heart" (2072).

PART FOUR: Christian Prayer (2558-2865)

Section One considers prayer in Christian life, underlining the relationship of this topic to the rest of the catechism: "The Church professes this mystery [of faith] in the Apostles' Creed (Part One) and celebrates it in the sacramental liturgy (Part Two), so that the life of the faithful may be conformed to Christ in the Holy Spirit to the glory of God the Father (Part Three). This mystery, then, requires that the faithful believe in it, that they celebrate it, and that they live from it in a vital and personal relationship with the living and true God. This relationship is prayer" (2558). The section then discusses the "revelation of prayer" in the Old Testament and now in the age of the Church, the tradition of prayer, and the life of prayer (kinds of prayer, problems and perseverance in prayer).

Section Two presents an extended reflection on the Our Father, considered as the model of prayer. Quoting Tertullian, the catechism says: "The Lord's Prayer 'is truly the summary of the whole Gospel.' 'Since the Lord. . . . after handing over the practice of prayer, said elsewhere, 'Ask and you will receive,' and since everyone has petitions which are peculiar to his circumstances, the regular and appropriate prayer [the Lord's Prayer] is said first, as the foundation of further desires'" (2761).

RECEPTION OF THE CATECHISM

Following the publication of the *Catechism of the Catholic Church*, Pope John Paul established an Interdicasterial Commission for the Catechism, under the chairmanship of Cardinal Ratzinger, responsible for overseeing translations of the volume and reviewing and approving suggested changes in the text. The commission approved the English translation of the catechism in February 1994, and it was published on June 22 of that year — in the United States, under the auspices of the National Conference of Catholic Bishops.

Pope John Paul presented the *editio typica* or normative Latin version of the catechism in a formal ceremony on September 8, 1997.

The following day, Cardinal Ratzinger presented the *editio typica* at a Vatican news conference. At the same time, he also introduced more than a hundred changes which had been approved for incorporation into the text. Most of the changes were of a minor, editorial nature. The most important was in paragraphs 2265-2267 of the catechism, where the treatment of capital punishment had been strengthened to reflect the discussion of the same topic in Pope John Paul's 1995 encyclical letter *Evangelium Vitae* (*The Gospel of Life*).

In the United States, the National Conference of Catholic Bishops in 1994 established an Ad Hoc Committee to Oversee the Use of the Catechism. It has an office and staff at NCCB headquarters in Washington, D.C. The committee reviews and approves materials that seek to make substantial direct use of the text of the *Catechism of the Catholic Church*, and also reviews catechetical series for their conformity with the catechism. In addition, the committee was mandated to conduct a feasibility study of a national catechism or catechetical series for the United States.

St. Basil

DOGMATIC CONSTITUTION ON THE CHURCH — *LUMEN GENTIUM*

Following are excerpts from the first two chapters of the "Dogmatic Constitution on the Church" (Lumen Gentium) *promulgated by the Second Vatican Council. They describe the relation of the Catholic Church to the Kingdom of God, the nature and foundation of the Church, the People of God, the necessity of membership and participation in the Church for salvation.*

I. MYSTERY OF THE CHURCH

By her relationship with Christ, the Church is a kind of sacrament or sign of intimate union with God, and of the unity of all mankind (No. 1).

He (the eternal Father) planned to assemble in the holy Church all those who would believe in Christ. Already from the beginning of the world the foreshadowing of the Church took place. She was prepared for in a remarkable way throughout the history of the people of Israel and by means of the Old Covenant. Established in the present era of time, the Church was made manifest by the outpouring of the Spirit. At the end of time she will achieve her glorious fulfillment. Then all just men from the time of Adam, "from Abel, the just one, to the last of the elect," will be gathered together with the Father in the universal Church (No. 2).

When the work which the Father had given the Son to do on earth (cf. Jn. 17:4) was accomplished, the Holy Spirit was sent on the day of Pentecost in order that he might forever sanctify the Church, and thus all believers would have access to the Father through Christ in the one Spirit (cf. Eph. 2:18).

The Spirit dwells in the Church and in the hearts of the faithful as in a temple (cf. 1 Cor. 3:16; 6:19). . . . The Spirit guides the Church into the fullness of truth (cf. Jn. 16:13) and gives her a unity of fellowship and service. He furnishes and directs her with various gifts, both hierarchical and charismatic, and adorns her with the fruits of His grace (cf. Eph. 4:11-12; 1 Cor. 12:4; Gal. 5:22). By the power of the Gospel he makes the Church grow, perpetually renews her, and leads her to perfect union with her Spouse (No. 4).

Foundation of the Church

The mystery of the holy Church is manifest in her very foundation, for the Lord Jesus inaugurated her by preaching the Good News, that is, the coming of God's Kingdom, which, for centuries, had been promised in the Scriptures. . . . In Christ's word, in his works, and in his presence this Kingdom reveals itself to men.

The miracles of Jesus also confirm that the Kingdom has already arrived on earth.

Before all things, however, the Kingdom is clearly visible in the very Person of Christ, Son of God and Son of Man.

When Jesus rose up again after suffering death on the cross for mankind, he manifested that he had been appointed Lord, Messiah, and Priest forever (cf. Acts 2:36; Heb. 5:6; 7:17-21), and he poured out on his disciples the Spirit promised by the Father (cf. Acts 2:33). The Church, consequently, equipped with the gifts of her Founder and faithfully guarding his precepts . receives the mission to proclaim and to establish among all peoples the Kingdom of Christ and of God. She becomes on earth the initial budding forth of that Kingdom. While she slowly grows, the Church strains toward the consummation of the Kingdom and, with all her strength, hopes and desires to be united in glory with her King (No. 5).

Figures of the Church

In the Old Testament the revelation of the Kingdom had often been conveyed by figures of speech. In the same way the inner nature of the Church was now to be made known to us through various images.

The Church is a sheepfold . . . a flock . . . a tract of land to be cultivated, the field of God . . . his choice vineyard . . . the true vine is Christ . . . the edifice of God . . . the house of God . . . the holy temple (whose members are) living stones . . . this holy city . . . a bride . . . our Mother . . . the spotless spouse of the spotless Lamb . . . an exile (No. 6).

In the human nature which he united to himself, the Son of God redeemed man and transformed him into a new creation (cf Gal. 6:15; 2 Cor. 5:17) by overcoming death through his own death and resurrection. By communicating his Spirit to his brothers, called together from all peoples, Christ made them mystically into his own body.

In that body, the life of Christ is poured into the believers, who, through the sacraments, are united in a hidden and real way to Christ who suffered and was glorified. Through baptism we are formed in the likeness of Christ.

Truly partaking of the body of the Lord in the breaking of the eucharistic bread, we are taken up into communion with him and with one another (No. 7).

One Body in Christ

As all the members of the human body, though they are many, form one body, so also are the faithful in Christ (cf. 1 Cor. 12:12). Also, in the building up of Christ's body there is a flourishing variety of members and functions. There is only one Spirit who . distributes his different gifts for the welfare of the Church (cf. 1 Cor. 12:1-11). Among these gifts stands out the grace given to the apostles. To their authority, the Spirit himself subjected even those who were endowed with charisms (cf. 1 Cor. 14). The head of this body is Christ (No. 7).

Mystical Body of Christ

Christ, the one Mediator, established and ceaselessly sustains here on earth his holy Church, the community of faith, hope, and charity, as a visible structure. Through her he communicates truth and grace to all. But the society furnished with hierarchical agencies and the Mystical Body of Christ are not to be considered as two realities, nor are the visible assembly and the spiritual community, nor the earthly Church and the Church enriched with heavenly things. Rather they form one interlocked reality which is comprised of a divine and a human element. For this reason, this reality is compared to the mystery of the incarnate Word. Just as the assumed nature inseparably united to the divine Word serves him as a living instrument of salvation, so, in a similar way, does the communal structure of the Church serve Christ's Spirit, who vivifies it by way of building up the body (cf. Eph. 4:16).

This is the unique Church of Christ which in the Creed we avow as one, holy, catholic, and apostolic. After his Resurrection our Savior handed her over to Peter to be shepherded (Jn. 21:17), commissioning him and the other apostles to propagate and govern her (cf. Mt. 28:18, ff.). Her he erected for all ages as "the pillar and mainstay of the truth" (1 Tm. 3:15). This Church, constituted and organized in the world as a society, subsists in the Catholic Church, which is governed by the successor of Peter and by the bishops in union with that successor, although many elements of sanctification and of truth can be found outside of her visible structure. These elements, however, as gifts properly belonging to the Church of Christ, possess an inner dynamism toward Catholic unity.

The Church, embracing sinners in her bosom, is at the same time holy and always in need of being purified, and incessantly pursues the path of penance and renewal.

The Church, "like a pilgrim in a foreign land, presses forward, announcing the cross and death of the Lord until he comes" (cf. 1 Cor. 11:26) (No. 8).

II. THE PEOPLE OF GOD

At all times and among every people, God has given welcome to whosoever fears him and does what is right (cf. Acts 10:35). It has pleased God, however, to make men holy and save them not merely as individuals without any mutual bonds, but by making them into a single people, a people which acknowledges him in truth and serves him in holiness. He therefore chose the race of Israel as a people unto himself. With it he set up a covenant. Step by step he taught this people by manifesting in its history both himself and the decree of his will, and by making it holy unto himself. All these things, however, were done by way of preparation and as a figure of that new and perfect covenant which was to be ratified in Christ.

Christ instituted this New Covenant, that is to say, the New Testament, in his blood (cf. 1 Cor. 11:25), by calling together a people made up of Jew and Gentile, making them one, not according to the flesh but in the Spirit.

This was to be the new People of God . . . reborn . . . through the Word of the living God (cf. 1 Pt. 1:23). from water and the Holy Spirit (cf. Jn. 3:5-6) . . . "a chosen race, a royal priesthood, a holy nation, a purchased people. You who in times past were not a people, but are now the People of God" (1 Pt. 2:9-10).

That messianic people has for its head Christ. Its law is the new commandment to love as Christ loved us (cf. Jn. 13:34). Its goal is the Kingdom of God, which has been begun by God himself on earth, and which is to be further extended until it is brought to perfection by him at the end of time.

This messianic people, although it does not actually include all men, and may more than once look like a small flock, is nonetheless a lasting and sure seed of unity, hope, and salvation for the whole human race. Established by Christ as a fellowship of life, charity, and truth, it is also used by him as an instrument for the redemption of all, and is sent forth into the whole world as the light of the world and the salt of the earth (cf. Mt. 5:13-16).

Israel according to the flesh . . . was already called the Church of God (Neh. 13:1; cf. Nm. 20:4; Dt. 23:1, ff.). Likewise the new Israel . . . is also called the Church of Christ (cf. Mt. 16:18). For he has bought it for himself with his blood (cf. Acts 20:28), has filled it with his Spirit, and provided it with those means which befit it as a visible and social unity. God has gathered together as one all those who in faith look upon Jesus as the author of salvation and the source of unity and peace, and has established them as the Church, that for each and all she may be the visible sacrament of this saving unity (No. 9).

Priesthood

The baptized, by regeneration and the anointing of the Holy Spirit, are consecrated into a holy priesthood.

[All members of the Church participate in the priesthood of Christ, through the common priesthood of the faithful. See Priesthood of the Laity.]

Though they differ from one another in essence and not only in degree, the common priesthood of the faithful and the ministerial or hierarchical priesthood are nonetheless interrelated. Each of them in its own special way is a participation in the one priesthood of Christ (No. 10).

It is through the sacraments and the exercise of the virtues that the sacred nature and organic structure of the priestly community is brought into operation (No. 11). (See Role of the Sacraments.)

Prophetic Office

The holy People of God shares also in Christ's prophetic office. It spreads abroad a living witness to him, especially by means of a life of faith and charity and by offering to God a sacrifice of praise. . . . The body of the faithful as a whole, anointed as they are by the Holy One (cf. Jn. 2:20, 27), cannot err in matters of belief. Thanks to a supernatural sense of faith which characterizes the People as a whole, it manifests this unerring quality when, "from the bishops down to the last member of the laity," it shows universal agreement in matters of faith and morals.

God's People accepts not the word of men but the very Word of God (cf. 1 Thes. 2:13). It clings without fail to the faith once delivered to the saints (cf. Jude 3), penetrates it more deeply by accurate insights, and applies it more thoroughly to life. All this it does under the lead of a sacred teaching authority to which it loyally defers.

It is not only through the sacraments and Church ministries that the same Holy Spirit sanctifies and leads the People of God. . . . He distributes special graces among the faithful of every rank. By these gifts he makes them fit and ready to undertake the various tasks or offices advantageous for the renewal and upbuilding of the Church. These charismatic gifts . . . are to be received with thanksgiving and consolation, for they are exceedingly suitable and useful for the needs of the Church.

Judgment as to their genuineness and proper use belongs to those who preside over the Church, and to whose special competence it belongs . . . to test all things and hold fast to that which is good (cf. 1 Thes. 5:12; 19-21) (No. 12).

All Are Called

All men are called to belong to the new People of God. Wherefore this People, while remaining one and unique, is to be spread throughout the whole world and must exist in all ages, so that the purpose of God's will may be fulfilled. In the beginning God made human nature one. After his children were scattered, he decreed that they should at length be united again (cf. Jn. 11:52). It was for this reason that God sent his Son. . . . that he might be Teacher, King, and Priest of all, the Head of the new and universal People of the sons of God. For this God finally sent his Son's Spirit as Lord and Lifegiver. He it is who, on behalf of the whole Church and each and every one of those who believe, is the principle of their coming together and remaining together in the teaching of the apostles and in fellowship, in the breaking of bread and in prayers (cf. Acts 2:42) (No. 13).

One People of God

It follows that among all the nations of earth there is but one People of God, which takes its citizens from every race, making them citizens of a Kingdom which is of a heavenly and not an earthly nature. For all the faithful scattered throughout the world are in communion with each other in the Holy Spirit. . . . the Church or People of God . foster(s) and take(s) to herself, insofar as they are good, the ability, resources and customs of each people. Taking them to herself, she purifies, strengthens, and ennobles them. . . . This characteristic of universality which adorns the People of God is a gift from the Lord himself. By reason of it, the Catholic Church strives energetically and constantly to bring all humanity with all its riches back to Christ its Head in the unity of his Spirit.

In virtue of this catholicity each individual part of the Church contributes through its special gifts to the good of the other parts and of the whole Church. Thus through the common sharing of gifts. The whole and each of the parts receive increase.

All men are called to be part of this catholic unity of the People of God. And there belong to it or are related to it in various ways, the Catholic faithful as well as all who believe in Christ, and indeed the whole of mankind. For all men are called to salvation by the grace of God (No. 13).

The Catholic Church

This sacred Synod turns its attention first to the Catholic faithful. Basing itself upon sacred Scripture and tradition, it teaches that the Church is necessary for salvation. For Christ, made present to us in his Body, which is the Church, is the one Mediator and the unique Way of salvation. In explicit terms he himself affirmed the necessity of faith and baptism (cf. Mk. 16:16; Jn.

3:5) and thereby affirmed also the necessity of the Church, for through baptism as through a door men enter the Church. Whosoever, therefore, knowing that the Catholic Church was made necessary by God through Jesus Christ, would refuse to enter her or to remain in her could not be saved.

They are fully incorporated into the society of the Church who, possessing the Spirit of Christ, accept her entire system and all the means of salvation given to her, and through union with her visible structure are joined to Christ, who rules her through the Supreme Pontiff and the bishops. This joining is effected by the bonds of professed faith, of the sacraments, of ecclesiastical government, and of communion. He is not saved, however, who, though he is part of the body of the Church, does not persevere in charity. He remains indeed in the bosom of the Church, but only in a "bodily" manner and not "in his heart."

Catechumens who, moved by the Holy Spirit, seek with explicit intention to be incorporated into the Church, are by that very intention joined to her. Mother Church already embraces them as her own (No. 14).

Other Christians, The Unbaptized

The Church recognizes that in many ways she is linked with those who, being baptized, are honored with the name of Christian, though they do not profess the faith in its entirety or do not preserve unity of communion with the successor of Peter.

We can say that in some real way they are joined with us in the Holy Spirit, for to them also he gives his gifts and graces, and is thereby operative among them with his sanctifying power (No. 15).

Finally, those who have not yet received the Gospel are related in various ways to the People of God. In the first place there is the people to whom the covenants and the promises were given and from whom Christ was born according to the flesh (cf. Rom. 9:4-5). On account of their fathers, this people remains most dear to God, for God does not repent of the gifts he makes nor of the calls he issues (cf. Rom. 11:28-29).

But the plan of salvation also includes those who acknowledge the Creator. In the first place among these are the Muslims. Nor is God himself far distant from those who in shadows and images seek the unknown God.

Those also can attain to everlasting salvation who through no fault of their own do not know the Gospel of Christ or his Church, yet sincerely seek God and, moved by grace, strive by their deeds to do his will as it is known to them through the dictates of conscience. Nor does divine Providence deny the help necessary for salvation to those who, without blame on their part, have not yet arrived at an explicit knowledge of God, but who strive to live a good life, thanks to his grace. Whatever goodness or truth is found among them is looked upon by the Church as a preparation for the Gospel. She regards such qualities as given by him who enlightens all men so that they may finally have life. (No. 16).

THE POPE, TEACHING AUTHORITY, COLLEGIALITY

The Roman Pontiff — the successor of St. Peter as the bishop of Rome and head of the Church on earth — has full and supreme authority over the universal Church in matters pertaining to faith and morals (teaching authority), discipline and government (jurisdictional authority).

The primacy of the pope is real and supreme power. It is not merely a prerogative of honor — that is, of his being regarded as the first among equals. Neither does primacy imply that the pope is just the presiding officer of the collective body of bishops. The pope is the head of the Church.

Catholic belief in the primacy of the pope was stated in detail in the dogmatic constitution on the Church, *Pastor Aeternus*, approved in 1870 by the fourth session of the First Vatican Council. Some elaboration of the doctrine was made in the Dogmatic Constitution on the Church which was approved and promulgated by the Second Vatican Council November 21, 1964. The

entire body of teaching on the subject is based on Scripture and tradition and the centuries-long experience of the Church.

Infallibility

The essential points of doctrine concerning infallibility in the Church and the infallibility of the pope were stated by the Second Vatican Council in the Dogmatic Constitution on the Church, as follows:

"This infallibility with which the divine Redeemer willed his Church to be endowed in defining a doctrine of faith and morals extends as far as extends the deposit of divine revelation, which must be religiously guarded and faithfully expounded. This is the infallibility which the Roman Pontiff, the head of the college of bishops, enjoys in virtue of his office, when, as the supreme shepherd and teacher of all the faithful who confirms his brethren in their faith (cf. Lk. 22:32), he proclaims by a definitive act some doctrine of faith or morals. Therefore his definitions, of themselves, and not from the consent of the Church, are justly styled irreformable, for they are pronounced with the assistance of the Holy Spirit, an assistance promised to him in blessed Peter. Therefore they need no approval of others, nor do they allow an appeal to any other judgment. For then the Roman Pontiff is not pronouncing judgment as a private person. Rather, as the supreme teacher of the universal Church, as one in whom the charism of the infallibility of the Church herself is individually present, he is expounding or defending a doctrine of Catholic faith.

"The infallibility promised to the Church resides also in the body of bishops when that body exercises supreme teaching authority with the successor of Peter. To the resultant definitions the assent of the Church can never be wanting, on account of the activity of that same Holy Spirit, whereby the whole flock of Christ is preserved and progresses in unity of faith.

"But when either the Roman Pontiff or the body of bishops together with him defines a judgment, they pronounce it in accord with revelation itself. All are obliged to maintain and be ruled by this revelation, which, as written or preserved by tradition, is transmitted in its entirety through the legitimate succession of bishops and especially through the care of the Roman Pontiff himself.

"Under the guiding light of the Spirit of truth, revelation is thus religiously preserved and faithfully expounded in the Church. The Roman Pontiff and the bishops, in view of their office and of the importance of the matter, strive painstakingly and by appropriate means to inquire properly into that revelation and to give apt expression to its contents. But they do not allow that there could be any new public revelation pertaining to the divine deposit of faith" (No. 25).

Authentic Teaching

The pope rarely speaks *ex cathedra* — that is, "from the chair" of St. Peter — for the purpose of making an infallible pronouncement. More often and in various ways he states authentic teaching in line with Scripture, tradition, the living experience of the Church, and the whole analogy of faith. Of such teaching, the Second Vatican Council said in its Dogmatic Constitution on the Church (No. 25):

"Religious submission of will and of mind must be shown in a special way to the authentic teaching authority of the Roman Pontiff, even when he is not speaking *ex cathedra*. That is, it must be shown in such a way that his supreme magisterium is acknowledged with reverence, the judgments made by him are sincerely adhered

to, according to his manifest mind and will. His mind and will in the matter may be known chiefly either from the character of the documents, from his frequent repetition of the same doctrine, or from his manner of speaking."

With respect to bishops, the constitution states: "They are authentic teachers, that is, teachers endowed with the authority of Christ, who preach to the people committed to them the faith they must believe and put into practice. By the light of the Holy Spirit, they make that faith clear, bringing forth from the treasury of revelation new things and old (cf. Mt. 13:52), making faith bear fruit and vigilantly warding off any errors which threaten their flock (cf. 2 Tm. 4:1-4).

"Bishops, teaching in communion with the Roman Pontiff, are to be respected by all as witnesses to divine and Catholic truth. In matters of faith and morals, the bishops speak in the name of Christ and the faithful are to accept their teaching and adhere to it with a religious assent of soul."

Magisterium — Teaching Authority

Responsibility for teaching doctrine and judging orthodoxy belongs to the official teaching authority of the Church.

This authority is personalized in the pope, the successor of St. Peter as head of the Church, and in the bishops together and in union with the pope, as it was originally committed to Peter and to the whole college of apostles under his leadership. They are the official teachers of the Church.

Others have auxiliary relationships with the magisterium: theologians, in the study and clarification of doctrine; teachers — priests, religious, lay persons — who cooperate with the pope and

Pope Gregory VII

bishops in spreading knowledge of religious truth; the faithful, who by their sense of faith and personal witness contribute to the development of doctrine and the establishment of its relevance to life in the Church and the world.

The magisterium, Pope Paul VI noted in an address at a general audience January 11, 1967, "is a subordinate and faithful echo and secure interpreter of the divine word." It does not reveal new truths, "nor is it superior to sacred Scripture." Its competence extends to the limits of divine revelation manifested in Scripture and tradition and the living experience of the Church, with respect to matters of faith and morals and related subjects. Official teaching in these areas is infallible when it is formally defined, for belief and acceptance by all members of the Church, by the pope, acting in the capacity of supreme shepherd of the flock of Christ; also, when doctrine is proposed and taught with moral unanimity of bishops with the pope in a solemn collegial manner, as in an ecumenical council, and/or in the ordinary course of events. Even when not infallibly defined, official teaching in the areas of faith and morals is authoritative and requires religious assent.

The teachings of the magisterium have been documented in creeds, formulas of faith, decrees and enactments of ecumenical and particular councils, various kinds of doctrinal statements, encyclical letters and other teaching instruments. They have also been incorporated into the liturgy, with the result that the law of prayer is said to be a law of belief.

Collegiality

The bishops of the Church, in union with the pope, have supreme teaching and pastoral authority over the whole Church in addition to the authority of office they have for their own dioceses.

This collegial authority is exercised in a solemn manner in an ecumenical council and can be exercised in other ways as well, "provided that the head of the college calls them to collegiate action, or at least so approves or freely accepts the united action of the dispersed bishops that it is made a true collegiate act."

This doctrine is grounded on the fact that: "Just as, by the Lord's will, St. Peter and the other apostles constituted one apostolic college, so in a similar way the Roman Pontiff as the successor of Peter, and the bishops as the successors of the apostles are joined together."

Doctrine on collegiality was stated by the Second Vatican Council in the Dogmatic Constitution on the Church (Nos. 22 and 23).

REVELATION

Following are excerpts from the "Dogmatic Constitution on Divine Revelation" (Dei Verbum) promulgated by the Second Vatican Council. They describe the nature and process of divine revelation, inspiration and interpretation of Scripture, the Old and New Testaments, and the role of Scripture in the life of the Church.

I. REVELATION ITSELF

God chose to reveal himself and to make known to us the hidden purpose of his will (cf. Eph. 1:9) by which through Christ, the Word made flesh, man has access to the Father in the Holy Spirit and comes to share in the divine nature (cf. Eph. 2:18; 2 Pt. 1:4). Through this revelation, therefore, the invisible God (cf. Col. 1:15; 1 Tm. 1:17). speaks to men as friends (cf. Ex. 33:11; Jn. 15:14-15) and lives among them (cf. Bar. 3:38) so that he may invite and take them into fellowship with himself. This plan of revelation is realized by deeds and words having an inner unity: the deeds wrought by God in the history of salvation manifest and confirm the teaching and realities signified by the words, while the words proclaim the deeds and clarify the mystery contained in them. By this revelation then, the deepest truth about God and the salvation of man is made clear to us in Christ, who is the Mediator and at the same time the fullness of all revelation (No. 2).

God from the start manifested himself to our first parents. Then after their fall his promise of redemption aroused in them the hope of being saved (cf. Gn. 3:15), and from that time on he ceaselessly kept the human race in his care, in order to give eternal life to those who perseveringly do good in search of salvation (cf. Rom. 2:6-7). He called Abraham in order to make of him a great nation (cf. Gn. 12:2). Through the patriarchs, and after them through Moses and the prophets, he taught this nation to acknowledge himself as the one living and true God and to wait for the Savior promised by him. In this manner he prepared the way for the Gospel down through the centuries (No. 3).

Revelation in Christ

Then, after speaking in many places and varied ways through the prophets, God "last of all in these days has spoken to us by his Son" (Heb. 1:1-2). Jesus perfected revelation by fulfilling it through his whole work of making himself present and manifesting himself: through his words and deeds, his signs and wonders, but especially through his death and glorious resurrection from the dead and final sending of the Spirit of truth. Moreover, he confirmed with divine testimony what revelation proclaimed: that God is with us to free us from the darkness of sin and death, and to raise us up to life eternal.

The Christian dispensation, therefore, as the new and definitive covenant, will never pass away, and we now await no further new public revelation before the glorious manifestation of our Lord Jesus Christ (cf. 1 Tm. 6:14; Ti. 2:13) (No. 4).

II. TRANSMISSION OF REVELATION

God has seen to it that what he had revealed for the salvation of all nations would abide perpetually in its full integrity and be handed on to all generations. Therefore Christ the Lord, in whom the full revelation of the supreme God is brought to completion (cf. 2 Cor. 1:20; 3:16; 4:6), commissioned the apostles to preach to all men that Gospel which is the source of all saving truth and moral teaching, and thus to impart to them divine gifts. This Gospel had been promised in former times through the prophets, and Christ himself fulfilled it and promulgated it with his own lips. This commission was faithfully fulfilled by the apostles who, by their oral preaching, by example, and by ordinances, handed on what they had received from Christ or what they had learned through the prompting of the Holy Spirit. The commission was fulfilled, too, by those apostles and apostolic men who under the inspi-

Cover of the Linderfarne Gospel
Early 9th Century

ration of the same Holy Spirit committed the message of salvation to writing (No. 7).

Tradition

But in order to keep the Gospel forever whole and alive within the Church, the apostles left bishops as their successors, "handing over their own teaching role" to them. This sacred tradition, therefore, and sacred Scripture of both the Old and the New Testament are like a mirror in which the pilgrim Church on earth looks at God (No. 7).

The apostolic preaching, which is expressed in a special way in the inspired books, was to be preserved by a continuous succession of preachers until the end of time. Therefore the apostles, handing on what they themselves had received, warn the faithful to hold fast to the traditions which they have learned. Now what was handed on by the apostles includes everything which contributes to the holiness of life, and the increase in faith of the People of God; and so the Church, in her teaching, life, and worship, perpetuates and hands on to all generations all that she herself is, all that she believes (No. 8).

Development of Doctrine

This tradition which comes from the apostles develops in the Church with the help of the Holy Spirit. For there is a growth in the understanding of the realities and the words which have been handed down. This happens through the contemplation and study made by believers through the intimate understanding of spiritual things they experience, and through the preaching of those who have received through episcopal succession the sure gift of truth. For, as the centuries succeed one another, the Church constantly moves forward toward the fullness of divine truth until the words of God reach their complete fulfillment in her.

The words of the holy Fathers witness to the living presence of this tradition, whose wealth is poured into the practice and life of the believing and praying Church. Through the same tradition the Church's full canon of the sacred books is known, and the sacred writings themselves are more profoundly understood and unceasingly made active in her; . . . and the Holy Spirit, through whom the living voice of the Gospel resounds in the Church, and through her, in the world, leads unto all truth those who believe and makes the word of Christ dwell abundantly in them (cf. Col. 3:16) (No. 8).

Tradition and Scripture

Hence there exist a close connection and communication between sacred tradition and sacred Scripture. For both of them, flowing from the same divine wellspring, in a certain way merge into a unity and tend toward the same end. For sacred Scripture is the word of God inasmuch as it is consigned to writing under the inspiration of the divine Spirit. To the successors of the apostles, sacred tradition hands on in its full purity God's word, which was entrusted to the apostles by Christ the Lord and the Holy Spirit. Thus, led by the light of the Spirit of truth, these successors can in their preaching preserve this word of God faithfully, explain it, and make it more widely known. Consequently, it is not from sacred Scripture alone that the Church draws her certainty about every thing which has been revealed. Therefore both sacred tradition and sacred Scripture are to be accepted and venerated with the same sense of devotion and reverence (No. 9).

Sacred tradition and sacred Scripture form one sacred deposit of the word of God, which is committed to the Church (No. 10).

Teaching Authority of the Church

The task of authentically interpreting the word of God, whether written or handed on, has been entrusted exclusively to the living teaching office of the Church, whose authority is exercised in the name of Jesus Christ. This teaching office is not above the word of God, but serves it, teaching only what has been handed on . . . it draws from this one deposit of faith everything which it presents for belief as divinely revealed.

It is clear, therefore, that sacred tradition, sacred Scripture, and the teaching authority of the Church . . . are so linked and joined together that one cannot stand without the others, and that all together and each in its own way under the action of the one Holy Spirit contribute effectively to the salvation of souls (No. 10).

III. INSPIRATION, INTERPRETATION

Those revealed realities contained and presented in sacred Scripture have been committed to writing under the inspiration of the Holy Spirit. Holy Mother Church, relying on the belief of the apostles, holds that the books of both the Old and New Testament in their entirety, with all their parts, are sacred and canonical because, having been written under the inspiration of the Holy Spirit (cf. Jn. 20:31; 2 Tm. 3:16; 2 Pt. 1:19-21; 3:15-16) they have God as their author and have been handed on as such to the Church herself. In composing the sacred books, God chose men and, while employed by him, they made use of their powers and abilities, so that, with him acting in them and through them, they, as true authors, consigned to writing everything and only those things which he wanted (No. 11).

Inerrancy

Therefore, since everything asserted by the inspired authors or sacred writers must be held to be asserted by the Holy Spirit, it follows that the books of Scripture must be acknowledged as teaching firmly, faithfully, and without error that truth which God wanted put into the sacred writings for the sake of our salvation. Therefore "all Scripture is inspired by God and useful for teaching, for reproving, for correcting, for instruction in justice; that the man of God may be perfect, equipped for every good work" (2 Tm. 3:16-17) (No. 11).

Literary Forms

However, since God speaks in sacred Scripture through men in human fashion, the interpreter of sacred Scripture, in order to see clearly what God wanted to communicate to us, should carefully investigate what meaning the sacred writers really intended, and what God wanted to manifest by means of their words.

The interpreter must investigate what meaning the sacred writer intended to express and actually expressed in particular circumstances as he used contemporary literary forms in accordance with the situation of his own time and culture. For the correct understanding of what the sacred author wanted to assert, due attention must be paid to the customary and characteristic styles of perceiving, speaking, and narrating which prevailed at the time of the sacred writer, and to the customs men normally followed at that period in their everyday dealings with one another (No. 12).

Analogy of Faith

No less serious attention must be given to the content and unity of the whole of Scripture, if the meaning of the sacred texts is to be correctly brought to light. The living tradition of the whole Church must be taken into account along with the harmony which exists between elements of the faith. All of what has been said about the way of interpreting Scripture is subject finally to the judgment of the Church, which carries out the divine commission and ministry of guarding and interpreting the word of God (No. 12).

IV. THE OLD TESTAMENT

In carefully planning and preparing the salvation of the whole human race, the God of supreme love, by a special dispensation, chose for himself a people to whom he might entrust his promises. First he entered into a covenant with Abraham (cf. Gn. 15:18) and, through Moses, with the people of Israel (cf. Ex. 24:8). To this people which he had acquired for himself, he so manifested himself through words and deeds as the one true and living God that Israel came to know by experience the ways of God with men. The plan of salvation, foretold by the sacred authors, recounted and explained by them, is found as the true word of God in the books of the Old Testament: these books, therefore, written under divine inspiration, remain permanently valuable (No. 14).

Principal Purpose

The principal purpose to which the plan of the Old Covenant was directed was to prepare for the coming both of Christ, the universal Redeemer, and of the messianic Kingdom. Now the books of the Old Testament, in accordance with the state of mankind before the time of salvation established by Christ, reveal to all men the knowledge of God and of man and the ways in which God deals with men. These books show us true divine pedagogy (No. 15).

The books of the Old Testament with all their parts, caught up into the proclamation of the Gospel, acquire and show forth their full meaning in the New Testament (cf. Mt. 5:17; Lk. 24:27; Rom. 16:25-26; 2 Cor. 3:14-16) and in turn shed light on it and explain it (No. 16).

V. THE NEW TESTAMENT

The word of God is set forth and shows its power in a most excellent way in the writings of the New Testament. For when the fullness of time

Holy Spirit Illumination from a 12th c. Missal

arrived (cf. Gal. 4:4), the Word was made flesh and dwelt among us in the fullness of grace and truth (cf. Jn. 12:32). This mystery had not been manifested to other generations as it was now revealed to his holy apostles and prophets in the Holy Spirit (cf. Eph. 3:4-6), so that they might preach the Gospel, stir up faith in Jesus, Christ and Lord, and gather the Church together. To these realities, the writings of the New Testament stand as a perpetual and divine witness (No. 17).

The Gospels and Other Writings

The Gospels have a special preeminence for they are the principal witness of the life and teaching of the incarnate Word, our Savior.

The Church has always and everywhere held and continues to hold that the four Gospels are of apostolic origin. For what the apostles preached afterwards they themselves and apostolic men, under the inspiration of the divine Spirit, handed on to us in writing: the foundation of faith, namely, the fourfold Gospel, according to Matthew, Mark, Luke, and John (No. 18).

The four Gospels . . . whose historical character the Church unhesitatingly asserts, faithfully hand on what Jesus Christ, while living among men, really did and taught for their eternal salvation until the day he was taken up into heaven (see Acts 1:1-2). Indeed, after the ascension of the Lord the apostles handed on to their hearers what he had said and done. The sacred authors wrote the four Gospels, selecting some things from the many which had been handed on by word of mouth or in writing, reducing some of them to a synthesis, explicating some things in view of the situation of their churches, and preserving the form of proclamation but always in such fashion that they told us the honest truth about Jesus. For their intention in writing was that we might know "the truth" concerning those matters about which we have been instructed (cf. Lk. 1:2-4) (No. 19).

Besides the four Gospels, the canon of the New Testament also contains the Epistles of St. Paul and other apostolic writings, composed under the inspiration of the Holy Spirit. In these writings those matters which concern Christ the Lord are confirmed, his true teaching is more and more fully stated, the saving power of the divine work of Christ is preached, the story is told of the beginnings of the Church and her marvelous growth, and her glorious fulfillment is foretold (No. 20).

VI. SCRIPTURE IN CHURCH LIFE

The Church has always venerated the divine Scriptures just as she venerates the body of the Lord. She has always regarded the Scriptures together with sacred tradition as the supreme rule of faith, and will ever do so. For, inspired by God and committed once and for all to writing, they impart the word of God himself without change, and make the voice of the Holy Spirit resound in the words of the prophets and apostles. Therefore, like the Christian religion itself, all the preaching of the Church must be nourished and ruled by sacred Scripture (No. 21).

Easy access to sacred Scripture should be provided for all the Christian faithful. That is why the Church from the very beginning accepted as her own that very ancient Greek translation of the Old Testament which is named after seventy men (the Septuagint); and she has always given a place of honor to other translations, Eastern and Latin, especially the one known as the Vulgate. But since the word of God should be available at all times, the Church with maternal concern sees to it that suitable and correct translations are made into different languages, especially from the original texts of the sacred books. And if, given the opportunity and the approval of Church authority, these translations are produced in cooperation with the separated brethren as well, all Christians will be able to use them (No. 22).

Biblical Studies, Theology

The constitution encouraged the development and progress of biblical studies "under the watchful care of the sacred teaching office of the Church."

It also noted: "Sacred theology rests on the written word of God, together with sacred tradition, as its primary and perpetual foundation," and that "the study of the sacred page is, as it were, the soul of sacred theology" (Nos. 23, 24).

THE BIBLE

The Canon of the Bible is the Church's official list of sacred writings. These works, written by men under the inspiration of the Holy Spirit, contain divine revelation and, in conjunction with the tradition and teaching authority of the Church, constitute the rule of Catholic faith. The Canon was fixed and determined by the tradition and teaching authority of the Church.

The Catholic Canon

The Old Testament Canon of 46 books is as follows.
- **The Pentateuch**, the first five books: Genesis (Gn.), Exodus (Ex.), Leviticus (Lv.), Numbers (Nm.), Deuteronomy (Dt.).
- **Historical Books**: Joshua (Jos.), Judges (Jgs.), Ruth (Ru.) 1 and 2 Samuel (Sm.), 1 and 2 Kings (Kgs.), 1 and 2 Chronicles (Chr.), Ezra (Ezr.), Nehemiah (Neh.), Tobit (Tb.), Judith (Jdt.), Esther (Est.), 1 and 2 Maccabees (Mc.).
- **Wisdom Books**: Job (Jb.), Psalms (Ps.), Proverbs (Prv.), Ecclesiastes (Eccl.), Song of Songs (Song), Wisdom (Wis.), Sirach (Sir.).
- **The Prophets**: Isaiah (Is.), Jeremiah (Jer.), Lamentations (Lam.), Baruch (Bar.), Ezekiel (Ez.), Daniel (Dn.), Hosea (Hos.), Joel (Jl.), Amos (Am.), Obadiah (Ob.), Jonah (Jon.), Micah (Mi.), Nahum (Na.), Habakkuk (Hb.), Zephaniah (Zep.), Haggai (Hg.), Zechariah (Zec.) Malachi (Mal.).

The New Testament Canon of 27 books is as follows.
- **The Gospels**: Matthew (Mt.), Mark (Mk.), Luke (Lk.), John (Jn.).
- **The Acts of the Apostles** (Acts).
- **The Pauline Letters**: Romans (Rom.), 1 and 2 Corinthians (Cor.), Galatians (Gal.), Ephesians (Eph.), Philippians (Phil.), Colossians (Col.), 1 and 2 Thessalonians (Thes.) 1 and 2 Timothy (Tm.), Titus (Ti.), Philemon (Phlm.), Hebrews (Heb.).
- **The Catholic Letters**: James (Jas.), 1 and 2 Peter (Pt.), 1, 2, and 3 John (Jn.), Jude (Jude).
- **Revelation** (Rv.).

Developments

The Canon of the Old Testament was firm by the fifth century despite some questioning by scholars. It was stated by a council held at Rome in 382, by African councils held in Hippo in 393 and in Carthage in 397 and 419, and by Innocent I in 405.

All of the New Testament books were generally known and most of them were acknowledged as inspired by the end of the second century. The Muratorian Fragment, dating from about 200, listed most of the books recognized as canonical in later decrees. Prior to the end of the fourth century, however, there was controversy over the inspired character of several works — the Letter to the Hebrews, James, Jude, 2 Peter, 2 and 3 John and Revelation. Controversy ended in the fourth century and these books, along with those about which there was no dispute, were enumerated in the canon stated by the councils of Hippo and Carthage and affirmed by Innocent I in 405.

The Canon of the Bible was solemnly defined by the Council of Trent in the dogmatic decree *De Canonicis Scripturis*, April 8, 1546.

Hebrew and Other Canons

The Hebrew Canon of sacred writings was fixed by tradition and the consensus of rabbis, probably by about 100 A.D. by the Synod or Council of Jamnia and certainly by the end of the second or early in the third century. It consists of the following works in three categories.

- **The Law** (Torah): the five books of Moses: Genesis, Exodus, Leviticus, Numbers, Deuteronomy.
- **The Prophets**: former prophets — Joshua, Judges, 1 and 2 Samuel, 1 and 2 Kings; latter prophets — Isaiah, Jeremiah, Ezekiel, and 12 minor prophets (Hosea, Joel, Amos, Obadiah, Jonah, Micah, Nahum, Habakkuk, Zephaniah, Haggai, Zechariah, Malachi).
- **The Writings**: 1 and 2 Chronicles, Ezra, Nehemiah, Job, Psalms, Proverbs, Ecclesiastes, Song of Songs, Ruth, Esther, Daniel.

This Canon, embodying the tradition and practice of the Palestine community, did not include a number of works contained in the Alexandrian version of sacred writings translated into Greek between 250 and 100 B.C. and in use by Greek-speaking Jews of the Dispersion (outside Palestine). The rejected works, called apocrypha and not regarded as sacred, are: Tobit, Judith, Wisdom, Sirach, Baruch, 1 and 2 Maccabees, the last six chapters of Esther and three passages of Daniel (3:24-90; 13; 14). These books have also been rejected from the Protestant Canon, although they are included in Bibles under the heading "Apocrypha."

The aforementioned books are held to be inspired and sacred by the Catholic Church. In Catholic usage, they are called deuterocanonical because they were under discussion for some time before questions about their canonicity were settled. Books regarded as canonical with little or no debate were called protocanonical. The status of both categories of books is the same in the Catholic Bible.

The Protestant Canon of the Old Testament is the same as the Hebrew.

The Old Testament Canon of some separated Eastern churches differs from the Catholic Canon.

Christians are in agreement on the Canon of the New Testament.

Languages

Hebrew, Aramaic and Greek were the original languages of the Bible. Most of the Old Testament books were written in Hebrew. Portions of Daniel, Ezra, Jeremiah, Esther, and probably the books of Tobit and Judith were written in Aramaic. The Book of Wisdom, 2 Maccabees and all the books of the New Testament were written in Greek.

Manuscripts and Versions

The original writings of the inspired authors have been lost. The Bible has been transmitted through ancient copies called manuscripts and through translations or versions.

Authoritative Greek manuscripts include the Sinaitic and Vatican manuscripts of the fourth century and the Alexandrine of the fifth century A.D. The Septuagint and Vulgate translations are in a class by themselves.

The Septuagint version, a Greek translation of the Old Testament for Greek-speaking Jews, was begun about 250 and completed about 100 B.C. The work of several Jewish translators at Alexandria, it differed from the Hebrew Bible in the arrangement of books and included several, later called deuterocanonical, which were not acknowledged as sacred by the community in Palestine.

The Vulgate was a Latin version of the Old and New Testaments produced from the original languages by St. Jerome from about 383 to 404. It became the most widely used Latin text for centuries and was regarded as basic long before the Council of Trent designated it as authentic and suitable for use in public reading, controversy, preaching and teaching. Because of its authoritative character, it became the basis for many translations into other languages. A critical revision was completed by a pontifical commission in 1977.

Hebrew and Aramaic manuscripts of great antiquity and value have figured more significantly than before in recent scriptural work by Catholic scholars, especially since their use was strongly encouraged, if not mandated, in 1943 by Pius XII in the encyclical *Divino Afflante Spiritu.*

The English translation of the Bible in general use among Catholics until well into the 20th century was the Douay-Rheims, so called because of the places where it was prepared and published, the New Testament at Rheims in 1582 and the Old Testament at Douay in 1609. The translation was made from the Vulgate text. As revised and issued by Bishop Richard Challoner in 1749 and 1750, it became the standard Catholic English version for about 200 years.

A revision of the Challoner New Testament, made on the basis of the Vulgate text by scholars of the Catholic Biblical Association of America, was published in 1941 in the United States under the sponsorship of the Episcopal Committee of the Confraternity of Christian Doctrine.

New American Bible

A new translation of the entire Bible, the first ever made directly into English from the original languages under Catholic auspices, was projected in 1944 and completed in the fall of 1970 with publication of the *New American Bible*. The Episcopal Committee of the Confraternity of Christian Doctrine sponsored the NAB. The translators were members of the Catholic Biblical Association of America and scholars of other faiths. The typical edition was produced by St. Anthony Guild Press, Paterson, NJ.

The *Jerusalem Bible*, published by Doubleday & Co., Inc., is an English translation of a French version based on the original languages.

Biblical translations approved for liturgical use by the National Conference of Catholic Bishops and the Holy See are the *New American Bible* (1970 edition), the *Revised Standard Version-Catholic Edition*, and the *Jerusalem Bible* (1966).

The Protestant counterpart of the *Douay-Rheims Bible* was the *King James Bible*, called the *Authorized Version* in England. Originally published in 1611 and in general use for more than three centuries, its several revisions include the *Revised Standard Version* and the *New Revised Standard Version*.

Biblical Federation

In November, 1966, Pope Paul VI commissioned the Secretariat for Promoting Christian Unity to start work for the widest possible distribution of the Bible and to coordinate endeavors toward the production of Catholic-Protestant Bibles in all languages.

The World Catholic Federation for the Biblical Apostolate, established in 1969, sponsors a program designed to create greater awareness among Catholics of the Bible and its use in everyday life.

The U. S. Center for the Catholic Biblical Apostolate is related to the Secretariat for Pastoral Research and Practices, National Conference of Catholic Bishops, 3211 Fourth St. N.E., Washington, DC 20017.

APOCRYPHA

In Catholic usage, Apocrypha are books which have some resemblance to the canonical books in subject matter and title but which have not been recognized as canonical by the Church. They are characterized by a false claim to divine authority; extravagant accounts of events and miracles alleged to be supplemental revelation; material favoring heresy (especially in "New Testament" apocrypha); minimal, if any, historical value. Among examples of this type of literature itemized by J. McKenzie, S.J., in *Dictionary of the Bible* are: the Books of Adam and Eve, Martyrdom of Isaiah, Testament of the Patriarchs, Assumption of Moses, Sibylline Oracles; Gos-

pel of James, Gospel of Thomas, Arabic Gospel of the Infancy, History of Joseph the Carpenter; Acts of John, Acts of Paul, Acts of Peter, Acts of Andrew, and numerous epistles.

Books of this type are called pseudepigrapha by Protestants.

In Protestant usage, some books of the Catholic Bible (deuterocanonical) are called apocrypha because their inspired character is rejected.

DEAD SEA SCROLLS

The Qumran Scrolls, popularly called the Dead Sea Scrolls, are a collection of manuscripts, all but one of them in Hebrew, found since 1947 in caves in the Desert of Juda west of the Dead Sea.

Among the findings were a complete text of Isaiah dating from the second century, B.C., more or less extensive fragments of other Old Testament texts (including the deuterocanonical Tobit), and a commentary on Habakkuk. Until the discovery of these materials, the oldest known Hebrew manuscripts were from the 10th century A.D.

Also found were messianic and apocalyptic texts, and other writings describing the beliefs and practices of the Essenes, a rigoristic Jewish sect.

The scrolls, dating from about the first century before and after Christ, are important sources of information about Hebrew literature, Jewish history during the period between the Old and New Testaments, and the history of Old Testament texts. They established the fact that the Hebrew text of the Old Testament was fixed before the beginning of the Christian era and have had definite effects in recent critical studies and translations of the Old Testament. Together with other scrolls found at Masada, they are still the subject of intensive study.

Illumination from the
Middle Ages

BOOKS OF THE BIBLE

OLD TESTAMENT BOOKS

Pentateuch

The Pentateuch is the collective title of the first five books of the Bible. Substantially, they identify the Israelites as Yahweh's Chosen People, cover their history from Egypt to the threshold of the Promised Land, contain the Mosaic Law and Covenant, and disclose the promise of salvation to come. Principal themes concern the divine promise of salvation, Yahweh's fidelity and the Covenant. Work on the composition of the Pentateuch was completed in the sixth century.

Genesis: The book of origins, according to its title in the Septuagint. In two parts, covers: religious prehistory, including accounts of the origin of the world and man, the original state of innocence and the fall, the promise of salvation, patriarchs before and after the Deluge, the Tower of Babel narrative, genealogies (first eleven chapters); the Covenant with Abraham and patriarchal history from Abraham to Joseph (balance of the 50 chapters). Significant are the themes of Yahweh's universal sovereignty and mercy.

Exodus: Named with the Greek word for departure, is a religious epic which describes the oppression of the 12 tribes in Egypt and their departure, liberation or passover therefrom under the leadership of Moses; Yahweh's establishment of the Covenant with them, making them his Chosen People, through the mediation of Moses at Mt. Sinai; instructions concerning the tabernacle, the sanctuary and Ark of the Covenant; the institution of the priesthood. The book is significant because of its theology of liberation and redemption. In Christian interpretation, the Exodus is a figure of baptism.

Leviticus: Mainly legislative in theme and purpose, contains laws regarding sacrifices, ceremonies of ordination and the priesthood of Aaron, legal purity, the holiness code, atonement, the redemption of offerings and other subjects. Summarily, Levitical laws provided directives for all aspects of religious observance and for the manner in which the Israelites were to conduct themselves with respect to Yahweh and each other. Leviticus was the liturgical handbook of the priesthood.

Numbers: Taking its name from censuses recounted at the beginning and near the end, is a continuation of Exodus. It combines narrative of the Israelites' desert pilgrimage from Sinai to the border of Canaan with laws related to and expansive of those in Leviticus.

Deuteronomy: The concluding book of the Pentateuch, recapitulates, in the form of a testament of Moses, the Law and much of the desert history of the Israelites; enjoins fidelity to the Law as the key to good or bad fortune for the people; gives an account of the commissioning of Joshua as the successor of Moses. Notable themes concern the election of Israel by Yahweh, observance of the Law, prohibitions against the worship of foreign gods, worship of and confidence in Yahweh, the power of Yahweh in nature. The Deuteronomic Code or motif, embodying all of these elements, was the norm for interpreting Israelite history.

Joshua, Judges, Ruth

Joshua: Records the fulfillment of Yahweh's promise to the Israelites in their conquest, occupation and division of Canaan under the leadership of Joshua. It also contains an account of the return of Transjordanian Israelites and of a renewal of the Covenant. It was redacted in final form probably in the sixth century or later.

Judges: Records the actions of charismatic leaders, called judges, of the tribes of Israel between the death of Joshua and the time of Samuel, and a crisis of idolatry among the people. The basic themes are sin and punishment, repentance and deliverance; its purpose was in line with the Deuteronomic motif, that the fortunes of the Israelites were related to their observance or non-observance of the Law and the Covenant. It was redacted in final form probably in the sixth century.

Ruth: Named for the Gentile (Moabite) woman who, through marriage with Boaz, became an Israelite and an ancestress of David (her son, Obed, became his grandfather). Themes are filial piety, faith and trust in Yahweh, the universality of messianic salvation. Dates ranging from c. 950 to the seventh century have been assigned to the origin of the book, whose author is unknown.

Historical Books

These books, while they contain a great deal of factual material, are unique in their preoccupation with presenting and interpreting it, in the Deuteronomic manner, in primary relation to the Covenant on which the nation of Israel was founded and in accordance with which community and personal life were judged.

The books are: Samuel 1 and 2, from the end of Judges (c. 1020) to the end of David's reign (c. 961); Kings 1 and 2, from the last days of David to the start of the Babylonian Exile and the destruction of the Temple (587); Chronicles 1 and 2, from the reign of Saul (c. 1020-1000) to the return of the people from the Exile (538); Ezra and Nehemiah, covering the reorganization of the Jewish community after the Exile (458-397); Maccabees 1 and 2, recounting the struggle against attempted suppression of Judaism (168-142).

Three of the books listed below — Tobit, Judith, and Esther — are categorized as religious novels.

Samuel 1 and 2: A single work in concept and contents, containing episodic history of the last two Judges, Eli and Samuel, the establishment and rule of the monarchy under Saul and David, and the political consequences of David's rule. The royal messianic dynasty of David was the subject of Nathan's oracle in 2 Sm. 7. The books were edited in final form probably late in the seventh century or during the Exile.

Kings 1 and 2: Cover the last days of David and the career of Solomon, including the building of the Temple and the history of the kingdom during his reign; stories of the prophets Elijah and Elisha; the history of the divided kingdom to the fall of Israel in the North (721) and the fall of Judah in the South (587), the destruction of Jerusalem and the Temple. They reflect the Deuteronomic motif in attributing the downfall of the people to corruption of belief and practice in public and private life. They were completed probably in the sixth century.

Chronicles 1 and 2: A collection of historical traditions interpreted in such a way as to present an ideal picture of one people governed by divine law and united in one Temple worship of the one true God. Contents include genealogical tables from Adam to David, the careers of David and Solomon, coverage of the kingdom of Judah to the Exile, and the decree of Cyrus permitting the return of the people and rebuilding of Jerusalem. Both are related to and were written about 400 by the same author, the Chronicler, who composed Ezra and Nehemiah.

Ezra and Nehemiah: A running account of the return of the people to their homeland after the Exile and of practical efforts, under the leadership of Ezra and Nehemiah, to restore and reorganize the religious and political community on the basis of Israelite traditions, divine worship and observance of the Law. Events of great significance were the building of the second Temple, the building of a wall around Jerusalem and the proclamation of the Law by Ezra. This restored community was the start of Judaism. Both are related to and were written about 400 by the same author, the Chronicler, who composed Chronicles 1 and 2.

Tobit: Written in the literary form of a novel and having greater resemblance to wisdom than to historical literature, narrates the personal his-

tory of Tobit, a devout and charitable Jew in exile, and persons connected with him, viz., his son Tobiah, his kinsman Raguel and Raguel's daughter Sarah. Its purpose was to teach people how to be good Jews. One of its principal themes is patience under trial, with trust in divine Providence which is symbolized by the presence and action of the angel Raphael. It was written about 200.

Judith: Recounts, in the literary form of a historical novel or romance, the preservation of the Israelites from conquest and ruin through the action of Judith. The essential themes are trust in God for deliverance from danger and emphasis on observance of the Law. It was written probably during the Maccabean period.

Esther: Relates, in the literary form of a historical novel or romance, the manner in which Jews in Persia were saved from annihilation through the central role played by Esther, the Jewish wife of Ahasuerus; a fact commemorated by the Jewish feast of Purim. Like Judith, it has trust in divine Providence as its theme and indicates that God's saving will is sometimes realized by persons acting in unlikely ways. It may have been written near the end of the fourth century.

Maccabees 1 and 2: While related to some extent because of common subject matter, are quite different from each other.

The first book recounts the background and events of the 40-year (175-135) struggle for religious and political freedom led by Judas Maccabaeus and his brothers against the Hellenist Seleucid kings and some Hellenophiles among the Jews. Victory was symbolized by the rededication of the Temple. Against the background of opposition between Jews and Gentiles, the author equated the survival of belief in the one true God with survival of the Jewish people, thus identifying religion with patriotism. It was written probably near the year 100.

The second book supplements the first to some extent, covering and giving a theological interpretation to events from 180 to 162. It explains the feast of the Dedication of the Temple, a key event in the survival of Judaism which is commemorated in the feast of Hanukkah; stresses the primacy of God's action in the struggle for survival; and indicates belief in an afterlife and the resurrection of the body. It was completed probably about 124.

Wisdom Books

With the exceptions of Psalms and the Song of Songs, the titles listed under this heading are called wisdom books because their purpose was to formulate the fruits of human experience in the context of meditation on sacred Scripture and to present them as an aid toward understanding the problems of life. The Hebrew wisdom literature was distinctive from pagan literature of the same type, but it had limitations; these were overcome in the New Testament, which added the dimensions of the New Covenant to those of the Old. Solomon was regarded as the archetype of the wise man.

Job: A dramatic, didactic poem consisting mainly of several dialogues between Job and his friends concerning the mystery involved in the coexistence of the just God, evil and the suffering of the just. It describes an innocent man's experience of suffering and conveys the truth that faith in and submission to God rather than complete understanding, which is impossible, make the experience bearable; also, that the justice of God cannot be defended by affirming that it is realized in this world. Of unknown authorship, it was composed between the seventh and fifth centuries.

Psalms: A collection of 150 religious songs or lyrics reflecting Israelite belief and piety dating from the time of the monarchy to the post-Exilic period, a span of well over 500 years. The psalms, which are a compendium of Old Testament theology, were used in the temple liturgy and for other occasions. They were of several types suitable for the king, hymns, lamentations, expressions of confidence and thanksgiving, prophecy, historical meditation and reflection, and the statement of wisdom. About one-half of them are attributed to David; many were composed by unknown authors.

Proverbs: The oldest book of the wisdom type in the Bible, consisting of collections of sayings attributed to Solomon and other persons regarding a wide variety of subjects including wisdom and its nature, rules of conduct, duties with respect to one's neighbor, the conduct of daily affairs. It reveals many details of Hebrew life. Its nucleus dates from the period before the Exile. The extant form of the book dates probably from the end of the fifth century.

Ecclesiastes: A treatise about many subjects whose unifying theme is the vanity of strictly human efforts and accomplishments with respect to the achievement of lasting happiness; the only things which are not vain are fear of the Lord and observance of his commandments. The pessimistic tone of the book is due to the absence of a concept of afterlife. It was written by an unknown author probably in the third century.

Song of Songs: A collection of love lyrics reflecting various themes, including the love of God for Israel and the celebration of ideal love and fidelity between man and woman. It was written by an unknown author after the Exile.

Wisdom: Deals with many subjects including the reward of justice; praise of wisdom, a gift

of Yahweh proceeding from belief in him and the practice of his Law; the part played by him in the history of his people, especially in their liberation from Egypt; the folly and shame of idolatry. Its contents are taken from the whole sacred literature of the Jews and represent a distillation of its wisdom based on the law, beliefs and traditions of Israel. The last of the Old Testament books, it was written in the early part of the first century before Christ by a member of the Jewish community at Alexandria.

Sirach: Resembling Proverbs, is a collection of sayings handed on by a grandfather to his grandson. It contains a variety of moral instruction and eulogies of patriarchs and other figures in Israelite history. Its moral maxims apply to individuals, the family and community, relations with God, friendship, education, wealth, the Law, divine worship. Its theme is that true wisdom consists in the Law. (It was formerly called Ecclesiasticus, the Church Book, because of its extensive use by the Church for moral instruction.) It was written in Hebrew between 200 and 175, during a period of strong Hellenistic influence, and was translated into Greek after 132.

The Prophets

These books and the prophecies they contain "express judgments of the people's moral conduct, on the basis of the Mosaic alliance between God and Israel. They teach sublime truths and lofty morals. They contain exhortations, threats, announcements of punishment, promises of deliverance. In the affairs of men, their prime concern is the interests of God, especially in what pertains to the Chosen People through whom the Messiah is to come; hence their denunciations of idolatry and of that externalism in worship which exclude the interior spirit of religion. They are concerned also with the universal nature of the moral law, with personal responsibility, with the person and office of the Messiah, and with the conduct of foreign nations" (*The Holy Bible, Prophetic Books*, CCD Edition, 1961; Preface). There are four major (Isaiah, Jeremiah, Ezekiel, Daniel) and twelve minor prophets (distinguished by the length of books), Lamentations and Baruch. Earlier prophets, mentioned in historical books, include Samuel, Gad, Nathan, Elijah, and Elisha.

Before the Exile, prophets were the intermediaries through whom God communicated revelation to the people. Afterwards, prophecy lapsed and the written word of the Law served this purpose.

Isaiah: Named for the greatest of the prophets whose career spanned the reigns of three Hebrew kings from 742 to the beginning of the seventh century, in a period of moral breakdown in Judah and threats of invasion by foreign enemies. It is an anthology of poems and oracles credited to him and a number of followers deeply influenced by him. Of special importance are the prophecies concerning Immanuel (6 to 12), including the prophecy of the virgin birth (7:14). Chapters 40 to 55, called Deutero-Isaiah, are attributed to an anonymous poet toward the end of the Exile; this portion contains the Songs of the Servant. The concluding part of the book (56-66) contains oracles by later disciples. One of many themes in Isaiah concerned the saving mission of the remnant of Israel in the divine plan of salvation.

Jeremiah: Combines history, biography and prophecy in a setting of crisis caused by internal and external factors, viz., idolatry and general infidelity to the Law among the Israelites and external threats from the Assyrians, Egyptians and Babylonians. Jeremiah prophesied the promise of a new covenant as well as the destruction of Jerusalem and the Temple. His career began in 626 and ended some years after the beginning of the Exile. The book, the longest in the Bible, was edited in final form after the Exile.

Lamentations: A collection of five laments or elegies over the fall of Jerusalem and the fate of the people in Exile, written by an unknown eyewitness. They convey the message that Yahweh struck the people because of their sins and reflect confidence in his love and power to restore his converted people.

Baruch: Against the background of the already-begun Exile, it consists of an introduction and several parts: an exile's prayer of confession and petition for forgiveness and the restoration of Israel; a poem praising wisdom and the Law of Moses; a lament in which Jerusalem, personified, bewails the fate of her people and consoles them with the hope of blessings to come; and a polemic against idolatry. Although ascribed to Baruch, Jeremiah's secretary, it was written by several authors, probably in the second century.

Ezekiel: Named for the priest-prophet who prophesied in Babylon from 593 to 571, during the first phase of the Exile. To prepare his fellow early exiles for the impending fall of Jerusalem, he reproached the Israelites for past sins and predicted woes to come upon them. After the destruction of the city, the burden of his message was hope and promise of restoration. Ezekiel had great influence on the religion of Israel after the Exile.

Daniel: The protagonist is a young Jew, taken early to Babylon where he lived until about 538, who figured in a series of edifying stories which originated in Israelite tradition. The stories, whose characters are not purely legendary but rest on historical tradition, recount the trials and triumphs of Daniel and his three companions, and other episodes including those concerning Susannah, Bel, and the Dragon. The book is more apocalyptic than prophetic: it envisions Israel in glory to come and conveys the message that men of faith can resist temptation and overcome adversity. It states the prophetic themes of right conduct, divine control of men and events, and the final triumph of the kingdom. It was written by an unknown author in the 160s to give moral support to Jews during the persecutions of the Maccabean period.

Hosea: Consists of a prophetic parallel between Hosea's marriage and Yahweh's relations with his people. As the prophet was married to a faithless wife whom he would not give up, Yahweh was bound in Covenant with an idolatrous and unjust Israel whom he would not desert but would chastise for purification. Hosea belonged to the Northern Kingdom of Israel and began his career about the middle of the eighth century. He inaugurated the tradition of describing Yahweh's relation to Israel in terms of marriage.

Joel: Is apocalyptic and eschatological regarding divine judgment, the Day of the Lord, which is symbolized by a ravaging invasion of locusts, the judgment of the nations in the Valley of Josaphat and the outpouring of the Spirit in the messianic era to come. Its message is that God will vindicate and save Israel, in view of the prayer and repentance of the people, and will punish their enemies. It was composed about 400.

Amos: Consists of an indictment against foreign enemies of Israel; a strong denunciation of the people of Israel, whose infidelity, idolatry and injustice made them subject to divine judgment and punishment; and a messianic oracle regarding Israel's restoration. Amos prophesied in the Northern Kingdom of Israel, at Bethel, in the first half of the eighth century; chronologically, he was the first of the canonical prophets.

Obadiah: A twenty-one-verse prophecy, the shortest and one of the sternest in the Bible, against the Edomites, invaders of southern Judah and enemies of those returning from the Exile to their homeland. It was probably composed in the fifth century.

Jonah: A parable of divine mercy with the theme that Yahweh wills the salvation of all, not just a few, men who respond to his call. Its protagonist is a disobedient prophet; forced by circumstances beyond his control to preach penance among Gentiles, he is highly successful in his mission but baffled by the divine concern for those who do not belong to the Chosen People. It was written after the Exile, probably in the fifth century.

Micah: Attacks the injustice and corruption of priests, false prophets, officials and people; announces judgment and punishment to come; foretells the restoration of Israel; refers to the saving remnant of Israel. Micah was a contemporary of Isaiah.

Nahum: Concerns the destruction of Nineveh in 612 and the overthrow of the Assyrian Empire by the Babylonians.

Habakkuk: Dating from about 605-597, concerns sufferings to be inflicted by oppressors on the people of Judah because of their infidelity to the Lord. It also sounds a note of confidence in the Lord, the Savior, and declares that the just will not perish.

Zephaniah: Exercising his ministry in the second half of the seventh century, during a time of widespread idolatry, superstition and religious degradation, he prophesied impending judgment and punishment for Jerusalem and its people. He prophesied too that a holy remnant of the people (*anawim*, mentioned also by Amos) would be spared. Zephaniah was a forerunner of Jeremiah.

Haggai: One of the first prophets after the Exile, Haggai in 520 encouraged the returning exiles to reestablish their community and to complete the second Temple (dedicated in 515), for which he envisioned greater glory, in a messianic sense, than that enjoyed by the original Temple of Solomon.

Zechariah: A contemporary of Haggai, he prophesied in the same vein. A second part of the book, called Deutero-Zechariah and composed by one or more unknown authors, relates a vision of the coming of the Prince of Peace, the Messiah of the Poor.

Malachi: Written by an anonymous author, presents a picture of life in the post-Exilic community between 516 and the initiation of reforms by Ezra and Nehemiah about 432. Blame for the troubles of the community is placed mainly on priests for failure to carry out ritual worship and to instruct the people in the proper manner; other factors were religious indifference and the influence of doubters who were scandalized at the prosperity of the wicked. The vision of a universal sacrifice to be offered to Yahweh (1:11) is interpreted in Catholic theology as a prophecy of the sacrifice of the Mass. Malachi was the last of the minor prophets.

DATES OF THE OLD TESTAMENT

c. 1800 - c. 1600 B.C.: Period of the patriarchs (Abraham, Isaac, Jacob).

c. 1600: Israelites in Egypt.

c. 1250: Exodus of Israelites from Egypt.

c. 1210: Entrance of Israelites into Canaan.

c. 1210-c. 1020: Period of the Judges.

c. 1020-c. 1000: Reign of Saul, first king.

c. 1000-c. 961: Reign of David.

c. 961-922: Reign of Solomon. Temple built during his reign.

922: Division of the Kingdom into Israel (North) and Judah (South).

721: Conquest of Israel by Assyrians.

587-538: Conquest of Judah by Babylonians.

Babylonian Captivity and Exile. Destruction of Jerusalem and the Temple, 587 (or 586). Captivity ended with the return of exiles, following the decree of Cyrus permitting the rebuilding of Jerusalem.

515: Dedication of the second Temple.

458-397: Restoration and reform of the Jewish religious and political community; building of the Jerusalem wall, 439. Leaders in the movement were Ezra and Nehemiah.

168-142: Period of the Maccabees; war against Syrians.

142: Independence granted to Jews by Demetrius II of Syria.

135-37: Period of the Hasmonean dynasty.

63: Beginning of Roman rule.

37-4: Period of Herod the Great.

NEW TESTAMENT BOOKS

Gospels

The term Gospel is derived from the Anglo-Saxon *god-spell* and the Greek *euangelion*, meaning good news, good tidings. In Christian use, it means the good news of salvation proclaimed by Christ and the Church, and handed on in written form in the Gospels of Matthew, Mark, Luke and John.

The initial proclamation of the coming of the kingdom of God was made by Jesus in and through his Person, teachings and actions, and especially through his passion, death and resurrection. This proclamation became the center of Christian faith and the core of the oral Gospel tradition with which the Church spread the good news by apostolic preaching for some 30 years before it was committed to writing by the Evangelists.

Nature of the Gospels

The historical truth of the Gospels was the subject of an instruction issued by the Pontifical Commission for Biblical Studies April 21, 1964.

- The sacred writers selected from the material at their disposal (the oral Gospel tradition, some written collections of sayings and deeds of Jesus, eyewitness accounts) those things which were particularly suitable to the various conditions (liturgical, catechetical, missionary) of the faithful and the aims they had in mind, and they narrated these things in such a way as to correspond with those circumstances and their aims.

- The life and teaching of Jesus were not simply reported in a biographical manner for the purpose of preserving their memory but were "preached" so as to offer the Church the basis of doctrine concerning faith and morals.
- In their works, the Evangelists presented the true sayings of Jesus and the events of his life in the light of the better understanding they had following their enlightenment by the Holy Spirit. They did not transform Christ into a "mythical" Person, nor did they distort his teaching. Passion narratives are the core of all the Gospels, covering the suffering, death and resurrection of Jesus as central events in bringing about and establishing the New Covenant. Leading up to them are accounts of the mission of John the Baptist and the ministry of Jesus, especially in Galilee and finally in Jerusalem before the Passion. The infancy of Jesus is covered by Luke and Matthew with narratives inspired in part by appropriate Old Testament citations.

Matthew, Mark and Luke, while different in various respects, have so many similarities that they are called Synoptic; their relationships are the subject of the Synoptic Problem.

Matthew: Written probably between 80 and 100 for Jewish Christians with clear reference to Jewish background and identification of Jesus as the divine Messiah, the fulfillment of the Old Testament. Distinctive are the use of Old Testament citations regarding the Person, activity and teaching of Jesus, and the presentation of doctrine in sermons and discourses.

Mark: Considered by most current Catholic exegetes to be most likely the first of the Gospels, dating from about 70. Written for Gentile Christians, it is noted for the realism and wealth of concrete details with which it reveals Jesus as Son of God and Savior more by his actions and miracles than by his discourses. Theologically, it is less refined than the other Gospels.

Luke: Written about 75 for Gentile Christians. It is noted for the universality of its address, the insight it provides into the Christian way of life, the place it gives to women, the manner in which it emphasizes Jesus' friendship with sinners and compassion for the suffering.

John: Edited and arranged in final form probably between 90 and 100, this is the most sublime and theological of the Gospels, and is different from the Synoptics in plan and treatment. Combining accounts of signs with longer discourses and reflections, it progressively reveals the Person and mission of Jesus — as Word, Way, Truth, Life, Light — in line with the purpose, "to help you believe that Jesus is the Messiah,

the Son of God, so that through this faith you may have life in his name" (Jn. 20:31). There are questions about the authorship but no doubt about the Johannine authority and tradition behind the Gospel.

Acts of the Apostles

Written by Luke about 75 as a supplement to his Gospel. It describes the origin and spread of Christian communities through the action of the Holy Spirit from the resurrection of Christ to the time when Paul was placed in custody in Rome in the early 60s.

Letters (Epistles)

These letters, many of which antedated the Gospels, were written in response to existential needs of the early Christian communities for doctrinal and moral instruction, disciplinary action, practical advice, and exhortation to true Christian living.

Pauline Letters

These letters, which comprise approximately one-fourth of the New Testament, are primary and monumental sources of the development of Christian theology. Several of them may not have had Paul as their actual author, but evidence of the Pauline tradition behind them is strong. The letters to the Colossians, Philippians, Ephesians and Philemon have been called the "Captivity Letters" because of a tradition that they were written while Paul was under house arrest or another form of detention.

Romans: Written about 57 probably from Corinth on the central significance of Christ and faith in him for salvation, and the relationship of Christianity to Judaism; the condition of mankind without Christ; justification and the Christian life; duties of Christians.

Corinthians 1: Written near the beginning of 57 from Ephesus to counteract factionalism and disorders, it covers community dissension, moral irregularities, marriage and celibacy, conduct at religious gatherings, the Eucharist, spiritual gifts (charisms) and their function in the Church, charity, the resurrection of the body.

Corinthians 2: Written later in the same year as 1 Cor., concerning Paul's defense of his apostolic ministry, and an appeal for a collection to aid poor Christians in Jerusalem.

Galatians: Written probably between 54 and 55 to counteract Judaizing opinions and efforts to undermine his authority, it asserts the divine origin of Paul's authority and doctrine, states that justification is not through Mosaic Law but through faith in Christ, insists on the practice of evangelical virtues, especially charity.

Ephesians: Written probably between 61 and

63, mainly on the Church as the Mystical Body of Christ.

Philippians: Written between 56 and 57 or 61 and 63 to warn the Philippians against enemies of their faith, to urge them to be faithful to their vocation and unity of belief, and to thank them for their kindness to him while he was being held in detention.

Colossians: Written probably while he was under house arrest in Rome from 61 to 63, to counteract the influence of self-appointed teachers who were watering down doctrine concerning Christ. It includes two highly important Christological passages, a warning against false teachers, and an instruction on the ideal Christian life.

Thessalonians 1 and 2: Written within a short time of each other probably in 51 from Corinth, mainly on doctrine concerning the *Parousia*, the second coming of Christ.

Timothy 1 and 2, Titus: Written between 65 and 67, or perhaps in the 70s, giving pastoral counsels to Timothy and Titus, who were in charge of churches in Ephesus and Crete, respectively. 1 Tm. emphasizes pastoral responsibility for preserving unity of doctrine; 2 Tm. describes Paul's imprisonment in Rome.

Philemon: A private letter written between 61 and 63 to a wealthy Colossian concerning a slave, Onesimus, who had escaped from him; Paul appealed for kind treatment of the man.

Hebrews: Dating from sometime between 70 and 96, a complex theological treatise on Christology, the priesthood and sacrifice of Christ, the New Covenant, and the pattern for Christian living. Critical opinion is divided as to whether it was addressed to Judaeo or Gentile Christians.

Catholic Letters

These seven letters have been called "catholic" because it was thought for some time, not altogether correctly, that they were not addressed to particular communities.

James: Written sometime before 62 in the spirit of Hebrew wisdom literature and the moralism of Tobit. An exhortation to practical Christian living, it is also noteworthy for the doctrine it states on good works and its citation regarding anointing of the sick.

Peter 1 and 2: The first letter may have been written between 64 and 67 or between 90 and 95; the second may date from 100 to 125. Addressed to Christians in Asia Minor, both are exhortations to perseverance in the life of faith despite trials and difficulties arising from pagan influences, isolation from other Christians and false teaching.

John 1: Written sometime in the 90s and addressed to Asian churches, its message is that God is made known to us in the Son and that fellowship with the Father is attained by living in the light, justice and love of the Son.

John 2: Written sometime in the 90s and addressed to a church in Asia, it commends the people for standing firm in the faith and urges them to perseverance.

John 3: Written sometime in the 90s, it appears to represent an effort to settle a jurisdictional dispute in one of the churches.

Jude: Written probably about 80, it is a brief treatise against erroneous teachings and practices opposed to law, authority and true Christian freedom.

Revelation

Written in the 90s along the lines of Johannine thought, it is a symbolic and apocalyptic treatment of things to come and of the struggle between the Church and evil combined with warning but hope and assurance to the Church regarding the coming of the Lord in glory.

APOSTLES AND EVANGELISTS

The Apostles were the men selected, trained and commissioned by Christ to preach the Gospel, to baptize, to establish, direct and care for his Church as servants of God and stewards of his mysteries. They were the first bishops of the Church.

St. Matthew's Gospel lists the Apostles in this order: Peter, Andrew, James the Greater, John, Philip, Bartholomew, Thomas, Matthew, James the Less, Jude, Simon and Judas Iscariot. Matthias was elected to fill the place of Judas. Paul became an Apostle by a special call from Christ. Barnabas was called an Apostle.

Two of the Evangelists, John and Matthew, were Apostles. The other two, Luke and Mark, were closely associated with the apostolic college.

Andrew: Born in Bethsaida, brother of Peter, disciple of John the Baptist, a fisherman, the first Apostle called; according to legend, preached the Gospel in northern Greece, Epirus and Scythia, and was martyred at Patras about 70; in art, is represented with an X-shaped cross, called St. Andrew's Cross; is honored as the patron of Russia and Scotland; November 30.

Barnabas: Originally called Joseph but named Barnabas by the Apostles, among whom he is ranked because of his collaboration with Paul; a Jew of the Diaspora, born in Cyprus; a cousin of Mark and member of the Christian community at Jerusalem, he influenced the Apostles to accept Paul, with whom he became a pioneer missionary outside Palestine and Syria, to Antioch, Cyprus, and southern Asia Minor; legend says he was martyred in Cyprus during the Neronian persecution; June 11.

Bartholomew (Nathaniel): A friend of Philip; according to various traditions, preached the Gospel in Ethiopia, India, Persia, and Armenia, where he was martyred by being flayed and beheaded; in art, is depicted holding a knife, an instrument of his death; August 24 (Roman Rite), August 25 (Byzantine Rite).

James the Greater: A Galilean, son of Zebedee, brother of John (with whom he was called a "Son of Thunder"), a fisherman; with Peter and John, witnessed the raising of Jairus's daughter to life, the transfiguration, the agony of Jesus in the Garden of Gethsemane; first of the Apostles to die, by the sword in 44 during the rule of Herod Agrippa; there is doubt about a journey legend says he made to Spain and also about the authenticity of relics said to be his at Santiago de Compostela; in art, is depicted carrying a pilgrim's bell; July 25 (Roman Rite), April 30 (Byzantine Rite).

James the Less: Son of Alphaeus, called "Less" because he was younger in age or shorter in stature than James the Greater; one of the Catholic Epistles bears his name; was stoned to death in 62 or thrown from the top of the temple in Jerusalem and clubbed to death in 66; in art, is depicted with a club or heavy staff; May 3 (Roman Rite), October 9 (Byzantine Rite).

John: A Galilean, son of Zebedee, brother of James the Greater (with whom he was called a "Son of Thunder"), a fisherman, probably a disciple of John the Baptist, one of the Evangelists, called the "Beloved Disciple"; with Peter and James the Greater, witnessed the raising of Jairus's daughter to life, the transfiguration, the agony of Jesus in the Garden of Gethsemane; Mary was commended to his special care by Christ; the fourth Gospel, three Catholic Epistles, and Revelation bear his name; according to various accounts, lived at Ephesus in Asia Minor for some time and died a natural death about 100; in art, is represented by an eagle, symbolic of the sublimity of the contents of his Gospel; December 27 (Roman Rite), May 8 (Byzantine Rite).

Jude Thaddeus: A brother of James and "servant of Jesus," the author of the shortest of the Catholic Epistles; various traditions say he preached the Gospel in Mesopotamia, Persia, and elsewhere, and was martyred; in art, is depicted with a halberd, the instrument of his death; October 28 (Roman Rite), June 19 (Byzantine Rite).

Luke: A Greek convert to the Christian community, called "our most dear physician" by Paul,

of whom he was a missionary companion; author of the third Gospel and Acts of the Apostles; the place — Achaia, Bithynia, Egypt — and circumstances of his death are not certain; in art, is depicted as a man, a writer, or an ox (because his Gospel starts at the scene of temple sacrifice); October 18.

Mark: A cousin of Barnabas and member of the first Christian community at Jerusalem; a missionary companion of Paul and Barnabas, then of Peter; author of the Gospel which bears his name; according to legend, founded the Church at Alexandria, was bishop there and was martyred in the streets of the city; in art, is depicted with his Gospel and a winged lion, symbolic of the voice of John the Baptist crying in the wilderness, at the beginning of his Gospel; April 25.

Matthew: A Galilean, called Levi by Luke and John and the son of Alphaeus by Mark, a tax collector, one of the Evangelists; according to various accounts, preached the Gospel in Judea, Ethiopia, Persia and Parthia, and was martyred; in art, is depicted with a spear, the instrument of his death, and as a winged man in his role as Evangelist; September 21 (Roman Rite), November 16 (Byzantine Rite).

Matthias: A disciple of Jesus whom the faithful eleven Apostles chose to replace Judas before the Resurrection; uncertain traditions report that he preached the Gospel in Palestine, Cappadocia or Ethiopia; in art, is represented with a cross and a halberd, the instruments of his death as a martyr; May 14 (Roman Rite), August 9 (Byzantine Rite).

Paul: Born at Tarsus, of the tribe of Benjamin, a Roman citizen; participated in the persecution of Christians until the time of his miraculous conversion on the way to Damascus; called by Christ, who revealed himself to him in a special way; became the Apostle of the Gentiles, among whom he did most of his preaching in the course of three major missionary journeys through areas north of Palestine, Cyprus, Asia Minor, and Greece; fourteen epistles bear his name; two years of imprisonment at Rome, following initial arrest in Jerusalem and confinement at Caesarea, ended with martyrdom, by beheading, outside the walls of the city in 64 or 67 during the Neronian persecution; in art, is depicted in various ways with St. Peter, with a sword, in the scene of his conversion; June 29 (with St. Peter), January 25 (Conversion).

Peter: Simon, son of Jonah, born in Bethsaida, brother of Andrew, a fisherman; called Cephas or Peter by Christ who made him the chief of the Apostles and head of the Church as his vicar; named first in the listings of Apostles in the Synoptic Gospels and the Acts of the Apostles; with

James the Greater and John, witnessed the raising of Jairus's daughter to life, the transfiguration, the agony of Jesus in the Garden of Gethsemane; was the first to preach the Gospel in and around Jerusalem and was the leader of the first Christian community there; established a local church in Antioch; presided over the Council of Jerusalem in 51; wrote two Catholic Epistles to the Christians in Asia Minor; established his see in Rome where he spent his last years and was martyred by crucifixion in 64 or 65 during the Neronian persecution; in art, is depicted carrying two keys, symbolic of his primacy in the Church; June 29 (with St. Paul), February 22 (Chair of Peter).

Philip: Born in Bethsaida; according to legend, preached the Gospel in Phrygia where he suffered martyrdom by crucifixion; May 3 (Roman Rite), November 14 (Byzantine Rite).

Simon: Called the Cananean or the Zealot; according to legend, preached in various places in the Middle East and suffered martyrdom by being sawed in two; in art, is depicted with a saw, the instrument of his death, or a book, symbolic of his zeal for the Law; October 28 (Roman Rite), May 10 (Byzantine Rite).

Thomas (Didymus): Notable for his initial incredulity regarding the Resurrection and his subsequent forthright confession of the divinity of Christ risen from the dead; according to legend, preached the Gospel in places from the Caspian Sea to the Persian Gulf and eventually reached India where he was martyred near Madras; Thomas Christians trace their origin to him; in art, is depicted kneeling before the risen Christ, or with a carpenter's rule and square; feast, July 3 (Roman Rite), October 6 (Byzantine Rite).

Judas: The Gospels record only a few facts about Judas, the Apostle who betrayed Christ. The only non-Galilean among the Apostles, he was from Carioth, a town in southern Judah. He was keeper of the purse in the apostolic band. He was called a petty thief by John. He voiced dismay at the waste of money, which he said might have been spent for the poor, in connection with the anointing incident at Bethany. He took the initiative in arranging the betrayal of Christ. Afterwards, he confessed that he had betrayed an innocent man and cast into the Temple the money he had received for that action. Of his death, Matthew says that he hanged himself; the Acts of the Apostles states that he swelled up and burst open; both reports deal more with the meaning than the manner of his death — the misery of the death of a sinner.

The consensus of speculation over the reason why Judas acted as he did in betraying Christ focuses on disillusionment and unwillingness to accept the concept of a suffering Messiah and personal suffering of his own as an Apostle.

APOSTOLIC FATHERS, FATHERS, DOCTORS OF THE CHURCH

The writers listed below were outstanding and authoritative witnesses to authentic Christian belief and practice, and played significant roles in giving them expression.

Apostolic Fathers

The Apostolic Fathers were Christian writers of the first and second centuries whose writings echo genuine apostolic teaching. Chief in importance are: St. Clement (d. c. 97), bishop of Rome and third successor of St. Peter in the papacy; St. Ignatius (50-c. 107), bishop of Antioch and second successor of St. Peter in that see, reputed to be a disciple of St. John; St. Polycarp (69-155), bishop of Smyrna and a disciple of St. John. The authors of the Didache and the Epistle of Barnabas are also numbered among the Apostolic Fathers.

Other early ecclesiastical writers included: St. Justin, martyr (100-165), of Asia Minor and Rome, a layman and apologist; St. Irenaeus (130-202), bishop of Lyons, who opposed Gnosticism; and St. Cyprian (210-258), bishop of Carthage, who opposed Novatianism.

Fathers and Doctors

The Fathers of the Church were theologians and writers of the first eight centuries who were outstanding for sanctity and learning. They were such authoritative witnesses to the belief and teaching of the Church that their unanimous acceptance of doctrines as divinely revealed has been regarded as evidence that such doctrines were so received by the Church in line with apostolic tradition and Sacred Scripture. Their unanimous rejection of doctrines branded them as heretical. Their writings, however, were not necessarily free of error in all respects.

The greatest of these Fathers were: Sts. Ambrose, Augustine, Jerome, and Gregory the Great in the West; Sts. John Chrysostom, Basil the Great, Gregory of Nazianzus, and Athanasius in the East.

The Doctors of the Church were ecclesiastical writers of eminent learning and sanctity who have been given this title because of the great advantage the Church has derived from their work. Their writings, however, were not necessarily free of error in all respects.

Albert the Great, St. (c. 1200-1280): Born in Swabia, Germany; Dominican; bishop of Regensburg (1260-1262); wrote extensively on logic, natural sciences, ethics, metaphysics, Scripture, systematic theology; contributed to development of Scholasticism; teacher of St. Thomas Aquinas; canonized and proclaimed doctor, 1931; named patron of natural scientists, 1941; called *Doctor Universalis, Doctor Expertus*; November 15.

Alphonsus Liguori, St. (1696-1787): Born near Naples, Italy; bishop of Saint Agatha of the Goths (1762-1775); founder of the Redemptorists; in addition to his principal work, *Theologiae Moralis*, wrote on prayer, the spiritual life and doctrinal subjects in response to controversy; canonized, 1839; proclaimed doctor, 1871; named patron of confessors and moralists, 1950; August 1.

Ambrose, St. (c. 340-397): Born in Trier, Germany; bishop of Milan (374-397); one of the strongest opponents of Arianism in the West; his homilies and other writings — on faith, the Holy Spirit, the Incarnation, the sacraments and other subjects — were pastoral and practical; influenced the development of a liturgy at Milan which was named for him; Father and Doctor of the Church; December 7.

Anselm, St. (1033-1109): Born in Aosta, Piedmont, Italy; Benedictine; archbishop of Canterbury (1093-1109); in addition to his principal work, *Cur Deus Homo*, on the atonement and reconciliation of man with God through Christ, wrote about the existence and attributes of God and defended the *Filioque* explanation of the procession of the Holy Spirit from the Father and the Son; proclaimed doctor, 1720; called Father of Scholasticism; April 21.

Anthony of Padua, St. (1195-1231): Born in Lisbon, Portugal; first theologian of the Franciscan Order; preacher; canonized, 1232; proclaimed doctor, 1946; called Evangelical Doctor; June 13.

Athanasius, St. (c. 297-373): Born in Alexandria, Egypt; bishop of Alexandria (328-373); participant in the Council of Nicaea I while still a deacon; dominant opponent of Arians, whose errors regarding Christ he refuted in *Apology Against the Arians*, Discourses against the Arians and other works; Father and Doctor of the Church; called Father of Orthodoxy; May 2.

Augustine, St. (354-430): Born in Tagaste, North Africa; bishop of Hippo (395-430) after conversion from Manichaeism; works include the autobiographical and mystical *Confessions, City of God*, treatises on the Trinity, grace, passages of the Bible and doctrines called into question and denied by Manichaeans, Pelagians and Donatists; had strong and lasting influence on Christian theology and philosophy; Father and Doctor of the Church; called Doctor of Grace; August 28.

Basil the Great, St. (c. 329-379): Born in Caesarea, Cappadocia, Asia Minor; bishop of Caesarea (370-379); wrote three books; *Contra Eunomium*, in refutation of Arian errors; a treatise on the Holy Spirit; many homilies; and several rules for monastic life, on which he had lasting influence; Father and Doctor of the Church; called Father of Monasticism in the East; January 2.

Bede the Venerable, St. (c. 673-735): Born in Northumberland, England; Benedictine; in addition to his principal work, *Ecclesiastical History* of the English Nation (covering the period 597-731), wrote scriptural commentaries; regarded as probably the most learned man in Western Europe of his time; called Father of English History; May 25.

Bernard of Clairvaux, St. (c. 1090-1153): Born near Dijon, France; abbot; monastic reformer, called the second founder of the Cistercian Order; mystical theologian with great influence on devotional life; opponent of the rationalism brought forward by Abélard and others; canonized, 1174; proclaimed doctor, 1830; called Mellifluous Doctor because of his eloquence; August 20.

Bonaventure, St. (c. 1217-1274): Born near Viterbo, Italy; Franciscan; bishop of Albano (1273-1274); cardinal; wrote *Itinerarium Mentis in Deum, De Reductione Artium ad Theologiam, Breviloquium*, scriptural commentaries, additional mystical works affecting devotional life, and a life of St. Francis of Assisi; canonized, 1482; proclaimed doctor, 1588; called Seraphic Doctor; July 15.

Catherine of Siena, St. (c. 1347-1380): Born in Siena, Italy; member of the Third Order of St. Dominic; mystic; authored a long series of letters, mainly concerning spiritual instruction and encouragement, to associates, and *Dialogue*, a spiritual testament in four treatises; was active in support of a crusade against the Turks and efforts to end war between papal forces and the Florentine allies; had great influence in inducing Gregory XI to return himself and the Curia to Rome in 1377, to end the Avignon period of the papacy; canonized, 1461; proclaimed the second woman doctor, October 4, 1970; named a co-patroness of Europe, with St. Edith Stein and St. Bridget of Sweden, on October 1, 1999; April 29.

Cyril of Alexandria, St. (c. 376-444): Born in Egypt; bishop of Alexandria (412-444); wrote treatises on the Trinity, the Incarnation and other subjects, mostly in refutation of Nestorian errors; made key contributions to the development of Christology; presided at the Council of Ephesus, 431; proclaimed doctor, 1882; June 27.

Cyril of Jerusalem, St. (c. 315-386): Bishop of Jerusalem from 350; vigorous opponent of Arianism; principal work, *Catecheses*, a pre-baptismal explanation of the creed of Jerusalem; proclaimed doctor, 1882; March 18.

Ephraem, St. (c. 306-373): Born in Nisibis, Mesopotamia; counteracted the spread of Gnostic and Arian errors with poems and hymns of his own composition; wrote also on the Eucharist and Mary; proclaimed doctor, 1920; called Deacon of Edessa and Harp of the Holy Spirit; June 9.

Francis de Sales, St. (1567-1622): Born in Savoy; bishop of Geneva (1602-1622); spiritual writer with strong influence on devotional life through treatises such as *Introduction to a Devout Life* and *The Love of God*; canonized, 1665; proclaimed doctor, 1877; patron of Catholic writers and the Catholic press; January 24.

Gregory Nazianzen, St. (c. 330-c. 390): Born in Arianzus, Cappadocia, Asia Minor; bishop of Constantinople (381-390); vigorous opponent of Arianism; in addition to five theological discourses on the Nicene Creed and the Trinity for which he is best known, wrote letters and poetry; Father and Doctor of the Church; called the Christian Demosthenes because of his eloquence and, in the Eastern Church, the Theologian; January 2.

Gregory I, the Great, St. (c. 540-604): Born in Rome; pope (590-604) wrote many scriptural commentaries, a compendium of theology in the *Book of Morals* based on Job, Dialogues concerning the lives of saints, the immortality of the soul, death, purgatory, heaven and hell, and fourteen books of letters; enforced papal supremacy and established the position of the pope vis-á-vis the emperor; worked for clerical and monastic reform and the observance of clerical celibacy; Father and Doctor of the Church; September 3.

Hilary of Poitiers, St. (c. 315-368): Born in Poitiers, France; bishop of Poitiers (c. 353-368); wrote *De Synodis*, with the Arian controversy in mind, and *De Trinitate*, the first lengthy study of the doctrine in Latin; introduced Eastern theology to the West; contributed to the development of hymnology; proclaimed doctor, 1851; called the Athanasius of the West because of his vigorous defense of the divinity of Christ against Arians; January 13.

Isidore of Seville, St. (c. 560-636): Born in Cartagena, Spain; bishop of Seville (c. 600-636); in addition to his principal work, *Etymologiae*, an encyclopedia of the knowledge of his day, wrote on theological and historical subjects; regarded as the most learned man of his time; proclaimed doctor, 1722; April 4.

Jerome, St. (c. 343-420): Born in Stridon, Dalmatia; translated the Old Testament from Hebrew into Latin and revised the existing Latin translation of the New Testament to produce the Vulgate version of the Bible; wrote scriptural commentaries and treatises on matters of controversy; regarded as Father and Doctor of the Church from the eighth century; called Father of Biblical Science; September 30.

John Chrysostom, St. (c. 347-407): Born in Antioch, Asia Minor; archbishop of Constantinople (398-407); wrote homilies, scriptural commentaries and letters of wide influence in addition to a classical treatise on the priesthood; proclaimed doctor by the Council of Chalcedon, 451; called the greatest of the Greek Fathers; named patron of preachers, 1909; called Golden-Mouthed because of his eloquence; September 13.

John Damascene, St. (c. 675-c. 749): Born in Damascus, Syria; monk; wrote Fountain of Wisdom, a three-part work including a history of heresies and an exposition of the Christian faith, three discourses against the Iconoclasts, homilies on Mary, biblical commentaries, and treatises on moral subjects; proclaimed doctor, 1890; called Golden Speaker because of his eloquence; December 4.

John of the Cross, St. (1542-1591): Born in Old Castile, Spain; Carmelite; founder of Discalced Carmelites; one of the greatest mystical theologians, wrote *The Ascent of Mt. Carmel*, *The Dark Night of the Soul*, *The Spiritual Canticle*, *The Living Flame of Love*; canonized, 1726; proclaimed doctor, 1926; called Doctor of Mystical Theology; December 14.

Lawrence of Brindisi, St. (1559-1619): Born in Brindisi, Italy; Franciscan (Capuchin); vigorous preacher of strong influence in the post-Reformation period; 15 tomes of collected works include scriptural commentaries, sermons, homilies and doctrinal writings; canonized, 1881; proclaimed doctor, 1959; July 21.

Leo I, the Great, St. (c. 400-461): Born in Tuscany, Italy; pope (440-461); wrote the *Tome of Leo*, to explain doctrine concerning the two natures and one Person of Christ, against the background of the Nestorian and Monophysite heresies; other works included sermons, letters, and writings against the errors of Manichaeism and Pelagianism; was instrumental in dissuading Attila from sacking Rome in 452; proclaimed doctor, 1574; November 10.

Peter Canisius, St. (1521-1597): Born in Nijmegen, Holland; Jesuit; wrote popular expositions of the Catholic faith in several catechisms which were widely circulated in 20 editions in his lifetime alone; was one of the moving figures in the Counter-Reformation period, especially in southern and western Germany; canonized and proclaimed doctor, 1925; December 21.

Peter Chrysologus, St. (c. 400-450): Born in Imola, Italy; served as archbishop of Ravenna (c. 433-450); his sermons and writings, many of which were designed to counteract Monophysitism, were pastoral and practical; proclaimed doctor, 1729; July 30.

Peter Damian, St. (1007-1072): Born in Ravenna, Italy; Benedictine; cardinal; his writings and sermons, many of which concerned ecclesiastical and clerical reform, were pastoral and practical; proclaimed doctor, 1828; February 21.

Robert Bellarmine, St. (1542-1621): Born in Tuscany, Italy; Jesuit; archbishop of Capua (1602-1605); wrote *Controversies*, a three-volume exposition of doctrine under attack during and after the Reformation, two catechisms and the spiritual work, *The Art of Dying Well*; was an authority on ecclesiology and Church-state relations; canonized, 1930; proclaimed doctor, 1931; September 17.

Teresa of Jesus (Ávila), St. (1515-1582): Born in Ávila, Spain; entered the Carmelite Order, 1535; in the early 1560s, initiated a primitive Carmelite reform which greatly influenced men and women religious, especially in Spain; wrote extensively on spiritual and mystical subjects; principal works included her *Autobiography*, *Way of Perfection*, *The Interior Castle*, *Meditations on the Canticle*, *The Foundations*, *Visitation of the Discalced Nuns*; canonized, 1622; proclaimed first woman doctor, September 27, 1970; October 15.

Thérèse of Lisieux, St. (1873-1897): Born in Alençon, Normandy, France; entered the Carmelites at Lisieux in 1888, lived for only nine more years, dying on September 30, 1897, from tuberculosis. Trusting completely in God, a path she described as the "little way," she lived a seemingly ordinary life of a nun, but her spiritual advancement was such that her superiors instructed her to write an autobiography in 1895 (*The Story of a Soul*). One of the most popular and respected saints throughout the 20th century, she was canonized on May 17, 1925. Pope John Paul II declared her the third woman doctor on October 20, 1997, in the letter *Divini amoris scientia*; October 1.

Thomas Aquinas, St. (1225-1274): Born near Naples, Italy; Dominican; teacher and writer on virtually the whole range of philosophy and theology; principal works were *Summa contra Gentiles*, a manual and systematic defense of Christian doctrine, and *Summa Theologiae*, a new (at that time) exposition of theology on philosophical principles; canonized, 1323; proclaimed doctor, 1567; called *Doctor Communis*, *Doctor Angelicus*, the Great Synthesizer because of the way in which he related faith and reason, theology and philosophy (especially that of Aristotle), and systematized the presentation of Christian doctrine; named patron of Catholic schools and education, 1880; January 28.

FATHERS OF THE CHURCH

Greek Fathers

St. Anastasius Sinaita (d. 700).
St. Andrew of Crete (d. 740).
Aphraates (fourth century).
St. Archelaus (d. 282).
St. Athanasius (d. 373).
Athenagoras (second century).
St. Basil the Great (d. 379).
St. Caesarius of Nazianzus (d. 369).
St. Clement of Alexandria (d. 215).
St. Clement I of Rome, pope (r. 88-97).
St. Cyril of Alexandria (d. 444).
St. Cyril of Jerusalem (d. 386).
Didymus the Blind (d. c. 398).
Diodore of Tarsus (d. 392).
St. Dionysius the Great (d. c. 264).
St. Epiphanius (d. 403).
Eusebius of Caesarea (d. 340).
St. Eustathius of Antioch (fourth century).
St. Firmillian (d. 268).
Gennadius I of Constantinople (fifth century).
St. Germanus (d. 732).
St. Gregory of Nazianzus (d. 390).
St. Gregory of Nyssa (d. 395).
St. Gregory Thaumaturgus (d. 268).
Hermas (second century).

Fathers of the Church Design

St. Hippolytus (d. 236).
St. Ignatius of Antioch (d. 107).
St. Isidore of Pelusium (d. c. 450).
St. John Chrysostom (d. 407).
St. John Climacus (d. 649).
St. John Damascene (d. 749), last Father of the East.
St. Julius I, Pope (r. 337-352).
St. Justin Martyr (d. 165).
St. Leontius of Byzantium (sixth century).
St. Macarius (d. c. 390).
St. Maximus the Confessor (d. 662).
St. Melito (d. c. 180).
St. Methodius of Olympus (d. 311?).
St. Nilus the Elder (d. c. 430).
Origen (d. 254).
St. Polycarp (d. c. 155?).
St. Proclus (d. c. 446).
Pseudo-Dionysius the Areopagite (sixth century)
St. Serapion (d. c. 370).
St. Sophronius (d. 638).
Tatian (second century).
Theodore of Mopsuestia (d. 428).
Theodoret of Cyrrhus (d. c. 458).
St. Theophilus of Antioch (second century).

Latin Fathers

St. Ambrose of Milan (d. 397).
Arnobius (d. 330).
St. Augustine of Hippo (d. 430)
St. Benedict of Nursia (d. c. 550).
St. Caesarius of Arles (d. 542).
St. John Cassian (d. 435).

St. Celestine I, pope (r. 422-432).
St. Cornelius, pope (r. 251-253).
St. Cyprian of Carthage (d. 258).
St. Damasus I, pope (r. 366-384).
St. Dionysius, pope (r. 259-268).
St. Ennodius (d. 521).
St. Eucherius of Lyons (d. c. 450).
St. Fulgentius (d. 533).
St. Gregory of Elvira (d. c. 392).
St. Gregory I the Great, pope (r. 590-604).
St. Hilary of Poitiers (d. 367).
St. Innocent I, pope (r. 401-417).
St. Irenaeus of Lyons (d. c. 202).
St. Isidore of Seville (d. 636), last Father of the West.
St. Jerome (d. 420).
Lactantius (d. 323).
St. Leo I the Great (r. 440-461).
Marius Mercator (d. 451).
Marius Victorinus (fourth century).
Minucius Felix (second century).
Novatian (d. c. 257).
St. Optatus (fourth century).
St. Pacian (d. c. 390).
St. Pamphilus (d. 309).
St. Paulinus of Nola (d. 431).
St. Peter Chrysologus (d. 450).
St. Phoebadius of Agen (fourth century).
Rufinus of Aquileia (d. 410).
Salvian (fifth century).
St. Siricius, pope (r. 384-399).
Tertullian (d. c. 222).
St. Vincent of Lérins (d. c. 450).

CREEDS

Creeds are formal and official statements of Christian doctrine. As summaries of the principal truths of faith, they are standards of orthodoxy and are useful for instructional purposes, for actual profession of the faith and for expression of the faith in the liturgy.

The classical creeds are the Apostles' Creed and the Creed of Nicaea-Constantinople. Two others are the Athanasian Creed and the Creed of Pius IV.

Apostles' Creed

Text: *I believe in God, the Father almighty, Creator of heaven and earth.*

And in Jesus Christ, his only Son, our Lord; who was conceived by the Holy Spirit, born of the Virgin Mary, suffered under Pontius Pilate, was crucified, died, and was buried. He descended into hell; the third day he arose again from the dead; he ascended into heaven, sits at the right hand of God, the Father almighty; from thence he shall come to judge the living and the dead.

I believe in the Holy Spirit, the holy Catholic Church, the communion of saints, the forgiveness of sins, the resurrection of the body, and life everlasting. Amen.

Background: The Apostles' Creed reflects the teaching of the Apostles but is not of apostolic origin. It probably originated in the second century as a rudimentary formula of faith professed by catechumens before the reception of baptism. Baptismal creeds in fourth-century use at Rome and elsewhere in the West closely resembled the present text, which was quoted in a handbook of Christian doctrine written between 710 and 724. This text was in wide use throughout the West by the ninth century. The Apostles' Creed is common to all Christian confessional churches in the West, but is not used in Eastern Churches.

Nicene Creed

The following translation of the Latin text of the creed was prepared by the International Committee on English in the Liturgy.

Text: *We believe in one God, the Father, the Almighty, maker of heaven and earth, of all that is seen and unseen.*

We believe in one Lord, Jesus Christ, the only Son of God, eternally begotten of the Father, God from God, Light from Light, true God from true God, begotten, not made, one in Being with the Father. Through him all things were made. For us men and for our salvation he came down from heaven: by the power of the Holy Spirit he was born of the Virgin Mary, and became man. For our sake he was crucified under Pontius Pilate; he suffered, died, and was buried. On the third day he rose again in fulfillment of the Scriptures; he ascended into heaven and is seated at the right hand of the Father. He will come again in glory to judge the living and the dead, and his kingdom will have no end.

We believe in the Holy Spirit, the Lord, the giver of life, who proceeds from the Father and the Son. With the Father and the Son he is worshiped and glorified. He has spoken through the prophets.

We believe in one holy catholic and apostolic Church. We acknowledge one baptism for the forgiveness of sins. We look for the resurrection of the dead, and the life of the world to come. Amen.

Background: The Nicene Creed (Creed of Nicaea-Constantinople) consists of elements of doctrine contained in an early baptismal creed of Jerusalem and enactments of the Council of Nicaea (325) and the Council of Constantinople (381).

Its strong trinitarian content reflects the doctrinal errors, especially of Arianism, it served to counteract. Theologically, it is much more sophisticated than the Apostles' Creed.

Since late in the fifth century, the Nicene Creed has been the only creed in liturgical use in the Eastern Churches. The Western Church adopted it for liturgical use by the end of the eighth century.

The Athanasian Creed

The Athanasian Creed, which has a unique structure, is a two-part summary of doctrine concerning the Trinity and the Incarnation-Redemption bracketed at the beginning and end with the statement that belief in the cited truths is necessary for salvation; it also contains a number of anathemas or condemnatory clauses regarding doctrinal errors. Although attributed to St. Athanasius, it was probably written after his death, between 381 and 428, and may have been authored by St. Ambrose. It is not accepted in the East; in the West, it formerly had place in the Roman-Rite Liturgy of the Hours and in the liturgy for the Solemnity of the Holy Trinity.

Creed of Pius IV

The Creed of Pius IV, also called the Profession of Faith of the Council of Trent, was promulgated in the bull *Injunctum Nobis,* November 13, 1564. It is a summary of doctrine defined by the council concerning: Scripture and tradition, original sin and justification, the Mass and sacraments, veneration of the saints, indulgences, the primacy of the See of Rome. It was slightly modified in 1887 to include doctrinal formulations of the First Vatican Council.

CHRISTIAN MORALITY
By Fr. Alfred McBride, O.Praem. [Numbers in brackets refer to footnotes.]

"Incorporated into Christ by Baptism, Christians are 'dead to sin and alive in Christ Jesus . . .'" (Rom. 6:11).

CHRISTIAN MORALITY IS LIFE IN CHRIST

The third part of the *Catechism* focuses on Christian morality. After the creed as faith professed, and sacraments as faith celebrated, the *Catechism* turns our attention to the faith lived. It deals with this issue in two major sections. The first section establishes the context for Christian morality. The second section analyzes the ten commandments. This approach preserves the *Catechism's* resolute insistence on the primacy of God's initiative through Revelation, salvation, and grace followed by our human response in faith, celebration, and Christian witness. Hence morality does not begin with the rules but with the call to life in Christ and the Holy Spirit.

Covenant love comes first, then the response of Christian affection in the life of the commandments. This saves us both from legalism and from piety without practical witness.

The following excerpt from the *Catechism of the Catholic Church* sets the vision for the Christian moral life:

LIFE IN CHRIST

1691 "Christian, recognize your dignity and, now that you share in God's own nature, do not return to your former base condition by sinning. Remember who is your head and of whose body you are a member. Never forget that you have been rescued from the power of darkness and brought into the light of the Kingdom of God."[1]

1692 The Symbol of the faith confesses the greatness of God's gifts to man in his work of creation, and even more in redemption and sanctification. What faith confesses, the sacraments communicate: by the sacraments of rebirth, Christians have become "children of God,"[2] "partakers of the divine nature."[3] Coming to see in the faith their new dignity, Christians are called to lead henceforth a life "worthy of the gospel of Christ."[4] They are made capable of doing so by the grace of Christ and the gifts of his Spirit, which they receive through the sacraments and through prayer.

1693 Christ Jesus always did what was pleasing to the Father,[5] and always lived in perfect communion with him. Likewise Christ's disciples are invited to live in the sight of the Father "who sees in secret,"[6] in order to become "perfect as your heavenly Father is perfect."[7]

1694 Incorporated into Christ by Baptism, Christians are "dead to sin and alive to God in Christ Jesus" and so participate in the life of the Risen Lord.[8] Following Christ and united with him,[9] Christians can strive to be "imitators of God as beloved children, and walk in love"[10] by conforming their thoughts, words and actions to the "mind . . . which is yours in Christ Jesus,"[11] and by following his example.[12]

1695 "Justified in the name of the Lord Jesus Christ and in the Spirit of our God,"[13] "sanctified . . . [and] called to be saints,"[14] Christians have become the temple of the Holy Spirit.[15] This "Spirit of the Son" teaches them to pray to the Father[16] and, having become their life, prompts them to act so as to bear "the fruit of the Spirit"[17] by charity in action. Healing the wounds of sin, the Holy Spirit renews us interiorly through a spiritual transformation.[18] He enlightens and strengthens us to live as "children of light" through "all that is good and right and true."[19]

1696 The way of Christ "leads to life"; a contrary way "leads to destruction."[20] The Gospel parable of the two ways remains ever present in the catechesis of the Church; it shows the importance of moral decisions for our salvation: "There are two ways, the one of life, the other of death; but between the two, there is a great difference."[21]

1697 Catechesis has to reveal in all clarity the joy and the demands of the way of Christ.[22] Catechesis for the "newness of life"[23] in him should be:

- a catechesis of the Holy Spirit, the interior Master of life according to Christ, a gentle guest and friend who inspires, guides, corrects, and strengthens this life;
- a catechesis of grace, for it is by grace that we are saved and again it is by grace that our works can bear fruit for eternal life;
- a catechesis of the beatitudes, for the way of Christ is summed up in the beatitudes,

the only path that leads to the eternal beatitude for which the human heart longs;
- a catechesis of sin and forgiveness, for unless man acknowledges that he is a sinner he cannot know the truth about himself, which is a condition for acting justly; and without the offer of forgiveness he would not be able to bear this truth;
- a catechesis of the human virtues which causes one to grasp the beauty and attraction of right dispositions towards goodness;
- a catechesis of the Christian virtues of faith, hope, and charity, generously inspired by the example of the saints; a catechesis of the twofold commandment of charity set forth in the Decalogue;
- an ecclesial catechesis, for it is through the manifold exchanges of "spiritual goods" in the "communion of saints" that Christian life can grow, develop, and be communicated.

1698 The first and last point of reference of this catechesis will always be Jesus Christ himself, who is "the way, and the truth, and the life."[24] It is by looking to him in faith that Christ's faithful can hope that he himself fulfills his promises in them, and that, by loving him with the same love with which he has loved them, they may perform works in keeping with their dignity: "I ask you to consider that our Lord Jesus Christ is your true head, and that you are one of his members. He belongs to you as the head belongs to its members; all that is his is yours: his spirit, his heart, his body and soul, and all his faculties. You must make use of all these as of your own, to serve, praise, love, and glorify God. You belong to him, as members belong to their head. And so he longs for you to use all that is in you, as if it were his own, for the service and glory of the Father."[25] "For to me, to live is Christ."[26]

Footnotes

1. *St. Leo the Great, Sermo 22 in nat. Dom. 3: PL 54, 192C.* 2. *Jn 1:12; 1 Jn 3:1.* 3. *2 Pet 1:4.* 4. *Phil 1:27.* 5. *Cf. Jn 8:29.* 6. *Mt 6:6.* 7. *Mt 5:48.* 8, *Rom 6:11 and cf. 6:5; cf. Col 2:12.* 9. *Cf. Jn 15:5.* 10. *Eph 5:1-2.* 11. *Phil 2:5.* 12. *Cf. Jn 13:12-16.* 13. *1 Cor 6:11.* 14. *1 Cor 1:2.* 15. *Cf. 1 Cor 6:19.* 16. *Cf. Gal 4:6.* 17. *Gal 5:22, 25.* 18. *Cf. Eph 4:23.* 19. *Eph 5:8, 9.* 20. *Mt 7:13; cf. Dt 30: 15-20.* 21. *Didache 1, 1: SCh 248, 140.* 22 .*Cf. John Paul II, CT 29.* 23. *Rom 6:4.* 24. *Jn 14:6.* 25. *St. John Eudes, Tract. de admirabili corde Jesu, 1, 5.* 26. *Phil 1:21.*

THE TEN COMMANDMENTS

Any discussions of the commandments should begin with the scene at Sinai where God gave them to us. Read Exodus 19:3-6; 20:1-17. The first event is a covenant experience. God tells Moses how much he has loved the Israelites, is delivering them from slavery by "raising them up on eagles' wings," and is bringing them to freedom. God then offers them a binding covenant of love. He will be their only God and they will be his chosen people. It's like a marriage experience, an exchange of vows between God and Israel.

The next section shows God telling them how to live out the love they have pledged. He gives them the Ten Commandments as the means to live the covenant, to express the love they have promised. The *Catechism* points out that the Ten Commandments are privileged expressions of the natural law, made known to us by reason as well as Divine Revelation. We are obliged in obedience to observe these laws of love, both in serious and light matters. Love is in the details as well as the large matters. We must remember that what God has commanded, he makes possible by his grace.

Jesus set the tone for understanding the importance of the commandments. When a rich young man came to him and asked him what he should do to enter eternal life, Jesus replied, "if you wish to enter into life, keep the commandments" (Mt 19:17). In another case, someone asked him which were the greatest commandments, Jesus replied, "you shall love the Lord, your God, with all your heart, with all your soul, and with all your mind. This is the greatest and first commandment. The second is like it: You shall love your neighbor as yourself" (Mt 22:37-39). The first three commandments deal with Christ's call to God with all our being. The last seven commandments show us how to love our neighbors as we love ourselves.

The following excerpt from the *Catechism of the Catholic Church* shows how Jesus taught the importance of the Ten Commandments:

"Teacher, what must I do . . .?"

2052 "Teacher, what good deed must I do, to have eternal life?" To the young man who asked this question, Jesus answers first by invoking the necessity to recognize God as the "One there is who is good," as the supreme Good and the source of all good. Then Jesus tells him: "If you would enter life, keep the commandments." And he cites for his questioner the precepts that concern love of neighbor: "You shall not kill, You shall not commit adultery, You shall not steal, You shall not bear false witness, Honor your father and mother." Finally Jesus sums up these commandments positively: "You shall love your neighbor as yourself."[1]

2053 To this first reply Jesus adds a second: "If you would be perfect, go, sell what you possess and give to the poor, and you will have treasure in heaven; and come, follow me."[2] This reply does not do away with the first: following Jesus Christ involves keeping the Commandments. The Law has not been abolished,[3] but rather man is invited to rediscover it in the person of his Master who is its perfect fulfillment. In the three synoptic Gospels, Jesus' call to the rich young man to follow him, in the obedience of a disciple and in the observance of the Commandments, is joined to the call to poverty and chastity.[4] The evangelical counsels are inseparable from the Commandments.

2054 Jesus acknowledged the Ten Commandments, but he also showed the power of the Spirit at work in their letter. He preached a "righteousness [which] exceeds that of the scribes and Pharisees"[5] as well as that of the Gentiles.[6] He unfolded all the demands of the Commandments. "You have heard that it was said to the men of old, 'You shall not kill.' . . . But I say to you that every one who is angry with his brother shall be liable to judgment."[7]

2055 When someone asks him, "Which commandment in the Law is the greatest?"[8] Jesus replies: "You shall love the Lord your God with all your heart, and with all your soul, and with all your mind. This is the greatest and first commandment. And a second is like it: You shall love your neighbor as yourself. On these two commandments hang all the Law and the prophets."[9] The Decalogue must be interpreted in light of this twofold yet single commandment of love, the fullness of the Law: "The commandments: 'You shall not commit adultery, You shall not kill, You shall not steal, You shall not covet,' and any other commandment, are summed up in this sentence: 'You shall love your neighbor as yourself.' Love does no wrong to a neighbor; therefore love is the fulfilling of the law."[10]

Footnotes

1. *Mt 19:16-19.* 2. *Mt 19:21.* 3. *Cf. Mt 5:17.* 4. *Cf. Mt 19:6-12, 21, 23-29.* 5. *Mt 5:20.* 6.*Cf. Mt 5:46-47.* 7. *Mt 5:21-22.* 8. *Mt 22:36.* 9. *Mt 22:37-40; cf. Dt 6:5; Lv 19:18.* 10. *Rom 13:9-10.*

In the traditional Catholic enumeration and according to Dt. 5:6-21, the Commandments are:

1. "I, the Lord, am your God. You shall not have other gods besides me. You shall not carve idols."
2. "You shall not take the name of the Lord, your God, in vain."
3. "Take care to keep holy the Sabbath day."
4. "Honor your father and your mother."
5. "You shall not kill."
6. "You shall not commit adultery."
7. "You shall not steal."
8. "You shall not bear dishonest witness against your neighbor."

9. "You shall not covet your neighbor's wife."

10. "You shall not desire your neighbor's house or field, nor his male or female slave, nor his ox or ass, nor anything that belongs to him" (summarily, his goods).

Another version of the Commandments, substantially the same, is given in Ex. 20:1-17.

The traditional enumeration of the Commandments in Protestant usage differs from the above. Thus: two commandments are made of the first, as above; the third and fourth are equivalent to the second and third, as above, and so on; and the 10th includes the ninth and 10th, as above.

Love of God and Neighbor

The first three of the commandments deal directly with man's relations with God, viz.: acknowledgment of one true God and the rejection of false gods and idols; honor due to God and his name; observance of the Sabbath as the Lord's day.

The rest cover interpersonal relationships, viz.: the obedience due to parents and, logically, to other persons in authority, and the obligations of parents to children and of persons in authority to those under their care; respect for life and physical integrity; fidelity in marriage, and chastity; justice and rights; truth; internal respect for faithfulness in marriage, chastity, and the goods of others.

Perfection in Christian Life

The moral obligations of the Ten Commandments are complemented by others flowing from the twofold law of love, the whole substance and pattern of Christ's teaching, and everything implied in full and active membership and participation in the community of salvation formed by Christ in his Church.

Precepts of the Church

The purpose of the precepts of the Church, according to the *Catechism of the Catholic Church*, is "to guarantee to the faithful the indispensable minimum in the spirit of prayer and moral effort, in the growth and love of God and neighbor" (No. 2041).

1. Attendance at Mass on Sundays and holy days of obligation. (Observance of Sundays and holy days of obligation involves refraining from work that hinders the worship due to God.)

2. Confession of sins at least once a year. (Not required by the precept in the absence of serious sin.)

3. Reception of the Eucharist at least during the Easter season (in the U.S., from the first Sunday of Lent to Trinity Sunday).

4. Keep holy the holy days of obligation.

5. Observance of specified days of fasting and abstinence.

There is also an obligation to provide for the material needs of the Church.

CATHOLIC MORAL TEACHINGS OF POPE JOHN PAUL II

On August 6, 1993, Pope John Paul II published his tenth encyclical, Veritatis Splendor (The Splendor of the Truth) *regarding the fundamental truths of the Church's moral teachings. On March 25, 1995, he published his eleventh encyclical,* Evangelium Vitae (The Gospel of Life), *concerning the value and inviolability of human life. The following material is adapted from* The Encyclicals of John Paul II, *with the kind permission of Rev. J. Michael Miller, C.S.B. [Numbers in brackets refer to footnote.]*

Veritatis Splendor (The Splendor of the Truth)

On August 6, 1993, John Paul II signed his tenth encyclical, *Veritatis Splendor*, regarding certain fundamental truths of the Church's moral teaching.[1] Undoubtedly it is the pope's most complex and most discussed document. Since its publication, the encyclical has generated a great deal of comment in the media and among theologians. This is not surprising, since *Veritatis Splendor* is the first-ever papal document on the theological and philosophical foundations of Catholic moral teaching. In this encyclical the pope affirms that divine revelation contains "a specific and determined moral content, universally valid and permanent" (§37.1), which the Magisterium has the competence to interpret and teach.

Six years before, in the apostolic letter *Spiritus Domini* (1987), John Paul had publicly announced his intention to publish a document which would treat "more fully and more deeply the issues regarding the very foundations of moral theology" (§5.1). For several reasons the encyclical's preparation took longer than was first anticipated. First, the pope widely consulted bishops and theologians throughout the world, and various drafts were drawn up. Second, he thought that it was fitting for the encyclical "to be preceded by the *Catechism of the Catholic Church*, which contains a complete and systematic exposition of Christian moral teaching" (§5.3). The *Catechism*, published in 1992, gives a full presentation of the Church's moral doctrine, including that on particular questions, and expounds it in a positive way. *Veritatis Splendor,* on the other hand, limits itself to dealing with the fundamental principles underlying all moral teaching.

John Paul sets several specific objectives for the encyclical. First, he wishes *"to reflect on the whole of the Church's moral teaching,* with the precise goal of recalling certain fundamental truths of Catholic doctrine which, in the present circumstances, risk being distorted or denied" (§4.2, cf. §30.1). Second, he aims to show the faithful "the inviting splendor of that truth which is Jesus Christ himself" (§83.2). Christ alone is the answer to humanity's questions, "the only response fully capable of satisfying the desire of the human heart" (§7.1). Third, if the present crisis is to be successfully resolved, the Magisterium must authoritatively discern *"interpretations of Christian morality which are not consistent with 'sound teaching'* (2 Tim 4:3)" (§29.4, cf. §27.4). This pastoral discernment of the pope and bishops is necessary as a way of assuring *"the right of the faithful* to receive Catholic doctrine in its purity and integrity" (§113.2).

Throughout the encyclical the pope repeatedly draws inspiration from the Bible. Chapter one, structured around the encounter of Jesus with the rich young man (Mt 19:16-21), establishes a biblical foundation for fundamental moral principles. In this chapter the pope wishes to apply the theological method proposed by the Second Vatican Council: "Sacred Scripture remains the living and fruitful source of the Church's moral doctrine" (§28.2, cf. §5.3). Chapter two, on the other hand, uses Scripture chiefly to corroborate positions advanced on the basis of the natural moral law. The beginning of chapter three returns to a more biblical approach; it discusses discipleship in terms of the Paschal Mystery and of martyrdom as the supreme expression of following Christ.

More so than in his other encyclicals, in *Veritatis Splendor* John Paul relies considerably on the teaching of Saint Thomas Aquinas, referring to him directly at least twenty times, and on the teaching of Saint Augustine, citing him sixteen times. The pope also mines extensively the documents of Vatican II, especially *Gaudium et Spes,* which he cites more than twenty times. Except for one reference to Saint Alphonsus Liguori and a single direct citation of John Henry Newman, the pope mentions no moral philosopher or theologian after the Middle Ages.

Footnotes

1. *Acta Apostolicae Sedis,* 85 (1993), 1133-1228.
2. Angelus, October 3, 1993, *L'Osservatore Romano,* 40 (1993), 1. 3. Angelus, October 17, 1993, *L'Osservatore Romano,* 42 (1993), 1.

Evangelium Vitae (The Gospel of Life)

"The *Gospel of life* is at the heart of Jesus' message" (§1.1). With these words Pope John Paul II begins his eleventh encyclical, *Evangelium Vitae,* published on March 25, 1995.[1] He aptly chose the feast of the Annunciation, which celebrates Mary's welcoming of the Son of God who took flesh in her womb, to issue a document dedicated to the value and inviolability of human life. By taking up the cause of the "great multitude of weak and defenseless human beings" (§5.4), especially unborn children and those at the end of life, the pope continues the defense of human dignity dealt with in his three social encyclicals. *Evangelium Vitae* is an anguished and vigorous response to *"scientifically and systematically programmed threats"* against life (§17.2), assaults which have repercussions on Church teaching, touching upon "the core of her faith in the redemptive Incarnation of the Son of God" (§3.1).

For John Paul, the cause of life is the cause of the Gospel entrusted to the Church, which is duty-bound to raise her voice in the defense of life. His encyclical is a "pressing appeal addressed to each and every person, in the name of God: *respect, protect, love and serve life, every human life!"* (§5.5).

Unlike *Veritatis Splendor,* which was directed primarily to bishops, John Paul intends *Evangelium Vitae* to be read also by the lay faithful, indeed by all people of good will. Concern for the sacredness of human life is not just a matter for Catholics. "The value at stake," writes the pope, "is one which every human being can grasp by the light of reason" (§101.2). The essential truths of the Gospel of life "are written in the heart of every man and woman," echoing in

Desiderii Mei

every human conscience "from the time of creation itself" (§29.3). He insists that anyone who is sincerely open to truth and goodness can discover "the sacred value of human life from its very beginning until its end, and can affirm the right of every human being to have this primary good respected to the highest degree" (§2.2).

Of particular significance in *Evangelium Vitae* are the pope's three authoritative doctrinal pronouncements: on the direct and voluntary killing of innocent human life (cf. §57.4), on abortion (cf. §62.3), and on euthanasia (cf. §65.3). In each of these formal statements John Paul recalls, through his ordinary magisterium, that a specific proposition is taught infallibly by the ordinary and universal Magisterium of the College of Bishops in communion with the Successor of Peter. He does not, therefore, call upon the charism which belongs to the Petrine ministry to teach infallibly, as this was defined at the First Vatican Council (1870). Rather, the pope "confirms" or "declares" (as in the case of abortion) a doctrine already taught by the bishops as belonging to the Catholic faith. Thus, there is nothing "new" in the Pope's affirmations, but merely the reiteration of teaching about which a consensus exists in the Episcopal College.

Footnotes

1. *Acta Apostolicae Sedis,* 87 (1995), 401-522.

CATHOLIC SOCIAL DOCTRINE

Nature of the Doctrine

Writing in *Christianity and Social Progress,* Pope John XXIII made the following statement about the nature and scope of the Church's social doctrine as stated in the encyclicals in particular and related writings in general:

"What the Catholic Church teaches and declares regarding the social life and relationships of men is beyond question for all time valid.

"The cardinal point of this teaching is that individual men are necessarily the foundation, cause, and end of all social institutions insofar as they are social by nature, and raised to an order of existence that transcends and subdues nature.

"Beginning with this very basic principle whereby the dignity of the human person is affirmed and defended, Holy Church — especially during the last century and with the assistance of learned priests and laymen, specialists in the field — has arrived at clear social teachings whereby the mutual relationships of men are ordered. Taking general norms into account, these principles are in accord with the nature of things and the changed conditions of man's social life, or with the special genius of our day. Moreover, these norms can be approved by all."

Background

While social concerns have always been a part of the Church's teachings, Catholic social doctrine has been the subject of much consideration since the end of the last century and has been formulated in a progressive manner in a number of authoritative documents starting with the encyclical *Rerum Novarum* ("On Capital and Labor") issued by Leo XIII in 1891. Owing to its significance, the encyclical was called by Pope John XXIII the *magna carta* of Catholic social doctrine.

Other outstanding examples are the encyclicals: *Quadragesimo Anno* ("On Reconstruction of the Social Order") by Pius XI in 1931; *Mater et Magistra* ("Christianity and Social Progress") and *Pacem in Terris* ("Peace on Earth"), by John XXIII in 1961 and 1963, respectively; *Populorum Progressio* ("Development of Peoples"), by Paul VI in 1967; *Laborem Exercens* ("On Human Work"), *Sollicitudo Rei Socialis* ("On Social Concerns") and *Centesimus Annus* ("The 100th Year") by John Paul II in 1981, 1987 and 1991, respectively. Among many other accomplishments of ideological importance in the social field, Pius XII made a distinctive contribution with his formulation of a plan for world peace and order in Christmas messages from 1939 to 1941, and in other documents.

Of particular significance to the contemporary application of social doctrine are the document *Gaudium et Spes* (Pastoral Constitution on the Church in the Modern World) issued by the Second Vatican Council and Pope John Paul II's encyclical letters, *Laborem Exercens* ("On Human Work"), *Sollicitudo Rei Socialis* ("On Social Concerns"), and *Centesimus Annus* ("The 100th Year").

These documents represent the most serious attempts in modern times to systematize the social implications of divine revelation as well as the socially relevant writings of the Fathers and Doctors of the Church. Their contents are theological penetrations into social life, with particular reference to human rights, the needs of the poor and those in underdeveloped countries, and humane conditions of life, freedom, justice and peace. In some respects, they read like juridical documents; essentially, however, they are Gospel-oriented and pastoral in intention.

Gaudium et Spes

Gaudium et Spes (Pastoral Constitution on the Church in the Modern World) was the last document issued by Vatican Council II (December 7, 1965). The document has as its purpose to search out the signs of God's presence and meaning in and through the events of this time in human history. Accordingly, it deals with the situation of men in present circumstances of profound change, challenge and crisis on all levels of life. It is evenly divided into two main parts: the Church's teaching on humanity in the modern era and urgent problems of the times.

Part One

The first part begins: "The joys and the hopes, the griefs and the anxieties of this age" (No. 1) — a clear indication that the Council Fathers were aware both of the positive nature of the modern world and its many dangers and travails. Further, the council places great emphasis throughout on the human existence, a stress that was quite innovative in its presentation: "According to the almost unanimous opinion of believers and unbelievers alike, all things on earth should be related to man as their center and crown" (No. 12). Having developed an analysis of humanity, the document then offered a thorough summary of traditional Church teaching on human life, complete with discussion of sin, the union of body and soul, and the moral conscience.

There is, as well, a genuinely realistic appraisal of contemporary society, noting the pervasiveness of atheism, adding that its spread can be attributed in part to the fault and carelessness of those within the Church whose actions and failures "must be said to conceal rather than reveal the authentic face of God and religion" (No. 19). Toward the fuller understanding of the place of the Church in the modern world, *Gaudium et Spes* emphasizes the harmony that should exist between the Catholic faith and scientific progress because "earthly matters and the concerns of faith derive from the same God" (No. 36). This does not mean, however, that there ought to be no qualifying elements or restraints to science; the Council Fathers add to this positive statement the provision that such research, "within every branch of learning," must be "carried out in a genuinely scientific manner and in accord with

moral norms" (No. 36). Finally, the first part makes an ecumenical gesture, noting that the Church "holds in high esteem the things which other Christian Churches or ecclesial communities have done. . . ." (No. 40).

Part Two

Part Two offers the practical application of the Church's teaching and message enunciated in Part One. Most pressing is the council's concern for the family, and its treatment of family life and marriage is the most detailed and extensive in the history of the councils of the Church. This leads to study of the deeply troubling presence of contraception. The council reiterates Church instruction in an affirmation of opposition to contraception that would receive even fuller expression in three years in the encyclical *Humanae Vitae*. In the matter of abortion, the document states clearly: ". . . from the moment of its conception life must be guarded with the greatest care, while abortion and infanticide are unspeakable crimes" (No. 51). In its study of culture, in which the council reminds all humanity that culture and civilization are creations of man, it points out his responsibility over it and his duty to seek that which is above, which entails an "obligation to work with all men in constructing a more human world" (No. 57). Here we have a powerful preface or introduction to the next concerns voiced in *Gaudium et Spes*: the questions of economic life, political systems, and war. In building upon earlier social encyclicals, *Gaudium et Spes* discusses economics as vital to human progress and social development, striking the important balance (developed so masterfully in the later writings of Pope John Paul II) between the rights of an individual to possess goods and the obligation to aid the poor (Nos. 63-72). While declaring the autonomous and independent nature of the Church and politics, the Council Fathers do acknowledge: "There are, indeed, close links between earthly affairs and those aspects of man's condition which transcend this world. The Church herself employs the things of time to the degree that her own proper mission demands" (No. 76). The document goes on to state that "the arms race is an utterly treacherous trap for humanity" (No. 81) and "It is our clear duty, then, to strain every muscle as we work for the time when all war can be completely outlawed by international consent" (No. 82).

SOCIAL DOCTRINE UNDER POPE JOHN PAUL II

Background

Throughout his pontificate, Pope John Paul II has traveled the globe speaking out on all matters of the Church's social teachings and has written a number of important encyclicals that are reflective not only of the Church's traditions of social doctrine but that seek to utilize the teachings of the faith to offer specific points of reflection and solutions to the many pressing problems of the late 20th century. Rooted in Christian anthropology and Tradition, Scripture, and Magisterium, John Paul's writings have encompassed economic ethics, the rights and dignity of the worker, the primacy of the human person, the place of the family in society and the Church, and the integrative teachings of the Church in the areas of moral and pastoral theology. The three main expressions of his social teachings have been the encyclicals: *Laborem Exercens* (1981); *Sollicitudo Rei Socialis* (1987); and *Centesimus Annus* (1991).

SOCIAL ENCYCLICALS OF POPE JOHN PAUL II

(The following material is adapted from The Encyclicals of John Paul II, *with the kind permission of the Rev. J. Michael Miller, C.S.B.)*

Laborem Exercens

Fascinated as he is by commemorative events, Pope John Paul II marked the ninetieth anniversary of Leo XIII's *Rerum Novarum* (1891) by publishing his first social encyclical, *Laborem Exercens*, on September 14, 1981.[1] Before him, Pius XI in *Quadragesimo Anno* (1931), John XXIII in *Mater et Magistra* (1961), and Paul VI in *Octogesima Adveniens* (1971) had observed the anniversary of Leo's ground-breaking encyclical with documents of their own.

Laborem Exercens is a very personal document. The encyclical has solid roots in the pope's own experience as a worker. It reflects his familiarity with various worlds of work: in mines and factories, in artistic and literary production, in scholarship and pastoral ministry. More particularly, *Laborem Exercens* has its origins in the long debate carried on by the Archbishop of Kracow with Marxist intellectuals. The topics chosen, which include the struggle between capital and labor, ownership of the means of production, and solidarity, as well as the terminology of the encyclical, bear ample witness to this background of controversy. Here, however, he is less concerned with economic systems than with the human person as a "worker." Furthermore, John Paul intended his letter to encourage the Solidarity union movement, which in the early 1980s was the primary motor for effecting social and political change in a Poland under a totalitarian regime.

Unlike earlier social encyclicals which dealt with a wide range of different questions, *Laborem Exercens* is sharply focused. John Paul chooses a very specific theme — the dignity and role of human work — and explores its many ramifications: "Through work man must earn his daily bread and contribute to the continual advance of science and technology and, above all, to elevating unceasingly the cultural and moral level of the society within which he lives in community with those who belong to the same family" (preface). At the present moment, he believes, the world is faced with important choices. It is "on the eve of new developments in technological, economic, and political conditions which, according to many experts, will influence the world of work and production no less than the industrial revolution of the last century" (§1.3).

A crisis in the meaning of human work is a crucial factor contributing to society's current plight. "Work, as human issue, is at the very center of the 'social question'" (§2.1). Moreover, the pope adds, "human work is *a key*, probably *the essential key*, to the whole social question" (§3.2). It is a problem with ramifications which extend beyond the so-called "working class"; the dimensions of the crisis are universal. Therefore he does not confine his encyclical to a reflection on the work only of industrial or agricultural workers. Instead, he extends it to encompass the work done by every sector of society: management, white-collar workers, scientists, intellectuals, artists, women in the home. "Each and every individual, to the proper extent and in an incalculable number of ways, takes part in the giant process whereby man 'subdues the earth' through his work" (§4.4). To use a favorite expression of the pope's, the world's "workbench" includes all those who labor for their daily bread — all men and women.

As in his two previous encyclicals, John Paul takes up the "way" of the human person, this time with regard to his fundamental activity of work. *Laborem Exercens* is yet another chapter in the pope's book on Christian anthropology. Moreover, since work is a great gift and good for humanity, his tone throughout the encyclical is constructive and exhortatory.

Footnotes

1. *Acta Apostolicae Sedis*, 73 (1981), 577-647.

Sollicitudo Rei Socialis

Although signed on December 30, 1987, Pope John Paul II's encyclical "on social concern" was not officially published until February 19, 1988.[1] Like *Laborem Exercens* (1981), this second social encyclical commemorates a previous papal document. *Sollicitudo Rei Socialis* marks the twentieth anniversary of Paul VI's *Populorum Progressio* (1967). But more than merely recalling the relevance and doctrine of Pope Paul's encyclical, it highlights new themes and responds to the problems of development in the Third World which had emerged in the intervening twenty years.

In some ways *Sollicitudo Rei Socialis* echoes *Laborem Exercens* (1981). John Paul's use of Sacred Scripture, for example, is similar in that he frequently quotes from the opening chapters of Genesis. The differences between the two social encyclicals, however, are noteworthy. Whereas in *Laborem Exercens* (1981) the pope never directly cites *Rerum Novarum* (1891), the encyclical of Leo XIII which it commemorates, throughout *Sollicitudo Rei Socialis* John Paul quotes or refers to *Populorum Progressio* more than forty times. It is his constant point of reference. Second, to support his presentation, the pope marshals statements taken from earlier writings and discourses of his own pontificate, as well as the social teaching of the Second Vatican Council expressed in *Gaudium et Spes*. Third, more than in any other encyclical, John Paul makes use of documents published by the Roman Curia. Especially notable are his six references to the *Instruction on Christian Freedom and Liberation* (1986) issued by the Congregation for the Doctrine of the Faith. He also cites two publications of the Pontifical Commission "Iustitia et Pax": *At the Service of the Human Community: An Ethical Approach to the International Debt Question* (1986) and *The Church and the Housing Problem* (1987).

While *Sollicitudo Rei Socialis* perceptively analyzes the economic, political, social, and cultural dimensions of world development, its perspective is primarily ethical and theological. John Paul rereads *Populorum Progressio* through a moral-spiritual lens. His main concern is to form the consciences of individual men and women, to help them in their task of promoting authentic development "in the light of faith and of the Church's Tradition" (§41.7).

Footnotes

1. *Acta Apostolicae Sedis*, 80 (1988), 513-586.

Centesimus Annus

Pope John Paul II issued his ninth encyclical, *Centesimus Annus*, on May 1, 1991.[1] Not surprisingly, the pope chose to mark the centenary of Leo XIII's *Rerum Novarum* (1891) with a document of his own. In the four years since the signing of *Sollicitudo Rei Socialis* (1987) the Berlin Wall had collapsed, and in the light of this event John Paul offers his "rereading" of Rerum Novarum. His purpose is twofold. He wishes to recall Leo's contribution to the development of the Church's social teaching and to honor the popes who drew upon the encyclical's "vital energies" in their social teaching.

Despite the opinions of some commentators, John Paul's primary interest is not to pass judgment on either failed socialism or contemporary capitalism. Above all, in keeping with his desire to articulate a Christian anthropology, he recalls the need for Catholic social doctrine to have a "correct view of the human person and of his unique value" (§11.3). Without such a view, he believes, it is impossible to solve today's social, economic, and political problems. The Church's distinctive contribution to meeting these challenges is her vision of the transcendent dignity of the human person created in God's image and redeemed by Christ's blood.

The pope's rereading of Leo XIII encompasses three time frames: "looking back" at *Rerum Novarum* itself, "looking around" at the contemporary situation, and "looking to the future" (§3.1). In looking back, John Paul confirms the enduring principles of Leo's encyclical, principles that belong to the Church's doctrinal inheritance. His "pastoral solicitude" also impels the pope to analyze recent political events from the perspective of the Gospel "in order to discern the new requirements of evangelization" (§3.5).

Even more clearly than in his two previous social encyclicals, *Laborem Exercens* (1981) and *Sollicitudo Rei Socialis* (1987), John Paul clearly distinguishes the authentic doctrine contained in the Church's social teaching from the analysis of contingent historical events. This analysis, he states, "is not meant to pass definitive judgments, since this does not fall per se within the Magisterium's specific domain" (§3.5). Whatever comes within the doctrinal sphere, however, "pertains to the Church's evangelizing mission and is an essential part of the Christian message" (§5.5).

Footnotes

1. *Acta Apostolicae Sedis*, 83 (1991), 793-867.

SOCIO-ECONOMIC STATEMENTS BY U.S. BISHOPS

Over a period of nearly 80 years, the bishops of the United States have issued a great number of socio-economic statements reflecting papal documents in a U.S. context.

One such statement, entitled "Economic Justice for All: Social Teaching and the U.S. Economy" was issued in November, 1986. It's contents are related in various ways with the subsequently issued encyclical letter, *Centesimus Annus*. Principles drawn from the bishops' document are given in the following excerpt entitled "A Catholic Framework for Economic Life." Another significant statement, entitled "The Harvest of Justice Is Sown in Peace" (1993) follows.

A Catholic Framework for Economic Life

As followers of Jesus Christ and participants in a powerful economy, Catholics in the United States, are called to work for greater economic justice in the face of persistent poverty, growing income gaps and increasing discussion of economic issues in the United States and around the world. We urge Catholics to use the following ethical framework for economic life as principles for reflection, criteria for judgment and directions for action. These principles are drawn directly from Catholic teaching on economic life.

1. The economy exists for the person, not the person for the economy.

2. All economic life should be shaped by moral principles. Economic choices and institutions must be judged by how they protect or undermine the life and dignity of the human person, support the family and serve the common good.

3. A fundamental moral measure of an economy is how the poor and vulnerable are faring.

4. All people have a right to life and to secure the basic necessities of life (e.g., food, clothing, shelter, education, health care, safe environment, economic security).

5. All people have the right to economic initiative, to productive work, to just wages and benefits, to decent working conditions as well as to organize and join unions or other associations.

6. All people, to the extent they are able, have a corresponding duty to work, a responsibility to provide for the needs of their families and an obligation to contribute to the broader society.

7. In economic life, free markets have both clear advantages and limits; government has essential responsibilities and limitations; voluntary groups have irreplaceable roles, but cannot substitute for the proper working of the market and the just policies of the state.

8. Society has a moral obligation, including governmental action where necessary, to assure opportunity, meet basic human needs and pursue justice in economic life.

9. Workers, owners, managers, stockholders, and consumers are moral agents in economic life. By our choices, initiative, creativity and investment, we enhance or diminish economic opportunity, community life and social justice.

10. The global economy has moral dimensions and human consequences. Decisions on investment, trade, aid and development should protect human life and promote human rights, especially for those most in need wherever they might live on this globe.

The Harvest of Justice Is Sown in Peace

The National Conference of Catholic Bishops, at a meeting November 17, 1993, issued a statement entitled "The Harvest of Justice Is Sown in Peace," marking the tenth anniversary of their earlier pastoral letter, "The Challenge of Peace: God's Promise and Our Response."

The Challenge of Peace

"The challenge of peace today is different, but no less urgent" than in 1983, and the threat of global nuclear war "may seem more remote than at any time in the nuclear age." Questions of peace and war, however, cannot be addressed "without acknowledging that the nuclear question remains of vital political and moral significance."

The statement outlines an agenda for action to guide future advocacy efforts of the bishops' national conference. It also urges that the cause of peace be reflected constantly in liturgical prayers of petition, preaching and Catholic education at all levels.

Confronting the temptation to isolationism in U.S. foreign policy is among "the major challenges peacemakers face in this new era."

Factors in a vision for peace include a commitment to the universal common good and recognition of the imperative of human solidarity.

Nonviolent revolutions in some countries "challenge us to find ways to take into full account the power of organized, active nonviolence."

With respect to just war criteria, the statement says that "important work needs to be done in refining, clarifying and applying the just war tradition to the choices facing our decision-makers in this still violent and dangerous world."

Subjects of concern include humanitarian intervention, deterrence, conscientious objection and the development of peoples.

Presumption against Force

"Our conference's approach, as outlined in 'The Challenge of Peace,' can be summarized in this way:

"1) In situations of conflict our constant commitment ought to be, as far as possible, to strive for justice through nonviolent means.

"2) But when sustained attempts at nonviolent action fail to protect the innocent against fundamental injustice, then legitimate political authorities are permitted as a last resort to employ limited force to rescue the innocent and establish justice."

Lethal Force

"Whether lethal force may be used is governed by the following criteria:

- "Just cause: Force may be used only to correct a grave, public evil, i.e., aggression or massive violation of the basic rights of whole populations.
- "Comparative justice: While there may be rights and wrongs on all sides of a conflict, to override the presumption against the use of force, the injustice suffered by one party must significantly outweigh that suffered by the other.
- "Legitimate authority: Only duly constituted public authorities may use deadly force or wage war.
- "Right intention: Force may be used only in a truly just cause and solely for that purpose.
- "Probability of Success: Arms may not be used in a futile cause or in a case where disproportionate measures are required to achieve success.
- "Proportionality: The overall destruction expected from the use of force must be outweighed by the good to be achieved.
- "Last Resort: Force may be used only after all peaceful alternatives have been seriously tried and exhausted.

"These criteria [of just war], taken as a whole, must be satisfied in order to override the strong presumption against the use of force."

Just War

"The just-war tradition seeks also to curb the violence of war through restraint on armed combat between the contending parties by imposing the following moral standards for the conduct of armed conflict:

- "Noncombatant Immunity: Civilians may not be the object of direct attack, and military personnel must take due care to avoid and minimize indirect harm to civilians.
- "Proportionality: In the conduct of hostilities, efforts must be made to attain military objectives with no more force than is militarily necessary and to avoid disproportionate collateral damage to civilian life and property.
- "Right Intention: Even in the midst of conflict, the aim of political and military leaders must be peace with justice so that acts of vengeance and indiscriminate violence, whether by individuals, military units or governments, are forbidden."

Structures for Justice and Peace

Quoting an address given by Pope John Paul in August 1993 in Denver, the statement said:

" 'The international community ought to establish more effective structures for maintaining and promoting justice and peace. This implies that a concept of strategic interest should evolve which is based on the full development of peoples — out of poverty and toward a more dignified existence, out of injustice and exploitation toward fuller respect for the human person and the defense of universal rights.'

"As we consider a new vision of the international community, five areas deserve special attention: (1) strengthening global institutions; (2) securing human rights; (3) promoting human development; (4) restraining nationalism and eliminating religious violence; and (5) building cooperative security."

Medieval Psalter Illustration

Part 6

THE BLESSED VIRGIN MARY

Hail Mary, full of grace, the Lord is with thee;
Blessed art thou among women and
Blessed is the fruit of thy womb, Jesus.
Holy Mary, Mother of God, pray for us sinners
now and at the hour of our death. Amen.

The Mother of God, Mother of Jesus, wife of St. Joseph, and the greatest of all Christian saints, the Blessed Virgin Mary "was, after her Son, exalted by divine grace above all angels and men" (Dogmatic Constitution of the Church, *Lumen Gentium*, n 66). Mary is venerated with a special cult, called by St. Thomas Aquinas, *hyperdulia*, as the highest of God's creatures. The principal events of her life are celebrated as liturgical feasts of the universal Church.

Mary's life and role in the history of salvation are prefigured in the Old Testament, while the events of her life are recorded in the New Testament. Traditionally, she was declared the daughter of Sts. Joachim and Anne. Born in Jerusalem, Mary was presented in the Temple and took a vow of virginity. Living in Nazareth, Mary was visited by the archangel Gabriel, who announced to her that she would become the Mother of Jesus, by the Holy Spirit (Lk. 1:31-35). She became betrothed to St. Joseph and went to visit her cousin, Elizabeth, who was bearing St. John the Baptist. Acknowledged by Elizabeth as the Mother of God, Mary intoned the Magnificat (Lk .1:46-55).

When Emperor Augustus (r. 37 B.C.-14 A.D.) declared a census throughout the vast Roman Empire, Mary and St. Joseph went to Bethlehem, his city of lineage, as he belonged to the House of David. There Mary gave birth to Jesus and lateer was visited by the Three Kings. Mary and Joseph presented Jesus in the Temple, where St. Simeon rejoiced and Mary received word of sorrows to come later. Warned to flee, St. Joseph and Mary went to Egypt to escape the wrath of King Herod. They remained in Egypt until King Herod died and then returned to Nazareth.

Nothing is known of Mary's life during the next years except for a visit to the Temple of Jerusalem, at which time Mary and Joseph sought the young Jesus, who was in the Temple with the learned elders. The first recorded miracle of Jesus was performed at a wedding in Cana (Jn. 2:1-5), and Mary was instrumental in calling Christ's attention to the need.

Mary was present at the Crucifixion in Jerusalem (Jn. 19:25-27), and there she was given into John's care. She was also with the disciples in the days before the Pentecost (Acts 1:14), and it is believed that she was present at the resurrection and Ascension. No scriptural reference concerns Mary's last years on earth. According to tradition, she went to Ephesus, where she experienced her "dormition." Another tradition states that she remained in Jerusalem.

The belief that Mary's body was assumed into heaven is one of the oldest traditions of the Catholic Church. Pope Pius XII declared this belief Catholic dogma in 1950. The feast of the Assumption is celebrated on August 15. The dogma of the Immaculate Conception – that Mary, as the Mother of the Second Person of the Holy Trinity, was free of original sin at the moment of her conception – was proclaimed by Pope Pius IX in 1854. The feast of the Immaculate Conception is celebrated on December 8.

The birthday of Mary is an old feast in the Church, celebrated on September 8 since the seventh century. Other feasts that commemorate events in the life of the Blessed Virgin Mary are listed in the Appendices. Pope Pius XII dedicated the entire human race to Mary in 1944.

The Church has long taught that Mary is truly the Mother of God (*Theotokos*). St. Paul observed (Gal. 4:4) that "God sent His Son, born of a woman," expressing the union of the human and the divine in Christ. As Christ possesses two natures, human and divine, Mary was the Mother of God in his human nature. This special role of Mary in salvation history is clearly depicted in the Gospel in which she is seen constantly at her son's side during his soteriological mission.

Because of this role – exemplified by her acceptance of Christ into her womb, her offering of him to God at the Temple, her urging him to perform his first miracle, and her standing at the foot of the Cross at Calvary – Mary was joined fully in the sacrifice by Christ of himself. Pope Benedict XV wrote in 1918: "To such an extent did Mary suffer and almost die with her suffering and dying Son; to such extent did she surrender her maternal rights over her Son for man's salvation, and immolated him – insofar as she could – in order to appease the justice of God, that we might rightly say she redeemed the human race together with Christ" *(Inter Sodalicia)*.

Mary is entitled to the title of Queen because, as Pope Pius XII expressed it in a 1946 radio speech, "Jesus is King throughout all eternity by nature and by right of conquest: through him, with him, and subordinate to him, Mary is Queen by grace, by divine relationship, by right of conquest, and by singular election." Mary possesses a unique relationship with all three Persons of the Trinity, thereby giving her a claim to the title of Queenship. She was chosen by God the Father to be the Mother of his Son; God the Holy Spirit chose her to be his virginal spouse for the Incarnation of the Son; and God the Son chose her to be his mother, the means of incarnating into the world for the purposes of the redemption of humanity.

This Queen is also our Mother. While she is not our Mother in the physical sense, she is called a spiritual mother, for she conceives, gives birth, and nurtures the spiritual lives of grace for each person. As Mediatrix of All Graces, she is ever present at the side of each person, giving nourishment and hope, from the moment of spiritual birth at Baptism to the moment of death. The confidence that each person should have in Mary was expressed by Pope Pius IX in the encyclical *Ubi primum* (1849): "The foundation of all our confidence . . . is found in the Blessed Virgin Mary. For God has committed to Mary the treasury of all good things, in order that everyone may know that through her are obtained every hope, every grace, and all salvation. For this is his will, that we obtain everything through Mary."

ROLE OF MARY IN THE MYSTERY OF CHRIST AND THE CHURCH

The following excerpts are from Chapter VIII of the Second Vatican Council's Constitution on the Church, Lumen Gentium.

Preface

Wishing in his supreme goodness and wisdom to effect the redemption of the world, "when the fullness of time came, God sent his Son, born of a woman, that we might receive the adoption of sons" (Gal. 4:4-5). "He for us men, and for our salvation, came down from heaven, and was incarnate by the Holy Spirit from the Virgin Mary." This divine mystery of salvation is revealed to us and continued in the Church, which the Lord established as his own body. In this Church, adhering to Christ the head and having communion with all his saints, the faithful must also venerate the memory "above all of the glorious and perpetual Virgin Mary. Mother of our God and Lord Jesus Christ." (52)

At the message of the angel, the Virgin Mary received the Word of God in her heart and in her body, and gave Life to the world. Hence, she is acknowledged and honored as being truly the Mother of God and Mother of the Redeemer. Redeemed in an especially sublime manner by reason of the merits of her Son, and united to him by a close and indissoluble tie, she is endowed with the supreme office and dignity of being the Mother of the Son of God. As a result, she is also the favorite daughter of the Father and the temple of the Holy Spirit. Because of this gift of sublime grace, she far surpasses all other creatures, both in heaven and on earth.

At the same time, however, because she belongs to the offspring of Adam, she is one with all human beings in their need for salvation. Indeed, she is "clearly the Mother of the members of Christ since she cooperated out of love so that there might be born in the Church the faithful, who are members of Christ their head. Therefore, she is also hailed as a pre-eminent and altogether singular member of the Church, and as the Church's model and excellent exemplar in faith and charity. Taught by the Holy Spirit, the Catholic Church honors her with filial affection and piety as a most beloved Mother. (53)

This sacred synod intends to describe with diligence the role of the Blessed Virgin in the mystery of the Incarnate Word and the Mystical Body. It also wishes to describe the duties of redeemed mankind toward the Mother of God, who is the Mother of Christ and Mother of men, particularly of the faithful.

The synod does not, however, have it in mind to give a complete doctrine on Mary, nor does it wish to decide those questions which have not yet been fully illuminated by the work of theologians. (54)

II. The Role of the Blessed Virgin in the Economy of Salvation

The Father of mercies willed that the consent of the predestined Mother should precede the Incarnation so that, just as a woman contributed to death, so also a woman should contribute to life. This contrast was verified in outstanding fashion by the Mother of Jesus. She gave to the world that very Life which renews all things, and she was enriched by God with gifts befitting such a role.

It is no wonder, then, that the usage prevailed among the holy Fathers whereby they called the Mother of God entirely holy and free from all stain of sin, fashioned by the Holy Spirit into a kind of new substance and new creature. Adorned from the first instant of her conception with the splendors of an entirely unique holiness, the Vir-

THE BLESSED VIRGIN MARY 191

gin of Nazareth is, on God's command, greeted by an angel messenger as "full of grace" (cf. Lk. 1:28). To the heavenly messenger she replies: "Behold the handmaid of the Lord; be it done to me according to thy word" (Lk. 1:38).

By thus consenting to the divine utterance, Mary, a daughter of Adam, became the Mother of Jesus. Embracing God's saving will with a full heart and impeded by no sin, she devoted herself totally as a handmaid of the Lord to the person and work of her Son. In subordination to him and along with him, by the grace of almighty God she served the mystery of redemption.

Rightly, therefore, the holy Fathers see her as used by God not merely in a passive way but as cooperating in the work of human salvation through free faith and obedience. (56)

This union of the Mother with the Son in the work of salvation was manifested from the time of Christ's virginal conception up to his death. It is shown first of all when Mary, arising in haste to go to visit Elizabeth, was greeted by her as blessed because of her belief in the promise of salvation, while the precursor leaped for joy in the womb of his mother (cf. Lk. 1.41-45). This association was shown also at the birth of our Lord, who did not diminish his Mother's virginal integrity but sanctified it, when the Mother of God joyfully showed her first-born Son to the shepherds and the Magi.

When she presented him to the Lord in the Temple, making the offering of the poor, she heard Simeon foretelling at the same time that her Son would be a sign of contradiction and that a sword would pierce the Mother's soul, that out of many hearts thoughts might be revealed (cf. Lk. 2:34-35). When the Child Jesus was lost and they had sought him sorrowing, his parents found him in the temple, taken up with things which were his Father's business. They did not understand the reply of the Son. But his Mother, to be sure, kept all these things to be pondered over in her heart (cf. Lk. 2:41-51). (57)

In the public life of Jesus, Mary made significant appearances. This was so even at the very beginning, when she was moved with pity at the marriage feast of Cana, and her intercession brought about the beginning of the miracles by Jesus the Messiah (Cf. Jn. 2:1-11). In the course of her Son's preaching, she received his praise when, in extolling a kingdom beyond the calculations and bonds of flesh and blood, he declared blessed (cf. Mk. 3:35 par.; Lk. 11:27-28) those who heard and kept the word of the Lord as she was faithfully doing (cf. Lk. 2:19, 51).

Thus, the Blessed Virgin advanced in her pilgrimage of faith and loyally persevered in her union with her Son unto the cross. There she stood, in keeping with the divine plan (cf. Jn. 19:25), suffering grievously with her only-begotten Son. There she united herself with a maternal heart to his sacrifice, and lovingly consented to the immolation of this Victim whom she herself had brought forth. Finally, the same Christ Jesus dying on the cross gave her as a mother to his disciple. This he did when he said: "Woman, behold your son" (Jn. 19:26-27). (58)

But since it pleased God not to manifest solemnly the mystery of the salvation of the human race until he poured forth the Spirit promised by Christ, we see the apostles before the day of Pentecost "continuing with one mind in prayer with the women and Mary, the Mother of Jesus, and with his brethren" (Acts 1:14). We see Mary prayerfully imploring the gift of the Spirit, who had already overshadowed her in the Annunciation.

Finally, preserved free from all guilt of original sin, the Immaculate Virgin was taken up body and soul into heavenly glory upon the completion of her earthly sojourn. She was exalted by the Lord as Queen of all, in order that she might be the more thoroughly conformed to her Son, the Lord of lords (cf. Rev. 19:16) and the conqueror of sin and death. (59)

III. The Blessed Virgin and the Church

We have but one Mediator, as we know from the words of the Apostle: "For there is one God, and one Mediator between God and men, himself man, Christ Jesus, who gave himself as a ransom for all" (1 Tim. 2:5-6). The maternal duty of Mary toward men in no way obscures or diminishes this unique mediation of Christ, but rather shows its power. For all the saving influences of the Blessed Virgin on men originate, not from some inner necessity, but from the divine pleasure. They flow forth from the superabundance of the merits of Christ, rest on his mediation, depend entirely on it, and draw all their power from it. In no way do they impede the immediate union of the faithful with Christ. Rather, they foster this union. (60)

In an utterly singular way, she (Mary) cooperated by her obedience, faith, hope and burning charity in the Savior's work of restoring supernatural life to souls. For this reason she is a mother to us in the order of grace. (61)

This maternity of Mary in the order of grace began with the consent which she gave in faith at the Annunciation and which she sustained without wavering beneath the cross. This maternity will last without interruption until the eternal fulfillment of all the elect. For, taken up to heaven, she did not lay aside this saving role, but by her manifold acts of intercession continues to win for us gifts of eternal salvation.

By her maternal charity, Mary cares for the brethren of her Son who still journey on earth surrounded by dangers and difficulties until they are led to their happy fatherland. Therefore, the Blessed Virgin is invoked by the Church under the titles of Advocate, Auxiliatrix, Adjutrix and Mediatrix. These, however, are to be so understood that they neither take away nor add anything to the dignity and efficacy of Christ the one Mediator.

For no creature could ever be classed with the Incarnate Word and Redeemer. But, just as the priesthood of Christ is shared in various ways both by sacred ministers and by the faithful; and as the one goodness of God is in reality communicated diversely to his creatures: so also the unique mediation of the Redeemer does not exclude but rather gives rise among creatures to a manifold cooperation which is but a sharing in this unique source.

The Church does not hesitate to profess this subordinate role of Mary. She experiences it continuously and commends it to the hearts of the faithful so that, encouraged by this maternal help, they may more closely adhere to the Mediator and Redeemer. (62)

Through the gift and role of divine maternity, Mary is united with her Son, the Redeemer, and with his singular graces and offices. By these, the Blessed Virgin is also intimately united with the Church. As St. Ambrose taught, the Mother of God is a model of the Church in the matter of faith, hope and charity, and perfect union with Christ. For in the mystery of the Church, herself rightly called Mother and Virgin, the Blessed Virgin stands out in eminent and singular fashion as exemplar of both virginity and motherhood. (63)

In the most holy Virgin, the Church has already reached that perfection whereby she exists without spot or wrinkle (cf. Eph. 5:27). Yet, the followers of Christ still strive to increase in holiness by conquering sin. And so they raise their eyes to Mary who shines forth to the whole community of the elect as a model of the virtues. Devotedly meditating on her and contemplating her in the light of the Word made man, the Church with reverence enters more intimately into the supreme mystery of the Incarnation and becomes ever increasingly like her Spouse. (64)

The Church in her apostolic work looks to her who brought forth Christ, conceived by the Holy Spirit and born of the Virgin, so that through the Church Christ may be born and grow in the hearts of the faithful also. The Virgin Mary in her own life lived as an example of that maternal love by which all should be fittingly animated who cooperate in the apostolic mission of the Church on behalf of the rebirth of men. (65)

IV. Devotion to the Blessed Virgin in the Church

Mary was involved in the mystery of Christ. As the most holy Mother of God she was, after her Son, exalted by divine grace above all angels and men. Hence, the Church appropriately honors her with special reverence. Indeed, from most ancient times the Blessed Virgin has been venerated under the title of "God-bearer." In all perils and needs, the faithful; have fled prayerfully to her protection. Especially after the Council of Ephesus the cult of the people of God toward Mary wonderfully increased in veneration and love, in invocation and imitation, according to her own prophetic words: "All generations shall call me blessed; because he who is mighty has done great things for me" (Lk. 1:48).

As it has always existed in the Church, this cult (of Mary) is altogether special, Still, it differs essentially from the cult of adoration which is offered to the Incarnate Word, as well as to the Father and the Holy Spirit. Yet, devotion to Mary is most favorable to this supreme cult. The Church has endorsed many forms of piety toward the Mother of God, provided that they were within the limits of sound and orthodox doctrine. These forms have varied according to the circumstances of time and place, and have reflected the diversity of native characteristics and temperament among the faithful. While honoring Christ's Mother, these devotions cause her Son to be rightly known, loved and glorified, and all his commands observed. Through him all things have their beginning (cf. Col. 1: 15-16) and in him "it has pleased (the eternal Father) that . all his fullness should dwell" (Col. 1:19). (66)

This most holy synod deliberately teaches this Catholic doctrine. At the same time, it admonishes all the sons of the Church that the cult, especially the liturgical cult, of the Blessed Virgin, be generously fostered. It charges that practices and exercises of devotion toward her be treasured as recommended by the teaching authority of the Church in the course of centuries.

This synod earnestly exhorts theologians and preachers of the divine word that, in treating of the unique dignity of the Mother of God, they carefully and equally avoid the falsity of exaggeration on the one hand and the excess of narrow-mindedness on the other.

Let the faithful remember, moreover, that true devotion consists neither in fruitless and passing emotion, nor in a certain vain credulity. Rather, it proceeds from the true faith, by which we are led to know the excellence of the Mother of God, and are moved to a filial love toward our Mother and to the imitation of her virtues. (67)

REDEMPTORIS MATER

Redemptoris Mater (*Mother of the Redeemer*), Pope John Paul II's sixth encyclical letter, is a "reflection on the role of Mary in the mystery of Christ and on her active and exemplary presence in the life of the Church." The letter was published March 25, 1987.

Central to consideration of Mary is the fact that she is the Mother of God (*Theotokos*), since by the power of the Holy Spirit she conceived in her virginal womb and brought into the world Jesus Christ, the Son of God, who is of one being with the Father and the Holy Spirit.

Mary was preserved from original sin in view of her calling to be the Mother of Jesus. She was gifted in grace beyond measure. She fulfilled her role in a unique pilgrimage of faith. She is the Mother of the Church and the spiritual mother of all people.

The following excerpts are from the English text provided by the Vatican and circulated by the CNS Documentary Service, *Origins*, April 9, 1987 (Vol. 16, No. 43). Subheads have been added. Quotations are from pertinent documents of the Second Vatican Council.

Mary's Presence in the Church

Mary, through the same faith which made her blessed, especially from the moment of the Annunciation, is present in the Church's mission, present in the Church's work of introducing into the world the kingdom of her Son.

This presence of Mary finds as many different expressions in our day just as it did throughout the Church's history. It also has a wide field of action: through the faith and piety of individual believers; through the traditions of Christian families or "domestic churches," of parish and missionary communities, religious institutes and dioceses; through the radiance and attraction of the great shrines where not only individuals or local groups, but sometimes whole nations and societies, even whole continents, seek to meet the Mother of the Lord, the one who is blessed because she believed, is the first among believers, and therefore became the Mother of Emmanuel.

Mary and Ecumenism

"In all of Christ's disciples the Spirit arouses the desire to be peacefully united, in the manner determined by Christ, as one flock under one shepherd." The journey of the Church, especially in our own time, is marked by the sign of ecumenism: Christians are seeking ways to restore that unity which Christ implored from the Father for his disciples on the day before his passion.

Christians must deepen in themselves and each of their communities that "obedience of faith" of which Mary is the first and brightest example.

Marian Mediation

The Church knows and teaches with St. Paul that there is only one mediator: "For there is one God, and there is one mediator between God and men, the man Christ Jesus, who gave himself as a ransom for all" (1 Tm. 2:5-6). "The maternal role of Mary toward people in no way obscures or diminishes the unique mediation of Christ, but rather shows its power." It is mediation in Christ.

Mediation and Motherhood

In effect, Mary's mediation is intimately linked with her motherhood. It possesses a specifically maternal character, which distinguishes it from the mediation of the other creatures who in various and always subordinate ways share in the one mediation of Christ, although her own mediation is also a shared mediation. In fact, while it is true that "no creature could ever be classed with the Incarnate Word and Redeemer," at the same time "the unique mediation of the Redeemer does not exclude but rather gives rise among creatures a manifold cooperation which is but a sharing in this unique source." Thus "the one goodness of God is in reality communicated diversely to his creatures."

Subordinate Mediation

The teaching of Vatican II presents the truth of Mary's mediation as "a sharing in the one unique source that is the mediation of Christ himself." Thus we read: "The Church does not hesitate to profess this subordinate role of Mary. She experiences it continuously and commends it to the hearts of the faithful so that, encouraged by this maternal help, they may more closely adhere to the Mediator and Redeemer."

This role is at the same time special and extraordinary. It flows from her divine motherhood and can be understood and lived in faith only on the basis of the full truth of this motherhood. Since by virtue of divine election Mary is the earthly Mother of the Father's consubstantial Son and his "generous companion" in the work of redemption, "she is a Mother to us in the order of grace." This role constitutes a real dimension of her presence in the saving mystery of Christ and the Church.

Mary is honored in the Church "with special reverence. Indeed, from most ancient times the Blessed Virgin Mary has been venerated under the title of 'God-bearer.' In all perils and needs, the faithful have fled prayerfully to her protection." This cult is altogether special; it bears in itself and expresses the profound link which exists between the Mother of Christ and the Church. As Virgin and Mother, Mary remains for the Church a "permanent model." It can therefore be said that, especially under this aspect, namely, as a model or rather as a "figure," Mary, present in the mystery of Christ, remains constantly present also in the mystery of the Church. For the Church too is "called mother and virgin," and these names have a profound biblical and theological justification.

APPARITIONS OF THE BLESSED VIRGIN MARY

Banneux, near Liège, Belgium: Mary appeared eight times between January 15 and March 2, 1933, to an eleven-year-old peasant girl, Mariette Beco, in a garden behind the family cottage in Banneux. She called herself the Virgin of the Poor, and has since been venerated as Our Lady of the Poor, the Sick, and the Indifferent. A small chapel was blessed August 15, 1933. Approval of devotion to Our Lady of Banneux was given in 1949 by Bishop Louis J. Kerkhofs of Liège, and a statue of that title was solemnly crowned in 1956.

Beauraing, Belgium: Mary appeared 33 times between November 29, 1932, and January 3, 1933, to five children in the garden of a convent school in Beauraing. A chapel was erected on the spot. Reserved approval of devotion to Our Lady of Beauraing was given February 2, 1943, and final approbation July 2, 1949, by Bishop Charue of Namur (d. 1977).

Fátima, Portugal: Mary appeared six times between May 13 and October 13, 1917, to three children (Lucia dos Santos, ten, who is now a Carmelite nun; Francisco Marto, nine, who died in 1919; and his sister Jacinta, 7, who died in 1920) in a field called Cova da Iria near Fátima. She recommended frequent recitation of the Rosary; urged works of mortification for the conversion of sinners; called for devotion to herself under the title of her Immaculate Heart; asked that the people of Russia be consecrated to her under this title, and that the faithful make a Communion of reparation on the first Saturday of each month.

The apparitions were declared worthy of belief in October 1930, and devotion to Our Lady of Fátima was authorized under the title of Our Lady of the Rosary. In October 1942, Pius XII consecrated the world to Mary under the title of her Immaculate Heart. Ten years later, in the first apostolic letter addressed directly to the peoples of Russia, he consecrated them in a special manner to Mary. See also below.

Guadalupe, Mexico: Mary appeared four times in 1531 to an Indian, Juan Diego (declared Blessed in 1990), on Tepeyac hill outside of Mexico City, and instructed him to tell Bishop Zumarraga of her wish that a church be built there. The bishop complied with the request about two years later, after being convinced of the genuineness of the apparition by the evidence of a miraculously painted life-size figure of the Virgin on the mantle of the Indian. The mantle bearing the picture has been preserved and is enshrined in the Basilica of Our Lady of Guadalupe. The shrine church, originally dedicated in 1709 and subsequently enlarged, has the title of basilica.

Benedict XIV, in a 1754 decree, authorized a Mass and Office under the title of Our Lady of Guadalupe for celebration on December 12, and named Mary the patroness of New Spain. Our Lady of Guadalupe was designated patroness of Latin America by St. Pius X in 1910 and of the Americas by Pius XII in 1945.

La Salette, France: Mary appeared as a sorrowing and weeping figure September 19, 1846, to two peasant children, Melanie Matthieu, fifteen, and Maximin Giraud, eleven, at La Salette. The message she confided to them, regarding the necessity of penance, was communicated to Pius IX in 1851 and has since been known as the "secret" of La Salette. Bishop de Bruillard of Grenoble declared in 1851 that the apparition was credible, and devotion to Mary under the title of Our Lady of La Salette was authorized. A Mass and Office with this title were authorized in 1942. The shrine church was given the title of minor basilica in 1879.

Lourdes, France: Mary, identifying herself as the Immaculate Conception, appeared eighteen times between February 11 and July 16, 1858, to fourteen-year-old Bernadette Soubirous (canonized in 1933) at the grotto of Massabielle near Lourdes. Her message concerned the necessity of prayer and penance for the conversion of peoples. Mary's request that a chapel be built at the grotto and spring was fulfilled in 1862. Devotion under the title of Our Lady of Lourdes was authorized, and a February 11 feast commemorating the apparitions was instituted by Leo XIII. St. Pius X extended this feast throughout the Church in 1907. The Church of Notre Dame was made a basilica in 1870, and the Church of the Rosary was built later. The underground Church of St. Pius X, with a capacity of 20,000 persons, was consecrated March 25, 1958. Plans were announced in 1994 for renovation and reconstruction of the Lourdes sanctuary.

Our Lady of the Miraculous Medal, France: Mary appeared three times in 1830 to Catherine Labouré (canonized in 1947) in the chapel of the motherhouse of the Daughters of Charity of St. Vincent de Paul, Rue de Bac, Paris. She commissioned Catherine to have made the medal of the Immaculate Conception, now known as the Miraculous Medal, and to spread devotion to her under this title. In 1832, the medal was struck.

THE "THIRD SECRET" OF FÁTIMA

On the morning of May 13, 2000, at the end of Mass at the Shrine of Fátima, Portugal, during which the Pope beatified the shepherd children Jacinta and Francisco, Cardinal Secretary of State Angelo Sodano read out, in Portuguese, a text concerning the third secret of Fátima. The text is given in full below:

"At the conclusion of this solemn celebration, I feel bound to offer to our beloved Holy Father John Paul II, on behalf of all present, heartfelt good wishes for his approaching eightieth birthday and to thank him for his significant pastoral ministry for the good of all God's Holy Church.

"On the solemn occasion of his visit to Fátima, His Holiness has directed me to make an announcement to you. As you know, the purpose of his visit to Fátima has been to beatify the two 'little shepherds'. Nevertheless he also wishes his pilgrimage to be a renewed gesture of gratitude to Our Lady for her protection during these years of his papacy. This protection seems also to be linked to the so-called 'third part' of the secret of Fátima.

"That text contains a prophetic vision similar to those found in Sacred Scripture, which do not describe with photographic clarity the details of future events, but rather synthesize and condense against a unified background events spread out over time in a succession and a duration which are not specified. As a result, the text must be interpreted in a symbolic key.

"The vision of Fátima concerns above all the war waged by atheist systems against the Church and Christians, and it describes the immense suffering endured by the witnesses to the faith in the last century of the second millennium. It is an interminable Way of the Cross led by the Popes of the twentieth century.

"According to the interpretation of the 'little shepherds,' which was also recently confirmed by Sister Lucia, the 'bishop clothed in white' who prays for all the faithful is the Pope. As he makes his way with great effort towards the Cross amid the corpses of those who were martyred (bishops, priests, men and women religious and many lay persons), he too falls to the ground, apparently dead, under a burst of gunfire.

"After the assassination attempt of May 13 1981, it appeared evident to His Holiness that it was 'a motherly hand which guided the bullet's path,' enabling the 'dying Pope' to halt 'at the threshold of death.' On the occasion of a visit to Rome by the then bishop of Leiria-Fátima, the Pope decided to give him the bullet which had remained in the jeep after the assassination attempt, so that it might be kept in the Shrine. At the behest of the bishop, the bullet was later set in the crown of the statue of Our Lady of Fátima.

"The successive events of 1989 led, both in the Soviet Union and in a number of countries of Eastern Europe, to the fall of the Communist regime which promoted atheism. For this too His Holiness offers heartfelt thanks to the Most Holy Virgin. In other parts of the world, however, attacks against the Church and against Christians, together with the burden of suffering which they involve, tragically continue. Even if the events to which the third part of the Secret of Fátima refers now seem part of the past, Our Lady's call to conversion and penance, issued at the beginning of the twentieth century, remains timely and urgent today. 'The Lady of the message seems to read the signs of the times - the signs of our time - with special insight . . . . The insistent invitation of Mary Most Holy to penance is nothing but the manifestation of her maternal concern for the fate of the human family, in need of conversion and forgiveness.'

"In order that the faithful may better receive the message of Our Lady of Fátima, the Pope has charged the Congregation for the Doctrine of the Faith with making public the third part of the secret, after the preparation of an appropriate commentary.

"Let us thank Our Lady of Fátima for her protection. To her maternal intercession let us entrust the Church of the Third Millennium.

'Sub tuum praesidium confugimus, Sancta Dei Genetrix!.' 'Intercede pro Ecclesia Dei! Intercede pro Sancto Patre Iohanne Paolo II! Amen.''

TRANSLATION OF THE THIRD SECRET

On June 26, 2000, the Holy See issued the complete translation of the original Portuguese text of the third part of the secret of Fátima, revealed to the three shepherd children at Cova da Iria-Fátima on July 13, 1917, and committed to paper by Sr. Lucia on January 3, 1944:

"I write in obedience to you, my God, who command me to do so through his Excellency the Bishop of Leiria and through your Most Holy Mother and mine.

"After the two parts which I have already explained, at the left of Our Lady and a little above, we saw an Angel with a flaming sword in his left hand; flashing, it gave out flames that looked as though they would set the world on fire; but they died out in contact with the splendor that Our Lady radiated towards him from her right hand: pointing to the earth with his right hand, the Angel cried out in a loud voice: 'Penance, Penance, Penance!' And we saw in an immense light that is God: 'something similar to how people appear in a mirror when they pass in front of it' a Bishop dressed in White 'we had the impression that it was the Holy Father.' Other Bishops, Priests, men and women Religious going up a steep mountain, at the top of which there was a big Cross of rough-hewn trunks as of a cork-tree with the bark; before reaching there the Holy Father passed through a big city half in ruins and half trembling with halting step, afflicted with pain and sorrow, he prayed for the souls of the corpses he met on his way; having reached the top of the mountain, on his knees at the foot of the big Cross he was killed by a group of soldiers who fired bullets and arrows at him, and in the same way there died one after another the other Bishops, Priests, men and women Religious, and various lay people of different ranks and positions. Beneath the two arms of the Cross there were two Angels each with a crystal aspersorium in his hand, in which they gathered up the blood of the Martyrs and with it sprinkled the souls that were making their way to God."

EVENTS AT MEDJUGORJE

The alleged apparitions of the Blessed Virgin Mary to six young people of Medjugorje, Bosnia-Herzogovina, have been the source of interest and controversy since they were first reported in June 1981, initially in the neighboring hillside field, subsequently in the village church of St. James and even in places far removed from Medjugorje.

Reports say the alleged visionaries have seen, heard, and even touched Mary during visions, and that they have variously received several or all of 10 secret messages related to coming world events and urging a quest for peace through penance and personal conversion. An investigative commission appointed by former local Bishop Pavao Zanic of Mostar-Duvno reported in March, 1984, that the authenticity of the apparitions had not been verified. He called the apparitions a case of "collective hallucination" exploited by local Franciscan priests at odds with him over control of a parish.

Former Archbishop Frane Franic of Split-Makarska, on the other hand, said in December, 1985: "Speaking as a believer and not as a bishop, my personal conviction is that the events at Medjugorje are of supernatural inspiration." He based his conviction on the observations of spiritual benefits related to the reported events, such as the spiritual development of the six young people, the increases in Mass attendance and sacramental practice at the scene of the apparitions, and the incidence of reconciliation among people.

On January 29, 1987, the bishops of Yugoslavia (by a vote of 19 to 1) declared: "On the basis of research conducted so far, one cannot affirm that supernatural apparitions are involved" at Medjugorje. Currently, the events at Medjugorje are under ongoing investigation by the Holy See to determine their authenticity. Nevertheless, the site of Medjugorje remains a popular destination for Catholic pilgrims from Europe and the United States.

Madonna and Christ Child

Part 7

THE CHURCH CALENDAR

The calendar of the Roman Church consists of an arrangement throughout the year of a series of liturgical seasons, commemorations of divine mysteries and commemorations of saints for purposes of worship.

The key to the calendar is the central celebration of the Easter Triduum, commemorating the supreme saving act of Jesus in his death and resurrection to which all other observances and acts of worship are related.

The purposes of this calendar were outlined in the Constitution on the Sacred Liturgy (*Sacrosanctum Concilium*, Nos. 102-105) promulgated by the Second Vatican Council.

"Within the cycle of a year . . . (the Church) unfolds the whole mystery of Christ, not only from his incarnation and birth until his ascension, but also as reflected in the day of Pentecost, and the expectation of a blessed, hoped-for return of the Lord.

Recalling thus the mysteries of redemption, the Church opens to the faithful the riches of her Lord's powers and merits, so that these are in some way made present at all times, and the faithful are enabled to lay hold of them and become filled with saving grace (No. 102).

In celebrating this annual cycle of Christ's mysteries, holy Church honors with special love the Blessed Mary, Mother of God" (No. 103).

The Church has also included in the annual cycle days devoted to the memory of the martyrs and the other saints (who) sing God's perfect praise in heaven and offer prayers for us. By celebrating the passage of these saints from earth to heaven the Church proclaims the paschal mystery as achieved in the saints who have suffered and been glorified with Christ; she proposes them to the faithful as examples who draw all to the Father through Christ, and through their merits she pleads for God's favors (No. 104).

In the various seasons of the year and according to her traditional discipline, the Church completes the formation of the faithful by means of pious practices for soul and body, by instruction, prayer, and works of penance and mercy (No. 105).

THE ROMAN CALENDAR

Norms for a revised calendar for the Western Church as decreed by the Second Vatican Council were approved by Paul VI in the *motu proprio Mysterii Paschalis* dated February 14, 1969. The revised calendar was promulgated a month later by a decree of the Congregation for Divine Worship and went into effect January 1, 1970, with provisional modifications. Full implementation of all its parts was delayed in 1970 and 1971, pending the completion of work on related liturgical texts. The U.S. bishops ordered the calendar into effect for 1972.

The Seasons

Advent: The liturgical year begins with the first Sunday of Advent, which introduces a season of four weeks or slightly less duration with the theme of expectation of the coming of Christ. During the first two weeks, the final coming of Christ as Lord and Judge at the end of the world is the focus of attention. From December 17 to 24, the emphasis shifts to anticipation of the celebration of his Nativity on the solemnity of Christmas.

Advent has four Sundays. Since the tenth century, the first Sunday has marked the beginning of the liturgical year in the Western Church. In the Middle Ages, a kind of pre-Christmas fast was in vogue during the season.

Christmas Season: The Christmas season begins with the vigil of Christmas and lasts until the Sunday after January 6, inclusive.

The period between the end of the Christmas season and the beginning of Lent belongs to the Ordinary Time of the year. Of variable length, the pre-Lenten phase of this season includes what were formerly called the Sundays after Epiphany and the suppressed Sundays of Septuagesima, Sexagesima and Quinquagesima.

Lent: The penitential season of Lent begins on Ash Wednesday, which occurs between February 4 and March 11, depending on the date of Easter, and lasts until the Mass of the Lord's Supper (Holy Thursday). It has six Sundays. The sixth Sunday marks the beginning of Holy Week and is known as Passion (formerly called Palm) Sunday.

The origin of Lenten observances dates back to the fourth century or earlier.

Easter Triduum: The Easter Triduum begins with evening Mass of the Lord's Supper and ends with Evening Prayer on Easter Sunday.

Easter Season: The Easter season whose theme is resurrection from sin to the life of grace, lasts for fifty days, from Easter to Pentecost. Easter, the first Sunday after the first full moon following the vernal equinox, occurs between March 22 and April 25. The terminal phase of the Easter season, between the solemnities of the Ascension of the Lord and Pentecost, stresses anticipation of the coming and action of the Holy Spirit.

Ordinary Time: The season of Ordinary Time begins on Monday (or Tuesday if the feast of the Baptism of the Lord is celebrated on that Monday) after the Sunday following January 6 and continues until the day before Ash Wednesday, inclusive. It begins again on the Monday after Pentecost and ends on the Saturday before the first Sunday of Advent. It consists of thirty-three or thirty-four weeks. The last Sunday is celebrated as the Solemnity of Christ the King. The overall purpose of the season is to elaborate the themes of salvation history.

The various liturgical seasons are characterized in part by the scriptural readings and Mass prayers assigned to each of them. During Advent, for example, the readings are messianic; during the Easter season, from the Acts of the Apostles, chronicling the Resurrection and the original proclamation of Christ by the Apostles, and from the Gospel of John; during Lent, baptismal and penitential passages. Mass prayers reflect the meaning and purpose of the various seasons.

Commemorations of Saints

The commemorations of saints are celebrated concurrently with the liturgical seasons and feasts of our Lord. Their purpose is to illustrate the paschal mysteries as reflected in the lives of saints, to honor them as heroes of holiness, and to appeal for their intercession.

In line with revised regulations, some former feasts were either abolished or relegated to observance in particular places by local option for one of two reasons: (1) lack of sufficient historical evidence for observance of the feasts; (2) lack of universal significance.

The commemoration of a saint, as a general rule, is observed on the day of death (*dies natalis*, day of birth to glory with God in heaven). Exceptions to this rule include the feasts of St. John the Baptist, who is honored on the day of his birth; Sts. Basil the Great and Gregory Nazianzen, and the brother Saints, Cyril and Methodius, who are commemorated in joint feasts. Application of this general rule in the revised calendar resulted in date changes of some observances.

Sundays and Other Holy Days

Sunday is the original Christian feast day and holy day of obligation because of the unusually significant events of salvation history which took place and are commemorated on the first day of the week viz., the Resurrection of Christ, the key event of his life and the fundamental fact of Christianity; and the descent of the Holy Spirit upon the Apostles on Pentecost, the birthday of the Church. The transfer of observance of the Lord's Day from the Sabbath to Sunday was made in apostolic times. The Mass and Liturgy of the Hours (Divine Office) of each Sunday reflect the themes and set the tones of the various liturgical seasons.

Holy days of obligation are special occasions on which Catholics who have reached the age of reason are seriously obliged, as on Sundays, to assist at Mass: they are also to refrain from work and involvement with business which impede participation in divine worship and the enjoyment of appropriate rest and relaxation.

The holy days of obligation observed in the United States are: Christmas, the Nativity of Jesus, December 25; Solemnity of Mary the Mother of God, January 1; Ascension of the Lord; Assumption of Blessed Mary the Virgin, August 15; All Saints' Day, November 1; Immaculate Conception of Blessed Mary the Virgin, December 8.

The precept to attend Mass is abrogated in the U.S. whenever the Solemnity of Mary, the Assumption, or All Saints falls on a Saturday or Monday (1991 decree of U.S. bishops; approved by Holy See July 4, 1992, and effective January 1, 1993).

In addition to these, there are four other holy days of obligation prescribed in the general law of the Church which are not so observed in the U.S.: Epiphany, January 6; St. Joseph, March 19; Corpus Christi; Sts. Peter and Paul, June 29. The solemnities of Epiphany and Corpus Christi are transferred to a Sunday in countries where they are not observed as holy days of obligation.

Solemnities, Feasts, Memorials

Categories of observances according to dignity and manner of observance are: solemnities, principal days in the calendar (observance begins with Evening Prayer I of the preceding day; some have their own vigil Mass); feasts (celebrated within the limits of the natural day); obligatory memorials (celebrated throughout the Church); optional memorials (observable by choice).

Fixed observances are those which are regularly celebrated on the same calendar day each year.

Movable observances are those which are not observed on the same calendar day each year. Examples of these are Easter (the first Sunday after the first full moon following the vernal equinox), Ascension (forty days after Easter), Pentecost (fifty days after Easter), Trinity Sunday (first after Pentecost), Christ the King (last Sunday of the liturgical year).

Weekdays, Days of Prayer

Weekdays are those on which no proper feast or vigil is celebrated in the Mass or Liturgy of the Hours (Divine Office). On such days, the Mass may be that of the preceding Sunday, which expresses the liturgical spirit of the season, an optional memorial, a votive Mass, or a Mass for the dead. Weekdays of Advent and Lent are in a special category of their own.

Days of Prayer: Dioceses, at times to be designated by local bishops, should observe "days or periods of prayer for the fruits of the earth, prayer for human rights and equality, prayer for world justice and peace, and penitential observance outside of Lent." So stated the Instruction on Particular Calendars (No. 331) issued by the Congregation for the Sacraments and Divine Worship June 24, 1970.

These days are contemporary equivalents of what were formerly called ember and rogation days.

Ember days originated at Rome about the fifth century, probably as Christian replacements for seasonal festivals of agrarian cults. They were observances of penance, thanksgiving, and petition for divine blessing on the various seasons; they also were occasions of special prayer for clergy to be ordained. These days were observed four times a year.

Rogation days originated in France about the fifth century. They were penitential in character and also occasions of prayer for a bountiful harvest and protection against evil.

Days and Times of Penance

Fridays throughout the year and the season of Lent are penitential times.

Abstinence: Catholics in the United States, from the age of fourteen throughout life, are obliged to abstain from meat on Ash Wednesday, the Fridays of Lent, and Good Friday. The law forbids the use of meat, but not of eggs, the products of milk, or condiments made of animal fat. Permissible are soup flavored with meat, meat gravy and sauces. The obligation to abstain from meat is not in force on days celebrated as solemnities (e.g., Christmas, Sacred Heart).

Fasting: Catholics in the United States, from the day after their eighteenth birthday to the day after their fifty-ninth birthday, are also obliged to fast on Ash Wednesday and Good Friday. The law allows only one full meal a day, but does not prohibit the taking of some food in the morning and evening, observing approved local custom as far as quantity and quality are concerned. The order of meals is optional, i.e., the full meal may be taken in the evening instead of at midday. Also: (1) The combined quantity of food taken at the two lighter meals should not exceed the quantity taken at the full meal. (2) The drinking of ordinary liquids does not break the fast.

Obligation: There is a general obligation to do penance for sins committed and for the remission of punishment due because of sin. Substantial observance of fasting and abstinence, prescribed for the community of the Church, is a matter of serious obligation; it allows, however, for alternate ways of doing penance (e.g., works of charity, prayer and prayer-related practices, almsgiving).

Readings at Mass

Scriptural readings for Mass on Sundays and holy days are indicated under the appropriate dates in the calendar pages for the year. For example, the B cycle is prescribed for Sunday Masses in liturgical year 2000, beginning December 3, 1999. The C cycle is prescribed for liturgical year 2001, beginning December 2, 2000. Weekday cycles of readings are the second and first, respectively, for liturgical years 2000 and 2001.

Monthly Prayer Intentions

Intentions chosen and recommended by Pope John Paul II to the prayers of the faithful and circulated by the Apostleship of Prayer are given for each month of the calendar. He has expressed his desire that all Catholics make these intentions their own "in the certainty of being united with the Holy Father and praying according to his intentions and desires."

Celebrations in U.S. Particular Calendar

The General Norms for the Liturgical Year and the Calendar, issued in 1969 and published along with the General Roman Calendar for the Universal Church, noted that the calendar consists of the General Roman Calendar used by the entire Church and of particular calendars used in particular churches (nations or dioceses) or in families of religious.

The particular calendar for the U.S. contains the following celebrations. **January:** 4, Elizabeth Ann Seton; 5, John Neumann; 6, Blessed André Bessette. **March:** 3, St. Katharine Drexel. **May:** 10, Blessed Damien DeVeuster; 15, Isidore the Farmer. **July:** 1, Blessed Junípero Serra; 4, Independence Day; 14, Blessed Kateri Tekakwitha. **August:** 18, Jane Frances de Chantal. **September:** 9, Peter Claver. **October:** 6, Blessed Marie-Rose Durocher; 19, Isaac Jogues and John de Brébeuf and Companions; 20, Paul of the Cross. **November:** 13, Frances Xavier Cabrini; 18, Rose Philippine Duchesne; 23, Blessed Miguel Agustín Pro; Fourth Thursday, Thanksgiving Day. **December:** 9, Blessed Juan Diego; 12, Our Lady of Guadalupe.

CALENDAR

JANUARY

1 Octave of Christmas, Solemnity of the Blessed Virgin Mary, Mother of God. The obligation to attend Mass is not in force this day.

2 Sts. Basil the Great and Gregory Nazianzen, bishops-doctors; memorial.

3

4 St. Elizabeth Ann Seton, religious; memorial.

5 St. John Neumann, bishop; memorial.

6 Blessed Andre Bessette, religious; optional memorial.

7 Epiphany of The Lord, solemnity.

8 Baptism of the Lord, feast.

9

10

11

12

13 St. Hilary, bishop-doctor; optional memorial.

14

15

16

17 St. Anthony, abbot; memorial.

18

19

20 St. Fabian, pope-martyr, or St. Sebastian, martyr; optional memorials.

21

22 St. Vincent, deacon-martyr; optional memorial.

23

24 St. Francis DeSales, bishop-doctor; memorial.

25 Conversion of St, Paul, apostle; feast.

26 Sts. Timothy and Titus, bishops; memorial.

27 St. Angela Merici, virgin; optional memorial.

28

29

30

31 St. John Bosco, priest; memorial.

FEBRUARY

1

2 Presentation of the Lord; feast.

3 St. Blase, bishop-martyr, or St. Ansgar, bishop; optional memorials

4

5 St. Agatha, virgin-martyr; memorial.

6 Sts. Paul Miki, priest-martyr, and Companions, martyrs; memorial.

7

8 St. Jerome Emiliani, priest; optional memorial.

9

10 St. Scholastica, virgin; memorial.

11

12

13

14 Sts. Cyril, monk, and Methodius, bishop; memorial.

15

16

17 Seven Founders of Order of Servites, religious; optional memorial.

18

19

20

21 St. Peter Damian, bishop-doctor; optional; memorial.

22 Chair of St. Peter, apostle; feast.

23 St. Polycarp, bishop-martyr; memorial.

24

25

26

27

28

MARCH

1

2

3 St. Katharine Drexel, virgin; optional memorial.

4

5

6

7 Sts. Perpetua and Felicity, martyrs; optional memorial.

St. John Neumann

8 St. John of God, religious; optional memorial.
9 St. Frances of Rome, religious; optional memorial.
10
11
12
13
14
15
16
17 St. Patrick bishop; optional memorial.
18
19 St. Joseph, husband of the Blessed Virgin Mary; solemnity.
20
21
22
23 St. Turibius de Mogrovejo, bishop; optional memorial.
24
25
26 Annunciation of the Lord; solemnity.
27
28
29
30
31

APRIL

1
2 St. Francis of Paola, hermit; optional memorial.
3
4 St. Isidore of Seville, bishop-doctor; optional memorial.
5 St. Vincent Ferrer, priest; optional memorial.
6
7 St. John Baptist de la Salle, priest; optional memorial.
8
9
10
11
12
13
14
15
16
17
18
19
20
21
22
23 St. George, martyr, or St. Adalbert, bishop-martyr; optional memorials.

24 St. Fidelis of Sigmaringen, priest-martyr; optional memorial.
25 St. Mark, evangelist; feast.
26
27
28 St. Peter Chanel, priest-martyr, or St. Louis de Montfort, priest; optional, memorials.
29
30 St. Pius V, pope; optional memorial.

MAY

1 St. Joseph the Worker; optional memorial.
2 St. Athanasius, bishop-doctor; memorial.
3 Sts. Philip and James, apostles; feast.
4
5
6
7
8
9
10
11
12 Sts. Nereus and Achilleus, martyrs, or St. Pancras, martyr; optional memorials.
13
14 St. Matthias, apostle; feast.
15 St. Isidore the Farmer; optional memorial.
16
17
18 St. John I, pope-martyr; optional memorial.
19
20
21
22
23
24
25 St. Bede the Venerable, priest-doctor; St. Gregory VII, pope, or St. Mary Magdalene de' Pazzi, virgin; optional memorials.
26 St. Philip Neri, priest; memorial.
27
28
29
30
31 Visitation of the Blessed Virgin Mary; feast.

JUNE

1 St. Justin Martyr; memorial
2 Sts. Marcellinus and Peter, martyrs; optional memorial.
3
4
5 St. Boniface, bishop-martyr; memorial.
6 St. Norbert, bishop; optional memorial.

7
8
9 St. Ephrem, deacon-doctor; optional memorial.
10
11 St. Barnabas, apostle; memorial.
12
13 St. Anthony of Padua, priest-doctor; memorial.
14
15
16
17
18
19 St. Romuald, abbot; optional memorial.
20
21 St. Aloysius Gonzaga, religious; memorial.
22 Most Sacred Heart of Jesus; solemnity.
23 Immaculate Heart of Mary; memorial.
24 Birth of John the Baptist; solemnity.
25
26
27 St. Cyril of Alexandria, bishop-doctor; optional memorial.
28 St. Irenaeus, bishop-martyr; memorial.
29 Sts. Peter and Paul, apostles; solemnity.
30 First Martyrs of the Church of Rome; optional memorial.

JULY

1
2
3 St. Thomas, apostle; feast
4 St. Elizabeth of Portugal; optional memorial. Independence Day, proper Mass in the United States.
5 St. Anthony Maria Zaccaria, priest; optional memorial.
6 St. Maria Goretti, virgin-martyr; optional memorial.
7
8
9
10
11 St. Benedict, abbot; memorial.
12
13 St. Henry; optional memorial.
14 Blessed Kateri Tekakwitha, virgin; memorial.
15
16 Our Lady of Mt. Carmel; optional memorial.
17
18 St. Camillus de Lellis, priest; optional memorial.
19
20

21 St. Lawrence of Brindisi, priest-doctor; optional memorial.
22
23 St. Bridget of Sweden, religious; optional memorial.
24
25 St. James, apostle; feast.
26 Sts. Joachim and Anne, parents of the Virgin Mary; memorial.
27
28
29
30 St. Peter Chrysologus, bishop-doctor; optional memorial.
31 St. Ignatius of Loyola, priest; memorial.

AUGUST

1 St. Alphonsus Liguori, bishop-doctor; memorial.
2 St. Eusebius of Vercelli, bishop, or St. Peter Julian Eymard, priest; optional memorials.
3
4 St. John Mary Vianney, priest; memorial.
5
6 Transfiguration of the Lord; feast
7 St. Sixtus II, pope-martyr, and Companions, martyrs, or St. Cajetan, priest; optional memorials.
8 St. Dominic, priest; memorial.
9
10 St. Lawrence, deacon-martyr; feast.
11 St. Clare, virgin; memorial.
12
13 Sts. Pontian, pope-martyr, and Hippolytus, priest-martyr; optional memorial
14 St. Maximilian Mary Kolbe, priest-martyr; memorial.
15 Assumption of the Blessed Virgin Mary; solemnity. Holy Day of Obligation.
16 St. Stephen of Hungary; optional memorial.
17
18 St. Jane Frances de Chantal, religious; optional memorial.
19
20 St. Bernard, abbot-doctor; memorial.
21 St. Pius X, pope; memorial.
22 Queenship of the Blessed Virgin Mary; memorial.
23 St. Rose of Lima, virgin; optional memorial.
24 St. Bartholomew, apostle; feast.
25 St. Louis of France, or St. Joseph Calasanz, priest; optional memorials.
26
27 St. Monica; memorial.
28 St. Augustine, bishop-doctor; memorial.

29 Martyrdom of St. John the Baptist; memorial.
30
31

SEPTEMBER

1
2
3 St. Gregory, pope-doctor; memorial.
4
5
6
7
8 Birth of the Blessed Virgin Mary; feast.
9
10
11
12
13 St. John Chrysostom, bishop-doctor; memorial
14 Exaltation of the Holy Cross; feast.
15 Our Lady of Sorrows; memorial.
16
17 St. Robert Bellarmine, bishop-doctor; optional memorial.
18
19 St. Januarius, bishop-martyr; optional memorial.
20 St. Andrew Kim Taegon, priest-martyr; St. Paul Chong Hasang, catechist and martyr, and Companions, martyrs; memorial.
21 St. Matthew, apostle-evangelist; feast.
22
23
24
25
26 Sts. Cosmas and Damian, martyrs; optional memorial.
27 St. Vincent de Paul, priest; memorial.
28 St. Wenceslaus, martyr, or St. Lawrence Ruiz and Companions, martyrs; optional memorials.
29 Sts. Michael, Gabriel, and Raphael, archangels; feast.
30

OCTOBER

1 St. Therese of the Child Jesus, virgin-doctor; memorial.
2 Guardian Angels, memorial.
3
4 St. Francis of Assisi, religious; memorial.
5
6 St. Bruno, priest, or Blessed Marie-Rose Durocher, virgin; optional memorials.
7
8
9 St. Denis, bishop-martyr, and Companions, martyrs, or St. John Leonard, priest; optional memorials.
10
11
12
13
14
15 St. Teresa of Jesus, virgin-doctor; memorial.
16 St. Hedwig, religious, or St. Margaret Mary Alacoque, virgin; optional memorials.
17 St. Ignatius of Antioch, bishop-martyr; memorial.
18 St. Luke, evangelist; feast
19 Sts Isaac Jogues and John de Brebeuf, priest-martyrs, and Companions, martyrs; memorial.
20 St. Paul of the Cross, priest; optional memorial.
21
22
23 St. John of Capistrano, priest; optional memorial.
24 St. Anthony Mary Claret, bishop; optional memorial.
25
26
27
28
29
30
31

NOVEMBER

1 All Saints; solemnity. Holy Day of Obligation.
2 Commemoration of All the Faithful Departed. (All Souls Day.)
3 St. Martin de Porres, religious; optional memorial.
4
5
6
7
8
9 Dedication of the Lateran Basilica in Rome; feast.
10 St. Leo the Great, pope-doctor; memorial.
11
12 St. Josaphat, bishop-martyr; memorial.
13 St. Frances Xavier Cabrini, virgin; memorial.
14
15 St. Albert the Great, bishop-doctor; optional memorial.
16 St. Margaret of Scotland or St. Gertrude the Great, virgin; optional memorials.

17 St. Elizabeth of Hungary, religious; memorial.
18
19
20
21 Presentation of the Blessed Virgin Mary; memorial.
22 St. Cecilia, virgin-martyr; memorial.
23 St. Clement I, pope-martyr; St. Columban, abbot; Blessed Miguel Agustin Pro, priest-martyr; optional memorials.
24 St. Andrew Dung-Lac, priest-martyr, and Companions, martyrs; memorial.
25 Christ the King; solemnity
26
27
28
29
30 St. Andrew, apostle; feast

DECEMBER

1
2
3 St. Francis Xavier, priest; memorial.
4 St. John of Damascus, priest-doctor; optional memorial.
5
6 St. Nicholas, bishop; optional memorial.
7 St. Ambrose, bishop-doctor; memorial.
8 Immaculate Conception of the Blessed Virgin Mary; solemnity. Holy Day of Obligation.

9
10
11 St. Damasus I, pope; optional memorial.
12 Our Lady of Guadalupe; feast.
13 St. Lucy, virgin-martyr; memorial.
14 St. John of the Cross, priest-doctor; memorial.
15
16
17
18
19
20
21 St. Peter Canisius, priest-doctor; optional memorial.
22
23
24
25 Christmas. Birth of the Lord; solemnity. Holy day of obligation. (Vigil — Is. 62:1-5; Acts 13:16-17, 22-25; Mt. 1:1-25. Midnight Mass — Is. 9:1-6; Ti. 2:11-14; Lk. 2:1-14. Mass at dawn — Is. 62:11-12; Ti. 3:4-7; Lk. 2:15-20. Mass during the day — Is. 52:7-10; Heb. 1:1-6; Jn. 1:1-18.)
26 St. Stephen, first martyr; feast.
27 St. John, apostle-evangelist; feast.
28 Holy Innocents, martyrs; feast.
29 St. Thomas Becket, bishop-martyr; optional memorial.
30 Holy Family of Jesus, Mary, and Joseph; feast.
31 St. Sylvester, pope; optional memorial.

HOLY DAYS AND OTHER OBSERVANCES

The following list includes the six holy days of obligation observed in the United States and additional observances of devotional and historical significance. The dignity or rank of observances is indicated by the terms: **solemnity** (highest in rank); **feast**; **memorial** (for universal observance); **optional memorial** (for celebration by choice).

All Saints, November 1, Holy Day of Obligation, solemnity. Commemorates all the blessed in heaven, and is intended particularly to honor the blessed who have no special feasts. The background of the feast dates to the fourth century when groups of martyrs, and later other saints, were honored on a common day in various places. In 609 or 610, the Pantheon, a pagan temple at Rome, was consecrated as a Christian church for the honor of Our Lady and the martyrs (later all saints). In 835, Gregory IV fixed November 1 as the date of observance.

All Souls, Commemoration of the Faithful Departed, November 2. The dead were prayed

for from the earliest days of Christianity. By the sixth century it was customary in Benedictine monasteries to hold a commemoration of deceased members of the order at Pentecost. A common commemoration of all the faithful departed on the day after All Saints was instituted in 998 by St. Odilo, of the Abbey of Cluny, and an observance of this kind was accepted in Rome in the 14th century.

Annunciation of the Lord (formerly, Annunciation of the Blessed Virgin Mary), March 25, solemnity. A feast of the Incarnation which commemorates the announcement by the Archangel Gabriel to the Virgin Mary that she was to become the Mother of Christ (Lk. 1:26-38), and the miraculous conception of Christ by her. The feast was instituted about 430 in the East. The Roman observance dates from the seventh century, when celebration was said to be universal.

Ascension of the Lord, movable observance held forty days after Easter, Holy Day of Obligation, solemnity. Commemorates the Ascension of

Christ into heaven 40 days after his Resurrection from the dead (Mk. 16:19; Lk. 24:51; Acts 1:2). The feast recalls the completion of Christ's mission on earth for the salvation of all people and his entry into heaven with glorified human nature. The Ascension is a pledge of the final glorification of all who achieve salvation. Documentary evidence of the feast dates from early in the fifth century, but it was observed long before that time in connection with Pentecost and Easter.

Ash Wednesday, movable observance, six and one-half weeks before Easter. It was set as the first day of Lent by Pope St. Gregory the Great (590-604) with the extension of an earlier and shorter penitential season to a total period including 40 weekdays of fasting before Easter. It is a day of fast and abstinence. Ashes, symbolic of penance, are blessed and distributed among the faithful during the day. They are used to mark the forehead with the Sign of the Cross, with the reminder: "Remember you are dust, and to dust you will return," or: "Turn away from sin and be faithful to the Gospel."

Assumption, August 15, holy day of obligation, solemnity. Commemorates the taking into heaven of Mary, soul and body, at the end of her life on earth, a truth of faith that was proclaimed a dogma by Pius XII on November 1, 1950. One of the oldest and most solemn feasts of Mary, it has a history dating back to at least the seventh century when its celebration was already established at Jerusalem and Rome.

Baptism of the Lord, movable, usually celebrated on the Sunday after January 6, feast. Recalls the baptism of Christ by John the Baptist (Mk. 1:9-11), an event associated with the liturgy of the Epiphany. This baptism was the occasion for Christ's manifestation of himself at the beginning of his public life.

Annunciation — Hood Design, Venetian Cape

Birth of Mary, September 8, feast. This is a very old feast which originated in the East and found place in the Roman liturgy in the seventh century.

Candlemas Day, February 2. See Presentation of the Lord.

Chair of Peter, February 22, feast. The feast, which has been in the Roman calendar since 336, is a liturgical expression of belief in the episcopacy and hierarchy of the Church.

Christmas, Birth of Our Lord Jesus Christ, December 25, Holy Day of Obligation, solemnity. Commemorates the birth of Christ (Lk. 2:1-20). This event was originally commemorated in the East on the feast of Epiphany or Theophany. The Christmas feast itself originated in the West; by 354 it was certainly kept on December 25. This date may have been set for the observance to offset pagan ceremonies held at about the same time to commemorate the birth of the sun at the winter solstice. There are texts for three Christmas Masses at midnight, dawn, and during the day.

Christ the King, movable, celebrated on the last Sunday of the liturgical year, solemnity. Commemorates the royal prerogatives of Christ and is equivalent to a declaration of his rights to the homage, service and fidelity of all people in all phases of individual and social life. Pius XI instituted the feast December 11, 1925.

Conversion of St. Paul, January 25, feast. An observance mentioned in some calendars from the 8th and 9th centuries. Pope Innocent III (1198-1216) ordered its observance with great solemnity.

Corpus Christi (The Body and Blood of Christ), movable, celebrated on the Thursday (or Sunday, as in the U.S.) following Trinity Sunday, solemnity. Commemorates the institution of the Holy Eucharist (Mt. 26:26-28). The feast originated at Liège in 1246 and was extended throughout the Church in the West by Urban IV in 1264. St. Thomas Aquinas composed the Liturgy of the Hours for the feast.

Cross, The Holy, September 14, feast. Commemorates the finding of the Cross on which Christ was crucified, in 326 through the efforts of St. Helena, mother of Constantine; the consecration of the Basilica of the Holy Sepulchre nearly 10 years later; and the recovery in 628 or 629 by Emperor Heraclius of a major portion of the cross which had been removed by the Persians from its place of veneration at Jerusalem. The feast originated in Jerusalem and spread through the East before being adopted in the West. General adoption followed the building at Rome of the Basilica of the Holy Cross "in Jerusalem," so called because it was the place of enshrinement of a major portion of the cross of crucifixion.

Dedication of St. John Lateran, November 9, feast. Commemorates the first public consecration of a church, that of the Basilica of the Most Holy Savior by Pope St. Sylvester about 324. The church, as well as the Lateran Palace, was the gift of Emperor Constantine. Since the 12th century it has been known as St. John Lateran, in honor of John the Baptist after whom the adjoining baptistery was named. It was rebuilt by Innocent X (1644-55), reconsecrated by Benedict XIII in 1726, and enlarged by Leo XIII (1878-1903). This basilica is regarded as the church of highest dignity in Rome and throughout the Roman Rite.

Dedication of St. Mary Major, August 5, optional memorial. Commemorates the rebuilding and dedication by Pope Sixtus III (432-40) of a church in honor of Blessed Mary the Virgin. This is the Basilica of St. Mary Major on the Esquiline Hill in Rome. An earlier building was erected during the pontificate of Liberius (352-66); according to legend, it was located on a site covered by a miraculous fall of snow seen by a nobleman favored with a vision of Mary.

Easter, movable celebration held on the first Sunday after the full moon following the vernal equinox (between March 22 and April 25), solemnity with an octave. Commemorates the Resurrection of Christ from the dead (Mk. 16:1-7). The observance of this mystery, kept since the first days of the Church, extends throughout the Easter season which lasts until the feast of Pentecost, a period of 50 days. Every Sunday in the year is regarded as a "little" Easter. The date of Easter determines the dates of movable feasts, such as Ascension and Pentecost, and the number of weeks before Lent and after Pentecost.

Easter Vigil, called by St. Augustine the "Mother of All Vigils," the night before Easter. Ceremonies are all related to the Resurrection and renewal-in-grace theme of Easter: blessing of the new fire, procession with the Easter Candle, singing of the Easter Proclamation (*Exsultet*), Liturgy of the Word with at least three Old Testament readings, the Litany of Saints, blessing of water, baptism of converts and infants, renewal of baptismal promises, Liturgy of the Eucharist. The vigil ceremonies are held after nightfall on Saturday.

Epiphany of the Lord, January 6 or (in the U.S.) a Sunday between January 2 and 8, solemnity. Commemorates the manifestations of the divinity of Christ. It is one of the oldest Christian feasts, with an Eastern origin traceable to the beginning of the third century and antedating the Western feast of Christmas. Originally, it commemorated the manifestations of Christ's

divinity — or Theophany — in his birth, the homage of the Magi, and baptism by John the Baptist. Later, the first two of these commemorations were transferred to Christmas when the Eastern Church adopted that feast between 380 and 430. The central feature of the Eastern observance now is the manifestation or declaration of Christ's divinity in his baptism and at the beginning of his public life. The Epiphany was adopted by the Western Church during the same period in which the Eastern Church accepted Christmas. In the Roman rite, commemoration is made in the Mass of the homage of the wise men from the East (Mt. 2:1-12).

Good Friday, the Friday before Easter, the second day of the Easter Triduum. Liturgical elements of the observance are commemoration of the Passion and Death of Christ in the reading of the Passion (according to John), special prayers for the Church and people of all ranks, the veneration of the Cross, and a Communion service. The celebration takes place in the afternoon, preferably at 3:00 p.m.

Guardian Angels, October 2, memorial. Commemorates the angels who protect people from spiritual and physical dangers and assist them in doing good. A feast in their honor celebrated in Spain in the 16th century was placed in the Roman calendar in 1615 and October 2 was set as the date of observance. Earlier, guardian angels were honored liturgically in conjunction with the feast of St. Michael.

Holy Family, movable observance on the Sunday after Christmas, feast. Commemorates the Holy Family of Jesus, Mary and Joseph as the model of domestic society, holiness and virtue. The devotional background of the feast was very strong in the 17th century. In the 18th century, in prayers composed for a special Mass, a Canadian bishop likened the Christian family to the Holy Family. Leo XIII consecrated families to the Holy Family. In 1921, Benedict XV extended the Divine Office and Mass of the feast to the whole Church.

Holy Innocents, December 28, feast. Commemorates the infants who suffered death at the hands of Herod's soldiers seeking to kill the child Jesus (Mt. 2:13-18). A feast in their honor has been observed since the fifth century.

Holy Saturday, the day before Easter. The Sacrifice of the Mass is not celebrated, and Holy Communion may be given only as Viaticum. If possible the Easter fast should be observed until the Easter Vigil.

Holy Thursday, the Thursday before Easter. Commemorates the institution of the sacraments of the Eucharist and holy orders, and the washing of the feet of the Apostles by Jesus at the Last Supper. The Mass of the Lord's Supper in the evening marks the beginning of the Easter Triduum. Following the Mass, there is a procession of the Blessed Sacrament to a place of reposition for adoration by the faithful. Usually at an earlier Mass of Chrism, bishops bless oils (of catechumens, chrism, the sick) for use during the year. (For pastoral reasons, diocesan bishops may permit additional Masses, but these should not overshadow the principal Mass of the Lord's Supper.)

Immaculate Conception, December 8, Holy Day of Obligation, solemnity. Commemorates the fact that Mary, in view of her calling to be the Mother of Christ and in virtue of his merits, was preserved from the first moment of her conception from original sin and was filled with grace from the very beginning of her life. She was the only person so preserved from original sin. The present form of the feast dates from December 8, 1854, when Pius IX defined the dogma of the Immaculate Conception An earlier feast of the Conception, which testified to long-existing belief in this truth, was observed in the East by the eighth century, in Ireland in the ninth, and subsequently in European countries. In 1846, Mary was proclaimed patroness of the U.S. under this title.

Immaculate Heart of Mary, Saturday following the second Sunday after Pentecost, memorial. On May 4, 1944, Pius XII ordered this feast observed throughout the Church in order to obtain Mary's intercession for "peace among nations, freedom for the Church, the conversion of sinners, the love of purity and the practice of virtue." Two years earlier, he consecrated the entire human race to Mary under this title. Devotion to Mary under the title of her Most Pure Heart originated during the Middle Ages. It was given great impetus in the seventeenth century by the preaching of St. John Eudes, who was the first to celebrate a Mass and Divine Office of Mary under this title. A feast, celebrated in various places and on different dates, was authorized in 1799.

Joachim and Ann, July 26, memorial. Commemorates the parents of Mary. A joint feast, celebrated September 9, originated in the East near the end of the sixth century. Devotion to Ann, introduced in the eighth century at Rome, became widespread in Europe in the 14th century; her feast was extended throughout the Latin Church in 1584. A feast of Joachim was introduced in the West in the fifteenth century.

John the Baptist, Birth, June 24, solemnity. The precursor of Christ, whose cousin he was, was commemorated universally in the liturgy by the fourth century. He is the only saint, except the Blessed Virgin Mary, whose birthday is observed as a feast. Another feast, on August 29, commemorates his passion and death at the order of Herod (Mk. 6:14-29).

Joseph, March 19, solemnity. Joseph is honored as the husband of the Blessed Virgin Mary, the patron and protector of the universal Church and workman. Devotion to him already existed in the eighth century in the East, and in the eleventh in the West. Various feasts were celebrated before the fifteenth century when March 19 was fixed for his commemoration; this feast was extended to the whole Church in 1621 by Gregory XV. In 1955, Pius XII instituted the feast of St. Joseph the Workman for observance May 1; this feast, which may be celebrated by local option, supplanted the Solemnity or Patronage of St. Joseph formerly observed on the third Wednesday after Easter. St. Joseph was proclaimed protector and patron of the universal Church in 1870 by Pius IX.

Michael, Gabriel and Raphael, Archangels, September 29, feast. A feast bearing the title of Dedication of St. Michael the Archangel formerly commemorated on this date the consecration in 530 of a church near Rome in honor of Michael, the first angel given a liturgical feast. For a while, this feast was combined with a commemoration of the Guardian Angels. The separate feasts of Gabriel (March 24) and Raphael (October 24) were suppressed by the calendar in effect since 1970 and this joint feast of the three archangels was instituted.

Octave of Christmas, January 1. See Solemnity of Mary, Mother of God.

Our Lady of Guadalupe, December 12, feast (in the U.S.). Commemorates under this title the appearances of the Blessed Virgin Mary in 1531 to an Indian, Juan Diego, on Tepeyac hill outside Mexico City (see Apparitions of the Blessed

Angel of the Noël

Virgin Mary). The celebration, observed as a memorial in the U.S., was raised to the rank of feast at the request of the National Conference of Catholic Bishops. Approval was granted in a decree dated January 8, 1988.

Our Lady of Sorrows, September 15, memorial. Recalls the sorrows experienced by Mary in her association with Christ: the prophecy of Simeon (Lk. 2:34-35), the flight into Egypt (Mt. 2:13-21), the three-day separation from Jesus (Lk. 2:41-50), and four incidents connected with the Passion: her meeting with Christ on the way to Calvary, the crucifixion, the removal of Christ's body from the cross, and his burial (Mt. 27:31-61; Mk. 15:20-47; Lk. 23:26-56; Jn. 19:17-42). A Mass and Divine Office of the feast were celebrated by the Servites, especially, in the 17th century, and in 1814 Pius VII extended the observance to the whole Church.

Our Lady of the Rosary, October 7, memorial. Commemorates the Virgin Mary through recall of the mysteries of the Rosary which recapitulate events in her life and the life of Christ. The feast was instituted in 1573 to commemorate a Christian victory over invading the forces of the Ottoman Empire at Lepanto in 1571, and was extended throughout the Church by Clement XI in 1716.

Passion Sunday (formerly called Palm Sunday), the Sunday before Easter. Marks the start of Holy Week by recalling the triumphal entry of Christ into Jerusalem at the beginning of the last week of his life (Mt. 21:1-9). A procession and other ceremonies commemorating this event were held in Jerusalem from very early Christian times and were adopted in Rome by the ninth century, when the blessing of palm for the occasion was introduced. Full liturgical observance includes the blessing of palm and a procession before the principal Mass of the day. The Passion, by Matthew, Mark, or Luke, is read during the Mass.

Pentecost, also called **Whitsunday**, movable celebration held fifty days after Easter, solemnity. Commemorates the descent of the Holy Spirit upon the Apostles, the preaching of Peter and the other Apostles to Jews in Jerusalem, the baptism and aggregation of some 3,000 persons to the Christian community (Acts 2:1-41). It is regarded as the birthday of the Catholic Church. The original observance of the feast antedated the earliest extant documentary evidence from the third century.

Peter and Paul, June 29, solemnity. Commemorates the martyrdoms of Peter by crucifixion and Paul by beheading during the Neronian persecution. This joint commemoration of the chief Apostles dates at least from 258 at Rome.

Presentation of the Lord (formerly called Purification of the Blessed Virgin Mary, also Candlemas), February 2, feast. Commemorates the presentation of Jesus in the Temple — according to prescriptions of Mosaic Law (Lv. 12:2-8; Ex. 13:2; Lk. 2:22-32) — and the purification of Mary 40 days after his birth. In the East, where the feast antedated fourth century testimony regarding its existence, it was observed primarily as a feast of Our Lord; in the West, where it was adopted later, it was regarded more as a feast of Mary until the calendar in effect since 1970. Its date was set for February 2 after the celebration of Christmas was fixed for December 25, late in the fourth century. The blessing of candles, probably in commemoration of Christ who was the Light to enlighten the Gentiles, became common about the eleventh century and gave the feast the secondary name of Candlemas.

Queenship of Mary, August 22, memorial. Commemorates the high dignity of Mary as Queen of heaven, angels and men. Universal observance of the memorial was ordered by Pius XII in the encyclical *Ad Caeli Reginam*, October 11, 1954, near the close of a Marian Year observed in connection with the centenary of the proclamation of the dogma of the Immaculate Conception and four years after the proclamation of the dogma of the Assumption. The original date of the memorial was May 31.

Resurrection. See **Easter**.

Sacred Heart of Jesus, movable observance held on the Friday after the second Sunday after Pentecost (Corpus Christi, in the U.S.), solemnity. The object of the devotion is the divine Person of Christ, whose heart is the symbol of his love for all people — for whom he accomplished the work of Redemption. The Mass and Office now used on the feast were prescribed by Pius XI in 1929. Devotion to the Sacred Heart was introduced into the liturgy in the 17th century through the efforts of St. John Eudes who composed an Office and Mass for the feast. It was furthered as the result of the revelations of St. Margaret Mary Alacoque after 1675 and by the work of St. Claude de la Colombière, S.J. In 1765, Clement XIII approved a Mass and Office for the feast, and in 1856 Pius IX extended the observance throughout the Roman rite.

Solemnity of Mary, Mother of God, January 1, Holy Day of Obligation, solemnity. The calendar in effect since 1970, in accord with Eastern tradition, reinstated the Marian character of this commemoration on the octave day of Christmas. The former feast of the Circumcision, dating at least from the first half of the sixth century, marked the initiation of Jesus (Lk. 2:21) in Judaism and by analogy focused attention on the initiation of persons in the Christian religion and their incorporation in Christ through baptism. The feast of the Solemnity supplants the former feast of the Maternity of Mary observed on October 11.

Transfiguration of the Lord, August 6, feast. Commemorates the revelation of his divinity by Christ to Peter, James and John on Mt. Tabor (Mt. 17:1-9). The feast, which is very old, was extended throughout the universal Church in 1457 by Callistus III.

Trinity, The Holy, movable observance held on the Sunday after Pentecost, solemnity. Commemorates the most sublime mystery of the Christian faith, i.e., that there are Three Divine Persons — Father, Son, and Holy Spirit — in one God (Mt. 28:18-20). A votive Mass of the Most Holy Trinity dates from the seventh century; an Office was composed in the 10th century; in 1334, John XXII extended the feast to the universal Church.

Visitation, May 31, feast. Commemorates Mary's visit to her cousin Elizabeth after the Annunciation and before the birth of John the Baptist, the precursor of Christ (Lk. 1:39-47). The feast had a medieval origin and was observed in the Franciscan Order before being extended throughout the Church by Urban VI in 1389. It is one of the feasts of the Incarnation and is notable for its recall of the *Magnificat*, one of the few New Testament canticles, which acknowledges the unique gifts of God to Mary because of her role in the redemptive work of Christ. The canticle is recited at Evening Prayer in the Liturgy of the Hours.

Antependium — Altar Frontal, Iceland, 13th c.

Part 8

LITURGICAL LIFE OF THE CHURCH

The nature and purpose of the liturgy, along with norms for its revision, were the subject matter of Sacrosanctum Concilium *(the Constitution on the Sacred Liturgy) promulgated by the Second Vatican Council. [Numbers in parentheses refer to citations from the document.]*

Nature and Purpose of Liturgy

The paragraphs under this and the following subhead are quoted directly from *Sacrosanctum Concilium* (Constitution on the Sacred Liturgy).

"It is through the liturgy, especially the divine Eucharistic Sacrifice, that 'the work of our redemption is exercised.' The liturgy is thus the outstanding means by which the faithful can express in their lives, and manifest to others, the mystery of Christ and the real nature of the true Church " (No. 2).

"The liturgy is considered as an exercise of the priestly office of Jesus Christ. In the liturgy the sanctification of man is manifested by signs perceptible to the senses, and is effected in a way which is proper to each of these signs; in the liturgy full public worship is performed by the Mystical Body of Jesus Christ, that is, by the Head and his members.

"From this it follows that every liturgical celebration, because it is an action of Christ the priest and of his Body the Church, is a sacred action surpassing all others. No other action of the Church can match its claim to efficacy, nor equal the degree of it" (No. 7).

"The liturgy is the summit toward which the activity of the Church is directed; at the same time it is the fountain from which all her power flows. For the goal of apostolic works is that all who are made sons of God by faith and baptism should come together to praise God in the midst of his Church, to take part in her sacrifice, and to eat the Lord's Supper.

"From the liturgy, therefore, and especially from the Eucharist, as from a fountain, grace is channeled into us; and the sanctification of men in Christ and the glorification of God, to which all other activities of the Church are directed as toward their goal, are most powerfully achieved" (No. 10).

Full Participation

"Mother Church earnestly desires that all the faithful be led to that full, conscious, and active participation in liturgical celebrations which is demanded by the very nature of the liturgy. Such participation by the Christian people as 'a chosen race, a royal priesthood, a holy nation, a purchased people' (1 Pt. 2:9; cf. 2:4-5), is their right and duty by reason of their baptism.

"In the restoration and promotion of the sacred liturgy, this full and active participation by all the people is the aim to be considered before all else; for it is the primary and indispensable source from which the faithful are to derive the true Christian spirit" (No. 14).

Norms

Norms regarding the reforms concern the greater use of Scripture; emphasis on the importance of the sermon or homily on biblical and liturgical subjects; use of vernacular languages for prayers of the Mass and for administration of the sacraments; provision for adaptation of rites to cultural patterns.

Approval for reforms of various kinds — in liturgical texts, rites, etc. — depends on the Holy See, regional conferences of bishops and individual bishops, according to provisions of law. No priest has authority to initiate reforms on his own. Reforms may not be introduced just for the sake of innovation, and any that are introduced in the light of present-day circumstances should embody sound tradition.

Sacramentals

Sacramentals, instituted by the Church, "are sacred signs which bear a resemblance to the sacraments: they signify effects, particularly of a spiritual kind, which are obtained through Church's intercession. By them men are disposed to receive the chief effect of the sacraments, and various occasions in life are rendered holy" (No. 60).

"Thus, for well-disposed members of the faithful, the liturgy of the sacraments and sacramentals sanctifies almost every event in their lives; they are given access to the stream of divine grace which flows from the paschal mystery of the passion, death, and resurrection of Christ, the fountain from which all sacraments and sacramentals draw their power. There is hardly any proper use of material things which cannot thus be directed toward the sanctification of men and the praise of God" (No. 61).

Some common sacramentals are priestly blessings, blessed palm, candles, holy water, medals, scapulars, prayers and ceremonies of the Roman Ritual.

Liturgy of the Hours

The Liturgy of the Hours (Divine Office) is the public prayer of the Church for praising God and sanctifying the day. Its daily celebration is required as a sacred obligation by men in holy orders and by men and women religious who have professed solemn vows. Its celebration by others is highly commended and is to be encouraged in the community of the faithful.

"By tradition going back to early Christian times, the Divine Office is arranged so that the whole course of the day and night is made holy by the praises of God. Therefore, when this wonderful song of praise is worthily rendered by priests and others who are deputed for this purpose by Church ordinance, or by the faithful praying together with the priest in an approved form, then it is truly the voice of the bride addressing her bridegroom; it is the very prayer which Christ himself, together with his Body, addresses to the Father" (No. 84).

"Hence all who perform this service are not only fulfilling a duty of the Church, but also are sharing in the greatest honor accorded to Christ's spouse, for by offering these praises to God they are standing before God's throne in the name of the Church their Mother" (No. 85).

Revised Hours

The Liturgy of the Hours, revised since 1965, was the subject of Pope Paul VI's apostolic constitution *Laudis Canticum*, dated November 1, 1970. The master Latin text was published in 1971; its four volumes have been published in authorized English translation since May 1975.

One-volume, partial editions of the Liturgy of the Hours containing Morning and Evening Prayer and other elements, have been published in approved English translation.

The revised Liturgy of the Hours consists of:
- Office of Readings, for reflection on the word of God. The principal parts are three psalms, biblical and non-biblical readings.
- Morning and Evening Prayer, called the "hinges" of the Liturgy of the Hours. The principal parts are a hymn, two psalms, an Old or New Testament canticle, a brief biblical reading, Zechariah's canticle (the *Benedictus*, morning) or Mary's canticle (the *Magnificat*, evening), responsories, intercessions and a concluding prayer.
- Daytime Prayer. The principal parts are a hymn, three psalms, a biblical reading and one of three concluding prayers corresponding to the time of day.
- Night Prayer: The principal parts are one or two psalms, a brief biblical reading, Simeon's canticle (*Nunc Dimittis*), a concluding prayer and an antiphon in honor of Mary.

The book used for recitation of the Office is the Breviary.

Sacred Music

"The musical tradition of the universal Church is a treasure of immeasurable value, greater even than that of any other art. The main reason for this pre-eminence is that, as sacred melody united to words, it forms a necessary or integral part of the solemn liturgy.

"Sacred music increases in holiness to the degree that it is intimately linked with liturgical action, winningly expresses prayerfulness, promotes solidarity, and enriches sacred rites with heightened solemnity. The Church indeed approves of all forms of true art, and admits them into divine worship when they show appropriate qualities" (No. 112).

The constitution decreed:
- Vernacular languages for the people's parts of the liturgy, as well as Latin, may be used.
- Participation in sacred song by the whole body of the faithful, and not just by choirs, is to be encouraged and brought about.
- Provisions should be made for proper musical training for clergy, religious and lay persons.
- While Gregorian Chant has a unique dignity and relationship to the Latin liturgy, other kinds of music are acceptable.
- Native musical traditions should be used, especially in mission areas.
- Various instruments compatible with the dignity of worship may be used.

Gregorian Chant: A form and style of chant called Gregorian was the basis and most highly regarded standard of liturgical music for centuries. It originated probably during the formative period of the Roman liturgy and developed in conjunction with Gallican and other forms of chant. Pope St. Gregory I the Great's connection with it is not clear, although it is known that he had great concern for and interest in church music. The earliest extant written versions of Gregorian Chant date from the ninth century. A thousand years later, the Benedictines of Solesmes, France, initiated a revival of chant which gave impetus to the modern liturgical movement.

Sacred Art and Furnishings

"Very rightly the fine arts are considered to rank among the noblest expressions of human genius. This judgment applies especially to religious art and to its highest achievement, which is sacred art. By their very nature both of the latter are related to God's boundless beauty, for this is the reality which these human efforts are trying to express in some way. To the extent that these works aim exclusively at turning men's thoughts to God persuasively and devoutly, they are dedicated to God and to the cause of his greater honor and glory" (No. 122).

The objective of sacred art is "that all things set apart for use in divine worship should be truly worthy, becoming, and beautiful, signs and symbols of heavenly realities. The Church has always reserved to herself the right to pass judgment upon the arts, deciding which of the works of artists are in accordance with faith, piety, and cherished traditional laws, and thereby suited to sacred purposes.

"Sacred furnishings should worthily and beautifully serve the dignity of worship" (No. 122).

RITES

Rites are the forms and ceremonial observances of liturgical worship coupled with the total expression of the theological, spiritual and disciplinary heritages of particular churches of the East and the West.

Different rites have evolved in the course of church history, giving to liturgical worship and church life in general forms and usages peculiar and proper to the nature of worship and the culture of the faithful in various circumstances of time and place. Thus, there has been development since apostolic times in the prayers and ceremonies of the Mass, in the celebration of the sacraments, sacramentals and the Liturgy of the Hours, and in observances of the liturgical calendar. The principal sources of rites in present use were practices within the patriarchates of Rome (for the West) and Antioch, Alexandria and Constantinople (for the East). Rites are identified as Eastern or Western on the basis of their geographical area of origin in the Roman Empire.

Eastern and Roman Rites

Eastern rites are proper to Eastern Catholic Churches (see separate entry). The principal rites are Byzantine, Alexandrian, Antiochene, Armenian and Chaldean.

The Latin or Roman rite prevails in the Western Church. It was derived from Roman practices and the use of Latin from the third century onward, and has been the rite in general use in the West since the eighth century. Other rites in limited use in the Western Church have been the Ambrosian (in the Archdiocese of Milan), the Mozarabic (in the Archdiocese of Toledo), the Lyonnais, the Braga, and rites peculiar to some religious orders like the Dominicans, Carmelites and Carthusians.

The purpose of the revision of rites in progress since the Second Vatican Council is to renew them, not to eliminate the rites of particular churches or to reduce all rites to uniformity. The Council reaffirmed the equal dignity and preservation of rites as follows.

"It is the mind of the Catholic Church that each individual church or rite retain its traditions whole and entire, while adjusting its way of life to various needs of time and place. Such individual churches, whether of the East or the West, although they differ somewhat among themselves in what are called rites (that is, in liturgy, ecclesiastical discipline and spiritual heritage), are, nevertheless, equally entrusted to the pastoral guidance of the Roman Pontiff, the divinely appointed successor of St. Peter in supreme government over the universal Church. They are, consequently, of equal dignity, so that none of them is superior to the others by reason of rite."

Determination of Rite

Determination of a person's rite is regulated by church law. Through baptism, a child becomes a member of the rite of his or her parents. If the parents are of different rites, the child's rite is decided by mutual consent of the parents; if there is lack of mutual consent, the child is baptized in the rite of the father. A candidate for baptism over the age of 14 can choose to be baptized in any approved rite. Catholics baptized in one rite may receive the sacraments in any of the approved ritual churches; they may transfer to another rite only with the permission of the Holy See and in accordance with other provisions of the Code of Canon Law.

Marble Relief — Life Tree and Peacocks
St. Sophia, Nicaea, 4th century

MASS, EUCHARISTIC SACRIFICE AND BANQUET

Declarations of Vatican II

The Second Vatican Council made the following declarations among others with respect to the Mass:

"At the Last Supper, on the night when he was betrayed, our Savior instituted the Eucharistic Sacrifice of his Body and Blood. He did this in order to perpetuate the Sacrifice of the Cross throughout the centuries until he should come again, and so to entrust to his beloved spouse, the Church, a memorial of his death and resurrection: a sacrament of love, a sign of unity, a bond of charity, a paschal banquet in which Christ is consumed, the mind is filled with grace, and a pledge of future glory is given to us" (*Sacrosanctum Concilium*, Constitution on the Sacred Liturgy, No. 47).

". . . As often as the Sacrifice of the Cross in which 'Christ, our Passover, has been sacrificed' (1 Cor. 5:7) is celebrated on an altar, the work of our redemption is carried on. At the same time, in the sacrament of the Eucharistic bread the unity of all believers who form one body in Christ (cf. 1 Cor. 10:17) is both expressed and brought about. All men are called to this union with Christ ." (*Lumen Gentium*, Dogmatic Constitution on the Church, No. 3).

". . . The ministerial priest, by the sacred power he enjoys, molds and rules the priestly people. Acting in the person of Christ, he brings about the Eucharistic Sacrifice, and offers it to God in the name of all the people. For their part, the faithful join in the offering of the Eucharist by virtue of their royal priesthood ." (Ibid., No. 10).

Declarations of Trent

Among its decrees on the Holy Eucharist, the Council of Trent stated the following points of doctrine on the Mass.

1. There is in the Catholic Church a true sacrifice, the Mass instituted by Jesus Christ. It is the sacrifice of his Body and Blood, Soul and Divinity, himself, under the appearances of bread and wine.

2. This Sacrifice is identical with the Sacrifice of the Cross, inasmuch as Christ is the Priest and Victim in both. A difference lies in the manner of offering, which was bloody upon the Cross and is bloodless on the altar.

3. The Mass is a propitiatory Sacrifice, atoning for the sins of the living and dead for whom it is offered.

4. The efficacy of the Mass is derived from the Sacrifice of the Cross, whose superabundant merits it applies to men.

5. Although the Mass is offered to God alone, it may be celebrated in honor and memory of the saints.

6. Christ instituted the Mass at the Last Supper.

7. Christ ordained the Apostles priests, giving them power and the command to consecrate his Body and Blood to perpetuate and renew the Sacrifice.

ORDER OF THE MASS

The Mass consists of two principal divisions called the **Liturgy of the Word**, which features the proclamation of the Word of God, and the **Eucharistic Liturgy**, which focuses on the central act of sacrifice in the Consecration and on the Eucharistic Banquet in Holy Communion. (Formerly, these divisions were called, respectively, the **Mass of the Catechumens** and the **Mass of the Faithful**.) In addition to these principal divisions, there are ancillary introductory and concluding rites.

The following description covers the Mass as celebrated with participation by the people. This Order of the Mass was approved by Pope Paul VI in the apostolic constitution *Missale Romanum* dated April 3, 1969, and promulgated in a decree issued April 6, 1969, by the Congregation for Divine Worship. The assigned effective date was November 30, 1969.

Introductory Rites

Entrance: The introductory rites begin with the singing or recitation of an entrance song consisting of one or more scriptural verses stating the theme of the mystery, season or feast commemorated in the Mass.

Greeting: The priest and people make the Sign of the Cross together. The priest then greets them in one of several alternative ways and they reply in a corresponding manner.

Introductory Remarks: At this point, the priest or another of the ministers may introduce the theme of the Mass.

Penitential Rite: The priest and people together acknowledge their sins as a preliminary step toward worthy celebration of the sacred mysteries.

This rite includes a brief examination of conscience, a general confession of sin and plea for divine mercy in one of several ways, and a prayer for forgiveness by the priest.

Glory to God: A doxology, a hymn of praise to God, sung or said on festive occasions.

Opening Prayer: A prayer of petition offered by the priest on behalf of the worshiping community.

I. Liturgy of the Word

Readings: The featured elements of this liturgy are readings of passages from the Bible. If three readings are in order, the first is usually from the Old Testament, the second from the New Testament (Letters, Acts, Revelation), and the third from one of the Gospels; the final reading is always a selection from a Gospel. The first reading(s) is (are) concluded with the formula, "The Word of the Lord" (effective February 28, 1993; optional before that date), to which the people respond, "Thanks be to God." The Gospel reading is concluded with the formula, "The Gospel of the Lord," (effective as above), to which the people respond, "Praise to you, Lord Jesus Christ." Between the readings, psalm verses are sung or recited. A Gospel acclamation is either sung or omitted.

Homily: An explanation, pertinent to the mystery being celebrated and the special needs of the listeners, of some point in either the readings from sacred Scripture or in another text from the Ordinary or Proper parts of the Mass; it is a proclamation of the Good News for a response of faith.

Creed: The Nicene profession of faith, by priest and people, on certain occasions.

Prayer of the Faithful: Litany-type prayers of petition, with participation by the people. Called general intercessions, they concern needs of the Church, the salvation of the world, public authorities, persons in need, the local community.

II. Eucharistic Liturgy

Presentation and Preparation of Gifts: Presentation to the priest of the gifts of bread and wine, principally, by participating members of the congregation. Preparation of the gifts consists of the prayers and ceremonies with which the priest offers bread and wine as the elements of the sacrifice to take place during the Eucharistic Prayer and of the Lord's Supper to be shared in Holy Communion.

Washing of Hands: After offering the bread and wine, the priest cleanses his fingers with water in a brief ceremony of purification.

Pray, Brothers and Sisters: Prayer that the sacrifice to take place will be acceptable to God. The first part of the prayer is said by the priest; the second, by the people.

Prayer over the Gifts: A prayer of petition offered by the priest on behalf of the worshipping community.

Eucharistic Prayer

Preface: A hymn of praise, introducing the Eucharistic Prayer or Canon, sung or said by the priest following responses by the people. The Order of the Mass contains a variety of prefaces, for use on different occasions.

Holy, Holy, Holy; Blessed is He: Divine praises sung or said by the priest and people.

Eucharistic Prayer (Canon): Its central portion is the Consecration, when the essential act of sacrificial offering takes place with the changing of bread and wine into the Body and Blood of Christ. The various parts of the prayer, which are said by the celebrant only, commemorate principal mysteries of salvation history and include petitions for the Church, the living and dead, and remembrances of saints.

Doxology: A formula of divine praise sung or said by the priest while he holds aloft the chalice containing the consecrated wine in one hand and the paten containing the consecrated host in the other.

Communion Rite

Lord's Prayer: Sung or said by the priest and people.

Prayer for Deliverance from evil: Called an embolism because it is a development of the final petition of the Lord's Prayer; said by the priest. It concludes with a memorial of the return of the Lord to which the people respond, "For the kingdom, the power, and the glory are yours, now and forever."

Prayer for Peace: Said by the priest, with corresponding responses by the people. The priest can, in accord with local custom, bid the people to exchange a greeting of peace with each other.

Lamb of God (*Agnus Dei*): A prayer for divine mercy sung or said while the priest breaks the consecrated host and places a piece of it into the consecrated wine in the chalice.

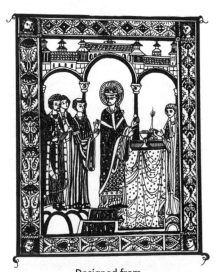

Designed from
The Mass — Weingarten School, 1190 – 1200

Communion: The priest, after saying a preparatory prayer, administers Holy Communion to himself and then to the people, thus completing the sacrifice-banquet of the Mass. (This completion is realized even if the celebrant alone receives the Eucharist.) On giving the Eucharist to each person under both species separately, the priest or eucharistic minister says, "The Body of Christ," "The Blood of Christ." The customary response is "Amen." If the Eucharist is given by intinction (in which the host is dipped into the consecrated wine), the priest says, "The Body and Blood of Christ."

Communion Song: Scriptural verses or a suitable hymn sung or said during the distribution of Holy Communion. After Holy Communion is received, some moments may be spent in silent meditation or in the chanting of a psalm or hymn of praise.

Prayer after Communion: A prayer of petition offered by the priest on behalf of the worshipping community.

Concluding Rite

Announcements: Brief announcements to the people are in order at this time.

Dismissal: Consists of a final greeting by the priest, a blessing, and a formula of dismissal. This rite is omitted if another liturgical action immediately follows the Mass; e.g., a procession, the blessing of the body during a funeral rite.

Some parts of the Mass are changeable with the liturgical season or feast, and are called the proper of the Mass. Other parts are said to be common because they always remain the same.

Additional Mass Notes

Catholics are seriously obliged to attend Mass in a worthy manner on Sundays and holy days of obligation. Failure to do so without a proportionately serious reason is gravely wrong.

It is the custom for priests to celebrate Mass daily whenever possible. To satisfy the needs of the faithful on Sundays and holy days of obligation, they are authorized to say Mass twice (**bination**) or even three times (**trination**). Bination is also permissible on weekdays to satisfy the needs of the faithful. On Christmas every priest may say three Masses.

The **fruits of the Mass**, which in itself is of infinite value, are: **general**, for all the faithful; **special (ministerial)**, for the intentions or persons specifically intended by the celebrant; **most special (personal)**, for the celebrant himself. On Sundays and certain other days pastors are obliged to offer Mass for their parishioners, or to have another priest do so. If a priest accepts a stipend or offering for a Mass, he is obliged in justice to apply the Mass for the intention of the donor. Mass may be applied for the living and the dead, or for any good intention.

Mass can be celebrated in several ways: e.g., with people present, without their presence (privately), with two or more priests as co-celebrants (con-celebration), with greater or less solemnity.

Some of the various types of Masses are: **for the dead** (Funeral Mass or Mass of Christian Burial, Mass for the Dead — formerly called Requiem Mass); **ritual,** in connection with celebration of the sacraments, religious profession, etc.; **nuptial,** for married couples, with or after the wedding ceremony; votive, to honor a Person of the Trinity, a saint, or for some special intention.

Places, Altars for Mass

The ordinary place for celebrating the Eucharist is a church or other sacred place, at a fixed or movable altar.

The altar is a table at which the Eucharistic Sacrifice is celebrated.

A fixed altar is attached to the floor of the church. It should be of stone, preferably, and should be consecrated. The Code of Canon Law orders observance of the custom of placing under a fixed altar relics of martyrs or other saints.

A movable altar can be made of any solid and suitable material, and should be blessed or consecrated.

Outside of a sacred place, Mass may be celebrated in an appropriate place at a suitable table covered with a linen cloth and corporal. An altar stone containing the relics of saints, which was formerly prescribed, is not required by regulations in effect since the promulgation April 6, 1969, of *Institutio Generalis Missalis Romani.*

LITURGICAL VESTMENTS

In the early years of the Church, vestments worn by the ministers at liturgical functions were the same as the garments in ordinary popular use. They became distinctive when their form was not altered to correspond with later variations in popular style. Liturgical vestments are symbolic of the sacred ministry and add appropriate decorum to divine worship.

Mass Vestments

Alb: A body-length tunic of white fabric; a vestment common to all ministers of divine worship.

Amice: A rectangular piece of white cloth worn about the neck, tucked into the collar and falling over the shoulders; prescribed for use when the alb does not completely cover the ordinary clothing at the neck.

Chasuble: Originally, a large mantle or cloak covering the body, it is the outer vestment of a

Dalmatic, Spain 15th c.

priest celebrating Mass or carrying out other sacred actions connected with the Mass.

Chasuble-Alb: A vestment combining the features of the chasuble and alb; for use with a stole by concelebrants and, by way of exception, by celebrants in certain circumstances.

Cincture: A cord which serves the purpose of a belt, holding the alb close to the body.

Dalmatic: The outer vestment worn by a deacon in place of a chasuble.

Stole: A long, band-like vestment worn by a priest about the neck and falling to about the knees. A deacon wears a stole over the left shoulder, crossed and fastened at his right side.

The material, form and ornamentation of the aforementioned and other vestments are subject to variation and adaptation, according to norms and decisions of the Holy See and concerned conferences of bishops. The overriding norm is that they should be appropriate for use in divine worship. The customary ornamented vestments are the chasuble, dalmatic and stole.

The minimal vestments required for a priest celebrating Mass are the alb, stole, and chasuble.

Liturgical Colors

The colors of outer vestments vary with liturgical seasons, feasts and other circumstances. The colors and their use are:

Green: For the season of Ordinary Time; symbolic of hope and the vitality of the life of faith.

Violet (Purple): For Advent and Lent; may also be used in Masses for the dead; symbolic of penance. (See below, Violet for Advent.)

Red: For the Sunday of the Passion, Good Friday, Pentecost; feasts of the Passion of Our Lord, the Apostles and Evangelists, martyrs; symbolic of the supreme sacrifice of life for the love of God.

Rose: May be used in place of purple on the Third Sunday of Advent (formerly called Gaudete Sunday) and the Fourth Sunday of Lent (formerly called Laetare Sunday); symbolic of anticipatory joy during a time of penance.

White: For the seasons of Christmas and Easter; feasts and commemorations of Our Lord, except those of the Passion; feasts and commemorations of the Blessed Virgin Mary, angels, saints who are not martyrs, All Saints (November 1), St. John the Baptist (June 24), St. John the Evangelist (December 27), the Chair of St. Peter (February 22), the Conversion of St. Paul (January 25). White, symbolic of purity and integrity of the life of faith, may generally be substituted for other colors, and can be used for funeral and other Masses for the dead.

Options are provided regarding the color of vestments used in offices and Masses for the dead. The newsletter of the U.S. Bishops' Committee on the Liturgy, in line with No. 308 of the General Instruction of the Roman Missal, announced in July 1970: "In the dioceses of the United States, white vestments may be used, in addition to violet (purple) and black, in offices and Masses for the dead."

On more solemn occasions, better than ordinary vestments may be used, even though their color (e.g., gold) does not match the requirements of the day.

Violet for Advent: Violet is the official liturgical color for the season of Advent, according to the September 1988, edition of the newsletter of the U.S. Bishops' Committee on the Liturgy. Blue was being proposed in order to distinguish between the Advent season and the specifically penitential season of Lent. The newsletter said, how-

Cingulum of Pope Benedict XIII

ever, that "the same effect can be achieved by following the official color sequence of the Church, which requires the use of violet for Advent and Lent, while taking advantage of the varying shades which exist for violet. Light blue vestments are not authorized for use in the United States."

Considerable freedom is permitted in the choice of colors of vestments worn for votive Masses.

Other Vestments

Cappa Magna: Flowing vestment with a train, worn by bishops and cardinals.

Cassock: A non-liturgical, full-length, close-fitting robe for use by priests and other clerics under liturgical vestments and in ordinary use; usually black for priests, purple for bishops and other prelates, red for cardinals, white for the pope. In place of a cassock, priests belonging to religious institutes wear the habit proper to their institute.

Cope: A mantle-like vestment open in front and fastened across the chest; worn by sacred ministers in processions and other ceremonies, as prescribed by appropriate directives.

Habit: The ordinary (non-liturgical) garb of members of religious institutes, analogous to the cassock of diocesan priests; the form of habits varies from institute to institute.

Humeral Veil: A rectangular vestment worn about the shoulders by a deacon or priest in Eucharistic processions and for other prescribed liturgical ceremonies.

Mitre: A headdress worn at some liturgical functions by bishops, abbots and, in certain cases, other ecclesiastics.

Pallium: A circular band of white wool about two inches wide, with front and back pendants, marked with six crosses, worn about the neck. It is a symbol of the fullness of the episcopal office.

Mitre with mixed lappets
France, late 12th c.

Pope Paul VI, in a document issued July 20, 1978, on his own initiative and entitled *Inter Eximia Episcopalis*, restricted its use to the pope and archbishops of metropolitan sees. In 1984, Pope John Paul II decreed that the pallium would ordinarily be conferred by the pope on the solemnity of Sts. Peter and Paul, June 29. The pallium is made from the wool of lambs blessed by the pope on the feast of St. Agnes (January 21).

Rochet: A knee-length, white linen-lace garment of prelates worn under outer vestments.

Surplice: a loose, flowing vestment of white fabric with wide sleeves. For some functions, it is interchangeable with an alb.

Zucchetto: A skullcap worn by bishops and other prelates.

SACRED VESSELS, LINENS

Vessels

Paten and Chalice: The principal sacred vessels required for the celebration of Mass are the paten (plate) and chalice (cup) in which bread and wine, respectively, are offered, consecrated and consumed. Both should be made of solid and noble material which is not easily breakable or corruptible. Gold coating is required of the interior parts of sacred vessels subject to rust. The cup of a chalice should be made of non-absorbent material.

Vessels for containing consecrated hosts (see below) can be made of material other than solid and noble metal — e.g., ivory, more durable woods — provided the substitute material is locally regarded as noble or rather precious and is suitable for sacred use.

Sacred vessels should be blessed, according to prescribed requirements.

Vessels, in addition to the paten, for containing consecrated hosts are:

Ciborium: Used to hold hosts for distribution to the faithful and for reservation in the tabernacle.

Luna, Lunula, Lunette: A small receptacle which holds the sacred host in an upright position in the monstrance.

Monstrance, Ostensorium: A portable receptacle so made that the sacred host, when enclosed therein, may be clearly seen, as at Benediction or during extended exposition of the Blessed Sacrament.

Pyx: A watch-shaped vessel used in carrying the Eucharist to the sick.

Linens

Altar Cloth: A white cloth, usually of linen, covering the table of an altar. One cloth is sufficient. Three were used according to former requirements.

Chalice of Pope Pius IX

Burse: A square, stiff flat case, open at one end, in which the folded corporal can be placed; the outside is covered with material of the same kind and color as the outer vestments of the celebrant.

Corporal: A square piece of white linen spread on the altar cloth, on which rest the vessels holding the Sacred Species — the consecrated host(s) and wine — during the Eucharistic Liturgy. The corporal is used whenever the Blessed Sacrament is removed from the tabernacle; e.g., during Benediction the vessel containing the Blessed Sacrament rests on a corporal.

Finger Towel: A white rectangular napkin used by the priest to dry his fingers after cleansing them following the offering of gifts at Mass.

Pall: A square piece of stiff material, usually covered with linen, which can be used to cover the chalice at Mass.

Purificator: A white rectangular napkin used for cleansing sacred vessels after the reception of Communion at Mass.

Veil: The chalice intended for use at Mass can be covered with a veil made of the same material as the outer vestments of the celebrant.

THE CHURCH BUILDING

A church is a building set aside and dedicated for purposes of divine worship, the place of assembly for a worshipping community.

A Catholic church is the ordinary place in which the faithful assemble for participation in the Eucharistic Liturgy and other forms of divine worship.

In the early years of Christianity, the first places of assembly for the Eucharistic Liturgy were private homes (Acts 2:46; Rom. 16:5; 1 Cor. 16:5; Col. 4:15) and, sometimes, catacombs. Church building began in the latter half of the second century during lulls in persecution and became widespread after enactment of the Edict of Milan in 313, when it finally became possible for the Church to emerge completely from the underground. The oldest and basic norms regarding church buildings date from about that time.

The essential principle underlying all norms for church building was reformulated by the Second Vatican Council, as follows: "When churches are to be built, let great care be taken that they be suitable for the celebration of liturgical services and for the active participation of the faithful" (*Sacrosanctum Concilium*, Constitution on the Sacred Liturgy, No. 124).

This principle was subsequently elaborated in detail by the Congregation for Divine Worship in a document entitled *Institutio Generalis Missalis Romani*, which was approved by Paul VI April 3 and promulgated by a decree of the congregation dated April 6, 1969. Coverage of the following items reflects the norms stated in Chapter V of this document.

Main Features

Sanctuary: The part of the church where the altar of sacrifice is located, the place where the ministers of the liturgy lead the people in prayer, proclaim the word of God and celebrate the Eucharist. It is set off from the body of the church by a distinctive structural feature — e.g., elevation above the main floor — or by ornamentation. (The traditional communion rail, removed in recent years in many churches, served this purpose of demarcation.) The customary location of the sanctuary is at the front of the church; it may, however, be centrally located.

Altar: The main altar of sacrifice and table of the Lord is the focal feature of the sanctuary and entire church. It stands by itself, so that the ministers can move about it freely, and is so situated that they face the people during the liturgical action. In addition to this main altar, there may also be others; in new churches, these are ideally situated in side chapels or alcoves removed to some degree from the body of the church.

Adornment of the Altar: The altar table is covered with a suitable linen cloth. Required candelabra and a cross are placed upon or near the altar in plain sight of the people and are so arranged that they do not obscure their view of the liturgical action.

Seats of the Ministers: The seats of the ministers should be so arranged that they are part of the seating arrangement of the worshipping congregation and suitably placed for the performance of ministerial functions. The seat of the celebrant or chief concelebrant should be in a presiding position.

Ambo, Pulpit, Lectern: The stand at which

scriptural lessons and psalm responses are read, the word of God preached, and the prayer of the faithful offered. It is so placed that the ministers can be easily seen and heard by the people.

Places for the People: Seats and kneeling benches (pews) and other accommodations for the people are so arranged that they can participate in the most appropriate way in the liturgical action and have freedom of movement for the reception of Holy Communion. Reserved seats are out of order.

Place for the Choir: Where it is located depends on the most suitable arrangement for maintaining the unity of the choir with the congregation and for providing its members maximum opportunity for carrying out their proper function and participating fully in the Mass.

Tabernacle: The best place for reserving the Blessed Sacrament is in a chapel suitable for the private devotion of the people. If this is not possible, reservation should be at a side altar or other appropriately adorned place. In either case, the Blessed Sacrament should be kept in a tabernacle, i.e., a safe-like, secure receptacle.

Statues: Images of the Lord, the Blessed Virgin Mary and the saints are legitimately proposed for the veneration of the faithful in churches. Their number and arrangement, however, should be ordered in such a way that they do not distract the people from the central celebration of the Eucharistic Liturgy. There should be only one statue of one and the same saint in a church.

General Adornment and Arrangement of Churches: Churches should be so adorned and fitted out that they serve the direct requirements of divine worship and the needs and reasonable convenience of the people.

Other Items

Ambry: A box containing the holy oils, attached to the wall of the sanctuary in some churches.

Baptistery: The place for administering baptism. Some churches have baptisteries adjoining or near the entrance, a position symbolizing the fact that persons are initiated in the Church and incorporated in Christ through this sacrament. Contemporary liturgical practice favors placement of the baptistery near the sanctuary and altar, or the use of a portable font in the same position, to emphasize the relationship of baptism to the Eucharist, the celebration in sacrifice and banquet of the death and resurrection of Christ.

Candles: Used more for symbolical than illuminative purposes, they represent Christ, the light and life of grace, at liturgical functions. They are made of beeswax. (See Index: Paschal Candle.)

Confessional, Reconciliation Room: A booth-like structure for the hearing of confessions, with separate compartments for the priest and penitents and a grating or screen between them. The use of confessionals became general in the Roman rite after the Council of Trent. Since the Second Vatican Council, there has been a trend in the U.S. to replace or supplement confessionals with small reconciliation rooms so arranged that priest and penitent can converse face-to-face.

Crucifix: A cross bearing the figure of the body of Christ, representative of the Sacrifice of the Cross.

Cruets: Vessels containing the wine and water used at Mass. They are placed on a credence table in the sanctuary.

Holy Water Fonts: Receptacles containing holy water, usually at church entrances, for the use of the faithful.

Sanctuary Lamp: A lamp which is kept burning continuously before a tabernacle in which the Blessed Sacrament is reserved, as a sign of the Real Presence of Christ.

Cope from Borgos, Spain, 1400

THE SACRAMENTS OF THE CHURCH

The sacraments are actions of Christ and his Church (itself a kind of sacrament) which signify grace, cause it in the act of signifying it, and confer it upon persons properly disposed to receive it. They perpetuate the redemptive activity of Christ, making it present and effective. They infallibly communicate the fruit of that activity — namely grace — to responsive persons with faith. Sacramental actions consist of the union of sensible signs (matter of the sacraments) with the words of the minister (form of the sacraments).

Christ himself instituted the seven sacraments of the New Law by determining their essence and the efficacy of their signs to produce the grace they signify.

Christ is the principal priest or minister of every sacrament; human agents — an ordained priest, baptized persons contracting marriage with each other, any person conferring emergency baptism in a proper manner — are secondary ministers. Sacraments have efficacy from Christ, not from the personal dispositions of their human ministers.

Each sacrament confers sanctifying grace for the special purpose of the sacrament; this is, accordingly, called sacramental grace. It involves a right to actual graces corresponding to the purposes of the respective sacraments.

Baptism, confirmation and the Eucharist are sacraments of initiation; penance (reconciliation) and anointing of the sick, sacraments of healing; order and matrimony, sacraments for service.

While sacraments infallibly produce the grace they signify, recipients benefit from them in proportion to their personal dispositions. One of these is the intention to receive sacraments as sacred signs of God's saving and grace-giving action. The state of grace is also necessary for fruitful reception of the Holy Eucharist, confirmation, matrimony, holy orders and anointing of the sick. Baptism is the sacrament in which grace is given in the first instance and original sin is remitted. Penance is the secondary sacrament of reconciliation, in which persons guilty of serious sin after baptism are reconciled with God and the Church, and in which persons already in the state of grace are strengthened in that state.

Role of Sacraments

The Second Vatican Council prefaced a description of the role of the sacraments with the following statement concerning participation by all the faithful in the priesthood of Christ and the exercise of that priesthood by receiving the sacraments (Dogmatic Constitution on the Church, *Lumen Gentium*, Nos. 10 and 11).

"The baptized by regeneration and the anointing of the Holy Spirit are consecrated into a spiritual house and a holy priesthood. Thus through all those works befitting Christian men they can offer spiritual sacrifice and proclaim the power of him who has called them out of darkness into his marvelous light (cf. 1 Pt. 2:4-10)."

"Though they differ from one another in essence and not only in degree, the common priesthood of the faithful and the ministerial or hierarchical priesthood (of those ordained to holy orders) are nonetheless interrelated. Each of them in its own special way is a participation in the one priesthood of Christ. The ministerial priest, by the sacred power he enjoys, molds and rules the priestly people. Acting in the Person of Christ, he brings about the Eucharistic Sacrifice, and offers it to God in the name of all the people. For their part, the faithful join in the offering of the Eucharist by virtue of their royal priesthood. They likewise exercise that priesthood by receiving the sacraments, by prayer and thanksgiving, by the witness of a holy life, and by self-denial and active charity."

"It is through the sacraments and the exercise of the virtues that the sacred nature and organic structure of the priestly community is brought into operation."

Baptism: "Incorporated into the Church through baptism, the faithful are consecrated by the baptismal character to the exercise of the cult of the Christian religion. Reborn as sons of God, they must confess before men the faith which they have received from God through the Church."

Confirmation: "Bound more intimately to the Church by the sacrament of confirmation, they are endowed by the Holy Spirit with special strength. Hence they are more strictly obliged to spread and defend the faith both by word and by deed as true witnesses of Christ."

Eucharist: "Taking part in the Eucharistic Sacrifice, which is the fount and apex of the whole Christian life, they offer the divine Victim to God, and offer themselves along with It. Thus, both by the act of oblation and through holy Communion, all perform their proper part in this liturgical service, not, indeed. all in the same way but each in that way which is appropriate to himself. Strengthened anew at the holy table by the Body of Christ, they manifest in a practical way that unity of God's People which is suitably signified and wondrously brought about by this most awesome sacrament."

Penance: "Those who approach the sacrament of penance obtain pardon from the mercy of God for offenses committed against him. They are at the same time reconciled with the Church, which they have wounded by their sins, and which by charity, example, and prayer seeks their conversion."

Anointing of the Sick: "By the sacred anointing of the sick and the prayer of her priests, the whole Church commends those who are ill to the suffering and glorified Lord, asking that he may lighten their suffering and save them (cf. Jas. 5:14-16). She exhorts them, moreover, to contribute to the welfare of the whole People of God by associating themselves freely with the passion and death of Christ (cf. Rom. 8:17; Col. 1:24; 2 Tm. 2:11-12; 1 Pt. 4:13)."

Holy Orders: "Those of the faithful who are consecrated by holy orders are appointed to feed the Church in Christ's name with the Word and the grace of God."

Matrimony: "Christian spouses, in virtue of the sacrament of matrimony, signify and partake of the mystery of that unity and fruitful love which exists between Christ and his Church (cf. Eph. 5:32). The spouses thereby help each other to attain to holiness in their married life and by the rearing and education of their children. And so, in their state and way of life, they have their own special gift among the People of God (cf. 1 Cor. 7:7).

"For from the wedlock of Christians there comes the family, in which new citizens of human society are born. By the grace of the Holy Spirit received in baptism these are made children of God, thus perpetuating the People of God through the centuries. The family is, so to speak, the domestic Church. In it parents should, by their word and example, be the first preachers of the faith to their children. They should encourage them in the vocation which is proper to each of them, fostering with special care any religious vocation."

"Fortified by so many and such powerful means of salvation, all the faithful, whatever their condition or state, are called by the Lord, each in his own way, to that perfect holiness whereby the Father himself is perfect."

Baptism

Baptism is the sacrament of spiritual regeneration by which a person is incorporated in Christ and made a member of his Mystical Body, given grace, and cleansed of original sin. Actual sins and the punishment due for them are remitted also if the person baptized was guilty of such sins (e.g., in the case of a person baptized

after reaching the age of reason). The theological virtues of faith, hope and charity are given with grace. The sacrament confers a character on the soul and can be received only once.

The matter is the pouring of water. The form is: "I baptize you in the name of the Father and of the Son and of the Holy Spirit."

The minister of solemn baptism is a bishop, priest or deacon, but in case of emergency anyone, including a non-Catholic, can validly baptize. The minister pours water on the forehead of the person being baptized and says the words of the form while the water is flowing. The water used in solemn baptism is blessed during the rite.

Baptism is conferred in the Roman Rite by immersion or infusion (pouring of water), depending on the directive of the appropriate conference of bishops, according to the Code of Canon Law. The Church recognizes as valid baptisms properly performed by non-Catholic ministers. The baptism of infants has always been considered valid and the general practice of infant baptism was well established by the fifth century. Baptism is conferred conditionally when there is doubt about the validity of a previous baptism.

Baptism is necessary for salvation. If a person cannot receive the baptism of water described above, this can be supplied by baptism of blood (martyrdom suffered for the Catholic faith or some Christian virtue) or by baptism of desire (perfect contrition joined with at least the implicit intention of doing whatever God wills that people should do for salvation).

A sponsor is required for the person being baptized. (See Godparents, below).

A person must be validly baptized before he or she can receive any of the other sacraments.

Christian Initiation of Infants: Infants should be solemnly baptized as soon after birth as conveniently possible. In danger of death, anyone may baptize an infant. If the child survives, the ceremonies of solemn baptism should be supplied.

The sacrament is ordinarily conferred by a priest or deacon of the parents' parish.

Catholics 16 years of age and over who have received the sacraments of confirmation and the Eucharist and are practicing their faith are eligible to be sponsors or godparents. Only one is required. Two, one of each sex, are permitted. A non-Catholic Christian cannot be a godparent for a Catholic child, but may serve as a witness to the baptism. A Catholic may not be a godparent for a child baptized in a non-Catholic religion, but may be a witness.

"Because of the close communion between the Catholic Church and the Eastern Orthodox churches," states the 1993 Directory on

Ecumenism, "it is permissible for a just cause for an Eastern faithful to act as godparent together with a Catholic godparent at the baptism of a Catholic infant or adult, so long as there is provision for the Catholic education of the person being baptized and it is clear that the godparent is a suitable one.

"A Catholic is not forbidden to stand as godparent in an Eastern Orthodox Church if he/she is so invited. In this case, the duty of providing for the Christian education binds in the first place the godparent who belongs to the church in which the child is baptized."

The role of godparents in baptismal ceremonies is secondary to the role of the parents. They serve as representatives of the community of faith and with the parents request baptism for the child and perform other ritual functions. Their function after baptism is to serve as proxies for the parents if the parents should be unable or fail to provide for the religious training of the child.

At baptism every child should be given a name with Christian significance, usually the name of a saint, to symbolize newness of life in Christ.

Christian Initiation of Adults: According to the *Ordo Initiationis Christianae Adultorum* ("Rite of the Christian Initiation of Adults") issued by the Congregation for Divine Worship under date of January 6, 1972, and put into effect in revised form September 1, 1988, adults are prepared for baptism and reception into the Church in several stages:

- An initial period of inquiry, instruction and evangelization.
- The catechumenate, a period of at least a year of formal instruction and progressive formation in and familiarity with Christian life. It starts with a statement of purpose and includes a rite of election.
- Immediate preparation, called a period of purification and enlightenment, from the beginning of Lent to reception of the sacraments of initiation — baptism, confirmation, Holy Eucharist — during ceremonies of the Easter Vigil. The period is marked by scrutinies, formal giving of the creed and the Lord's Prayer, the choice of a Christian name, and a final statement of intention.
- A mystagogic phase whose objective is greater familiarity with Christian life in the Church through observances of the Easter season and association with the community of the faithful, and through extended formation for about a year.

National Statutes for the Catechumenate were approved by the National Conference of Catholic Bishops November 11, 1986, and were subsequently ratified by the Vatican.

The priest who baptizes a catechumen can also administer the sacrament of confirmation.

A sponsor is required for the person being baptized.

The *Ordo* also provides a simple rite of initiation for adults in danger of death and for cases in which all stages of the initiation process are not necessary, and guidelines for: (1) the preparation of adults for the sacraments of confirmation and Holy Eucharist in cases where they have been baptized but have not received further formation in the Christian life; (2) for the formation and initiation of children of catechetical age.

The Church recognizes the right of anyone over the age of seven to request baptism and to receive the sacrament after completing a course of instruction and giving evidence of good will. Practically, in the case of minors in a non-Catholic family or environment, the Church accepts them when other circumstances favor their ability to practice the faith — e.g., well-disposed family situation, the presence of another or several Catholics in the family. Those who are not in such favorable circumstances are prudently advised to defer reception of the sacrament until they attain the maturity necessary for independent practice of the faith.

Reception of Baptized Christians: Procedure for the reception of already baptized Christians into full communion with the Catholic Church is distinguished from the catechumenate, since they have received some Christian formation. Instruction and formation are provided as necessary, however; and conditional baptism is administered if there is reasonable doubt about the validity of the person's previous baptism.

In the rite of reception, the person is invited to join the community of the Church in professing the Nicene Creed and is asked to state: "I believe and profess all that the holy Catholic Church believes, teaches, and proclaims as revealed by God." The priest places his hand on the head of the person, states the formula of admission to full communion, confirms (in the absence of a bishop), gives a sign of peace, and administers Holy Communion during a Eucharistic Liturgy.

Confirmation

Confirmation is the sacrament by which a baptized person, through anointing with chrism and the imposition of hands, is endowed with the fullness of baptismal grace; is united more intimately to the Church; is enriched with the special power of the Holy Spirit; is committed to be an authentic witness to Christ in word and action. The sacrament confers a character on the soul and can be received only once.

According to the apostolic constitution

Divinae Consortium Naturae dated August 15, 1971, in conjunction with the *Ordo Confirmationis* ("Rite of Confirmation"): "The sacrament of confirmation is conferred through the anointing with chrism on the forehead, which is done by the imposition of the hand (matter of the sacrament), and through the words: *'N, receive the seal of the Holy Spirit, the Gift of the Father'*" (form of the sacrament). On May 5, 1975, bishops' conferences in English-speaking countries were informed by the Congregation for Divine Worship that Pope Paul had approved this English version of the form of the sacrament: *"Be sealed with the gift of the Holy Spirit."*

The ordinary minister of confirmation in the Roman rite is a bishop. Priests may be delegated for the purpose. A pastor can confirm a parishioner in danger of death, and a priest can confirm in ceremonies of Christian initiation and at the reception of a baptized Christian into union with the Church.

Ideally, the sacrament is conferred during the Eucharistic Liturgy. Elements of the rite include renewal of the promises of baptism, which confirmation ratifies and completes, and the laying on of hands by the confirming bishop and priests participating in the ceremony.

"The entire rite," according to the *Ordo*; "has a twofold meaning. The laying of hands upon the candidates, done by the bishop and the concelebrating priests, expresses the biblical gesture by which the gift of the Holy Spirit is invoked. The anointing with chrism and the accompanying words clearly signify the effect of the Holy Spirit. Signed with the perfumed oil

Last Supper Plaque, 6th c.
Coptic — St. Sergius-Caire

by the bishop's hand, the baptized person receives the indelible character, the seal of the Lord, together with the Spirit who is given and who conforms the person more perfectly to Christ and gives him the grace of spreading the Lord's presence among men."

A sponsor is required for the person being confirmed. Eligible is any Catholic 16 years of age or older who has received the sacraments of confirmation and the Eucharist and is practicing the faith. The baptismal sponsor, preferably, can also be the sponsor for confirmation. Parents may present their children for confirmation but cannot be sponsors.

In the Roman rite, it has been customary for children to receive confirmation within a reasonable time after first Communion and confession. There is a trend, however, to defer confirmation until later when its significance for mature Christian living becomes more evident. In the Eastern rites, confirmation is administered at the same time as baptism.

Eucharist

The Holy Eucharist is a sacrifice (see The Mass) and the sacrament in which Christ is present and is received under the appearances of bread and wine.

The matter is bread of wheat, unleavened in the Roman rite and leavened in the Eastern rites, and wine of grape. The form consists of the words of consecration said by the priest at Mass: "This is my body. This is the cup of my blood" (according to the traditional usage of the Roman rite).

Only a priest can consecrate bread and wine so they become the body and blood of Christ. After consecration, however, the Eucharist can be administered by deacons and, for various reasons, by religious and lay persons.

Priests celebrating Mass receive the Eucharist under the species of bread and wine. In the Roman rite, others receive under the species of bread only, i.e., the consecrated host, or in some circumstances they may receive under the species of both bread and wine. In Eastern-rite practice, the faithful generally receive a piece of consecrated leavened bread which has been dipped into consecrated wine (i.e., by intinction).

Conditions for receiving the Eucharist, commonly called Holy Communion, are the state of grace, the right intention and observance of the Eucharistic fast.

The faithful of Roman Rite are required by a precept of the Church to receive the Eucharist at least once a year, ordinarily during the Easter time.

(See Eucharistic Fast, Mass, Transubstantiation, Viaticum.)

First Communion and Confession: Children are to be prepared for and given opportunity for receiving both sacraments (Eucharist and reconciliation, or penance) on reaching the age of discretion, at which time they become subject to general norms concerning confession and Communion. This, together with a stated preference for first confession before first Communion, was the central theme of a document entitled *Sanctus Pontifex* and published May 24, 1973, by the Congregation for the Discipline of the Sacraments and the Congregation for the Clergy, with the approval of Pope Paul VI.

What the document prescribed was the observance of practices ordered by St. Pius X in the decree *Quam Singulari* of August 8, 1910. Its purpose was to counteract pastoral and catechetical experiments virtually denying children the opportunity of receiving both sacraments at the same time. Termination of such experiments was ordered by the end of the 1972-73 school year.

At the time the document was issued, two- or three-year experiments of this kind — routinely deferring reception of the sacrament of penance until after the first reception of Holy Communion — were in effect in more than half of the dioceses of the U.S. They have remained in effect in many places, despite the advisory from the Vatican.

One reason stated in support of such experiments is the view that children are not capable of serious sin at the age of seven or eight, when Communion is generally received for the first time, and therefore prior reception of the sacrament of penance is not necessary. Another reason is the purpose of making the distinctive nature of the two sacraments clearer to children.

The Vatican view reflected convictions that the principle and practice of devotional reception of penance are as valid for children as they are for adults, and that sound catechetical programs can avoid misconceptions about the two sacraments.

A second letter on the same subject and in the same vein was released May 19, 1977, by the aforementioned congregations. It was issued in response to the question:

" 'Whether it is allowed after the declaration of May 24, 1973, to continue to have, as a general rule, the reception of first Communion precede the reception of the sacrament of penance in those parishes in which this practice developed in the past few years.'

"The Sacred Congregations for the Sacraments and Divine Worship and for the Clergy, with the approval of the Supreme Pontiff, reply: Negative, and according to the mind of the declaration.

"The mind of the declaration is that one year after the promulgation of the same declaration, all experiments of receiving first Communion without the sacrament of penance should cease so that the discipline of the Church might be restored, in the spirit of the decree, *Quam Singulari*."

The two letters from the Vatican congregations have not produced uniformity of practice in this country. Simultaneous preparation for both sacraments is provided in some dioceses where a child has the option of receiving either sacrament first, with the counsel of parents, priests and teachers. Programs in other dioceses are geared first to reception of Communion and later to reception of the sacrament of reconciliation.

Commentators on the letters note that: they are disciplinary rather than doctrinal in content; they are subject to pastoral interpretation by bishops; they cannot be interpreted to mean that a person who is not guilty of serious sin must be required to receive the sacrament of penance before (even first) Communion.

Canon 914 of the Code of Canon Law states that sacramental confession should precede first Communion.

Holy Communion under the Forms of Bread and Wine (by separate taking of the consecrated bread and wine or by intinction, the reception of the host dipped in the wine): Such reception is permitted under conditions stated in instructions issued by the Congregation for Divine Worship (May 25, 1967; June 29, 1970), the General Instruction on the Roman Missal (No. 242), and directives of bishops' conferences and individual bishops.

Accordingly, Communion can be administered in this way to: persons being baptized, received into communion with the Church, confirmed, receiving anointing of the sick; couples at their wedding or jubilee; religious at profession or renewal of profession; lay persons receiving an ecclesiastical assignment (e.g., lay missionaries); participants at concelebrated Masses, retreats, pastoral commission meetings, daily Masses and, in the U.S., Masses on Sundays and holy days of obligation.

A communicant has the option of receiving the Eucharist under the form of bread alone or under the forms of bread and wine.

Holy Communion More Than Once a Day: A person who has already received the Eucharist may receive it (only) once again on the same day only during a Eucharistic celebration in which the person participates. A person in danger of death who has already received the Eucharist once or twice is urged to receive Communion again as Viaticum. Pope John Paul approved this decision, in accord with Canon 917, and ordered it published July 11, 1984.

Holy Communion and Eucharistic Devotion outside of Mass: These were the subjects of an instruction (*De Sacra Communione et de Cultu Mysterii Eucharistici extra Missam*) dated June 21 and made public October 18, 1973, by the Congregation for Divine Worship.

Holy Communion can be given outside of Mass to persons unable for a reasonable cause to receive it during Mass on a given day. The ceremonial rite is modeled on the structure of the Mass, consisting of a penitential act, a scriptural reading, the Lord's Prayer, a sign or gesture of peace, giving of the Eucharist, prayer and final blessing. Viaticum and Communion to the sick can be given by extraordinary ministers (authorized lay persons) with appropriate rites.

Forms of devotion outside of Mass are exposition of the Blessed Sacrament (by men or women religious, especially, or lay persons in the absence of a priest; but only a priest can give the blessing), processions and congresses with appropriate rites.

Intercommunion: Church policy on intercommunion was stated in an "Instruction on the Admission of Other Christians to the Eucharist," dated June 1 and made public July 8, 1972, against the background of the Decree on Ecumenism approved by the Second Vatican Council, and the Directory on Ecumenism issued by the Secretariat for Promoting Christian Unity in 1967, 1970, and 1993.

Basic principles related to intercommunion are:

• "There is an indissoluble link between the mystery of the Church and the mystery of the Eucharist, or between ecclesial and Eucharistic communion; the celebration of the Eucharist of itself signifies the fullness of profession of faith and ecclesial communion" (1972 Instruction).

• "Eucharistic communion practiced by those who are not in full ecclesial communion with each other cannot be the expression of that full unity which the Eucharist of its nature signifies and which in this case does not exist; for this reason such communion cannot be regarded as a means to be used to lead to full ecclesial communion" (1972 Instruction).

• The question of reciprocity "arises only with those churches which have preserved the substance of the Eucharist, the sacrament of orders and apostolic succession" (1967 Directory).

• "A Catholic cannot ask for the Eucharist except from a minister who has been validly ordained" (1967 Directory).

The policy distinguishes between separated Eastern Christians and other Christians.

With Separated Eastern Christians (e.g., Orthodox): These may be given the Eucharist (as well as penance and anointing of the sick) at their request. Catholics may receive these same sacraments from priests of separated Eastern churches if they experience genuine spiritual necessity, seek spiritual benefit, and access to a Catholic priest is morally or physically impossible. This policy (of reciprocity) derives from the facts that the separated Eastern churches have apostolic succession through their bishops, valid priests, and sacramental beliefs and practices in accord with those of the Catholic Church.

With Other Christians (e.g., members of Reformation-related churches, others): Admission to the Eucharist in the Catholic Church, according to the Directory on Ecumenism, "is confined to particular cases of those Christians who have a faith in the sacrament in conformity with that of the Church, who experience a serious spiritual need for the Eucharistic sustenance, who for a prolonged period are unable to have recourse to a minister of their own community and who ask for the sacrament of their own accord; all this provided that they have proper dispositions and lead lives worthy of a Christian." The spiritual need is defined as "a need for an increase in spiritual life and a need for a deeper involvement in the mystery of the Church and its unity."

Circumstances under which Communion may be given to other properly disposed Christians are danger of death, imprisonment, persecution, grave spiritual necessity coupled with no chance of recourse to a minister of their own community.

Catholics cannot ask for the Eucharist from ministers of other Christian churches who have not been validly ordained to the priesthood.

Penance

Penance is the sacrament by which sins committed after baptism are forgiven and a person is reconciled with God and the Church.

Individual and integral confession and absolution are the only ordinary means for the forgiveness of serious sin and for reconciliation with God and the Church.

(Other than ordinary means are perfect contrition and general absolution without prior confession, both of which require the intention of subsequent confession and absolution.)

A revised ritual for the sacrament — *Ordo Paenitentiae*, published by the Congregation of Divine Worship February 7, 1974, and made mandatory in the U.S. from the first Sunday of Lent, 1977 — reiterates standard doctrine concerning the sacrament; emphasizes the social (communal and ecclesial) aspects of sin and conversion, with due regard for personal aspects and individual reception of the sacrament; prescribes three forms for celebration of the sacrament; and presents models for community penitential services.

The basic elements of the sacrament are sorrow for sin because of a supernatural motive, confession (of previously unconfessed mortal or grave sins, required; of venial sins also, but not of necessity), and reparation (by means of prayer or other act enjoined by the confessor), all of which comprise the matter of the sacrament; and absolution, which is the form of the sacrament.

The traditional words of absolution — *"I absolve you from your sins in the name of the Father, and of the Son, and of the Holy Spirit"* — remain unchanged at the conclusion of a petition in the new rite that God may grant pardon and peace through the ministry of the Church.

The minister of the sacrament is an authorized priest — i.e., one who, besides having the power of orders to forgive sins, also has faculties of jurisdiction granted by an ecclesiastical superior and/or by canon law.

The sacrament can be celebrated in three ways.

• For individuals, the traditional manner remains acceptable but is enriched with additional elements including: reception of the penitent and making of the Sign of the Cross; an exhortation by the confessor to trust in God; a reading from Scripture; confession of sins; manifestation of repentance; petition for God's forgiveness through the ministry of the Church and the absolution of the priest; praise of God's mercy, and dismissal in peace. Some of these elements are optional.

• For several penitents, in the course of a community celebration including a Liturgy of the Word of God and prayers, individual confession and absolution, and an act of thanksgiving.

• For several penitents, in the course of a community celebration, with general confession and general absolution. In extraordinary cases, reconciliation may be attained by general absolution without prior individual confession as, for example, under these circumstances: (1) danger of death, when there is neither time nor priests available for hearing confessions; (2) grave necessity of a number of penitents who, because of a shortage of confessors, would be deprived of sacramental grace or Communion for a lengthy period of time through no fault of their own. Persons receiving general absolution are obliged to be properly disposed and resolved to make an individual confession of the grave sins from which they have been absolved; this confession should be made as soon as the opportunity to confess presents itself and before any second reception of general absolution.

Norms regarding general absolution, issued by the Congregation for the Doctrine of the Faith in 1972, are not intended to provide a basis for convoking large gatherings of the faithful for the purpose of imparting general absolution, in the absence of extraordinary circumstances. Judgment about circumstances that warrant general absolution belongs principally to the bishop of the place, with due regard for related decisions of appropriate episcopal conferences.

Communal celebrations of the sacrament are not held in connection with Mass.

The place of individual confession, as determined by episcopal conferences in accordance with given norms, can be the traditional confessional or another appropriate setting.

A precept of the Church obliges the faithful guilty of grave sin to confess at least once a year.

The Church favors more frequent reception of the sacrament not only for the reconciliation of persons guilty of serious sins but also for reasons of devotion. Devotional confession — in which venial sins or previously forgiven sins are confessed — serves the purpose of confirming persons in penance and conversion.

Penitential Celebrations: Communal penitential celebrations are designed to emphasize the social dimensions of Christian life — the community aspects and significance of penance and reconciliation.

Elements of such celebrations are community prayer, hymns and songs, scriptural and other readings, examination of conscience, general confession and expression of sorrow for sin, acts of penance and reconciliation, and a form of non-sacramental absolution resembling the one in the penitential rite of the Mass.

If the sacrament is celebrated during the service, there must be individual confession and absolution of sin.

Anointing of the Sick

This sacrament, promulgated by St. James the Apostle (Jas. 5:13-15), can be administered to the faithful after reaching the age of reason who begin to be in danger because of illness or old age. By the anointing with blessed oil and the prayer of a priest, the sacrament confers on the person comforting grace; the remission of venial sins and inculpably unconfessed mortal sins, together with at least some of the temporal punishment due for sins; and, sometimes, results in an improved state of health.

The matter of this sacrament is the anointing with blessed oil (of the sick — olive oil, or vegetable oil if necessary) of the forehead and hands; in cases of necessity, a single anointing of another portion of the body suffices. The form is: "Through this holy anointing and his most loving mercy, may the Lord assist you by the grace of the Holy Spirit so that, when you have been freed from your sins, he may save you and in his goodness raise you up."

Anointing of the sick, formerly called extreme unction, may be received more than once, e.g., in new or continuing stages of serious illness. Ideally, the sacrament should be administered while the recipient is conscious and in conjunction with the sacraments of penance and the Eucharist. It should be administered in cases of doubt as to whether the person has reached the age of reason, is dangerously ill or dead.

The sacrament can be administered during a communal celebration in some circumstances, as in a home for the aged.

Holy Orders

Orders is the sacrament by which the mission given by Christ to the Apostles continues to be exercised in the Church until the end of time; it is the sacrament of apostolic mission. It has three grades: episcopacy, priesthood and diaconate. The sacrament confers a character on the soul and can be received only once. The minister of the sacrament is a bishop.

Orders, like matrimony but in a different way, is a social sacrament. As the Second Vatican Council declared in *Lumen Gentium*, the Dogmatic Constitution on the Church:

"For the nurturing and constant growth of the People of God, Christ the Lord instituted in his Church a variety of ministries, which work for the good of the whole body. For those ministers who are endowed with sacred power are servants of their brethren, so that all who are of the People of God, and therefore enjoy a true Christian dignity, can work toward a common goal freely and in an orderly way, and arrive at salvation" (No. 18).

Bishop: The fullness of the priesthood belongs to those who have received the order of bishop. Bishops, in hierarchical union with the pope and their fellow bishops, are the successors of the Apostles as pastors of the Church: they have individual responsibility for the care of the local churches they serve and collegial responsibility for the care of the universal Church (see Collegiality). In the ordination or consecration of bishops, the essential form is the imposition of hands by the consecrator(s) and the assigned prayer in the preface of the rite of ordination.

"With their helpers, the priests and deacons, bishops have taken up the service of the community presiding in place of God over the flock whose shepherds they are, as teachers of doctrine, priests of sacred worship, and officers of good order" (No. 20).

Priests: A priest is an ordained minister with the power to celebrate Mass, administer the sacraments, preach and teach the word of God, impart blessings, and perform additional pastoral functions, according to the mandate of his ecclesiastical superior.

Concerning priests, the Second Vatican Council stated in *Lumen Gentium* (No. 28):

"The divinely established ecclesiastical ministry is exercised on different levels by those who from antiquity have been called bishops, priests, and deacons. Although priests do not possess the highest degree of the priesthood, and although they are dependent on the bishops in the exercise of their power, they are nevertheless united with the bishops in sacerdotal dignity. By the power of the sacrament of orders, and in the image of Christ the eternal High Priest (Heb. 5:1-10; 7:24; 9:11-28), they are consecrated to preach the Gospel, shepherd the faithful, and celebrate divine worship as true priests of the New Testament.

"Priests, prudent cooperators with the episcopal order as well as its aides and instruments, are called to serve the People of God. They constitute one priesthood with their bishop, although that priesthood is comprised of different functions."

In the ordination of a priest of Roman rite, the essential matter is the imposition of hands on the heads of those being ordained by the ordaining bishop. The essential form is the accompanying prayer in the preface of the ordination ceremony. Other elements in the rite are the presentation of the implements of sacrifice — the chalice containing the wine and the paten containing a host — with accompanying prayers.

Deacon: There are two kinds of deacons: those who receive the order and remain in it permanently, and those who receive the order while advancing to priesthood. The following quotation — from Vatican II's Dogmatic Constitution on the Church (*Lumen Gentium*, No. 29) — describes the nature and role of the diaconate, with emphasis on the permanent diaconate.

"At a lower level of the hierarchy are deacons, upon whom hands are imposed 'not unto the priesthood, but unto a ministry of service.' For strengthened by sacramental grace, in communion with the bishop and his group of priests, they serve the People of God in the ministry of the liturgy, of the word, and of charity. It is the duty of the deacon, to the extent that he has been authorized by competent authority, to administer baptism solemnly, to be custodian and dispenser of the Eucharist, to assist at and bless marriages in the name of the Church, to bring Viaticum to the dying, to read the sacred Scripture to the faithful, to instruct and exhort the people, to preside at the worship and prayer of the faithful, to administer sacramentals, and to officiate at funeral and burial services. (Deacons are) dedicated to duties of charity and administration."

"The diaconate can in the future be restored as a proper and permanent rank of the hierarchy. It pertains to the competent territorial bodies of bishops, of one kind or another, to decide, with the approval of the Supreme Pontiff, whether and where it is opportune for such deacons to be appointed for the care of souls. With the consent of the Roman Pontiff, this diaconate will be able to be conferred upon men of more mature age, even upon those living in the married state. It may also be conferred upon suitable young men. For them, however, the law of celibacy must remain intact" (No. 29).

The Apostles ordained the first seven deacons (Acts 6:1-6): Stephen, Philip, Prochorus, Nicanor, Timon, Parmenas, Nicholas.

Former Orders, Ministries: With the revision of the sacrament of orders, which began in 1971, the orders of subdeacon, acolyte, exorcist, lector and porter were abolished because they and their respective functions had fallen into disuse or did not require ordination. The Holy See started revision of the sacrament of orders in 1971. In virtue of an indult of October 5 of that year, the bishops of the United States were permitted to discontinue ordaining porters and exorcists. Another indult, dated three days later, permitted the use of revised rites for ordaining acolytes and lectors.

To complete the revision, Pope Paul VI abolished September 14, 1972, the orders of porter, exorcist and subdeacon; decreed that laymen, as well as candidates for the diaconate and priesthood, can be installed (rather than ordained) in the ministries (rather than orders) of acolyte and lector; reconfirmed the suppression of tonsure and its replacement with a service of dedication to God and the Church; and stated that a man enters the clerical state on ordination to the diaconate.

The abolished orders were:

- Subdeacon, with specific duties in liturgical worship, especially at Mass. The order, whose first extant mention dates from about the middle of the third century, was regarded as minor until the thirteenth century; afterwards, it was called a major order in the West but not in the East.
- Acolyte, to serve in minor capacities in liturgical worship; a function now performed by Mass servers.
- Exorcist, to perform services of exorcism for expelling evil spirits; a function which came to be reserved to specially delegated priests.
- Lector, to read scriptural and other passages during liturgical worship; a function now generally performed by lay persons.
- Porter, to guard the entrance to an assembly of Christians and to ward off undesirables who tried to gain admittance; an order of early origin and utility but of present insignificance.

Permanent Diaconate

Restoration of the permanent diaconate in the Roman rite — making it possible for men to become deacons permanently, without going on to the priesthood — was promulgated by Pope Paul VI June 18, 1967, in a document entitled *Sacrum Diaconatus Ordinem* ("Sacred Order of the Diaconate").

The Pope's action implemented the desire expressed by the Second Vatican Council for reestablishment of the diaconate as an independent order in its own right not only to supply ministers for carrying on the work of the Church but also to complete the hierarchical structure of the Church of Roman rite.

Permanent deacons have been traditional in the Eastern Church. The Western Church, however, since the fourth or fifth century, generally followed the practice of conferring the diaconate only as a sacred order preliminary to the priesthood, and of restricting the ministry of deacons to liturgical functions.

The Pope's document, issued on his own initiative, provided:

- Qualified unmarried men twenty-five years of age or older may be ordained deacons. They cannot marry after ordination.
- Qualified married men thirty-five years of age or older may be ordained deacons. The consent of the wife of a prospective deacon is required. A married deacon cannot remarry after the death of his wife.
- Preparation for the diaconate includes a course of study and formation over a period of at least three years.
- Candidates who are not members of religious institutes must be affiliated with a diocese. Reestablishment of the diaconate among religious is reserved to the Holy See.
- Deacons will practice their ministry under the direction of a bishop and with the priests with whom they will be associated. (For functions, see also the description of deacon, under Holy Orders.)

Restoration of the permanent diaconate in the United States was approved by the Holy See in October 1968. Shortly afterwards the U.S. bishops established a committee for the permanent diaconate. The committee operates through a secretariat, with offices at 3211 Fourth St. N. E., Washington, D.C. 20017.

Status and Functions

Training programs of spiritual, theological and pastoral formation are based on guidelines emanating from the National Conference of Catholic Bishops.

Deacons have various functions, depending on the nature of their assignments. Liturgically, they can officiate at baptisms, weddings, wake services and funerals, can preach and distribute Holy Communion. Some are engaged in religious education work. All are intended to carry out works of charity and pastoral service of one kind or another.

The majority of deacons, the majority of whom are married, continue in their secular work. Their ministry of service is developing in three dimensions: of liturgy, of the word, and of charity. Depending on the individual deacon's abilities and preference, he is assigned by his bishop to either a parochial ministry or to another field of service. Deacons are active in a variety of ministries including those to prison inmates and their families, the sick in hospitals, nursing homes and homes for the aged, alienated youth, the elderly and the poor, and in various areas of legal service to the indigent, of education and campus ministry.

National Association of Diaconate Directors: Membership organization of directors, vicars and other staff personnel of diaconate programs. Established in 1977 to promote effective communication and facilitate the exchange of information and resources of members; to develop professional expertise and promote research, training and self evaluation; to foster accountability and seek ways to promote means of implementing solutions to problems. The association is governed by an executive board of elected officers.

Ordination of Women

The Catholic Church believes and teaches that, in fidelity to the will of Christ, it cannot ordain women to the priesthood. This position has been set out over the last quarter-century in a series of authoritative documents published by or with the authority of Pope Paul VI and Pope John Paul II.

The first of these, *Inter Insigniores* ("Among the Characteristics"), was issued by the Congregation for the Doctrine of the Faith in October, 1976. Its central statement is: "The Sacred Congregation for the Doctrine of the Faith judges it necessary to recall that the Church, in fidelity to the example of the Lord, does not consider herself authorized to admit women to priestly ordination."

In support of this, the document cited the constant tradition of the Church, the fact that Christ called only men to be Apostles and the continuation of this practice by the Apostles themselves, and the sacramental appropriateness of a male priesthood acting *in persona Christi*— in the person of Christ.

Pope Paul reaffirmed the teaching set out in *Inter Insigniores* in an address the following year, calling it part of the Church's "fundamental constitution" as it is given by Christ.

In light of continuing discussion, Pope John Paul II returned to the subject in the apostolic letter *Ordinatio Sacerdotalis* ("Priestly Ordination"), issued May 29, 1994. He reaffirmed the position stated by Paul VI, and said the fact that the Blessed Virgin was not ordained a priest makes it clear that restricting ordination to men does not lessen the dignity of women or discriminate against them. Ordination is not a means of access to power, he pointed out; rather, the Church's hierarchical structure is entirely oriented to the "holiness of the faithful."

John Paul continued: "Wherefore, in order that all doubt may be removed regarding a matter of great importance, a matter which pertains to the Church's divine constitution itself, in virtue of my ministry of confirming the brethren (cf. Luke 22.32) I declare that the Church has no authority whatsoever to confer priestly ordination on women and that this judgment is to be definitively held by all the Church's faithful."

The Congregation for the Doctrine of the Faith followed this on October 28, 1995, with a response, published over the signature of its Prefect, Cardinal Joseph Ratzinger, to a bishop's inquiry concerning how "to be held definitively" should be understood. The response was:

"This teaching requires definitive assent, since, founded on the written Word of God and from the beginning constantly preserved and applied in the Tradition of the Church, it has been set forth infallibly by the ordinary and universal Magisterium (cf. Second Vatican Council, Dogmatic Constitution on the Church *Lumen Gentium*, 25, 2). Thus, in the present circumstances, the Roman Pontiff, exercising his proper office of confirming the brethren (cf. Luke 22.32), has handed on this same teaching by a formal declaration, explicitly stating that it is to be held always, everywhere, and by all, as belonging to the deposit of faith."

Apparently it remains an open question at this time whether women could be ordained as deacons.

MATRIMONY

Marriage Doctrine

The following excerpts, stating key points of doctrine on marriage, are from *Gaudium et Spes*, (Nos. 48 to 51) promulgated by the Second Vatican Council:

Conjugal Covenant

The intimate partnership of married life and love has been established by the Creator and qualified by his laws. It is rooted in the conjugal covenant of irrevocable personal consent. God himself is the author of matrimony, endowed as it is with various benefits and purposes. All of these have a very decisive bearing on the continuation of the human race, on the personal development and eternal destiny of the individual members of a family, and on the dignity, stability, peace, and prosperity of the family itself and of human society as a whole. By their very nature, the institution of matrimony itself and conjugal love are ordained for the procreation and education of children, and find in them their ultimate crown.

Thus a man and a woman render mutual help and service to each other through an intimate union of their persons and of their actions. Through this union they experience the meaning of their oneness and attain to it with growing perfection day by day. As a mutual gift of two persons, this intimate union, as well as the good of the children, imposes total fidelity on the spouses and argues for an unbreakable oneness between them (No. 48).

Sacrament of Matrimony

Christ the Lord abundantly blessed this many-faceted love. The Savior of men and the Spouse of the Church comes into the lives of married Christians through the sacrament of matrimony. He abides with them thereafter so that, just as he loved the Church and handed himself over on her behalf, the spouses may love each other with perpetual fidelity through mutual self-bestowal.

Graced with the dignity and office of fatherhood and motherhood, parents will energetically acquit themselves of a duty which devolves primarily on them; namely, education, and especially religious education.

The Christian family, which springs from marriage as a reflection of the loving covenant uniting Christ with the Church, and as a participation in that covenant, will manifest to all men the Savior's living presence in the world, and the genuine nature of the Church (No. 48).

Conjugal Love

The biblical Word of God several times urges the betrothed and the married to nourish and develop their wedlock by pure conjugal love and undivided affection.

This love is an eminently human one since it is directed from one person to another through an affection of the will. It involves the good of the whole person. Therefore it can enrich the expressions of body and mind with a unique dignity, ennobling these expressions as special ingredients and signs of the friendship distinctive of marriage. This love the Lord has judged worthy of special gifts, healing, perfecting, and exalting gifts of grace and of charity.

Such love, merging the human with the divine, leads the spouses to a free and mutual gift of themselves, a gift proving itself by gentle affection and by deed. Such love pervades the whole of their lives. Indeed, by its generous activity it grows better and grows greater. Therefore it far excels mere erotic inclination, which, selfishly pursued, soon enough fades wretchedly away.

This love is uniquely expressed and perfected through the marital act. The actions within marriage by which the couple are united intimately and chastely are noble and worthy ones. Expressed in a manner which is truly human, these actions signify and promote that mutual self-giving by which spouses enrich each other with a joyful and a thankful will.

Sealed by mutual faithfulness and hallowed above all by Christ's sacrament, this love remains steadfastly true in body and in mind, in bright days or dark. It will never be profaned by adultery or divorce. Firmly established by the Lord, the unity of marriage will radiate from the equal personal dignity of wife and husband, a dignity acknowledged by mutual and total love.

The steady fulfillment of the duties of this Christian vocation demands notable virtue. For this reason, strengthened by grace for holiness of life, the couple will painstakingly cultivate and pray for constancy of love, largeheartedness, and the spirit of sacrifice (No. 49).

Fruitfulness of Marriage

Marriage and conjugal love are by their nature ordained toward the begetting and educating of children. Children are really the supreme gift of marriage and contribute very substantially to the welfare of their parents. God himself wished to share with man a certain special participation in his own creative work. Thus he blessed male and female, saying: "Increase and multiply" (Gn. 1:28).

Hence, while not making the other purposes of matrimony of less account, the true practice of conjugal love, and the whole meaning of the family life which results from it, have this aim: that the couple be ready with stout hearts to cooperate with the love of the Creator and the Savior, who through them will enlarge and enrich his own family day by day.

Parents should regard as their proper mission the task of transmitting human life and educating those to whom it has been transmitted. They should realize that they are thereby cooperators with the love of God the Creator, and are, so to speak, the interpreters of that love. Thus they will fulfill their task with human and Christian responsibility (No. 50).

Norms of Judgment

They will thoughtfully take into account both their own welfare and that of their children, those already born and those who may be foreseen. For this accounting they will reckon with both the material and the spiritual conditions of the times as well as of their state in life. Finally, they will consult the interests of the family group, of temporal society, and of the Church herself.

The parents themselves should ultimately make this judgment in the sight of God. But in their manner of acting, spouses should be aware that they cannot proceed arbitrarily. They must always be governed according to a conscience dutifully conformed to the divine law itself, and should be submissive toward the Church's teaching office, which authentically interprets that law in the light of the Gospel. That divine law reveals and protects the integral meaning of conjugal love, and impels it toward a truly human fulfillment.

Marriage, to be sure, is not instituted solely for procreation. Rather, its very nature as an unbreakable compact between persons, and the welfare of the children, both demand that the mutual love of the spouses, too, be embodied in a rightly ordered manner, that it grow and ripen. Therefore, marriage persists as a whole manner and communion of life, and maintains its value and indissolubility, even when offspring are lacking — despite, rather often, the very intense desire of the couple (No. 50).

Love and Life

This Council realizes that certain modern conditions often keep couples from arranging their married lives harmoniously, and that they find themselves in circumstances where at least temporarily the size of their families should not be increased. As a result, the faithful exercise of love and the full intimacy of their lives are hard to maintain. But where the intimacy of married life is broken off, it is not rare for its faithfulness to be imperiled and its quality of fruitfulness ruined. For then the upbringing of the children and the courage to accept new ones are both endangered.

To these problems there are those who presume to offer dishonorable solutions. Indeed, they do not recoil from the taking of life. But the Church issues the reminder that a true contradiction cannot exist between the divine laws pertaining to the transmission of life and those pertaining to the fostering of authentic conjugal love.

Church Teaching

For God, the Lord of Life, has conferred on men the surpassing ministry of safeguarding life — a ministry which must be fulfilled in a manner which is worthy of men. Therefore from the moment of its conception life must be guarded with the greatest care, while abortion and infanticide are unspeakable crimes. The sexual characteristics of man and the human faculty of reproduction wonderfully exceed the dispositions of lower forms of life. Hence the acts themselves which are proper to conjugal love and which are exercised in accord with genuine human dignity must be honored with great reverence (No. 51).

Therefore when there is question of harmonizing conjugal love with the responsible transmission of life, the moral aspect of any procedure does not depend solely on the sincere intentions or on an evaluation of motives. It must be determined by objective standards. These, based on the nature of the human person and his acts, preserve the full sense of mutual self-giving and human

Ojibwa Tabernacle — Arbre Cross (Cross Village)
Michigan, 1846

procreation in the context of true love. Such a goal cannot be achieved unless the virtue of conjugal chastity is sincerely practiced. Relying on these principles, sons of the Church may not undertake methods of regulating procreation which are found blameworthy by the teaching authority of the Church in its unfolding of the divine law.

Everyone should be persuaded that human life and the task of transmitting it are not realities bound up with this world alone. Hence they cannot be measured or perceived only in terms of it, but always have a bearing on the eternal destiny of men (No. 51).

Humanae Vitae

Marriage doctrine and morality were the subjects of the encyclical letter *Humanae Vitae* ("Of Human Life"), issued by Pope Paul VI, July 29, 1968. *Humanae Vitae* was given reaffirmation and its teaching restated and defended by Pope John Paul II in his encyclical *Evangelium Vitae* (*The Gospel of Life*, 1995). Following are a number of key excerpts from *Humanae Vitae*, which was framed in the pattern of traditional teaching and statements by the Second Vatican Council.

Each and every marriage act (*"quilibet matrimonii usus"*) must remain open to the transmission of life (No. 11).

Indeed, by its intimate structure, the conjugal act, while most closely uniting husband and wife, capacitates them for the generation of new lives according to laws inscribed in the very being of man and of woman. By safeguarding both these essential aspects, the unitive and the procreative, the conjugal act preserves in its fullness the sense of true mutual love and its ordination toward man's most high calling to parenthood (No. 12).

It is, in fact, justly observed that a conjugal act imposed upon one's partner without regard for his or her condition and lawful desires is not a true act of love, and therefore denies an exigency of right moral order in the relationships between husband and wife. Hence, one who reflects well must also recognize that a reciprocal act of love which jeopardizes the responsibility to transmit life — which God the Creator, according to particular laws, inserted therein — is in contradiction with the design constitutive of marriage and with the will of the Author of life. To use this divine gift, destroying, even if only partially, its meaning and its purpose, is to contradict the nature both of man and of woman and of their most intimate relationship, and therefore it is to contradict also the plan of God and his will (No. 13).

Forbidden Actions

The direct interruption of the generative process already begun, and, above all, directly willed and procured abortion, even if for therapeutic reasons, are to be absolutely excluded as licit means of regulating birth.

Equally to be excluded is direct sterilization, whether perpetual or temporary, whether of the man or of the woman. Similarly excluded is every action which, either in anticipation of the conjugal act, or in its accomplishment, or in the development of its natural consequences, proposes, whether as an end or as a means, to render procreation impossible.

To justify conjugal acts made intentionally infecund, one cannot invoke as valid reasons the lesser evil, or the fact that such acts would constitute a whole together with the fecund acts already performed or to follow later and hence would share in one and the same moral goodness. In truth, if it is sometimes licit to tolerate a lesser evil in order to avoid a greater evil or to promote a greater good, it is not licit, even for the gravest reasons, to do evil so that good may follow therefrom; that is, to make into the object of a positive act of the will something which is intrinsically disorder, and hence unworthy of the human person, even when the intention is to safeguard or promote individual, family or social well-being.

Consequently, it is an error to think that a conjugal act which is deliberately made infecund, and so is intrinsically dishonest, could be made honest and right by the ensemble of a fecund conjugal life (No. 14).

If, then, there are serious motives to space out births, which derive from the physical or psychological conditions of husband and wife, or from external conditions, the Church teaches that it is then licit to take into account the natural rhythms immanent in the generative functions, for the use of marriage in the infecund periods only, and in this way to regulate birth without offending earlier stated principles (No. 16).

Pastoral Concerns

We do not at all intend to hide the sometimes serious difficulties inherent in the life of Christian married persons; for them, as for everyone else, "the gate is narrow and the way is hard that leads to life." But the hope of that life must illuminate their way, as with courage they strive to live with wisdom, justice and piety in this present time, knowing that the figure of this world passes away.

Let married couples then, face up to the efforts needed, supported by the faith and hope which "do not disappoint because God's love has been poured into our hearts through the Holy Spirit, who has been given to us." Let them implore divine assistance by persevering prayer; above all, let them draw from the source of grace and charity in the Eucharist. And, if sin should still keep its hold over them, let them not be discouraged but rather have recourse with humble perseverance to the mercy of God, which is poured forth in the sacrament of penance (No. 25).

Marriage Laws

The Catholic Church claims jurisdiction over its members in matters pertaining to marriage. which is a sacrament. Church legislation on the subject is stated principally in 111 canons of the Code of Canon Law.

Catholics are bound by all marriage laws of the Church. Non-Catholics, whether baptized or not, are not considered bound by these ecclesiastical laws except in cases of marriage with a Catholic. Certain natural laws, in the Catholic view, bind all men and women, irrespective of their religious beliefs; accordingly, marriage is prohibited before the time of puberty, without knowledge and free mutual consent, in the case of an already existing valid marriage bond, in the case of antecedent and perpetual impotence.

Premarital instructions are the subject matter of Pre-Cana Conferences.

Marital Consent

Matrimonial consent can be invalidated by an essential defect, substantial error, the strong influence of force and fear, the presence of a condition or intention against the nature of marriage.

Form of Marriage

A Catholic is required, for validity and lawfulness, to contract marriage — with another Catholic or with a non-Catholic — in the presence of a competent priest or deacon and two witnesses.

There are two exceptions to this law. A Roman-rite Catholic (since March 25, 1967) or an Eastern Rite Catholic (since November 21, 1964) can contract marriage validly in the presence of a priest of a separated Eastern-rite Church, provided other requirements of law are complied with. With permission of the competent Roman Rite or Eastern Rite bishop, this form of marriage is lawful, as well as valid. (See Eastern-rite Laws, below.)

With these two exceptions, and aside from cases covered by special permission, the Church does not regard as valid any marriages involving Catholics which take place before non-Catholic ministers of religion or civil officials.

(An excommunication formerly in force against Catholics who celebrated marriage before a non-Catholic minister was abrogated in a decree issued by the Sacred Congregation for the Doctrine of the Faith on March 18, 1966.)

The ordinary place of marriage is the parish of either Catholic party or of the Catholic party in case of a mixed marriage.

Church law regarding the form of marriage does not affect non-Catholics in marriages among themselves. The Church recognizes as valid the marriages of non-Catholics before ministers of religion and civil officials, unless they are rendered null and void on other grounds.

The canonical form is not to be observed in the case of a marriage between a non-Catholic and a baptized Catholic who has left the Church by a formal act.

Impediments

Diriment Impediments to marriage are factors which render a marriage invalid.

- age, which obtains before completion of the fourteenth year for a woman and the sixteenth year for a man;
- impotency, if it is antecedent to the marriage and permanent (this differs from sterility, which is not an impediment);
- the bond of an existing valid marriage;
- disparity of worship, which obtains when one party is a Catholic and the other party is unbaptized;
- sacred orders;
- religious profession of the perpetual vow of chastity;
- abduction, which impedes the freedom of the person abducted;
- crime, variously involving elements of adultery, promise or attempt to marry, conspiracy to murder a husband or wife;
- blood relationship in the direct line (father-daughter, mother-son, etc.) and to the fourth degree inclusive of the collateral line (brother-sister, first cousins);
- affinity, or relationship resulting from a valid marriage, in any degree of the direct line;
- public honesty, arising from an invalid marriage or from public or notorious concubinage; it renders either party incapable of marrying blood relatives of the other in the first degree of the direct line.
- legal relationship arising from adoption; it renders either party incapable of marrying relatives of the other in the direct line or in the second degree of the collateral line.

Dispensations from Impediments: Persons hindered by impediments cannot marry unless they are dispensed therefrom in view of reasons recognized in canon law. Local bishops can dispense from the impediments most often encountered (e.g., disparity of worship) as well as others.

Decision regarding some dispensations is reserved to the Holy See.

Separation

A valid and consummated marriage of baptized persons cannot be dissolved by any human authority or any cause other than the death of one of the persons.

In other circumstances:

1. A valid but unconsummated marriage of baptized persons, or of a baptized and an unbaptized person, can be dissolved:
   a. by the solemn religious profession of one of the persons, made with permission of the pope. In such a case, the bond is dissolved at the time of profession, and the other person is free to marry again.
   b. by dispensation from the pope, requested for a grave reason by one or both of the persons. If the dispensation is granted, both persons are free to marry again.

   Dispensations in these cases are granted for reasons connected with the spiritual welfare of the concerned persons.

2. A legitimate marriage, even consummated, of unbaptized persons can be dissolved in favor of one of them who subsequently receives the sacrament of baptism. This is the Pauline Privilege, so called because it was promulgated by St. Paul (1 Cor. 7:12-15) as a means of protecting the faith of converts. Requisites for granting the privilege are:
   a. marriage prior to the baptism of either person;
   b. reception of baptism by one person;
   c. refusal of the unbaptized person to live in peace with the baptized person and without interfering with his or her freedom to practice the Christian faith. The privilege does not apply if the unbaptized person agrees to these conditions.

3. A legitimate and consummated marriage of a baptized and an unbaptized person can be dissolved by the pope in virtue of the Privilege of Faith, also called the Petrine Privilege.

Civil Divorce

Because of the unity and the indissolubility of marriage, the Church denies that civil divorce can break the bond of a valid marriage, whether the marriage involves two Catholics, a Catholic and a non-Catholic, or non-Catholics with each other.

In view of serious circumstances of marital distress, the Church permits an innocent and aggrieved party, whether wife or husband, to seek and obtain a civil divorce for the purpose of acquiring title and right to the civil effects of divorce, such as separate habitation and maintenance, and the custody of children. Permission for this kind of action should be obtained from proper church authority. The divorce, if obtained, does not break the bond of a valid marriage.

Under other circumstances — as would obtain if a marriage was invalid (see Annulment, below) — civil divorce is permitted for civil effects and as a civil ratification of the fact that the marriage bond really does not exist.

Annulment

This is a decision by a competent church authority — e.g., a bishop, a diocesan marriage tribunal, the Roman Rota — that an apparently valid marriage was actually invalid from the beginning because of the unknown or concealed existence, from the beginning, of a diriment impediment, an essential defect in consent, radical incapability for marriage, or a condition placed by one or both of the parties against the very nature of marriage.

Eastern-rite Laws

Marriage laws of the Eastern Church differ in several respects from the legislation of the Roman rite. The regulations in effect since May 2, 1949, were contained in the *motu proprio Crebre Allatae* issued by Pius XII the previous February.

According to both the Roman Code of Canon Law and the Oriental Code, marriages between Roman-rite Catholics and Eastern-rite Catholics ordinarily take place in the rite of the groom and have canonical effects in that rite.

Regarding the form for the celebration of marriages between Eastern Catholics and baptized Eastern non-Catholics, the Second Vatican Council declared:

"By way of preventing invalid marriages between Eastern Catholics and baptized Eastern non-Catholics, and in the interests of the permanence and sanctity of marriage and of domestic harmony, this sacred Synod decrees that the canonical 'form' for the celebration of such marriages obliges only for lawfulness. For their validity, the presence of a sacred minister suffices, as long as the other requirements of law are honored" (Decree on Eastern Catholic Churches, No. 18).

Marriages taking place in this manner are lawful, as well as valid, with permission of a competent Eastern-rite bishop.

The Rota

The Roman Rota is the ordinary court of appeal for marriage, and some other cases, which are appealed to the Holy See from lower church courts. Appeals are made to the Rota if decisions by diocesan and archdiocesan courts fail to settle the matter in dispute. Pope John Paul II, at annual meetings with Rota personnel, speaks about the importance of the court's actions in providing norms of practice for other tribunals.

Mixed Marriages

"Mixed Marriages" (*Matrimonia Mixta*) was the subject of: (1) a letter issued under this title by Pope Paul VI March 31, 1970, and (2) a statement, Implementation of the Apostolic Letter on Mixed Marriages, approved by the National Conference of Catholic Bishops November 16, 1970.

One of the key points in the bishops' statement referred to the need for mutual pastoral care by ministers of different faiths for the sacredness of marriage and for appropriate preparation and continuing support of parties to a mixed marriage.

Pastoral experience, which the Catholic Church shares with other religious bodies, confirms the fact that marriages of persons of different beliefs involve special problems related to the continuing religious practice of the concerned persons and to the religious education and formation of their children.

Pastoral measures to minimize these problems include instruction of a non-Catholic party in essentials of the Catholic faith for purposes of understanding. Desirably, some instruction should also be given the Catholic party regarding his or her partner's beliefs.

Requirements

The Catholic party to a mixed marriage is required to declare his (her) intention of continuing practice of the Catholic faith and to promise to do all in his (her) power to share his (her) faith with children born of the marriage by having them baptized and raised as Catholics. No declarations or promises are required of the non-Catholic party, but he (she) must be informed of the declaration and promise made by the Catholic.

Notice of the Catholic's declaration and promise is an essential part of the application made to a bishop for (1) permission to marry a baptized non-Catholic, or (2) a dispensation to marry an unbaptized non-Catholic.

A mixed marriage can take place with a Nuptial Mass. (The bishops' statement added this caution: "To the extent that Eucharistic sharing is not permitted by the general discipline of the Church, this is to be considered when plans are being made to have the mixed marriage at Mass or not.")

The ordinary minister at a mixed marriage is an authorized priest or deacon, and the ordinary place is the parish church of the Catholic party. A non-Catholic minister may not only attend the marriage ceremony but may also address, pray with and bless the couple.

For appropriate pastoral reasons, a bishop can grant a dispensation from the Catholic form of marriage and can permit the marriage to take place in a non-Catholic church with a non-Catholic minister as the officiating minister. A priest may not only attend such a ceremony but may also address, pray with and bless the couple.

"It is not permitted," however, the bishops' statement declared, "to have two religious services or to have a single service in which both the Catholic marriage ritual and a non-Catholic marriage ritual are celebrated jointly or successively."

Pastoral Ministry for Divorced and Remarried

Ministry to divorced and remarried Catholics is a difficult field of pastoral endeavor, situated as it is in circumstances tantamount to the horns of a dilemma.

At Issue

On the one side is firm church teaching on the permanence of marriage and norms against reception of the Eucharist and full participation in the life of the Church by Catholics in irregular unions.

On the other side are men and women with broken unions followed by second and perhaps happier attempts at marriage which the Church does not recognize as valid and which may not be capable of being validated because of the existence of an earlier marriage bond.

Factors involved in these circumstances are those of the Church, upholding its doctrine and practice regarding the permanence of marriage, and those of many men and women in irregular second marriages who desire full participation in the life of the Church.

Sacramental participation is not possible for those whose first marriage was valid, although there is no bar to their attendance at Mass, to sharing in other activities of the Church, or to their efforts to have children baptized and raised in the Catholic faith.

An exception to this rule is the condition of a divorced and remarried couple living in a brother-sister relationship.

There is no ban against sacramental participation by separated or divorced persons who have not attempted a second marriage, provided the usual conditions for reception of the sacraments are in order.

Unverified estimates of the number of U.S. Catholics who are divorced and remarried vary between six and eight million.

Tribunal Action

What can the Church do for them and with them in pastoral ministry, is an old question charged with new urgency because of the rising number of divorced and remarried Catholics.

One way to help is through the agency of marriage tribunals charged with responsibility for investigating and settling questions concerning the validity or invalidity of a prior marriage. There are reasons in canon law justifying the Church in declaring a particular marriage null and void from the beginning, despite the short- or long-term existence of an apparently valid union.

Decrees of nullity (annulments) are not new in the history of the Church. If such a decree is issued, a man or woman is free to validate a second marriage and live in complete union with the Church.

Reasons behind Decrees

Pastoral experience reveals that some married persons, a short or long time after contracting an apparently valid marriage, exhibit signs that point back to the existence, at the time of marriage, of latent and serious personal deficiencies which made them incapable of valid consent and sacramental commitment.

Such deficiencies might include gross immaturity and those affecting in a serious way the capacity to love, to have a true interpersonal and conjugal relationship, to fulfill marital obligations, to accept the faith aspect of marriage.

Psychological and behavioral factors like these have been given greater attention by tribunals in recent years and have provided grounds for numerous decrees of nullity.

Decisions of this type do not indicate any softening of the Church's attitude regarding the permanence of marriage. They affirm, rather, that some persons who have married were really not capable of doing so.

Serious deficiencies in the capacity for real interpersonal relationship in marriage were the reasons behind a landmark decree of nullity issued in 1973 by the Roman Rota, the Vatican high court of appeals in marriage cases. Pope John Paul referred to such deficiencies — the "grave lack of discretionary judgment," incapability of assuming "essential matrimonial rights and obligations," for example — in an address January 26, 1984, to personnel of the Rota.

The tribunal way to a decree of nullity regarding a previous marriage, however, is not open to many persons in second marriages — because grounds are either lacking or, if present, cannot be verified in tribunal process.

Unacceptable Solutions

One unacceptable solution of the problem, called "good conscience procedure," involves administration of the sacraments of penance and the Eucharist to divorced and remarried Catholics unable to obtain a decree of nullity for a first marriage who are living in a subsequent marriage "in good faith."

This procedure, despite the fact that it has no standing or recognition in church law, is being advocated and practiced by some priests and remarried Catholics.

Conditions for Receiving Communion

Practically speaking, "when for serious reasons — for example, for the children's upbringing — a man and a woman cannot satisfy the obligation to separate," they may be admitted to Communion if "they take on themselves the duty to live in complete continence, that is, by abstinence from the acts proper to married couples. In such a case they may receive holy Communion as long as they respect the obligation to avoid giving scandal."

The teaching of the Church on this subject "does not mean that the Church does not take to heart the situation of those faithful who, moreover, are not excluded from ecclesial communion. She is concerned to accompany them pastorally and invite them to share in the life of the Church in the measure that is compatible with the dispositions of divine law, from which the Church has no power to dispense. On the other hand, it is necessary to instruct these faithful so that they do not think their participation in the life of the Church is reduced exclusively to the question of the reception of the Eucharist. The faithful are to be helped to deepen their understanding of the value of sharing in the sacrifice of Christ in the Mass, or spiritual communion, of prayer, of meditation on the word of God, and of works of charity and justice."

Part 9

THE COMMUNION OF SAINTS

The sheer magnitude of saints in the Church demonstrates not only the universality of the Catholic faith but the centuries of mortal time in which men and women have confessed their beliefs and imitated Christ in their activities. These saints stand as representatives of entire generations of human beings who went to the far-flung corners of the world to preach the "Good News" of the Gospel, to care for the abandoned, the sick, and the poor, or to remain in cloisters to offer unceasing praise to Almighty God.

The panoramas of genuine heroism, perseverance, endurance, and loyalty that come to life in these entries about the saints is staggering. The saints were rich or poor, titled or unknown, living on every continent in all of the ages of the Christian era in the world.

The Process of Canonization

Through the process of beatification and canonization, a deceased member of the Church is granted definitive recognition of his or her heroic sanctity. Beatification is the tentative decision to permit limited veneration and culminates in full canonization, by which an irrevocable decree is issued by the pope prescribing universal veneration. In canonizing a person, the pope speaks infallibly and for the whole Church, under the guidance of the Holy Spirit. The person's name is entered in the canon of the saints, listing all who are to receive veneration universally in the Church. Canonization is an earthly decision, which means that it has nothing to do with the actual entry of a saint into heaven. The act merely removes all doubt about the validity of honoring the saint on earth.

Liturgical law definitely determines the acts of public cult by which a canonized saint may receive veneration. Specifically, the saints may be invoked in the public and official prayers of the Church offered for them; churches may be built in their honor; altars dedicated in their honor; the Mass celebrated; the Divine Office recited; a feast day is set aside to their memory; and they may be designated as special patrons.

Owing to the deep spiritual significance of the saints and their roles as models of Christian life and intercessors with God, the steps by which a person becomes a saint are carefully executed by the Church and follow a meticulous investigation. This scrutiny is called the process of canonization. It is an ancient custom and has undergone many changes and reforms through the centuries.

The process of canonization has its origins in the very early formulation of the Christian doctrines of worship (*cultus*), invocation, and intercession. Catholics give adoration to God alone, called worship or *latria*. Honor and reverence, *dulia*, is accorded the saints, and an elevated form of this honor and reverence, *hyperdulia*, is given to the Blessed Virgin Mary.

St. Paul and the other apostles beseeched men on earth to pray for them, and the Church gradually began to invoke the prayers of the saints and martyrs in heaven. In 451, at the council of Chalcedon, the Fathers announced: "Flavianus lives after death! May the martyr pray for us." The Church in Smyrna (modern Izmir, Turkey), celebrated February 23 as the day on which St. Polycarp suffered martyrdom, stating:

We have at last gathered his bones, which are dearer than priceless gems and purer than gold, and laid them to rest where it was befitting they should lie . . . may God grant us to celebrate the birthday of his martyrdom with gladness, thus to recall the memory of those who fought in the glorious combat, and to teach and strengthen by his example, those who shall come after us. . . .

While St. Polycarp and other victors of the "glorious combat" were venerated privately, such public displays required ecclesiastical approval. The increased public veneration required some central authority to insure that the respect paid to the saints was not improperly conducted or that veneration was not given to someone of imperfect sanctity. The technical term for this proper authority is vindication, denoting the approval of the bishop, which was bestowed – after some inquiry – upon some cults within a diocese and withheld from others. Vindication became the forerunner of the process of beatification.

In time, the local worship of the saints and martyrs passed from one region to another with the permission of those jurisdictions. Indeed, St. Lawrence, St. Cyprian of Carthage, and Pope St. Sixtus I of Rome (r. 115-125) were revered universally almost from the start, as their cults spread rapidly from one Christian community to another with ecclesiastical support. The veneration of saints and martyrs eventually became the concern of the Holy See, which took upon itself the proper determination of saints' cults for the universal

Church, an assumption which became the foundation for the modern process of canonization.

In the fourth century, men and women called "confessors," those who died peacefully after a life of heroic virtue, were honored in public displays alongside the martyrs. Originally these "confessors" were individuals who preached the faith before tyrants and enemies of Christ, suffering punishment as a result. By the fourth century, the "confessors" included those who had displayed sanctity and had died in holy peace. This definition is still in use.

By 848, the feasts of such "confessors" as Sts. Martin and Remigius were listed by the council of Mainz. Missals and breviaries from that early period contain public commemorations of "confessors" and ascetics. Local observances spread, and in time, the acceptance of the cults by the Bishop of Rome made them universal in their applications. The first formal canonization for the entire Church came in 993, when Pope John XV (r. 985-996) raised Ulric of Augsburg to the altars during a synod at the Lateran Basilica. Further centralization by papal authority proved necessary in succeeding centuries owing to laxity in local vindications in which individuals, after further investigation, were found to be of imperfect sanctity.

In early periods, the process was concerned with little more than a cursory examination of a person's life and miracles. In 1512, Julius II (r. 1503-1513) made formal the difference between beatification and canonization. In 1634, Pope Urban VIII (r. 1623-1644) decreed that the Holy See alone maintained the right of beatification and canonization. During the eleventh century, the acceptance of miracles became dependent upon eyewitness accounts. Even more legal requirements were instituted during the Middle Ages. Pope Urban II (r. 1088-1099), and a little later Popes Callixtus II (r. 1119-1124), and Eugenius III (r. 1145-1153) ruled that the virtues and miracles of individuals proposed for public veneration should be examined in episcopal councils.

The basic process of canonization laid down during this period and codified by Pope Benedict XIV (r. 1740-1758) remained unchanged in most particulars into modern times. The oversight of the process was placed in 1588 into the hands of the Congregation of Rites which was established by Pope Sixtus V (r. 1585-1590) as part of his extensive reforms of the Roman Curia and his foundation of the so-called Sacred Congregations. The Congregation of Rites was renamed the Congregation for the Causes of Saints (*Congregatio de Causis Sanctorum*) and reorganized in 1969 by Pope Paul VI (r. 1963-1978) through the apostolic constitution *Regimini Ecclesiae Universae*. Further reforms were implemented by Pope John Paul II (r. 1978-) through his 1983 apostolic constitution *Divinus Prefectionis Magistro*. One of the chief reforms introduced by the pope was to widen the authority and role of local bishops in the initial determination of candidates for canonization.

Local bishops, the heads of the individual dioceses around the world, now initiate investigations and the gathering of proper sanctity. Each bishop does so in consultation with other bishops of the region, appointing officials to study the life and/or martyrdom and the virtues of the proposed candidate. Eyewitness accounts are taken as to the life, labors, and purity of the individual being considered. All phases of the individual's existence are documented, and such findings are submitted to Rome.

If the Congregation for the Causes of Saints agrees with the local findings, the man or woman being considered is given the title "Servant of God." The cause is opened in Rome, and two officials are appointed: The realtor and the postulator. The realtor (or relator, reporter, and also called the *advocatus diaboli*, or devil's advocate) is assigned the task of assembling the historic documentation of the particular location and era of the candidate. In other words, the realtor must research the history of each place, era, and social milieu pertinent to the candidate's life. The postulator, taken from the Latin for *postulare*, asking or requesting, serves as the guiding force of the cause, moving it through the various stages of the process.

Sts. Francis and Clare

The Congregation reviews the documentation presented, and a panel under the direction of the *Promotore Generale della Fide*, the prelate theologian, studies the cause. The *Promotore* then submits the approval of the panel to a group of thirty prelates for their consideration. Miracles are required for each step of the process, from venerable status to canonization, and these miracles must be authenticated by competent sources, such as medical practitioners and competent consultations. Pope John Paul II has revised the necessity for a martyr's canonization. Other aspects involved in the consideration include study of prior beatification of a candidate for sainthood, instances of heroic faith, and special circumstances involving discrepancies or inconsistencies in the candidate's life or preserved writings. Normally these investigations and studies require a considerable amount of time, although the pontificate of Pope John Paul II has provided a certain impetus to beatification and canonization.

Since 1969, some cults have been confined to local calendars or discontinued entirely. This is an effort to update causes and cults and to bring them into line with modern scientific and historical verifications. Some saints, popular as they may have been over the centuries, were not recorded with any verifiable authenticity. Legends, mistaken identities, repetitions, and local folk tales have blurred the facts in some of the individuals from truly ancient eras. The changes thus made do not imply a lack of veneration, but a new approach to saints that demands clearer authenticity and proof.

SAINTS OF THE CHURCH

An asterisk with a feast date indicates that the saint is listed in the General Roman Calendar or the proper calendar for U.S. dioceses.

Adalbert (956-997): Born in Bohemia; bishop of Prague; Benedictine; missionary in Poland, Prussia and Hungary; martyred by Prussians near Danzig; April 23.*

Adjutor (d. 1131): Norman knight; fought in First Crusade; monk-recluse after his return; April 30.

Agatha (d. c. 250): Sicilian virgin-martyr; her intercession credited in Sicily with stilling eruptions of Mt. Etna; patron of nurses; February 5.*

Agnes (d. c. 304): Roman virgin-martyr; martyred at age of 10 or 12; patron of young girls; January 21.*

Aloysius Gonzaga (1568-1591): Italian Jesuit; died while nursing plague-stricken; canonized 1726; patron of youth; June 21.*

Amand (d. c. 676): Apostle of Belgium; b. France; established monasteries throughout Belgium; February 6.

André Bessette, Blessed (Bro. André) (1845-1937): Canadian Holy Cross Brother; prime mover in building of St. Joseph's Oratory, Montreal; beatified May 23, 1982; January 6* (U.S.).

André Grasset de Saint Sauveur, Blessed (1758-1792): Canadian priest; martyred in France, September 2, 1792, during the Revolution; one of a group called the Martyrs of Paris who were beatified in 1926; September 2.

Andrew Bobola (1592-1657): Polish Jesuit; joined Jesuits at Vilna; worked for return of Orthodox to union with Rome; martyred; canonized 1938; May 16.

Andrew Corsini (1302-1373): Italian Carmelite; bishop of Fiesoli; mediator between quarrelsome Italian states; canonized 1629; February 4.

Andrew Dung-Lac and Companions (d. 18th-19th c.): Martyrs of Vietnam. Total of 117 included 96 Vietnamese, 11 Spanish and 10 French missionaries (8 bishops; 50 priests, including Andrew Dung-Lac, 1 seminarian, 58 lay persons). Canonized June 19, 1988; inscribed in General Roman Calendar, 1989, as a memorial. November 24.*

Andrew Fournet (1752-1834): French priest; co-founder with St. Jeanne Elizabeth Bichier des Anges of the Daughters of the Holy Cross of St. Andrew; canonized 1933; May 13.

Andrew Kim, Paul Chong and Companions (d. between 1839-1867): Korean martyrs (103) killed in persecutions of 1839, 1846, 1866, and 1867; among them were Andrew Kim, the first Korean priest, and Paul Chong, lay apostle; canonized May 6, 1984, during Pope John Paul II's visit to Korea; entered into General Roman Calendar, 1985, as a memorial. September 20.*

Angela Merici (1474-1540): Italian secular Franciscan; foundress of Company of St. Ursula, 1535, the first teaching order of women Religious in the Church; canonized 1807, January 27.*

Angelico, Blessed (Fra Angelico; John of Faesulis) (1387-1455): Dominican; Florentine painter of early Renaissance; proclaimed blessed by John Paul II, February 3, 1982; patron of artists; February 18.

Anne Marie Javouhey, Blessed (1779-1851): French virgin; foundress of Institute of St. Joseph of Cluny, 1812; beatified 1950; July 15.

Ansgar (801-865): Benedictine monk; b. near Amiens; archbishop of Hamburg; missionary in Denmark, Sweden, Norway and northern Germany; apostle of Scandinavia; February 3.*

Anthony (c. 251-c. 354): Abbot; Egyptian hermit; patriarch of all monks; established communities for hermits which became models for monastic life, especially in the East; friend and supporter of St. Athanasius in the latter's struggle with the Arias; January 17.*

Anthony Claret (1807-1870): Spanish bishop; founder of Missionary Sons of the Immaculate Heart of Mary (Claretians), 1849; archbishop of Santiago, Cuba, 1851-57; canonized 1950; October 24.*

Anthony Gianelli (1789-1846): Italian bishop; founded the Daughters of Our Lady of the Garden, 1829; bishop of Bobbio, 1838; canonized 1951; June 7.

Anthony Zaccaria (1502-1539): Italian priest; founder of Barnabites (Clerks Regular of St. Paul), 1530; canonized 1897; July 5.*

Apollonia (d. 249): Deaconess of Alexandria; martyred during persecution of Decius; her patronage of dentists and those suffering from toothaches probably rests on tradition that her teeth were broken by her persecutors; February 9.

Augustine of Canterbury (d. 604 or 605): Italian missionary; apostle of the English; sent by Pope Gregory I with 40 monks to evangelize England; arrived there 597; first archbishop of Canterbury; May 27.*

Bartolomea Capitania (1807-1833): Italian foundress with Vincenza Gerosa of the Sisters of Charity of Lovere; canonized 1950; July 26.

Beatrice da Silva Meneses (1424-1490): Foundress, b. Portugal; founded Congregation of the Immaculate Conception, 1484, in Spain; canonized 1976; September 1.

Benedict Joseph Labré (1748-1783): French layman; pilgrim-beggar; noted for his piety and love of prayer before the Blessed Sacrament; canonized 1883; April 16.

Benedict of Nursia (c. 480-547): Abbot; founder of monasticism in Western Europe; established monastery at Monte Cassino; proclaimed patron of Europe by Paul VI in 1964; July 11.*

Benedict the Black *(il Moro)* (1526-1589): Sicilian Franciscan; born a slave; joined Franciscans as lay brother; appointed guardian and novice master; canonized 1807; April 3.

Bernadette Soubirous (1844-1879): French peasant girl favored with series of visions of Blessed Virgin Mary at Lourdes (see Lourdes Apparitions); joined Institute of Sisters of Notre Dame at Nevers, 1866; canonized 1933; April 16.

Bernard of Montjoux (or Menthon) (d. 1081): Augustinian canon; probably born in Italy; founded Alpine hospices near the two passes named for him; patron of mountaineers; May 28.

Bernardine of Feltre, Blessed (1439-1494): Italian Franciscan preacher; a founder of *montes pietatis*; September 28.

Bernardine of Siena (1380-1444): Italian Franciscan; noted preacher and missioner; spread of devotion to Holy Name is attributed to him; represented in art holding to his breast the monogram IHS; canonized 1450; May 20.*

Blase (d. c. 316): Armenian bishop; martyr; the blessing of throats on his feast day derives from tradition that he miraculously saved the life of a boy who had half-swallowed a fish bone; February 3.*

Boniface (Winfrid) (d. 754): English Benedictine; bishop; martyr; apostle of Germany; established monastery at Fulda which became center of missionary work in Germany; archbishop of Mainz; martyred near Dukkum in Holland; June 5.*

Brendan (c. 489-583): Irish abbot; founded monasteries; his patronage of sailors probably rests on a legend that he made a seven-year voyage in search of a fabled paradise; called Brendan the Navigator; May 16.

Bridget (Brigid) (c. 450-525): Irish nun; founded religious community at Kildare, the first in Ireland; patron, with Sts. Patrick and Columba, of Ireland; February 1.

Bridget (Birgitta) (c. 1303-1373): Swedish mystic; widow; foundress of Order of Our Savior (Brigittines); canonized 1391; patroness of Sweden; July 23.*

Bruno (1030-1101): German monk; founded Carthusians, 1084, in France; October 6.*

Cabrini, Mother: See Frances Xavier Cabrini.

Cajetan (Gaetano) **of Thiene** (1480-1547): Italian lawyer; religious reformer; a founder of Oratory of Divine Love, forerunner of the Theatines; canonized 1671; August 7.*

Callistus I (d. 222): Pope, 217-222; martyr; condemned Sabellianism and other heresies; advocated a policy of mercy toward repentant sinners; October 14.*

Camillus de Lellis (1550-1614): Italian priest; founder of Camillians (Ministers of the Sick); canonized 1746; patron of the sick and of nurses; July 14.*

Casimir (1458-1484): Polish prince; grand duke of Lithuania; noted for his piety; buried at cathedral in Vilna, Lithuania; canonized 1521; patron of Poland and Lithuania; March 4.*

Cassian of Tangier (d. 298): Roman martyr; an official court stenographer who declared himself a Christian; patron of stenographers; December 3.

Catherine Labouré (1806-1876): French Religious; favored with series of visions soon after she joined Sisters of Charity of St. Vincent de Paul in Paris in 1830; first Miraculous Medal (see Index) struck in 1832 in accord with one of the visions; canonized 1947; November 28.

Catherine of Bologna (1413-1463): Italian Poor Clare; mystic, writer, artist canonized 1712; patron of artists; May 9.

Cecilia (2nd-3rd century): Roman virgin-martyr; traditional patroness of musicians; November 22.*

Charles Borromeo (1538-1584): Italian cardinal; nephew of Pope Pius IV; cardinal bishop of Milan; influential figure in Church reform in Italy; promoted education of clergy; canonized 1610; November 4.*

Charles Lwanga and Companions (d. between 1885 and 1887): Twenty-two Martyrs of Uganda, many of them pages of King Mwanga of Uganda, who were put to death because they denounced his corrupt lifestyle; canonized 1964; first martyrs of black Africa; June 3.*

Charles of Sezze (1616-1670): Italian Franciscan lay brother who served in humble capacities; canonized 1959; January 6.

Christopher (3rd cent.): Early Christian martyr inscribed in Roman calendar about 1550; feast relegated to particular calendars because of legendary nature of accounts of his life; traditional patron of travelers; July 25.

Clare (1194-1253): Foundress of Poor Clares; b. at Assisi; was joined in religious life by her sisters, Agnes and Beatrice, and eventually her widowed mother Ortolana; canonized 1255; patroness of television; August 11.*

Claude de la Colombière (1641-1682): French Jesuit; spiritual director of St. Margaret Mary Alacoque; instrumental in spreading devotion to the Sacred Heart; beatified, 1929; canonized May 31, 1992; February 15.

Clement Hofbauer (1751-1820): Redemptorist priest, missionary; born in Moravia; helped spread Redemptorists north of the Alps; canonized 1909; March 15.

Clement I (d. c. 100): Pope, 88-97; third successor of St. Peter; wrote important letter to Church in Corinth settling disputes there; venerated as a martyr; November 23.*

Columba (521-597): Irish monk; founded monasteries in Ireland; missionary in Scotland; established monastery at Iona which became the center for conversion of Picts, Scots, and Northern English; Scotland's most famous saint; patron saint of Ireland (with Sts. Patrick and Brigid); June 9.

Columban (545-615): Irish monk; scholar; founded monasteries in England and Brittany (famous abbey of Luxeuil), forced into exile because of his criticism of Frankish court; spent last years in northern Italy where he founded abbey at Bobbio; November 23.*

Conrad of Parzham (1818-1894): Bavarian Capuchin lay brother; served as porter at the Marian shrine of Altotting in Upper Bavaria for 40 years; canonized 1934; April 21.

Contardo Ferrini, Blessed (1859-1902): Italian secular Franciscan; model of the Catholic professor; beatified 1947; patron of universities; October 20.

Cornelius (d. 253): Pope, 251-253; promoted a policy of mercy with respect to readmission of repentant Christians who had fallen away during the persecution of Decius (*lapsi*); banished from Rome during persecution of Gallus; regarded as a martyr; September 16 (with Cyprian).*

Cosmas and Damian (d. c. 303): Arabian twin brothers, physicians; martyred during Diocletian persecution; patrons of physicians; September 26.*

Crispin and Crispinian (3rd century): Early Christian martyrs; said to have met their deaths in Gaul; patrons of shoemakers, a trade they pursued; October 25.

Crispin of Viterbo (1668-1750): Capuchin brother; canonized June 20, 1982; May 21.

Cyprian (d. 258): Early ecclesiastical writer; b. Africa; bishop of Carthage, 249-258; supported Pope St. Cornelius concerning the readmission of Christians who had apostatized in time of persecution; erred in his teaching that baptism administered by heretics and schismatics was invalid; wrote *De Unitate*; September 16 (with St. Cornelius).*

Cyril and Methodius (9th century): Greek missionaries, bothers; venerated as apostles of the Slavs; Cyril (d. 869) and Methodius (d. 885) began their missionary work in Moravia in 863; developed a Slavonic alphabet; used the vernacular in the liturgy, a practice that was eventually approved; declared patrons of Europe with St. Benedict, December 31, 1980; February 14.*

Damasus I (d. 384): Pope, 366-384; opposed Arians and Apollinarians; commissioned St. Jerome to work on Bible translation; developed Roman liturgy; December 11.*

Damian: See Cosmas and Damian.

Damien of Molokai (d. 1889): The so-called leper priest of Molokai; originally from Belgium, Damien devoted over twenty years to the care of the lepers in Hawaii, ultimately dying of the same disease. He was beatified by Pope John Paul II in 1996.

David (5th or 6th century): Nothing for certain known of his life; said to have founded monastery at Menevia; patron saint of Wales; March 1.

Denis and Companions (d. 3rd century): Denis, bishop of Paris, and two companions identified by early writers as Rusticus, a priest, and Eleutherius, a deacon; martyred near Paris; Denis is popularly regarded as the apostle and a patron saint of France; October 9.*

Dismas (1st cent.): Name given to repentant thief (Good Thief) to whom Jesus promised salvation (Lk. 23:40-43); regarded as patron of prisoners; March 25 (observed on second Sunday of October in U.S. prison chapels).

Dominic (Dominic de Guzman) (1170-1221): Spanish priest; founded the Order of Preachers (Dominicans), 1215, in France; preached against the Albigensian heresy; a contemporary of St. Francis of Assisi; canonized 1234; August 8.*

Dominic Savio (1842-1857): Italian youth; pupil of St. John Bosco; died before his 15th birthday; canonized 1954; patron of choir boys; May 6.

Duns Scotus, John (d. 1308): Scottish Franciscan; theologian; advanced theological arguments for doctrine of the Immaculate Conception; proclaimed blessed; cult solemnly confirmed by John Paul II, March 20, 1993; November 8.

Dunstan (c. 910-988): English monk; archbishop of Canterbury; initiated reforms in religious life; counselor to several kings; considered one of greatest Anglo-Saxon saints; patron of goldsmiths, locksmiths, jewelers (trades in which he is said to have excelled); May 19.

Dymphna (dates unknown): Nothing certain known of her life; according to legend, she was an Irish maiden murdered by her heathen father at Gheel near Antwerp, Belgium, where she had fled to escape his advances; her relics were discovered there in the 13th century; since that time cures of mental illness and epilepsy have been attributed to her intercession; patron of those suffering from mental illness; May 15.

Edith Stein, St. (1891-1942): German Carmelite (Teresa Benedicta of the Cross); born of Jewish parents; author and lecturer; baptized in Catholic Church, 1922; arrested with her sister Rosa in 1942 and put to death at Auschwitz; beatified 1987, by Pope John Paul II during his visit to West Germany. She was canonized by Pope John Paul II on October 11, 1998. August 10.

Edmund Campion (1540-1581): English Jesuit; convert 1573; martyred at Tyburn; canonized 1970, one of the Forty English and Welsh Martyrs; December 1.

Edward the Confessor (d. 1066): King of England, 1042-66; canonized 1161; October 13.

Eligius (c. 590-660): Bishop; born in Gaul; founded monasteries and convents; bishop of Noyon and Tournai; famous worker in gold and silver; December 1.

Elizabeth Ann Seton (1774-1821): American foundress; convert, 1805; founded Sisters of Charity in the U.S.; beatified 1963; canonized September 14, 1975; the first American-born saint; January 4 (U.S.).*

Elizabeth of Hungary (1207-1231): Became secular Franciscan after death of her husband in 1227; devoted life to poor and destitute; a patron of the Secular Franciscan Order; canonized 1235; November 17.*

Elizabeth of Portugal (1271-1336): Queen of Portugal; b. Spain; retired to Poor Clare convent as a secular Franciscan after the death of her husband; canonized 1626; July 4.*

Emily de Rodat (1787-1852): French foundress of the Congregation of the Holy Family of Villefranche; canonized 1950; September 19.

Emily de Vialar (1797-1856): French foundress of the Sisters of St. Joseph of the Apparition; canonized 1951; June 17.

Erasmus (Elmo) (d. 303): Life surrounded by legend; martyred during Diocletian persecution; patron of sailors; June 2.

Ethelbert (552-616): King of Kent, England; baptized by St. Augustine of Canterbury, 597; issued legal code; furthered spread of Christianity; February 26.

Euphrasia Pelletier (1796-1868): French Religious; founded Sisters of the Good Shepherd at Angers, 1829; canonized 1940; April 24.

Eusebius of Vercelli (283-370): Italian bishop; exiled from his see (Vercelli) for a time because of his opposition to Arianism; considered a martyr because of sufferings he endured; August 2.*

Fabian (d. 250): Pope, 236-250; martyred under Decius; January 20.*

St. Elizabeth of Hungary

Felicity: See Perpetua and Felicity.

Ferdinand III (1198-1252): King of Castile and Leon; waged successful crusade against Muhammadans in Spain; founded university at Salamanca; canonized 1671; May 30.

Fiacre (Fiachra) (d. c. 670): Irish hermit; patron of gardeners; August 30.

Fidelis of Sigmaringen (Mark Rey) (1577-1622): German Capuchin; lawyer before he joined the Capuchins; missionary to Swiss Protestants; stabbed to death by peasants who were told he was agent of Austrian emperor; April 24.*

Frances of Rome (1384-1440): Italian model for housewives and widows; happily married for 40 years; after death of her husband in 1436 joined community of Benedictine Oblates she had founded; canonized 1608; patron of motorists; March 9.*

Frances Xavier Cabrini (Mother Cabrini) (1850-1917): American foundress; b. Italy; founded the Missionary Sisters of the Sacred Heart, 1877; settled in the U.S. 1889; became an American citizen at Seattle 1909; worked among Italian immigrants; canonized 1946, the first American citizen so honored; November 13 (U.S.).*

Francis Borgia (1510-1572): Spanish Jesuit; joined Jesuits after death of his wife in 1546; became general of the Order, 1565; October 10.

Francis Caracciolo (1563-1608): Italian priest; founder with Father Augustine Adorno of the Clerics Regular Minor (Adorno Fathers); canonized 1807; declared patron of Italian chefs, 1996; June 4.

Francis Fasani (1681-1742): Italian Conventual Franciscan; model of priestly ministry, especially in service to poor and imprisoned; canonized 1986; November 27.

Francis of Assisi (Giovanni di Bernardone) (1181/82-1226): Founder of the Franciscans, 1209; received stigmata 1224; canonized 1228; one of best known and best loved saints; patron of Italy, Catholic Action, and ecologists; October 4.*

Francis of Paola (1416-1507): Italian hermit: founder of Minim Friars; April 2.*

Francis Xavier (1506-1552): Spanish Jesuit; missionary to Far East; canonized 1602; patron of foreign missions; considered one of greatest Christian missionaries; December 3.*

Francis Xavier Bianchi (1743-1815): Italian Barnabite; acclaimed apostle of Naples because of his work there among the poor and abandoned; canonized 1951; January 31.

Gabriel of the Sorrowful Mother (Francis Possenti) (1838-1862): Italian Passionist; died while a scholastic; canonized 1920; February 27.

Gaspar (Caspar) **del Bufalo** (1786-1836): Italian priest; founded Missionaries of the Precious Blood, 1815; canonized 1954; January 2.

Gemma Galgani (1878-1903): Italian laywoman; visionary; subject of extraordinary religious experiences; canonized 1940; April 11.

Genesius (d. c. 300): Roman actor; according to legend, was converted while performing a burlesque of Christian baptism and was subsequently martyred; patron of actors; August 25.

Geneviève (422-500): French nun; a patroness and protectress of Paris; events of her life not authenticated; January 3.

George (d. c. 300): Martyr, probably during Diocletian persecution in Palestine; all other incidents of his life, including story of the dragon, are legendary; patron of England; April 23.*

Gerard Majella (1725-1755): Italian Redemptorist lay brother; noted for supernatural occurrences in his life including bilocation and reading of consciences; canonized 1904; patron of mothers; October 16.

Gertrude (1256-1302): German mystic; writer; helped spread devotion to the Sacred Heart; November 16.*

Gregory VII (Hildebrand) (1020?-1085): Pope, 1075-1085; Benedictine monk; adviser to several popes; as pope, strengthened interior life of Church and fought against lay investiture; driven from Rome by Henry IV; died in exile; canonized 1584; May 25.*

Gregory Barbarigo (1626-1697): Italian cardinal; noted for his efforts to bring about reunion of separated Christians; canonized 1960; June 18.

Gregory of Nyssa (c. 335-395): Bishop; theologian; younger brother of St. Basil the Great; March 9.

Gregory Thaumaturgus (c. 213-268): Bishop of Neocaesarea; missionary, famed as wonder worker; November 17.

Gregory the Illuminator (257-332): Martyr; bishop; apostle and patron saint of Armenia; helped free Armenia from the Persians; September 30.

Hedwig (1174-1243): Moravian noblewoman; married duke of Silesia, head of Polish royal family; fostered religious life in country; canonized 1266; October 16.*

Helena (250-330): Empress; mother of Constantine the Great; associated with discovery of the True Cross; August 18.

Henry (972-1024): Bavarian emperor; cooperated with Benedictine abbeys in restoration of ecclesiastical and social discipline; canonized 1146; July 13.*

Herman Joseph (1150-1241): German Premonstratensian; his visions were the subjects of artists; writer; cult approved, 1958; April 7.

Hippolytus (d. c. 236): Roman priest; opposed Pope St. Callistus I in his teaching about the readmission to the Church of repentant Christians who had apostatized during time of persecution; elected antipope; exiled to Sardinia; reconciled before his martyrdom; important ecclesiastical writer; August 13* (with Pontian).

Hubert (d. 727): Bishop; his patronage of hunters is based on legend that he was converted while hunting; November 3.

Hugh of Cluny (the Great) (1024-1109): Abbot of Benedictine foundation at Cluny; supported popes in efforts to reform ecclesiastical abuses; canonized 1120; April 29.

Ignatius of Antioch (d. c. 107): Early ecclesiastical writer; martyr; bishop of Antioch in Syria for 40 years; October 17.*

Ignatius of Laconi (1701-1781): Italian Capuchin lay brother whose 60 years of religious life were spent in Franciscan simplicity; canonized 1951; May 11.

Ignatius of Loyola (1491-1556): Spanish soldier; renounced military career after recovering from wounds received at siege of Pampeluna (Pamplona) in 1521; founded Society of Jesus (Jesuits), 1534, at Paris; wrote *The Book of Spiritual Exercises*; canonized 1622; July 31.*

Irenaeus of Lyons (130-202): Early ecclesiastical writer; opposed Gnosticism; bishop of Lyons; traditionally regarded as a martyr; June 28.*

Isidore the Farmer (d. 1170): Spanish layman; farmer; canonized 1622; patron of farmers; May 15 (U.S.).*

Jane Frances de Chantal (1572-1641): French widow; foundress, under guidance of St. Francis de Sales, of Order of the Visitation; canonized 1767; December 12* (General Roman Calendar); August 18* (U.S.).

Januarius (Gennaro) (d. 304): Bishop of Benevento; martyred during Diocletian persecution; fame rests on liquefaction of some of his blood preserved in a phial at Naples, an unexplained phenomenon which has occurred regularly several times each year for over 400 years; September 19.*

Jeanne Delanoue (1666-1736): French foundress of Sisters of St. Anne of Providence, 1704; canonized 1982; August 16.

Jeanne (Joan) **de Lestonnac** (1556-1640): French foundress; widowed in 1597; founded the Religious of Notre Dame 1607; canonized 1947; February 2.

Jeanne de Valois (Jeanne of France) (1464-1505): French foundress; deformed daughter of King Louis XI; was married in 1476 to Duke Louis of Orleans who had the marriage annulled when he ascended the throne as Louis XII; Jeanne retired to life of prayer; founded contemplative Annonciades of Bourges, 1504; canonized 1950; February 5.

Jeanne-Elizabeth Bichier des Ages (1773-1838): French Religious; co-founder with

St. Andrew Fournet of Daughters of the Cross of St. Andrew, 1807; canonized 1947; August 26.

Jeanne Jugan, Blessed (1792-1879): French Religious; foundress of Little Sisters of the Poor; beatified October 3, 1982; August 30.

Jerome Emiliani (1481-1537): Venetian priest; founded Somascan Fathers, 1532, for care of orphans; canonized 1767; patron of orphans and abandoned children; February 8.*

Joan Antida Thouret (1765-1826): French Religious; founded, 1799, congregation now known as Sisters of Charity of St. Joan Antida; canonized 1934; August 24.

Joan of Arc (1412-1431): French heroine, called The Maid of Orleans, La Pucelle; led French army in 1429 against English invaders besieging Orleans; captured by Burgundians the following year; turned over to ecclesiastical court on charge of heresy, found guilty and burned at the stake; her innocence was declared in 1456; canonized 1920; patroness of France; May 30.

Joaquina de Vedruna de Mas (1783-1854): Spanish foundress; widowed in 1816; after providing for her children, founded the Carmelite Sisters of Charity; canonized 1959; August 28.

John I (d. 526): Pope, 523-526; martyr; May 18.*

John Baptist de la Salle (1651-1719): French priest; founder of Brothers of the Christian Schools, 1680; canonized 1900; patron of teachers; April 7.*

John Berchmans (1599-1621): Belgian Jesuit scholastic; patron of Mass servers; canonized 1888; August 13.

John (Don) Bosco (1815-1888): Italian priest; founded Salesians, 1859, for education of boys; cofounder of Daughters of Mary Help of Christians for education of girls; canonized 1934; January 31.*

John Capistran (1386-1456): Italian Franciscan; preacher; papal diplomat; canonized 1690; declared patron of military chaplains, February 10, 1984. October 23.*

John de Ribera (1532-1611): Spanish bishop and statesman; archbishop of Valencia, 1568-1611, and viceroy of that province; canonized 1960; January 6.

John Eudes (1601-1680): French priest; founder of Sisters of Our Lady of Charity of Refuge, 1642, and Congregation of Jesus-Mary (Eudists), 1643; canonized 1925; August 19.*

John Fisher (1469-1535): English prelate; theologian; martyr; bishop of Rochester, cardinal; refused to recognize validity of Henry VIII's marriage to Anne Boleyn; upheld supremacy of the pope; beheaded for refusing to acknowledge Henry as head of the Church; canonized 1935; June 22 (with St. Thomas More).*

John Francis Regis (1597-1640): French Jesuit priest; preached missions among poor and unlettered; canonized 1737; patron of social workers, particularly medical social workers, because of his concern for poor and needy and sick in hospitals; July 2.

John Gualbert (d. 1073): Italian priest; founder of Benedictine congregation of Vallombrosians, 1039; canonized 1193; July 12.

John Kanty (Cantius) (1395-1473): Polish theologian; canonized 1767; December 23.*

John Leonardi (1550-1609): Italian priest; worked among prisoners and the sick; founded Clerics Regular of the Mother of God; canonized 1938; October 9.*

John Nepomucene (1345-1393): Bohemian priest; regarded as a martyr; canonized 1729; patron of Czechoslovakia; May 16.

John Nepomucene Neumann (1811-1860): American prelate; b. Bohemia; ordained in New York 1836; missionary among Germans near Niagara Falls before joining Redemptorists, 1840; bishop of Philadelphia, 1852; first bishop in U.S. to prescribe Forty Hours devotion in his diocese; beatified 1963; canonized June 19, 1977; January 5 (U.S.).*

John of Ávila (1499-1569): Spanish priest; preacher; ascetical writer; spiritual adviser of St. Teresa of Jesus (Ávila); canonized 1970; May 10.

John of Britto (1647-1693): Portuguese Jesuit; missionary in India where he was martyred; canonized 1947; February 4.

John of God (1495-1550): Portuguese founder; his work among the sick poor led to foundation of Brothers Hospitallers of St. John of God, 1540, in Spain; canonized 1690; patron of sick, nurses, hospitals; March 8.*

John of Matha (1160-1213): French priest; founder of the Order of Most Holy Trinity, whose original purpose was the ransom of prisoners from the Muslims; February 8.

John Ogilvie (1579-1615): Scottish Jesuit; martyr; canonized 1976, the first canonized Scottish saint since 1250 (Margaret of Scotland); March 10.

John Vianney (Curé of Ars) (1786-1859): French parish priest; noted confessor, spent 16 to 18 hours a day in confessional; canonized 1925; patron of parish priests; August 4.*

Josaphat Kuncevyc (1584-1623): Basilian monk; b. Poland; archbishop of Polotsk, Lithuania; worked for reunion of separated Eastern Christians with Rome; martyred by mob of schismatics; canonized 1867; November 12.*

Joseph Benedict Cottolengo (1786-1842): Italian priest; established Little Houses of Divine Providence (*Piccolo Casa*) for care of orphans and the sick; canonized 1934; April 30.

Joseph Cafasso (1811-1860): Italian priest; renowned confessor; promoted devotion to Blessed Sacrament; canonized 1947; June 23.

Joseph Calasanz (1556-1648): Spanish priest; founder of Piarists (Order of Pious Schools); canonized 1767; August 25.*

Joseph of Cupertino (1603-1663): Italian Franciscan; noted for remarkable incidents of levitation; canonized 1767; September 18.

Joseph Pignatelli (1737-1811): Spanish Jesuit; left Spain when Jesuits were banished in 1767; worked for revival of the Order; named first superior when Jesuits were reestablished in Kingdom of Naples, 1804; canonized 1954; November 28.

Juan Diego, Blessed (16th cent.): Mexican Indian, convert; indigenous name according to tradition Cuauhtlatohuac ("The eagle who speaks"); favored with apparitions of Our Lady (see Index: Our Lady of Guadalupe) on Tepeyac hill; beatified, 1990; December 9* (U.S.).

Julia Billiart (1751-1816): French foundress; founded Sisters of Notre Dame de Namur, 1804; canonized 1969; April 8.

Justin de Jacobis (1800-1860): Italian Vincentian; bishop; missionary in Ethiopia; canonized 1975; July 31.

Justin Martyr (100-165): Early ecclesiastical writer; Apologies for the Christian Religion, Dialog with the Jew Tryphon; martyred at Rome; June 1.*

Kateri Tekakwitha, Blessed (1656-1680): "Lily of the Mohawks"; Indian maiden born at Ossernenon (Auriesville), N.Y.; baptized Christian, Easter, 1676, by Jesuit missionary Father Jacques de Lambertville; lived life devoted to prayer, penitential practices and care of sick and aged in Christian village of Caughnawaga near Montreal where her relics are now enshrined; beatified June 22, 1980; July 14* (in U.S.).

Katharine Drexel (1858-1955): Philadelphia-born heiress; devoted wealth to founding schools and missions for Indians and Blacks; foundress of Sisters of Blessed Sacrament for Indians and Colored People, 1891; beatified 1988; canonized on October 1, 2000; March 3* (U.S.).

Ladislaus (1040-1095): King of Hungary; supported Pope Gregory VII against Henry IV; canonized 1192; June 27.

Lawrence (d. 258): Widely venerated martyr who suffered death, according to a long-standing but unverifiable legend, by fire on a gridiron; August 10.*

Lawrence (Lorenzo) **Ruiz and Companions** (d. 1630s): Martyred in or near the city of Nagasaki, Japan; Lawrence Ruiz, first Filipino saint, and 15 Companions (nine Japanese, four Spaniards, one Italian and one Frenchman); canonized 1987; September 28.*

Leonard Murialdo (1828-1900): Italian priest; educator; founder of Pious Society of St. Joseph of Turin, 1873; canonized 1970; March 30.

Leonard of Port Maurice (1676-1751): Italian Franciscan; ascetical writer; preached missions throughout Italy; canonized 1867; patron of parish missions; November 26.

Leopold Mandic (1866-1942): Croatianborn Franciscan priest, noted confessor; spent most of his priestly life in Padua, Italy; canonized 1983; July 30.

Louis IX (1215-1270): King of France, 1226-1270; participated in Sixth Crusade; patron of Secular Franciscan Order; canonized 1297; August 25.*

Louis de Montfort (1673-1716): French priest; founder of Sisters of Divine Wisdom, 1703, and Missionaries of Company of Mary, 1715; wrote *True Devotion to the Blessed Virgin*; canonized 1947; April 28.*

Louis Zepherin Moreau, Blessed (d. 1901): Canadian bishop; headed St. Hyacinthe, Que., diocese, 1876-1901; beatified 1987; May 24.

Louise de Marillac (1591-1660): French foundress, with St. Vincent de Paul, of the Sisters of Charity; canonized 1934; March 15.

Lucy (d. 304): Sicilian maiden; martyred during Diocletian persecution; one of most widely venerated early virgin-martyrs; patron of Syracuse, Sicily; invoked by those suffering from eye diseases; December 13.*

Lucy Filippini (1672-1732): Italian educator, helped improve status of women through education; considered a founder of the Religious Teachers Filippini, 1692; canonized 1930; March 25.

Madeleine Sophie Barat (1779-1865): French foundress of the Society of the Sacred Heart of Jesus; canonized 1925; May 25.

Malachy (1095-1148): Irish bishop; instrumental in establishing first Cistercian house in Ireland, 1142; canonized 1190; November 3 (See Index: Prophecies of St. Malachy).

Marcellinus and Peter (d.c. 304): Early Roman martyrs; June 2.*

Margaret Clitherow (1556-1586): English martyr; convert shortly after her marriage; one of Forty Martyrs of England and Wales; canonized 1970; March 25.

Margaret Mary Alacoque (1647-1690): French Religious; spread devotion to Sacred Heart in accordance with revelations made to her in 1675 (see Sacred Heart); canonized 1920; October 16.*

Margaret of Cortona (1247-1297): Secular Franciscan; reformed her life in 1273 following the violent death of her lover; canonized 1728; May 16.

Margaret of Hungary (1242-1270): Contemplative; daughter of King Bela IV of Hungary; lived a life of self-imposed penances; canonized 1943; January 18.

Margaret of Scotland (1050-1093): Queen of Scotland; noted for solicitude for the poor and promotion of justice; canonized 1250; November 16.*

Maria Goretti (1890-1902): Italian virginmartyr; a model of purity; canonized 1950; July 6.*

Mariana Paredes of Jesus (1618-1645): South American recluse; Lily of Quito; canonized, 1950; May 28.

Marie-Leonie Paradis, Blessed (1840-1912): Canadian Religious; founded Little Sisters of the Holy Family, 1880; beatified 1984; May 4.

Marie-Rose Durocher, Blessed (1811-1849): Canadian Religious; foundress of Sisters of Holy Names of Jesus and Mary; beatified 1982; October 6* (in U.S.).

Martha (1st cent.): Sister of Lazarus and Mary of Bethany; Gospel accounts record her concern for homely details; patron of cooks; July 29.*

Martin I (d. 655): Pope, 649-55; banished from Rome by emperor in 653 because of his condemnation of Monothelites; considered a martyr; April 13.*

Martin of Tours (316-397): Bishop of Tours; opposed Arianism and Priscillianism; pioneer of Western monasticism, before St. Benedict; November 11.*

Mary Domenica Mazzarello (1837-1881): Italian foundress, with St. John Bosco, of the Daughters of Mary Help of Christians, 1872; canonized 1951; May 14.

Mary Josepha Rossello (1811-1881): Italian-born foundress of the Daughters of Our Lady of Mercy; canonized 1949; December 7.

Mary Magdalen Postel (1756-1846): French foundress of the Sisters of Christian Schools of Mercy, 1807; canonized 1925; July 16.

Mary Magdalene (1st cent.): Gospels record her as devoted follower of Christ to whom he appeared after the Resurrection; her identification with Mary of Bethany (sister of Martha and Lazarus) and the woman sinner (Lk. 7:36-50) has been questioned; July 22.*

Mary Magdalene dei Pazzi (1566-1607): Italian Carmelite nun; recipient of mystical experiences; canonized 1669; May 25.*

Mary Michaela Desmaisières (1809-1865): Spanish-born foundress of the Institute of the Handmaids of the Blessed Sacrament, 1848; canonized 1934; August 24.

Maximilian Kolbe (1894-1941): Polish Conventual Franciscan; prisoner at Auschwitz who heroically offered his life in place of a fellow prisoner; beatified 1971, canonized 1982; August 14.*

Methodius: See Cyril and Methodius.

Miguel Febres Cordero (1854-1910): Ecuadorean Christian Brother; educator; canonized 1984; February 9.

Miguel Pro, Blessed (1891-1927): Mexican Jesuit; joined Jesuits, 1911; forced to flee because of religious persecution; ordained in Belgium, 1925; returned to Mexico, 1926, to minister to people despite government prohibition; unjustly accused of assassination plot against president; arrested and executed; beatified 1988. November 23* (U.S.).

Monica (332-387): Mother of St. Augustine; model of a patient mother; her feast is observed in the Roman calendar the day before her son's; August 27.*

Nereus and Achilleus (d. c. 100): Early Christian martyrs; soldiers who, according to legend, were baptized by St. Peter; May 12.*

Nicholas of Flüe (1417-1487): Swiss layman; at the age of 50, with the consent of his wife and 10 children, he retreated from the world to live as a hermit; called Brother Claus by the Swiss; canonized 1947; March 21.

Nicholas of Myra (4th cent.): Bishop of Myra in Asia Minor; one of most popular saints in both East and West; most of the incidents of his life are based on legend; patron of Russia; December 6.*

Nicholas of Tolentino (1245-1305): Italian hermit; famed preacher; canonized 1446; September 10.

Nicholas Tavelic and Companions (Deodatus of Aquitaine, Peter of Narbonne, Stephen of Cuneo) (d. 1391): Franciscan missionaries; martyred by Muslims in the Holy Land: canonized 1970; November 14.

Norbert (1080-1134): German bishop; founded Canons Regular of Premontre (Premonstratensians, Norbertines), 1120; promoted reform of the clergy, devotion to Blessed Sacrament; canonized 1582; June 6.*

Odilia (d. c. 720): Benedictine abbess; according to legend she was born blind, abandoned by her family and adopted by a convent of nuns where her sight was miraculously restored; patroness of blind; December 13.

Oliver Plunket (1629-1681): Irish martyr; theologian; archbishop of Armagh and primate of Ireland; beatified 1920; canonized, 1975; July 1.

Pancras (d. c. 304): Roman martyr; May 12.*

Paola Frassinetti (1809-1882): Italian Religious; foundress, 1834, of Sisters of St. Dorothy; canonized 1984; June 11.

Paschal Baylon (1540-1592): Spanish Franciscan lay brother; spent life as doorkeeper in various Franciscan friaries; defended doctrine of Real Presence in Blessed Sacrament; canonized 1690; patron of all Eucharistic confraternities and congresses, 1897; May 17.

Patrick (389-461): Famous missionary of Ireland; began missionary work in Ireland about 432; organized the Church there and established it on a lasting foundation; patron of Ireland, with Sts. Bridget and Columba; March 17.*

Paul Miki and Companions (d. 1597): Martyrs of Japan; Paul Miki, Jesuit, and twenty-five other priests and laymen were martyred at Nagasaki; canonized 1862, the first canonized martyrs of the Far East; February 6.*

Paul of the Cross (1694-1775): Italian Religious; founder of the Passionists; canonized 1867; Oct 19* (October 20, U.S.*).

Paulinus of Nola (d. 451): Bishop of Nola (Spain); writer; June 22.*

Peregrine (1260-1347): Italian Servite; invoked against cancer (he was miraculously cured of cancer of the foot after a vision); canonized 1726; May 1.

Perpetua and Felicity (d. 203): Martyrs; Perpetua was a young married woman; Felicity was a slave girl; March 7.*

Peter Chanel (1803-1841): French Marist; missionary to Oceania, where he was martyred; canonized 1954; April 28.*

Peter Fourier (1565-1640): French priest; co-founder with Alice LeClercq (Mother Teresa of Jesus) of the Augustinian Canonesses of Our Lady, 1598; canonized 1897; December 9.

Peter Gonzalez (1190-1246): Spanish Dominican; worked among sailors; court chaplain and confessor of King St. Ferdinand of Castile; patron of sailors; April 14.

Peter Julian Eymard (1811-1868): French priest; founder of the Congregation of the Blessed Sacrament (men), 1856, and Servants of the Blessed Sacrament (women), 1864; dedicated to Eucharistic apostolate; canonized 1962; August 2.*

Peter Nolasco (c. 1189-1258): Born in Langueduc area of present-day France; founded the Mercedarians (Order of Our Lady of Mercy), 1218, in Spain; canonized 1628; January 31.

Peter of Alcántara (1499-1562): Spanish Franciscan; mystic; initiated Franciscan reform; confessor of St. Teresa of Jesus (Ávila); canonized 1669; October 22 (in U.S.).

Philip Benizi (1233-1285): Italian Servite; noted preacher, peacemaker; canonized 1671; August 23.

Philip Neri (1515-1595): Italian Religious; founded Congregation of the Oratory; considered a second apostle of Rome because of his mission activity there; canonized 1622; May 26.*

Philip of Jesus (1517-1597): Mexican Franciscan; martyred at Nagasaki, Japan; canonized 1862; patron of Mexico City; February 6.*

Pio, Blessed Padre, (1887-1968): Italian Capuchin Franciscan, mystic, and stigmatic; assisted souls from all over the world who came to him for counsel and guidance; September 23.

Pius V (1504-1572): Pope, 1566-1572; enforced decrees of Council of Trent; organized expedition against Turks resulting in victory at Lepanto; canonized 1712; April 30.*

Polycarp (2nd cent.): Bishop of Smyrna; ecclesiastical writer; martyr; February 23.*

Pontian (d. c. 235): Pope, 230-235; exiled to Sardinia by the emperor; regarded as a martyr; August 13 (with Hippolytus).*

Rafaela Maria Porras y Ayllon (1850-1925): Spanish Religious; founded the Handmaids of the Sacred Heart, 1877; canonized 1977; January 6.

Raymond Nonnatus (d. 1240): Spanish Mercedarian; cardinal; devoted his life to ransoming captives from the Moors; August 31.

Raymond of Peñafort (1175-1275): Spanish Dominican; confessor of Gregory IX; systematized and codified canon law, in effect until 1917; master general of Dominicans, 1238; canonized 1601; January 7.*

Rita of Cascia (1381-1457): Widow; cloistered Augustinian Religious of Umbria; invoked in impossible and desperate cases; May 22.

Robert Southwell (1561-1595): English Jesuit; poet; martyred at Tyburn; canonized 1970, one of the Forty English and Welsh Martyrs; February 21.

Roch (1350-1379): French layman; pilgrim; devoted life to care of plague-stricken; widely venerated; invoked against pestilence; August 17.

Romuald (951-1027): Italian monk; founded Camaldolese Benedictines; June 19.*

Rose of Lima (1586-1617): Peruvian Dominican tertiary; first native-born saint of the New World; canonized 1671; August 23.*

Scholastica (d. c. 559): Sister of St. Benedict; regarded as first nun of the Benedictine Order; February 10.*

Sebastian (3rd cent.): Roman martyr; traditionally pictured as a handsome youth with arrows; martyred; patron of athletes, archers; January 20.*

Seven Holy Founders of the Servants of Mary (Buonfiglio Monaldo, Alexis Falconieri, Benedict dell'Antello, Bartholomew Amidei, Ricovero Uguccione, Gerardino Sostegni, John Buonagiunta Monetti): Florentine youths who founded Servites, 1233, in obedience to a vision; canonized 1888; February 17.*

Sharbel Makhlouf (1828-1898): Lebanese Maronite monk-hermit; canonized 1977; December 24.

Sixtus II and Companions (d. 258): Sixtus, pope 257-258, and four deacons, martyrs; August 7.*

Stanislaus (1030-1079): Polish bishop; martyr; canonized 1253; April 11.*

Stephen (d. c. 33): First Christian martyr; chosen by the Apostles as the first of the seven deacons; stoned to death; December 26.*

Stephen (975-1038): King; apostle of Hungary; welded Magyars into national unity; canonized 1083; August 16.*

Sylvester I (d. 335): Pope 314-335; first ecumenical council held at Nicaea during his pontificate; December 31.*

Tarcisius (d. 3rd cent.): Early martyr; according to tradition, was martyred while carrying the Blessed Sacrament to some Christians in prison; patron of first communicants; August 15.

Teresa Margaret Redi (1747-1770): Italian Carmelite; lived life of prayer and austere penance; canonized 1934; March 11.

Teresa of Jesus Jornet Ibars (1843-1897): Spanish Religious; founded the Little Sisters of the Abandoned Aged, 1873; canonized 1974; August 26.

Thérèse Couderc (1805-1885): French Religious; foundress of the Religious of Our Lady of the Retreat in the Cenacle, 1827; canonized 1970; September 26.

Thomas Becket (1118-1170): English martyr; archbishop of Canterbury; chancellor under Henry II; murdered for upholding rights of the Church; canonized 1173; December 29.*

Thomas More (1478-1535): English martyr; statesman, chancellor under Henry VIII; author of Utopia; opposed Henry's divorce, refused to renounce authority of the papacy; beheaded; canonized 1935; June 22 (with St. John Fisher). Pope John Paul II declared him patron saint of politicians on October 31, 2000.*

Thorlac (1133-1193): Icelandic bishop; instituted reforms; although his cult was never officially approved, he was declared patron of Iceland, January 14, 1984; December 23.

Timothy (d. c. 97): Bishop of Ephesus; disciple and companion of St. Paul; martyr; January 26.*

Titus (d. c. 96): Bishop; companion of St. Paul; recipient of one of Paul's epistles; January 26.*

Titus Brandsma, Blessed (1881-1942): Dutch Carmelite priest; professor, scholar, journalist; denounced Nazi persecution of Jews; arrested by Nazis, January 19, 1942; executed by lethal injection at Dachau, July 26, 1942; beatified 1985; July 26.

Valentine (d. 269): Priest; physician; martyred at Rome; legendary patron of lovers; February 14.

Vicenta Maria Lopez y Vicuna (1847-1896): Spanish foundress of the Daughters of Mary Immaculate for domestic service; canonized 1975; December 26.

Vincent (d. 304): Spanish deacon; martyr; January 22.*

Vincent de Paul (1581?-1660): French priest; founder of Congregation of the Mission (Vincentians, Lazarists) and co-founder of Sisters of Charity; declared patron of all charitable organizations and works by Leo XIII; canonized 1737; September 27.*

Vincent Ferrer (1350-1418): Spanish Dominican; famed preacher; April 5.*

Vincent Pallotti (1795-1850): Italian priest; founded Society of the Catholic Apostolate (Pallottines), 1835; January 22.

Vincent Strambi (1745-1824): Italian Passionist; bishop; reformer; canonized 1950; September 25.

Vincenza Gerosa (1784-1847): Italian co-foundress of the Sisters of Charity of Lovere; canonized 1950; June 28.

Vitus (d.c. 300): Martyr; died in Lucania, southern Italy; regarded as protector of epileptics and those suffering from St. Vitus Dance (chorea); June 15.

Walburga (d. 779): English-born Benedictine Religious; belonged to group of nuns who established convents in Germany at the invitation of St. Boniface; abbess of Heidenheim; February 25.

Wenceslaus (d. 935): Duke of Bohemia; martyr; patron of Bohemia; September 28.*

Zita (1218-1278): Italian maid; noted for charity to poor; patron of domestics; April 27.

SAINTS — PATRONS AND INTERCESSORS

A patron is a saint who is venerated as a special intercessor before God. Most patrons have been so designated as the result of popular devotion and long-standing custom. In many cases, the fact of existing patronal devotion is clear despite historical obscurity regarding its origin. The Church has made official designation of relatively few patrons; in such cases, the dates of designation are given in parentheses in the list below. The theological background of the patronage of saints includes the dogmas of the Mystical Body of Christ and the Communion of Saints. Listed are patron saints of occupations and professions, and saints whose intercession is sought for special needs.

Academics: Thomas Aquinas.
Accomodations: Gertrude of Nivelles.
Accountants: Matthew.
Actors: Genesius.
Adopted children: Clotilde; Thomas More.
Advertisers: Bernardine of Siena (May 20, 1960).
Alcoholics: John of God; Monica.
Alpinists: Bernard of Montjoux (or Menthon) (August 20, 1923).
Altar servers: John Berchmans.
Anesthetists: René Goupil.
Animals: Francis of Assisi.
Archaeologists: Damasus.
Archers: Sebastian.
Architects: Thomas, Apostle.
Art: Catherine of Bologna.
Artists: Luke, Catherine of Bologna, Blessed Angelico (February 21, 1984).
Astronauts: Joseph Cupertino.
Astronomers: Dominic.
Athletes: Sebastian.

Authors: Francis de Sales.
Aviators: Our Lady of Loreto (1920), Thérèse of Lisieux, Joseph of Cupertino.
Bakers: Elizabeth of Hungary, Nicholas.
Bankers: Matthew.
Barbers: Cosmas and Damian, Louis.
Barren women: Anthony of Padua, Felicity.
Basket-makers: Anthony, Abbot.
Bees: Ambrose.
Birth: Margaret.
Beggars: Martin of Tours.
Blacksmiths: Dunstan.
Blind: Odilia, Raphael.
Blood banks: Januarius.
Bodily ills: Our Lady of Lourdes.
Bookbinders: Peter Celestine.
Bookkeepers: Matthew.
Booksellers: John of God.
Boy Scouts: George.
Brewers: Augustine of Hippo, Luke, Nicholas of Myra.
Bricklayers: Stephen.
Brides: Nicholas of Myra.
Bridges: John of Nepomucene.
Broadcasters: Gabriel.
Brushmakers: Anthony, Abbot.
Builders: Vincent Ferrer.
Bus drivers: Christopher.
Butchers: Anthony (Abbot), Luke.
Butlers: Adelelm.
Cabdrivers: Fiacre.
Cabinetmakers: Anne.
Cancer patients: Peregrine.
Canonists: Raymond of Peñafort.
Carpenters: Joseph.

Catechists: Viator, Charles Borromeo, Robert Bellarmine.

Catholic Action: Francis of Assisi (1916).

Catholic Press: Francis de Sales.

Chandlers: Ambrose, Bernard of Clairvaux.

Chaplains: John of Capistrano.

Charitable societies: Vincent de Paul (May 12, 1885).

Chastity: Thomas Aquinas.

Childbirth: Raymond Nonnatus, Gerard Majella.

Children: Nicholas of Myra.

Children of Mary: Agnes, Maria Goretti.

Choirboys: Dominic Savio (June 8, 1956), Holy Innocents.

Church: Joseph (December 8, 1870).

Circus people: Julian the Hospitaller.

Clerics: Gabriel of the Sorrowful Mother.

Colleges: Thomas Aquinas.

Comedians: Vitus.

Communications personnel: Bernardine.

Confessors: Alphonsus Liguori (April 26, 1950), John Nepomucene.

Converts: Helena; Vladimir.

Convulsive children: Scholastica.

Cooks: Lawrence, Martha.

Coopers: Nicholas of Myra.

Coppersmiths: Maurus.

Dairy workers: Brigid.

Dancers: Vitus.

Deaf: Francis de Sales.

Dentists: Apollonia.

Desperate situations: Gregory of Neocaesarea, Jude Thaddeus, Rita of Cascia.

Dietitians (in hospitals): Martha.

Diplomats: Gabriel.

Divorce: Helena.

Drug addiction: Maximilian Kolbe.

Dyers: Maurice, Lydia.

Dying: Joseph.

Ecologists: Francis of Assisi (November 29, 1979).

Ecumenists: Cyril and Methodius.

Editors: John Bosco.

Emigrants: Frances Xavier Cabrini (September 8, 1950).

Endurance: Pantaleon.

Engineers: Ferdinand III.

Epilepsy, Motor Diseases: Vitus, Willibrord.

Eucharistic congresses and societies: Paschal Baylon (November 28, 1897).

Expectant mothers: Raymond Nonnatus, Gerard Majella.

Eye diseases: Lucy.

Falsely accused: Raymond Nonnatus.

Farmers: George, Isidore.

Farriers: John the Baptist.

Firemen: Florian.

Fire prevention: Catherine of Siena.

First communicants: Tarcisius.

Fishermen: Andrew.

Florists: Thérèse of Lisieux.

Forest workers: John Gualbert.

Foundlings: Holy Innocents.

Friendship: John the Divine.

Fullers: Anastasius the Fuller, James the Less.

Funeral directors: Joseph of Arimathea, Dismas.

Gardeners: Adelard, Tryphon, Fiacre, Phocas.

Glassworkers: Luke.

Goldsmiths: Dunstan, Anastasius.

Gravediggers: Anthony, Abbot.

Greetings: Valentine.

Grocers: Michael.

Grooms: King Louis IX of France.

Hairdressers: Martin de Porres.

Happy meetings: Raphael.

Hatters: Severus of Ravenna, James the Less.

Headache sufferers: Teresa of Jesus (Ávila).

Heart patients: John of God.

Homeless: Margaret of Cortona, Benedict Joseph Labré.

Horses: Giles, Hippolytus.

Housekeepers: Zita.

Hospital administrators: Basil the Great, Frances X. Cabrini.

Hospitals: Camillus de Lellis and John of God (June 22, 1886), Jude Thaddeus.

Housewives: Anne.

Hunters: Hubert, Eustachius.

Infantrymen: Maurice.

Innkeepers: Amand, Martha, Julian the Hospitaller.

Innocence: Hallvard.

Invalids: Roch.

Janitors: Theobald.

Jewelers: Eligius, Dunstan.

Journalists: Francis de Sales (April 26, 1923).

Jurists: John Capistran.

Laborers: Isidore, James, John Bosco.

Lawyers: Ivo (Yves Helory), Genesius, Thomas More.

Learning: Ambrose.

Librarians: Jerome.

Lighthouse keepers: Venerius (March 10, 1961).

Linguists: Gottschalk.

Locksmiths: Dunstan.

Lost souls: Nicholas of Tolentino.

Lovers: Raphael; Valentine.
Lunatics: Christina.
Maids: Zita.
Marble workers: Clement I.
Mariners: Michael, Nicholas of Tolentino.
Medical record librarians: Raymond of Peñafort.
Medical social workers: John Regis.
Medical technicians: Albert the Great.
Mentally ill: Dymphna.
Merchants: Francis of Assisi, Nicholas of Myra.
Messengers: Gabriel.
Metal workers: Eligius.
Military chaplains: John Capistran (February 10, 1984).
Millers: Arnulph, Victor.
Missions, foreign: Francis Xavier (March 25, 1904), Thérèse of Lisieux (December 14, 1927).
Missions, black: Peter Claver (1896, Leo XIII), Benedict the Black.
Missions, parish: Leonard of Port Maurice (March 17, 1923).
Monks: Benedict of Nursia.
Mothers: Monica.
Motorcyclists: Our Lady of Grace.
Motorists: Christopher, Frances of Rome.
Mountaineers: Bernard of Montjoux (or Menthon).
Musicians: Gregory the Great, Cecilia, Dunstan.
Mystics: John of the Cross.
Notaries: Luke, Mark.
Nuns: Bridget.
Nurses: Camillus de Lellis and John of God (1930, Pius XI), Agatha, Raphael.
Nursing and nursing service: Elizabeth of Hungary, Catherine of Siena.
Orators: John Chrysostom (July 8, 1908).
Organ builders: Cecilia.
Orphans: Jerome Emiliani.
Painters: Luke.
Paratroopers: Michael.
Pawnbrokers: Nicholas.
Plumbers: Vincent Ferrer.
Pharmacists: Cosmas and Damian, James the Greater.
Pharmacists (in hospitals): Gemma Galgani.
Philosophers: Justin.
Physicians: Pantaleon, Cosmas and Damian, Luke, Raphael.
Pilgrims: James the Greater.
Plasterers: Bartholomew.
Poets: David, Cecilia.
Poison sufferers: Benedict.

Policemen: Michael.
Politicians: Thomas More.
Poor: Lawrence, Anthony of Padua.
Poor souls: Nicholas of Tolentino.
Popes: Gregory I the Great.
Porters: Christopher.
Possessed: Bruno, Denis.
Postal employees: Gabriel.
Priests: Jean-Baptiste Vianney (April 23, 1929).
Printers: John of God, Augustine of Hippo, Genesius.
Prisoners: Dismas, Joseph Cafasso.
Protector of crops: Ansovinus.
Public relations: Bernardine of Siena (May 20, 1960).
Public relations (of hospitals): Paul, Apostle.
Publishers: John the Divine.
Race relations: Martin de Porres.
Radiologists: Michael (January 15, 1941).
Radio workers: Gabriel.
Refugees: Alban.
Retreats: Ignatius Loyola (July 25, 1922).
Rheumatism: James the Greater.
Saddlers: Crispin and Crispinian.
Sailors: Cuthbert, Brendan, Eulalia, Christopher, Peter Gonzalez, Erasmus, Nicholas.
Scholars: Bede the Venerable, Brigid.
Schools, Catholic: Thomas Aquinas (August 4, 1880), Joseph Calasanz (August 13, 1948).
Scientists: Albert (August 13, 1948).
Sculptors: Four Crowned Martyrs.
Seamen: Francis of Paola.
Searchers of lost articles: Anthony of Padua.
Secretaries: Genesius.
Secular Franciscans: Louis of France, Elizabeth of Hungary.
Seminarians: Charles Borromeo.
Servants: Martha, Zita.
Shepherds: Drogo.
Shoemakers: Crispin and Crispinian.
Sick: Michael, John of God, Camillus de Lellis (June 22, 1886).
Silversmiths: Andronicus.
Singers: Gregory, Cecilia.
Single mothers: Margaret of Cortona.
Single women: Catherine of Alexandria.
Skaters: Lidwina.
Skiers: Bernard of Montjoux (or Menthon).
Social workers: Louise de Marillac (February 12, 1960).
Soldiers: Hadrian, George, Ignatius, Sebastian, Martin of Tours, Joan of Arc.
Speleologists: Benedict.

Stamp collectors: Gabriel.
Stenographers: Genesius, Cassian.
Stonecutters: Clement.
Stonemasons: Stephen.
Stress: Walter of Portnoise.
Students: Thomas Aquinas.
Surgeons: Cosmas and Damian, Luke.
Swimmers: Adjutor.
Swordsmiths: Maurice.
Tailors: Homobonus.
Tanners: Crispin and Crispinian, Simon.
Tax collectors: Matthew.
Teachers: Gregory the Great, John Baptist de la Salle (May 15, 1950).
Telecommunications workers: Gabriel (January 12, 1951).
Television: Clare of Assisi (February 14, 1958).
Television workers: Gabriel.
Thieves: Dismas.
Theologians: Augustine, Alphonsus Liguori.
Throat ailments: Blase.
Torture victims: Alban, Eustachius, Regina, Vincent, Victor of Marseilles.
Toymakers: Claude.
Travelers: Anthony of Padua, Nicholas of Myra, Christopher, Raphael.
Travel hostesses: Bona (March 2, 1962).
Truck drivers: Christopher.
Universities: Blessed Contardo Ferrini.
Veterinarians: Blaise.
Vocations: Alphonsus.
Whales: Brendan the Voyager.
Watchmen: Peter of Alcantara.
Weavers: Paul the Hermit, Anastasius the Fuller, Anastasia.
Wine merchants: Amand.
Wineries: Morand; Vincent.
Women in labor: Anne.
Workingmen: Joseph.
Writers: Francis de Sales (April 26, 1923), Lucy.
Yachtsmen: Adjutor.
Young girls: Agnes.
Youth: Aloysius Gonzaga (1729, Benedict XIII; 1926, Pius XI), John Berchmans, Gabriel of the Sorrowful Mother.

PATRON SAINTS OF PLACES

Albania: Our Lady of Good Counsel.
Alsace: Odilia.
Americas: Our Lady of Guadalupe, Rose of Lima.
Angola: Immaculate Heart of Mary (November 21, 1984).
Argentina: Our Lady of LuJan.
Armenia: Gregory Illuminator.
Asia Minor: John, Evangelist.
Australia: Our Lady Help of Christians.
Belgium: Joseph.
Bohemia: Wenceslaus, Ludmilla.
Bolivia: Our Lady of Copacabana, *"Virgen de la Candelaria."*
Borneo: Francis Xavier.
Brazil: Nossa Señora de Aparecida, Immaculate Conception, Peter of Alcantara.
Canada: Joseph, Anne.
Chile: James the Greater, Our Lady of Mt. Carmel.
China: Joseph.
Colombia: Peter Claver, Louis Bertran.
Corsica: Immaculate Conception.
Cuba: Our Lady of Charity.
Czechoslovakia: Wenceslaus, John Nepomucene, Procopius.
Denmark: Ansgar, Canute.
Dominican Republic: Our Lady of High Grace, Dominic.
East Indies: Thomas, Apostle.
Ecuador: Sacred Heart.
El Salvador: Our Lady of Peace (October 10, 1966).
England: George.
Equatorial Guinea: Immaculate Conception (May 25, 1986).
Europe: Benedict (1964), Cyril and Methodius, co-patrons (December 31, 1980), Sts. Catherine of Siena, Bridget of Sweden, and Edith Stein, co-patronesses (October 1, 1999).
Finland: Henry.
France: Our Lady of the Assumption, Joan of Arc, Thérèse (May 3, 1944).
Germany: Boniface, Michael.
Gibraltar: Blessed Virgin Mary under title, "Our Lady of Europe" (May 31, 1979).
Greece: Nicholas, Andrew.
Holland: Willibrord.
Hungary: Blessed Virgin, "Great Lady of Hungary," Stephen, King.
Iceland: Thorlac (January 14, 1984).
India: Our Lady of Assumption.
Ireland: Patrick, Brigid and Columba.
Italy: Francis of Assisi, Catherine of Siena.
Japan: Peter Baptist.
Korea: Joseph and Mary, Mother of the Church.
Lesotho: Immaculate Heart of Mary.
Lithuania: Casimir, Blessed Cunegunda.

Luxembourg: Willibrord.
Malta: Paul, Our Lady of the Assumption.
Mexico: Our Lady of Guadalupe.
Monaco: Devota.
Moravia: Cyril and Methodius.
New Zealand: Our Lady Help of Christians.
Norway: Olaf.
Papua New Guinea (including northern Solomon Islands): Michael the Archangel (May 31, 1979).
Paraguay: Our Lady of Assumption (July 13, 1951).
Peru: Joseph (March 19, 1957).
Philippines: Sacred Heart of Mary.
Poland: Casimir, Blessed Cunegunda, Stanislaus of Krakow, Our Lady of Czestochowa.
Portugal: Immaculate Conception, Francis Borgia, Anthony of Padua, Vincent of Saragossa, George.
Russia: Andrew, Nicholas of Myra, Thérèse of Lisieux.
Scandinavia: Ansgar.
Scotland: Andrew, Columba.
Silesia: Hedwig.
Slovakia: Our Lady of Sorrows.
South Africa: Our Lady of Assumption (March 15, 1952).
South America: Rose of Lima.
Solomon Islands: BVM, under title Most Holy Name of Mary (September 4, 1991).
Spain: James the Greater, Teresa.
Sri Lanka (Ceylon): Lawrence.
Sweden: Bridget, Eric.
Tanzania: Immaculate Conception (December 8, 1964).
United States: Immaculate Conception (1846).
Uruguay: Blessed Virgin Mary, under title *"La Virgen de los Treinte y Tres"* (November 21, 1963).
Venezuela: Our Lady of Coromoto.
Wales: David.
West Indies: Gertrude.

EMBLEMS, PORTRAYALS OF SAINTS

Agatha: Tongs, veil.
Agnes: Lamb.
Ambrose: Bees, dove, ox, pen.
Andrew: Transverse cross.
Anne, Mother of the Blessed Virgin: Door.
Anthony of Padua: Infant Jesus, bread, book, lily.
Augustine of Hippo: Dove, child, shell, pen.
Bartholomew: Knife, flayed and holding his skin.
Benedict: Broken cup, raven, bell, crosier, bush.

Bernard of Clairvaux: Pen, bees, instruments of the Passion.
Bernardine of Siena: Tablet or sun inscribed with IHS.
Blase: Wax, taper, iron comb.
Bonaventure: Communion, ciborium, cardinal's hat.
Boniface: Oak, ax, book, fox, scourge, fountain, raven, sword.
Bridget of Sweden: Book, pilgrim's staff.
Bridget of Kildare: Cross, flame over her head, candle.
Catherine of Ricci: Ring, crown, crucifix.
Catherine of Siena: Stigmata, cross, ring, lily.
Cecilia: Organ.
Charles Borromeo: Communion, coat of arms with word "Humilitas."
Christopher: Giant, torrent, tree, Child Jesus on his shoulders.
Clare of Assisi: Monstrance.
Cosmas and Damian: A phial, box of ointment.
Cyril of Alexandria: Blessed Virgin holding the Child Jesus, pen.
Cyril of Jerusalem: Purse, book.
Dominic: Rosary, star.
Edmund the Martyr: Arrow, sword.
Elizabeth of Hungary: Alms, flowers, bread, the poor, a pitcher.
Francis of Assisi: Wolf, birds, fish, skull, the Stigmata.
Francis Xavier: Crucifix, bell, vessel.
Genevieve: Bread, keys, herd, candle.
George: Dragon.
Gertrude: Crown, taper, lily.
Gervase and Protase: Scourge, club, sword.
Gregory I (the Great): Tiara, crosier, dove.
Helena: Cross.
Ignatius of Loyola: Communion, chasuble, book, apparition of Our Lord.
Isidore: Bees, pen.
James the Greater: Pilgrim's staff, shell, key, sword.
James the Less: Square rule, halberd, club.
Jerome: Lion.
John Berchmans: Rule of St. Ignatius, cross, rosary.
John Chrysostom: Bees, dove, pen.
John of God: Alms, a heart, crown of thorns.
John the Baptist: Lamb, head on platter, skin of an animal.
John the Evangelist: Eagle, chalice, kettle, armor.
Josaphat Kuncevyc: Chalice, crown, winged deacon.

Joseph, Spouse of the Blessed Virgin: Infant Jesus, lily, rod, plane, carpenter's square.

Jude: Sword, square rule, club.

Justin Martyr: Ax, sword.

Lawrence: Cross, book of the Gospels, gridiron.

Leander of Seville: A pen.

Liberius: Pebbles, peacock.

Longinus: In arms at foot of the cross.

Louis IX of France: Crown of thorns, nails.

Lucy: Cord, eyes on a dish.

Luke: Ox, book, brush, palette.

Mark: Lion, book.

Martha: Holy water sprinkler, dragon.

Mary Magdalene: Alabaster box of ointment.

Matilda: Purse, alms.

Matthew: Winged man, purse, lance.

Matthias: Lance.

Maurus: Scales, spade, crutch.

Meinrad: Two ravens.

Michael: Scales, banner, sword, dragon.

Monica: Girdle, tears.

Nicholas: Three purses or balls, anchor or boat, child.

Patrick: Cross, harp, serpent, baptismal font, demons, shamrock.

Paul: Sword, book or scroll.

Peter: Keys, boat, cock.

Philip, Apostle: Column.

Philip Neri: Altar, chasuble, vial.

Rita of Cascia: Rose, crucifix, thorn.

Roch: Angel, dog, bread.

Rose of Lima: Crown of thorns, anchor, city.

Sebastian: Arrows, crown.

Simon Stock: Scapular.

Teresa of Jesus (Ávila): Heart, arrow, book.

Thérèse of Lisieux: Roses entwining a crucifix.

Thomas, Apostle: Lance, ax.

Thomas Aquinas: Chalice, monstrance, dove, ox, person trampled under foot.

Vincent de Paul: Children.

Vincent Ferrer: Pulpit, cardinal's hat, trumpet, captives.

Katchkar Cross 12th Century

Part 10

ECUMENISM AND INTERRELIGIOUS DIALOGUE

ECUMENISM

The modern ecumenical movement, meaning the relationship of the Church with other Christian denominations, has roots among nineteenth-century scholars and individuals, began its institutional life in 1910 among Protestants and Orthodox, and led to formation of the World Council of Churches in 1948. The movement developed largely outside the mainstream of Catholic interest for many years. It has now become for Catholics one of the great religious facts of our time.

The *magna carta* of ecumenism for Catholics is a complex of several documents which include, in the first place, *Unitatis Redintegratio*, the Decree on Ecumenism, promulgated by the Second Vatican Council November 21, 1964. Other enactments underlying and expanding this decree are *Lumen Gentium* (Dogmatic Constitution on the Church), *Orientalium Ecclesiarum* (Decree on Eastern Catholic Churches), and *Gaudium et Spes* (Pastoral Constitution on the Church in the Modern World).

The Holy See has more recently brought together Catholic ecumenical priorities in *Directory for the Application of Principles and Norms on Ecumenism* (1993) and *The Ecumenical Dimension in the Formation of Pastoral Workers* (1998). These, in addition to Pope John Paul II's encyclical letter, *Ut Unum Sint* (1995), provide a guide for Catholic ecumenical initiatives.

VATICAN II DECREE

The following excerpts from *Unitatis Redintegratio* cover the broad theological background and principles and indicate the thrust of the Church's commitment to ecumenism, under the subheads: Elements Common to Christians, Unity Lacking, What the Movement Involves, Primary Duty of Catholics. [Numbers in parentheses refer to citations.]

Men who believe in Christ and have been properly baptized are brought into a certain, though imperfect, communion with the Catholic Church. Undoubtedly, the differences that exist in varying degrees between them and the Catholic Church — whether in doctrine and sometimes in discipline, or concerning the structure of the Church — do indeed create many and sometimes serious obstacles to full ecclesiastical communion. These the ecumenical movement is striving to overcome (No. 3).

Elements Common to Christians

Moreover some, even very many, of the most significant elements or endowments which together go to build up and give life to the Church herself can exist outside the visible boundaries of the Catholic Church: the written word of God; the life of grace; faith, hope, and charity, along with other interior gifts of the Holy Spirit and visible elements. All of these, which come from Christ and lead back to Him, belong by right to the one Church of Christ (No. 3).

[In a later passage, the decree singled out a number of elements which the Catholic Church and other churches have in common but not in complete agreement: confession of Christ as Lord and God and as mediator between God and man; belief in the Trinity; reverence for Scripture as the revealed word of God; baptism and the Lord's Supper; Christian life and worship; faith in action; concern with moral questions.]

The brethren divided from us also carry out many of the sacred actions of the Christian religion. Undoubtedly, in ways that vary according to the condition of each church or community, these actions can truly engender a life of grace, and can be rightly described as capable of providing access to the community of salvation.

It follows that these separated Churches and Communities, though we believe they suffer from defects already mentioned, have by no means been deprived of significance and importance in the mystery of salvation. For the Spirit of Christ has not refrained from using them as means of salvation which derive their efficacy from the very fullness of grace and truth entrusted to the Catholic Church (No. 3).

Unity Lacking

Nevertheless, our separated brethren, whether considered as individuals or as Communities and Churches, are not blessed with that unity which

Jesus Christ wished to bestow on all those whom he has regenerated and vivified into one body and newness of life – that unity which the holy Scriptures and the revered tradition of the Church proclaim. For it is through Christ's Catholic Church alone, which is the all-embracing means of salvation, that the fullness of the means of salvation can be obtained. It was to the apostolic college alone, of which Peter is the head, that we believe our Lord entrusted all the blessings of the New Covenant, in order to establish on earth the one Body of Christ into which all those should be fully incorporated who already belong in any way to God's People (No. 3).

What the Movement Involves

Today, in many parts of the world, under the inspiring grace of the Holy Spirit, multiple efforts are being expended through prayer, word, and action to attain that fullness of unity which Jesus Christ desires. This sacred Synod, therefore, exhorts all the Catholic faithful to recognize the signs of the times and to participate skillfully in the work of ecumenism.

The "ecumenical movement" means those activities and enterprises which, according to various needs of the Church and opportune occasions, are started and organized for the fostering of unity among Christians. These are:

- First, every effort to eliminate words, judgments, and actions which do not respond to the condition of separated brethren with truth and fairness and so make mutual relations between them more difficult.
- Then, "dialogue" between competent experts from different Churches and Communities [scholarly ecumenism].
- In addition, these Communions cooperate more closely in whatever projects a Christian conscience demands for the common good [social ecumenism].
- They also come together for common prayer, where this is permitted [spiritual ecumenism].
- Finally, all are led to examine their own faithfulness to Christ's will for the Church and, wherever necessary, undertake with vigor the task of renewal and reform.

It is evident that the work of preparing and reconciling those individuals who wish for full Catholic communion is of its nature distinct from ecumenical action. But there is no opposition between the two, since both proceed from the wondrous providence of God (No. 4).

Primary Duty of Catholics

In ecumenical work, Catholics must assuredly be concerned for their separated brethren, praying for them, keeping them informed about the Church, making the first approaches toward them. But their primary duty is to make an honest and careful appraisal of whatever needs to be renewed and achieved in the Catholic household itself, in order that its life may bear witness more loyally and luminously to the teachings and ordinances which have been handed down from Christ through the Apostles.

Every Catholic must aim at Christian perfection (cf. Jas. 1:4; Rom. 12:1-2) and, each according to his station, play his part so that the Church may daily be more purified and renewed, against the day when Christ will present her to himself in all her glory, without spot or wrinkle (cf. Eph. 5:27).

Catholics must joyfully acknowledge and esteem the truly Christian endowments from our common heritage which are to be found among our separated brethren.

Nor should we forget that whatever is wrought by the grace of the Holy Spirit in the hearts of our separated brethren can contribute to our own edification. Whatever is truly Christian never conflicts with the genuine interests of the faith; indeed, it can always result in a more ample realization of the very mystery of Christ and the Church (No. 4).

Participation in Worship

Norms concerning participation by Catholics in the worship of other Christian Churches were sketched in this conciliar decree and elaborated in a number of other documents such as: the Decree on Eastern Catholic Churches, promulgated by the Second Vatican Council in 1964; Interim Guidelines for Prayer in Common, issued June 18, 1965, by the U.S. Bishops' Committee for Ecumenical and Interreligious Affairs; a Directory on Ecumenism, published in 1967, 1970, and 1993 by the Pontifical Council for Promoting Christian Unity; additional communications from the U.S. Bishops' Committee, and numerous sets of guidelines issued locally by and for dioceses throughout the U.S.

The norms encourage common prayer services for Christian unity and other intentions. Beyond that, they draw a distinction between separated churches of the Reformation tradition and of the Anglican Communion, and separated Eastern churches, in view of doctrine and practice the Catholic Church has in common with the separated Eastern churches concerning the apostolic succession of bishops, holy orders, liturgy and other credal matters.

Full participation by Catholics in official Protestant liturgies is prohibited, because it implies profession of the faith expressed in the liturgy. Intercommunion by Catholics at

Protestant liturgies is prohibited. Under certain conditions, Protestants may be given Holy Communion in the Catholic Church. A Catholic may stand as a witness, but not as a sponsor, in baptism, and as a witness in the marriage of separated Christians. Similarly, a Protestant may stand as a witness, but not as a sponsor, in a Catholic baptism, and as a witness in the marriage of Catholics.

The principal norms regarding liturgical participations with separated Eastern Churches are included under Eastern Ecumenism.

DIRECTORY ON ECUMENISM

A *Directory for the Application of the Principles and Norms of Ecumenism* was approved by Pope John Paul II on March 25, 1993, and published early in June. The Pontifical Council for Promoting Christian Unity said on release of the document that revision of Directories issued in 1967 and 1970 was necessary in view of subsequent developments. These included promulgation of the Code of Canon Law for the Latin Church in 1983 and of the Code of Canons of the Eastern Churches in 1990; publication of the *Catechism of the Catholic Church* in 1992; additional documents and the results of theological dialogues. In 1998, *The Ecumenical Dimension in the Formation of Pastoral Workers* was published by the Holy See to give practical and detailed guidance in the implementation of Chapter 3 of the *Directory*.

The following excerpts are from the text published in the June 16, 1993, English edition of *L'Osservatore Romano*.

Address and Purpose

"The Directory is addressed to the pastors of the Catholic Church, but it also concerns all the faithful, who are called to pray and work for the unity of Christians, under the direction of their bishops."

"At the same time, it is hoped that the Directory will also be useful to members of churches and ecclesial communities that are not in full communion with the Catholic Church."

"The new edition of the Directory is meant to be an instrument at the service of the whole Church, and especially of those who are directly engaged in ecumenical activity in the Catholic Church. The Directory intends to motivate, enlighten and guide this activity, and in some particular cases also to give binding directives in accordance with the proper competence of the Pontifical Council for Promoting Christian Unity."

Outline

Principles and norms of the document are covered in five chapters.

"I. The Search for Christian Unity. The ecumenical commitment of the Catholic Church based on the doctrinal principles of the Second Vatican Council.

"II. Organization in the Catholic Church at the Service of Christian Unity. Persons and structures involved in promoting ecumenism at all levels, and the norms that direct their activity.

"III. Ecumenical Formation in the Catholic Church. Categories of people to be formed, those responsible for formation; the aims and methods of formation; its doctrinal and practical aspects.

"IV. Communion in Life and Spiritual Activity among the Baptized. The communion that exists with other Christians on the basis of the sacramental bond of baptism, and the norms for sharing in prayer and other spiritual activities, including, in particular cases, sacramental sharing.

"V. Ecumenical Cooperation, Dialogue and Common Witness. Principles, different forms and norms for cooperation between Christians with a view to dialogue and common witness in the world."

ECUMENICAL AGENCIES

Pontifical Council

The top-level agency for Catholic ecumenical efforts is the Pontifical Council for Promoting Christian Unity (formerly the Secretariat for Promoting Christian Unity), which originated in 1960 as a preparatory commission for the Second Vatican Council. Its purposes are to provide guidance and, where necessary, coordination for ecumenical endeavor by Catholics, and to establish and maintain relations with representatives of other Christian Churches for ecumenical dialogue and action.

The council, under the direction of Cardinal Edward I. Cassidy (successor to Cardinal Johannes Willebrands), has established firm working relations with representative agencies of other churches and the World Council of Churches. It has joined in dialogue with Orthodox Churches, the Anglican Communion, the Lutheran World Federation, the World

Alliance of Reformed Churches, the World Methodist Council and other religious bodies. In the past several years, staff members and representatives of the council have been involved in one way or another in nearly every significant ecumenical enterprise and meeting held throughout the world.

While the council and its counterparts in other churches have focused primary attention on theological and other related problems of Christian unity, they have also begun, and in increasing measure, to emphasize the responsibilities of the churches for greater unity of witness and effort in areas of humanitarian need.

Bishops' Committee

The U.S. Bishops' Committee for Ecumenical and Interreligious Affairs was established by the American hierarchy in 1964. Its purposes are to maintain relationships with other Christian churches and other religious communities at the national level, to advise and assist dioceses in developing and applying ecumenical policies, and to maintain liaison with corresponding Vatican offices — the Pontifical Councils for Christian Unity and for Interreligious Dialogue. Operationally, the committee is assisted by a secretariat.

The committee co-sponsors several national consultations with other churches and confessional families. These bring together Catholic representatives and their counterparts from the Episcopal Church, the Lutheran Church, the Polish National Catholic Church, the United Methodist Church, the Orthodox Churches, the Oriental Orthodox Churches, the Alliance of Reformed Churches (North American area), the Interfaith Witness Department of the Home Mission Board of the Southern Baptist Convention. (See Ecumenical Dialogues.)

The committee relates with the National Council of Churches of Christ, through membership in the Faith and Order Commission and through observer relationship with the Commission on Regional and Local Ecumenism, and has sponsored a joint study committee investigating the possibility of Roman Catholic membership in that body.

Advisory and other services are provided by the committee to ecumenical commissions and agencies in dioceses throughout the country.

Through its Section for Catholic-Jewish Relations, the committee is in contact with several national Jewish agencies and bodies. Issues of mutual interest and shared concern are reviewed for the purpose of furthering deeper understanding between the Catholic and Jewish communities.

Through its Section for Interreligious Relations, the committee promotes activity in wider areas of dialogue with other religions, notably, with Muslims, Buddhists and Hindus. Offices of the committee are located at 3211 Fourth St. N.E., Washington, D.C. 20017.

World Council of Churches

The World Council of Churches is a fellowship of churches which acknowledge "Jesus Christ as Lord and Savior." It is a permanent organization providing constituent members — 330 churches with some 450 million communicants in 100 countries — with opportunities for meeting, consultation and cooperative action with respect to doctrine, worship, practice, social mission, evangelism and missionary work, and other matters of mutual concern.

The WCC was formally established August 23, 1948, in Amsterdam with ratification of a constitution by 147 communions. This action merged two previously existing movements — Life and Work (social mission), Faith and Order (doctrine) — which had initiated practical steps toward founding a fellowship of Christian churches at meetings held in Oxford, Edinburgh and Utrecht in 1937 and 1938. A third movement for cooperative missionary work, which originated about 1910 and, remotely, led to formation of the WCC, was incorporated into the council in 1971 under the title of the International Missionary Council.

Additional general assemblies of the council have been held since the charter meeting of 1948: in Evanston, Ill. (1954), New Delhi, India (1961), Uppsala, Sweden (1968), Nairobi, Kenya (1975), Vancouver, British Columbia, Canada (1983) and Canberra, Australia (1991). The 1998 general assembly was held in Harare, Zimbabwe, with the regular Catholic delegation in attendance, led by Bishop Mario Conti from St. Andrew's, Scotland.

The council continues the work of the International Missionary Council, the Commission on Faith and Order, and the Commission on Church and Society. The work of the council is carried out through four program units: unity and renewal; mission, education and witness; justice, peace and creation; sharing and service.

Liaison between the council and the Vatican has been maintained since 1966 through a joint working group. Roman Catholic membership in the WCC is a question officially on the agenda of this body. The Joint Commission on Society, Development and Peace (SODEPAX) was an agency of the council and the Pontifical Commission for Justice and Peace from 1968 to December 31, 1980, after which another working group was formed. Roman Catholics serve individually as full members of the Commission on Faith and Order and in various capacities on other program committees of the council.

WCC headquarters are located in Geneva, Switzerland. The United States Conference for the World Council of Churches at 475 Riverside Drive, Room 915, New York, New York. 10115, provides liaison between the U.S. churches and Geneva, a communications office for secular and church media relations, and a publications office. The WCC also maintains fraternal relations with regional, national and local councils of churches throughout the world.

National Council of Churches

The National Council of the Churches of Christ in the U.S.A., the largest ecumenical body in the United States, is an organization of 35 Protestant, Orthodox and Anglican communions, with an aggregate membership of about 52 million.

The NCC, established by the churches in 1950, was structured through the merger of twelve separate cooperative agencies. Presently, the NCC carries on work in behalf of member churches in overseas ministries, Christian education, domestic social action, communications, disaster relief, refugee assistance, rehabilitation and development, biblical translation, international affairs, theological dialogue, interfaith activities, worship and evangelism, and other areas.

Policies of the NCC are determined by a general board of approximately 270 members appointed by the constituent churches. The board meets once a year.

NCC headquarters are located at 475 Riverside Drive, New York, New York 10115.

Consultation on Church Union

The Consultation on Church Union, officially begun in 1962, is a venture of American churches seeking a united church "truly catholic, truly evangelical, and truly reformed." The churches engaged in this process, representing 25 million Christians, are the African Methodist Episcopal Church, the African Methodist Episcopal Zion Church, the Christian Church (Disciples of Christ), the Christian Methodist Episcopal Church, the Episcopal Church, the Presbyterian Church (U.S.A); the United Church of Christ, the United Methodist Church and the International Council of Community Churches.

At a plenary assembly of COCU in December, 1988, a plan of church unity was unanimously approved for submission to member churches for their action. The plan is contained in a 102-page document entitled "Churches in Covenant Communion: The Church of Christ Uniting." It proposes the formation of a covenant communion of the churches which, while remaining institutionally autonomous, would embrace together eight elements of ecclesial communion: claiming unity in faith, commitment to seek unity with wholeness, mutual recognition of members in one baptism, mutual recognition of each other as churches, mutual recognition and reconciliation of ordained ministries, celebrating the Eucharist together, engaging together in Christ's mission, and the formation together of covenanting councils at each level (national, regional, and local). At its January 1999 plenary in St. Louis, the churches proposed a 2002 decision to come into full communion as the *Churches Uniting in Christ*.

Graymoor Institute

The Graymoor Ecumenical and Interreligious Institute is a forum where issues that confront the Christian Churches are addressed, the spiritual dimensions of ecumenism are fostered, and information, documentation and developments within the ecumenical movement are published through *Ecumenical Trends*, a monthly journal.

INTERNATIONAL BILATERAL COMMISSIONS

Anglican-Roman Catholic International Commission, sponsored by the Pontifical Council for Promoting Christian Unity and the Lambeth Conference, from 1970 to 1981; succeeded by a **Second Anglican-Roman Catholic International Commission**, called into being by the Common Declaration of Pope John Paul and the Archbishop of Canterbury in 1982.

The International Theological Colloquium between Baptists and Catholics, established in 1984 by the Pontifical Council for Promoting Christian Unity and the Commission for Faith and Interchurch Cooperation of the Baptist World Alliance.

The Disciples of Christ-Roman Catholic Dialogue, organized by the Council of Christian Unity of the Christian Church (Disciples of Christ) and the U.S. Bishops' Committee for Ecumenical and Interreligious Affairs, along with participation by the Disciples' Ecumenical Consultative Council and the Unity Council; since 1977.

The Evangelical-Roman Catholic Dialogue on Mission, organized by Evangelicals and the Pontifical Council for Promoting Christian Unity; from 1977.

The Lutheran-Roman Catholic Commission on Unity, established by the Pontifical Council for

Promoting Christian Unity and the Lutheran World Federation; from 1967.

The Joint International Commission for Theological Dialogue between the Orthodox Church and the Catholic Church, established by the Holy See and 14 autocephalous Orthodox Churches, began its work at a first session held at Patmos/Rhodes in 1980. Subsequent sessions have been held at Munich (1982), Crete (1984), Bari (1987), Valamo (1988), Freising (1990), Balamand (1993), and Emmitsburg, Maryland (2000).

Pentecostal-Roman Catholic Conversations, since 1966.

The Reformed-Roman Catholic Conversations, inaugurated in 1970 by the Pontifical Council for Promoting Christian Unity and the World Alliance of Reformed Churches.

The International Joint Commission between the Catholic Church and the Coptic Orthodox Church, since 1974. Established officially in the Common Declaration signed by Pope Paul VI and Coptic Pope Shenouda III in Rome in 1973.

The Joint International Commission between the Roman Catholic Church and the Malankara Orthodox Syrian Church, since 1989.

The Joint Commission between the Catholic Church and the Malankara Jacobite Syrian Orthodox Church, since 1990.

The Assyrian Church of the East-Roman Catholic Dialogue, officially established in the Common Declaration signed by Pope John Paul II and Mar Dinkha IV in November 1994. Has been meeting annually since 1995.

U.S. ECUMENICAL DIALOGUES

Representatives of the Bishops' Committee for Ecumenical and Interreligious Affairs, National Conference of Catholic Bishops, have met in dialogue with representatives of other churches since the 1960s, for discussion of a wide variety of subjects related to the quest for unity among Christians. Following is a list of dialogue groups and the years in which dialogue began.

Anglican-Roman Catholic Consultation, 1965; North American Orthodox-Catholic Theological Consultation, 1965; Joint Committee of Orthodox and Catholic Bishops, 1981; Lutheran Consultation, 1965; Oriental Orthodox Consultation (with Armenian, Coptic, Ethiopian, Indian Malabar and Syrian Orthodox Churches), 1978; Polish National-Catholic Consultation, 1984; Presbyterian/Reformed Consultation, 1965; Southern Baptist Conversations, 1969; United Methodist Consultation, 1966; Faith and Order National Council of Churches.

ANGLICAN-ROMAN CATHOLIC FINAL REPORT

The Anglican-Roman Catholic International Commission issued a Final Report in 1982 on 12 years of dialogue on major issues of concern, especially the Eucharist and ordained ministry.

In 1988 the Lambeth Conference called parts of the report on these two subjects "consonant in substance with the faith of Anglicans." In 1991 the Congregation for the Doctrine of the Faith and the Pontifical Council for Promoting Christian Unity called the Report a significant milestone not only in relations between the Catholic Church and the Anglican Communion but in the ecumenical movement as a whole. They said, however, that it was not yet possible to state that substantial agreement had been reached on all the questions studied by the commission, and that important differences still remained with respect to essential matters of Catholic doctrine regarding the Eucharist, ordination and other subjects. Clarifications were requested.

The Anglican-Roman Catholic Commission II responded in 1994, saying that its members were in agreement regarding:

- the substantial and sacramental presence of Christ in the Eucharist;
- the propitiatory nature of the Eucharistic Sacrifice, which can also be applied to the deceased;
- institution of the sacrament of order from Christ;
- the character of priestly ordination, implying configuration to the priesthood of Christ.

In 1994 Cardinal Edward I. Cassidy, president of the Pontifical Council for Interreligious Dialogue addressed a letter to the Catholic and Anglican co-chairmen of the commission, responding to the clarifications, stating that "no further work" seems to be necessary at this time on Eucharist and ministry. Questions still remained to be answered about a number of subjects, including the authority in the Church, ordination of women, infallibility and Marian doctrine.

JOINT DECLARATION ON JUSTIFICATION
(By Russell Shaw)

Hailed by Pope John Paul II as a "milestone" on the road to Christian unity, a Lutheran-Catholic Joint Declaration on the Doctrine of Justification was signed October 31, 1999, in Augsburg, Germany, by representatives of the Catholic Church and the Lutheran World Federation.

"This document represents a sound basis for continuing the ecumenical theological research and for addressing the remaining problems with a better founded hope of resolving them in the future," Pope John Paul said the same day in Rome in a talk accompanying the recitation of the Angelus. "It is also a valuable contribution to the purification of historical memory and to our common witness."

The Joint Declaration states a "consensus" shared by the signers regarding the doctrine of justification. The key passage formulating this consensus says:

"In faith we together hold the conviction that justification is the work of the triune God. The Father sent his Son into the world to save sinners. The foundation and presupposition of justification is the incarnation, death, and resurrection of Christ. Justification thus means that Christ himself is our righteousness, in which we share through the Holy Spirit in accord with the will of the Father.

"Together we confess: By grace alone, in faith in Christ's saving work and not because of any merit on our part, we are accepted by God and receive the Holy Spirit, who renews our hearts while equipping and calling us to good works."

The signers of the Joint Declaration were Cardinal Edward I. Cassidy, President of the Vatican's Pontifical Council for Promoting Christian Unity, and Bishop Christian Krause, President of the Lutheran World Federation, which represents 58 million of the world's 61 million Lutherans. Most, but not all, of the churches within the federation have accepted the Joint Declaration.

Both the date and the place of the signing had symbolic significance. October 31 is observed by Protestants as Reformation Day, commemorating Martin Luther's nailing of his Ninety-five Theses on the castle church door in Wittenberg on that date in 1517. The city of Augsburg is associated with the Augsburg Confession, a document authored in 1530 by the Protestant Reformer Philipp Melancthon in an attempt to bring about a reconciliation between Lutherans and Catholics.

From a theological perspective, the doctrine of justification was of central importance in the Reformation and in the mutual condemnations exchanged by Catholics and Lutherans in the 16th century via the Council of Trent and the Lutheran Confessions.

The Joint Declaration stresses that the churches "neither take the condemnations lightly nor do they disavow their own past." But, it insists, as a result of ecumenical dialogue during the last 30 years, they have come to "new insights" that transcend the mutual polemics of the Reformation era and make it clear that neither party's understanding of justification, as it is expressed in the Joint Declaration, now merits condemnation by the other, while the differences about the doctrine that continue to exist between them "are acceptable."

The Council for Promoting Christian Unity and the Lutheran World Federation reached basic agreement on the document in June, 1998, but further clarifications were required on both sides before official approval was forthcoming. These clarifications are embodied in an "Annex" to the text.

Cardinal Cassidy listed "three basic truths" that he said were central to the doctrine of justification and to the Lutheran-Catholic consensus expressed in the Joint Declaration. They are:

"Firstly, justification is a free gift bestowed by the Trinitarian God and centers on the person of Christ who became incarnate, died and rose.

St. Saba — "The Great Laura"

In being related to the person of Christ through the work of the Holy Spirit, we enter into a condition of righteousness. . . .

"Secondly, we receive this salvation in faith. . . . [T]he reality of justification is linked to faith, but not simply as an intellectual assent of the mind. Rather the believer is to give him/herself over to Christ in the renewal of life.

"Thirdly, justification points to the heart of the Gospel message, but must be seen in an organic unity with all the other truths of faith: Trinity, Christology, Ecclesiology and Sacraments."

The Joint Declaration begins with a Preamble that includes this statement of the document's intention: ". . . to show that on the basis of their dialogue the subscribing Lutheran churches and the Roman Catholic Church are now able to articulate a common understanding of our justification by God's grace through faith in Christ. It does not cover all that either church teaches about justification; it does encompass a consensus on basic truths of the doctrine of justification and shows that the remaining differences in its explication are no longer the occasion for doctrinal condemnations."

Following an overview of significant scriptural passages on the doctrine (section one), the document notes that, historically, justification has been an ecumenical problem between the Catholic Church and the Reformation churches and that differences focusing on it were the "principal cause" of their division and mutual condemnations in the 16th century. But in the ecumenical dialogue since the Second Vatican Council (1962-1965), it says, a "notable convergence" has emerged (section two).

The Joint Declaration then states the "consensus" on the basic truths of the doctrine, quoted above (section three). Justification is said to be "more than just one part of Christian doctrine. It stands in an essential relation with all truths of faith, which are to be seen as internally related to each other."

The fourth section of the Declaration ("Explicating the Common Understanding of Justification") is the document's longest section. It identifies, one by one, seven particular questions relating to the doctrine, states the consensus shared by Lutherans and Catholics regarding these seven questions, and then sets out distinctive Catholic and Lutheran perspectives on each.

The seven topics treated in this manner are: "Human Powerlessness and Sin in Relation to Justification," "Justification as Forgiveness of Sins and Making Righteous," "Justification by Faith and through Grace," "The Justified as Sinner," "Law and Gospel," "Assurance of Salvation," and "The Good Works of the Justified."

The Joint Declaration closes by once again underlining the "consensus in basic truths" regarding justification and stating its "significance and scop."

In particular, Cardinal Cassidy said, "Catholics are not able to share the Eucharist with their Lutheran brothers and sisters. . . . Our common participation in the Eucharist awaits the full ecclesial communion which we seek."

Nevertheless, Cardinal Cassidy added, the limitations of what has been accomplished in reaching this agreement should not cause it to be underestimated. "Serious difficulties remain, but they are secondary to what we hold in common. No longer may we look upon our different expressions of faith as being like two huge cannons drawn up in battle line and facing each other. . . . We need, above all, to give thanks to God for this achievement."

THE RELATIONSHIP OF ANGLICANS AND ROMAN CATHOLICS

(By Dr. John Borelli, associate director, Secretariat for Ecumenical and Interreligious Affairs, National Conference of Catholic Bishops)

A special consultation of Roman Catholic and Anglican bishops from thirteen regions around the world met in Mississauga, Ontario, May 14-20, 2000, to review and evaluate the accomplishment of thirty years of dialogue between the two traditions and to reflect on how the special relationship has been developing in various parts of the world. Bishops attended from New Zealand, Canada, England, United States, Ireland, India, Nigeria, Papua New Guinea, Southern Africa, Uganda, Australia, Brazil and the West Indies.

The meeting was convened by His Eminence Edward Cardinal Cassidy, President of the Pontifical Council Promoting Christian Unity, and His Grace Archbishop George Carey of Canterbury. Also participating were the two recently appointed co-chairman for the Anglican-Roman Catholic International Commission: the Most Rev. Frank T. Griswold, Presiding Bishop of the Episcopal Church (U. S.) and Most Rev. Alexander J. Brunett, Archbishop of Seattle.

On May 20, 2000, Cardinal Cassidy and Archbishop Carey released two short documents resulting from the meeting and a press release: "Communion in Mission" and "Action Plan to

Implement 'Communion in Mission.'" They reported that the bishops had spent a week in prayer together, worship, and reflection. They focused on the relationship between their communions which the Second Vatican Council said "occupies a special place" (*Decree on Ecumenism* 13). They also reported how the participants came to see that the relationship is no longer to be viewed in minimal terms but has reached a significant new place. The texts acknowledge unresolved differences and challenges, but they felt that these did not compare with all that Anglicans and Catholics hold in common. They also list the essentials of the faith and common practices to which the faithful hold fast and noted areas of theological convergence that have been achieved. They also express a common vision of full and visible unity.

The strength of the texts resulting from the special consultation lies in the recommendations. First, as a sign of the new stage in relations, they recommend the signing and celebration of a Joint Declaration of Agreement. This may turn out to be something on the scale of the joint declaration between Catholics and Lutherans on the doctrine of justification. To prepare the joint declaration and promote and monitor the reception of theological agreements, they recommend the formation of a Joint Unity Commission. They go into some detail how the bishops at the meeting believed the membership, accountability and mandate of the commission should be defined as well as how the participants themselves and how the Anglican-Roman Catholic International Commission for dialogue might follow up to this meeting.

Much has been achieved in thirty five years of dialogue both on the international commission and on various national Anglican-Roman Catholic commissions, but now a special effort will be made to incorporate these theological agreements into the lives of the churches. Also, in more formal ways, Anglicans and Catholics will be encouraged to spend more time together in prayer, study, consultation, teaching, preparation of educational and liturgical materials, marriage preparation, and common action. Bishops of both churches will be asked to gather more frequently and to work together and consult more often, especially prior to one church making decisions on matters of faith and morals which would affect the other church. Catholics and Anglicans will be asked to live more visibly the unity they already share in service and witness to the gospel. As they strive to participate together in the mission of the Church, Catholics and Anglicans will inevitably return to the unresolved differences and challenges and may be able to address them in a renewed spirit of unity and guided by the results of the ecumenical dialogue which will continue. The shape of how Anglicans and Catholics will live together in full visible unity has yet to be discerned fully, but for the present there seems to be a reinvigorated effort to live more visibly the unity they already have.

SEPARATED EASTERN CHURCHES

THE ORTHODOX CHURCH

This is a group of Eastern churches of the Byzantine tradition that were in full communion with Rome during the first millennium, and which all recognize the Patriarch of Constantinople as the first Orthodox bishop. In spite of the division between Catholics and Orthodox, often symbolized by the mutual excommunications of 1054, the Catholic Church considers itself to be in almost full communion with the Orthodox Churches. According to Vatican II, they "are still joined to us in closest intimacy" in various ways, especially in the priesthood and Eucharist. The Orthodox Churches recognize the first seven ecumenical councils as normative for their faith, along with the Scriptures and other local councils that took place in later centuries.

The Orthodox Churches are organized in approximately 15 autocephalous (independent) churches that correspond in most cases to nations or ethnic groups. The Ecumenical Patriarch of Constantinople (modern Istanbul) has a primacy of honor among the patriarchs, but his actual jurisdiction is limited to his own patriarchate. As the spiritual head of worldwide Orthodoxy, he serves as a point of unity, and has the right to call Pan-Orthodox assemblies.

Top-level relations between the Churches have improved in recent years through the efforts of Ecumenical Patriarch Athenagoras I, John XXIII, Paul VI, and Patriarch Dimitrios I. Pope Paul met with Athenagoras three times before the latter's death in 1972. The most significant action of both spiritual leaders was their mutual nullification of excommunications imposed by the two Churches on each other in 1054. Development of better relations with the Orthodox has been a priority of John Paul II since the beginning of his pontificate. Both he and Orthodox Ecumenical Patriarch Bartholomew have made known their commitment to better relations, despite contentions between Eastern Catholic and Orthodox Churches over charges of proselytism and rival property claims in places liberated from anti-religious communist control in the recent past.

The largest Orthodox body in the United States is the Greek Orthodox Archdiocese of America consisting of nine dioceses; it has an estimated membership of 1.9 million. The second largest is the Orthodox Church in America, with more than one million members; it was given autocephalous status by the Patriarchate of Moscow May 18, 1970, without the consent of the Patriarchate of Constantinople. An additional 650,000 or more Orthodox belong to smaller national and language jurisdictions. Heads of orthodox jurisdictions in this hemisphere hold membership in the Standing Conference of Canonical Orthodox Bishops in the Americas.

JURISDICTIONS

The Autocephalous Orthodox Churches

Patriarchate of Constantinople (Ecumenical Patriarchate), with jurisdiction in Turkey, Crete, the Dodecanese, and Greeks in the rest of the world outside Greece and Africa. Autonomous churches linked to the Ecumenical Patriarchate exist in Finland and Estonia. Several other jurisdictions of various ethnicities in the diaspora are also directly under the Patriarchate.

Patriarchate of Alexandria, with jurisdiction in Egypt and the rest of Africa; it includes a native African Orthodox Church centered in Kenya and Uganda.

Patriarchate of Antioch, with jurisdiction in Syria, Lebanon, Iraq, Australia, the Americas.

Patriarchate of Jerusalem, with jurisdiction in Israel and Jordan. The autonomous church of Mount Sinai is linked to the Jerusalem Patriarchate.

Russian Orthodox Church, the Patriarchate of Moscow with jurisdiction over most of the former

Soviet Union. Autonomous churches in Japan and China are linked to the Moscow Patriarchate, and since the breakup of the Soviet Union, a certain autonomy has been granted to the Orthodox churches in the newly independent republics of Ukraine, Belarus, Estonia, Moldova and Latvia.

The Serbian Orthodox Church, a patriarchate with jurisdiction in all of former Yugoslavia, Western Europe, North America and Australia.

The Romanian Orthodox Church, a patriarchate with jurisdiction in Romania, Western Europe and North America.

The Bulgarian Orthodox Church, a patriarchate with jurisdiction in Bulgaria, Western Europe and North America.

The Georgian Orthodox Church, a patriarchate with jurisdiction in the republic of Georgia.

The Orthodox Church of Cyprus, an archbishopric with jurisdiction in Cyprus.

The Orthodox Church of Greece, an archbishopric with jurisdiction in most of Greece.

The Orthodox Church of Poland, a metropolitanate with jurisdiction in Poland.

The Orthodox Church of Albania, an archbishopric with jurisdiction in Albania.

The Orthodox Church in the Czech and Slovak Republics, a metropolitanate with jurisdiction in the Czech and Slovak Republics. Its autocephalous status was granted by Moscow in 1951 but by Constantinople only in 1998.

The Orthodox Church in America, a metropolitanate with jurisdiction in North America and a few parishes in Latin America and Australia. Its autocephalous status was granted by Moscow in 1970; Constantinople and most other Orthodox churches have not recognized this.

Population

The Division of Archives and Statistics of the Eastern Orthodox World Foundation reported a 1970 estimate of more than 200 million Orthodox Church members throughout the world. A contemporary estimate put the number close to 220 million. Many Orthodox today claim a total membership of about 300 million.

Conference of Orthodox Bishops

The Standing Conference of Canonical Orthodox Bishops in the Americas was established in 1960 to achieve cooperation among the various Orthodox jurisdictions in the Americas. Office: 8-10 East 79th St., New York, NY 10021.

Member churches are the: Albanian Orthodox Diocese of America (Ecumenical Patriarchate), American Carpatho-Russian

From a Moscow Pantocrator Illumination

Orthodox Greek Catholic Diocese in the U.S.A. (Ecumenical Patriarchate), Antiochian Orthodox Christian Archdiocese of North America, Bulgarian Eastern Orthodox Church, Greek Orthodox Archdiocese of America (Ecumenical Patriarchate), Orthodox Church in America, Romanian Orthodox Archdiocese in America and Canada, Serbian Orthodox Church in the United States and Canada, Ukrainian Orthodox Church in the United States (Ecumenical Patriarchate), Ukrainian Orthodox Church of Canada (Ecumenical Patriarchate).

ANCIENT CHURCHES OF THE EAST

The Ancient Eastern Churches, which are distinct from the Orthodox Churches, were the subject of an article by Gerard Daucourt published in the February 16, 1987, English edition of *L'Osservatore Romano*. Following is an adaptation:

By Ancient Eastern Churches one means: the Assyrian Church of the East (formerly called Nestorian), the Armenian Apostolic Church, the Coptic Orthodox Church, the Ethiopian Orthodox Church, the Syrian Orthodox Church (sometimes called Jacobite) and the Malankara Orthodox Syrian Church of India.

After the Council of Ephesus (431), the Assyrian Church of the East did not maintain communion with the rest of the Christian world. For reasons as much and perhaps more political than doctrinal, it did not accept the Council's teaching (that Mary is the Mother of God, in opposition to the opinion of Nestorius; see Nestorianism. For this reason, the Assyrian Church of the East came to be called Nestorian.) It is well known that in the 16th century a great segment of the faithful of this Church entered into communion with the See of Rome and constitutes today, among the Eastern Catholic Churches, the Chaldean Patriarchate. The Patriarch of the Assyrian Church of the East, His Holiness Mar Dinkha IV, in the course of his visit to the Holy Father and to the Church of Rome of November 7-9, 1984, requested that people stop using the term "Nestorian" to designate his Church and expressed the desire that a declaration made jointly by the Pope of Rome and himself may one day serve to express the common faith of the two Churches in Jesus Christ, Son of God incarnate, born of the Virgin Mary. The labors of Catholic historians and theologians have, moreover, already contributed to showing that such a declaration would be possible.

The other Ancient Churches of the East (today known as the Oriental Orthodox Churches) for a long time have been designated by the term "Monophysite Churches" (see Monophysitism). It is regrettable to find this name still employed sometimes in certain publications, since already in 1951, in the encyclical *Sempiternus Rex*, on the occasion of the 15th centenary of the Council of Chalcedon, Pius XII declared with regard to the Christians of these Churches: "They depart from the right way only in terminology, when they expound the doctrine of the Incarnation of the Lord. This may be deduced from their liturgical and theological books."

In this same encyclical, Pius XII expressed the view that the separation at the doctrinal level came about "above all, through a certain ambiguity of terminology that occurred at the beginning." Since then, two important declarations have been arrived at in line with the ecumenical stance taken by the Church at the Second Vatican Council and the labors of the theologians (particularly in the framework of the Foundation "Pro Oriente" of Vienna). One was signed by Pope Paul VI and Coptic Patriarch Shenouda III on May 10, 1973, and the other by Pope John Paul II and the Syrian Patriarch Ignatius Zakka II was, on June 23, 1984. In both of these texts, the hierarchies of the respective Churches confess one and the same faith in the mystery of the Word Incarnate. After such declarations, it is no longer possible to speak in general terms of the "Monophysite" Churches. The Armenian Apostolic Church has communicants in the former Soviet Union, the Middle and Far East, the Americas. The Coptic Orthodox Church is centered in Egypt and has a growing diaspora overseas. The Syrian Orthodox Church has communicants in the Middle East, the Americas, and India. Members of the Assyrian Church of the East are scattered throughout the world, and the Patriarch now resides near Chicago, Illinois.

It is estimated that there are approximately ten million or more members of these other Eastern Churches throughout the world. For various reasons, a more accurate determination is not possible.

EASTERN ECUMENISM

The Second Vatican Council, in *Orientalium Ecclesiarum*, the Decree on Eastern Catholic Churches, pointed out the special role they have to play "in promoting the unity of all Christians." The document also stated in part as follows.

The Eastern Churches in communion with the Apostolic See of Rome have a special role to play in promoting the unity of all Christians, particularly Easterners, according to the principles of this sacred Synod's Decree on Ecumenism first of all by prayer, then by the example of their lives, by religious fidelity to ancient Eastern traditions, by greater mutual knowledge, by collaboration, and by a brotherly regard for objects and attitudes (No. 24).

If any separated Eastern Christian should, under the guidance of grace of the Holy Spirit, join himself to Catholic unity, no more should be required of him than what a simple profession of the Catholic faith demands. A valid priesthood is preserved among Eastern clerics. Hence, upon joining themselves to the unity of the Catholic Church, Eastern clerics are permitted to exercise the orders they possess, in accordance with the regulations established by the competent authority (No. 25).

Divine Law forbids any common worship (*communicatio in sacris*) which would damage the unity of the Church, or involve formal acceptance of falsehood or the danger of deviation in the faith, of scandal, or of indifferentism. At the same time, pastoral experience clearly shows that with respect to our Eastern brethren there should and can be taken into consideration various circumstances affecting individuals, wherein the unity of the Church is not jeopardized nor are intolerable risks involved, but in which salvation itself and the spiritual profit of souls are urgently at issue.

Hence, in view of special circumstances of time, place, and personage, the Catholic Church has often adopted and now adopts a milder policy, offering to all the means of salvation and an example of charity among Christians through participation in the sacraments and in other sacred functions and objects. With these considerations in mind, and "lest because of the harshness of our judgment we prove an obstacle to those seeking salvation," and in order to promote closer union with the Eastern Churches separated from us, this sacred Synod lays down the following policy:

In view of the principles recalled above, Eastern Christians who are separated in good faith from the Catholic Church, if they ask of their own accord and have the right dispositions, may be granted the sacraments of penance, the Eucharist, and the anointing of the sick. Furthermore, Catholics may ask for these same sacraments from those non-Catholic ministers whose Churches possess valid sacraments, as often as necessity or a genuine spiritual benefit recommends such a course of action, and when access to a Catholic priest is physically or morally impossible (Nos. 26, 27).

Again, in view of these very same principles, Catholics may for a just cause join with their separated Eastern brethren in sacred functions, things, and places (No. 28). Bishops decide when and if to follow this lenient policy.

Recent Documents

Three recent documents of importance with respect to relations between Catholic and separated Eastern Churches are the apostolic letter, *Orientale Lumen*, issued May 5, 1995; the encyclical letter, *Ut Unum Sint*, issued May 30, 1995; and the Christological Declaration signed November 11, 1994, by Pope John Paul and His Holiness Mar Dinkha IV, Catholicos-Patriarch of the Assyrian Church of the East. The text of the Christological Document follows.

CHRISTOLOGICAL DECLARATION

Following is the text of the "Common Christological Declaration" between the Catholic Church and the Assyrian Church of the East, signed November 11, 1994, by Pope John Paul II and His Holiness Mar Dinkha IV, Catholicos-Patriarch of the Assyrian Church of the East. The declaration acknowledges that, despite past differences, both churches profess the same faith in the real union of divine and human natures in the divine Person of Christ. Providing background to the declaration was the Assyrian Church's adherence to the teaching of Nestorius who, in the fifth century, denied the real unity of divine and human natures in the single divine Person of Christ.

The text was published in the November 16, 1994, English edition of *L'Osservatore Romano*:

As heirs and guardians of the faith received from the Apostles as formulated by our common Fathers in the Nicene Creed, we confess one Lord Jesus Christ, the only Son of God, begotten of the Father from all eternity who, in the fullness of time, came down from heaven and became man for our salvation. The Word of God, second

Person of the Holy Trinity, became incarnate by the power of the Holy Spirit in assuming from the Virgin Mary a body animated by a rational soul, with which he was indissolubly united from the moment of conception.

Unity of Two Natures in One Person

Therefore our Lord Jesus Christ is true God and true man, perfect in his divinity and perfect in his humanity, consubstantial with the Father and consubstantial with us in all things but sin. His divinity and his humanity are united in one person, without confusion or change, without division or separation. In him has been preserved the difference of the natures of divinity and humanity, with all their properties, faculties and operations. But far from constituting "one and another," the dignity and humanity are united in the person of the same and unique Son of God and Lord Jesus Christ, who is the object of a single adoration. Christ therefore is not an "ordinary man" whom God adopted in order to reside in him and inspire him, as in the righteous ones and the prophets. But the same God the Word, begotten of his Father before all worlds without beginning according to his divinity, was born of a mother without a father in the last times according to his humanity. The humanity to which the Blessed Virgin Mary gave birth always was that of the Son of God himself. That is the reason the Assyrian Church of the East is praying the Virgin Mary as "the Mother of Christ our God and Savior." In the light of this same faith the Catholic tradition addresses the Virgin Mary

The Resurrection — The Three Marys

as "the Mother of God" and also as "the Mother of Christ." We both recognize the legitimacy and rightness of these expressions of the same faith and we both respect the preference of each Church in her liturgical life and piety.

Confession of the Same Faith

This is the unique faith that we profess in the mystery of Christ. The controversies of the past led to anathemas, bearing on persons and on formulas. The Lord's Spirit permits us to understand better today that the divisions brought about in this way were due in large part to misunderstandings. Whatever our Christological divergences have been, we experience ourselves united today in the confession of the same faith in the Son of God who became man so that we might become children of God by his grace. We wish from now on to witness together to this faith in the One who is the Way, the Truth and the Life, proclaiming it in appropriate ways to our contemporaries, so that the world may believe in the Gospel of salvation. The mystery of the Incarnation which we profess in common is not an abstract and isolated truth. It refers to the Son of God sent to save us. The economy of salvation, which has its origin in the mystery of communion of the Holy Trinity — Father, Son and Holy Spirit — is brought to its fulfillment through the sharing in this communion, by grace, within the one, holy, catholic and apostolic Church, which is the People of God, the Body of Christ and the Temple of the Spirit.

The Sacraments

Believers become members of this Body through the sacrament of Baptism, through which, by water and the working of the Holy Spirit, they are born again as new creatures. They are confirmed by the seal of the Holy Spirit who bestows the sacrament of anointing. Their communion with God and among themselves is brought to full realization by the celebration of the unique offering of Christ in the sacrament of the Eucharist. This communion is restored for the sinful members of the Church when they are reconciled with God and with one another through the sacrament of Forgiveness. The sacrament of Ordination to the ministerial priesthood in the apostolic succession assures the authenticity of the faith, the sacraments and the communion in each local Church.

Sister Churches But Not Full Communion

Living by this faith and these sacraments, it follows as a consequence that the particular Catholic Churches and the particular Assyrian Churches can recognize each other as sister

Churches. To be full and entire, communion presupposes the unanimity concerning the content of the faith, the sacraments and the constitution of the Church. Since this unanimity for which we aim has not yet been attained, we cannot unfortunately celebrate together the Eucharist which is the sign of the ecclesial communion already fully restored. Nevertheless, the deep spiritual communion in the faith and the mutual trust already existing between our Churches entitles us from now on to consider witnessing together to the gospel message and cooperating in particular pastoral situations, including especially the areas of catechesis and the formation of future priests.

Commitment to Unity Efforts

In thanking God for having made us rediscover what already unites us in the faith and the sacraments, we pledge ourselves to do everything possible to dispel the obstacles of the past which still prevent the attainment of full communion between our Churches, so that we can better respond to the Lord's call for the unity of his own, a unity which has of course to be expressed visibly. To overcome these obstacles, we now establish a Mixed Committee for theological dialogue between the Catholic Church and the Assyrian Church of the East. Given at Saint Peter's on November 11, 1994.

INTERRELIGIOUS DIALOGUE

JUDAISM

Judaism is the religion of the Hebrew Bible and of contemporary Jews. Divinely revealed and with a patriarchal background (Abraham and Sarah, Isaac and Jacob), it originated with the Mosaic Covenant, was identified with the Israelites, and achieved distinctive form and character as the religion of the Torah (Law, "The Teaching") from this Covenant and reforms initiated by Ezra and Nehemiah after the Babylonian Exile.

Judaism does not have a formal creed but its principal points of belief are clear. Basic is belief in one transcendent God who reveals himself through the Torah, the prophets, the life of his people and events of history. The fatherhood of God involves the brotherhood of all humanity. Religious faith and practice are equated with just living according to God's Law. Moral conviction and practice are regarded as more important than precise doctrinal formulation and profession. Formal worship, whose principal act was sacrifice from the Exodus times to 70 A.D., is by prayer, reading and meditating upon the sacred writings, and observance of the Sabbath and festivals.

Judaism has messianic expectations of the complete fulfillment of the Covenant, the coming of God's kingdom, the ingathering of his people, and final judgment and retribution for all. Views differ regarding the manner in which these expectations will be realized — through a person, the community of God's people, an evolution of historical events, an eschatological act of God himself. Individual salvation expectations also differ, depending on views about the nature of immortality, punishment and reward, and related matters.

Catholic-Jewish Relations

The Second Vatican Council, in addition to the Decree on Ecumenism (concerning the movement for unity among Christians, stated the mind of the Church on a similar matter in *Nostra Aetate*, a Declaration on the Relationship of the Church to Non-Christian Religions. This document, as the following excerpts indicate, backgrounds the reasons and directions of the Church's regard for the Jews. (Other portions of the document refer to Hindus, Buddhists and Muslims.)

Spiritual Bond

As this sacred Synod searches into the mystery of the Church, it recalls the spiritual bond linking the people of the New Covenant with Abraham's stock.

For the Church of Christ acknowledges that, according to the mystery of God's saving design, the beginnings of her faith and her election are already found among the patriarchs, Moses, and the prophets. She professes that all who believe in Christ, Abraham's sons according to faith (cf. Gal. 3:7), are included in the same patriarch's call, and likewise that the salvation of the Church was mystically foreshadowed by the Chosen People's exodus from the land of bondage.

The Church, therefore, cannot forget that she received the revelation of the Old Testament through the people with whom God in his inexpressible mercy deigned to establish the Ancient Covenant. Nor can she forget that she draws sustenance from the root of that good olive tree onto which have been grafted the wild olive branches of the Gentiles (cf. Rom. 11:17-24).

Indeed, the Church believes that by his cross Christ, our Peace, reconciled Jew and Gentile, making them both one in himself (cf. Eph. 2:14-16).

The Jews still remain most dear to God because of their fathers, for he does not repent of the gifts he makes nor of the calls he issues (cf. Rom. 11:28-29). In company with the prophets and the same Apostle (Paul), the Church awaits that day, known to God alone, on which all peoples will address the Lord in a single voice and "serve him with one accord" (Zeph. 3:9; cf. Is. 66:23; Ps. 65:4; Rom. 11:11-32).

Since the spiritual patrimony common to Christians and Jews is thus so great, this sacred Synod wishes to foster and recommend that mutual understanding and respect which is the fruit above all of biblical and theological studies, and of brotherly dialogues.

No Anti-Semitism

True, authorities of the Jews and those who followed their lead pressed for the death of Christ (cf. Jn. 19:6); still, what happened in his passion cannot be blamed upon all the Jews then living, without distinction, nor upon the Jews of today. Although the Church is the new People of God, the Jews should not be presented as repudiated or cursed by God, as if such views followed from the holy Scriptures. All should take pains, then, lest in catechetical instruction and in the preaching of God's Word they teach anything out of harmony with the truth of the Gospel and the spirit of Christ.

The Church repudiates all persecutions against any person. Moreover, mindful of her common patrimony with the Jews, and motivated by the Gospel's spiritual love and by no political considerations, she deplores the hatred, persecutions, and displays of anti-Semitism directed against the Jews at any time and from any source (No. 4).

The Church rejects, as foreign to the mind of Christ, any discrimination against men or harassment of them because of their race, color, condition of life, or religion (No. 5).

Bishops' Secretariat

The American hierarchy's first move toward implementation of the Vatican II Declaration on the Relationship of the Church to Non-Christian Religions (*Nostra Aetate*) was to establish, in 1965, a Subcommission for Catholic-Jewish Relations in the framework of its Commission for Ecumenical and Interreligious Affairs.

According to the key norm of a set of guidelines issued by the secretariat March 16, 1967, and updated April 9, 1985: "The general aim of all Catholic-Jewish meetings (and relations) is to increase our understanding both of Judaism and the Catholic faith, to eliminate sources of tension and misunderstanding, to initiate dialogue or conversations on different levels, to multiply intergroup meetings between Catholics and Jews, and to promote cooperative social action."

Vatican Guidelines

In a document issued January 3, 1975, the Vatican Commission for Religious Relations with the Jews offered a number of suggestions and guidelines for implementing the Christian-Jewish portion of the Second Vatican Council's Declaration on Relations with Non-Christian Religions.

Among "suggestions from experience" were those concerning dialogue, liturgical links between Christian and Jewish worship, the interpretation of biblical texts, teaching and education for the purpose of increasing mutual understanding, and joint social action.

Notes on Preaching and Catechesis

On June 24, 1985, the Vatican Commission for Religious Relations with the Jews promulgated its "Notes on the Correct Way to Present Jews and Judaism in Preaching and Catechesis in the Roman Catholic Church," with the intent of providing "a helpful frame of reference for those who are called upon in the course of their teaching assignments to speak about Jews and Judaism and who wish to do so in keeping with the current teaching of the Church in this area."

The document states emphatically that, since the relationship between the Church and the Jewish people is one "founded on the design of the God of the Covenant," Judaism does not occupy "an occasional and marginal place in catechesis," but an "essential" one that "should be organically integrated" throughout the curriculum on all levels of Catholic education.

The Notes discuss the relationship between the Hebrew Scriptures and the New Testament, focusing especially on typology, which is called "the sign of a problem unresolved." Underlined is the "eschatological dimension," that "the people of God of the Old and the New Testament are tending toward a like end in the future: the coming or return of the Messiah." Jewish witness to God's Kingdom, the Notes declare, challenges Christians to "accept our responsibility to prepare the world for the coming of the Messiah by working together for social justice and reconciliation."

The Notes emphasize the Jewishness of Jesus' teaching, correct misunderstandings concerning the portrayal of Jews in the New Testament and describe the Jewish origins of Christian liturgy.

One section addresses the "spiritual fecundity" of Judaism to the present, its continuing "witness — often heroic — of its fidelity to the one God," and mandates the development of Holocaust curricula and a positive approach in Catholic education to the "religious attachment which finds its roots in biblical tradition" between the Jewish people and the Land of Israel, affirming the "existence of the State of Israel" on the basis of "the common principles of international law."

Papal Statements

(Courtesy of Dr. Eugene Fisher, associate director of the Bishops' Committee for Ecumenical and Interreligious Affairs.)

Pope John Paul II, in a remarkable series of addresses beginning in 1979, has sought to promote and give shape to the development of dialogue between Catholics and Jews.

In a homily delivered June 7, 1979, at Auschwitz, which he called the "Golgotha of the Modern World," he prayed movingly for "the memory of the people whose sons and daughters were intended for total extermination."

International Liaison Committee

The International Catholic-Jewish Liaison Committee was formed in 1971 and is the official link between the Commission for Religious Relations with the Jewish People and the International Jewish Committee for Interreligious Consultations. The committee meets every 18 months to examine matters of common interest.

Topics under discussion have included: mission and witness (Venice, 1977), religious education (Madrid, 1978), religious liberty and pluralism (Regensburg, 1979), religious commitment (London, 1981), the sanctity of human life in an age of violence (Milan, 1982), youth and faith (Amsterdam, 1984), the Vatican Notes on Preaching and Catechesis (Rome, 1985), the Holocaust (Prague, 1990), education and social action (Baltimore, Md., 1992), family and ecology (Jerusalem, 1994).

Pope John Paul II, addressing in Rome a celebration of *Nostra Aetate* (the Second Vatican Council's "Declaration on the Relationship of the Church to Non-Christian Religions") by the Liaison Committee, stated: "What you are celebrating is nothing other than the divine mercy which is guiding Christians and Jews to mutual awareness, respect, cooperation and solidarity. The universal openness of *Nostra Aetate* is anchored in and takes its orientation from a high sense of the absolute singularity of God's choice of a particular people. The Church is fully aware that Sacred Scripture bears witness that the Jewish people, this community of faith and custodian of a tradition thousands of years old, is an intimate part of the mystery of revelation and of salvation."

Family Rights and Obligations

The Liaison Committee, at its May 1994, meeting in Jerusalem, issued its first joint statement, on the family — in anticipation of the UN Cairo Conference subsequently held in September.

The statement affirmed that "the rights and obligations of the family do not come from the State but exist prior to the State and ultimately have their source in God the Creator. The family is far more than a legal, social or economic unit. For both Jews and Christians, it is a stable community of love and solidarity based on God's covenant."

Caring for God's Creation

During its March 23-26, 1998 meeting in the Vatican, the Liaison Committee issued its second joint statement, on the environment. Drawing deeply on the shared sacred text of Genesis, the Committee affirmed that "concern for the environment has led both Catholics and Jews to reflect on the concrete implications of their belief in God, creator of all things," especially "a recognition of the mutual dependence between the land and the human person." The document concluded, "Care for creation is also a religious act."

Vatican-Israel Accord

On December 30, 1993, a year of dramatic developments in the Middle East was capped by the signing in Jerusalem of a "Fundamental Agreement" between representatives of the Holy See and the State of Israel. The agreement acknowledged in its preamble that the signers were "aware of the unique nature of the relationship between the Catholic Church and the Jewish people, and of the historic process of reconciliation and growth in mutual understanding and friendship between Catholics and Jews." Archbishop (later Cardinal) William H. Keeler, president of the National Conference of Catholic Bishops, welcomed the accord together with the Israeli Ambassador to the United States at a ceremony at the NCCB headquarters in Washington. (See also News Events for recent developments.)

In 1996, the Anti-Defamation League published a set of documents related to the accord, entitled "A Challenge Long Delayed," edited by Eugene Fisher and Rabbi Klenicki.

U.S. Dialogue

The National Workshop on Christian-Jewish Relations, begun in 1973 by the NCCB

Secretariat, draws more than 1,000 participants from around the world. Recent workshops have been held in Baltimore (1986), Minneapolis (1987), Charleston, South Carolina (1989), Chicago (1990), Pittsburgh (1992), Tulsa (1994), Stamford (1996), and Houston (1999).

In October 1987, the Bishops' Committee for Ecumenical and Interreligious Affairs began a series of twice-yearly consultations with representatives of the Synagogue Council of America. Topics of discussion have included education, human rights, respect for life, the Middle East. The consultation has issued several joint statements: "On Moral Values in Public Education" (1990), "On Stemming the Proliferation of Pornography" (1993), "On Dealing with Holocaust Revisionism" (1994).

Ongoing relationships are maintained by the NCCB Secretariat with such Jewish agencies as the American Jewish Committee, the Anti-Defamation League, B'nai B'rith International, and the National Jewish Council for Public Affairs.

In June, 1988, the Bishops' Committee for Ecumenical and Interreligious Affairs published in Spanish and English Criteria for the Evaluation of Dramatizations of the Passion, providing for the first time Catholic guidelines for passion plays.

In January, 1989, the Bishops' Committee for the Liturgy issued guidelines for the homiletic presentation of Judaism under the title, "God's Mercy Endures Forever."

When the Synagogue Council of America dissolved in 1995, the Bishops' Committee for Ecumenical and Interreligious Affairs initiated separate consultations with the new National Council of Synagogues (Reform and Conservative), chaired by Cardinal William H. Keeler, and the Orthodox Union/Rabbinical Council, chaired by Cardinal John J. O'Connor, of blessed memory. The bishops have issued two joint statements with the National Council of Synagogues: "Reflections on the Millennium" (1998) and "To End the Death Penalty" (1999).

WE REMEMBER: A Reflection on the Shoah

On March 16, 1998, the Commission for Religious Relations with the Jews under Cardinal Edward Idris Cassidy, issued a long-awaited white paper on the Holocaust, entitled "We Remember: Reflections on the Shoah."

The document was ten years in preparation, and, at its heart, it seeks to offer repentance for the failures of many Christians to oppose the policies of Nazi Germany and to resist the extermination of the Jews during the years of the Third Reich. It analyzes the history of anti-Semitism in the Church, but differentiates between historical anti-Semitism in the Christian community that may have led some Christians to ignore or even participate in the terrible persecutions of Jews in Nazi Germany or Occupied Europe, and the ideology of Nazism that climaxed with the Holocaust.

Defense of Pope Pius XII and Acknowledgment of Responsibility

"We Remember" defends Pope Pius XII and his numerous efforts on behalf of the Jews during World War II. "We Remember" is equally unequivocal in seeking repentance for the failure of Catholics to do more: ". . . alongside . . . courageous men and women, the spiritual resistance and concrete action of other Christians was not that which might have been expected from Christ's followers. . . . For Christians, this heavy burden of conscience of their brothers and sisters during the Second World War must be a call to penitence . . . We deeply regret the errors and failures of those sons and daughters of the Church."

Five-Part Document

"We Remember" begins with a letter from Pope John Paul II expressing his hope that the document "will indeed help to heal the wounds of past misunderstandings and injustices" and "enable memory to play its necessary part in the process of shaping a future in which the unspeakable iniquity of the Shoah will never again be possible."

Angel from a French Plaque

Part I, "The Tragedy of the Shoah and the Duty of Remembrance," looks at the call by Pope John Paul II in *Tertio Millennio Adveniente*: "The Church should become more fully conscious of the sinfulness of her children," lamenting that the 20th century "has witnessed an unspeakable tragedy which can never be forgotten: the attempt by the Nazi regime to exterminate the Jewish people . . . We ask all Christians to join us in meditating on the catastrophe which befell the Jewish people, and on the moral imperative to ensure that never again will selfishness and hatred grow to the point of sowing such suffering and death."

Part II, "What We Must Remember," declares that "such an event cannot be fully measured by the ordinary criteria of historical research alone," requiring a "reflection" on the conditions that made it possible. One important point is that the Shoah was perpetrated in Europe, raising the question of a relationship between Nazism and historical Christian anti-Semitism.

Part III, "Relations Between Jews and Christians," traces the "tormented" history of Christian-Jewish relations. The section explores the historical failure of Christians to follow Christ's teachings right up to the 19th century. It is noted that in that century, "there began to spread in varying degrees throughout most of Europe an anti-Judaism that was essentially more sociological and political than religious," in connection with ideas that "denied the unity of the human race." Of these, National Socialism was the most extreme expression, an ideology resisted, as the paper documents, by Church leaders in Germany and by Pope Pius XI.

Part IV, "Nazi Anti-Semitism and the Shoah," stresses that Nazism's anti-Semitism "had its roots outside of Christianity and, in pursuing its aims, it did not hesitate to oppose the Church and persecute her members also." Further, "the Nazi Party not only showed aversion to the ideas of divine Providence . . . but gave proof of a definite hatred directed at God . . .

such an attitude led to a rejection of Christianity, and a desire to see the Church destroyed. . . ."

Part V, "Looking Together to a Common Future," expresses Catholic hopes that by this act of repentance (*teshuva*), a new relationship will be possible. It calls upon all peoples to reflect upon the Shoah and resolve that "the spoiled seeds of anti-Judaism and anti-Semitism must never again be allowed to take root in any human heart."

Reactions

Response to the paper was mixed, with many prominent rabbis and Jewish leaders expressing disappointment that the Church did not go far enough in making a full apology or in admitting greater complicity on the part of Catholics. One notable dissenting opinion was that of Professor Marc Saperstein, of George Washington University, who wrote in the *Washington Post* that Nazi ideology had a non-Christian origin and the Catholic Church was limited in its capacity to prevent the Nazis — then dominating Europe — from massacring any who opposed its policies: "The fundamental responsibility for the Holocaust lies with the Nazi perpetrators. Not with Pope Pius XII. Not with the Church. Not with the teachings of the Christian faith."

Recent Developments

In December 1999 the Holy See's Commission and the International Jewish Committee for Interreligious Consultations announced the establishment of a committee of three Catholic and three Jewish scholars to look into the many complex historical and moral issues involving the Church and the Shoah beginning with an analysis of the thousands of archival documents for the period of World War II already made public by the Holy See in its 12 volume *Actes et Documents* (1965-1980).The Committee met in New York in December 1999, in London in May 2000, and in Baltimore in July 2000.

ISLAM

(Courtesy of Dr. John Borelli, executive secretary for Interreligious Relations, NCCB.)

Islam, meaning grateful surrender (to God), originated with Muhammad and the revelation he is believed to have received. Muslims acknowledge that this revelation, recorded in the *Qu'ran*, is from the one God and do not view Islam as a new religion. They profess that Muhammad was the last in a long series of prophets, most of whom are named in the Hebrew Bible and the New Testament,

beginning with Adam and continuing through Noah, Abraham, Moses, Jesus and down to Muhammad.

Muslims believe in the one God, Allah in Arabic, and cognate with the Hebrew Elohim and the ancient Aramaic Elah. According to the *Qu'ran*, God is one and transcendent, Creator and Sustainer of the universe, all-merciful and all-compassionate Ruler and Judge. God possesses numerous other titles, known collectively as the 99 names of God. The profession of faith states: "There is no god but the God and Muhammad is the messenger of God."

The essential duties of Muslims are to: witness the faith by daily recitation of the profession of faith; worship five times a day facing in the direction of the holy city of Mecca; give alms; fast daily from dawn to dusk during the month of Ramadan; make a pilgrimage to Mecca once if possible.

Muslims believe in final judgment, heaven and hell. Morality and following divinely revealed moral norms are extremely important to Muslims. Some dietary regulations are in effect. On Fridays, the noon prayer is a congregational (juma) prayer which should be said in a mosque. The general themes of prayer are adoration and thanksgiving. Muslims do not have an ordained ministry.

The basis of Islamic belief is the *Qu'ran*, the created word of God revealed to Muhammad through the angel Gabriel over a period of 23 years. The contents of this sacred book are complemented by the Sunna, a collection of sacred traditions from the life of the prophet Muhammad, and reinforced by Ijma, the consensus of Islamic scholars of Islamic Law (*Shariah*) which guarantees them against errors in matters of belief and practice

Conciliar Statement

The attitude of the Church toward Islam was stated as follows in the Second Vatican Council's Declaration on the Relation of the Church to Non-Christian Religions (*Nostra Aetate*, No. 3).

"The Church has a high regard for the Muslims. They worship God, who is one, living and subsistent, merciful and almighty, the Creator of heaven and earth, who has also spoken to men. They strive to submit themselves without reserve to the hidden decrees of God, just as Abraham submitted himself to God's plan, to whose faith Muslims eagerly link their own. Although not acknowledging him as God, they venerate Jesus as a prophet, his virgin Mother they also honor, and even at times devoutly invoke. Further, they await the day of judgment and the reward of God following the resurrection of the dead, For this reason, they highly esteem an upright life and worship God, especially by way of prayer, alms-deeds and fasting.

"Over the centuries many quarrels and dissensions have arisen between Christians and Muslims. The sacred Council now pleads with all to forget the past, and urges that a sincere effort be made to achieve mutual understanding; for the benefit of all men, let them together preserve and promote peace, liberty, social justice and moral values."

Dialogue

Pope John Paul II has met with Muslim leaders and delegations both in Rome and during his trips abroad. He has addressed large gatherings of Muslims in Morocco, Indonesia, Mali and elsewhere. In *Tertio Millennio Adveniente*, he recommended for the year 1999 that "the dialogue with Jews and the Muslims ought to have a pre-eminent place" and "meetings in places of significance for the great monotheistic religions." On February 24, 2000, John Paul II traveled to Egypt as part of his Jubilee Year pilgrimages and was received by Grand Sheik Mohammed Sayyid Tantawi at al-Azhar University, the most influential Islamic university in the world. The Pontifical Council for Interreligious Dialogue holds formal dialogues with several Islamic organizations on a regular basis. In the U.S., the bishops' Committee for Ecumenical and Interreligious Affairs holds consultations on relations with Muslims and several special dialogues with Muslims related to international issues. Dialogue with participation of Catholics and Muslims from several U.S. cities was initiated in October 1991. These continue on a regional basis. In 1996, an annual regional dialogue in the Midwest with the co-sponsorship of the Islamic Society of North America in Indianapolis was initiated. In 1998, an annual dialogue in the Mid-Atlantic region with the co-sponsorship of the Islamic Circle of North America in Queens, New York held its first meeting. In 1999, the West Coast Dialogue of Muslims and Catholics began meeting in Orange, California, with the co-sponsorship of several Islamic councils. Also in 1996 a dialogue between representatives of the ministry of W.D. Mohammed and the National Conference of Catholic Bishops began.

In 1995, the American Muslim Council presented its Mahmoud Abu-Saud Award for Excellence to Cardinal William H. Keeler for his leadership in promoting Christian-Muslim relations during his term as president of the National Conference of Catholic Bishops/United States Catholic Conference.

HINDUISM AND BUDDHISM
(Courtesy of Dr. John Borelli.)

In its Declaration on the Relation of the Church to Non-Christian Religions, the Second Vatican Council stated: "In Hinduism men explore the divine mystery and express it both in the limitless riches of myth and the accurately defined insights of philosophy. They seek release from the trials of the present life by ascetical practices, profound meditation and recourse to God in confidence and love." (2)

Catholics, especially in India, have sought good relations with Hindus and have engaged in numerous dialogues and conferences. In papal visits to India, Paul VI in 1964 and John Paul II in 1986 and 1999, popes have addressed words of respect for Indian, particularly Hindu, religious leaders. Pope John Paul II said to Hindus in India in 1986: "Your overwhelming sense of the primacy of religion and of the greatness of the Supreme Being has been a powerful witness against a materialistic and atheistic view of life." In 1987, he said of Hinduism: "I hold in esteem your concern for inner peace and for the peace of the world, based not on purely mechanistic or materialistic political considerations, but on self-purification, unselfishness, love and sympathy for all."

In 1995, the Pontifical Council for Interreligious Dialogue began sending a general message to Hindus on the occasion of Diwali, a feast commemorating the victory of light over darkness. In 1999, John Paul II was in India during the celebration and said these words to the religious leaders of India: "On the occasion of Diwali, the festival of lights, which symbolizes the victory of life over death, good over evil, I express the hope that this meeting will speak ot the world of the things that unite us all: our common human origin and destiny, our shared responsibility for people's well-being and progress, our need of the light and strength that we seek in our religious convictions." In the United States, there are a few dialogues between Catholics and Hindus.

"Buddhism in its multiple forms acknowledges the radical insufficiency of this shifting world. It teaches a path by which men, in a devout and confident spirit, can either reach a state of absolute freedom or attain supreme enlightenment by their own efforts or by higher assistance." So stated the Second Vatican Council in its Declaration on the Relation of the Church to Non-Christian Religions.

Numerous delegations of Buddhists and leading monks have been received by the popes, and John Paul II has met with Buddhist leaders on many of his trips. Paul VI said to a group of Japanese Buddhists in 1973: "Buddhism is one of the riches of Asia: you teach men to seek truth and peace in the kingdom of the Eternal, beyond the horizon of visible things. You likewise strive to encourage the qualities of goodness, meekness and non-violence." In 1995, while in Sri Lanka, John Paul II said to Buddhists: "I express my highest regard for the followers of Buddhism, . . . with its four great values of loving kindness, compassion, sympathy, and equanimity; with its ten transcendental virtues and the joys of the Sangha [the monastic community]. . . . At the 1986 World Day of Prayer for Peace at Assisi, the Dalai Lama, principal teacher of the Gelugpa lineage, was placed immediately to the Holy Father's left. Numerous dialogues and good relations between Catholics and Buddhists exist in many countries.

In 1995, the Pontifical Council for Interreligious Dialogue organized a Buddhist-Christian colloquium hosted by the Fo Kuang Shan Buddhist order in Taiwan. A second colloquium was held in Bangalore, India, in 1998. These grew out of the perceived need for greater ongoing contact between the Pontifical Council and Buddhist leaders and scholars. Each of these meetings has produced a report. Also in 1995, the council began sending a message to Buddhists on the feast of Vesakh, the celebration of Gautama Buddha's life.

A meeting of great significance between Buddhist and Catholic monastics took place at Our Lady of Gethsemani Abbey, Kentucky, in July 1996, which was organized and facilitated by Monastic Interreligious Dialogue, a network formed in 1981 of mostly monasteries of men and women following the rule of St. Benedict. "The Gethsemani Encounter," the result of several formal visits and hospitality between Catholic and Buddhist monks and nuns, focused on various aspects of monastic life. There were twenty-five participants on each side with numerous observers. The Buddhists represented the Theravada, Tibetan, and Zen traditions.

In 1998, an ongoing dialogue between Buddhists and Catholics in Los Angeles hosted a retreat dialogue for 50 Catholic and Buddhist participants from different regions of the U.S. The retreat/dialogue was co-planned with the Faiths in the World Committee of the National Association of Diocesan Ecumenical Officers, a network of Catholic diocesan staff responsible for ecumenical and interreligious relations.

In 1996, Cardinal Arinze, in a letter to "Dear Buddhist Friends," wrote: "The pluralistic society in which we live demands more than mere tolerance. Tolerance is usually thought of as putting up with the other or, at best, as a code of public conduct. Yet, this resigned, lukewarm attitude does not create the right atmosphere for true harmonious coexistence. The spirit of our religions challenges us to go beyond this. We are commanded, in fact, to love our neighbors as ourselves." The cardinal wrote in the same vein to Muslims on the occasion of their 1996 celebration of Id al-Fitr.

Formal dialogues continue in the Archdiocese of Los Angeles and formal relations are developing in a few other dioceses. In 1989, the Bishops' Committee for Ecumenical and Interreligious Affairs convened its first national consultation on relations with Buddhists; a second consultation was held in 1990. Committee staff meet with Monastic Interreligious Dialogue and participate in other activities bringing Christians and Buddhists together.

Mosque o al-Azhar, Egypt

APPENDICES

GLOSSARY

A

Abbacy Nullius: A non-diocesan territory whose people are under the pastoral care of an abbot acting in general in the manner of a bishop.

Abbess: The female superior of a monastic community of nuns, e.g., Benedictines, Poor Clares, some others. Elected by members of the community, an abbess has general authority over her community but no sacramental jurisdiction.

Abbey: See Monastery.

Abbot: The male superior of a monastic community of men religious, e.g., Benedictines, Cistercians, some others. Elected by members of the community, an abbot has ordinary jurisdiction and general authority over his community. Eastern Rite equivalents of an abbot are a hegumen and an archimandrite. A regular abbot is the head of an abbey or monastery. An abbot general or archabbot is the head of a congregation consisting of several monasteries. An abbot primate is the head of the modern Benedictine Confederation.

Abiogenesis: The term used to describe the spontaneous generation of living matter from nonliving matter.

Ablution: A term derived from Latin, meaning washing or cleansing, and referring to the cleansing of the hands of a priest celebrating Mass, after the offering of gifts; and to the cleansing of the chalice with water and wine after Communion.

Abnegation: The spiritual practice of self-denial (or mortification), in order to atone for past sins or in order to join oneself to the passion of Christ. Mortification can be undertaken through fasting, abstinence, or refraining from legitimate pleasure.

Abortion: Abortion is not only "the ejection of an immature fetus" from the womb, but is "also the killing of the same fetus in whatever way at whatever time from the moment of conception it may be procured." (This clarification of Canon 1398, reported in the December 5, 1988, edition of *L'Osservatore Romano*, was issued by the Pontifical Council for the Interpretation of Legislative Texts — in view of scientific developments regarding ways and means of procuring abortion.) Accidental expulsion, as in cases of miscarriage, is without moral fault. Direct abortion, in which a fetus is intentionally removed from the womb, constitutes a direct attack on an innocent human being, a violation of the Fifth Commandment. A person who procures a completed abortion is automatically excommunicated (Canon 1398 of the *Code of Canon Law*); also excommunicated are all persons involved in a deliberate and successful effort to bring about an abortion. Direct abortion is not justifiable for any reason, e.g., therapeutic, for the physical and/or psychological welfare of the mother; preventive, to avoid the birth of a defective or unwanted child; social, in the interests of family and/or community. Indirect abortion, which occurs when a fetus is expelled during medical or other treatment of the mother for a reason other than procuring expulsion, is permissible under the principle of double effect for a proportionately serious reason, e.g., when a medical or surgical procedure is necessary to save the life of the mother. Such a procedure should not be confused with the purportedly "medical" procedure of the partial-birth abortion, a particularly cruel form of abortion.

Abrogation: The abolition or elimination of a law by some official action. In Canon Law, abrogation occurs through a direct decree of the Holy See or by the enactment of a later or subsequent law contrary to the former law.

Absolute: (1) A term in philosophy, first introduced at the end of the 18th century and used by Scholasticism, that signifies the "perfect being" (i.e., God), who relies upon no one for existence. Modern philosophical thought has added two new concepts: a) the Absolute is the sum of all being; b) the Absolute has no relationship with any other things; the Absolute is thus unknowable. These concepts are agnostic and contrary to Catholicism, which holds that God is the cause of all being (and hence not the sum) and is knowable by his creatures, at least in part. (2) Certain truths, revealed by God, which are unchanging.

Absolution, Sacramental: The act by which bishops and priests, acting as agents of Christ and ministers of the Church, grant forgiveness of sins in the sacrament of penance. The essential formula of absolution is: "I absolve you from your sins; in the name of the Father, and of the Son, and of the Holy Spirit. Amen." The power to absolve is given with ordination to the priesthood and episcopate. Priests exercise this power in virtue of authorization (faculties) granted by a bishop, a religious superior or canon law. Authorization can be limited or restricted regarding certain sins and penalties or censures. In cases of necessity, and also in cases of the absence of their own confessors, Eastern and Latin Rite Catholics may ask for and receive sacramental absolution from an Eastern or Latin Rite priest; so may Polish National Catholics, according to a Vatican decision issued in May 1993. Any priest can absolve a person in danger of death; in the absence of a priest with the usual faculties, this includes a laicized priest or a priest under censure.

Abstinence: (1) The deliberate deprivation by a person of meat or of foods prepared with meat on those days prescribed by the Church as penitential (Ash Wednesday, Good Friday, and all Fridays of the year which are not solemnities; in the United States, not all Fridays of the year but only the Fridays of Lent). Those fourteen years of age and above are bound by the discipline. (2) Sexual abstinence is the willing refrain from sexual intercourse; total abstinence is observed in obedience to the Sixth Commandment by single persons and couples whose marriages are not recognized by the Church as valid; periodic abstinence or periodic continence is observed by a married couple for regulating conception by natural means or for ascetical motives.

Adoration: The highest act and purpose of religious worship, which is directed in love and reverence to God alone in acknowledgment of his infinite perfection and goodness, and of his total dominion over creatures. Adoration, which is also called latria, consists of internal and external elements, private and social prayer, liturgical acts and ceremonies, and especially sacrifice.

Adultery: Marital infidelity. Sexual intercourse between a married person and another to whom one is not married, a violation of the obligations of the marital covenant, chastity and justice; any sin of impurity (thought, desire, word, action) involving a married person who is not one's husband or wife has the nature of adultery.

Advent Wreath: A wreath of laurel, spruce, or similar foliage with four candles which are lighted successively in the weeks of Advent to symbolize the approaching celebration of the birth of Christ, the Light of the World, at Christmas. The wreath originated among German Protestants.

Agape: A Greek word, meaning love, love feast, designating the meal of fellowship eaten at some gatherings of early Christians. Although held in some places in connection with the Mass, the agape was not part of the Mass, nor was it of universal institution and observance. It was infrequently observed by the fifth century and disappeared altogether between the sixth and eighth centuries.

Age of Reason: (1) The time of life when one begins to distinguish between right and wrong, to understand an obligation and take on moral responsibility; seven years of age is the presumption in church law. (2) Historically, the eighteenth century period of Enlightenment in England and France, the age of the Encyclopedists and Deists. According to a basic thesis of the Enlightenment, human experience and reason are the only sources of certain knowledge of truth; consequently, faith and revelation are discounted as valid sources of knowledge, and the reality of supernatural truth is called into doubt and/or denied.

Aggiornamento: An Italian word having the general meaning of bringing up to date, renewal, revitalization, descriptive of the processes of spiritual renewal and institutional reform and change in the Church; fostered by the Second Vatican Council.

Agnosticism: A theory that holds that a person cannot have certain knowledge of immaterial reality, especially the existence of God and things pertaining to him. Immanuel Kant, one of the philosophical fathers of agnosticism, stood for the position that God, as well as the human soul, is unknowable on speculative grounds; nevertheless, he found practical imperatives for acknowledging God's existence, a view shared by many agnostics. The First Vatican Council declared that the existence of God and some of his attributes can be known with certainty by human reason, even without divine revelation. The word agnosticism was first used, in the sense given here, by T. H. Huxley in 1869.

Agnus Dei: A Latin phrase, meaning Lamb of God. (1) A title given to Christ, the Lamb (victim) of the Sacrifice of the New Law (on Calvary and in Mass). (2) A prayer said at Mass before the reception of Holy Communion. (3) A sacramental. It is a round paschal-candle fragment blessed by the pope. On one side it bears the impression of a lamb, symbolic of Christ. On the reverse side, there may be any one of a number of impressions, e.g., the figure of a saint, the name and coat of arms of the reigning pope. The *agnus dei* may have originated at Rome in the fifth century. The first definite mention of it dates from about 820.

Akathist Hymn: The most profound and famous expression of Marian devotion in churches of the Byzantine Rite. It consists of twenty-four sections, twelve of which relate to the Gospel of the Infancy and twelve to the mysteries of the Incarnation and the virginal motherhood of Mary. In liturgical usage, it is sung in part in Byzantine churches on the first four Saturdays of Lent and in toto on the fifth Saturday; it is also recited in private devotion. It is of unknown origin prior to 626, when its popularity increased as a hymn of thanksgiving after the successful defense and liberation of Constantinople, which had been under siege by Persians and Avars. Akathist means "without sitting," indicating that the hymn is recited or sung while standing. Pope John Paul, in a decree dated May 25, 1991, granted a plenary indulgence to the faithful of any rite who recite the hymn in a church or oratory, as a family, in a religious community or in a pious association — in conjunction with the usual conditions of freedom from attachment to sin, reception of the sacraments of penance and the Eucharist, and prayers for the intention of the pope (e.g., an Our Father, the Apostles' Creed, and an aspiration). A partial indulgence can be gained for recitation of the hymn in other circumstances.

Alleluia: An exclamation of joy derived from Hebrew, "All hail to him who is, praise God," with various use in the liturgy and other expressions of worship.

Allocution: A formal type of papal address, as distinguished from an ordinary sermon or statement of views.

Alms: An act, gift or service of compassion, motivated by love of God and neighbor, for the help of persons in need; an obligation of charity, which is measurable by the ability of one person to give assistance and by the degree of another's need. Almsgiving, along with prayer and fasting, is regarded as a work of penance as well as an exercise of charity. (See Mercy, Works of.)

Alpha and Omega: The first and last letters of the Greek alphabet, used to symbolize the eternity of God (Rv. 1:8) and the divinity and eternity of Christ, the beginning and end of all things (Rv. 21:6; 22:13). Use of the letters as a monogram of Christ originated in the fourth century or earlier.

Amen: A Hebrew word meaning truly, it is true. In the Gospels, Christ used the word to add a note of authority to his statements. In other New Testament writings, as in Hebrew usage, it was the concluding word to doxologies. As the concluding word of prayers, it expresses assent to and acceptance of God's will.

Anamnesis: A prayer recalling the saving mysteries of the death and resurrection of Jesus, following the consecration at Mass in the Latin Rite.

Anaphora: A Greek term for the Canon or Eucharistic Prayer of the Mass.

Anathema: A Greek word with the root meaning of cursed or separated and the adapted meaning of excommunication, used in church documents, especially the canons of ecumenical councils, for the condemnation of heretical doctrines and of practices opposed to proper discipline.

Anchorite: A kind of hermit living in complete isolation and devoting himself exclusively to exercises of religion and severe penance according to a rule and way of life of his own devising. In early Christian times, anchorites were the forerunners of the monastic life. The closest contemporary approach to the life of an anchorite is that of Carthusian and Camaldolese hermits.

Angels: Purely spiritual beings with intelligence and free will whose name indicates their mission as servants and messengers of God. They were created before the creation of the visible universe. Good angels enjoy the perfect good of the beatific vision. They can intercede for persons. The doctrine of guardian angels, although not explicitly defined as a matter of faith, is rooted in long-standing tradition. No authoritative declaration has ever been issued regarding choirs or various categories of angels: seraphim, cherubim, thrones, dominations, principalities, powers, virtues, archangels and angels. Archangels commemorated in the liturgy are: Michael,

leader of the angelic host and protector of the synagogue; Raphael, guide of Tobiah and healer of his father; Gabriel, angel of the Incarnation. Fallen angels, the chief of whom is called the Devil or Satan, rejected the love of God and were therefore banished from heaven to hell. They can tempt persons to commit sin.

Angelus: A devotion which commemorates the Incarnation of Christ. It consists of three versicles, three Hail Marys and a special prayer, and recalls the announcement to Mary by the Archangel Gabriel that she was chosen to be the Mother of Christ, her acceptance of the divine will, and the Incarnation (Lk. 1:26-38). The Angelus is recited in the morning, at noon and in the evening. The practice of reciting the Hail Mary in honor of the Incarnation was introduced by the Franciscans in 1263. The *Regina Caeli*, commemorating the joy of Mary at Christ's Resurrection, replaces the Angelus during the Easter season.

Anger (Wrath): Passionate displeasure arising from some kind of offense suffered at the hands of another person, frustration or other cause, combined with a tendency to strike back at the cause of the displeasure; a violation of the Fifth Commandment and one of the capital sins if the displeasure is out of proportion to the cause and/ or if the retaliation is unjust.

Anglican Orders: Holy orders conferred according to the rite of the Anglican Church, which Leo XIII declared null and void in the bull *Apostolicae Curae*, September 13, 1896. The orders were declared null because they were conferred according to a rite that was substantially defective in form and intent, and because of a break in apostolic succession that occurred when Matthew Parker became head of the Anglican hierarchy in 1559. In making his declaration, Pope Leo cited earlier arguments against validity made by Julius III in 1553 and 1554 and by Paul IV in 1555. He also noted related directives requiring absolute ordination, according to the Catholic ritual, of convert ministers who had been ordained according to the Anglican Ordinal.

Anglican Use Parishes: In line with Vatican-approved developments since 1980, several Anglican use parishes have been established in the United States with the right to continue using some elements of Anglican usage in their liturgical celebrations. A Vatican document dated March 31, 1981, said: "In June 1980, the Holy See, through the Congregation for the Doctrine of the Faith, agreed to the request presented by the bishops of the United States of America in behalf of some clergy and laity formerly or actually belonging to the Episcopal (Anglican) Church for full communion with the Catholic Church. The Holy See's response to the initiative of these Episcopalians includes the possibility of a 'pastoral provision' which will provide, for those who desire it, a common identity reflecting certain elements of their own heritage."

Annulment: A decree issued by an appropriate

Church authority or tribunal that a sacrament or ecclesiastical act is invalid and therefore lacking in all legal or canonical consequences.

Antichrist: The "deceitful one," the "antichrist" (2 Jn. 7), adversary of Christ and the kingdom of God, especially in the end time before the second coming of Christ. The term is also used in reference to anti-Christian persons and forces in the world.

Antiphon: (1) A short verse or text, generally from Scripture, recited in the Liturgy of the Hours before and after psalms and canticles. (2) Any verse sung or recited by one part of a choir or congregation in response to the other part, as in antiphonal or alternate chanting.

Anti-Semitism: A prejudice against Jews, and often accompanied by persecution. The prejudice has existed historically from the time of the ancient Persian Empire and survives even to the present day. It has been condemned consistently by the Church as being in opposition to scriptural principles and Christian charity.

Apologetics: The science and art of developing and presenting the case for the reasonableness of the Christian faith, by a wide variety of means including facts of experience, history, science, philosophy. The constant objective of apologetics, as well as of the total process of pre-evangelization, is preparation for response to God in faith; its ways and means, however, are subject to change in accordance with the various needs of people and different sets of circumstances.

Apostasy: (1) The total and obstinate repudiation of the Christian faith. An apostate automatically incurs a penalty of excommunication. (2) Apostasy from orders is the unlawful withdrawal from or rejection of the obligations of the clerical state by a man who has received major orders. An apostate from orders is subject to a canonical penalty. (3) Apostasy from the religious life occurs when a Religious with perpetual vows unlawfully leaves the community with the intention of not returning, or actually remains outside the community without permission. An apostate from religious life is subject to a canonical penalty.

Apostolate: The ministry or work of an apostle. In Catholic usage, the word is an umbrella-like term covering all kinds and areas of work and endeavor for the service of God and the Church and the good of people. Thus, the apostolate of bishops is to carry on the mission of the Apostles as pastors of the People of God: of priests, to preach the word of God and to carry out the sacramental and pastoral ministry for which they are ordained; of religious, to follow and do the work of Christ in conformity with the evangelical counsels and their rule of life; of lay persons, as individuals and/or in groups, to give witness to Christ and build up the kingdom of God through practice of their faith, professional competence and the performance of good works in the concrete circumstances of daily life. Apos-

tolic works are not limited to those done within the Church or by specifically Catholic groups, although some apostolates are officially assigned to certain persons or groups and are under the direction of church authorities. Apostolate derives from the commitment and obligation of baptism, confirmation, holy orders, matrimony, the duties of one's state in life, etc.

Apostolic Succession: Bishops of the Church, who form a collective body or college, are successors to the Apostles by ordination and divine right; as such they carry on the mission entrusted by Christ to the Apostles as guardians and teachers of the deposit of faith, principal pastors and spiritual authorities of the faithful. The doctrine of apostolic succession is based on New Testament evidence and the constant teaching of the Church, reflected as early as the end of the first century in a letter of Pope St. Clement to the Corinthians. A significant facet of the doctrine is the role of the pope as the successor of St. Peter, the vicar of Christ and head of the college of bishops. The doctrine of apostolic succession means more than continuity of apostolic faith and doctrine; its basic requisite is ordination by the laying on of hands in apostolic succession.

Archives: Documentary records, and the place where they are kept, of the spiritual and temporal government and affairs of the Church, a diocese, church agencies like the departments of the Roman Curia, bodies like religious institutes, and individual parishes. The collection, cataloguing, preserving, and use of these records are governed by norms stated in canon law and particular regulations. The strictest secrecy is always in effect for confidential records concerning matters of conscience, and documents of this kind are destroyed as soon as circumstances permit.

Ark of the Covenant: The sacred chest of the Israelites in which were placed and carried the tablets of stone inscribed with the Ten Commandments, the basic moral precepts of the Old Covenant (Ex. 25: 10-22; 37:1-9). The Ark was also a symbol of God's presence. The Ark was probably destroyed with the Temple in 586 B.C.

Asceticism: The practice of self-discipline. In the spiritual life, asceticism — by personal prayer, meditation, self-denial, works of mortification, and outgoing interpersonal works — is motivated by love of God and contributes to growth in holiness.

Ashes: Religious significance has been associated with their use as symbolic of penance since Old Testament times. Thus, ashes of palm blessed on the previous Sunday of the Passion are placed on the foreheads of the faithful on Ash Wednesday to remind them to do works of penance, especially during the season of Lent, and that they are dust and unto dust will return. Ashes are a sacramental.

Aspergillum: A vessel or device used for sprinkling holy water. The ordinary type is a metallic rod with a bulbous tip which absorbs the water and discharges it at the motion of the user's hand.

Aspersory: A portable metallic vessel, similar to a pail, for carrying holy water.

Aspiration (Ejaculation): Short exclamatory prayer, e.g., My Jesus, mercy.

Atheism: Denial of the existence of God, finding expression in a system of thought (speculative atheism) or a manner of acting (practical atheism) as though there were no God. The Second Vatican Council, in its Pastoral Constitution on the Church in the Modern World (*Gaudium et Spes*, Nos. 19 to 21), noted that a profession of atheism may represent an explicit denial of God, the rejection of a wrong notion of God, an affirmation of man rather than of God, an extreme protest against evil. It said that such a profession might result from acceptance of such propositions as: there is no absolute truth; man can assert nothing, absolutely nothing, about God; everything can be explained by scientific reasoning alone; the whole question of God is devoid of meaning.

Atonement: The redemptive activity of Christ, who reconciled man with God through his Incarnation and entire life, and especially by his suffering and Resurrection. The word also applies to prayer and good works by which persons join themselves with and take part in Christ's work of reconciliation and reparation for sin.

Attributes of God: Perfections of God. God possesses — and is — all the perfections of being, without limitation. Because he is infinite, all of these perfections are one, perfectly united in him. Because of the limited power of human intelligence, divine perfections — such as omnipotence, truth, love — are viewed separately, as distinct characteristics, even though they are not actually distinct in God.

Authority, Ecclesiastical: The authority exercised by the Church, and particularly by the pope and the bishops; it is delegated by Jesus Christ to St. Peter. This authority extends to all those matters entrusted to the Apostles by Christ, including teaching of the Faith, the liturgy and sacraments, moral guidance, and the administration of discipline.

Avarice (Covetousness): A disorderly and unreasonable attachment to and desire for material things; called a capital sin because it involves preoccupation with material things to the neglect of spiritual goods and obligations of justice and charity.

Ave Maria: See **Hail Mary**.

B

Baldacchino: A canopy over an altar.

Baptism: See Sacraments.

Beatification: A preliminary step toward canonization of a saint. It begins with an investigation of the candidate's life, writings and heroic practice of virtue, and, except in the case of martyrs, the certification of one miracle worked by God through his or her intercession. If the findings of the investigation so indicate, the pope decrees that the Servant of God may be called Blessed and may be honored locally or in a limited way in the liturgy. Additional procedures lead to canonization (see separate entry).

Beatific Vision: The intuitive, immediate and direct vision and experience of God enjoyed in the light of glory by all the blessed in heaven. The vision is a supernatural mystery.

Beatitude: A literary form of the Old and New Testaments in which blessings are promised to persons for various reasons. Beatitudes are mentioned 26 times in the Psalms, and in other books of the Old Testament. The best known Beatitudes — identifying blessedness with participation in the kingdom of God and his righteousness, and descriptive of the qualities of Christian perfection — are those recounted in Mt. 5:3-12 and Lk. 6:20-23. The Beatitudes are of central importance in the teaching of Jesus.

Benedictus: The canticle or hymn of Zechariah at the circumcision of St. John the Baptist (Lk. 1:68-79). It is an expression of praise and thanks to God for sending John as a precursor of the Messiah. The Benedictus is recited in the Liturgy of the Hours as part of the Morning Prayer.

Biglietto: A papal document of notification of appointment to the cardinalate.

Biretta: A stiff, square hat with three ridges on top worn by clerics in church and on other occasions.

Blasphemy: Any internal or external expression of hatred, reproach, insult, defiance or contempt with respect to God and the use of his name, principally, and to the Church, saints and sacred things, secondarily; a serious sin, directly opposed to the second commandment. Blasphemy against the Spirit is the deliberate refusal to accept divine mercy, rejection of forgiveness of sins and of the promise of salvation. The sin that is unforgivable because a person refuses to seek or accept forgiveness.

Blessing: Invocation of God's favor, by official ministers of the Church or by private individuals. Blessings are recounted in the Old and New Testaments, and are common in the Christian tradition. Many types of blessings are listed in the Book of Blessings of the Roman Ritual. Private blessings, as well as those of an official kind, are efficacious. Blessings are imparted with the Sign of the Cross and appropriate prayer.

Bride of Christ: A metaphorical title that denotes the intimate union that Christ enjoys with his Church; the title is mentioned specifically in the New Testament (2 Cor. 11:2).

Brief, Apostolic: A papal letter, less formal than a bull, signed for the pope by a secretary and impressed with the seal of the Fisherman's Ring. Simple apostolic letters of this kind are issued for beatifications and with respect to other matters.

Bull, Apostolic: Apostolic letter, a solemn form of papal document, beginning with the name and title of the pope (e.g., John Paul II, Servant of the Servants of God), dealing with an important subject, sealed with a *bulla* or red-ink imprint of the device on the *bulla*. Bulls are issued to confer the titles of bishops and cardinals, to promulgate canonizations, to proclaim Holy Years and for other purposes. A collection of bulls is called a *bullarium*.

Burial, Ecclesiastical: Interment with ecclesiastical rites, a right of the Christian faithful. The Church recommends burial of the bodies of the dead, but cremation is permissible if it does not involve reasons against church teaching. Ecclesiastical burial is in order for catechumens; for unbaptized children whose parents intended to have them baptized before death; and even, in the absence of their own ministers, for baptized non-Catholics unless it would be considered against their will.

Burse, Financial: A special fund maintained by a diocese, religious institute, or private foundation usually endowed by a private benefactor; it often has the purpose of making possible the education of candidates for the priesthood.

C

Calumny (Slander): Harming the name and good reputation of a person by lies; a violation of obligations of justice and truth. Restitution is due for calumny.

Calvary: A knoll about 15 feet high just outside the western wall of Jerusalem where Christ was crucified, so called from the Latin *calvaria* (skull) which described its shape.

Canon: A Greek word meaning rule, norm, standard, measure. (1) The word designates the Canon of Sacred Scripture, which is the list of books recognized by the Church as inspired by the Holy Spirit. (2) The term also designates the canons (Eucharistic Prayers, anaphoras) of the Mass, the core of the eucharistic liturgy. (3) Certain dignitaries of the Church have the title of Canon, and some religious are known as Canons. (See Bible.)

Canonization: An infallible declaration by the pope that a person, who died as a martyr and/or practiced Christian virtue to a heroic degree, is now in heaven and is worthy of honor and imitation by all the faithful. Such a declaration is preceded by the process of beatification and another detailed investigation concerning the person's reputation for holiness, writings, and (except in the case of martyrs) a miracle ascribed to his or her intercession after death. The pope can dispense with some of the formalities ordinarily required in canonization procedures (equivalent canonization), as Pope John XXIII did in the canonization of St. Gregory Barbarigo on May 26, 1960. A saint is worthy of honor in liturgical worship throughout the universal Church. From its earliest years the Church has venerated saints. Public official honor always required the approval of the bishop of the place. Martyrs were the first to be honored. St. Martin of Tours, who died in 397, was an early non-martyr venerated as a saint. The earliest canonization by a pope with positive documentation was that of St. Ulrich (Uldaric) of Augsburg by John XV in 993. Alexander III reserved the process of canonization to the Holy See in 1171. In 1588 Sixtus V established the Sacred Congregation of Rites for the principal purpose of handling causes for beatification and canonization: this function is now the work of the Congregation for the Causes of Saints. The official listing of saints and blessed is contained in the Roman Martyrology (being revised and updated) and related decrees issued after its last publication. Butler's unofficial *Lives of the Saints* (1956) contains 2,565 entries. The Church regards all persons in heaven as saints, not just those who have been officially canonized. (See Beatification, Saints, Canonizations by Leo XIII and His Successors.)

Canon Law: The Code of Canon Law (*Corpus Iuris Canonici*) enacted and promulgated by ecclesiastical authority for the orderly and pastoral administration and government of the Church. A revised Code for the Latin Rite, effective November 27, 1983, consists of 1,752 canons in seven books under the titles of general norms, the people of God, the teaching mission of the Church, the sanctifying mission of the Church, temporal goods of the Church, penal law and procedural law. The antecedent of this Code was promulgated in 1917 and became effective in 1918; it consisted of 2,414 canons in five books covering general rules, ecclesiastical persons, sacred things, trials, crimes and punishments. There is a separate Code of the Canons of Eastern Churches, in effect since October 1, 1991.

Canticle: A scriptural chant or prayer differing from the psalms. Three of the canticles prescribed for use in the Liturgy of the Hours are: the *Magnificat*, the Canticle of Mary (Lk. 1:46-55); the *Benedictus*, the Canticle of Zechariah (Lk. 1:68-79); and the *Nunc Dimittis*, the Canticle of Simeon (Lk. 2:29-32).

Capital Punishment: Punishment for crime by means of the death penalty. The political community, which has authority to provide for the common good, has the right to defend itself and its members against unjust aggression and may in extreme cases punish with the death penalty persons found guilty before the law of serious crimes against individuals and a just social order. Such punishment is essentially vindictive. Its value as a crime deterrent is a matter of perennial debate. The prudential judgment as to whether or not there should be capital punishment belongs to the civic community. The U.S. Supreme Court, in a series of decisions dating from June 29, 1972, ruled against the constitutionality of statutes on capital punishment except in specific cases and with appropriate consideration, with respect to sentence, of mitigating circumstances of the crime. Pope John Paul II, in his encyclical letter *Evangelium Vitae* ("The

Gospel of Life"), wrote: "There is a growing tendency, both in the Church and in civil society, to demand that it (capital punishment) be applied in a very limited way or even that it be abolished completely." Quoting the *Catechism of the Catholic Church*, the pope wrote: "'If bloodless means are sufficient to defend human lives against an aggressor and to protect public order and the safety of persons, public authority must limit itself to such means, because they better correspond to the concrete conditions of the common good and are more in conformity to the dignity of the human person.'"

Capital Sins: Sins which give rise to other sins: pride, avarice, lust, wrath (anger), gluttony, envy, sloth.

Cardinal Virtues: The four principal moral virtues are prudence, justice, temperance and fortitude.

Casuistry: In moral theology, the application of moral principles to specific cases. Casuistry can be of assistance because it takes the abstract and makes it practical in a particular situation. It has definite limitations and does not replace the conscience in the decision-making process; additionally, it must be aligned with the cardinal virtue of prudence.

Catacombs: Underground Christian cemeteries in various cities of the Roman Empire and Italy, especially in the vicinity of Rome; the burial sites of many martyrs and other Christians.

Catechesis: The whole complex of church efforts to make disciples of Christ, involving doctrinal instruction and spiritual formation through practice of the faith.

Catechism: A systematic presentation of the fundamentals of Catholic doctrine regarding faith and morals. Sources are Sacred Scripture, tradition, the magisterium (teaching authority of the Church), the writings of Fathers and Doctors of the Church, liturgy. The new *Catechism of the Catholic Church*, published October 11, 1992, consists of four principal sections: the profession of faith, (the Creed), the sacraments of faith, the life of faith (the Commandments) and the prayer of the believer (the Lord's Prayer). The sixteenth century Council of Trent mandated publication of the *Roman Catechism*. Catechisms such as these two are useful sources for other catechisms serving particular needs of the faithful and persons seeking admission to the Catholic Church.

Catechumen: A person preparing in a program (catechumenate) of instruction and spiritual formation for baptism and reception into the Church. The Church has a special relationship with catechumens. It invites them to lead the life of the Gospel, introduces them to the celebration of the sacred rites, and grants them various prerogatives that are proper to the faithful (one of which is the right to ecclesiastical burial). (See Rite of Christian Initiation of Adults, under Baptism.)

Cathedra: A Greek word for chair, designating the chair or seat of a bishop in the principal church of his diocese, which is therefore called a cathedral.

Cathedraticum: The tax paid to a bishop by all churches and benefices subject to him for the support of episcopal administration and for works of charity.

Catholic: A Greek word, meaning universal, first used in the title Catholic Church in a letter written by St. Ignatius of Antioch about 107 to the Christians of Smyrna.

Celebret: A Latin word, meaning "Let him celebrate," the name of a letter of recommendation issued by a bishop or other superior stating that a priest is in good standing and therefore eligible to celebrate Mass or perform other priestly functions.

Celibacy: The unmarried state of life, required in the Roman Church of candidates for holy orders and of men already ordained to holy orders, for the practice of perfect chastity and total dedication to the service of people in the ministry of the Church. Celibacy is enjoined as a condition for ordination by church discipline and law, not by dogmatic necessity. In the Roman Church, a consensus in favor of celibacy developed in the early centuries while the clergy included both celibates and men who had been married once. The first local legislation on the subject was enacted by a local council held in Elvira, Spain, about 306; it forbade bishops, priests, deacons and other ministers to have wives. Similar enactments were passed by other local councils from that time on, and by the 12th century particular laws regarded marriage by clerics in major orders to be not only unlawful but also null and void. The latter view was translated by the Second Lateran Council in 1139 into what seems to be the first written universal law making holy orders an invalidating impediment to marriage. In 1563 the Council of Trent ruled definitely on the matter and established the discipline in force in the Roman Church. Some exceptions to this discipline have been made in recent years. A number of married Protestant and Episcopalian (Anglican) clergymen who became converts and were subsequently ordained to the priesthood have been permitted to continue in marriage. Married men over the age of 35 can be ordained to the permanent diaconate. Eastern Church discipline on celibacy differs from that of the Roman Church. In line with legislation enacted by the Synod of Trullo in 692 and still in force, candidates for holy orders may marry before becoming deacons and may continue in marriage thereafter, but marriage after ordination is forbidden. Bishops of Eastern Catholic Churches in the U.S., however, do not ordain married candidates for the priesthood. Bishops of Eastern Catholic Churches are unmarried.

Cenacle: The upper room in Jerusalem where Christ ate the Last Supper with his Apostles.

Censer: A metal vessel with a perforated cover and suspended by chains, in which incense is burned. It is used at some Masses, Benediction of the Blessed Sacrament and other liturgical functions.

Censorship of Books: An exercise of vigilance by the Church for safeguarding authentic religious teaching. Pertinent legislation in a decree issued by the Congregation for the Doctrine of the Faith April 9, 1975, is embodied in the Code of Canon Law (Book III, Title IV). The legislation deals with requirements for pre-publication review and clearance of various types of writings on religious subjects. Permission to publish works of a religious character, together with the apparatus of reviewing them beforehand, falls under the authority of the bishop of the place where the writer lives or where the works are published. Clearance for publication is usually indicated by the terms *Nihil obstat* ("Nothing stands in the way") issued by the censor and *Imprimatur* ("Let it be printed") authorized by the bishop. The clearing of works for publication does not necessarily imply approval of an author's viewpoint or his manner of handling a subject.

Censures: Sanctions imposed by the Church on baptized Roman Catholics eighteen years of age or older for committing certain serious offenses and for being or remaining obstinate therein: (1) excommunication (exclusion from the community of the faithful, barring a person from sacramental and other participation in the goods and offices of the community of the Church), (2) suspension (prohibition of a cleric to exercise orders) and (3) interdict (deprivation of the sacraments and liturgical activities). The intended purposes of censures are to correct and punish offenders; to deter persons from committing sins which, more seriously and openly than others, threaten the common good of the Church and its members; and to provide for the making of reparation for harm done to the community of the Church. Censures may be incurred automatically (*ipso facto*) on the commission of certain offenses for which fixed penalties have been laid down in church law (*latae sententiae*); or they may be inflicted by sentence of a judge (*ferendae sententiae*). Automatic excommunication is incurred for the offenses of abortion, apostasy, heresy and schism. Obstinacy in crime — also called contumacy, disregard of a penalty, defiance of church authority — is presumed by law in the commission of offenses for which automatic censures are decreed. The presence and degree of contumacy in other cases, for which judicial sentence is required, is subject to determination by a judge. Absolution can be obtained from any censure, provided the person repents and desists from obstinacy. Absolution may be reserved to the pope, the bishop of a place, or the major superior of an exempt clerical religious institute. In danger of death, any priest can absolve from all censures; in other cases, faculties to absolve from reserved censures can be exercised by competent authorities or given to other priests. The penal law of the Church is contained in Book VI of the Code of Canon Law.

Ceremonies, Master of: One who directs the proceedings of a rite or ceremony during the function.

Chamberlain (*Camerlengo*): (1) the Chamberlain of the Holy Roman Church is a cardinal with special responsibilities, especially during the time between the death of one pope and the election of his successor; among other things, he safeguards and administers the goods and revenues of the Holy See and heads particular congregations of cardinals for special purposes. (See also Papal Election.) (2) the Chamberlain of the College of Cardinals has charge of the property and revenues of the College and keeps the record of business transacted in consistories. (3) the Chamberlain of the Roman Clergy is the president of the secular clergy of Rome.

Chancellor: Notary of a diocese, who draws up written documents used in the government of the diocese; takes care of, arranges and indexes diocesan archives, records of dispensations and ecclesiastical trials.

Chancery: (1) A branch of church administration that handles written documents used in the government of a diocese. (2) The administrative office of a diocese, a bishop's office.

Chant: A type of sacred singing. It is either recitative in nature with a short two-to-six tones for an accentus, or melodic in one of three styles (syllabic, neumatic, or melismatic).

Chapel: A building or part of another building used for divine worship; a portion of a church set aside for the celebration of Mass or for some special devotion.

Chaplain: A priest — or, in some instances, a properly qualified religious or lay person — serving the pastoral needs of particular groups of people and institutions, such as hospitals, schools, correctional facilities, religious communities, the armed forces, etc.

Chaplet: A term, meaning little crown, applied to a rosary or, more commonly, to a small string of beads used for devotional purposes, e.g., the Infant of Prague chaplet.

Chapter: A general meeting of delegates of religious orders for elections and the handling of other important affairs of their communities.

Charismatic Renewal: A movement which originated with a handful of Duquesne University students and faculty members in the 1966-67 academic year and spread from there to Notre Dame, Michigan State University, the University of Michigan, other campuses and cities throughout the U.S., and to well over 100 other countries. Scriptural keys to the renewal are: Christ's promise to send the Holy Spirit upon the Apostles; the description, in the Acts of the Apostles, of the effects of the coming of the Holy Spirit upon the Apostles on Pentecost; St. Paul's explanation, in the Letter to the Romans and 1 Corinthians, of the charismatic gifts (for the good of the Church and persons) the Holy Spirit would bestow on Christians; New Testament evidence concerning the effects of charismatic gifts in and through the early Church. The personal key to the renewal is baptism in the Holy Spirit. This is not a new sacrament but the personally experienced actualization of grace already sacramentally received, principally in baptism and confirmation. The experience of baptism in the Holy Spirit is often accompanied by the reception of one or more charismatic gifts. A characteristic form of the renewal is the weekly prayer meeting, a gathering which includes periods of spontaneous prayer, singing, sharing of experience and testimony, fellowship and teaching.

Charisms: Gifts or graces given by God to persons for the good of others and the Church. Examples are special gifts for apostolic work, prophecy, healing, discernment of spirits, the life of evangelical poverty, here-and-now witness to faith in various circumstances of life. The Second Vatican Council made the following statement about charisms in the Dogmatic Constitution on the Church (No. 12): "It is not only through the sacraments and Church ministries that the same Holy Spirit sanctifies and leads the People of God and enriches it with virtues. Allotting his gifts 'to everyone according as he will' (1 Cor. 12:11), he distributes special graces among the faithful of every rank. By these gifts he makes them fit and ready to undertake the various tasks or offices advantageous for the renewal and upbuilding of the Church, according to the words of the Apostle: 'The manifestation of the Spirit is given to everyone for profit' (1 Cor. 12:7). These charismatic gifts, whether they be the most outstanding or the more simple and widely diffused, are to be received with thanksgiving and consolation, for they are exceedingly suitable and useful for the needs of the Church. Still, extraordinary gifts are not to be rashly sought after, nor are the fruits of apostolic labor to be presumptuously expected from them. In any case, judgment as to their genuineness and proper use belongs to those who preside over the Church, and to whose special competence it belongs, not indeed to extinguish the Spirit, but to test all things and hold fast to that which is good" (cf. 1 Thes. 5:12; 19-21).

Charity: Love of God above all things for his own sake, and love of one's neighbor as oneself because and as an expression of one's love for God; the greatest of the three theological virtues. The term is sometimes also used to designate sanctifying grace.

Chastity: Properly ordered behavior with respect to sex. In marriage, the exercise of the procreative power is integrated with the norms and purposes of marriage. Outside of marriage, the rule is self-denial of the voluntary exercise and enjoyment of the procreative faculty in thought, word or action. The vow of chastity, which reinforces the virtue of chastity with the virtue of religion, is one of the three vows professed publicly by members of institutes of consecrated life.

Chirograph or Autograph Letter: A letter written by a pope himself, in his own handwriting.

Chrism: A mixture of olive or other vegetable oil and balsam (or balm), that is consecrated by a bishop for use in liturgical anointings: baptism, confirmation, holy orders, the blessing of an altar.

Christ: The title of Jesus, derived from the Greek translation *Christos* of the Hebrew term Messiah, meaning the Anointed of God, the Savior and Deliverer of his people. Christian use of the title is a confession of belief that Jesus is the Savior.

Christianity: The sum total of things related to belief in Christ — the Christian religion, Christian churches, Christians themselves, society based on and expressive of Christian beliefs, culture reflecting Christian values.

Christians: The name first applied about the year 43 to followers of Christ at Antioch, the capital of Syria. It was used by the pagans as a contemptuous term. The word applies to persons who profess belief in the divinity and teachings of Christ and who give witness to him in life.

Circumcision: A ceremonial practice symbolic of initiation and participation in the covenant between God and Abraham.

Circumincession: The indwelling of each divine Person of the Holy Trinity in the others.

Clergy: Men ordained to holy orders and commissioned for sacred ministries and assigned to pastoral and other duties for the service of the people and the Church. (1) Diocesan or secular clergy are committed to pastoral ministry in parishes and in other capacities in a particular church (diocese) under the direction of their bishop, to whom they are bound by a promise of obedience. (2) Regular clergy belong to religious institutes (orders, congregations, societies — institutes of consecrated life) and are so called because they observe the rule (*regula*, in Latin) of their respective institutes. They are committed to the ways of life and apostolates of their institutes. In ordinary pastoral ministry, they are under the direction of local bishops as well as their own superiors.

Clericalism: A term generally used in a derogatory sense to mean action, influence and interference by the Church and the clergy in matters with which they allegedly should not be concerned. Anticlericalism is a reaction of antipathy, hostility, distrust and opposition to the Church and clergy arising from real and/or alleged faults of the clergy, overextension of the role of the laity, or for other reasons.

Cloister: Part of a monastery, convent or other house of religious reserved for use by members of the institute. Houses of contemplative Religious have a strict enclosure.

Code: A digest of rules or regulations, such as the Code of Canon Law.

Code of Canon Law: See Canon Law.

Collegiality: A term in use especially since the Second Vatican Council to describe the authority exercised by the College of Bishops. The bishops of the Church, in union with and subordinate to the pope — who has full, supreme and universal power over the Church which he can always exercise independently — have supreme teaching and pastoral authority over the whole Church. In addition to their proper authority of office for the good of the faithful in their respective dioceses or other jurisdictions, the bishops have authority to act for the good of the universal Church. This collegial authority is exercised in a solemn manner in an ecumenical council and can also be exercised in other ways sanctioned by the pope. Doctrine on collegiality was set forth by the Second Vatican Council in *Lumen Gentium* (the Dogmatic Constitution on the Church). (See separate entry.) By extension, the concept of collegiality is applied to other forms of participation and co-responsibility by members of a community.

Communicatio in Sacris: The reception of the Church's sacraments by non-members or the reception by Catholics of sacraments in non-Catholic Churches.

Communion of Saints: "The communion of all the faithful of Christ, those who are pilgrims on earth, the dead who are being purified, and the blessed in heaven, all together forming one Church; in this communion, the merciful love of God and his saints is always (attentive) to our prayers" (Paul VI, *Creed of the People of God*).

Communism: The substantive principles of modern communism, a theory and system of economics and social organization, were stated about the middle of the 19th century by Karl Marx, author of *The Communist Manifesto* and, with Friedrich Engels, *Das Kapital*. The elements of communist theory include: radical materialism; dialectical determinism; the inevitability of class struggle and conflict, which is to be furthered for the ultimate establishment of a worldwide, classless society; common ownership of productive and other goods; the subordination of all persons and institutions to the dictatorship of the collective; denial of the rights, dignity and liberty of persons; militant atheism and hostility to religion, utilitarian morality. Communism in theory and practice has been the subject of many papal documents and statements. Pius IX condemned it in 1846. Leo XIII dealt with it at length in the encyclical letter *Quod Apostolici Muneris* in 1878 and *Rerum Novarum* in 1891. Pius XI wrote on the same subject in the encyclicals *Quadragesimo Anno* in 1931 and *Divini Redemptoris* in 1937. These writings have been updated and developed in new directions by Pius XII, John XXIII, Paul VI, and John Paul II.

Compline: The night prayer of the Church that completes the daily cursus (course) of the Liturgy of the Hours (Divine Office).

Concelebration: The liturgical act in which several priests, led by one member of the group, offer Mass together, all consecrating the bread and wine. Concelebration has always been common in churches of Eastern Rite. In the Roman Rite, it was long restricted, taking place only at the ordination of bishops and the ordination of priests. The Constitution on the Sacred Liturgy issued by the Second Vatican Council set new norms for concelebration, which is now relatively common in the Roman Rite.

Concordance, Biblical: An alphabetical verbal index enabling a user knowing one or more words of a scriptural passage to locate the entire text.

Concordat: A Church-State treaty with the force of law concerning matters of mutual concern — e.g., rights of the Church, arrangement of ecclesiastical jurisdictions, marriage laws, education. Approximately 150 agreements of this kind have been negotiated since the Concordat of Worms in 1122.

Concupiscence: Any tendency of the sensitive appetite. The term is most frequently used in reference to desires and tendencies for sinful sense pleasure.

Confession: Sacramental confession is the act by which a person tells or confesses his sins to a priest who is authorized to give absolution in the sacrament of penance.

Confessor: A priest who administers the sacrament of penance. The title of confessor, formerly given to a category of male saints, was suppressed with publication of the calendar reform of 1969.

Confraternity: An association whose members practice a particular form of religious devotion and/or are engaged in some kind of apostolic work.

Congregation: (1) The collective name for the people who form a parish. (2) One of the chief administrative departments of the Roman Curia. (3) An unofficial term for a group of men and women who belong to a religious community or institute of consecrated life.

Conscience: Practical judgment concerning the moral goodness or sinfulness of an action (thought, word, desire). In the Catholic view, this judgment is made by reference of the action, its attendant circumstances and the intentions of the person to the requirements of moral law as expressed in the Ten Commandments, the summary law of love for God and neighbor, the life and teaching of Christ, and the authoritative teaching and practice of the Church with respect to the total demands of divine Revelation. A person is obliged: (1) to obey a certain and correct conscience; (2) to obey a certain conscience even if it is inculpably erroneous; (3) not to obey, but to correct, a conscience known to be erroneous or lax; (4) to rectify a scrupulous conscience by following the advice of a confessor and by other measures; (5) to resolve doubts of conscience before acting. It is legitimate to act for solid and probable reasons when a question of moral responsibility admits of argument (see Probabiliorism and Probabilism).

Conscience, Examination of: Self-examination to determine one's spiritual state before God, regarding one's sins and faults. It is recommended as a regular practice and is practically necessary in preparing for the sacrament of penance. The particular examen is a regular examination to assist in overcoming specific faults and imperfections.

Consequentialism: A moral theory, closely associated with proportionalism and utilitarianism, that holds that the preferable action is one that brings about the best consequences. Preferred results, rather than the objective truth and intentionality, are the object of actions based on consequentialism. While traditional moral theology acknowledges that consequences are important in determining the rightness of an act, importance is also placed on the intrinsic morality of the act and the agent's intention.

Consistory: An assembly of cardinals presided over by the pope.

Constitution: (1) An apostolic or papal constitution is a document in which a pope enacts and promulgates law. (2) A formal and solemn document issued by an ecumenical council on a doctrinal or pastoral subject, with binding force in the whole Church; e.g., the four constitutions issued by the Second Vatican Council on the Church, liturgy, Revelation, and the Church in the modern world. (3) The constitutions of institutes of consecrated life and societies of apostolic life spell out details of and norms drawn from the various rules for the guidance and direction of the life and work of their members.

Consubstantiation: A theory which holds that the Body and Blood of Christ coexist with the substance of bread and wine in the Holy Eucharist. This theory, also called impanation, is incompatible with the doctrine of transubstantiation.

Contraception: Anything done by positive interference to prevent sexual intercourse from resulting in conception. Direct contraception is against the order of nature. Indirect contraception — as a secondary effect of medical treatment or other action having a necessary, good, non-contraceptive purpose — is permissible under the principle of the double effect. The practice of periodic continence is not contraception because it does not involve positive interference with the order of nature. (See *Humanae Vitae*, other entries.)

Contrition: Sorrow for sin coupled with a purpose of amendment. Contrition arising from a supernatural motive is necessary for the forgiveness of sin. (1) Perfect contrition is total sorrow for and renunciation of attachment to sin, arising from the motive of pure love of God. Perfect contrition, which implies the intention of doing all God wants done for the forgiveness of sin (including confession in a reasonable period of time), is sufficient for the forgiveness of serious sin and the remission of all temporal punishment due for sin. (The intention to receive the sacrament of penance is implicit — even if unrealized, as in the case of some persons — in perfect contrition.) (2) Imperfect contrition or attrition is sorrow arising from a quasi-selfish supernatural motive, e.g., the fear of losing heaven, suffering the pains of hell, etc. Imperfect contrition is sufficient for the forgiveness

of serious sin when joined with absolution in confession, and sufficient for the forgiveness of venial sin even outside of confession.

Contumely: Personal insult, reviling a person in his presence by accusation of moral faults, by refusal of recognition or due respect; a violation of obligations of justice and charity.

Conversion: In a general sense, the turning away from someone or something and the moving toward another person or thing. In Christian belief, conversion is the embrace of Jesus Christ and a rejection of all that keeps one from God.

Corpus Iuris Canonici: See Canon Law.

Council: A formal meeting of Church leaders, summoned by a bishop or appropriate Church leader, with the general purpose of assisting the life of the Church through deliberations, decrees, and promulgations. Different councils include: **diocesan** councils (synod), a gathering of the officials of an individual diocese; **provincial** councils, the meeting of the bishops of a province; **plenary** councils, the assembly of the bishops of a country; and **ecumenical** councils, a gathering of all the bishops in the world under the authority of the Bishop of Rome.

Counsels, Evangelical: Gospel counsels of perfection, especially voluntary poverty, perfect chastity and obedience, which were recommended by Christ to those who would devote themselves exclusively and completely to the immediate service of God. Religious (members of institutes of consecrated life) bind themselves by public vows to observe these counsels in a life of total consecration to God and service to people through various kinds of apostolic works.

Counter-Reformation: The period of approximately 100 years following the Council of Trent (1545-63), which witnessed a reform within the Church to stimulate genuine Catholic life and to counteract effects of the Reformation.

Covenant: A bond of relationship between parties pledged to each other. God-initiated covenants in the Old Testament included those with Noah, Abraham, Moses, Levi, David. The Mosaic (Sinai) covenant made Israel God's Chosen People on terms of fidelity to true faith, true worship, and righteous conduct according to the Decalogue. The New Testament covenant, prefigured in the Old Testament, is the bond people have with God through Christ. All people are called to be parties to this perfect and everlasting covenant, which was mediated and ratified by Christ. The marriage covenant seals the closest possible relationship between a man and a woman.

Creation: The production by God of something out of nothing. The biblical account of creation is contained in the first two chapters of Genesis.

Creator: God, the supreme, self-existing Being, the absolute and infinite First Cause of all things.

Creature: Everything in the realm of being is a creature, except God.

Cremation: The reduction of a human corpse to ashes by means of fire. Cremation is not in line with Catholic tradition and practice, even though it is not opposed to any article of faith. The Congregation for the Doctrine of the Faith, under date of May 8, 1963, circulated among bishops an instruction which upheld the traditional practices of Christian burial but modified anti-cremation legislation. Cremation may be permitted for serious reasons, of a private as well as public nature, provided it does not involve any contempt of the Church or of religion, or any attempt to deny, question, or belittle the doctrine of the resurrection of the body. In a letter dated March 21, 1997, and addressed to Bishop Anthony M. Pilla, president of the National Conference of Catholic Bishops, the Congregation for Divine Worship and the Discipline of the Sacraments granted "a particular permission to the diocesan bishops of the United States of America. By this, local Ordinaries (heads of dioceses) are authorized . . . to permit that the funeral liturgy, including where appropriate the celebration of the Eucharist, be celebrated in the presence of the cremated remains instead of the natural body." Bishop Pilla asked bishops not to use this indult until appropriate texts and ritual directives are approved by the Vatican. (See Burial, Ecclesiastical).

Crib: Also Crèche, a devotional representation of the birth of Jesus. The custom of erecting cribs is generally attributed to St. Francis of Assisi, who in 1223 obtained from Pope Honorius III permission to use a crib and figures of the Christ Child, Mary, St. Joseph, and others, to represent the mystery of the Nativity.

Crosier: The bishop's staff, symbolic of his pastoral office, responsibility and authority; used at liturgical functions.

Crypt: An underground or partly underground chamber, e.g., the lower part of a church used for worship and/or burial.

Cura Animarum: A Latin phrase, meaning care of souls, designating the pastoral ministry and responsibility of bishops and priests.

Curia: The personnel and offices through which (1) the pope administers the affairs of the universal Church, the Roman Curia, or (2) a bishop the affairs of a diocese, diocesan curia. The principal officials of a diocesan curia are the vicar general of the diocese, the chancellor, officials of the diocesan tribunal or court, examiners, consultors, auditors, notaries.

Custos: A religious superior who presides over a number of convents collectively called a custody. In some institutes of consecrated life a custos may be the deputy of a higher superior.

D

Dean: (1) A priest with supervisory responsibility over a section of a diocese known as a deanery. The post-Vatican II counterpart of a dean is an episcopal vicar. (2) The senior or ranking member of a group.

Decision: A judgment or pronouncement on a cause or suit, given by a church tribunal or official with judicial authority. A decision has the force of law for concerned parties.

Declaration: (1) An ecclesiastical document which presents an interpretation of an existing law. (2) A position paper on a specific subject, e.g., the three declarations issued by the Second Vatican Council on religious freedom, non-Christian religions, and Christian education.

Decree: An edict or ordinance issued by a pope and/or by an ecumenical council, with binding force in the whole Church; by a department of the Roman Curia, with binding force for concerned parties; by a territorial body of bishops, with binding force for persons in the area; by individual bishops, with binding force for concerned parties until revocation or the death of the bishop. The nine decrees issued by the Second Vatican Council were combinations of doctrinal and pastoral statements with executive orders for action and movement toward renewal and reform in the Church.

Dedication of a Church: The ceremony whereby a church is solemnly set apart for the worship of God. The custom of dedicating churches had an antecedent in Old Testament ceremonies for the dedication of the Temple, as in the times of Solomon and the Maccabees. The earliest extant record of the dedication of a Christian church dates from early in the fourth century, when it was done simply by the celebration of Mass. Other ceremonies developed later. A church can be dedicated by a simple blessing or a solemn consecration. The rite of consecration is generally performed by a bishop.

Deposit of the Faith: The body of saving truth, entrusted by Christ to the Apostles and handed on by them to the Church to be preserved and proclaimed. As embodied in Revelation and Tradition the term is very nearly coextensive with objective revelation, in that it embraces the whole of Christ's teaching. But the term of deposit highlights particular features of the apostolic teaching implying that this teaching is an inexhaustible store that rewards and promotes reflection and study so that new insights and deeper penetration might be made into the mystery of the divine economy of salvation. Although our understanding of this teaching can develop, it can never be augmented in its substance; the teaching is a divine trust, that cannot be altered, modified, or debased. The term *depositum fidei* first entered official Catholic teaching with the Council of Trent, but its substance is well-attested in the Scriptures and the Fathers.

Despair: Abandonment of hope for salvation arising from the conviction that God will not provide the necessary means for attaining it, that following God's way of life for salvation is impossible, or that one's sins are unforgivable; a serious sin against the Holy Spirit and the theological virtues of hope and faith, involving distrust in the mercy and goodness of God and a denial of the truths that God wills the salvation of all persons and provides sufficient grace for it. Real despair is distinguished from unreasonable fear with respect to the difficulties of attaining salvation, from morbid anxiety over the demands of divine justice, and from feelings of despair.

Detraction: Revelation of true but hidden faults of a person without sufficient and justifying reason; a violation of requirements of justice and charity, involving the obligation to make restitution when this is possible without doing more harm to the good name of the offended party. In some cases, e.g., to prevent evil, secret faults may and should be disclosed.

Devil: (1) Lucifer, Satan, chief of the fallen angels who sinned and were banished from heaven. Still possessing angelic powers, he can cause such diabolical phenomena as possession and obsession, and can tempt men to sin. (2) Any fallen angel.

Devotion: (1) Religious fervor, piety; dedication. (2) The consolation experienced at times during prayer; a reverent manner of praying.

Devotions: Pious practices of members of the Church include not only participation in various acts of the liturgy but also in other acts of worship generally called popular or private devotions. Concerning these, the Second Vatican Council said in the Constitution on the Sacred Liturgy (*Sacrosanctum Concilium*, No. 13): "Popular devotions of the Christian people are warmly commended, provided they accord with the laws and norms of the Church. Such is especially the case with devotions called for by the Apostolic See. Devotions proper to the individual churches also have a special dignity. These devotions should be so drawn up that they harmonize with the liturgical seasons, accord with the sacred liturgy, are in some fashion derived from it, and lead the people to it, since the liturgy by its very nature far surpasses any of them." Devotions of a liturgical type are Exposition of the Blessed Sacrament, recitation of Evening Prayer and Night Prayer of the Liturgy of the Hours. Examples of paraliturgical devotion are a Bible Service or Vigil, and the Angelus, Rosary and Stations of the Cross, which have a strong scriptural basis.

Diocese: A particular church, a fully organized ecclesiastical jurisdiction under the pastoral direction of a bishop as local Ordinary.

Discalced: Of Latin derivation and meaning without shoes, the word is applied to religious orders or congregations whose members go barefoot or wear sandals.

Disciple: A term used sometimes in reference to the Apostles but more often to a larger number of followers (70 or 72) of Christ mentioned in Lk. 10:1.

Disciplina Arcani: A Latin phrase, meaning discipline of the secret and referring to a practice of the early Church, especially during the Roman persecutions, to: (1) conceal Christian truths

from those who, it was feared, would misinterpret, ridicule and profane the teachings, and persecute Christians for believing them; (2) instruct catechumens in a gradual manner, withholding the teaching of certain doctrines until the catechumens proved themselves of good faith and sufficient understanding.

Dispensation: The relaxation of a law in a particular case. Laws made for the common good sometimes work undue hardship in particular cases. In such cases, where sufficient reasons are present, dispensations may be granted by proper authorities. Bishops, religious superiors and others may dispense from certain laws; the pope can dispense from all ecclesiastical laws. No one has authority to dispense from obligations of the divine law.

Divination: Attempting to foretell future or hidden things by means of things like dreams, necromancy, spiritism, examination of entrails, astrology, augury, omens, palmistry, drawing straws, dice, cards, etc. Practices like these attribute to created things a power which belongs to God alone and are violations of the First Commandment.

Divine Praises: Fourteen praises recited or sung at Benediction of the Blessed Sacrament in reparation for sins of sacrilege, blasphemy and profanity. Some of these praises date from the end of the 18th century: Blessed *be God.* / Blessed *be his holy Name.* / Blessed *be Jesus Christ, true God and true Man.* / Blessed *be the Name of Jesus.* / Blessed *be his most Sacred Heart.* / Blessed *be his most Precious Blood.* / Blessed *be Jesus in the most holy Sacrament of the Altar.* / Blessed *be the Holy Spirit, the Paraclete.* / Blessed *be the great Mother of God, Mary most holy.* / Blessed *be her holy and Immaculate Conception.* / Blessed *be her glorious Assumption.* / Blessed *be the name of Mary, Virgin and Mother.* / Blessed *be St. Joseph, her most chaste Spouse.* / Blessed *be God in his Angels and in his Saints.*

Double Effect Principle: Actions sometimes have two effects closely related to each other, one good and the other bad, and a difficult moral question can arise: Is it permissible to place an action from which two such results follow? It is permissible to place the action if: the action is good in itself and is directly productive of the good effect; the circumstances are good; the intention of the person is good; the reason for placing the action is proportionately serious to the seriousness of the indirect bad effect.

Doxology: (1) The lesser doxology, or ascription of glory to the Trinity, is the Glory be to the Father. The first part dates back to the third or fourth century, and came from the form of baptism. The concluding words, As it was in the beginning, etc., are of later origin. (2) The greater doxology, Glory to God in the highest, begins with the words of angelic praise at the birth of Christ recounted in the Infancy Narrative (Lk. 2:14). It is often recited at Mass. Of early Eastern origin, it is found in the Apostolic Constitutions in a form much like the present. (3) The formula of praise at the end of the Eucharistic Prayer at Mass, sung or said by the celebrant while he holds aloft the paten containing the consecrated host in one hand and the chalice containing the consecrated wine in the other.

Dulia: A Greek term meaning the veneration or homage, different in nature and degree from that given to God, paid to the saints. It includes honoring the saints and seeking their intercession with God.

Duty: A moral obligation deriving from the binding force of law, the exigencies of one's state in life, and other sources.

E

Easter Controversy: A three-phase controversy over the time for the celebration of Easter. Some early Christians in the Near East, called Quartodecimans, favored the observance of Easter on the fourteenth day of Nisan, the spring month of the Hebrew calendar, whenever it occurred. Against this practice, Pope St. Victor I, about 190, ordered a Sunday observance of the feast. The Council of Nicaea, in line with usages of the Church at Rome and Alexandria, decreed in 325 that Easter should be observed on the Sunday following the first full moon of spring. Uniformity of practice in the West was not achieved until several centuries later, when the British Isles, in delayed compliance with measures enacted by the Synod of Whitby in 664, accepted the Roman date of observance. Unrelated to the controversy is the fact that some Eastern Christians, in accordance with traditional calendar practices, celebrate Easter at a different time than the Roman and Eastern Churches.

Easter Duty: The serious obligation binding Catholics of Roman Rite, to receive the Eucharist during the Easter season (in the U.S., from the first Sunday of Lent to and including Trinity Sunday).

Easter Water: Holy water blessed with special ceremonies and distributed on the Easter Vigil; used during Easter Week for blessing the faithful and homes.

Ecclesiology: Study of the nature, constitution, members, mission, functions, etc., of the Church.

Ecology: The natural environment of the total range of creation — mineral, vegetable, animal, human — entrusted to people for respect, care and appropriate use as well as conservation and development for the good of present and future generations.

Ecstasy: An extraordinary state of mystical experience in which a person is so absorbed in God that the activity of the exterior senses is suspended.

Economy, Divine: The fulfillment of God's plan of salvation. It was fully developed in his divine mind from eternity, and fully revealed in Jesus Christ. Before the Incarnation it was known only

obscurely, but after the ascension of Christ and the coming of the Holy Spirit at Pentecost, it became the substance of apostolic preaching and is preserved in its integrity for each new generation.

Ecumenism: The movement of Christians and their churches toward the unity willed by Christ. The Second Vatican Council called the movement "those activities and enterprises which, according to various needs of the Church and opportune occasions, are started and organized for the fostering of unity among Christians" (Decree on Ecumenism, No. 4). Spiritual ecumenism, i.e., mutual prayer for unity, is the heart of the movement. The movement also involves scholarly and pew-level efforts for the development of mutual understanding and better interfaith relations in general, and collaboration by the churches and their members in the social area.

Elevation: The raising of the host after consecration at Mass for adoration by the faithful. The custom was introduced in the Diocese of Paris about the close of the 12th century to offset an erroneous teaching of the time which held that transubstantiation of the bread did not take place until after the consecration of the wine in the chalice. The elevation of the chalice following the consecration of the wine was introduced in the 15th century.

Encyclical: The highest form of papal teaching document. It is normally addressed to all the bishops and/or to all the faithful.

Envy: Sadness over another's good fortune because it is considered a loss to oneself or a detraction from one's own excellence; one of the seven capital sins, a violation of the obligations of charity.

Epiclesis: An invocation of the Holy Spirit, to bless the offerings consecrated at Mass; before the consecration in the Latin Rite, after the consecration in Eastern usage.

Epikeia: A Greek word meaning reasonableness and designating a moral theory and practice, a mild interpretation of the mind of a legislator who is prudently considered not to wish positive law to bind in certain circumstances.

Episcopate: (1) The office, dignity and sacramental powers bestowed upon a bishop at his ordination. (2) The body of bishops collectively.

Equivocation: (1) The use of words, phrases, or gestures having more than one meaning in order to conceal information which a questioner has no strict right to know. It is permissible to equivocate (have a broad mental reservation) in some circumstances. (2) A lie, i.e., a statement of untruth. Lying is intrinsically wrong. A lie told in joking, evident as such, is not wrong.

Eschatology: Doctrine concerning the last things: death, judgment, heaven and hell, and the final state of perfection of the people and kingdom of God at the end of time.

Eternity: The interminable, perfect possession of life in its totality without beginning or end; an attribute of God, who has no past or future but always is. Man's existence has a beginning but no end and is, accordingly, called immortal.

Ethics: Moral philosophy, the science of the morality of human acts deriving from natural law, the natural end of man, and the powers of human reason. It includes all the spheres of human activity — personal, social, economic, political, etc. Ethics is distinct from but can be related to moral theology, whose primary principles are drawn from divine revelation.

Euthanasia: Mercy killing, the direct causing of death for the purpose of ending human suffering. Euthanasia is murder and is totally illicit, for the natural law forbids the direct taking of one's own life or that of an innocent person. The use of drugs to relieve suffering in serious cases, even when this results in a shortening of life as an indirect and secondary effect, is permissible under conditions of the double-effect principle. It is also permissible for a seriously ill person to refuse to follow — or for other responsible persons to refuse to permit — extraordinary medical procedures even though the refusal might entail shortening of life.

Evangelization: Proclamation of the Gospel, the Good News of salvation in and through Christ, among those who have not yet known or received it; and efforts for the progressive development of the life of faith among those who have already received the Gospel and all that it entails. Evangelization is the primary mission of the Church, in which all members of the Church are called to participate.

Evolution: Scientific theory concerning the development of the physical universe from unorganized matter (inorganic evolution) and, especially, the development of existing forms of vegetable, animal and human life from earlier and more primitive organisms (organic evolution). Various ideas about evolution were advanced for some centuries before scientific evidence in support of the main-line theory of organic evolution, which has several formulations, was discovered and verified in the second half of the 19th century and afterwards. This evidence — from the findings of comparative anatomy and other sciences — confirmed evolution of species and cleared the way to further investigation of questions regarding the processes of its accomplishment. While a number of such questions remain open with respect to human evolution, a point of doctrine not open to question is the immediate creation of the human soul by God. For some time, theologians regarded the theory with hostility, considering it to be in opposition to the account of creation in the early chapters of Genesis and subversive of belief in such doctrines as creation, the early state of man in grace, and the fall of man from grace. This state of affairs and the tension it generated led to considerable controversy regarding an alleged conflict between religion and science. Gradually, however, the tension was diminished with the development of biblical studies from the latter part of the 19th century onwards, with clari-

fication of the distinctive features of religious truth and scientific truth, and with the refinement of evolutionary concepts. So far as the Genesis account of creation is concerned, the Catholic view is that the writer(s) did not write as a scientist but as the communicator of religious truth in a manner adapted to the understanding of the people of his time. He used anthropomorphic language, the figure of days and other literary devices to state the salvation truths of creation, the fall of man from grace, and the promise of redemption. It was beyond the competency and purpose of the writer(s) to describe creation and related events in a scientific manner.

Excommunication: A penalty or censure by which a baptized Roman Catholic is excluded from the communion of the faithful, for committing and remaining obstinate in certain serious offenses specified in canon law, e.g. heresy, schism, apostasy, abortion. As by baptism a person is made a member of the Church in which there is a communication of spiritual goods, so by excommunication he is deprived of the same spiritual goods until he repents and receives absolution. Even though excommunicated, a person is still responsible for fulfillment of the normal obligations of a Catholic. (See Censures).

Ex Opere Operantis: A term in sacramental theology meaning that the effectiveness of sacraments depends on the moral rectitude of the minister or participant. This term was applied to rites of the Old Testament in contrast with those of the New Testament when it was first advanced in the thirteenth century.

Ex Opere Operato: A term in sacramental theology meaning that sacraments are effective by means of the sacramental rite itself and not because of the worthiness of the minister or participant.

Exorcism: (1) Driving out evil spirits; a rite in which evil spirits are charged and commanded on the authority of God and with the prayer of the Church to depart from a person or to cease causing harm to a person suffering from diabolical possession or obsession. The sacramental is officially administered by a priest delegated for the purpose by the bishop of the place. Elements of the rite include the Litany of Saints; recitation of the Our Father, one or more creeds, and other prayers; specific prayers of exorcism; the reading of Gospel passages and use of the Sign of the Cross. On January 26, 1999, the Congregation for Divine Worship and the Discipline of the Sacraments published a new rite of exorcism in the Roman Ritual. (2) Exorcisms which do not imply the conditions of either diabolical possession or obsession form part of the ceremony of baptism and are also included in formulas for various blessings; e.g., of water.

Exposition of the Blessed Sacrament: "In churches where the Eucharist is regularly reserved, it is recommended that solemn exposition of the Blessed Sacrament for an extended period of time should take place once a year, even though the period is not strictly continuous. Shorter expositions of the Eucharist (Benediction) are to be arranged in such a way that the blessing with the Eucharist is preceded by a reasonable time for readings of the word of God, songs, prayers and a period for silent prayer." So stated Vatican directives issued in 1973.

F

Faculties: Grants of jurisdiction or authority by the law of the Church or superiors (pope, bishop, religious superior) for exercise of the powers of holy orders, e.g., priests are given faculties to hear confessions, officiate at weddings; bishops are given faculties to grant dispensations, etc.

Faith: In religion, faith has several aspects. Catholic doctrine calls faith the assent of the mind to truths revealed by God, the assent being made with the help of grace and by command of the will on account of the authority and trustworthiness of God revealing. The term faith also refers to the truths that are believed (content of faith) and to the way in which a person, in response to Christ, gives witness to and expresses belief in daily life (living faith). All of these elements, and more, are included in the following statement: "'The obedience of faith' (Rom. 16:26; 1:5; 2 Cor. 10:5-6) must be given to God who reveals, an obedience by which man entrusts his whole self freely to God, offering 'the full submission of intellect and will to God who reveals' (First Vatican Council, Dogmatic Constitution on the Catholic Faith, Chap. 3), and freely assenting to the truth revealed by him. If this faith is to be shown, the grace of God and the interior help of the Holy Spirit must precede and assist, moving the heart and turning it to God, opening the eyes of the mind, and giving 'joy and ease to everyone in assenting to the truth and believing it'" (Second Council of Orange, Canon 7, Second Vatican Council, Constitution on Revelation, *Dei Verbum*, No. 5). Faith is necessary for salvation.

Faith, Rule of: The norm or standard of religious belief. The Catholic doctrine is that belief must be professed in the divinely revealed truths in the Bible and tradition as interpreted and proposed by the infallible teaching authority of the Church.

Fast, Eucharistic: Abstinence from food and drink, except water and medicine, is required for one hour before the reception of the Eucharist. Persons who are advanced in age or suffer from infirmity or illness, together with those who care for them, can receive Holy Communion even if they have not abstained from food and drink for an hour. A priest celebrating two or three Masses on the same day can eat and drink something before the second or third Mass without regard for the hour limit.

Father: A title of priests, who are regarded as spiritual fathers because they are the ordinary ministers of baptism, by which persons are born to supernatural life, and because of their pastoral service to people.

First Friday: A devotion consisting of the reception of Holy Communion on the first Friday of nine consecutive months in honor of the Sacred Heart of Jesus and in reparation for sin. (See Sacred Heart, Promises.)

First Saturday: A devotion tracing its origin to the apparitions of the Blessed Virgin Mary at Fátima in 1917. Those practicing the devotion go to confession and, on the first Saturday of five consecutive months, receive Holy Communion, recite five decades of the Rosary, and meditate on the mysteries for fifteen minutes.

Fisherman's Ring: A signet ring (termed in Italian the *pescatorio*) engraved with the image of St. Peter fishing from a boat, and encircled with the name of the reigning pope. It is not worn by the pope. It is used to seal briefs, and is destroyed after each pope's death.

Forgiveness of Sin: Catholics believe that sins are forgiven by God through the mediation of Christ in view of the repentance of the sinner and by means of the sacrament of penance. (See Penance, Contrition).

Fortitude: Courage to face dangers or hardships for the sake of what is good; one of the four cardinal virtues and one of the seven gifts of the Holy Spirit.

Forty Hours Devotion: A Eucharistic observance consisting of solemn exposition of the Blessed Sacrament coupled with special Masses and forms of prayer, for the purposes of making reparation for sin and praying for God's blessings of grace and peace. The devotion was instituted in 1534 in Milan. St. John Neumann of Philadelphia was the first bishop in the U.S. to prescribe its observance in his diocese. For many years in this country, the observance was held annually on a rotating basis in all parishes of a diocese. Simplified and abbreviated Eucharistic observances have taken the place of the devotion in some places.

Forum: The sphere in which ecclesiastical authority or jurisdiction is exercised. (1) External: Authority is exercised in the external forum to deal with matters affecting the public welfare of the Church and its members. Those who have such authority because of their office (e.g., diocesan bishops) are called ordinaries. (2) Internal: Authority is exercised in the internal forum to deal with matters affecting the private spiritual good of individuals. The sacramental forum is the sphere in which the sacrament of penance is administered; other exercises of jurisdiction in the internal forum take place in the non-sacramental forum.

Freedom, Religious: The Second Vatican Council declared that the right to religious freedom in civil society "means that all men are to be immune from coercion on the part of individuals or of social groups and of any human power, in such wise that in matters religious no one is to be forced to act in a manner contrary to his own beliefs. Nor is anyone to be restrained from acting in accordance with his own beliefs, whether privately or publicly, whether alone or in association with others, within due limits" of requirements for the common good. The foundation of this right in civil society is the "very dignity of the human person" (Declaration on Religious Freedom, *Dignitatis Humanae*, No. 2). The conciliar statement did not deal with the subject of freedom within the Church. It noted the responsibility of the faithful "carefully to attend to the sacred and certain doctrine of the Church" (No. 14).

Free Will: The faculty or capability of making a reasonable choice among several alternatives. Freedom of will underlies the possibility and fact of moral responsibility.

Friar: Term applied to members of mendicant orders to distinguish them from members of monastic orders. (See Mendicants.)

Fruits of the Holy Spirit: Charity, joy, peace, patience, kindness, goodness, generosity, gentleness, faithfulness, modesty, self-control, chastity.

Fruits of the Mass: The spiritual and temporal blessings that result from the celebration of the Holy Sacrifice of the Mass. The general fruits are shared by all the faithful, living and departed, while the special fruits are applied to the priest who celebrates it, to those for whose intention it is offered, and to all those who participate in its celebration.

Fundamental Option: The orientation of one's life either to God by obedience or against Him through disobedience. Catholic Tradition acknowledges that one free and deliberate act with knowledge renders one at odds with God. A prevalent and vague moral theory today asserts that one act cannot change one's option to God — no matter how grave — unless the action comes from the person's "center." Pope John Paul II cautioned against this ambiguous position in the encyclical *Veritatis Splendor* (1993).

G

Gehenna: Greek form of a Jewish name, Gehinnom, for a valley near Jerusalem, the site of Moloch worship; used as a synonym for hell.

Genuflection: Bending of the knee, a natural sign of adoration or reverence, as when persons genuflect with the right knee in passing before the tabernacle to acknowledge the Eucharistic presence of Christ.

Gethsemane: A Hebrew word meaning oil press, designating the place on the Mount of Olives where Christ prayed and suffered in agony the night before he died.

Gifts of the Holy Spirit: Supernatural habits disposing a person to respond promptly to the inspiration of grace; promised by Christ and communicated through the Holy Spirit, especially in the sacrament of confirmation. They are: wisdom, understanding, counsel, knowledge, fortitude, piety, and fear of the Lord.

Glorified Body: The definitive state of humanity in eternity. The risen Christ calls humanity to the glory of his resurrection; this is a theological premise that presupposes that, like Christ, all of his brothers and sisters will be transformed physically.

Gluttony: An unreasonable appetite for food and drink; one of the seven capital sins.

God: The infinitely perfect Supreme Being, uncaused and absolutely self-sufficient, eternal, the Creator and final end of all things. The one God subsists in three equal Persons, the Father and the Son and the Holy Spirit. God, although transcendent and distinct from the universe, is present and active in the world in realization of his plan for the salvation of human beings, principally through Revelation, the operations of the Holy Spirit, the life and ministry of Christ, and the continuation of Christ's ministry in the Church. The existence of God is an article of faith, clearly communicated in divine Revelation. Even without this Revelation, however, the Church teaches, in a declaration by the First Vatican Council, that human beings can acquire certain knowledge of the existence of God and some of his attributes. This can be done on the bases of principles of reason and reflection on human experience. Non-revealed arguments or demonstrations for the existence of God have been developed from the principle of causality; the contingency of human beings and the universe; the existence of design, change and movement in the universe; human awareness of moral responsibility; widespread human testimony to the existence of God.

Goods of Marriage: Three blessings — children, faithful companionship, and permanence — that were first enumerated by St. Augustine in a work on marriage.

Grace: A free gift of God to persons (and angels), grace is a created sharing or participation in the life of God. It is given to persons through the merits of Christ and is communicated by the Holy Spirit. It is necessary for salvation. The principal means of grace are the sacraments (especially the Eucharist), prayer and good works. (1) **Sanctifying or habitual grace** makes persons holy and pleasing to God, adopted children of God, members of Christ, temples of the Holy Spirit, heirs of heaven capable of supernaturally meritorious acts. With grace, God gives persons the supernatural virtues and gifts of the Holy Spirit. The sacraments of baptism and penance were instituted to give grace to those who do not have it; the other sacraments, to increase it in those already in the state of grace. The means for growth in holiness, or the increase of grace, are prayer, the sacraments, and good works. Sanctifying grace is lost by the commission of serious sin. Each sacrament confers sanctifying grace for the special purpose of the sacrament; in this context, grace is called sacramental grace. (2) **Actual grace** is a supernatural help of God which enlightens and strengthens a person to do good and to avoid evil. It is not a permanent quality, like sanctifying grace. It is necessary for the performance of supernatural acts. It can be resisted and refused. Persons in the state of serious sin are given actual grace to lead them to repentance.

Grace at Meals: Prayers said before meals, asking a blessing of God, and after meals, giving thanks to God. In addition to traditional prayers for these purposes, many variations suitable for different occasions are possible, at personal option.

Guilt: The condition of an individual who has committed some moral wrong and is liable to receive punishment.

H

Habit: (1) A disposition to do things easily, given with grace (and therefore supernatural) and/or acquired by repetition of similar acts. (2) The garb worn by Religious.

Hagiography: Writings or documents about saints and other holy persons.

Hail Mary: A prayer addressed to the Blessed Virgin Mary; also called the *Ave Maria* (Latin equivalent of Hail Mary) and the Angelic Salutation. In three parts, it consists of the words addressed to Mary by the Archangel Gabriel on the occasion of the Annunciation, in the Infancy Narrative (*Hail Mary, full of grace, the Lord is with you,* Blessed *are you among women.*); the words addressed to Mary by her cousin Elizabeth on the occasion of the Visitation (*Blessed is the fruit of your womb.*); a concluding petition (*Holy Mary, Mother of God, pray for us sinners now and at the hour of our death. Amen.*). The first two salutations were joined in Eastern rite formulas by the sixth century, and were similarly used at Rome in the seventh century. Insertion of the name of Jesus at the conclusion of the salutations was probably made by Urban IV about 1262. The present form of the petition was incorporated into the breviary in 1514.

Heaven: The state of those who, having achieved salvation, are in glory with God and enjoy the beatific vision. The phrase, kingdom of heaven, refers to the order or kingdom of God, grace, salvation.

Hell: The state of persons who die in mortal sin, in a condition of self-alienation from God which will last forever.

Heresy: The obstinate post-baptismal denial or doubt by a Catholic of any truth which must be believed as a matter of divine and Catholic faith (Canon 751, of the Code of Canon Law). Formal heresy involves deliberate resistance to the authority of God who communicates revelation through Scripture and tradition and the teaching authority of the Church. Heretics automatically incur the penalty of excommunication (Canon 1364 of the Code of Canon Law). Heresies have been significant not only as disruptions of unity of faith but also as occasions for the clarification and development of doctrine. Heresies from the beginning of the Church to the thirteenth century are described in Dates and Events in Church History.

Hermeneutics: See under the section Interpretation of the Bible.

Hermit: See Anchorite.

Heroic Act of Charity: The completely unselfish offering to God of one's good works and merits for the benefit of the souls in purgatory rather than for oneself. Thus a person may offer to God for the souls in purgatory all the good works he performs during life, all the indulgences he gains, and all the prayers and indulgences that will be offered for him after his death. The act is revocable at will, and is not a vow. Its actual ratification depends on the will of God.

Heroic Virtue: The exemplary practice of the four cardinal virtues and three theological virtues; such virtue is sought in persons considered for sainthood.

Heterodoxy: False doctrine teaching or belief; a departure from truth.

Hierarchy: The hierarchy of order who carry out the sacramental, teaching, and pastoral ministry of the Church; the hierarchy consists of the pope, bishops, priests, and deacons; the pope and the bishops give pastoral governance to the faithful.

Holy Father: A title used for the pope; it is a shortened translation of the Latin title *Beatissimus Pater,* "Most Blessed Father" and refers to his position as the spiritual father of all the Christian faithful.

Holy See: (1) The diocese of the pope, Rome. (2) The pope himself and/or the various officials and bodies of the Church's central administration at Vatican City — the Roman Curia — which act in the name and by authority of the pope.

Holy Spirit: God the Holy Spirit, third Person of the Holy Trinity, who proceeds from the Father and the Son and with whom he is equal in every respect; inspirer of the prophets and writers of sacred Scripture; promised by Christ to the Apostles as their advocate and strengthener; appeared in the form of a dove at the baptism of Christ and as tongues of fire at his descent upon the Apostles; soul of the Church and guarantor, by his abiding presence and action, of truth in doctrine; communicator of grace to human beings, for which reason he is called the sanctifier.

Holy Water: Water blessed by the Church and used as a sacramental, a practice which originated in apostolic times.

Holy Year: A year during which the pope grants the plenary Jubilee Indulgence to the faithful who fulfill certain conditions. For those who make a pilgrimage to Rome during the year, the conditions are reception of the sacraments of penance and the Eucharist, visits and prayer for the intention of the pope in the basilicas of St. Peter, St. John Lateran, St. Paul, and St. Mary Major. For those who do not make a pilgrimage to Rome, the conditions are reception of the sacraments and prayer for the pope during a visit or community celebration in a church designated by the bishop of the locality. Pope Boniface VIII formally proclaimed the first Holy Year on February 22, 1300, and the first three Holy Years were observed in 1300, 1350, and 1390. Subsequent ones were celebrated at 25-year intervals except in 1800 and 1850 when, respectively, the French invasion of Italy and political turmoil made observance impossible. Pope Paul II (1464-1471) set the 25-year timetable. In 1500, Pope Alexander VI prescribed the start and finish ceremonies — the opening and closing of the Holy Doors in the major basilicas on successive Christmas Eves. All but a few of the earlier Holy Years were classified as ordinary. Several — like those of 1933 and 1983-84 to commemorate the 1900th and 1950th anniversaries of the death and resurrection of Christ — were in the extraordinary category. Pope John Paul II designated Jubilee Year 2000 to be a Holy Year ending the second and beginning the third millennium of Christianity.

Homosexuality: The condition of a person whose sexual orientation is toward persons of the same rather than the opposite sex. The condition is not sinful in itself. Homosexual acts are seriously sinful in themselves; subjective responsibility for such acts, however, may be conditioned and diminished by compulsion and related factors.

Hope: The theological virtue by which a person firmly trusts in God for the means and attainment salvation.

Hosanna: A Hebrew word, meaning *O Lord, save, we pray.*

Host, The Sacred: The bread under whose appearances Christ is and remains present in a unique manner after the consecration which takes place during Mass. (See Transubstantiation.)

Human Dignity: The inherent worth of all human persons as they are made in God's image and likeness and they alone — of all God's creatures on earth — have an immortal soul.

Humanism: A world view centered on man. Types of humanism which exclude the supernatural are related to secularism.

Humility: A virtue which induces a person to evaluate himself or herself at his or her true worth, to recognize his or her dependence on God, and to give glory to God for the good he or she has and can do.

Hyperdulia: The special veneration accorded the Blessed Virgin Mary because of her unique role in the mystery of Redemption, her exceptional gifts of grace from God, and her pre-eminence among the saints. Hyperdulia is not adoration; only God is adored.

Hypostatic Union: The union of the human and divine natures in the one divine Person of Christ.

I

Icons: Byzantine-style paintings or representations of Christ, the Blessed Virgin and other saints, venerated in the Eastern Churches where they take the place of statues.

Idolatry: Worship of any but the true God; a violation of the First Commandment.

IHS: In Greek, the first three letters of the name of Jesus — Iota, Eta, Sigma.

Immaculate Conception: The doctrine that affirms that "the Blessed Virgin Mary was preserved, in the first instant of her conception, by a singular grace and privilege of God omnipotent and because of the merits of Jesus Christ the Savior of the human race, free from all stain of Original Sin," as stated by Pope Pius IX in his declaration of the dogma, December 8, 1854. Thus, Mary was conceived in the state of perfect justice, free from original sin and its consequences, in virtue of the redemption achieved by Christ on the cross.

Immortality: The survival and continuing existence of the human soul after death.

Imprimatur: See Censorship of Books.

Impurity: Unlawful indulgence in sexual pleasure. See Chastity.

Imputability: A canonical term for the moral responsibility of a person for an act that he or she has performed.

Incardination: The affiliation of a priest to his diocese. Every secular priest must belong to a certain diocese. Similarly, every priest of a religious community must belong to some jurisdiction of his community; this affiliation, however, is not called incardination.

Incarnation: (1) The coming-into-flesh or taking of human nature by the Second Person of the Trinity. He became human as the Son of Mary, being miraculously conceived by the power of the Holy Spirit, without ceasing to be divine. His divine Person hypostatically unites his divine and human natures. (2) The supernatural mystery coextensive with Christ from the moment of his human conception and continuing through his life on earth; his sufferings and death; his resurrection from the dead and ascension to glory with the Father; his sending, with the Father, of the Holy Spirit upon the Apostles and the Church; and his unending mediation with the Father for the salvation of human beings.

Incense: A granulated substance which, when burnt, emits an aromatic smoke. It symbolizes the zeal with which the faithful should be consumed, the good odor of Christian virtue, the ascent of prayer to God. An incense boat is a small vessel used to hold incense which is to be placed in the censer.

Incest: Sexual intercourse with relatives by blood or marriage; a sin of impurity and also a grave violation of the natural reverence due to relatives. Other sins of impurity, desire, etc. concerning relatives have the nature of incest.

Inculturation: The correct and entirely appropriate adaptation of the Catholic liturgy and institutions to the culture, language, and customs of an indigenous or local people among whom the Gospel is first proclaimed. Pope John Paul II February 15, 1982, at a meeting in Lagos with the bishops of Nigeria proclaimed: "An important aspect of your own evangelizing role is the whole dimension of the inculturation of the Gospel into the lives of your people. The Church truly respects the culture of each people. In offering the Gospel message, the Church does not intend to destroy or to abolish what is good and beautiful. In fact, she recognizes many cultural values and, through the power of the Gospel, purifies and takes into Christian worship certain elements of a people's customs."

Index of Prohibited Books: A list of books which Catholics were formerly forbidden to read, possess or sell, under penalty of excommunication. The books were banned by the Holy See after publication because their treatment of matters of faith and morals and related subjects were judged to be erroneous or serious occasions of doctrinal error. Some books were listed in the Index by name; others were covered under general norms. The Congregation for the Doctrine of the Faith declared June 14, 1966, that the Index and its related penalties of excommunication no longer had the force of law in the Church. Persons are still obliged, however, to take normal precautions against occasions of doctrinal error.

Indifferentism: A theory that any one religion is as true and good — or false — as any other religion, and that it makes no difference, objectively, what religion one professes, if any. The theory is completely subjective, finding its justification entirely in personal choice without reference to or respect for objective validity. It is also self-contradictory, since it regards as equally acceptable — or unacceptable — the beliefs of all religions, which in fact are not only not all the same but are in some cases opposed to each other.

Indulgence: According to The Doctrine and Practice of Indulgences, an apostolic constitution issued by Paul VI January 1, 1967, an indulgence is the remission before God of the temporal punishment due for sins already forgiven as far as their guilt is concerned, which a follower of Christ — with the proper dispositions and under certain determined conditions — acquires through the intervention of the Church. An indulgence is partial or plenary, depending on whether it does away with either part or all of the temporal punishment due for sin. Both types of indulgences can always be applied to the dead by way of suffrage; the actual disposition of indulgences applied to the dead rests with God. Only one plenary indulgence can be gained in a single day. The Apostolic Penitentiary issued a decree December 14, 1985, granting diocesan bishops the right to impart — three times a year on solemn feasts of their choice — the papal blessing with a plenary indulgence to those who cannot be physically present but who follow the sacred rites at which the blessing is imparted by radio or television transmission. In July, 1986, publication was announced of a new and simplified *Enchiridion Indulgentiarum*, in accord with provisions of the revised Code of Canon Law.

Indult: A favor or privilege granted by competent ecclesiastical authority, giving permission to do something not allowed by the common law of the Church.

Infallibility: 1) The inability of the Church to err in its teaching, in that she preserves and teaches the deposit of truth as revealed by Christ; 2) The inability of the Roman Pontiff to err when he teaches *ex cathedra* in matters of faith or morals, and indicates that the doctrine is to be believed by all the faithful; and 3) the inability of the college of bishops to err when speaking in union with the pope in matters of faith and morals, agreeing that a doctrine must be held by the universal Church, and the doctrine is promulgated by the Pontiff.

Infused Virtues: The theological virtues of faith, hope, and charity; principles or capabilities of supernatural action, they are given with sanctifying grace by God rather than acquired by repeated acts of a person. They can be increased by practice; they are lost by contrary acts. Natural-acquired moral virtues, like the cardinal virtues of prudence, justice, temperance, and fortitude, can be considered infused in a person whose state of grace gives them supernatural orientation.

Inquisition: A tribunal for dealing with heretics, authorized by Gregory IX in 1231 to search them out, hear and judge them, sentence them to various forms of punishment, and in some cases to hand them over to civil authorities for punishment. The Inquisition was a creature of its time when crimes against faith, which threatened the good of the Christian community, were regarded also as crimes against the state, and when heretical doctrines of such extremists as the Cathari and Albigensians threatened the very fabric of society. The institution, which was responsible for many excesses, was most active in the second half of the 13th century.

Inquisition, Spanish: An institution peculiar to Spain and the colonies in Spanish America. In 1478, at the urging of King Ferdinand, Pope Sixtus IV approved the establishment of the Inquisition for trying charges of heresy brought against Jewish (*Marranos*) and Moorish (*Moriscos*) converts. It acquired jurisdiction over other cases as well, however, and fell into disrepute because of irregularities in its functions, cruelty in its sentences, and the manner in which it served the interests of the Spanish crown more than the accused persons and the good of the Church. Protests by the Holy See failed to curb excesses of the Inquisition, which lingered in Spanish history until early in the 19th century.

I N R I: The first letters of words in the Latin inscription atop the cross on which Christ was crucified: *(I)esus (N)azaraenus, (R)ex (I)udaeorum* — Jesus of Nazareth, King of the Jews.

Insemination, Artificial: The implanting of human semen by some means other than consummation of natural marital intercourse. In view of the principle that procreation should result only from marital intercourse, donor insemination is not permissible.

In Sin: The condition of a person called spiritually dead because he or she does not possess sanctifying grace, the principle of supernatural life, action and merit. Such grace can be regained through repentance.

Instruction: A document containing doctrinal explanations, directive norms, rules, recommendations, admonitions, issued by the pope, a department of the Roman Curia or other competent authority in the Church. To the extent that they so prescribe, instructions have the force of law.

Intercommunion, Eucharistic Sharing: The common celebration and reception of the Eucharist by members of different Christian churches; a pivotal issue in ecumenical theory and practice. Catholic participation and intercommunion in the Eucharistic liturgy of another church without a valid priesthood and with a variant Eucharistic belief is out of order. Under certain conditions, other Christians may receive the Eucharist in the Catholic Church. (See additional Intercommunion entry). Intercommunion is acceptable to some Protestant churches and unacceptable to others.

Interdict: A censure imposed on persons for certain violations of church law. Interdicted persons may not take part in certain liturgical services, administer or receive certain sacraments.

Intinction: A method of administering Holy Communion under the dual appearances of bread and wine, in which the consecrated host is dipped in the consecrated wine before being given to the communicant. The administering of Holy Communion in this manner, which has been traditional in Eastern-Rite liturgies, was authorized in the Roman Rite for various occasions by the Constitution on the Sacred Liturgy promulgated by the Second Vatican Council.

Irenicism: Peace-seeking, conciliation, as opposed to polemics; an important element in ecumenism, provided it furthers pursuit of the Christian unity willed by Christ without degenerating into a peace-at-any-price disregard for religious truth.

Irregularity: A permanent impediment to the lawful reception or exercise of holy orders. The Church instituted irregularities — which include apostasy, heresy, homicide, attempted suicide — out of reverence for the dignity of the sacraments.

J

Jehovah: The English equivalent of the Hebrew *Adonai* ("my Lord") used out of fear and reverence for the Holy Name of Yahweh. *Jehovah* uses the consonants YHWH and the vowels of *Adonai* (a, o, a). Scholars today maintain that *Jehovah* is a false derivation.

Jesus: The name of Jesus, meaning "God saves," expressing the identity and mission of the second Person of the Trinity become man; derived from the Aramaic and Hebrew Yeshua and Joshua, meaning Yahweh is salvation.

Jesus Prayer: A prayer of Eastern origin, dating back to the fifth century: *"Lord Jesus Christ, Son of God, have mercy on me (a sinner)."*

Judgment: (1) **Last or final judgment:** Final judgment by Christ, at the end of the world and the general resurrection. (2) **Particular judgment:** The judgment that takes place immediately after a person's death, followed by entrance into heaven, hell or purgatory.

Jurisdiction: Right, power, authority to rule. Jurisdiction in the Church is of divine institution; has pastoral service for its purpose; includes legislative, judicial and executive authority; can be exercised only by persons with the power of orders. (1) Ordinary jurisdiction is attached to ecclesiastical offices by law; the officeholders, called Ordinaries, have authority over those who are subject to them. (2) Delegated jurisdiction is that which is granted to persons rather than attached to offices. Its extent depends on the terms of the delegation.

Justice: One of the four cardinal virtues by which a person gives to others what is due to them as a matter of right. (See Cardinal Virtues.)

Justification: The act by which God makes a person just, and the consequent change in the spiritual status of a person, from sin to grace; the remission of sin and the infusion of sanctifying grace through the merits of Christ and the action of the Holy Spirit.

K

Kenosis: A term from the Greek for "emptying" that denotes Christ's emptying of Himself in his free renunciation of his right to divine status, by reason of the Incarnation, particularly as celebrated in the kenotic hymn (Phil 2:6-11), where it is said that Christ "emptied himself," taking the form of a slave, born in the likeness of man totally integrated with his divinity.

Kerygma: Proclaiming the word of God, in the manner of the Apostles, as here and now effective for salvation. This method of preaching or instruction, centered on Christ and geared to the facts and themes of salvation history, is designed to dispose people to faith in Christ and/or to intensify the experience and practice of that faith in those who have it.

Keys, Power of the: Spiritual authority and jurisdiction in the Church, symbolized by the keys of the kingdom of heaven. Christ promised the keys to St. Peter, as head-to-be of the Church (Mt. 16:19), and commissioned him with full pastoral responsibility to feed his lambs and sheep (Jn. 21:15-17), The pope, as the successor of St. Peter, has this power in a primary and supreme manner. The bishops of the Church also have the power, in union with and subordinate to the pope. Priests share in it through holy orders and the delegation of authority. Examples of the application of the Power of the Keys are the exercise of teaching and pastoral authority by the pope and bishops, the absolving of sins in the sacrament of penance, the granting of indulgences, the imposing of spiritual penalties on persons who commit certain serious sins.

Kingdom of God: God's sovereign lordship or rule over salvation history, leading to the eschatological goal of eternal life with God.

Koinonia: A term from the Greek word for "community, fellowship, or association" that was used by St. Luke for the fellowship of believers who worshipped together and held all their possessions in common (Acts 2:42-47); it is also used of fellowship with God (1 Jn. 1:3, 6), with the Son (1 Cor. 1:9), and with the Holy Spirit (2 Cor. 13:13; Phil. 2:1). St. Paul used *koinonia* to denote the intimate union of the believer with Christ and the community that exists among all the faithful themselves (Rom. 15:26; 2 Cor. 6:14).

L

Laicization: The process by which a man ordained to holy orders is relieved of the obligations of orders and the ministry and is returned to the status of a lay person.

Languages of the Church: The languages in which the Church's liturgy is celebrated. These include Ge'ez, Syriac, Greek, Arabic, and Old Slavonic in the Eastern Churches. In the West, there is, of course, Latin and the various vernaculars. The Eastern Rites have always had the vernacular. The first language in church use, for divine worship and the conduct of ecclesiastical affairs, was Aramaic, the language of the first Christians in and around Jerusalem. As the Church spread westward, Greek was adopted and prevailed until the third century when it was supplanted by Latin for official use in the West. In the Western Church, Latin prevailed as the general official language until the promulgation on December 4, 1963, of the Constitution on the Sacred Liturgy (*Sacrosanctum Concilium*) by the second session of the Second Vatican Council. Since that time, vernacular languages have come into use in the Mass, administration of the sacraments, and the Liturgy of the Hours. Latin, however, remains the official language for documents of the Holy See, administrative and procedural matters.

Latria: Greek-rooted Latin term that refers to the form of praise due to God alone.

Law: An ordinance or rule governing the activity of things. (1) **Natural law**: Moral norms corresponding to man's nature by which he orders his conduct toward God, neighbor, society and himself. This law, which is rooted in human nature, is of divine origin, can be known by the use of reason, and binds all persons having the use of reason. The Ten Commandments are declarations and amplifications of natural law. The primary precepts of natural law, to do good and to avoid evil, are universally recognized, despite differences with respect to understanding and application resulting from different philosophies of good and evil. (2) **Divine positive law**: That which has been revealed by God. Among its essentials are the twin precepts of love of God and love of neighbor, and the Ten Commandments. (3) **Ecclesiastical law**: That which is established by the Church for the spiritual welfare of the faithful and the orderly conduct of ecclesiastical affairs. (See Canon Law.) (4) **Civil law**: That which is established by a socio-political community for the common good.

Liberalism: A multiphased trend of thought and movement favoring liberty, independence and progress in moral, intellectual, religious, social, economic and political life. Traceable to the Renaissance, it developed through the Enlightenment, the rationalism of the 19th century, and modernist- and existentialist-related theories of the 20th century. Evaluations of various kinds of liberalism depend on the validity of their underlying principles. Extremist positions — regarding subjectivism, libertinarianism, naturalist denials of the supernatural, and the alienation of individuals and society from God and the Church — were condemned by Gregory XVI in the 1830s, Pius IX in 1864, Leo XIII in 1899, and St. Pius X in 1907. There is, however, nothing objectionable about forms of liberalism patterned according to sound principles of Christian doctrine.

Liberation Theology: Deals with the relevance of Christian faith and salvation — and, therefore, of the mission of the Church — to efforts for the promotion of human rights, social justice and human development. It originated in the religious, social, political and economic environment of Latin America, with its contemporary need for a theory and corresponding action by the Church, in the pattern of its overall mission, for human rights and integral personal and social development. Some versions of liberation theology are at variance with the body of church teaching because of their ideological concept of Christ as liberator, and also because they play down the primary spiritual nature and mission of the Church. Instructions from the Congregation for the Doctrine of the Faith — "On Certain Aspects of the Theology of Liberation" (September 3, 1984) and "On Christian Freedom and Liberation" (April 5, 1986) — contain warnings against translating sociology into theology and advocating violence in social activism.

Life in Outer Space: Whether rational life exists on other bodies in the universe besides earth, is a question for scientific investigation to settle. The possibility can be granted, without prejudice to the body of revealed truth.

Limbo: The limbo of the fathers was the state of rest and natural happiness after death enjoyed by the just of pre-Christian times until they were admitted to heaven following the Ascension of Christ.

Litany: A prayer in the form of responsive petition, e.g., St. Joseph, pray for us, etc. Examples are the litanies of Loreto (Litany of the Blessed Mother), the Holy Name, All Saints, the Sacred Heart, the Precious Blood, St. Joseph, Litany for the Dying.

Logos: A Greek term for "word, speech, or reason." It is most commonly identified with the title given to Jesus in John's Gospel, though not exclusive to that Gospel; In the New Testament, however, the term reflects more the influence of Hellenistic philosophy: St. Paul uses logos as interchangeable with *sophia*, wisdom (1 Cor. 1:24). The *Logos* is the Wisdom of God made manifest in the Son. As a name for the Second Person of the Trinity, the Incarnate Word, the term receives new meaning in the light of the life, death, and resurrection of Jesus Christ.

Loreto, House of: A Marian shrine in Loreto, Italy, consisting of the home of the Holy Family which, according to an old tradition, was transported in a miraculous manner from Nazareth to Dalmatia and finally to Loreto between 1291 and 1294. Investigations conducted shortly after the appearance of the structure in Loreto revealed that its dimensions matched those of the house of the Holy Family missing from its place of enshrinement in a basilica at Nazareth. Among the many popes who regarded it with high honor was John XXIII, who went there on pilgrimage October 4, 1962. The house of the Holy Family is enshrined in the Basilica of Our Lady.

Love: A devotion to a person or object that has been categorized by Greek philosophy into four types: *storge* (one loves persons and things close to him); *philia* (the love of friends); *eros* (sexual love and that of a spiritual nature); *agape* (a self-giving to one in need). Christian charity is love, but not all love is true charity.

Lust: A disorderly desire for sexual pleasure; one of the seven capital sins.

M

Magi: In the Infancy Narrative of St. Matthew's Gospel (2:1-12), three wise men from the East whose visit and homage to the Child Jesus at Bethlehem indicated Christ's manifestation of himself to non-Jewish people. The narrative teaches the universality of salvation. The traditional names of the Magi are Caspar, Melchior, and Balthasar.

Magisterium: The Church's teaching authority, instituted by Christ and guided by the Holy Spirit, which seeks to safeguard and explain the truths of the faith. The Magisterium is exercised in two ways. The extraordinary Magisterium is exercised when the pope and ecumenical councils infallibly define a truth of faith or morals that is necessary for one's salvation and that has been constantly taught and held by the Church. Ordinary Magisterium is exercised when the Church infallibly defines truths of the Faith as taught universally and without dissent; which must be taught or the Magisterium would be failing in its duty; is connected with a grave matter of faith or morals; and which is taught authoritatively. Not everything taught by the Magisterium is done so infallibly; however, the exercise of the Magisterium is faithful to Christ and what he taught.

Magnificat: The canticle or hymn of the Virgin Mary on the occasion of her visitation to her cousin Elizabeth (Lk. 1:46-55). It is an expression of praise, thanksgiving, and acknowledgment of the great blessings given by God to Mary, the Mother of the Second Person of the Blessed Trinity made Man. The *Magnificat* is recited in the Liturgy of the Hours as part of the Evening Prayer.

Martyr: A Greek word, meaning witness, denoting one who voluntarily suffered death for the faith or some Christian virtue.

Martyrology: A catalogue of martyrs and other saints, arranged according to the calendar. The Roman Martyrology contains the official list of saints venerated by the Church. Additions to the list are made in beatification and canonization decrees of the Congregation for the Causes of Saints.

Mass for the People: On Sundays and certain feasts throughout the year pastors are required to offer Mass for the faithful entrusted to their care. If they cannot offer the Mass on these days, they must do so at a later date or provide that another priest offer the Mass.

Materialism: Theory which holds that matter is the only reality, and everything in existence is merely a manifestation of matter; there is no such thing as spirit, and the supernatural does not exist. Materialism is incompatible with Christian doctrine.

Meditation: Mental, as distinguished from vocal, prayer, in which thought, affections, and resolutions of the will predominate. There is a meditative element to all forms of prayer, which always involves the raising of the heart and mind to God.

Mendicants: A term derived from Latin and meaning beggars, applied to members of religious orders without property rights; the members, accordingly, worked or begged for their support. The original mendicants were Franciscans and Dominicans in the early thirteenth century; later, the Carmelites, Augustinians, Servites, and others were given the mendicant title and privileges, with respect to exemption from episcopal jurisdiction and wide faculties for preaching and administering the sacrament of penance. The practice of begging is limited at the present time, although it is still allowed with the permission of competent superiors and bishops. Mendicants are supported by free will offerings and income received for spiritual services and other work.

Mercy, Divine: The love and goodness of God, manifested particularly in a time of need.

Mercy, Works of: Works of corporal or spiritual assistance, motivated by love of God and neighbor, to persons in need. (1) **Corporal works**: feeding the hungry, giving drink to the thirsty, clothing the naked, visiting the imprisoned, sheltering the homeless, visiting the sick, burying the dead. (2) **Spiritual works**: counseling the doubtful, instructing the ignorant, admonishing sinners, comforting the afflicted, forgiving offenses, bearing wrongs patiently, praying for the living and the dead.

Merit: In religion, the right to a supernatural reward for good works freely done for a supernatural motive by a person in the state of and with the assistance of grace. The right to such reward is from God, who binds himself to give it. Accordingly, good works, as described above, are meritorious for salvation.

Metanoia: A term from the Greek *metanoein* ("to change one's mind, repent, be converted") that is used in the New Testament for conversion. It entails the repentance of sin and the subsequent turning toward the Lord. *Metanoia* is fundamental to the Christian life and is necessary for spiritual growth.

Metaphysics: The branch of philosophy (from the Greek *meta* — after + *physika* — physics) dealing with first things, including the nature of being (ontology), the origin and structure of the world (cosmology), and the study of the reality and attributes of God (natural theology). Metaphysics has long been examined by Catholic philosophers, most especially in the writings of St. Augustine and St. Thomas Aquinas.

Millennium: A thousand-year reign of Christ and the just upon earth before the end of the world. This belief of the Millenarians, Chiliasts, and some sects of modern times is based on an erroneous interpretation of Rv. 20.

Miracles: Observable events or effects in the physical or moral order of things, with reference to salvation, which cannot be explained by the ordinary operation of laws of nature and which, therefore, are attributed to the direct action of God. They make known, in an unusual way, the concern and intervention of God in human affairs for the salvation of men.

Mission: (1) Strictly, it means being sent to perform a certain work, such as the mission of Christ to redeem mankind, the mission of the Apostles and the Church and its members to perpetuate the prophetic, priestly and royal mission of Christ. (2) A place where: the Gospel has not been proclaimed; the Church has not been firmly established; the Church, although established, is weak. (3) An ecclesiastical territory with the simplest kind of canonical organization, under the jurisdiction of the Congregation for the Evangelization of Peoples. (4) A church or chapel without a resident priest. (5) A special course of sermons and spiritual exercises conducted in parishes for the purpose of renewing and deepening the spiritual life of the faithful and for the conversion of lapsed Catholics.

Modernism: The "synthesis of all heresies," which appeared near the beginning of the twentieth century. It undermines the objective validity of religious beliefs and practices which, it contends, are products of the subconscious developed by mankind under the stimulus of a religious sense. It holds that the existence of a personal God cannot be demonstrated, the Bible is not inspired, Christ is not divine, nor did he establish the Church or institute the sacraments. A special danger lies in modernism, which is still influential, because it uses Catholic terms with perverted meanings. St. Pius X condemned 65 propositions of modernism in 1907 in the decree *Lamentabili* and issued the encyclical *Pascendi* to explain and analyze its errors.

Monastery: The dwelling place, as well as the community thereof, of monks belonging to the Benedictine and Benedictine-related orders like the Cistercians and Carthusians; also, the Augustinians and Canons Regular. Distinctive of monasteries are: their separation from the world; the enclosure or cloister; the permanence or stability of attachment characteristic of their members; autonomous government in accordance with a monastic rule, like that of St. Benedict in the West or of St. Basil in the East; the special dedication of its members to the community celebration of the liturgy as well as to work that is suitable to the surrounding area and the needs of its people. Monastic superiors of men have such titles as abbot and prior; of women, abbess and prioress. In most essentials, an abbey is the same as a monastery.

Monk: A member of a monastic order — e.g., the Benedictines, the Benedictine-related Cistercians and Carthusians, and the Basilians, who bind themselves by religious profession to stable attachment to a monastery, the contemplative life and the work of their community. In popular use, the title is wrongly applied to many men religious who really are not monks.

Monotheism: Belief in and worship of one God.

Morality: Conformity or difformity of behavior to standards of right conduct. See Moral Obligations, Commandments of God, Precepts of the Church, Conscience, Law.

Mortification: Acts of self-discipline, including prayer, hardship, austerities and penances undertaken for the sake of progress in virtue.

Motu Proprio: A Latin phrase designating a document issued by a pope on his own initiative. Documents of this kind often concern administrative matters.

Mystagogy: Experience of the mystery of Christ, especially through participation in the liturgy and the sacraments.

Mysteries of Faith: Supernatural truths whose existence cannot be known without revelation by God and whose intrinsic truth, while not contrary to reason, can never be wholly understood even after revelation. These mysteries are above reason, not against reason. Among them are the divine mysteries of the Trinity, Incarnation and Eucharist. Some mysteries — e.g., concerning God's attributes — can be known by reason without revelation, although they cannot be fully understood.

N

Natural Law: See Law.

Natural Theology: The field of knowledge that relies upon human reason and the observation of nature, instead of revelation, to determine the existence and attributes of God.

Necromancy: Supposed communication with the dead; a form of divination.

Neo-Scholasticism: A movement begun in the late nineteenth century that had as its aim the restoration of Scholasticism for use in contemporary philosophy and theology. Great emphasis was placed upon the writings of such Scholastic masters as Peter Lombard, St. Albert the Great, St. Anselm, St. Bonaventure, Blessed John Duns Scotus, and especially St. Thomas Aquinas. The movement began at the Catholic University of Louvain, in Belgium, and then found its way into theological centers in Italy, France, and Germany. Particular attention was given to the philosophical and theological works of St. Thomas Aquinas, from which arose a particular school of neo-Thomism; the movement was strongly reinforced by Pope Leo XIII who issued the encyclical *Aeterni Patris* (1879) mandating that Scholasticism, in particular Thomism, be the foundation for all Catholic philosophy and theology taught in Catholic seminaries, universities, and colleges. Neo-Scholasticism was responsible for a true intellectual renaissance in twentieth-century Catholic philosophy and theology. Among its foremost modern leaders were Jacques Maritain, Étienne Gilson, M. D. Chenu, Henri de Lubac, and Paul Claudel.

Nihil Obstat: See **Censorship of Books**.

Non-Expedit: A Latin expression. It is not expedient (fitting, proper), used to state a prohibition or refusal of permission.

Novena: A term designating public or private devotional practices over a period of nine consecutive days; or, by extension, over a period of nine weeks, in which one day a week is set aside for the devotions.

Novice: A man or woman preparing, in a formal period of trial and formation called a novitiate, for membership in an institute of consecrated life. The novitiate lasts a minimum of twelve and a maximum of twenty-four months; at its conclusion, the novice professes temporary promises or vows of poverty, chastity and obedience. Norms require that certain periods of time be spent in the house of novitiate; periods of apostolic work are also required, to acquaint the novice with the apostolate(s) of the institute. A novice is not bound by the obligations of the professed members of the institute, is free to leave at any time, and may be discharged at the discretion of competent superiors. The superior of a novice is a master of novices or director of formation.

Nun: (1) Strictly, a member of a religious order of women with solemn vows (*moniales*). (2) In general, all women religious, even those in simple vows who are more properly called sisters.

Nunc Dimittis: The canticle or hymn of Simeon at the sight of Jesus at the Temple on the occasion of his presentation (Lk. 2:29-32). It is an expression of joy and thanksgiving for the blessing of having lived to see the Messiah. It is prescribed for use in the Night Prayer of the Liturgy of the Hours.

O

Oath: Calling upon God to witness the truth of a statement. Violating an oath, e.g., by perjury in court, or taking an oath without sufficient reason, is a violation of the honor due to God.

Obedience: Submission to one in authority. General obligations of obedience fall under the Fourth Commandment. The vow of obedience professed by religious is one of the evangelical counsels.

Obsession, Diabolical: The extraordinary state of one who is seriously molested by evil spirits in an external manner. Obsession is more than just temptation.

Occasion of Sin: A person, place, or thing that is a temptation to sin. An occasion may be either a situation that always leads to sin or one that usually leads to sin.

Octave: A period of eight days given over to the celebration of a major feast such as Easter.

Oils, Holy: The oils blessed by a bishop at the Chrism Mass on Holy Thursday or another suitable day, or by a priest under certain conditions. (1) The oil of catechumens (olive or vegetable oil), used at baptism; also, poured with chrism into the baptismal water blessed in Easter Vigil ceremonies. (2) Oil of the sick (olive or vegetable oil) used in anointing the sick. (3) Chrism (olive or vegetable oil mixed with balm), which is ordinarily consecrated by a bishop, for use at baptism, in confirmation, at the ordination of a priest and bishop, in the dedication of churches and altars.

Ontologism: A philosophical theory (the name is taken from the Greek for being and study) that posits that knowledge of God is immediate and intuitive; it stipulates further that all other human knowledge is dependent upon this. It was condemned in 1861 by Pope Pius IX. See also Ontology.

Ontology: A branch of metaphysics that studies the nature and relations of existence.

Oratory: A chapel.

Ordinariate: An ecclesiastical jurisdiction for special purposes and people. Examples are military ordinariates for armed services personnel (in accord with provisions of the apostolic constitution *Spirituali militum curae*, April 21, 1986) and Eastern-Rite ordinariates in places where Eastern-Rite dioceses do not exist.

Ordination: The consecration of sacred ministers for divine worship and the service of people in things pertaining to God. The power of ordination comes from Christ and the Church, and must be conferred by a minister capable of communicating it.

Organ Transplants: The transplanting of organs from one person to another is permissible provided it is done with the consent of the concerned parties and does not result in the death or essential mutilation of the donor. Advances in methods and technology have increased the range of transplant possibilities in recent years.

Original Sin: The sin of Adam (Gn. 2:8-3:24), personal to him and passed on to all persons as a state of privation of grace. Despite this privation and the related wounding of human nature and weakening of natural powers, original sin leaves unchanged all that man himself is by nature. The scriptural basis of the doctrine was stated especially by St. Paul in 1 Cor. 15:21ff., and Rom. 5:12-21. Original sin is remitted by baptism and incorporation in Christ, through whom grace is given to persons. Pope John Paul, while describing original sin during a general audience October 1, 1986, called it "the absence of sanctifying grace in nature which has been diverted from its supernatural end."

O Salutaris Hostia: The first three Latin words, *O Saving Victim,* of a Benediction hymn.

Ostpolitik: Policy adopted by Pope Paul VI in an attempt to improve the situation of Eastern European Catholics through diplomatic negotiations with their governments.

Oxford Movement: A movement in the Church of England from 1833 to about 1845 which had for its objective a threefold defense of the Church as a divine institution, the apostolic succession of its bishops, and the *Book of Common Prayer* as the rule of faith. The movement took its name from Oxford University and involved a number of intellectuals who authored a series of influential Tracts for Our Times. Some of its leading figures — e.g., F. W. Faber, John Henry Newman, and Henry Edward Manning — became converts to the Catholic Church. In the Church of England, the movement affected the liturgy, historical and theological scholarship, the status of the ministry, and other areas of ecclesiastical life.

P

Paganism: A term referring to non-revealed religions, i.e., religions other than Christianity, Judaism, and Islam.

Palms: Blessed palms are a sacramental. They are blessed and distributed on the Sunday of the Passion in commemoration of the triumphant entrance of Christ into Jerusalem. Ashes of the burnt palms are used on Ash Wednesday.

Pange Lingua: First Latin words, *Sing, my tongue,* of a hymn in honor of the Holy Eucharist, used particularly on Holy Thursday and in Eucharistic processions.

Pantheism: Theory that all things are part of God, divine, in the sense that God realizes himself as the ultimate reality of matter or spirit through being and/or becoming all things that have been, are, and will be. The theory leads to hopeless confusion of the Creator and the created realm of being, identifies evil with good, and involves many inherent contradictions.

Papal Election: The pope is elected by the College of Cardinals during a secret conclave which begins no sooner than fifteen days and no later than twenty days after the death of his predecessor. Cardinals under the age of eighty, totaling no more than 120, are eligible to take part in the election by secret ballot. Election is by a two-thirds vote of participating cardinals. New legislation regarding papal elections and church government during a vacancy of the Holy See was promulgated by Pope John Paul February 23, 1996, in the apostolic constitution *Universi Dominici Gregis* ("Shepherd of the Lord's Whole Flock").

Paraclete: A title of the Holy Spirit meaning, in Greek, Advocate, Consoler.

Parental Duties: All duties related to the obligation of parents to provide for the welfare of their children. These obligations fall under the Fourth Commandment.

Parish: A community of the faithful served by a pastor charged with responsibility for providing them with full pastoral service. Most parishes are territorial, embracing all of the faithful in a certain area of a diocese: some are personal or national, for certain classes of people, without strict regard for their places of residence.

Parousia: The coming, or saving presence, of Christ which will mark the completion of salvation history and the coming to perfection of God's kingdom at the end of the world.

Particular Church: A term used since Vatican II that denotes certain divisions of the Universal Church. Examples include dioceses, vicariates, and prelatures.

Paschal Candle: A large candle, symbolic of the risen Christ, blessed and lighted on the Easter Vigil and placed at the altar until Pentecost. It is ornamented with five large grains of incense, representing the wounds of Christ, inserted in the form of a cross; the Greek letters Alpha and Omega, symbolizing Christ the beginning and end of all things, at the top and bottom of the shaft of the cross; and the figures of the current year of salvation in the quadrants formed by the cross.

Paschal Precept: Church law requiring reception of the Eucharist in the Easter season (see separate entry) unless, for a just cause, once-a-year reception takes place at another time.

Passion of Christ: Sufferings of Christ, recorded in the four Gospels.

Pastor: An ordained minister charged with responsibility for the doctrinal, sacramental and related service of people committed to his care, e.g., a bishop for the people in his diocese, a priest for the people of his parish.

Pater Noster: The initial Latin words, *Our Father,* of the Lord's Prayer.

Peace, Sign of: A gesture of greeting, e.g., a handshake, exchanged by the ministers and participants at Mass.

Pectoral Cross: A cross worn on a chain about the neck and over the breast by bishops and abbots as a mark of their office.

Penance or Penitence: (1) The spiritual change or conversion of mind and heart by which a person turns away from sin, and all that it implies, toward God, through a personal renewal under the influence of the Holy Spirit. Penance involves sorrow and contrition for sin, together with other internal and external acts of atonement. It serves the purposes of reestablishing in one's life the order of God's love and commandments, and of making satisfaction to God for sin. (2) Penance is a virtue disposing a person to turn to God in sorrow for sin and to carry out works of amendment and atonement. (3) The sacrament of penance and sacramental penance.

People of God: A name for the Church in the sense that it is comprised by a people with Christ as its head, the Holy Spirit as the condition of its unity, the law of love as its rule, and the kingdom of God as its destiny. Although it is a scriptural term, it was given new emphasis by the Second Vatican Council's Dogmatic Constitution on the Church (*Lumen Gentium*).

Perjury: Taking a false oath, lying under oath, a violation of the honor due to God.

Persecution, Religious: A campaign waged against a church or other religious body by persons and governments intent on its destruction. The best known campaigns of this type against the Christian Church were the Roman persecutions which occurred intermittently from about fifty-four to the promulgation of the Edict of Milan in 313. More Catholics have been persecuted in the twentieth century than in any other period in history.

Personal Prelature: A special-purpose jurisdiction — for particular pastoral and missionary work, etc. — consisting of secular priests and deacons and open to lay persons willing to dedicate themselves to its apostolic works. The prelate in charge is an Ordinary, with the authority of office; he can establish a national or international seminary, incardinate its students and promote them to holy orders under the title of service to the prelature. The prelature is constituted and governed according to statutes laid down by the Holy See. Statutes define its relationship and mode of operation with the bishops of territories in which members live and work. Opus Dei is a personal prelature.

Peter's Pence: A collection made each year among Catholics for the maintenance of the pope and his works of charity. It was originally a tax of a penny on each house, and was collected on St. Peter's day, whence the name. It originated in England in the 8th century.

Petition: One of the four purposes of prayer. In prayers of petition, persons ask of God the blessings they and others need.

Pharisees: Influential class among the Jews, referred to in the Gospels, noted for their self-righteousness, legalism, strict interpretation of the Law, acceptance of the traditions of the elders as well as the Law of Moses, and beliefs regarding angels and spirits, the resurrection of the dead and judgment. Most of them were laymen, and they were closely allied with the Scribes; their opposite numbers were the Sadducees. The Pharisaic and rabbinical traditions had a lasting influence on Judaism following the destruction of Jerusalem in 70 A.D.

Pious Fund: Property and money originally accumulated by the Jesuits to finance their missionary work in Lower California. When the Jesuits were expelled from the territory in 1767, the fund was appropriated by the Spanish Crown and used to support Dominican and Franciscan missionary work in Upper and Lower California. In 1842 the Mexican government took over administration of the fund, incorporated most of the revenue into the national treasury, and agreed to pay the Church interest of six per cent a year on the capital so incorporated. From 1848 to 1967 the fund was the subject of lengthy negotiations between the U.S. and Mexican governments because of the latter's failure to make payments as agreed. A lump-sum settlement was made in 1967 with payment by Mexico to the U.S. government of more than $700,000, to be turned over to the Archdiocese of San Francisco.

Polytheism: Belief in and worship of many gods or divinities, especially prevalent in pre-Christian religions.

Poor Box: Alms-box; found in churches from the earliest days of Christianity.

Pope: A title from the Italian word *papa* (from Greek *pappas*, father) used for the Bishop of Rome, the Vicar of Christ and successor of St. Peter, who exercises universal governance over the Church.

Portiuncula: (1) Meaning little portion (of land), the Portiuncula was the chapel of Our Lady of the Angels near Assisi, Italy, which the Benedictines gave to St. Francis early in the thirteenth century. He repaired the chapel and made it the first church of the Franciscan Order. It is now enshrined in the Basilica of St. Mary of the Angels in Assisi. (2) The plenary Portiuncula Indulgence, or Pardon of Assisi, was authorized by Honorius III. Originally, it could be gained for the souls in purgatory only in the chapel of Our Lady of the Angels; by later concessions, it could be gained also in other Franciscan and parish churches. The indulgence (applicable to the souls in purgatory) can be gained from noon of August 1 to midnight of August 2, once each day. The conditions are, in addition to freedom from attachment to sin: reception of the sacraments of penance and the Eucharist on or near the day and a half; a visit to a parish church within the day and a half, during which the Our Father, the Creed, and another prayer are offered for the intentions of the pope.

Positivism: The philosophy that teaches that the

only reality is that which is perceived by the senses; the only truth is that which is empirically verified. It asserts that ideas about God, morality, or anything else that cannot be scientifically tested are to be rejected as unknowable.

Possession, Diabolical: The extraordinary state of a person who is tormented from within by evil spirits who exercise strong influence over his powers of mind and body. (See also Exorcism.)

Postulant: One of several names used to designate a candidate for membership in a religious institute during the period before novitiate.

Poverty: (1) The quality or state of being poor, in actual destitution and need, or being poor in spirit. In the latter sense, poverty means the state of mind and disposition of persons who regard material things in proper perspective as gifts of God for the support of life and its reasonable enrichment, and for the service of others in need. It means freedom from unreasonable attachment to material things as ends in themselves, even though they may be possessed in small or large measure. (2) One of the evangelical counsels professed as a public vow by members of an institute of consecrated life. It involves the voluntary renunciation of rights of ownership and of independent use and disposal of material goods; or, the right of independent use and disposal, but not of the radical right of ownership. Religious institutes provide their members with necessary and useful goods and services from common resources. The manner in which goods are received and/or handled by religious is determined by poverty of spirit and the rule and constitutions of their institute.

Pragmatism: Theory that the truth of ideas, concepts and values depends on their utility or capacity to serve a useful purpose rather than on their conformity with objective standards; also called utilitarianism.

Prayer: The raising of the mind and heart to God in adoration, thanksgiving, reparation and petition. Prayer, which is always mental because it involves thought and love of God, may be vocal, meditative, private and personal, social, and official. The official prayer of the Church as a worshipping community is called the liturgy.

Precepts: Commands or orders given to individuals or communities in particular cases; they establish law for concerned parties. Preceptive documents are issued by the pope, departments of the Roman Curia and other competent authority in the Church.

Presence of God: A devotional practice of increasing one's awareness of the presence and action of God in daily life.

Presumption: A sin against hope, by which a person striving for salvation (1) either relies too much on his own capabilities or (2) expects God to do things which he cannot do, in keeping with his divine attributes, or does not will to do, according to his divine plan. Presumption is the opposite of despair.

Preternatural Gifts: Exceptional gifts, beyond the exigencies and powers of human nature, enjoyed by Adam in the state of original justice: immunity from suffering and death, superior knowledge, integrity or perfect control of the passions. These gifts were lost as the result of original sin; their loss, however, implied no impairment of the integrity of human nature.

Pride: Unreasonable self-esteem; one of the seven capital sins.

Prie-Dieu: A French phrase, meaning pray God, designating a kneeler or bench suitable for kneeling while at prayer.

Priesthood: (1) The common priesthood of the non-ordained faithful. In virtue of baptism and confirmation, the faithful are a priestly people who participate in the priesthood of Christ through acts of worship, witness to the faith in daily life, and efforts to foster the growth of God's kingdom. (2) The ordained priesthood, in virtue of the sacrament of orders, of bishops, priests and deacons, for service to the common priesthood.

Primary Option: The life-choice of a person for or against God which shapes the basic orientation of moral conduct. A primary option for God does not preclude the possibility of serious sin.

Prior: A superior or an assistant to an abbot in a monastery.

Privilege: A favor, an exemption from the obligation of a law. Privileges of various kinds, with respect to ecclesiastical laws, are granted by the pope, departments of the Roman Curia and other competent authority in the Church.

Probabiliorism: The moral system asserting that the more probable opinion of a varied set of acceptable positions regarding the binding character of a law should be accepted. If the reasons for being free from a law are more probably true, one is freed from the law's obligations. Probabiliorism, however, maintained that if it was probable that the law did not bind, one still had to follow it unless it was more probable that the law did not bind.

Probabilism: A moral system for use in cases of conscience which involve the obligation of doubtful laws. There is a general principle that a doubtful law does not bind. Probabilism, therefore, teaches that it is permissible to follow an opinion favoring liberty, provided the opinion is certainly and solidly probable. Probabilism may not be invoked when there is question of: a certain law or the certain obligation of a law; the certain right of another party; the validity of an action; something which is necessary for salvation.

Pro-Cathedral: A church used as a cathedral.

Promoter of the Faith (*Promotor fidei*): An official of the Congregation for the Causes of Saints, whose role in beatification and canonization procedures is to establish beyond reasonable doubt the validity of evidence regarding the holiness of prospective saints and miracles attributed to their intercession.

Prophecy: (1) The communication of divine revelation by inspired intermediaries, called prophets, between God and his people. Old Testament prophecy was unique in its origin and because of its ethical and religious content, which included disclosure of the saving will of Yahweh for the people, moral censures and warnings of divine punishment because of sin and violations of the Law and Covenant, in the form of promises, admonitions, reproaches and threats. Although Moses and other earlier figures are called prophets, the period of prophecy is generally dated from the early years of the monarchy to about 100 years after the Babylonian Exile. From that time on, the written Law and its interpreters supplanted the prophets as guides of the people. Old Testament prophets are cited in the New Testament, with awareness that God spoke through them and that some of their oracles were fulfilled in Christ. John the Baptist is the outstanding prophetic figure in the New Testament. Christ never claimed the title of prophet for himself, although some people thought he was one. There were prophets in the early Church, and St. Paul mentioned the charism of prophecy in 1 Cor. 14:1-5. Prophecy disappeared after New Testament times. Revelation is classified as the prophetic book of the New Testament. (2) In contemporary non-scriptural usage, the term is applied to the witness given by persons to the relevance of their beliefs in everyday life and action.

Proportionalism: The moral theory that asserts that an action is judged on whether the evils resulting are proportionate to the goods that result. If the evils outweigh the goods, the act is objectionable; if the opposite is true, the act is permissible. Proportionalism differs from consequentialism in that the former admits that the inherent morality of the act and the agent's intention must also be considered. Proportionalism is rejected by critics as it does not offer an objective criterion for determining when evils are proportionate or disproportionate. It also fails to consider the intrinsic nature of human acts and does nothing to assist Christians to grow in virtue.

Province: (1) A territory comprising one archdiocese called the metropolitan see and one or more dioceses called suffragan sees. The head of the archdiocese, an archbishop, has metropolitan rights and responsibilities over the province. (2) A division of a religious order under the jurisdiction of a provincial superior.

Prudence: Practical wisdom and judgment regarding the choice and use of the best ways and means of doing good; one of the four cardinal virtues.

Punishment Due for Sin: The punishment which is a consequence of sin. It is of two kinds: (1) Eternal punishment is the punishment of hell, to which one becomes subject by the commission of mortal sin. Such punishment is remitted when mortal sin is forgiven. (2) Temporal punishment is a consequence of venial sin and/or

forgiven mortal sin; it is not everlasting and may be remitted in this life by means of penance. Temporal punishment unremitted during this life is remitted by suffering in purgatory.

Purgatory: The state or condition of those who have died in the state of grace but with some attachment to sin, and are purified for a time before they are admitted to the glory and happiness of heaven. In this state and period of passive suffering, they are purified of unrepented venial sins, satisfy the demands of divine justice for temporal punishment due for sins, and are thus converted to a state of worthiness of the beatific vision.

Q

Quadragesima: From the Latin for fortieth, the name given to the forty penitential days of Lent.

Quinquennial Report: A report on the current state of a diocese that must be compiled and submitted by a bishop to the Holy See every five years in anticipation of the *ad liminal* visit.

Quinque Viae: From the Latin for the "five ways," the five proofs for the existence of God that were proposed by St. Thomas Aquinas in his *Summa Theologiae* (Part I, question 2, article 3). The five ways are: 1) all the motion in the world points to an unmoved Prime Mover; 2) the subordinate agents in the world imply the First Agent; 3) there must be a Cause Who is not perishable and Whose existence is underived; 4) the limited goodness in the world must be a reflection of Unlimited Goodness; 5) all things tend to become something, and that inclination must have proceeded from some Rational Planner.

R

Racism: A theory which holds that any one or several of the different races of the human family are inherently superior or inferior to any one or several of the others. The teaching denies the essential unity of the human race, the equality and dignity of all persons because of their common possession of the same human nature, and the participation of all in the divine plan of redemption. It is radically opposed to the virtue of justice and the precept of love of neighbor. Differences of superiority and inferiority which do exist are the result of accidental factors operating in a wide variety of circumstances, and are in no way due to essential defects in any one or several of the branches of the one human race. The theory of racism, together with practices related to it, is incompatible with Christian doctrine.

Rash Judgment: Attributing faults to another without sufficient reason; a violation of the obligations of justice and charity.

Rationalism: A theory which makes the mind the measure and arbiter of all things, including religious truth. A product of the Enlightenment, it rejects the supernatural, divine revelation, and authoritative teaching by any church.

Recollection: Meditation, attitude of concentration or awareness of spiritual matters and things pertaining to salvation and the accomplishment of God's will.

Relativism: Theory which holds that all truth, including religious truth, is relative, i.e., not absolute, certain or unchanging; a product of agnosticism, indifferentism, and an unwarranted extension of the notion of truth in positive science. Relativism is based on the tenet that certain knowledge of any and all truth is impossible. Therefore, no religion, philosophy or science can be said to possess the real truth; consequently, all religions, philosophies and sciences may be considered to have as much or as little of truth as any of the others.

Relics: The physical remains and effects of saints, which are considered worthy of veneration inasmuch as they are representative of persons in glory with God. Catholic doctrine proscribes the view that relics are not worthy of veneration. In line with norms laid down by the Council of Trent and subsequent enactments, discipline concerning relics is subject to control by the Congregations for the Causes of Saints and for Divine Worship and the Discipline of the Sacraments.

Religion: The adoration and service of God as expressed in divine worship and in daily life. Religion is concerned with all of the relations existing between God and human beings, and between humans themselves because of the central significance of God. Objectively considered, religion consists of a body of truth which is believed, a code of morality for the guidance of conduct, and a form of divine worship. Subjectively, it is a person's total response, theoretically and practically, to the demands of faith; it is living faith, personal engagement, self-commitment to God. Thus, by creed, code and cult, a person orders and directs his or her life in reference to God and, through what the love and service of God implies, to all people and all things.

Reliquary: A vessel for the preservation and exposition of a relic; sometimes made like a small monstrance.

Reparation: The making of amends to God for sin committed; one of the four ends of prayer and the purpose of penance.

Requiem: A Mass offered for the repose of the soul of one who has died in Christ. Its name is derived from the first word of the Gregorian (Latin) entrance chant (or Introit) at Masses for the dead: *Requiem aeternam dona eis, Domine* ("Eternal rest grant unto them, O Lord"). The revised Rite for Funerals refers to the requiem as the Mass of Christian Burial; however, it would not be uncommon to hear people employ the former usage.

Rescript: A written reply by an ecclesiastical superior regarding a question or request; its provisions bind concerned parties only. Papal dispensations are issued in the form of rescripts.

Reserved Censure: A sin or censure, absolution from which is reserved to religious superiors, bishops, the pope, or confessors having special faculties. Reservations are made because of the serious nature and social effects of certain sins and censures.

Restitution: An act of reparation for an injury done to another. The injury may be caused by taking and/or retaining what belongs to another or by damaging either the property or reputation of another. The intention of making restitution, usually in kind, is required as a condition for the forgiveness of sins of injustice, even though actual restitution is not possible.

Ring: In the Church a ring is worn as part of the insignia of bishops, abbots, et al.; by sisters to denote their consecration to God and the Church. The wedding ring symbolizes the love and union of husband and wife.

Ritual: A book of prayers and ceremonies used in the administration of the sacraments and other ceremonial functions. In the Roman Rite, the standard book of this kind is the Roman Ritual.

Rogito: The official notarial act or document testifying to the burial of a pope.

Rosary: A form of mental and vocal prayer centered on mysteries or events in the lives of Jesus and Mary. Its essential elements are meditation on the mysteries and the recitation of a number of decades of Hail Marys, each beginning with the Lord's Prayer. Introductory prayers may include the Apostles' Creed, an initial Our Father, three Hail Marys, and a Glory Be to the Father; each decade is customarily concluded with a Glory be to the Father; at the end, it is customary to say the Hail, Holy Queen and a prayer from the liturgy for the feast of the Blessed Virgin Mary of the Rosary. The Mysteries of the Rosary, which are the subject of meditation, are: (1) *Joyful* — the Annunciation to Mary that she was to be the Mother of Christ, her visit to Elizabeth, the birth of Jesus, the presentation of Jesus in the Temple, the finding of Jesus in the Temple. (2) *Sorrowful* —Christ's agony in the Garden of Gethsemani, scourging at the pillar, crowning with thorns, carrying of the cross to Calvary, and crucifixion. (3) *Glorious* — the Resurrection and Ascension of Christ, the descent of the Holy Spirit upon the Apostles, Mary's Assumption into heaven and her crowning as Queen of angels and men. The complete Rosary, called the Dominican Rosary, consists of fifteen decades. In customary practice, only five decades are usually said at one time. Rosary beads are used to aid in counting the prayers without distraction. The Rosary originated through the coalescence of popular devotions to Jesus and Mary from the twelfth century onward. Its present form dates from about the fifteenth century. Carthusians contributed greatly toward its development; Dominicans have been its greatest promoters.

S

Sabbath: The seventh day of the week, observed by Jews and Sabbatarians as the day for rest and religious observance.

Sacrarium: A basin with a drain leading directly into the ground; standard equipment of a sacristy.

Sacred Heart, Enthronement of the: An acknowledgment of the sovereignty of Jesus Christ over the Christian family, expressed by the installation of an image or picture of the Sacred Heart in a place of honor in the home, accompanied by an act of consecration.

Sacred Heart, Promises: Twelve promises to persons having devotion to the Sacred Heart of Jesus, which were communicated by Christ to St. Margaret Mary Alacoque in a private revelation in 1675: (1) *I will give them all the graces necessary in their state in life.* (2) *I will establish peace in their homes.* (3) *I will comfort them in all their afflictions.* (4) *I will be their secure refuge during life and, above all, in death.* (5) *I will bestow abundant blessing upon all their undertakings.* (6) *Sinners shall find in my Heart the source and the infinite ocean of mercy.* (7) *By devotion to my Heart tepid souls shall grow fervent.* (8) *Fervent souls shall quickly mount to high perfection.* (9) *I will bless every place where a picture of my Heart shall be set up and honored.* (10) *I will give to priests the gift of touching the most hardened hearts.* (11) *Those who promote this devotion shall have their names written in my Heart, never to be blotted out.* (12) *I will grant the grace of final penitence to those who communicate (receive Holy Communion) on the first Friday of nine consecutive months.*

Sacrilege: Violation of and irreverence toward a person, place or thing that is sacred because of public dedication to God; a sin against the virtue of religion. Personal sacrilege is violence of some kind against a cleric or religious, or a violation of chastity with a cleric or religious. Local sacrilege is the desecration of sacred places. Real sacrilege is irreverence with respect to sacred things, such as the sacraments and sacred vessels.

Sacristy: A utility room where vestments, church furnishings and sacred vessels are kept and where the clergy vest for sacred functions.

Sadducees: The predominantly priestly party among the Jews in the time of Christ, noted for extreme conservatism, acceptance only of the Law of Moses, and rejection of the traditions of the elders. Their opposite numbers were the Pharisees.

Saints, Cult of: The veneration, called *dulia*, of holy persons who have died and are in glory with God in heaven; it includes honoring them and petitioning them for their intercession with God. Liturgical veneration is given only to saints officially recognized by the Church; private veneration may be given to anyone thought to be in heaven. The veneration of saints is essentially different from the adoration given to God alone; by its very nature, however, it terminates in the worship of God. (See also *Dulia* and *Latria*.)

Salvation: The liberation of persons from sin and its effects, reconciliation with God in and through Christ, the attainment of union with God forever in the glory of heaven as the supreme purpose of life and as the God-given reward for fulfillment of his will on earth. Salvation-in-process begins and continues in this life through union with Christ in faith professed and in action; its final term is union with God and the whole community of the saved in the ultimate perfection of God's kingdom. The Church teaches that: God wills the salvation of all men; men are saved in and through Christ; membership in the Church established by Christ, known and understood as the community of salvation, is necessary for salvation; men with this knowledge and understanding who deliberately reject this Church, cannot be saved. The Catholic Church is the Church founded by Christ. (See below, Salvation outside the Church.)

Salvation History: The facts and the record of God's relations with human beings, in the past, present and future, for the purpose of leading them to live in accordance with his will for the eventual attainment after death of salvation, or everlasting happiness with him in heaven. The essentials of salvation history are: God's love for all human beings and will for their salvation; his intervention and action in the world to express this love and bring about their salvation; the revelation he made of himself and the covenant he established with the Israelites in the Old Testament; the perfecting of this revelation and the new covenant of grace through Christ in the New Testament; the continuing action-for-salvation carried on in and through the Church; the communication of saving grace to people through the merits of Christ and the operations of the Holy Spirit in the here-and-now circumstances of daily life and with the cooperation of people themselves.

Salvation outside the Church: The Second Vatican Council covered this subject summarily in the following manner: "Those also can attain to everlasting salvation who through no fault of their own do not know the Gospel of Christ or his Church, yet sincerely seek God and, moved by grace, strive by their deeds to do his will as it is known to them through the dictates of conscience. Nor does divine Providence deny the help necessary for salvation to those who, without blame on their part, have not yet arrived at an explicit knowledge of God, but who strive to live a good life, thanks to his grace. Whatever good or truth is found among them is looked upon by the Church as a preparation for the Gospel. She regards such qualities as given by him who enlightens all men so that they may finally have life" (Dogmatic Constitution on the Church, *Lumen Gentium*, No. 16).

Sanctifying Grace: See Grace.

Satanism: Worship of the devil, a blasphemous inversion of the order of worship which is owed to God alone.

Scandal: Conduct that is the occasion of sin to another person.

Scapular: (1) A part of the habit of some religious orders like the Benedictines and Dominicans; a nearly shoulder-wide strip of cloth worn over the tunic and reaching almost to the feet in front and behind. Originally a kind of apron, it came to symbolize the cross and yoke of Christ. (2) Scapulars worn by lay persons as a sign of association with religious orders and for devotional purposes are an adaptation of monastic scapulars. Approved by the Church as sacramentals, they consist of two small squares of woolen cloth joined by strings and are worn about the neck. They are given for wearing in a ceremony of investiture or enrollment. There are nearly 20 scapulars for devotional use: the five principal ones are generally understood to include those of Our Lady of Mt. Carmel (the brown Carmelite Scapular), the Holy Trinity, Our Lady of the Seven Dolors, the Passion, the Immaculate Conception.

Scapular Medal: A medallion with a representation of the Sacred Heart on one side and of the Blessed Virgin Mary on the other. Authorized by St. Pius X in 1910, it may be worn or carried in place of a scapular by persons already invested with a scapular.

Scapular Promise: According to a legend of the Carmelite Order, the Blessed Virgin Mary appeared to St. Simon Stock in 1251 at Cambridge, England, and declared that wearers of the brown Carmelite Scapular would be the beneficiaries of her special intercession. The scapular tradition has never been the subject of official decision by the Church. Essentially, it expresses belief in the intercession of Mary and the efficacy of sacramentals in the context of truly Christian life.

Schism: Derived from a Greek word meaning separation, the term designates formal and obstinate refusal by a baptized Catholic, called a schismatic, to be in communion with the pope and the Church. The canonical penalty is excommunication. One of the most disastrous schisms in history resulted in the definitive separation of the Church in the East from union with Rome about 1054.

Scholasticism: The term usually applied to the Catholic theology and philosophy which developed in the Middle Ages. (See also Neo-Scholasticism.)

Scribes: Hebrew intellectuals noted for their knowledge of the Law of Moses, influential from the time of the Exile to about 70 A.D. Many of them were Pharisees. They were the antecedents of rabbis and their traditions, as well as those o the Pharisees, had a lasting influence on Judaism following the destruction of Jerusalem in 70 A.D.

Scruple: A morbid, unreasonable fear and anxiety that one's actions are sinful when they are not, or more seriously sinful than they actually are. Compulsive scrupulosity is quite different from the transient scrupulosity of persons of tender or highly sensitive conscience, or of persons with faulty moral judgment.

Seal of Confession: The obligation of secrecy which must be observed regarding knowledge of things learned in connection with the confession of sin in the sacrament of penance. The seal covers matters whose revelation would make the sacrament burdensome. Confessors are prohibited, under penalty of excommunication, from making any direct revelation of confessional matter; this prohibition holds, outside of confession, even with respect to the person who made the confession unless the person releases the priest from the obligation. Persons other than confessors are obliged to maintain secrecy, but not under penalty of excommunication. General, non-specific discussion of confessional matter does not violate the seal.

Secularism: A school of thought, a spirit and manner of action which ignores and/or repudiates the validity or influence of supernatural religion with respect to individual and social life.

See: Another name for diocese or archdiocese.

Seminary: A house of study and formation for men, called seminarians, preparing for the priesthood. Traditional seminaries date from the Council of Trent in the middle of the 16th century; before that time, candidates for the priesthood were variously trained in monastic schools, universities under church auspices, and in less formal ways.

Sermon on the Mount: A compilation of sayings of Our Lord in the form of an extended discourse in Matthew's Gospel (5:1 to 7:27) and, in a shorter discourse, in Luke (6:17-49). The passage in Matthew, called the "Constitution of the New Law," summarizes the living spirit of believers in Christ and members of the kingdom of God. Beginning with the Beatitudes and including the Lord's Prayer, it covers the perfect justice of the New Law, the fulfillment of the Old Law in the New Law of Christ, and the integrity of internal attitude and external conduct with respect to love of God and neighbor, justice, chastity, truth, trust and confidence in God.

Seven Last Words of Christ: Words of Christ on the cross. (1) *"Father, forgive them; for they do not know what they are doing."* (2) To the penitent thief: *"I assure you: today you will be with me in Paradise."* (3) To Mary and his Apostle John: *"Woman, there is your son. There is your mother."* (4) *"My God, my God, why have you forsaken me?"* (5) *"I am thirsty."* (6) *"Now it is finished."* (7) *"Father, into your hands I commend my spirit."*

Shrine, Crowned: A shrine approved by the Holy See as a place of pilgrimage. The approval permits public devotion at the shrine and implies that at least one miracle has resulted from devotion at the shrine. Among the best known crowned shrines are those of the Virgin Mary at Lourdes and Fátima. Shrines with statues crowned by Pope John Paul in 1985 in South America were those of Our Lady of Coromoto, patroness of Venezuela, in Caracas, and Our Lady of Carmen of Paucartambo in Cuzco, Peru.

Shroud of Turin: A strip of brownish linen cloth, fourteen feet, three inches in length and three feet, seven inches in width, bearing the front and back imprint of a human body. A tradition dating from the seventh century, which has not been verified beyond doubt, claims that the shroud is the fine linen in which the body of Christ was wrapped for burial. The early history of the shroud is obscure. It was enshrined at Lirey, France, in 1354 and was transferred in 1578 to Turin, Italy, where it has been kept in the cathedral down to the present time. Scientific investigation, which began in 1898, seems to indicate that the markings on the shroud are those of a human body. The shroud, for the first time since 1933, was placed on public view from August 27 to October 8, 1978, and was seen by an estimated 3.3 million people. Scientists conducted intensive studies of it thereafter, finally determining that the material of the shroud dated from between 1260 and 1390. The shroud, which had been the possession of the House of Savoy, was willed to Pope John Paul II in 1983.

Sick Calls: When a person is confined at home by illness or other cause and is unable to go to church for reception of the sacraments, a parish priest should be informed and arrangements made for him to visit the person at home. Such visitations are common in pastoral practice, both for special needs and for providing persons with regular opportunities for receiving the sacraments. If a priest cannot make the visitation, arrangements can be made for a deacon or Eucharistic minister to bring Holy Communion to the homebound or bedridden person.

Sign of the Cross: A sign, ceremonial gesture or movement in the form of a cross by which a person confesses faith in the Holy Trinity and Christ, and intercedes for the blessing of himself or herself, other persons and things. In Roman-Rite practice, a person making the sign touches the fingers of the right hand to forehead, below the breast, left shoulder and right shoulder while saying: *"In the name of the Father, and of the Son, and of the Holy Spirit."* The sign is also made with the thumb on the forehead, the lips, and the breast. For the blessing of persons and objects, a large sign of the cross is made by movement of the right hand. In Eastern-Rite practice, the sign is made with the thumb and first two fingers of the right hand joined together and touching the forehead, below the breast, the right shoulder and the left shoulder; the formula generally used is the doxology, *"O Holy God, O Holy Strong One, O Immortal One."* The Eastern manner of making the sign was general until the first half of the 13th century; by the 17th century, Western practice involved the whole right hand and the reversal of direction from shoulder to shoulder.

Signs of the Times: Contemporary events, trends and features in culture and society, the needs and aspirations of people, all the factors that form the context in and through which the Church has to carry on its saving mission. The Second Vatican Council spoke on numerous occasions about these signs and the relationship between them and a kind of manifestation of God's will, positive or negative, and about subjecting them to judgment and action corresponding to the demands of divine revelation through Scripture, Christ, and the experience, tradition and teaching authority of the Church.

Simony: The deliberate intention and act of selling and/or buying spiritual goods or material things so connected with the spiritual that they cannot be separated therefrom; a violation of the virtue of religion, and a sacrilege, because it wrongfully puts a material price on spiritual things, which cannot be either sold or bought. In church law, actual sale or purchase is subject to censure in some cases. The term is derived from the name of Simon Magus, who attempted to buy from Sts. Peter and John the power to confirm people in the Holy Spirit (Acts 8:4-24).

Sin: (1) Actual sin is the free and deliberate violation of God's law by thought, word or action. (a) Mortal sin — involving serious matter, sufficient reflection and full consent — results in the loss of sanctifying grace and alienation from God, and renders a person incapable of performing meritorious supernatural acts and subject to everlasting punishment. (b) Venial sin — involving less serious matter, reflection and consent — does not have such serious consequences. (2) Original sin is the sin of Adam, with consequences for all human beings. (See separate entry.)

Sins against the Holy Spirit: Despair of salvation, presumption of God's mercy, impugning the known truths of faith, envy at another's spiritual good, obstinacy in sin, final impenitence. Those guilty of such sins stubbornly resist the influence of grace and, as long as they do so, cannot be forgiven.

Sins, Occasions of: Circumstances (persons, places, things, etc.) which easily lead to sin. There is an obligation to avoid voluntary proximate occasions of sin, and to take precautions against the dangers of unavoidable occasions.

Sins That Cry to Heaven for Vengeance: Willful murder, sins against nature, oppression of the poor, widows and orphans, defrauding laborers of their wages.

Sister: Any woman religious, in popular speech; strictly, the title applies only to women religious belonging to institutes whose members never professed solemn vows. Most of the institutes whose members are properly called Sisters were established during and since the nineteenth century. Women religious with solemn vows, or belonging to institutes whose members formerly professed solemn vows, are properly called nuns.

Sisterhood: A generic term referring to the whole institution of the life of women religious in the Church, or to a particular institute of women religious.

Situation Ethics: A subjective, individualistic ethical theory which denies the binding force of ethical principles as universal laws and preceptive norms of moral conduct, and proposes that morality is determined only by situational conditions and considerations and the intention of the person. It has been criticized for ignoring the principles of objective ethics. (See also Consequentialism and Proportionalism.)

Slander: Attributing to a person faults which he or she does not have; a violation of the obligations of justice and charity, for which restitution is due.

Sloth (Acedia): One of the seven capital sins; spiritual laziness, involving distaste and disgust for spiritual things; spiritual boredom, which saps the vigor of spiritual life. Physical laziness is a counterpart of spiritual sloth.

Sorcery: A kind of black magic in which evil is invoked by means of diabolical intervention; a violation of the virtue of religion.

Soteriology: The division of theology which treats of the mission and work of Christ as Redeemer.

Species, Sacred: The appearances of bread and wine (color, taste, smell, etc.) that remain after the substance has been changed at the Consecration of the Mass into the Body and Blood of Christ. (See Transubstantiation.)

Spiritism: Attempts to communicate with spirits and departed souls by means of seances, table tapping, ouija boards, and other methods; a violation of the virtue of religion. Spiritualistic practices are noted for fakery.

Stational Churches, Days: Churches, especially in Rome, where the clergy and lay people were accustomed to gather with their bishop on certain days for the celebration of the liturgy. The 25 early titular or parish churches of Rome, plus other churches, each had their turn as the site of divine worship in practices which may have started in the third century. The observances were rather well developed toward the latter part of the 4th century, and by the fifth they included a Mass concelebrated by the pope and attendant priests. On some occasions, the stational liturgy was preceded by a procession from another church called a *collecta*. There were forty-two Roman stational churches in the eighth century, and eighty-nine stational services were scheduled annually in connection with the liturgical seasons. Stational observances fell into disuse toward the end of the Middle Ages. Some revival was begun by John XXIII in 1959 and continued by Paul VI and John Paul II.

Stations (Way) of the Cross: A form of devotion commemorating the Passion and death of Christ, consisting of a series of meditations (stations): (1) his condemnation to death, (2) taking up of the cross, (3) the first fall on the way to Calvary, (4) meeting his Mother, (5) being assisted by Simon of Cyrene and (6) by the woman Veronica who wiped his face, (7) the second fall, (8) meeting the women of Jerusalem, (9) the third fall, (10) being stripped and (11) nailed to the cross, (12) his death, (13) the removal of his body from the cross and (14) his burial. Depictions of these scenes are mounted in most churches, chapels and in some other places, beneath small crosses. A person making the Way of the Cross passes before these stations, or stopping points, pausing at each for meditation. If the stations are made by a group of people, only the leader has to pass from station to station. A plenary indulgence is granted to the faithful who make the stations, under the usual conditions: freedom from all attachment to sin, reception of the sacraments of penance and the Eucharist, and prayers for the intentions of the pope. Those who are impeded from making the stations in the usual manner can gain the same indulgence if, along with the aforementioned conditions, they spend at least a half hour in spiritual reading and meditation on the passion and death of Christ. The stations originated remotely from the practice of Holy Land pilgrims who visited the actual scenes of incidents in the Passion of Christ. Representations elsewhere of at least some of these scenes were known as early as the fifth century. Later, the stations evolved in connection with and as a consequence of strong devotion to the Passion in the twelfth and thirteenth centuries. Franciscans, who were given custody of the Holy Places in 1342, promoted the devotion widely; one of them, St. Leonard of Port Maurice, became known as the greatest preacher of the Way of the Cross in the eighteenth century. The general features of the devotion were fixed by Clement XII in 1731.

Statutes: Virtually the same as decrees (see separate entry), they almost always designate laws of a particular council or synod rather than pontifical laws.

Stigmata: Marks of the wounds suffered by Christ in his crucifixion, in hands and feet by nails, and side by the piercing of a lance. Some persons, called stigmatists, have been reported as recipients or sufferers of marks like these. The Church, however, has never issued any infallible declaration about their possession by anyone, even in the case of St. Francis of Assisi whose stigmata seem to be the best substantiated and may be commemorated in the Roman-Rite liturgy. Ninety percent of some 300 reputed stigmatists have been women. Judgment regarding the presence, significance, and manner of causation of stigmata would depend, among other things, on irrefutable experimental evidence.

Stipend, Mass: An offering given to a priest for applying the fruits of the Mass according to the intention of the donor. The offering is a contribution to the support of the priest. The disposition of the fruits of the sacrifice, in line with doctrine concerning the Mass in particular and prayer in general, is subject to the will of God. Mass offerings and intentions were the subjects of a decree approved by John Paul II and made public March 22, 1991: (1) Normally, no more than one offering should be accepted for a Mass; the Mass should be offered in accord with the donor's intention; the priest who accepts the offering should celebrate the Mass himself or have another priest do so. (2) Several Mass intentions, for which offerings have been made, can be combined for a "collective" application of a single Mass only if the previous and explicit consent of the donors is obtained. Such Masses are an exception to the general rule.

Stole Fee: An offering given on certain occasions; e.g., at a baptism, wedding, funeral, for the support of the clergy who administer the sacraments and perform other sacred rites.

Stoup: A vessel used to contain holy water.

Suffragan See: Any diocese, except the archdiocese, within a province.

Suicide: The taking of one's own life; a violation of God's dominion over human life. Ecclesiastical burial is denied to persons while in full possession of their faculties; it is permitted in cases of doubt.

Supererogation: Actions which go beyond the obligations of duty and the requirements enjoined by God's law as necessary for salvation. Examples of these works are the profession and observance of the evangelical counsels of poverty, chastity, and obedience, and efforts to practice charity to the highest degree.

Supernatural: Above the natural; that which exceeds and is not due or owed to the essence, exigencies, requirements, powers and merits of created nature. While human beings have no claim on supernatural things and do not need them in order to exist and act on a natural level, they do need them in order to exist and act in the higher order or economy of grace established by God for their salvation. God has freely given them certain things which are beyond the powers and rights of their human nature. Examples of the supernatural are: grace, a kind of participation by human beings in the divine life, by which they become capable of performing acts meritorious for salvation; divine revelation by which God manifests himself to them and makes known truth that is inaccessible to human reason alone; faith, by which they believe divine truth because of the authority of God who reveals it through Sacred Scripture and tradition and the teaching of his Church.

Suspension: A censure by which a cleric is forbidden to exercise some or all of his powers of orders and jurisdiction, or to accept the financial support of his benefices.

Syllabus, The: (1) When not qualified, the term refers to the list of eighty errors accompanying Pope Pius IX's encyclical *Quanta Cura*, issued in 1864. (2) The Syllabus of St. Pius X in the decree *Lamentabili*, issued by the Holy Office July 4, 1907, condemning sixty-five heretical propositions of Modernism. This schedule of errors was followed shortly by that pope's encyclical *Pascendi*, the principal ecclesiastical document against modernism, issued September 8, 1907.

Synod, Diocesan: Meeting of representative persons of a diocese — priests, religious, lay persons — with the bishop, called by him for the purpose of considering and taking action on matters affecting the life and mission of the Church in the diocese. Persons taking part in a synod have consultative status; the bishop alone is the legislator, with power to authorize synodal decrees. According to canon law, every diocese should have a synod every ten years.

T

Tabernacle: The receptacle in which the Blessed Sacrament is reserved in churches, chapels, and oratories. It is to be immovable, solid, locked, and located in a prominent place.

Te Deum: The opening Latin words, *Thee, God,* of a hymn of praise and thanksgiving prescribed for use in the Office of Readings of the Liturgy of the Hours on many Sundays, solemnities and feasts.

Temperance: Moderation, one of the four cardinal virtues.

Temptation: Any enticement to sin, from any source: the strivings of one's own faculties, the action of the devil, other persons, circumstances of life, etc. Temptation itself is not sin. Temptation can be avoided and overcome with the use of prudence and the help of grace.

Thanksgiving: An expression of gratitude to God for his goodness and the blessings he grants; one of the four ends of prayer.

Theism: A philosophy which admits the existence of God and the possibility of divine revelation; it is generally monotheistic and acknowledges God as transcendent and also active in the world. Because it is a philosophy rather than a system of theology derived from revelation, it does not include specifically Christian doctrines, like those concerning the Trinity, the Incarnation and Redemption.

Theodicy: From the Greek for God (*theos*) and judgment (*dike*), the study of God as he can be known by natural reason, rather than from supernatural revelation. First used by Gottfried Leibnitz (1646-1716), its primary objective is to make God's omnipotence compatible with the existence of evil.

Theological Virtues: The virtues which have God for their direct object: faith, or belief in God's infallible teaching; hope, or confidence in divine assistance; charity, or love of God. They are given to a person with grace in the first instance, through baptism and incorporation in Christ.

Theology: Knowledge of God and religion, deriving from and based on the data of divine Revelation, organized and systematized according to some kind of scientific method. It involves systematic study and presentation of the truths of divine Revelation in Sacred Scripture, tradition, and the teaching of the Church. Theology has been divided under various subject headings. Some of the major fields have been: dogmatic (systematic theology), moral, pastoral, historical, ascetical (the practice of virtue and means of attaining holiness and perfection), sacramental, and mystical (higher states of religious experience). Other subject headings include ecumenism (Christian unity, interfaith relations), ecclesiology (the nature and constitution of the Church), and Mariology (doctrine concerning the Blessed Virgin Mary), etc.

Theotokos: From the Greek for God-bearer, the preeminent title given to the Blessed Mother in the Oriental Church. This title has very ancient roots, stretching as far back as the third century but it did not became official in the Church until the Council of Ephesus in 431.

Thomism: The philosophy based on St. Thomas Aquinas (1224/5-1274), which is mandated to be the dominant philosophy used in Catholic educational institutions. (See also Neo-Scholasticism and Scholasticism.)

Tithing: Contribution of a portion of one's income, originally one-tenth, for purposes of religion and charity. The practice is mentioned 46 times in the Bible. In early Christian times, tithing was adopted in continuance of Old Testament practices of the Jewish people, and the earliest positive church legislation on the subject was enacted in 567. Catholics are bound in conscience to contribute to the support of their church, but the manner in which they do so is not fixed by law. Tithing, which amounts to a pledged contribution of a portion of one's income, has aroused new attention in recent years in the United States.

Titular Sees: Dioceses where the Church once flourished but which now exist only in name or title. Bishops without a territorial or residential diocese of their own, e.g., auxiliary bishops, are given titular sees. There are more than 2,000 titular sees; sixteen of them are in the United States.

Transfinalization, Transignification: Terms coined to express the sign value of consecrated bread and wine with respect to the presence and action of Christ in the Eucharistic sacrifice and the spiritually vivifying purpose of the Eucharistic banquet in Holy Communion. The theory behind the terms has strong undertones of existential and "sign" philosophy, and has been criticized for its openness to interpretation at variance with the doctrine of transubstantiation and the abiding presence of Christ under the appearances of bread and wine after the sacrifice of the Mass and Communion have been completed. The terms, if used as substitutes for transubstantiation, are unacceptable; if they presuppose transubstantiation, they are acceptable as clarifications of its meaning.

Transubstantiation: "The way Christ is made present in this sacrament (Holy Eucharist) is none other than by the change of the whole substance of the bread into his Body, and of the whole substance of the wine into his Blood (in the Consecration at Mass), this unique and wonderful change the Catholic Church rightly calls transubstantiation" (encyclical *Mysterium Fidei* of Paul VI, September 3, 1965). The first official use of the term was made by the Fourth Council of the Lateran in 1215. Authoritative teaching on the subject was issued by the Council of Trent.

Treasury of the Church: The superabundant merits of Christ and the saints from which the Church draws to confer spiritual benefits, such as indulgences.

Triduum: A three-day series of public or private devotions.

U-Z

Ultramontanism: The movement found primarily in France during the nineteenth century that advocated a strong sense of devotion and service to the Holy See. Generally considered a reaction to the anti-papal tendencies of Gallicanism, its name was derived from the Latin for "over the mountains," a reference to the Alps, beyond which rested Rome and the Holy See.

Unction: From the Latin, *ungere*, meaning to anoint or smear, a term used to denote the Sacrament of the Sick (or the Anointing of the Sick); it was more commonly termed Extreme Unction and was given as an anointing to a person just before death.

Universal Law: See Law.

Urbi et Orbi: A Latin phrase meaning "To the City and to the World" that is a blessing given by the Holy Father. Normally, the first *Urbi et Orbi* delivered by a pontiff is immediately after his election by the College of Cardinals. This is a blessing accompanied by a short address to the crowds in St. Peter's Square and to the world; frequently, as with Pope John Paul II in 1978, it is delivered in as many languages as possible. The pope also delivers an *Urbi et Orbi* each year at Christmas and at Easter.

Usury: Excessive interest charged for the loan and use of money; a violation of justice.

Vagi: A Latin word meaning wanderers that is used to describe any homeless person with no fixed residence.

Veni Creator Spiritus: A Latin phrase, meaning "Come, Creator Spirit" that is part of a hymn sung to the Holy Spirit. The hymn invokes the presence of the Holy Spirit and was perhaps first composed by Rabanus Maurus (776-856). The hymn is commonly sung as part of the Divine Office, papal elections, episcopal consecrations, ordinations, councils, synods, canonical elections, and confirmations.

Venial Sin: See under Sin.

Veronica: A word resulting from the combination of

a Latin word for true, *vera*, and a Greek word for image, *eikon*, designating a likeness of the face of Christ or the name of a woman said to have given him a cloth on which he caused an imprint of his face to appear. The veneration at Rome of a likeness depicted on cloth dates from about the end of the tenth century; it figured in a popular devotion during the Middle Ages, and in the Holy Face devotion practiced since the nineteenth century. A faint, indiscernible likeness said to be of this kind is preserved in St. Peter's Basilica. The origin of the likeness is uncertain, and the identity of the woman is unknown. Before the fourteenth century, there were no known artistic representations of an incident concerning a woman who wiped the face of Christ with a piece of cloth while he was carrying the cross to Calvary.

Vespers: From the Latin for evening, the evening service of the Divine Office, also known as Evening Prayer, or among Anglicans as Evensong.

Viaticum: Holy Communion given to those in danger of death. The word, derived from Latin, means provision for a journey through death to life hereafter.

Vicar Forane: A Latin term meaning "deputy outside" that is applied to the priest given authority by the local bishop over a certain area or region of the diocese.

Vicar General: A priest or bishop appointed by the bishop of a diocese to serve as his deputy, with ordinary executive power, in the administration of the diocese.

Vicar, Judicial: The title given to the chief judge and head of the tribunal of a diocese.

Virginity: Observance of perpetual sexual abstinence. The state of virginity, which is embraced for the love of God by religious with a public vow or by others with a private vow, was singled out for high praise by Christ (Mt. 19:10-12) and has always been so regarded by the Church. In the encyclical *Sacra Virginitas*, Pius XII stated: "Holy virginity and that perfect chastity which is consecrated to the service of God is without doubt among the most perfect treasures which the founder of the Church has left in heritage to the society which he established." Paul VI approved in 1970 a rite in which women can consecrate their virginity "to Christ and their brethren" without becoming members of a religious institute. The *Ordo Consecrationis Virginum*, a revision of a rite promulgated by Clement VII in 1596, is traceable to the Roman liturgy of about 50.

Virtue: A habit or established capability for performing good actions. Virtues are natural (acquired and increased by repeating good acts) and/or supernatural (given with grace by God).

Visions: A charism by which a specially chosen individual is able to behold a person or something that is naturally invisible. A vision should not be confused with an illusion or hallucination. Like other charisms, a vision is granted for the good of people; it should be noted, however, that they are not essential for holiness or salvation. Many saints throughout history have beheld visions, among them St. Thomas Aquinas, St. Teresa of Ávila, St. John of the Cross, and St. Francis of Assisi.

Vocation: A call to a way of life. Generally, the term applies to the common call of all persons, from God, to holiness and salvation. Specifically, it refers to particular states of life, each called a vocation, in which response is made to this universal call; viz., marriage, the religious life and/or priesthood, the single state freely chosen or accepted for the accomplishment of God's will. The term also applies to the various occupations in which persons make a living. The Church supports the freedom of each individual in choosing a particular vocation, and reserves the right to pass on the acceptability of candidates for the priesthood and religious life. Signs or indicators of particular vocations are many, including a person's talents and interests, circumstances and obligations, invitations of grace and willingness to respond thereto.

Vow: A promise made to God with sufficient knowledge and freedom, which has as its object a moral good that is possible and better than its voluntary omission. A person who professes a vow binds himself or herself by the virtue of religion to fulfill the promise. The best known examples of vows are those of poverty, chastity and obedience professed by religious (see Evangelical Counsels, individual entries). Public vows are made before a competent person, acting as an agent of the Church, who accepts the profession in the name of the Church, thereby giving public recognition to the person's dedication and consecration to God and divine worship. Vows of this kind are either solemn, rendering all contrary acts invalid as well as unlawful; or simple, rendering contrary acts unlawful. Solemn vows are for life; simple vows are for a definite period of time or for life. Vows professed without public recognition by the Church are called private vows. The Church, which has authority to accept and give public recognition to vows, also has authority to dispense persons from their obligations for serious reasons.

Witness, Christian: Practical testimony or evidence given by Christians of their faith in all circumstances of life — by prayer and general conduct, through good example and good works, etc.; being and acting in accordance with Christian belief; actual practice of the Christian faith.

Zeal: The expression of charity that permits one to serve God and others fully with the objective of furthering the Mystical Body of Christ.

Zucchetto: A small skullcap worn by ecclesiastics, most notably prelates and derived from the popular Italian vernacular term *zucca*, meaning a pumpkin, and used as slang for head. The Holy Father wears a white zucchetto made of watered silk; cardinals use scarlet, and bishops use purple. Priests of the monsignorial rank may wear black with purple piping. All others may wear simple black.

PRAYERS OF THE CATHOLIC CHURCH

COMMON PRAYERS

The Sign of the Cross

In the name of the Father,
and of the Son,
and of the Holy Spirit.
Amen.

The Lord's Prayer

Our Father, who art in heaven,
hallowed be thy name;
thy kingdom come;
thy will be done
on earth as it is in heaven.
Give us this day our daily bread;
and forgive us our trespasses
as we forgive those
who trespass against us;
and lead us not into temptation,
but deliver us from evil.
Amen.

The Glory Be

Glory be to the Father,
and to the Son,
and to the Holy Spirit,
as it was in the beginning,
is now,
and ever shall be,
world without end.
Amen.

Act of Contrition

O my God,
I am heartily sorry
for having offended you.
I detest all my sins
because of your just punishments,
but most of all because they offend you,
my God,
who are all good
and deserving of all my love.
I firmly resolve,
with the help of your grace,
to sin no more
and to avoid the occasions of sin.
Amen.

I Confess

I confess to almighty God,
and to you, my brothers and sisters,
that I have sinned through my own fault
in my thoughts and in my words,
in what I have done,
and in what I have failed to do;
and I ask blessed Mary, ever virgin,
all the angels and saints,
and you, my brothers and sisters,
to pray for me to the Lord our God.
May almighty God have mercy on us,
forgive us our sins,
and bring us to everlasting life.
Amen.

Act of Faith

O my God,
I firmly believe that you are one God
in three divine Persons,
Father, Son and Holy Spirit.
I believe that your divine Son
became man and died for our sins.
and that he will come again
to judge the living and the dead.
I believe these and all the truths
that the holy Catholic Church teaches
because you revealed them
who cannot deceive nor be deceived.
Amen.

Act of Hope

O my God,
relying on your infinite mercy and promises,
I hope to obtain the pardon of my sins,
the help of your grace,
and life everlasting,
through the merits of Jesus Christ,
my Lord and my Redeemer.
Amen.

The Universal Prayer

(attributed to Pope Clement XI)

Lord, I believe in you: increase my faith.
  I trust in you: strengthen my trust.
  I love you: let me love you more and more.
  I am sorry for my sins: deepen my sorrow.
I worship you as my first beginning,
  I long for you as my last end,
  I praise you as my constant helper,
  and call on you as my loving protector.
Guide me by your wisdom,
  correct me with your justice,
  comfort me with your mercy,
  protect me with your power.
I offer you, Lord, my thoughts: to be fixed on
    you;
  my words: to have you for their theme;
  my actions: to reflect my love for you;
  my sufferings: to be endured for your
    greater glory.
I want to do what you ask of me:
  in the way you ask,
  for as long as you ask,
  because you ask it.
Lord, enlighten my understanding,
  strengthen my will,
  purify my heart,
  and make me holy.
Help me to repent of my past sins
  and to resist temptation in the future.
  Help me to rise above my human weakness
  and to grow stronger as a Christian.
Let me love you, my Lord and my God,
  and see myself as I really am:
  a pilgrim in this world,
  a Christian called to respect and love
  all whose lives I touch,
  those in authority over me
  or those under my authority,
  my friends and my enemies.
Help me to conquer anger by gentleness,
  greed by generosity, apathy by fervor.
  Help me to forget myself
  and reach out toward others.
Make me prudent in planning,
  courageous in taking risks.
  Make me patient in suffering,
  unassuming in prosperity.
Keep me, Lord, attentive in prayer,
  temperate in food and drink,
  diligent in my work,
  firm in my good intentions.
Let my conscience be clear,
  my conduct without fault,
  my speech blameless,
  my life well-ordered.
Put me on guard against my human
    weaknesses.

Let me cherish your love for me,
  keep your law,
  and come at last to your salvation.
Teach me to realize that this world is passing,
  that my true future is the happiness of
    heaven,
  that life on earth is short,
  and the life to come eternal.
Help me to prepare for death
  with a proper fear of judgment,
  but a greater trust in your goodness.
  Lead me safely through death
  to the endless joy of heaven.
  Grant this through Christ our Lord.
  Amen.

Te Deum

To you, our God, be praise!
We acknowledge you as Lord.
In you the whole earth worships
its everliving Father.
All the angels cry to you,
and heaven and all its mighty Powers;
the Cherubim and Seraphim
continually cry aloud:
Holy, holy, holy are you,
Lord God of hosts;
your sovereign glory fills all heaven
and earth.
The triumphant band of the apostles,
the prophets, that noble company,
the white-robed throng of martyrs,
all sing your praise.
Throughout the world, holy Church proclaims
    you,
the Father of majesty unbounded;
your worshipful, true, and only Son;
and the Holy Spirit, who befriends us.
You, Christ, are the King of glory,
you, the Father's everliving Son.
To set us free you took on our flesh,
not shrinking from the Virgin's womb.
You have conquered the pangs of death
and opened the kingdom of heaven
to all believers.
You sit at the right hand of God,
in your Father's glory.
We believe that you will come
and judge the world.
Help us, then, we entreat you:
help your servants
whom you have ransomed
with your precious blood.
Cause them to be numbered with your saints
in everlasting glory.
Save your people, Lord,
and bless your heritage.
Govern them, and evermore uphold them.

Day by day we bless you
and praise your name forever,
world without end.
Lord, be pleased to keep us this day
from all sin.
Have mercy on us, Lord, have mercy.
Lord, let your mercy rest upon us,
for we put our trust in you.
In you, O Lord, we place our hope.
Let us never be put to confusion.
Amen.

Morning Offering

Most Holy and Adorable Trinity, one God in three Persons, I firmly believe that You are here present; I adore You with the most profound humility; I praise You and give You thanks with all my heart for the favors You have bestowed on me. Your Goodness has brought me safely to the beginning of this day. Behold, O Lord, I offer You my whole being and in particular all my thoughts, words and actions, together with such crosses and contradictions as I may meet with in the course of this day. Give them, O Lord, Your blessing; may Your divine Love animate them and may they tend to the greater honor and glory of Your Sovereign Majesty. Amen.

Prayer to One's Guardian Angel

Angel of God,
whom God has appointed to be my protector
against all things evil:
be always at my side,
and keep me aware of your presence
as God's messenger to me
all the days of my life,
for my good.
Pray for me this day
and every day of my life
in this world.
Amen.

Prayer to the Blessed Trinity

(For priests)

May the tribute of my humble ministry be pleasing to you, Holy Trinity. Grant that the sacrifice which I — unworthy as I am — have offered in the presence of your majesty, may be acceptable to you. Through your mercy may it bring forgiveness to me and to all for whom I have offered it: through Christ our Lord. Amen.

Prayer for the Pope

Heavenly Father, guide and strengthen Pope
N.,
chief pastor of your Church on earth.
May he by word and example
lead your people to eternal life.
Amen.

Prayer to St. Michael

Saint Michael the Archangel,
defend us in battle.
Be our protection against the wickedness
and snares of the devil.
May God rebuke him, we humbly pray,
and do you, O prince of the heavenly hosts,
by the power of God,
cast into hell Satan
and all other evil spirits
who prowl about the world
for the ruin of souls.
Amen.

Design of Cana Miracle
Chartres window panel

CREEDS

The Apostles' Creed

I believe in God, the Father almighty,
creator of heaven and earth.
I believe in Jesus Christ, his only Son, our
Lord.
He was conceived by the power of the Holy
Spirit
and born of the virgin Mary.
He suffered under Pontius Pilate,
was crucified, died, and was buried.
He descended into hell.
On the third day he rose again.
He ascended into heaven,
and is seated at the right hand of the Father.
He will come again to judge the living and the
dead.
I believe in the Holy Spirit,
the holy catholic Church,
the communion of saints,
the forgiveness of sins,
the resurrection of the body,
and the life everlasting. Amen.

Athanasian Creed

Whoever wants to be saved should above all
cling to the catholic faith.
Whoever does not guard it whole and
inviolable will doubtless perish eternally.
Now this is the catholic faith: We worship one
God in trinity and the Trinity in unity,
neither confusing the persons nor dividing
the divine being.
For the Father is one person, the Son is
another, and the Spirit is still another.
But the deity of the Father, Son, and Holy
Spirit is one, equal in glory, coeternal in
majesty.
What the Father is, the Son is, and so is the
Holy Spirit.
Uncreated is the Father; uncreated is the Son;
uncreated is the Spirit.
The Father is infinite; the Son is infinite; the
Holy Spirit is infinite.
Eternal is the Father; eternal is the Son;
eternal is the Spirit:
And yet there are not three eternal beings, but
one who is eternal;
as there are not three uncreated and unlimited
beings, but one who is uncreated and
unlimited.
Almighty is the Father; almighty is the Son;
almighty is the Spirit:
And yet there are not three almighty beings,
but one who is almighty.

Thus the Father is God; the Son is God; the
Holy Spirit is God:
And yet there are not three gods, but one God.
Thus the Father is Lord; the Son is Lord; the
Holy Spirit is Lord:
And yet there are not three lords, but one
Lord.
As Christian truth compels us to acknowledge
each distinct person as God and Lord, so
catholic religion forbids us to say that there
are three gods or lords.
The Father was neither made nor created nor
begotten;
the Son was neither made nor created, but was
alone begotten of the Father;
the Spirit was neither made nor created, but is
proceeding from the Father and the Son.
Thus there is one Father, not three fathers; one
Son, not three sons; one Holy Spirit, not
three spirits.
And in this Trinity, no one is before or after,
greater or less than the other;
but all three persons are in themselves,
coeternal and coequal; and so we must
worship the Trinity in unity and the one
God in three persons.
Whoever wants to be saved should think thus
about the Trinity.
It is necessary for eternal salvation that one
also faithfully believe that our Lord Jesus
Christ became flesh.
For this is the true faith that we believe and
confess: That our Lord Jesus Christ, God's
Son, is both God and man.
He is God, begotten before all worlds from the
being of the Father, and he is man, born in
the world from the being of his mother —
existing fully as God, and fully as man with a
rational soul and a human body;
equal to the Father in divinity, subordinate to
the Father in humanity.
Although he is God and man, he is not
divided, but is one Christ.
He is united because God has taken humanity
into himself; he does not transform deity
into humanity.
He is completely one in the unity of his
person, without confusing his natures.
For as the rational soul and body are one
person, so the one Christ is God and man.
He suffered death for our salvation.
He descended into hell and rose again from
the dead.
He ascended into heaven and is seated at the
right hand of the Father.

He will come again to judge the living and the dead.

At his coming all people shall rise bodily to give an account of their own deeds.

Those who have done good will enter eternal life,

those who have done evil will enter eternal fire.

This is the catholic faith.

One cannot be saved without believing this firmly and faithfully.

PRAYERS TO THE BLESSED VIRGIN MARY

Hail Mary

Hail, Mary, full of grace.
The Lord is with you.
Blessed are you among women,
and blessed is the fruit of your womb,
Jesus.
Holy Mary, mother of God,
pray for us sinners,
now and at the hour of our death.
Amen.

Salve Regina

Hail, holy Queen,
Mother of Mercy:
Hail, our life, our sweetness and our hope:
To you do we cry,
poor banished children of Eve:
to you do we send up our sighs,
mourning and weeping
in this vale of tears.
Turn, then, most gracious advocate,
your eyes of mercy toward us;
and after this, our exile,
show unto us the blessed fruit of your womb,
Jesus.
O clement, O loving, O sweet Virgin Mary.

The Angelus

The angel of the Lord declared unto Mary:
And she conceived of the Holy Spirit.
Hail Mary . . .
Behold the handmaid of the Lord:
Be it done unto me according to thy word.
Hail Mary . . .
And the Word was made flesh:
And dwelt among us.
Hail Mary . . .
Pray for us, O holy Mother of God:
That we may be made worthy
of the promises of Christ.
Pour forth, we beseech thee, O Lord,
thy grace into our hearts,
that we, to whom the Incarnation

of Christ, thy Son,
was made known by the message of an angel,
may, by his Passion and Cross,
be brought to the glory of his resurrection.
Through the same Christ our Lord.
Amen.

The *Regina Caeli*

O Queen of Heaven, rejoice;
alleluia!
For he whom thou didst merit to bear —
alleluia! —
Has risen as he said;
alleluia!
Pray for us to God;
alleluia!
V. Rejoice and be glad, O Virgin Mary;
alleluia!
R. For the Lord has risen indeed; alleluia!
O God, who gayest joy to the world
through the resurrection of thy Son,
our Lord Jesus Christ:
grant that we may obtain,
through his Virgin Mother, Mary,
the joys of everlasting life.
Through the same Christ our Lord. Amen.

Prayer to the Virgin Mary

Mary, holy virgin mother,
I have received your Son, Jesus Christ.
With love you became his mother,
gave birth to him, nursed him,
and helped him grow to manhood.
With love I return him to you,
to hold once more,
to love with all your heart,
and to offer to the Holy Trinity
as our supreme act of worship
for your honor and for the good
of all your pilgrim brothers and sisters.
Mother, ask God to forgive my sins
and to help me serve him more faithfully.
Keep me true to Christ until death,
and let me come to praise him with you
for ever and ever. Amen.

The *Memorare*

Remember, O most gracious Virgin Mary,
that never was it known
that anyone who fled to your protection,
implored your help,
or sought your intercession
was left unaided.
Inspired by this confidence,
I fly to you,
O virgin of virgins, my mother.
To you I come,
before you I stand,
sinful and sorrowful.
O Mother of the Word Incarnate,
do not ignore my petitions,
but in your mercy hear and pray for me.
Amen.

Alma Redemptoris Mater

An Evening Prayer
Gentle Mother of our Redeemer,
ever-open Gate of Heaven,
Star of the Sea,
come to our aid.
Help the fallen who strive to rise again.
While nature marveled,
you gave birth to
your own most holy Creator,
before and after still a virgin.
Now hear again the angel's greeting
and show your compassion

for sinners.
Lord, into your hands I commend my spirit.
Grant me a quiet night
and a worthy dying at the end of my days.
May the souls of all the faithful departed,
through the mercy of God,
rest in peace.
Amen.

Ave Regina Caelorum

Hail, Queen of the heavens!
Hail, Empress of the angels!
Hail, the source . . . the gate . . .
the dawn of this world's light.
Rejoice, glorious Virgin,
More lovely than all other virgins
in heaven.
Receive our evening farewell,
O Mother of beauty,
and for us plead with Christ your Son.
Amen.

Consecration to the Blessed Virgin

Hail Mary, . . .
My Queen! my Mother! I give you all of
myself, and, to show my devotion to you, I
consecrate to you my eyes, my ears, my mouth,
my heart, my entire self. Therefore, O loving
Mother, as I am your own, keep me, defend me,
as your property and possession.

Saint-Riquier Abbey, 6th century

INDEX

ABOUT THE AUTHOR

Matthew Bunson was born in Germany and grew up in Hawaii. He is the author or co-author of more than twenty books, including **Our Sunday Visitor's Encyclopedia of Catholic History, Encyclopedia of the Roman Empire, Encyclopedia of the Middle Ages, Papal Wisdom, Words of Hope and Inspiration from Pope John Paul II,** and **The Angelic Doctor: The Life and World of St. Thomas Aquinas**. He is also general editor of the **Our Sunday Visitor's Catholic Almanac**. In addition to delivering lectures on a variety of topics related to his books, he has also appeared on many radio and television programs.

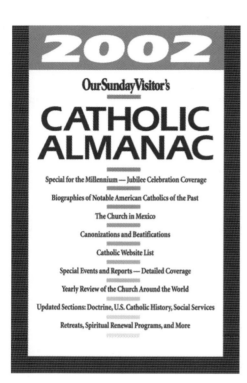

Our Sunday Visitor's 2002 Catholic Almanac

Matthew Bunson, General Editor

THE SINGLE BEST CATHOLIC RESOURCE ON THE MARKET

It is simply *the* source you turn to for information on virtually every subject of Catholic interest in the United States and the world. With annually updated facts and figures, this only-one-of-its-kind resource book brings you not only topical events and developments of headline importance, but a sweeping variety of biblical, historical, doctrinal, and secular subjects as we proceed in the new millennium. Features include the Church calendar; hundreds of biographical sketches of saints, cardinals, and bishops; listings of Catholic associations, religious orders, social-service facilities, as well as a full range of national and international statistics.

0-87973-974-6, (974) paper, 608 pages

0-87973-975-4, (975) hardcover, 608 pages

To order: Call toll-free 1-800-348-2440, or e-mail us at osvbooks@osv.com. Order securely online on the web: www.osvbooks.com.

Availability of books and CDs subject to change without notice.

Now On-line

Visit the *Catholic Almanac* on-line at www.catholicalmanac.com. Searchable sections of the *Almanac* plus information not included in the book, such as Catholic Bishops of the Past.

www.catholicalmanac.com

Our Sunday Visitor's Encyclopedia of Saints

by Matthew Bunson, Margaret Bunson, and Stephen Bunson

Virtually every person ever declared a saint by the Catholic Church is in this exhaustive reference.

Hardcover book:
0-87973-588-0, 800 pages

Or on CD-ROM:
0-87973-291-1, for Windows or Mac

To order: Call toll-free 1-800-348-2440, or e-mail us at osvbooks@osv.com. Order securely online on the web: www.osvbooks.com.

Availability of books and CDs subject to change without notice.